Personnel Administration:

An Experiential / Skill-Building Approach

Gary L. Shores   RAF Mildenhall, United Kingdom

Course Completed 19 May 1981

Instructor: Robin Jacobs
University of Maryland

Personnel Administration:

An Experiential / Skill-Building Approach

RICHARD W. BEATTY
Graduate School of Business Administration
University of Colorado

CRAIG ERIC SCHNEIER
College of Business and Management
University of Maryland

ADDISON–WESLEY PUBLISHING COMPANY
Reading, Massachusetts • Menlo Park, California • London
Amsterdam • Don Mills, Ontario • Sydney

ISBN 0-201-00436-4
FGHIJKLMNO-MU-89876543210

TO:

Dena

Nancy

Otis Lipstreu

Preface

During our early teaching experiences in personnel administration, students often seemed to ask the same question at the end of the course: "But what do people in personnel really *do*?" This book is the culmination of our efforts to answer that question, and the activities included in it enable students to experience first hand what is required of those in personnel today.

Our experiential approach to personnel shifts the responsibility for learning to the participant, while the implementor retains responsibility for structuring and managing the learning environment and for serving as a resource person. When this division of labor occurs, there is an excellent opportunity for learning — both about the subject matter and about oneself — and for interest to develop. We continue to find it exciting to witness a classroom transform from a collection of passive *listeners* to a group of involved, active *learners* — "learn" is an action verb.

This book is also the culmination of our efforts to upgrade the personnel curriculum in order to better reflect current challenges and complexities. Personnel is a field which has changed dramatically in recent years. Equal employment opportunity, government legislation, rising expectations of the labor force, and advancements in the behavioral sciences, among many other developments, have transformed practice regarding human-resource management in all types and sizes of organizations. There is now an enormous and growing body of substantive knowledge which personnel practitioners are expected to use as the basis for human-

resource programs. The activities in this book were developed to build skill in designing, implementing, and evaluating these programs, for those in personnel are now being called on to reinforce knowledge with specific skills.

Our experiential/skill-building approach to personnel was thus written to facilitate learning through participation in the college and university classroom and to build skill in the management development seminar, the workshop, or the training program. It was born of the apathy of those students in the former setting who could not see their learning transfer into action and of the frustration of the personnel specialists in the latter setting who were searching for material that emphasized program implementation. Both the student and the practicing personnel professional are intended audiences for this book. Moreover, the exercises each contain activities that vary in complexity and can be used for graduate and undergraduate courses in personnel, human-resource management, human relations, and industrial/organizational psychology. Because those in all types of managerial and administrative positions must themselves make important personnel decisions, such as selecting subordinates or evaluating their performance, this book has been very useful to them as well.

All of the activities in the text have been developed, used, and evaluated over a period of four years by innumerable students and professionals. The book has been used in colleges and universities, both large and small; in business schools, psychology departments, and public-administration departments; and in day and evening divisions. It has been used in military, government, educational, health care, and business organizations by first-level supervisors to vice presidents. While extensive previous use of this material has eliminated many problems and greatly enhanced the book's ability to facilitate learning, an experientially oriented book is an emerging learning tool. We realize no amount of testing can eliminate each error or each potential snag that may arise in any unique learning setting. Yet some flexibility must be built into any set of experiential materials in order to allow users to adapt them to their own learning settings.

We emphasize the experiential/skill-building approach, but recognize the necessity of a sound conceptual foundation in order to gain the maximum benefit from one's experiences — to tie them to other ideas, techniques, and previous experience; to predict and prepare for future contingencies; to reflect on and test one's own hypotheses. We have prepared conceptual introductions to each exercise. Although their length and complexity depend on the topic, each provides a basic conceptual framework and an admittedly selective introduction to prepare participants for activities and to bridge the gap between concrete experience and abstract conceptualization. The conceptual material enables the book to be used as a primary text as well as a supplemental one. Most important, however, is that the text can make learning come alive.

In a way, a book is a process of laying out one's values and biases about an academic discipline for all to see — and criticize. We may have made errors; we certainly made assumptions about conceptual material and relied on previous work, which we have attempted to acknowledge.

We especially wish to acknowledge the contributions of the late Otis Lipstreu who taught personnel administration at the University of Colorado. Professor Lipstreu realized the importance of learning through participation long before experiential learning became fashionable. He also felt that personnel courses should teach skills. His enthusiasm and far-sighted views on pedagogy were an inspiration to us. The materials he prepared for the classroom were a model for us and we are indebted to him.

Many persons contribute to the effort that culminates in a completed book. At the risk of omitting some, many should be mentioned by name. The reviewers of the entire text helped point out errors and presented countless suggestions that contributed significantly to the book. They are George Milkovich (University of Minnesota), Tom De-Cotiis (Cornell University), Doug Durand (University of Missouri–St. Louis), and John Bernardin (Old Dominion University). Contributors and/or reviewers for specific exercises whose ideas benefited us include Milt Hakel, Fred Luthans, Tony Kulisch, Fran Coyne, Jim Beatty, Earl Vinson, Maxine Kurtz, Harvey Wilson, Patricia Smith, Walt Nord, W. R. Johnston, Robert Comerford, David Van Fleet, Herbert Heneman, Allan Nash, Thomas Gutteridge, and the Civil Service Commission (Denver Federal Region). We also owe a great debt of gratitude to the Business Research Division (University of Colorado), Faculty Services (University of Maryland), Polly Jackson, Sidney Summers, and Mary Triollo for their competent assistance in the preparation of the manuscript. The staff of Addison-Wesley believed in the project from the very beginning. Their support and encouragement helped us get through many drafts of the manuscript.

The biggest acknowledgment must, however, go to two groups. The many students and professionals who used the manuscript provided us with comments and suggestions that made the book actually "work" in the classroom. We learned a great deal from them and thank them. Our families — Dena, Nancy, Sarah, and Arthur — sacrificed as families of authors often do, yet gave us the patience and understanding we needed to complete the project.

College Park, Maryland   CES
Boulder, Colorado   RWB
November 1976

Contents

Introduction   **1**

Section 1 The Personnel Administrator   **7**

    Exercise 1 Hiring a Personnel Administrator: An Exploration of Job Duties
           and Roles   8

Section 2 Planning for an Effective Human-Resource System   **23**

    Exercise 2 Human-Resource Planning and Forecasting   24
    Exercise 3 Analyzing Jobs and Writing Job Descriptions   55

Section 3 Identifying, Observing, and Appraising Performance in Organizations   **77**

    Exercise 4 Appraising Job Performance: General Methods   78
    Exercise 5 Designing Behaviorally Anchored Rating Scales: A
           Performance-Appraisal System Built around Ratee Job Behavior   103
    Exercise 6 Designing and Implementing a Management-By-Objectives
           (MBO) Program: Measuring Employee Contributions   153

Section 4 Human-Resource Selection and Staffing   **175**

    Exercise 7 Biographical Data as a Predictor of Job Success   177
    Exercise 8 Interviewing as a Predictor of Job Success   207
    Exercise 9 Work Sampling and Simulation as Predictors of Job Success   221
    Exercise 10 Testing Personnel and Validating Selection Procedures   257

Section 5 Building Human-Resource Skills: Training and Development   **285**

    Exercise 11 Assessing Training and Development Needs   287
    Exercise 12 Designing and Implementing Training and Development
           Programs   309
    Exercise 13 Evaluating the Effectiveness of Training and Development
           Programs   329

Section 6 Maintaining and Improving Commitment, Performance, and Productivity   **349**

    Exercise 14 Job Satisfaction: Its Meaning and Its Measurement   350
    Exercise 15 Designing and Implementing Job Enrichment Programs   369
    Exercise 16 Improving Performance through Positive Reinforcement   395
    Exercise 17 Job Evaluation and Wage and Salary Administration   415

**Section 7 Personnel Administration and Human-Resource Management in the
Contemporary Environment**   **449**

    Exercise 18 Issues in Equal Employment Opportunity and Affirmative
                Action   450
    Exercise 19 The Impact of Unions on Personnel Administration and
                Human-Resource Management: Constraints and Opportunities   515

Index   **559**

Introduction

PERSONNEL ADMINISTRATION: THE PROCUREMENT, DEVELOPMENT, AND UTILIZATION OF HUMAN RESOURCES

Personnel administration refers broadly to the procurement, development, and utilization of an organization's human resources. Regardless of what product or service an organization provides and no matter what its size, age, or location, it must procure human resources in order to remain viable. Further, if the organization is to survive, it must design programs to develop its human resources to their fullest capacities and to maintain ongoing worker commitment.

Obviously, organizations differ in their degree of reliance on the three above-mentioned processes. The relative importance of any one process may also vary both within an organization and over time. For example, a prestigious accounting firm with branches in several cities may not have problems procuring or attracting human resources, but may exhaust a great deal of time, effort, and expense in developing these resources. A voluntary organization, on the other hand, may see procurement as a problem, but due to the nature of most tasks, may expend only minimal effort in human-resource development. A new university may initially experience a faculty procurement problem in some academic departments; however, after a few decades in which academic prestige builds, this aspect of personnel administration may become less problematic than utilizing its faculty efficiently and/or maintaining a high level of instructor performance.

Personnel administration, as opposed to person-nel management, refers more to the design, implementation, evaluation, and administration of human-resource programs. While the personnel manager's job may typically be one of supervising and directing his or her staff, the personnel administrator's job routinely consists of problem identification through program design, implementation, and evaluation. Clearly, these two titles are quite similar and duties often may overlap, but the approach taken here emphasizes the administration of human-resource programs.

Personnel is a rapidly changing profession and job. This is due in part to the changing external environment in which organizations operate. Labor legislation, rising expectations of workers, unionization, and foreign competition are but a few examples of environmental forces shaping the personnel profession. Internal environmental conditions are also creating challenges for those in personnel. These include organizations' size, complexity, and interdependence, as well as coordination problems between various subunits or functional areas, such as production, marketing, finance, and research and development.

In one sense, personnel must be all things to all people in an organization. As a staff or advisory function, it supports other line (or producing) areas, such as manufacturing. It also services other staff areas, such as the legal or public-relations departments. "Service" in this context refers to record keeping, data gathering, advising, auditing, evaluating, and other support functions. In addition, the personnel department is often given responsibility for helping to solve the organization's most difficult problems: absenteeism, poor performance, turnover, inadequate incentive systems, lack of coordination and planning, and forecasting future needs.

Thus, personnel faces three general demands. First, it must help the organization cope with a changing environment—with constraints and opportunities developed externally, such as those stemming from government legislation and labor unions. Second, it must cooperate with other line and staff areas to achieve the organization's goals. It must secure the respect, trust, and confidence of the members of these units in order to effectively implement its programs—in short, to do its own job. Third, it is required to respond to certain serious human-resource-management problems organizations face.

These demands involve complex human behavior, as well as complex laws, technologies, and interrelationships between groups. To succeed in personnel administration one must possess substantial knowledge and skill in the areas of human behavior, interpersonal relations, organization structure and process, labor relations, general administration and supervision, and in such technical areas as psychological testing, learning theory, employment legislation, statistics, and human motivation and performance. In other words, personnel work has become more and more demanding and, accordingly, those in the field are granted increased prestige, respect, and compensation, as well as a powerful central position in many organizations.

TOWARD A RATIONAL AND INTEGRATED PERSONNEL SYSTEM

All of the many different personnel programs are related in that their ultimate goal is the improvement of organizational effectiveness through the use of human resources. Organizational effectiveness refers to the results or outcomes of activity in an organizational setting. These results can be defined in terms of profit, cost, services provided, sales volume, interest earned, money raised, patients discharged, test score improvements, etc. Each type of organization (e.g., educational, industrial, voluntary, military, governmental, professional) would measure its results differently and each may use several measures.

How do personnel programs impact on organizational effectiveness? Such impacts are many and complex. Personnel programs that are able to select successful performers, increase skills and abilities through training, secure commitment through wage and salary administration, measure human performance, and identify desired behaviors obviously will improve a system's efficacy. The ultimate link between

these programs and organizational effectiveness is, of course, also determined by such additional factors as organizational policies, individual preferences and desires, and general economic conditions. Nevertheless, the personnel department does control a major determinant of organizational effectiveness—an organization's human resources.

The personnel system explained here must be discussed in its proper context; as Fig. 1 shows, a personnel system does not operate in isolation. It is influenced by and influences its environment significantly. On the one hand, the personnel system of programs to procure, develop, and utilize human resources lies within an environment *external* to the organization and affected by general economic, sociocultural, and political conditions (e.g., a period of high unemployment). Two aspects of this environment, Equal Employment Opportunity (EEO) laws and guidelines and labor unions, have had such a pervasive effect on personnel that they are noted explicitly in Fig. 1. On the other hand, the personnel system is actually one of a number of other coexisting *internal* organizational systems, which determine organizational effectiveness and are served by the personnel department. The interface between the personnel system and these other organizational systems ultimately determines the effectiveness of the programs the personnel department implements.

Working with line managers is sometimes the most difficult task in personnel, as personnel's staff position typically precludes complete authority and autonomy for its programs. Certainly those in personnel must be able to work very well with others, present their ideas clearly and concisely, and realize that the success of their programs often ultimately rests on their relationship with line managers. More will be said about interfaces between line managers and personnel staffs throughout the exercises in this book. The other systems with which personnel works may include functional areas, such as marketing, finance, manufacturing, research and development, etc.

The uppermost box in Fig. 1 depicts the internal and external environmental influences on the personnel system and is directly connected to each of the core personnel programs (shown in the boxes). The five core personnel programs form the base of the personnel system. They are typically sequentially developed, although they certainly interact with each other and are dependent on each other. Each core program corresponds to a section in this book and specific exercises in each section are indicated by their numbers in Fig. 1.

A first task in personnel is planning. Personnel

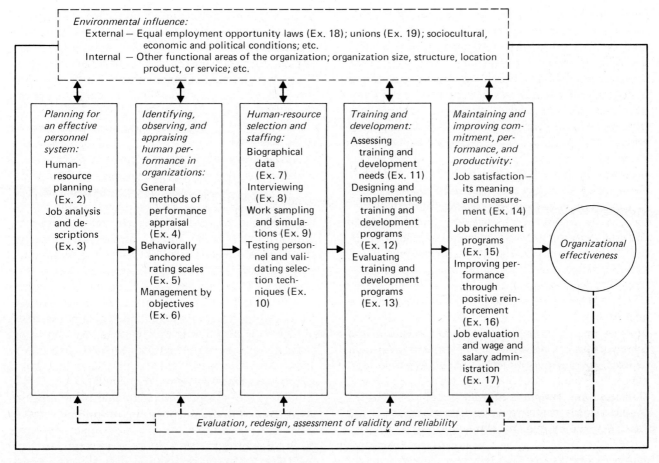

Fig. 1.   Toward a Rational and Integrated Personnel System

planning involves forecasting for future human-resource needs in light of a changing environment and long- and short-run organizational objectives. Planning also consists of analyses of jobs in the organization in order to determine their tasks and convert them into human requirements and characteristics. Such planning enables the personnel staff to gather the data required to make subsequent personnel decisions and forms the foundation for all personnel programs. It enables us to answer such questions as, "How many managers are needed to produce the new product line?" and "What are the responsibilities given to a person holding that job?"

The second core personnel program is that of identifying, observing, and appraising human performance. In a way, this program, like the previous one, is a preliminary step before human resources can be procured, developed, or utilized effectively. However, it is an extremely vital process. Desired performance must be defined before people are selected in order to establish a standard for appraising their on-the-job effectiveness. Further, setting standards and developing performance-appraisal scales or formats to help in the observation and evaluation of performance redirects attention to job behavior—what people are expected to do on the job. While job analyses may identify job tasks (e.g., operating a machine), the performance identification and appraisal process can identify actual standards or desired behaviors (e.g., operating the machine at a rate of fifty pieces per hour).

Both types of information are required—that is, we would not only want to select someone who could operate the machine, but someone who could operate it at the desired rate. Further, once we know what desired behavior is, we can develop training and/or motivation programs when performance is too low. The performance appraisal system thus facilitates performance measurement and improvement.

Selection and staffing, the third core personnel program, refers broadly to the process of matching people to jobs. Selection is actually decision making under uncertainty. We are attempting to predict future job performance based on information from past and present performance. Obviously, as much information as is practical is gathered in order to improve this decision-making process. However, once future human-resource needs have been forecasted, jobs have been analyzed and described, and desired performance has been identified, the information gathered about job applicants can be related to a standard or to a set of job and person requirements. Hence personnel decision making becomes more rational.

The fourth core personnel process is training and development. Certainly, we cannot improve or augment skill, ability, or knowledge unless we have selected persons and observed and evaluated their performance, compared it to standards, and concluded that any deviance is due to lack of ability. Training, actually learning in the organizational context, is aimed at improving present job performance and preparing persons to assume higher-level positions in the future. Due to the dynamic nature of the job environment, it is important for the organization to maintain a pool of potential replacements for key jobs.

Personnel staffs are given the responsibility, in coordination with managers and supervisors in other functional areas, of maintaining and improving commitment, performance, and productivity. This fifth core personnel system can really become effective only after commitment or performance problems have been noted and inadequate training has been eliminated as a cause. Numerous types of specific motivational, incentive, or wage and salary programs are in use, often in combination. Although their assumptions may differ, their common objective is to insure that the level of performance and commitment required is maintained and, if possible, improved. This core personnel program recognizes that individuals require certain inducements, by no means limited to financial, to insure their contributions to organizational effectiveness.

Figure 1 also indicates that the five core personnel programs, as well as those programs developed to meet environmental constraints and opportunities, need continual evaluation and redesign. All personnel programs must be subjected to a rigorous evaluation, perhaps through a cost/benefit analysis. The provision for evaluation must be built into program design and costs must be estimated and benefits measured. When program objectives are not met, as in, for example, a selection program that fails to predict the desired percentage of successful performers from a group of applicants, or when program costs are judged

to outweigh economic and/or noneconomic benefits, programs must be altered. Redesign is also called for when previously effective programs become outmoded as jobs, people, organization objectives, and organizational environments change. The most detailed job description must be revised if new machinery changes the nature of the job.

A significant part of the evaluation process of personnel programs concerns assessing their validity and reliability. While these terms will be explained in their many specific contexts throughout this book,[1] a brief definition can be given here. Validity refers to the accuracy of a program: Did it accomplish what it was intended to accomplish? Did it contribute to organizational effectiveness? Reliability refers to consistency and repeatability: Were similar, predictable, accurate results obtained over time?

Both validity and reliability relate to the evaluation of a program's effectiveness, but they are very difficult to measure. As noted above, many variables influence organizational effectiveness and often it is defined itself by several different measures. Reliability and validity are also related and a program that is not valid will in many cases not be reliable.

Because of the great difficulty in ascertaining reliability and validity, it is tempting to settle for "soft" criteria in evaluating success. For example, a training program may be termed valid because people reacted favorably to it. But did the program achieve its real purpose? Were objectives for the program ever set and later met? Are people's reactions accurate? These are tough questions. So many factors can account for the outcome of any personnel program that they are difficult to sort out.

For some programs, such as testing, detailed validity and reliability are sometimes required by law. A valid test for leadership ability would be able to predict, on the basis of its results, successful and unsuccessful future job performance of test takers. Validity would also be inferred if scores attained by a group of people correlated highly with scores the same people received on another test also designed to measure leadership ability and if their scores did not correlate highly with scores from a test measuring "need for followership." A reliable test would be one on which individuals achieved similar scores from one administration of the test to another. That is, if they scored high initially on the test, they would also score high on the second administration.

But how do we validate a human-resource forecasting effort or plan? Clearly, ascertaining whether

---

[1] See Exercise 10.

or not the effort accomplished what it set out to do would be difficult unless we were sure of the original objectives. But this standard may be too unrealistic or subjective.

Thus, the evaluation and reliability of entire personnel programs is a difficult problem, and becomes even more acute if programs are closely related. This is because the validity or reliability of one is often difficult to separate from the others. Attempts at assessing validity and reliability are necessary, however, for several reasons: they facilitate the effective evaluation of personnel programs' impact on organizational effectiveness; their demonstration is often required by law; and their determination pinpoints weaknesses in programs, which helps facilitate program redesign.

PERSONNEL ADMINISTRATION FROM AN EXPERIENTIAL/SKILL-BUILDING PERSPECTIVE

In writing this book, we took a different approach than do most textbook authors. Typically, a book's content is decided by answering the question: What should people *know* at the end of this course? We asked that question too. But we also asked another question: What should people be able to *do* at the end of the course? In answering this second question, we developed a set of exercises designed to build participants' skill, as well as their knowledge, in the field of personnel administration. These exercises all require participants to take an active part in the learning process—to learn by doing.

While many textbooks contain much of the information required in personnel administration, they have no provision for *skill acquisition*. This set of exercises will hopefully provide you with the experiences necessary to begin to build skills in the areas of, for example, training, selection, and performance appraisal. You can thus move from the learning environment into the organizational environment with not only some knowledge of what to do, but also some expertise on *how* to do it.

Experiential Learning. Experiential learning differs from more traditional classroom learning in several ways. First, the learner is active. You must participate in the learning situation, rather than merely sitting back and absorbing material. Second, the implementor acts more as a coach, director, or resource person than as an evaluator or transmitter of information. The instructor is thus a manager of the learning environment. Third, learning takes place not only while you participate directly, but also while you observe others participate. They can act as your models for both ineffective and effective behavior. Fourth, experiential learning involves your behavior and your emotions or attitudes, as well as your thought processes. You must act as well as think and your actions and those of others may affect you in a positive or negative way. But if you are perceptive, you may learn much about yourself, about the way you behave in groups, about your preferences for certain tasks or for amounts of authority, in addition to course content. Finally, once you have experienced something, have actually done it, your learning has a much higher probability of transferring from the classroom environment to the environment in which you will be required to use the skill and knowledge.

The Role of the Participant in Experiential Learning. In order to maximize the learning from these exercises, a few hints are offered. Participate seriously. Try to place yourself in the situation described and act accordingly. Use the information given in the exercises as a jumping-off point for your own extrapolation and improvisation. Make assumptions you think are necessary according to your own perception of the situation, recognizing that these assumptions may differ from those of others (as is often the case in actual situations).

Try to incorporate the conceptual material from the *Introductions* of the exercises, from lectures, and from other sources into your experiences. Concepts, ideas, and theories you gather will help to integrate the exercises, make them a richer experience, and allow you to predict their outcomes more accurately. After you have completed each exercise, reflect on your learning and try to pinpoint precisely what new information you possess and particularly what skills you have begun to develop. A form for this self-assessment process follows each exercise. Finally, try to be an effective group or team member. As many of the tasks require small-group effort, you must work with others closely and cooperatively in order to perform well. As noted above, you can learn much from your team members' behavior as well as from your own.

THE ORGANIZATION AND CONTENTS OF THIS TEXT

This book contains nineteen exercises. Each topic and the activities in each exercise were chosen to reflect the important personnel programs currently in use in all types of modern organizations. The exercises are grouped into seven broad sections, each preceded by a statement of introduction to the topic area. Each section contains one or more exercises.

Section 1 contains one exercise designed to familiarize you with the roles and duties of people in personnel work. Sections 2 through 6 each include two or more exercises pertaining to each of the five core personnel programs explained above. As shown in Fig. 1, the five core programs are presented in order. The two exercises in Section 7 deal with environmental impacts on personnel.

USING THE TEXT

Each exercise contains all of the information you will need to complete it. All forms required are also included and the perforated pages enable you to tear out certain forms your implementor may ask you to hand in.

Each exercise begins with a *Preview*, to give you a glimpse of the exercise's content. Next, *Objectives* spell out the aims of the exercise in some detail and the *Premeeting Assignment* informs you of reading tasks to be completed before you begin or parts you are not to read until told to do so. The *Introduction* serves as a brief summary of the topic and will provide a set of relevant terms, concepts, and issues that can be used to facilitate your understanding of the exercise and enable you to integrate it with others. The *Procedure* explains your tasks in a step-by-step fashion. As with any other experience, having all of the terms, concepts, rules, and procedures firmly in mind *before you begin* will aid your performance, understanding, and enjoyment. Careful reading and study of the *Procedure* and your serious attempts at staying within time guidelines will facilitate learning.

For Further Reading suggests a good number of related sources of information to be used by those who want to learn about a topic in more depth or for those seeking material for term papers and other projects. The references were chosen to provide a representative sample of the many different levels and types of literature, very current ideas and classic issues, research, and practical guidelines.

The forms follow the reading list. The lettered parts of the exercise and the numbered forms correspond to those explained in the procedure. The instructions for filling out the forms are detailed in the *Procedure*. Finally, an *Assessment of Learning* form is placed at the end of each exercise. The first three questions on the form are the same for every exercise; subsequent questions pertain to each particular exercise. The last statement on the form provides a space for any additional questions supplied by your implementor.

A FINAL NOTE

Now that you are familiar with the organization and content of this book, you can more readily see how we answered the question posed above: What should people be able to *do* at the end of this course? Simply put, they should be able to begin to *design, implement,* and *evaluate* personnel programs in order to procure, develop, and utilize human resources in organizations. This emphasis on design, implementation, and evaluation was incorporated into each exercise and, coupled with knowledge you glean from this book, the exercises facilitate skill building in personnel. Hopefully, you can thus learn not only what to do, but you can begin to learn *how* to do it.

The activities offered here cannot, of course, substitute for actual experience in organizations. Nor were they meant to incorporate every variable, consideration, problem, or complexity you may encounter in an actual organizational setting. Simply following these guidelines will not assure an effective personnel system. The activities do, however, incorporate the most important and pervasive considerations and problems you would typically encounter in an organization and, while they are simulations, they were all designed around actual organizational practices. They enable you to gain valuable experience and try out your ideas, thereby developing an understanding of how personnel programs are implemented and how they can impact on organizational effectiveness.

Remember that the responsibility for your learning ultimately rests with *you*, the learner, not with your implementor. Be prepared to take an active role in learning, be prepared to experience, observe, experiment, assess, and evaluate your own learning. And be prepared to have some fun, for fun and learning need not be mutually exclusive.

Section 1
The Personnel Administrator

This section of the book contains one exercise, yet serves many purposes. For participants unfamiliar with the duties and roles of people in the personnel field, Exercise 1 can provide information about the type of work expected from those in personnel, human-resources, or employee-relations departments. In addition, the first exercise allows participants to gain some practice in using this book. You will become familiar with the format, how various parts are arranged, and how specific assignments in exercises are made. By completing Exercise 1, you can also gain practice in analyzing cases, in role playing, and in group discussion—activities that are all required in subsequent exercises.

Therefore, Section 1 is a preview to the personnel administrator's (PA's) job as well as to the experiential/skill-building method of learning used in this book. Try to reflect back on this exercise as you participate in other exercises and think about two questions. As you finish each exercise, ask yourself how your perception of the duties and role of the PA has changed. Are you developing a clearer picture of what organizations do to attend to their human-resource needs? Secondly, consider your own skill development. Are you picking up new skills that would enable you to design, implement, and evaluate human-resource programs?

Personnel administration or human-resource management is a dynamic, challenging academic field of study and profession. As Exercise 1 points out, the role of the PA in an organization is becoming quite technical and increasingly important. He or she is typically responsible for making many decisions that influence people's lives and the organization significantly, for controlling information vital to the organization's functioning, and for helping to solve one of an organization's most difficult problems—how to procure, develop, and utilize its human resources most effectively.

Exercise 1

HIRING A PERSONNEL ADMINISTRATOR: AN EXPLORATION OF JOB DUTIES AND ROLES

PREVIEW

In this exercise you simulate the process of interviewing and hiring a personnel administrator (PA) for a small manufacturing company. As you participate in the exercise, you are able to discover the duties and responsibilities of PA's, as well as their roles in an organization. Three applicants for the job of PA are interviewed by a company's board of directors and one of them is eventually chosen. As the exercise proceeds, try to identify the combination of education, experience, knowledge, and personal characteristics which would be desirable for a prospective PA job applicant and how these would change as characteristics of the organization change.

OBJECTIVES

1. To become acquainted with the job duties and roles of a personnel administrator in an organization.
2. To gain experience in the interviewing process and begin to appreciate its strengths and weaknesses.
3. To begin thinking about job performance—how it can be described, measured, and predicted.

PREMEETING PREPARATION

Read the *Introduction* and Forms 1, 2, and 3. Do not read past Form 3 until you are assigned a role by the implementor.

INTRODUCTION

The Job Duties and Roles of the Personnel Administrator

The Traditional Role. Traditionally, the personnel administrator (PA) had responsibility for staffing the organization, for selection, for benefit administration, and for interfacing with unions on a day-to-day basis. These activities were part of the staff or advisory role of the personnel departments during the early part of the twentieth century. The PA typically had little or no direct authority over the decisions made by managers and supervisors involved in the actual production of a product or service. These "line" managers had the authority to hire, fire, or promote their workers and the personnel staff attempted to advise them in these matters. In addition, there was little government interference in the form of laws and guidelines as the PA carried out his or her duties. Decisions regarding selection methods, promotions, etc. were left primarily to top management, with advice from the PA. The union was the primary constraint on management decision making in the personnel area in the period before World War I.

External Environmental Influences on the Role of the PA. This "laissez-faire" era for management and the PA began to change, however, as several external influences emerged to affect their roles.[1] The foremost of these influences was the federal government. Due to a series of legislation enacted in the past few decades, the PA's role has permanently changed. Among these acts are the Manpower Training and Development Act (MTDA) of 1962, Title VII of the Civil Rights Act of 1964, the Occupational Safety and Health Act (OSHA) of 1970, and the Equal Employment Opportunity (EEO) Act of 1972. These laws, coupled with major labor laws and the numerous other manpower laws, set guidelines, quotas, and often strict rules for the PA and the organization in all areas of personnel.[2]

One of the most notable ramifications of these laws was the illegality of discrimination in hiring practices. This forced all concerned with the personnel function to take a hard look at, for example, their selection tests, in order to ensure their "fairness." Finding selection tests that do not discriminate against certain groups is a difficult and controversial task for the PA, but one which makes the role even more challenging. Research and new technical developments are required to meet this challenge and many such techniques and implications of the complex laws and guidelines are discussed in later exercises.

Beside government influence, several other factors have contributed to the changing nature of the role of the PA. Among these have been shifts in the composition of the labor force toward more white-collar workers, a more highly educated labor force, and more skilled-labor and managerial positions. These trends have made it more difficult for the PA to recruit people for certain jobs. The changes in attitudes, values, and the rising expectations of many workers today also make motivation programs and wage, salary, and benefit administration more challenging and difficult. General economic conditions and unemployment rates certainly affect the PA's job by altering the supply of labor available to an organization.

Finally, the role of the PA is being influenced by changes in the internal environment of the organization itself. Not only are physical environments beginning to reflect people's needs (e.g., bright colors, recreation facilities, etc.), but organization structure and technology are also rapidly changing. More authority is given to lower-level workers and many decisions are made by a work group or team. Looser organizational structures and less-formal authority

are becoming more pervasive. Thus, to accommodate these changes, the PA is forced to revise training methods to emphasize interpersonal and group relations. The computer and its technology are also pervasive in organizations and the PA may be required not only to staff and train those who will work with computers, but also to use computers effectively in his or her own department.

A New Role for the PA. The environmental influences noted above, both external and internal to the organization, have vastly expanded the role of the PA. The PA essentially has responsibility for obtaining, utilizing, and developing the human resources of an organization. In this role, he or she must still carry out traditional activities such as selection, training, and wage and salary administration. But even these activities must conform to the reporting and legal requirements of the government. The role of developing human resources requires the PA to take a much broader view of training, which may encompass career development and interpersonal relations in addition to skill building. The PA must now anticipate the changes in the labor force and in the human-resource requirements of the organization and attempt to mesh the two with sophisticated planning and forecasting techniques. Finally, the PA is now often seen as the primary change agent or catalyst for change in the organization.[3] He or she often has responsibility for changing the structure of the organization and the people in it in order to adapt to the rapid pace of change in our society.

These new roles for the PA have added significantly to his or her status and importance in the organization. What has traditionally been a staff function is now becoming a vital part of the central decision-making and goal-setting processes in an organization. The PA now has considerable authority based upon (a) his or her possession of vital information regarding laws, the labor force, and the current manpower inventory of the organization; and (b) his or her control over such vital organizational functions as selection, training, and wage and salary administration. In fact, personnel administrators are being chosen as chief executive officers in organizations with increasing regularity.[4]

---

[1] T. H. Patton, "Personnel Management in the 1970's: The End of Laissez Faire," *Human Resource Management* 12, no. 3 (Fall 1973): 7–11.

[2] See Exercises 10 and 18 for discussions of laws relating to hiring practices. Major labor laws are outlined in Exercise 19.

[3] S. H. Applebaum, "Contemporary Personnel Administrators: Agents of Change," *Personnel Journal* 53, no. 11 (November 1974): 835–837.

[4] D. Henning and W. French, "The Mythical Personnel Manager," *California Management Review* 3, no. 4 (Summer 1961): 33–45; H. E. Meyer, "Personnel Directors are the New Corporate Heroes," *Fortune* 93, no. 2 (February 1976): 86–88+; "Personnel: Fast Track to the Top," *Dun's Review* 105, no. 4 (April 1975): 74–77.

Challenges for the PA. The changes and complexities in the role of the PA offer considerable challenge for those in this position. The PA is now challenged to devise valid and fair selection tests, to develop relevant and job-related selection tools in addition to the interview and biographical data, to make training programs more effective and transferable to actual job situations, and to motivate people on the job by using rewards and programs rather than strictly monetary inducements. Increasingly, the challenge for the PA is to *develop* people in their jobs to their fullest potential, rather than merely *place* them in jobs.

Simultaneously fulfilling the demands of government, management, employees, and unions is the major challenge facing the PA. Merging organizational efficiency and productivity with individual and career development will require extremely creative efforts.

Background, Training, and Experience of the PA. What type of person is able to meet the challenges discussed above? What experience and training should they have? What specific duties will they be asked to perform? The answers to these questions are the concern of this exercise. As you prepare criteria for selection of a PA and/or interview prospective candidates, you will be confronted with these issues.

In selecting a person for any job, several types of standards or criteria may be used to help make the decision. Based on what you now know about the role of the PA, we may group these criteria into the following four broad categories:

1. General management skills and abilities;
2. Specific job skills and abilities;
3. Technical information and knowledge; and
4. Specific job behaviors.

Because the PA will have broad administrative and managerial duties as he or she develops and implements programs, some skill and ability in planning, organizing, controlling, and general supervision seems essential. The PA must implement specific programs in the areas of, for example, training and wage and salary administration, and thus some specific skills in these content areas is desirable. A PA today must also be familiar with the content of the many laws that affect the job, as well as with other technical information, such as safety standards, in his or her industry. Finally, certain specific behaviors may be desirable for a PA—for example, facility in verbal and/or written communication.

Remember ① The selection of any job applicant will depend on the candidate's current ability in each of these four areas, as well as on the competence he or she can be expected to obtain through postselection training. ② In addition, the selection decision will rest on the specific nature of the job and the organization. As you develop selection criteria for the PA in this exercise, try to keep these two points in mind.

PROCEDURE

Overview. Several of you will be asked to play the role of a candidate for the job of a PA of a small firm, while others are asked to be the owners and officers of the firm who comprise its board of directors. The remaining participants form groups whose task is to devise a list of criteria for selecting the candidate and to decide on a method for weighting these criteria.

PART A

STEP 1: Everyone should read all of the information in Forms 1–3.

STEP 2: Three people are chosen to be the candidates for the job of PA. They are to prepare their personal resumes for the board of directors and to read Forms 1–3 carefully.

PART B

STEP 3: A group is chosen to be the company's board of directors and each is given one of the seven roles in Form 4. The board will discuss its interview strategy and prepare for the interview.

PART C

STEP 4: Remaining participants form small groups to determine the criteria each would use to select a PA for the company and how these criteria would be used or weighted to evaluate candidates in an interview. These groups are also to design a scale (see Form 5) to use as they observe the candidates being interviewed. As candidates are interviewed, they will rate them in various areas using this scale. The criteria are not to be known to the interviewers or interviewees.

TIME: Each group should take about 30 minutes to prepare (Parts A, B, and C).

STEP 5: The candidates for the job of PA are interviewed by the board. Candidates should not observe another interview unless they have already been interviewed.

TIME: About 10 minutes per interview.

PART D

STEP 6: After the interviews are completed:

   a) The board should select one candidate (the "best" person for the job in question) and compose letters to the person selected and to those rejected informing the candidates of their decision. These letters are then delivered to the appropriate candidates.

   b) Each group that composed selection criteria and observed the interviewing process should also select a candidate and prepare a rationale for their choice.

   c) The candidates decide among themselves who should be selected and discuss their strengths and weaknesses during the interview.

TIME: About 25 minutes.

STEP 7: Each of the three groups (candidates, interviewers, and groups that observed the process and developed criteria) reveal their decisions and their rationales for the decision to all other groups. Emphasis should be placed on the reasons for the choice and whether these reasons could withstand possible litigation initiated by rejected candidates who might feel they were victims of prejudice.

STEP 8: Each of the candidates is permitted to respond briefly to the letter received.

FOR FURTHER READING

Each reference is followed by either the roman numeral I or II, meant to indicate the general level of difficulty of the reference. Those followed by the numeral I are introductory references that can be read and understood by those with little or no background in the specific topic, other than what is contained in the exercise itself. These are also sources that contain information especially useful to practitioners and professionals, as they develop guidelines, suggestions, etc. They are not, however, overly simplistic or unrealistic. References followed by the numeral II are at a somewhat higher level of complexity and may require previous knowledge of the topic if the reader is to derive their full benefit. These can be very useful to those wishing more detailed information on a particular topic. References followed by an R are research articles or books containing primarily research. They of course contain data analyses and research-methodology discussions and are typically also noted with the numeral II, as they may require

some background in research statistics and methods. The categories of references are certainly somewhat subjective and the codes should therefore not restrict users of these exercises from exploring any reference that seems appropriate for their needs. All references were chosen on the basis of their content, and we have attempted to provide a representative sample of the various types of literature available for each subject.

American Management Association. *The Personnel Job in a Changing World*. New York: American Management Association, 1964. (I)

"An Interview with Bob Berra". *The Personnel Administrator* 21, no. 2 (February 1976): 29–33. (I)

Applebaum, S. H. "Contemporary Personnel Administrators: Agents of Change." *Personnel Journal* 53, no. 11 (November 1974): 835–837. (I)

Appley, L. A. "Management *Is* Personnel Administration." *Personnel* 46 (March–April 1969): 8–15. (I)

Barrett, G. V. "Research Models of the Future for Industrial and Organizational Psychology." *Personnel Psychology* 25 (1972): 1–18. (II)

Bass, B. M. "Organizational Life in the 1970s and Beyond." *Personnel Psychology* 25 (1972): 19–30. (II)

Beatty, R. W. "Personnel Systems and Human Performance." *Personnel Journal* 54 (1973): 307–312. (I)

Burack, E. H., and E. L. Miller. "The Personnel Function in Transition." *California Management Review*, 1976, in press. (I)

Cassell, F. H. "A New Role in Corporate Management." *Personnel Administration* 34, no. 6 (November–December 1971): 33–37. (I)

Coleman, C. J. "Personnel: The Changing Function." *Public Personnel Management* 2 (May–June 1973): 186–193. (I)

Dunnette, M. D. "Research Needs of the Future in Industrial and Organizational Psychology." *Personnel Psychology* 25 (1972): 31–40. (II)

Dunnette, M. D., and B. M. Bass. "Behavioral Scientists and Personnel Management." *Industrial Relations* 2 (1963): 115–130. (I)

French, W. "The Contemporary and Emerging Role of the Personnel Department." In W. French, *The Personnel Management Process*, 3d ed. Boston: Houghton Mifflin, 1974, Chap. 30. (I)

French, W., and A. D. Ebling. "Predictions for Personnel and Industrial Relations in 1985." *Personnel Journal* 40, no. 6 (1961): 249–253. (I)

Fowlkes, F. K. "The Expanding Role of the Personnel Function." *Harvard Business Review* 53, no. 2 (March–April 1975): 71–84. (I)

Guthrie, R. R. "Personnel's Emerging Role." *Personnel Journal* 53, no. 9 (September 1974): 657–664. (I)

Henning, D., and W. French. "The Mythical Personnel Manager." *California Management Review* 3, no. 4 (Summer 1961): 33–45. (I)

Hunt, T. "Critical Issues Facing Personnel Administrators Today." *Public Personnel Management* 3, no. 6 (November–December 1974): 464–472. (I)

Johnson, R. J. "The Personnel Administrator of the 1970's." *Personnel Journal* 50, no. 4 (April 1971): 298–305. (I)

Ling, C. C. *The Management of Personnel Relations: History and Origins.* Homewood, Ill.: Irwin, 1965. (I)

Meyer, H. E. "Personnel Directors Are the New Corporate Heroes." *Fortune* 93, no. 2 (February 1976): 86–88+. (I)

Meyer, H. H. "The Future of Industrial and Organizational Psychology." *American Psychologist* 27 (1972): 608–614. (II)

Miner, J. B., and M. G. Miner. "Careers in Personnel and Industrial Relations," In J. B. Miner and M. G. Miner, *Personnel and Industrial Relations,* 2d. ed. New York: Macmillan, 1973, Chap. 23. (I)

Mitchell, J. M., and R. E. Schroeder. "Future Shock for Personnel Administration." *Public Personnel Management* 3, no. 4 (July–August 1974): 265–69. (I)

Myers, C. A. "New Frontiers for Personnel Management." *Personnel* 41, no. 3 (May–June 1964): 381–384. (I)

Nash, A. N., and J. B. Miner. *Personnel and Labor Relations, An Historical Approach.* New York: Macmillan, 1973. (I)

Patton, T. H. "Personnel Management in the 1970's: The End of Laissez Faire." *Human Resource Management* 12 (Fall 1973): 7–19. (I)

Patton, T. H. "Is Personnel Administration a Profession?" *Personnel Administration* 31, no. 2 (March–April 1968): 4+. (I)

"Personnel—Fast Track to the Top." *Dun's Review* 105, no. 4 (April 1975): 74–77. (I)

Ritzer, G., and H. M. Trice. *An Occupation in Conflict: A Study of the Personnel Manager.* Ithaca, New York: New York State School of Industrial and Labor Relations, Cornell University, 1969. (II-R)

Sloane, A. R. "Creative Personnel Management." *Personnel Journal* 53, no. 9 (September 1974): 662–666. (I)

PART A

Form 1 Letter to Personnel Administrator Candidates

Date_____

Dear_____

We are happy to inform you that you are one of the finalists for the position of Personnel Administrator of Acme Precision Planter Company. The Board of Directors has reviewed the resumes of many well qualified applicants. We have a few questions relative to your education or experience, but our main concern is how well we feel you personally mesh with our personal values and our organization's needs. Accordingly, we invite you to meet with the Board for a final interview.

Some of the things we would like to explore are: (1) your general concept of the role of personnel in an organization of some 600 employees (after expansion); (2) how the personnel function fits into the general function pattern of an organization; (3) generally what the personnel department should do and roughly the priority of activities you would emphasize; (4) how formalizing personnel would affect the presently decentralized personnel authority; (5) examples of how a personnel function could add to the profitability of our firm and provide relief for our operating executives without impairing their control over personnel; (6) your attitudes relative to labor unions, hiring the disadvantaged, including Mexican Americans, relationships with employees, expectations of employees; and (7) your plans for avoiding litigation problems in personnel activities.

We are looking forward to visiting with you for an hour or so on _____ at _____ in the Board Room. If you have any questions about our operations which may facilitate our interview with you, please do not hesitate to give us a call.

Please bring copies of your latest resume with you to give to our Directors.

Sincerely,

Vice President

PART A

Form 2 The Company

The company is a relatively young organization having been founded five years ago by the current president. It is located in a city having an estimated population of 13,500, located some thirty miles due north of a major midwestern city.

The company became a reality when the president invented an exceptionally sophisticated product which could position various seedlings at optimal depths for growth and spacing, thus minimizing the need for expensive tree-thinning operations. The product chassis is of conventional design, hardly distinguishable from those of major producers. But the outstanding competitive advantage of the product is in the precision positioning mechanism. From its initial appearance on the market five years ago, it has had an amazing market performance, only limited by problems of a developing organization and "debugging" of a new invention.

The president invented the product in his machine shop when he became dissatisfied with the performance of standard products. It worked so well on his farm that he interested a local mechanic, the present general manager of the firm, in the development phase. Together with a friend, another mechanic and now the production manager, they improved the product until they were satisfied that it was marketable.

The three incorporated the organization and leased an abandoned, former assembly manufacturing building in a downtown area (see Form 3). They immediately enlarged the board of directors to include the president of the First City Bank, a wealthy local cattle feeder, and the wife of the general manager, a former commercial-science teacher in Beetland High School who also serves as secretary-treasurer-office manager of the Company.

The almost incredible initial market performance of the product indicated a fabulous success for the company. However, as so frequently occurs with a new invention, "debugging" problems occurred to dim early promise. The difficulty arose when a shipment to northern California failed to perform effectively. The succeeding six months resulted in a large expenditure for the services of experts from a nearby university, and subsequent modifications of the product. This financial setback plus the inexperience of the new managers in organizing and operating a fairly complex manufacturing enterprise very nearly resulted in economic disaster.

The president, general manager, and the production manager, recognized their inexperience and agreed to the recruitment of a production manager from a successful Cleveland, Ohio, assembly plant who had relatives in the area and usually visited the area on his vacations. He had become acquainted with the president and the bank president.

The production manager was elected to the board of directors, given stock options, and designated as vice president of the organization. This proved to be a turning point since he moved immediately to smooth out production irregularities and to upgrade the skills of the work force. However, the company still had the persisting problem of lack of financial liquidity.

To further complicate the problem, a certain type of metal alloy which had proved essential in the effective performance of the product's precision mechanism had recently been severly limited by government requisistioning for use in missile and aircraft manufacturing. This cutback in supply of the essential material resulted in a recent layoff within the past month of 100 personnel, leaving the present work force at 250.

The vice president anticipated cutback problems soon after his arrival and began negotiations with the Northwest Aircraft Manufacturing Company for a subcontract to produce a subassembly. Landing-gear subassemblies made by Northwest were similar to that of the present product. Only two special-purpose machines would be required for the new operation and both of these would enhance machining operations and reduce contract-out work on the planter. The eighteen-month contract for $5,000,000 could net as much as $300,000 profits, providing both financial liquidity as well as releasing sufficient supplies of government stores of the metal alloy for use in the present product.

Current product production would be continued on the first shift with its hours moved to a 6:00 A.M. starting time. With a thirty-minute brunch break, the second shift, landing-gear subassemblies, could begin after a thirty-minute conversion period, at 3:00 P.M., using the same assembly lines. This would enable the second shift to terminate by 11:00 P.M., including a half-hour supper break. No formal rest periods were scheduled for either shift. A small third shift of maintenance and housekeeping personnel would begin at 11:00 P.M., overlapping briefly the last thirty minutes of the second shift and the initial hour of the first shift.

In order to man the additional shifts, approximately 400 new personnel would be needed, 100 to bring the planter operation up to full scale production, and 300 for the new landing-gear assembly. Thus the company projected 650 employees. It was planned that upon completion of the government contract, the company will continue planter production on a two-shift basis, retaining the majority of the work force.

This "dream" became a reality when the company was awarded a subcontract for $5,000,000 to be initiated from the first of the ensuing month. The contract has a $2,500 a day penalty provision. The vice president anticipates that the minimum production time required to complete the contract will be sixteen months, giving a maximum of two months to develop a pilot operation and a try-out operation. Hopefully, in six weeks from the first of the coming month, both operations will be in full production.

The vice president has convinced the board of directors that a formalized personnel department is essential for satisfactorily affecting the expansion and the ultimate success of the organization. He has been authorized to hire as soon as possible, with the approval of the board of directors, a personnel administrator to assume the personnel activities presently handled by the secretary-treasurer and to develop a complete program commensurate with the needs of a plant of 650 personnel.

PART A

Form 3 The City

Altitude: 1200 feet   *Population:* (latest census estimates) 13,500

Annual mean temperature: 53° F   *Annual precipitation:* 16 inches

Location: The city is located thirty miles north of a major metropolitan area. The city is connected by four-lane highway with the metropolitan area and is near major universities and colleges.

Industry: The city is located in the center of one of the state's most productive irrigated agricultural areas. Farms are about 80 percent irrigated and 20 percent dry land and grazing. Major crops are sugar beets, corn, wheat, beans, alfalfa, etc. Cattle feeding, dairy farming, and poultry raising are important occupations. Products from industries include beet sugar, livestock feeds, frozen foods, electronic equipment, brass, aluminum and iron and steel castings, irrigation equipment, and sausage.

Educational facilities: Total school enrollment in schools is 4,500. The high school is fully accredited. A new high school under construction will be occupied soon.

Employment: Persons interested in employment should contact the State Office of Employment. Although Beetland is growing rapidly, employers do not offer employment as an inducement for people to move to this area, since there are generally more people seeking employment than there are jobs.

Housing: Generally speaking, rental housing is in short supply—depending on the time of year. Rental housing and apartments can usually be obtained within a few days to a week. Again this depends on the taste of the home seeker. New homes are available in both quantity and variety. A list of local realty firms will be forwarded on request. The local newspaper want-ad section lists both rentals and homes for sale. Subscription rate is $1.50 per month by mail.

Business opportunities: There are always a few businesses for sale in the area, as well as farm property. Please make inquiries of this nature to local real-estate firms. A list of firms is available on request.

Cost of living: No specific information available. Due to the city's close proximity to the metropolitan area, prices here must be competitive with those areas. Recent figures show the city's cost of living to be approximately 5 percent below that of the metropolitan area.

Taxes and mill levies: The overall tax rate per $1,000 of assessed valuation (1974) is 80 mills. Property is assessed at 100 percent of 1941 replacement cost, less depreciation. This would average 30 percent of today's value.

Miscellaneous: The city has council-manager type government. Municipal utilities owned include electricity, water, and sewer. Rates among lowest in area. Natural gas supplied by Public Service Company. The city has two hospitals, a community hospital (80 bed), a community osteopathic hospital (25 bed), and twenty medical doctors. There are thirty-two active churches (list available on request), including most denominations. One daily paper, *The Bugle,* and a radio station KMOO serve the area. Television reception is excellent from five stations. Three city parks provide a variety of facilities for recreation and family use. A Carnegie library with approximately 30,000 volumes and a museum provide plenty of reading and information. An excellent year-round recreation program is co-sponsored by city and schools. A nine-hole municipal golf course is rated "tops" by area golfers. Local citizens and visitors are able to avail themselves of hunting, fishing hiking, camping, and sightseeing only thirty minutes away. Surfaced, all-weather roads lead to resorts and scenic areas.

Additional information: The company has the single largest payroll in the city. A beet-sugar mill on the city outskirts employs 150 people at the height of the season (the fall). The remainder of the year its personnel requirements fluctuate from 15–50. An electronics firm has broken ground on the outskirts of the city with an estimated employment in two years of 2,000. The firm will be in pilot operation within six months, employing by that time approximately 50, predominantly women. The population is 80 percent Anglo-American with about 12 percent Spanish-American, 7 percent Negro, and 2 percent Japanese ethnic minorities. The company has no ethnic minority employees at this time. In fact, the implied hiring policy of the company has been to hire only Anglos. It hires women only in the office. None are hired on the assembly lines or in the plant.

PART B

Form 4 The Board Members

The board of directors consists of the chairman of the board (president of the company), the treasurer (president of the First City Bank), the secretary (the secretary-treasurer of the company), a wealthy cattle feeder-rancher, the vice president, general manager, and production manager of the company. The stock is held among the members of the board, with the president of the company retaining 51 percent.

President. The president has been a successful farmer-rancher all of his adult life. He inherited one section (640 acres) of irrigated agricultural land from his parents and, through his skill and energy, has added four additional sections of agricultural and grazing land to his holdings. As previously indicated, he invented the current product. His interest in mechanics was stimulated during his two years in the nearby state agricultural and mechanical college. He did not finish his education, leaving school on the death of his father to operate the farm, since he was an only child. He is an exceptionally intelligent, alert man in his late fifties. As a manager, he is a good farmer, with little interest in organizational theory, delegation, and the like. His managerial style, if it can be so-called, is exceedingly informal, characterized by general disregard for any formal lines of communication. This has proved distressing to those managerial personnel who require more orderly and formalized structure and exercise of authority. He is happily married, has no children, and enjoys frequent Florida vacations, especially during the winter months. The president is extremely active in all activities of the enterprise. In the president's absence, the vice president is the nominal head of the firm and typically serves as executive vice president.

Vice president. The vice president joined the company three years ago. He is in his late thirties, an engineering graduate of the Case Institute of Technology. Immediately after graduation he was employed in the production-control department of a large manufacturing plant in the Cleveland area. After becoming manager of production control, he resigned to take the position of general manager of a middle-sized Cleveland assembly plant. From this position he was recruited for his present position. He is progressive, personable, technically capable, perceptive, and a student of managerial practices, having a particularly keen interest in the application of the behavioral sciences to management. He is divorced, has no children, and is devoted to the task of developing the company into a major producer. If he is successful, he stands to become quite well-to-do as a result of stock options which were a major attraction, along with the growth potential, for his joining the company.

General manager. The general manager is a former machine-shop operator and the codeveloper with the president of the current product. He is a high-school graduate and the husband of the secretary-treasurer. His knowledge of managerial practices is limited and he tends to be an intuitive manager of some skill. He is not enthusiastic about newer ideas of motivation, but relies basically on the "carrot and the stick" approach. Although tough-minded, he is considered to be a good boss, fair and consistent. Although he has the title of general manager, he tends to operate as a first-line supervisor. His ability to keep the machinery working, to innovate, and to operate efficiently on a shoe string, has earned him the admiration of his colleagues and employees. He tends to be impatient in group meetings and with what he calls "gobbledegook," red tape, and discussions that solve no problems. Next to the president, he and his wife own the largest block of stock in the company.

Secretary-treasurer. The secretary-treasurer, formerly the head of the commercial-science department in Beetland High School, is the wife of the general manager and the mother of two boys, one in junior high and the other in the agricultural and mechanical college nearby. As office manager and financial manager, she is thorough but relatively uninformed concerning more progressive and complex aspects of financial management. Although limited in her understanding of personnel management, she has performed a record-keeping function relative to personnel and is proud of her informational system. She is chairman of the personnel committee of the company, comprised of the operating executives of the board. In addition to managing the office and what centralized personnel activities are considered requisite (mainly record keeping, recruitment, rough screening, induction, and changes in employment status), she handles the wage administration function, including payroll. As secretary to the board, she plays a key role in many major decisions, and realizes it. She is not adverse to "throwing her weight around." Of the board members, she could be expected to be the least cooperative with the new personnel director.

Production manager. The production manager was formerly a mechanic in the machine shop of the general manager and assisted in the development of the planter. He is a skilled mechanic (not a machinist) who dropped out of school in the fifth grade to help support his family on the death of his father. He is without doubt the weakest link in the management team. He does not operate as a manager, but rather as a mechanical troubleshooter, leaving most of the organization and management to the general manager and vice president. He has extremely close relations with the employees, and on several occasions when union organizers appeared to be making headway in the company, he was instrumental in aborting election attempts. He is a slow-thinking, happy-go-lucky, somewhat superficial individual, often overimbibing, even on the job—an individual who has achieved status above his aspiration level. The president is extremely fond of him, having known him since he was "a little tyke." He is in his early fifties, married, and the father of seven children, varying in age from seven through thirty. None of the children has attended an institution of higher learning.

Banker. The banker member of the board is president of the First City Bank and chairman of the financial committee of the board. She is a dignified, somewhat pompous, "self-styled" financial expert. Although she never attended college, she has completed, through self-study, most of the American Institute of Banking courses. An excellent financial advisor for farming and ranching operations, she has little understanding of modern financial operations in manufacturing. Her bank has loaned the company over $100,000 and she was elected to the board more to "ride herd" on the loan than to bring any financial expertise. She is extremely conservative, having been a member of the Daughters of the American Revolution in the early days of that organization's prominence. At seventy, she is a sharp, outspoken little woman.

Rancher. The last member of the board is a rancher—a local millionaire who operates one of the largest cattle-feeding operations in the West. He is an unimpressive-looking gentleman, normally wearing ranch clothing and cowboy boots. He has the third largest block of stock. Although he got his start from inherited land, he became a self-made millionaire by sheer hard work, and is an exponent of the Horatio Alger philosophy and the Protestant Ethic, using the flimsiest of excuses to expound at some length on how America is going to the devil, aided and abetted by the Democrats. He attended the state Agricultural College for one year, quitting in disgust because, as he frequently comments, "I knew more than the professors."

Section 2
Planning for an Effective Human-Resource System

An effective system of human-resource programs requires advance planning and information gathering. The specific decisions made concerning human resources, such as who should receive a promotion or how to improve performance, depend on the coordination of several types of information about the organization, the environment in which it operates, its workers, and its jobs.

Section 2 contains two exercises which describe the major personnel-planning and data-gathering processes. First, planning at the organizational, or macro, level is required in order to ascertain the numbers and types of people required by an organization for various periods into the future. These human-resource forecasts are vital because as future expansion, merger, acquisition, product, or service changes, etc. are anticipated or planned, a statement of the levels and types of human resources available is required in order to help decide whether or not these changes are feasible, given existing human resources and where deficiencies lie. Further, an organizational fact of life is worker succession (i.e., persons leaving

and their positions being taken by others). As the dynamic nature of staffing an organization is considered, plans are required to point to appropriate successors, to their successors, and so on. Human-resource plans and forecasts, examined in Exercise 2, provide the data to facilitate organizational decision making under uncertain environmental conditions and succession.

Planning and data gathering is also required at the individual job, or micro, level. Here jobs must be analyzed in order to decide what worker characteristics, skills, abilities, and knowledge are required and to define successful performance in the job. This job information is then transformed into selection standards, performance standards, and training needs, and forms the foundation for a host of other human-resource programs. Probably no single personnel activity is so fundamental and basic to all others as job analysis. Exercise 3 describes the job-analysis process, how resultant job descriptions are derived from such an analysis, and how job performance is thus identified.

Exercise 2

HUMAN-RESOURCE PLANNING AND FORECASTING

PREVIEW

In order to help assure that the future human-resource needs of organizations are fulfilled with high-quality personnel, considerable planning and analysis may be required. This type of planning is often either initiated or facilitated by the personnel administrator and his or her own staff. To utilize the skills of present human resources most effectively, as well as to plan for future personnel needs in light of the rapidly changing external environments in which many organizations operate, all phases of personnel work must be coordinated and integrated. For example, without an accurate performance-appraisal system an organization would not be able to identify its most promotable workers, those who must assume its top positions in the future. Without an effective training program, necessary skills cannot be added to workers' repertoires to enable them to assume more responsibility. Therefore, human-resource planning is, in a way, an activity that utilizes and depends on the other personnel programs.

It is also, however, an activity on which the other personnel programs depend as well. Once the number and type of workers are known, their selection can be made more effectively. Once the skill levels an organization would require in the future due to product or technology changes are forecasted, training programs can be designed to impart these skills and prepare workers for future demands. Human-resource planning and forecasting is thus very much related to other personnel programs. If done properly, it enables the personnel specialist to achieve a broad, overall view of where his or her organization is headed in terms of human-resource utilization. This overall forecast can then be related to each specific area or personnel program, beginning with job analyses.

This exercise enables you to simulate the human-resource planning process for an organization by assessing its current skills; by developing a forecast of human-resource requirements for up to five years in the future after analyzing the organization's goals and environment; and finally by deciding who, from amongst the organization's current pool of workers, should assume anticipated future openings based on their present performance levels and their potential. The *Introduction* provides an overview of human-resource planning, including its purposes, its importance, and the process of implementing plans.

OBJECTIVES

1. To gain an understanding of the purpose and importance of accurately forecasting future human-resource requirements of organizations.
2. To analyze current personnel skill inventories and to make forecasts of future human-resource needs.
3. To analyze present performance and potential of managers and use this data to decide who should fill future forecasted vacancies.

PREMEETING PREPARATION

Read the entire exercise, paying careful attention to the *Procedure.*

INTRODUCTION

Planning for Future Human-Resource Requirements

Organizations exist in environments that are dynamic to various degrees. These environments contain elements that present uncertainties to organizations because they change—often very rapidly and unpredictably. For example, due to changing societal values and norms, consumers' tastes change, in turn causing certain products' sales to decline and others to rise. Or the earth's supply of resources, such as oil and natural gas, changes, in turn causing shifts in technology and numbers of job openings in specific industries. Organizations can never be totally accurate in predicting what effects various environmental changes will have on them, but to the extent that they can anticipate and plan for changes, they are better able to diminish possible adverse effects and/or turn new circumstances into opportunities.

One of the most crucial areas in which organizations must plan and anticipate changes concerns its human resources. No employee can be counted on forever. Eventually, all personnel change or "turnover," and must be replaced due to promotions, retirements, job changes, expansions, mergers, terminations, etc. In addition to employees leaving organizations to find better or different jobs, external environmental changes like those noted above, as well as planned expansion, contraction, merger, and acquisitions, all contribute to changing human resources in an organization. These changes must be anticipated. Plans to recruit, train, and place new human resources must be made in order to assure the smooth and continued functioning of an organization.

Further uncertainties are presented as the composition of the United States labor force changes. Numbers of workers in service-oriented industries are increasing, as are demands for scientific and engineering personnel, while percentages of blue-collar workers are declining. Women are comprising an ever-larger percentage of the work force, as are younger people, and the average educational levels for workers are certainly increasing.[1] These changes are augmented by changes in job content. Computers and other technological advances have changed how many people do their jobs. Further, migrations of workers—for example, from rural to urban areas—have been observed for some time.

All of these changes are compounded by the belief of some that an upcoming shortage in managerial resources is imminent. John Miner, who has studied the supply of managers and college graduates' inclinations to be managers, stated:

> It seems likely, then, that by the mid-1980's the major constraint on corporate growth will not necessarily be a shortage of monetary or material resources, but rather a shortage of managerial resources—there will not be enough good managers around . . . .[2]

The forecasting of future human-resource needs is beset by uncertainty. However, this very uncertainy now makes human-resource planning as important to the success of an organization as inventory, financial, or product planning have been in the past. Essentially, human-resource-planning efforts have as their goal the estimation and recognition of future human-resource requirements and the development of strategies to insure that these requirements will be met by securing a supply of human resources from outside the organization and by developing the organization's present supply of human resources.

Human-resource plans are most often coordinated and begun at top levels of an organization—for example, the chief executive officer may "groom" a replacement. Typically, many managers have a large say in determining their replacement as they retire or are promoted. However, planning exists at all levels in most larger organizations.

Plans are also made for various time periods. These range from immediate plans, which forecast needs in the next few months, to long-range plans, which involve forecasts ten or more years hence. Obviously, the certainty and accuracy of the plans declines as the time interval increases, but long-range plans are still necessary in order to assure, for example, adequate staffing for tasks involving technology now only in its infancy but which may eventually become commonplace.

The strategies or plans actually developed to meet human-resource requirements are closely related to other personnel programs, as noted above in the *Preview.* Job analyses and descriptions enable planners to zero in on the type of tasks in which openings will arise, performance appraisals allow for accurate identification of potential promotees to fill future vacancies, selection techniques help bring in valuable human resources from sources external to the organi-

---

[1] See various annual issues of the *Manpower Report of the President* (Washington, D.C.: U.S. Government Printing Office).

[2] J. B. Miner, "The Real Crunch in Managerial Manpower," *Harvard Business Review* (November–December 1973): 147.

zation, training and development programs prepare personnel for future assignments, and motivation programs help provide the incentive to workers to add skills and abilities and/or to perform well enough to be included in the lists of replacements for those now at upper levels.

The Sequential Process of Human-Resource Planning. The most important broad tasks required in order to design and implement a human-resource planning system are pictured as a sequential process in Fig. 1. Each of the major steps in the process is discussed briefly below.

Inputs. In order to develop plans and forecasts of future needs, planners must identify and analyze the goals or intentions of organizations. For example: Is expansion or contraction intended? Are new products or services requiring new technologies intended? In addition, various aspects of the external environment must be measured and used to make plans. These might include general economic conditions, societal norms and values, the political and legal climate, or the size and composition of the labor supply. All of these data form the inputs into the planning system and thus are the rationale for the plans and forecasts themselves.

Analysis of current human-resource skills. The second phase of the planning process would be an analysis of what is currently available within the organization in terms of human resources. This process might result in an inventory of skills, potential, age, time in current position, and salary for each employee. Obviously, adequate performance-appraisal systems, discussed in Exercises 4, 5, and 6, would be required to measure current skill levels accurately. Further, Assessment Centers (see Exercise 9) or other similar techniques might be required to evaluate the potential of workers. This data is used to form a baseline or current level of human-resource abilities which would be available for future requirements. Differences between the eventual forecast of numbers, types, and skill levels of future human resources and the levels represented by the current inventory must be either developed from existing personnel, based on their potential, or secured from sources external to the organization.

Forecasts. Armed with the intended goals of the organization, other external environmental inputs, and what is currently available in terms of human resources, planners can begin to synthesize all of this data into forecasted requirements for different time periods. They extrapolate from past environmental trends and intended future goals; estimate the pro-

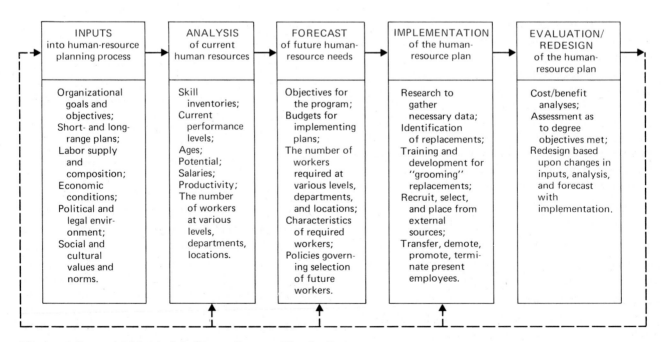

Fig. 1.   A Sequential Model of the Human-Resource Planning Process

gression of employees in terms of skills and movement through levels of the hierarchy; account for retirement, turnover, etc.; and use any other relevant data in order to come up with a forecast of the number and type of human resources required for various future periods, such as one, two, or five years hence.

Planners must then develop budgets that reflect the costs of securing or developing the necessary workers. Costs might include recruiting new personnel, orientation and training programs, and retraining and developing current workers. Policies and guidelines are also necessary in order to advise decision makers regarding such matters as how future replacements will be selected, whether full- or part-time workers will be needed, or how career development should proceed. The specific data needed in order to implement plans must be identified. This might include current performance levels, ages, turnover ratios, or salary levels.

Implementation. Once the forecasts of future needs for various time periods have been made, the plan must be implemented. Implementation of the plan may involve actually conducting research to gather the necessary data on which to base decisions; the recruitment of human resources to fill vacancies; the appraisal of performance to determine strengths, deficiencies, and promotability potential; training and development to prepare employees to meet future needs; and transfers, terminations, promotions, and other placement changes designed to minimize the match between job requirements and workers' abilities.

Implementation of human-resource plans is very difficult and must be closely coordinated with line personnel, as they help supply necessary data and make decisions. The time period of this phase, of course, depends on the time frame for which the plan was intended. For example, a plan designed to meet staffing requirements for a new plant scheduled to begin operations in twelve months must be completed before that time.

Evaluation and redesign. No plans are perfect and no forecasts are completely accurate, simply because they are based on imperfect information about the future. Of the many things that can change during the course of a human-resource planning effort, changes in organizational goals, turnover of key personnel, and changes in economic conditions are but a few.

Therefore, plans must be monitored, evaluated, and redesigned to assure their effectiveness by correcting errors and amending details as changes in

inputs or forecasts occur. Plans should also be carefully evaluated as to their ability to attain their stated objectives. A plan designed to upgrade the skills of twenty military officers and recruit officers to take their places would be evaluated on the basis of whether all the officers were able to successfully perform their new jobs, whether all twenty replacements were found and trained within the desired time period, and, of course, whether this was all done at the least possible cost.

Evaluation and redesign thus involve gathering data about the effectiveness of plans and amending them accordingly. The dotted feedback-loop lines in Fig. 1 represent this notion, as well as the idea that human-resource planning is a continual organizational process rather than a one-time event, as those recurring changes in an organization's goals and environment provide the uncertainties for which plans must be developed.

Other Issues in Human-Resource Planning. This brief introduction has been quite selective. Actually, many other considerations, which can only be noted here, would be important in human-resource planning.[3]

Career development is closely related to human-resource planning and involves the provisions an organization (or an individual) makes in order to upgrade skills, abilities, and knowledge such that the individual can progress through several jobs in an occupation over time. A career orientation is important for the organization, for it helps assure loyalty and a source of experienced personnel. An opportunity for periodic promotion is also a powerful incentive to individuals. Many organizations have adopted a career orientation to certain classes of jobs and design training and development programs which, when coupled with human-resource planning, identify "paths" workers follow throughout their careers.

In order to predict further into the future and to better anticipate the consequences of specific human-resource plans, a technique known as simulation is often employed. A model, representation, or abstraction of some type (e.g., mathematical or schematic) is made of a set of circumstances which describes a forecasted future state of an organization. The model defines the essential characteristics of the situation and the relationship between them. For example, a model of an intended merger might depict the relative number of workers in departments of one organization to those in similar departments of the other organi-

---

[3] Refer to *For Further Reading* for more information on these and other topics.

zation. Then different possible alternative outcomes (e.g., transfers, layoffs, etc.) are set and the model helps predict, often with the aid of a computer, the consequences of the different outcomes.

The actual process of our merger is thus simulated, so that its possible consequences can be observed. If we wanted to determine how many workers might be required in five years in a certain department of the newly merged organization, we could put values in our model for the relationships between key variables. These might include the relative numbers of employees in the relevant departments of each separate organization before the merger, their past rates of growth, their past turnover rates, anticipated technology changes, etc. We could then, through mathematical manipulation or on a computer, arrive at an estimated number of workers. We could also put in other values for our variables and come out with an estimate of the number of workers required in other departments, in the entire merged organization, or at different time periods.

Of course, the accuracy of our estimates depends on the accuracy of the data the model uses and the accuracy of the relationships between the variables. But simulation can allow us to anticipate consequences of various alternatives without actually having to manipulate employees or resources. Simulation can provide planners with important information, provided it is based on accurate data.

The final consideration in this discussion of human-resource planning is its relation to the public-policy goals of eliminating unemployment and of increasing and upgrading the employment situation of minority-group members.

Public policy regarding human-resource planning on a national level has changed considerably over the years. One of the most striking changes is the nature of vocational education in the United States as it has evolved into new uses for developing human resources at all levels in American society. Vocational education (i.e., training people for employment in trades) is no longer confined to the secondary-school level. Programs such as the Model Cities Program, the Special Impact Program, the New Careers Program, Operation Mainstream, the Concentrated Employment Program (CEP), and the Work Incentive Program (WIN) are all aspects of contemporary human-resources development and planning, as well as poverty fighting, which illustrate the federal government's and other organizations' concern with these issues.

The federal government has realized that it cannot single-handedly solve all of the complicated social problems involved in human-resource planning and development, and has increasingly asked industry to intervene. Industry, in turn, has shown willingness to participate widely in administering Job Corps centers, in accepting on-the-job trainees under the Manpower Training and Development Act (MDTA), and in making proposals for the expansion of vocational curricula in junior colleges and in high schools where funds from the Vocational Education Act of 1963 and 1968 amendments are being expended.

There is little doubt that the human-resources "revolution" of the 1960s (i.e., all of the legislation enacted during that decade) will continue to influence education, employment, and planning. The emphasis on federal government programs in education and human resources continues to influence school administrators at state and local levels to use human-resource planners in their organizations in order to reassess their own human-resource plans in light of federal programs and objectives.

While there is still very much work to be done in coordinating and formulating federal programs, school programs, and organization programs into a cohesive human-resources plan incorporating the goals of individuals, organizations, and the government, some progress has been made. However, the uncertainty and change which surround the planning process will no doubt become more prevalent in the future, thus making human-resource planning not only more important but also more difficult. This area presents one of the greatest challenges to those beginning personnel careers in the near future.

PROCEDURE

Overview. You are to determine the managerial resource needs of the organization described in the exercise and develop a plan as to how these needs will be met. Skill inventories and projected human requirements and needs are provided to help you develop a human-resource forecast.

PART A

STEP 1: Several forms are necessary in order to complete Step 1. Form 1 provides information about Happyday Corporation, the company for which your human-resource plan is to be written. Form 2 provides current employment estimates, an estimated annual average of job openings, and an estimate of whether the openings can be filled with qualified applicants for the next ten years relative to certain job statistics for the southern United States. Form 3 is an example of the file kept on each Happyday manager, which provides data for the skill inventory the personnel department maintains. A summary of the vital data contained in each of the manager's skill inventory data sheets is found on Form 4, the personnel department's skill inventory for the entire group of ninety-six managers in Happyday Corporation.

Using Forms 1–4, answer all of the questions on Form 5. Then, based solely on current performance, *not* on potential (i.e., do not use the column entitled "Potential Level Rating" of Form 4), decide how many people will be required to fill positions in any one of the departments of Happyday (except manufacturing) for each of the periods listed on Form 5. Also decide how many people are available now to fill these vacancies and who should fill them (i.e., fill in names of actual workers from Form 4). If any positions cannot be filled from internal organizational sources, indicate where the use of sources external to the organization are necessary. Form 5 should reflect the new department at each of the three time periods. That is, all of the people in the department and their organizational levels should be listed. For example, if you feel that the accounting department would have twenty managers in the short-range period (i.e., six months to two years), then names of twenty people, and/or "X's" representing external requirements, must be placed on Form 5. Remember that some promotions are likely over the three time periods indicated on Form 5. Therefore, a manager listed as level 5 in your immediate plan may move up to level 4 by the time his or her name appears on your long-run plan.

TIME: About 50 minutes.

PART B

STEP 2: Form 6 contains the skill inventory of managerial *potential* kept for each of Happyday's ninety-six managers. Using this data, the skill-potential scores given for each manager on Form 4, and the rest of the data on Form 4, complete Part II of Form 5 again (reproduced now as Form 7). This time, however, complete the Human Resource Forecast for each of the three periods and the department

you chose earlier by using current performance *and potential* to make your forecasts as to the names of those who should fill vacant slots and their intended organizational level. How do you account for any differences between forecasts based only on current performance levels and those based on performance *and* potential?

TIME: About 50 minutes.

PART C

STEP 3: In this part, you are required to make a "Managerial Progress Forecast" for the manufacturing department of Happyday. This forecast indicates all of the potential replacements (and their ages) for each current employee, or job incumbent; lists the replacements in order of their readiness to assume the incumbent's position; and indicates how many years before they will be ready to assume the incumbent's position. Here you are required to indicate specifically *who* could assume each job in place of the current job holder; thus you are concerned with the level of each person in the hierarchy. Only prepare the forecast for Levels 1–6. Remember that Happyday has a policy of promoting from within. Therefore, use people from within the current group of ninety-six managers to develop your list of possible replacements. You need not identify replacements solely from within the manufacturing department, of course. Form 8 is a sample of a Managerial Progression Forecast to use as a model in completing yours (use Form 9). Notice how, in some cases, the replacements are from the next lowest managerial level and sometimes they are not. The information required (e.g., current incumbents' names, ages, departments, managerial level, and possible replacements' ages, performance ratings, etc.) are given on Form 4. Begin by filling in the names for each managerial level in the manufacturing department. Then search for replacements (typically at lower levels) inside and outside of the manufacturing department. Note ages and performance and potential levels as you make your selections.

TIME: About 1 hour.

FOR FURTHER READING*

Alfred, T. M. "Checkers or Choice in Manpower Management." *Harvard Business Review* 45 (1967): 157–169. (I)

Bright, W. E. "How One Company Manages Its Human Resources." *Harvard Business Review* 54 (January–February 1976): 81–93. (I)

Brummet, R. L., W. C. Pyle, and E. G. Flamholtz. "Human Resource Accounting in Industry." *Personnel Administration* 32 (July–August 1969): 34–46. (I)

Burak, E. H. *Manpower Planning and Programming.* Morristown, New York: General Teaming Press, 1971. (II)

Burak, E. H., and J. W. Walker, eds. *Manpower Planning and Programming.* Boston: Allyn and Bacon, 1972. (II)

Burak, E. H., and T. J. McNichols. *Human Resource Planning.* Kent, Ohio: Kent State University, Comparative Administration Research Institute, 1973. (II)

Clough, D. J. et al., eds. *Manpower Planning Models.* New York: Crane Russak, 1974. (II)

Coleman, B. "An Integrated System for Manpower Planning." *Business Horizons* 13 (October 1970): 89–95. (I)

Crites, J. O. *Vocational Psychology.* New York: McGraw-Hill, 1969. (II)

Davies, G. K. "Needed: A National Job Matching Network." *Harvard Business Review* 47 (1969): 63–72. (I)

Deckard, N. S., and K. W. Lessey. "A Model for Understanding Management Manpower: Forecasting and Planning." *Personnel Journal* 54 (1975): 169–173+. (I)

Dill, W. R., D. P. Gavar, and W. C. Weber. "Models and Modeling for Manpower Planning." *Management Science* 13 (1966): B142–B167. (II)

Drandell, M. "A Composite Forecasting Methodology for Manpower Planning Using Objective and Subjective Criteria." *Academy of Management Journal* 18 (1975): 510–519. (II–R)

Dukes, C. W. "EDP Personnel File Searching: A Variable Parameter Approach." *Personnel* 44 (July–August 1972): 20–26. (I)

Glickman, A. S. et al. *Top Management Development and Succession.* Supplementary paper #27, Committee for Economic Development, November 1968. (II)

Holland, J. L. "Vocational Preferences." In M. D. Dunnette, ed., *Handbook of Industrial/Organizational Psychology.* Chicago: Rand McNally, 1976. (II)

Kelley, S. C. et al. *Manpower Forecasting in the United States: An Evaluation of the State of the Art.* Columbus: Ohio State University Center for Human Resource Research, 1975. (II)

Lenninger, R. A. "Personnel Management and the Computer." *Personnel Administrator* 20, no. 1 (January 1975): 54–55. (I)

Lester, R. A. *Manpower Planning in a Free Society.* Princeton, N.J: Princeton University Press, 1966. (I)

Levitan, S. A., and J. K. Zickler. *The Quest for a Federal Manpower Partnership.* Cambridge, Mass.: Harvard University Press, 1974. (I)

Livingston, J. Sterling. "The Myth of the Well-Educated Manager." *Harvard Business Review,* January–February 1971. (I)

Mace, Myles L. *The Growth and Development of Executives.* Boston: Graduate School of Business Administration, Harvard University, 1950. (I)

Mahoney, T. A., and G. T. Milkovich. "Computer Simulation: A Training Tool for Manpower Managers." *Personnel Journal* 54 (December 1975): 609–612+. (II)

Mangum, G. *The Emergence of Manpower Policy.* New York: Holt, 1969. (I)

Manpower Report of the President. Washington, D.C.: U.S. Government Printing Office (annually). (II)

Martin, R. "Skills Inventories." *Personnel Journal* 48 (1967): 28–30. (I)

Miner, J. B. *Studies in Management Education.* New York: Springer, 1965. (I)

Miner, J. B. *The Human Constraint: The Coming Shortage of Managerial Talent.* Washington, D.C.: Bureau of National Affairs, 1974. (I)

Patten, T. J., Jr. *Manpower Planning and the Development of Human Resources.* New York: Wiley, 1972. (II)

Pinto, P. R. et al. *Career Planning and Career Management: Perspectives of the Individual and the Organization. An Annotated Research Bibliography.* Minneapolis, Minn.: Industrial Relations Center Bulletin No. 62. University of Minnesota, 1975. (I)

"Plotting a Route to the Top." *Business Week,* Personal Business Supplement, 12 October 1974.

Singleton, W. T., and P. Spurgeon, eds. *Measurement of Human Resources.* New York: Halsted, 1975. (I)

---

* See also references listed in Exercise 12 pertaining to career planning and development.

Snyder, R. J., and G. Herman. *Manpower Planning: A Research Bibliography*. Minneapolis, Minn.: Industrial Relations Center, Bulletin No. 45, University of Minnesota, 1967. (I)

Staszak, F. J., and N. J. Mathys. "Organization Gap: Implications for Manpower Planning." *California Management Review* 17 (Spring 1975): 32–38. (I)

Steiner, G. A. *Top Management Planning*. New York: Macmillan, 1969. (I)

Vetter, E. W. *Manpower Planning for High Talent Personnel*. Ann Arbor, Mich.: University of Michigan, Bureau of Industrial Relations, 1967. (II)

Walker, J. W. "Forecasting Manpower Needs." *Harvard Business Review* 47 (1969): 152–164. (I)

Walker, J. W. "Problems in Managing Manpower Change." *Business Horizons* 13 (1970): 63–68. (I)

Wickstrom, W. S. *Manpower Planning: Evolving Systems*. New York: Conference Board, 1971. (I)

Wortman, M. "Manpower: The Management of Human Resources. *Academy of Management Journal* 13 (1970): 198–208. (I)

Yoder, D. "Manpower Management Planning." In D. Yoder, *Personnel Management and Industrial Relations*. 6th ed. Englewood Cliffs, N.J.: Prentice-Hall, 1970, Chapter 8. (I)

Zaleznick, A. et al., eds. *Orientation and Conflict in Career*. Cambridge, Mass.: Harvard Business School, 1970. (II–R)

PART A

Form 1 Descriptive Information for the Happyday Corporation

Happyday, located in a large southern city, is a small to medium-sized manufacturer of consumer goods relating to sports and recreation activities. It is a family-controlled organization begun about twenty-five years ago. In the late 1970s, Happyday was considering a major expansion of facilities and product lines to tap the rapidly growing and diversified recreational market.

The five-year outlook for obtaining and developing key managerial personnel was not especially bright in the light of technological changes and corporate expansion plans which would require much technical expertise and innovative ability. Basically, the production techniques, the products, and the consumers themselves had grown very sophisticated in the last decade and in order to maintain a competitive advantage in an industry dominated by huge companies, Happyday had to be extremely creative and current regarding the technology required to produce its products. The plan for modernizing and expanding existing facilities indicated substantial redefinition of job roles, requiring innovative human-resource planning and organization design. It was predicted that future business needs would create demands for new specializations (particularly those in engineering).

Currently, Happyday has ninety-six persons in managerial positions. The managers are divided among departments as follows:

Manufacturing	35
Accounting	16
Finance	6
Marketing	13
Engineering	21
Personnel	5
	96

However, because Happyday still plans to greatly increase its productive capacity, based on continued optimistic demand data for recreation and leisure products, they will need to add human resources in some areas and perhaps decrease them in other areas within the next five years in order to facilitate the expansion.

Specifically, Happyday is planning to begin increasing productive capacity within the next few months. Initially, contractors, architects, etc., will be needed as management has already decided the expansion is wise. Market research, new-product development, financial planning, and production planning and scheduling have each conducted independent analyses and have all agreed that expansion is feasible, desirable, and necessary at this time. Only personnel has not yet given its plan for future human-resource requirements and the feasibility of obtaining them.

Areas of planned expansion

The planned expansion includes additions to the engineering department for new product development and prototypes, to manufacturing for new work processes and scheduling, and to marketing for added sales capability and advertising. Of course, since new products will be designed, manufactured, and (hopefully) sold, these areas must grow. However, support areas would seem to grow also to serve the needs of the larger manufacturing organization.

Within the next three years, productive capacity is projected to increase by 20 percent and to increase another 25 percent within the next five to six years. Physical facilities are already being finished to house manufacturing and administration expansion. The executive committee's estimate of sales five years from now, allowing for inflation, is $58,700,000.

Happyday has had a policy of promoting qualified personnel from within the organization before seeking outside candidates. This policy further implies consideration of the best-qualified people from all departments within the company rather than simply promoting only from within that department in which an opening occurs. This, according to the top management, fosters morale and better assures that the company promotes the best person from among all of its employees. It also affords the varied experience deemed necessary for top positions.

Typically, the personnel department provides assistance in locating qualified candidates and takes pride in its "Skill Inventory" (see Forms 3 and 4) of all personnel, an extremely current, and therefore valuable, selection and planning aid. A standard procedure in the past has been to consider at least two candidates from outside a department, as well as one or more from within, before a selection decision is made to fill a position. If no adequate applicants are found in this search, the organization turns to external labor sources, but stays within the southern United States for such recruiting efforts and usually enlists the aid of an executive search organization. The mandatory retirement age at Happyday is 65.

Each departmental vice president thus has the responsibility for seeking opportunities for promotion of qualified personnel, both in and out of his or her own department. While Happyday has always been concerned with human-resource planning and development, it has never before actually formulated an explicit human-resource plan for a future five-year period. However, due to the importance and size of the planned expansion (including physical facilities, product lines, marketing capability, and technological advances), a formal plan of human-resource needs seems vital.

The financial picture of Happyday has been consistently bright and improving. The organization, witnessed by the historical balance-sheet data (see Exhibit A), has a sound capital structure and relatively small debt obligations. Sales volume and net income have also increased in eight of the last ten years.

Exhibit A: Historical Abbreviated Financial Data for Happyday Company (in thousands of dollars)

Assets	Two years ago	Last year	This year
Cash	49	48	53
Marketable securities	150	165	170
Receivables, net	199	205	208
Inventories	300	310	324
Net Plant and equipment	1300	1280	1273
Total assets	2000	2008	2028

Claims on Assets			
Accounts payable	60	59	63
Notes payable	100	97	106
Accruals	9	9	9
Federal income taxes accrued	131	135	140
Mortgage bonds	500	495	500
Stock	600	620	632
Retained earnings	600	593	578
Total claims on assets	1998	2008	2028

	Two years ago	Last year	This year
Net sales volume	30,000	32,500	36,000
Net income (after taxes)	921	1235	1386

Additional vital information on Happyday concerns its specific departments. These are reasonably autonomous units and their director or vice president typically has considerable authority for the departments' activities. However, due to Happyday's policy of attempting to fill a vacancy in any department with members of other departments before it resorts to external selection, the best people of various departments sometimes get "picked off" by others, thus leaving some with weak personnel at the top. Additional information about each department follows.

Manufacturing. The largest and most powerful department, it contains the two top (i.e., level one) members of the organization. They are brothers. Directors or vice presidents are no higher than second-level officers, subordinates to the two persons at the top of the manufacturing department. The department lacks direction, as its senior people must take charge of the entire operation and their reluctance to delegate any authority in manufacturing is the reason for their failure to promote anyone to challenge their authority in the manufacturing department. Equipment is modern, but expertise in production planning and control is shallow. Ties to engineering are weak.

Accounting. Accounting is not a large group, but is very professional. It boasts graduates from very prestigious business schools and people from the "Big Eight" public accounting firms. The goals of the department are to educate managers in accounting practices and set up Happyday as an example in the industry of an organization that is able to implement the latest accounting conventions and rules correctly and efficiently.

Finance. This department is quite small, perhaps due to the family-owned nature of the company. One member of the department is a member of the family of the founders and owners of Happyday. The remainder of the department consists of managers with little power.

Marketing. This department is very viable and visible. It has a pool of creative people who have developed a very effective sales network. Their goals are to expand and begin to develop in-house advertising capability.

Engineering. The engineering department is large, but contains many people who direct the maintenance system for machinery and other tangible assets. Liaison with the manufacturing department is poor, and this hinders morale in engineering. The best people hope for transfers to manufacturing where things actually happen. Engineering contains a small research and development (R-and-D) group who are given excellent physical resources and who are quite visible. However, their work is seldom advanced through manufacturing where the ideas for new products always seem to originate. R-and-D has been called a public-relations gimmick by some. The director of engineering was recently hired to develop the department into a viable force, particularly R-and-D, but is having problems retaining people. Turnover is a huge problem.

Personnel. Personnel is the smallest department as far as number of managers, but has several clerks because of its record-keeping functions. Personnel is involved in an affirmative-action program, in union negotiations, and in contract administration almost exclusively. Selection and training are primarily decentralized (i.e., left to line managers). Performance appraisal and career development are the department's strong points. The assessment-center method for spotting future managers is used very heavily.

PART A

Form 2 Current and Projected Employment Data for Selected Job Classes in the Southern United States*

Job class	Latest employment estimate	Predicted annual average job openings for next decade
ADMINISTRATION		
Accountants[†]	143,000	8,380
City managers	500	30
Credit officers	22,800	1,500
Personnel workers	48,000	4,160
Public relations workers	17,400	3,480
Total	231,700	17,550
COUNSELING		
Employment counselors[†]	1,700	160
Rehabilitation counselors[†]	3,200	340
School counselors	8,600	580
Total	13,500	1,080
OTHER SELECTED PROFESSIONS		
Architects	7,400	660
Commercial artists	8,000	600
Industrial designers	2,000	800
Landscape architects	2,500	200
Lawyers	61,000	4,000
Photographers	12,000	700
Programmers[†]	37,200	2,600
Systems analysts[†]	20,100	2,000
Total	150,200	11,560
MANAGERS		
Bank officers	45,000	4,000
Administrative officers	26,600	3,750
Office managers[†]	33,000	6,500
Supervisors (first level)	200,000	20,500
Total	304,600	34,750
ENGINEERS		
Aerospace[†]	12,400	340
Agricultural[†]	2,400	100
Ceramic	2,000	100
Chemical	9,400	300
Civil	35,400	1,700
Electrical	46,200	2,200
Industrial[†]	25,000	1,480
Mechanical	41,800	1,780
Metallurgical	2,000	100
Mining[†]	800	20
Total	177,400	8,120
PHYSICAL SCIENCES		
Chemists	26,800	1,360
Food scientists[†]	1,250	60
Physicists	9,800	300
Total	37,850	1,720

Job class	Latest employment estimate	Predicted annual average job openings for next decade
TECHNICIANS		
Computer servicepersons[†]	9,000	820
Draftspersons[†]	65,400	3,580
Engineering/science workers[†]	141,400	7,320
Total	215,800	11,720
SALES		
Manufacturers' salespersons[†]	106,700	5,000
Retail trade salespersons	576,000	43,000
Wholesale trade salespersons	125,600	6,200
Total	808,300	54,200

* Illustrative data.
† Jobs for which estimated number of qualified applicants will be smaller than number of openings.

PART A

Form 3 Sample Skill-Inventory Data Sheet Kept for Each Happyday Manager

Name _____ Employee No. _____ Age _____ Current position _____

Began current position _____ Evaluated by _____ Title _____ Date _____

I. **SKILLS:**   Estimate current skill levels by checking the appropriate boxes below.

   A. **Personal Independence:**   Rate the amount of supervisory time required by individual. Consider time and assistance required in areas of problem solving, decision making, flexibility, creativity, initiative, follow-through.
      [   ] 1. Seeks a great deal of supervisor's time.
      [   ] 2. Occasionally requires attention beyond nature of assignments.
      [   ] 3. Follows directions and instructions easily. Requires only routine checks on performance.
      [   ] 4. Performs most tasks independently and requires help only in difficult situations.
      [   ] 5. Can operate without direct supervision and can be left to complete assignments independently.

   B. **Interpersonal Skills:**   Evaluate individual's ability to work constructively with others without causing hard feelings. Measure tactfulness and human relation skills.
      [   ] 1. Relations with co-workers and business associates is often poor.
      [   ] 2. Gains moderate acceptance over time, but is not particularly active.
      [   ] 3. Generally achieves good acceptance from co-workers and business associates.
      [   ] 4. Actively establishes good interpersonal relations with associates.
      [   ] 5. Is extremely successful at gaining quick and lasting acceptance from others.

   C. **Oral and Written Communications:**   Evaluate this individual's ability to express thoughts and ideas and have them understood by others.
      [   ] 1. Fails to communicate with satisfactory clarity and organization.
      [   ] 2. Occasional lack of clarity and conciseness in communications.
      [   ] 3. Quite acceptable communication skills in the tasks associated with current assignment.
      [   ] 4. Noticeably well organized in communication of thoughts, reports, and comments.
      [   ] 5. Outstanding communicating skills, extremely well-organized reports and messages that are clear, concise, and timely.

   D. **Priorities:**   Does this individual recognize the most important demands of assignment, and plan and organize to meet these demands?
      [   ] 1. Shows little or no recognition of priorities in accomplishing work.
      [   ] 2. Shows a fair understanding of priority needs, is not consistent in actually meeting them.
      [   ] 3. Generally meets priority needs of regular assignments.
      [   ] 4. Consistently meets priority needs of regular assignments. Usually adjusts to changing demands as they occur.
      [   ] 5. Consistently meets priority needs of regular job. Anticipates changing demands and adjusts appropriately.

   E. **Thoroughness:**   Indicate thoroughness with which individual performs work assignments. Are all relevant factors considered?
      [   ] 1. Overlooks important details.
      [   ] 2. Covers most important factors but slights some of the less-obvious or critical ones.
      [   ] 3. Is usually thorough and recognizes most of the relevant factors.
      [   ] 4. Is thorough in carrying out assignments. Rarely misses any factors that affect assignments.
      [   ] 5. Completely covers all aspects of work assignments and overlooks no possibilities.

   F. **Leadership:**   Evaluate ability or potential to obtain results through others. Consider willingness to lead and acceptance by others.
      [   ] 1. Does not have desire to lead, or is not accepted as a leader.
      [   ] 2. Occasionally evidences leadership ability, receives some acceptance.
      [   ] 3. Generally assumes a leadership role, and is accepted as a leader.
      [   ] 4. Evident leader when in a group; very well accepted.
      [   ] 5. Outstanding leadership skills; demands and receives everyone's attention and respect.

Skill Summary: total of the six categories _____

II. **PERFORMANCE:**   This judgment should be based on how well individual met objectives, or position requirements.

[   ] 1. *Marginal or unsatisfactory.* Below standard, corrective action needed.
[   ] 2. *Adequate.* Below average, and below normally expected standards for position.
[   ] 3. *Competent.* Performance is average and meets all position requirements.
[   ] 4. *Superior.* Above average, performance is consistently above requirements.
[   ] 5. *Outstanding.* Clearly recognized and exceptional performance, much more than position requires.

Comments _____

_____

_____

_____

_____

PART A

Form 4 Summary of Skills Inventory of Managerial Skills, Performance, and Potential in Happyday Corporation

Top is level 1

Name of employee	Depart- ment	Current per- form- ance level (1 to 5; 5 is highest)	Age	Present manage- ment level (1–7) in heirarchy (1 is highest)	Current mana- gerial skill level (6–30; see Form 3)	Educa- tion (highest degree)	Assess- ment center report (rank in one of four groups of 24 each)*	Poten- tial level rating (1–10; see Form 6)	Current salary ($/yr.)	Time in present job (mos.)	Minority status (minor- ity = M)	Sex (M–F)
	(1)	(2)	(3)	(4)	(5)	(6)	(7)	(8)	(9)	(10)	(11)	(12)
Walter C. Adams	MFG	3	61	3	6	BS	10	3	46700	62		M
Stanley F. Allen	ACC	2	38	4	10	BS	17	2	37700	43		M
Valentine Allen	MKT	4	39	5	22	BA	7	6	27000	23	M	F
Allen Anderson	PER	5	33	6	28	MBA	1	10	23000	9		M
C. Beryl Anderson	ENG	3	51	2	17	BS	15	4	26500	14		M
Lucas Anthony	ACC	2	45	6	9	MS/CPA	19	3	24000	28	M	M
Roy Arneson	MFG	4	53	6	24	BS	21	4	24700	100		M
Elino Baus	MFG	4	46	7	23	HS	19	6	20500	144		M
Lester Belcheff	PER	4	50	3	21	MBA	9	6	43300	8		M
Bernard T. Benson	FIN	3	50	5	18	BS	24	3	34700	82		M
William Bickle	MFG	3	47	7	16	HS	23	3	23000	102		M
R. Ludvig Biros	MKT	2	43	7	8	BS	16	4	18000	1		M
Howard Bloom	MFG	4	40	5	26	HS	11	6	33200	72		M
Marilyn Sass Burberton	ENG	5	37	6	29	PhD	5	7	23500	3	M	F
Dayton Caroon	ENG	5	31	7	30	MBA	1	10	14000	2	M	M
Carl K. Cayou	ENG	5	33	4	27	MS	3	10	37000	8		M
James Chapmen	ENG	5	38	7	26	BS	4	9	18100	11		M
E. Michel Conway	ACC	3	43	7	19	BS	13	6	20600	133		M
U. W. Craig	ENG	2	34	7	10	BS	N/A	4	11400	24		M
Herman Enslow	MFG	4	29	6	25	BS	22	2	23500	63		M
Helen C. Eytcheson	PER	3	31	6	14	MBA	23	2	24700	82	M	F
William Fehlman	ENG	4	53	5	23	BS	11	7	38700	89		M
T. R. H. Foster	MFG	4	59	6	21	HS	14	6	23400	136	M	M
Marvin A. Fredericks	ENG	4	45	7	26	BS	9	8	19900	69		M
Julian Galpin	MKT	5	33	7	28	MBA	6	9	13800	44		M
Pamela Jil Gamble	ENG	4	54	3	23	MBA	2	10	43400	21	M	F
Diane Kay Bensky	MFG	4	34	7	23	BA	24	2	14000	71	M	F
Walter C. Goodwin	ACC	5	58	7	28	HS	6	7	25700	150		M
Warren L. Griggs	MFG	5	63	7	29	HS	3	10	18000	8		M
Curtis Hack	ACC	5	42	6	30	HS	1	10	24600	20		M
Wilbur Hall	FIN	4	36	4	21	BS	15	4	38000	91		M
Ralph Hanson	MFG	4	27	7	21	MBA	7	7	15700	11		M
Harvey H. Hanson	ENG	3	23	7	16	BS	16	5	12500	9		M
Charles R. Harry	MFG	3	56	6	13	BS	20	3	27500	183		M
Perry Henrich	ACC	3	36	7	12	BS	17	4	16600	28		M
William Hernandez	FIN	2	48	3	7	BS	9	7	37500	14	M	M
Carl Hesselgrave	ENG	4	48	4	22	MS	13	6	35000	43		M
Gabriel Hill	MKT	5	51	5	29	BS	10	7	33400	106	M	M
Boyd Hill	MFG	5	61	6	29	HS	5	9	26500	49		M
Don I. Ingle	MKT	4	52	3	25	HS	5	10	39700	34		M
Arthur B. Jackson	MFG	3	39	7	19	MBA	14	6	15700	8		M
Harry Jackson	MFG	2	33	7	12	BS	15	4	13000	2		M
Dena B. Johnson	MFG	5	23	7	29	MBA	12	5	16000	3	M	F
Michael Kennelly	ACC	5	36	4	28	MBA	4	9	39400	83		M
Roy Kiefel	MFG	5	53	7	30	BS	11	6	19500	53		M
Pando Kiiski	FIN	4	43	5	22	MS	8	7	31500	26		M
Nancy Kimble	MFG	3	32	7	18	BS	18	8	18500	120	M	F
Oscar Kirchoffner	ACC	4	34	7	18	BS/CPA	7	7	16000	8		M
O. W. Knapp	MFG	5	55	5	27	BS	11	8	33400	123		M
Harlon Knoll	ENG	5	35	6	29	PhD	2	10	27600	3		M
Dan Kron	MKT	4	26	7	27	MBA	13	3	15900	14		M
Conrad W. Laboy	MFG	3	38	7	18	HS	19	5	14700	37		M

Name of employee	Depart-ment (1)	Current per-form-ance level (1 to 5; 5 is highest) (2)	Age (3)	Present manage-ment level (1–7) in heirarchy (1 is highest) (4)	Current mana-gerial skill level (6–30; see Form 3) (5)	Educa-tion (highest degree) (6)	Assess-ment center report (rank in one of four groups of 24 each)* (7)	Poten-tial level rating (1–10; see Form 6) (8)	Current salary ($/yr.) (9)	Time in present job (mos.) (10)	Minority status (minor-ity = M) (11)	Sex (M–F) (12)
J. E. Larson	ACC	3	59	6	17	BS	17	4	25700	82		M
Harold S. Larson	ACC	3	48	7	20	BS	20	3	16000	18		M
L. C. Lennon	MFG	4	60	1	27	MS	2	N/A	97500	180		M
Alec Leusick	MFG	5	48	7	28	BS	5	9	15000	18		M
J. E. McConnell	MFG	5	61	1	28	HS	3	10	97000	173		M
Jeffrey Neal Marks	ACC	1	42	3	9	MBA/CPA	21	4	44800	92		M
George R. Merrill	ENG	2	46	6	11	BS	22	3	19700	43		M
Louis Miller	MKT	5	64	4	27	BA	6	7	37000	14	M	M
Lloyd W. Miller	ENG	4	29	7	22	BS	12	5	16500	12		M
Avald R. Murray	ENG	4	40	7	28	BS	9	5	17400	3		M
Roy L. Muta	MFG	3	38	7	22	BS	19	3	17500	3		M
Robert N. Nilsen	ACC	4	61	5	26	HS	13	5	35700	81		M
Wendy Sue Nuntley	MFG	1	37	6	9	BA	22	3	24700	21		F
Paul Olson	MKT	5	34	7	29	BA	4	8	18400	36		M
Bernard A. Ortiz	MFG	5	58	5	28	MBA	7	8	36700	3	M	M
Edward F. Pederson	ACC	3	52	6	20	MBA/CPA	17	4	28500	68		M
Leo J. Petrykows	MFG	2	51	7	12	BS	20	2	16700	4		M
Natalie (Nikki) Potter	MKT	3	56	5	19	MS	16	3	29700	12		F
Albert Ranallo	PER	1	58	7	9	MBA	21	2	26000	91	M	M
H. C. Reeves	MFG	3	41	7	13	HS	24	2	18700	2		M
Thaddeus Reitan	ENG	4	53	4	26	BS	14	5	21600	48		M
Henry Ringler	MFG	2	37	7	17	BA	20	6	19600	18		M
Pedro Robison	ACC	3	33	7	21	MBA	N/A	7	17000	6	M	M
Maurice Rydberg	FIN	3	55	5	20	BA	22	3	35000	106		M
Clarence Schmidt	MFG	3	49	7	19	HS	18	2	18700	36		M
Bert S. Schneider	ENG	3	45	6	16	HS	23	2	27700	93		M
Lester Schoeben	MKT	4	40	4	23	BS	10	5	33400	9		M
Frank R. Shanks	ACC	5	43	2	28	BA	2	10	54700	61		M
C. W. E. Simpson	MFG	5	26	7	29	MBA	8	3	17000	19		M
R. Edmund Smith	MKT	5	42	7	27	BA	10	5	18400	31		M
James Sorenson	MFG	5	41	6	27	MBA	4	9	26700	3		M
William Spiker	MFG	4	36	7	21	MBA	18	3	11300	3		M
Donald D. Steinmetz	ENG	5	38	4	29	MBA	1	10	37700	50		M
Stephen Paul Streeter	MKT	4	44	7	28	MBA	10	5	21500	62		M
J. C. Swartout	MKT	5	61	2	26	MS	3	9	63700	6		M
Harmon E. Tower	MFG	5	29	7	25	BS	8	6	19800	4		M
N. F. Traudt	ENG	3	34	6	17	BS	18	2	21900	91		M
Theodore W. Traudt	PER	5	48	5	29	BS	8	7	28700	3		M
Harry C. Ulrey	MFG	3	63	7	18	BA	16	4	20000	13		M
G. J. Upton	ENG	3	47	3	20	BS	14	4	41700	3		M
Sarah K. Vest	MFG	4	47	6	21	BS	12	3	23400	11	M	F
Herbert Walden	FIN	5	46	2	30	MBA	6	8	50700	18		M
Lance W. Weintraub	ACC	4	52	5	24	MBA	15	4	32700	46		M
Edward B. Young	ENG	3	50	4	13	BS	12	4	39400	21		M

* Ties were possible. N/A = not available. An assessment center is an intensive one-, two-, or three-day program whereby managers are evaluated with several types of techniques in order to arrive at an overall performance level (see also Exercise 9). A rank of 1 is the highest possible.

Name _Gary L. Shores_ _____   Group Number _____

Date _11 April 1981_ _____   Class Section _____   Hour _____   Score _____

PART A

Form 5 Supporting Comments and Assumptions for Human-Resource Forecast of Happyday Corporation

Answer these questions based on the next five-year period.

1. **What basic changes do you see for Happyday?**

① In view of the proposed expansion and subsequent increase in production utilizing the most modern technology, I foresee possible organization design changes in the managerial structure, and a need for new specialization positions. There will be a need for increased recruitment outside the firm, and the manufacturing and engineering departments will need re-structuring to improve liaison between the two, provide new direction, and to correct a turnover problem plaguing R & D. Advancement from within will continue, but should not lead to any department being left weak at the top.

2. **What major assumptions have you made in developing your changes?**

We assumed that production will increase as planned, that the expansion will be successful and result in the anticipated increase in sales. Also, that there will be an adequate work force both quantitatively and qualitatively to fill the new specific skill positions, as well as those required to run and manage the various departments within the company.

3. **What specific human-resource skills are likely to be in more demand? Why?**

Engineering skills relating to the current technology in the means of production.
Key managerial personnel who will possess the necessary abilities and expertise to manage a highly technical and expanding operation.
All departments will be affected by the changes. Manufacturing, Engineering, and Personnel in particular. The marketing department will also need the skills of advertising, sales, and product managers. Production planning and control is greatly needed in manufacturing.

4. **What specific human-resource skills are likely to be in less demand? Why?**

In an expanding operation such as Happydays' most all skills will be in more demand, except those whose skills have become obsolete due to the advancement of technology. The new production processes may make some workers redundant, and increased computerization may make some clerical workers jobs less secure.

5. **What departments will gain the most people and power? Why?**

The manufacturing department will probably have to increase personnel, unless the new production process vastly improves efficiency and requires less human participation. Perhaps a delegation of some of the power & authority in the department by its heads, would result in a more efficient production process. (Improve overall coordination).

Engineering will require additional personnel & should gain more power in the organization & become a more integral part of the production process.

The marketing department will also expand its operation with the anticipated increase in production.

The Finance department should probably also gain personnel & The personnel department will grow.

6. What departments will lose the most people and power (or remain static)? Why?

The manufacturing department may lose people with the improved production methods, and stands to lose power to the engineering department. With the large number of people, some might also be recruited to other departments.

~~Personnel dept will gain~~ *Acct & Fin will probably remain about the same due to present efficiency.*

7. What is the average current salary in Happyday by hierarchical level and by department? The average number of months in current jobs by level and department? The average age by level and department?

Manufacturing	Average Current Salary	- $25,937	Hierarchical level 1	average current salary	- $97,250
Accounting	" " "	- 28,731	2	" " "	- 48,900
Finance	" "	- 37,900	3		- 42,443
Marketing	" "	- 28,454	4		- 35,620
Engineering	" "	- 26,248	5		- 33,108
Personnel	" "	- 29,140	6		- 24,805
			7		- 17,478

8. What additional information would be useful to you as you develop your human-resource plans?

Average number of months in job by level: (5 highest)

5 -	37 months
4 -	53 "
3 -	54 "
2 -	20 "
1 -	68 "

Performance

Average Age by hierarchical level:

7 -	40
6 -	44
5 -	51
4 -	44
3 -	51
2 -	50
1 -	60.5

<u>5</u>

0-6

2 level 3, 4, 5, 6

Ranallo should be dropped.

Recruit MBA from engineering

Anderson } 3.
Belcher }

        4

        5

recruit the six outside

Consider Carson   choose 1 as 5 level.
Dena B. Johnson

<u>6</u>

6 mos - 2 yrs

1 more level 4

2 3's 2 4's 1 5 1-6

<u>7</u>

2 - 5 yrs.

a level 2 - 2 level 5's - no 7's

2   2 3's   2 4's   2 5's

PART B

Form 6 Sample Skill Inventory of Managerial Potential Data Sheet Kept for Each Happyday Manager

Name _____ Employee No. _____ Age _____ Current position _____

Began current position _____ Evaluated by _____ Title _____ Date _____

I. *Potential Rating:*   Check one box only.

Promote now

10 [   ] Extremely promotable *NOW*. Top executive potential very high.

9 [   ] Promotable now; top executive potential.

8 [   ] Promotable now; can assume more responsibility.

Potential, needs time, training

7 [   ] Promotable; needs more time to develop (6–12 months)

6 [   ] Promotable; needs more time to develop (1–2 years)

5 [   ] Possibly promotable; requires considerable training and development.

Not promotable

4 [   ] Probably not promotable; could be effective in present job with some training and development.

3 [   ] Not promotable; possibly effective in present job with extensive retraining.

2 [   ] Definitely not promotable; effectiveness in present job not probable; consider transfer/discharge.

1 [   ] Definitely not promotable; ineffective in present job; consider discharge.

II. *Comments:*   Indicate major strengths, weaknesses, training plans and needs, areas of competence, etc.

_____
_____
_____
_____
_____
_____
_____
_____
_____
_____
_____
_____
_____
_____
_____
_____
_____
_____
_____
_____
_____
_____

Name _____   Group Number _____

Date _____   Class Section _____   Hour _____   Score _____

PART B

Form 7 Human-Resources Forecast Based Upon Performance and Potential

Insert as many names as necessary and indicate proposed managerial level (1–7) in parentheses for each name.

Department: _____

	Immediate needs (0–6 mos.) Total required: _____			Short-range needs (6 mos.–2 years) Total required: _____			Intermediate needs (2–5 years) Total required: _____		
	Available in dept.	Available out of dept.	Required— external?	Available in dept.	Available out of dept.	Required— external?	Available in dept.	Available out of dept.	Required— external?
1.									
2.									
3.									
4.									
5.									
6.									
7.									
8.									
9.									
10.									
11.									
12.									
13.									
14.									
15.									
16.									
17.									
18.									
19.									
20.									

PART C

Form 8 Sample Managerial Progression Forecast

Organization: Division A of Denancy Clothing Co., Inc. (executive operating committee levels only)

Managerial level	Position incumbent (age)	Replacement(s) (age)	Years until ready to move	Performance (1–5)	Potential (1–10)
Level 1	President, T. R. Jones (62)	1. Robert T. Malone (57)	Now	5	10
		2. C. Charles McGinn (57)	1–2	5	9
		3. Harvey N. Max (53)	2–3	5	8
Level 2	V.P. Finance/ Accounting, C. Charles McGinn (57)	1. C. P. Smith (48)	2–3	5	8
	V.P. Marketing, Robert T. Malone (57)	1. Earl J. Franks (55)	Now	5	10
		2. Maxwell N. Roberts (48)	2–3	4	8
		3. Simon Brown (49)	3–4	4	7
	V.P. Manufacturing, C.E.S. Sloane (51)	1. Robert P. Weiss (41)	½–1	5	9
		2. Spencer R. Brod (46)	½	5	8
	V.P. Organization/ Employee Relations, Steven Adams, Jr. (48)	1. Wendell R. Jones (48)	Now	5	10
		2. Louis C. Vries (44)	2–3	4	7
Level 3	Director of Corporate Planning, Earl J. Franks (55)	1. Edwin R. Kopinski (53)	½–1	5	9
		2. Carl O. Schmidt (50)	1–2	4	8
		3. Martin Genelli (46)	3–4	5	7
	Director of Fiber Research and Development, Robert Weiss (41)	1. T. Lawrence Wheeler (43)	½–1	5	9
		2. William R. Davidson (40)	1–2	5	9
		3. G. I. Gordon (40)	2–3	4	8
		4. Richard W. Grant (37)	3–4	5	7
	Director of Foreign Operations, Harvey N. Max (45)	(no potentially qualified replacement found in organization)			
	Director of Fashion and Design, Alexa (Bunny) Schneider (39)	1. Susan Jay (41)	Now	5	10
		2. Wendy R. Gold (36)	1–2	4	9
		3. Clair P. Podal (37)	2–3	4	8
	Chief Legal Counsel and Director of Consumer Affairs, Louis C. Vries (44)	1. Jim Bershon	1–2	4	8

Name _____ Group Number _____

Date _____ Class Section _____ Hour _____ Score _____

PART C

Form 9 Managerial Progression Forecast for Happyday Corporation

Organization: Happyday Co.   Department: Manufacturing (levels 1–6 only)

Managerial level	Position incumbent (age)	Replacement(s) (age)	Years until ready to move	Performance* (1–5)	Potential* (1–10)
Level 1	1. L.C. Lennon (60)				
	2. J.E. McConnell (61)				
Level 2	None presently				
Level 3	1. Walter C. Adams (61)				
Level 4	None presently				
Level 5	1. Bloom (40)				
	2. Knapp (55)				
	3. Ortiz (58)				
Level 6	1. Arneson (53)				
	2. Enslow (29)				
	3. Foster (59				
	4. Harry (56)				
	5. Hill (61)				
	6. Nurtley (37)				
	7. Sorenson (41)				
	8. Vest (47)				

_____
* See Form 4 for this data.

Exercise 3

ANALYZING JOBS AND WRITING JOB DESCRIPTIONS

PREVIEW*

This exercise enables you to actually analyze jobs using a variation of a technique used by the U.S. Civil Service Commission (and the United States Training and Employment Service). In order to write a description of a job, a few job holders are selected and instructed to fill out a questionnaire that indicates how they spend their time on the job. People then interview the job holder in order to learn more about the job. Finally, job descriptions are written from the data obtained in the interviews. The description, which includes a statement of duties, responsibilities, background, personal characteristics, education, etc., can then be used to develop other personnel programs, such as selection procedures, performance appraisals, and wage and salary programs. A systematic job analysis thus can be the foundation on which many programs in personnel are built.

INTRODUCTION

Job Analysis and the Identification of Job Performance

Many of the decisions made in personnel administration are based on what people *do* in an organization. When we select someone for a job, we want to know what activities this person would have to perform. Before we can train someone, we want to know what we are training them to do. How do we obtain this information?

OBJECTIVES

1. To become familiar with the different methods of job analysis and to understand the importance of and uses of job descriptions.

2. To gain experience and develop skill both in interviewing job incumbents to gather information about jobs and in writing job descriptions from this information.

3. To become aware of the nature of job performance and how it differs both from behavior on the job and job effectiveness.

PREMEETING PREPARATION

Read the entire exercise.

The type of information we need in order to make "job related" decisions in personnel administration can be derived from a job analysis. Decisions are job related if they are based on a systematic process of collecting information about what a "job calls for in employee behaviors."[1] If we can identify the *desired behaviors* called for in a job and then design our selection, training, motivation, and other personnel

* The help of Region VIII of the U.S. Civil Service Commission, especially Steven Shikes, Evy Milstein, and George Dwyer, is gratefully acknowledged.

[1] M. D. Dunnette, *Personnel Selection* (Belmont, Cal.: Wadsworth, 1966), p. 69.

systems around these behaviors, we can begin to make more rational and effective decisions in these areas. Decisions should be based on what people do in their jobs, not on attitudes or personality factors unrelated to job performance.

What Is Job Performance?   As we attempt to identify what people do in their jobs, we must define job performance. *Performance* is simply behavior that has been evaluated in an organization. *Behavior*, such as setting up machinery, talking to others, or writing reports, is constantly evaluated by members of an organization as to its value to the organization. After behaviors are evaluated, they can be described as performance—either good, fair, poor, etc. Often we develop indices, or measures of performance, to help judge whether the performance contributes to organizational outcomes. Such measures could be absenteeism ratios, profit, or sales volumes.[2] But these *effectiveness measures* can be quite removed from behavior and performance. For instance, an employee may engage in certain behaviors (e.g., calling on customers regularly) and these behaviors may be evaluated by the organization as desired performance. But effectiveness ratios based on these behaviors (e.g., sales volume) may be low because of external factors, such as product demand. Thus, when we concentrate on effectiveness, we may miss some important things that people actually *do* on the job. When we select, appraise, or train people, we want to have what people do to get job results—their behaviors and/or activities—clearly in mind.

It is also essential to keep in mind that job performance is multidimensional—that is, there is more than one type of activity a person performs on a job. An individual's job performance may consist of running a machine, monitoring a control panel, filling out log sheets, and instructing others. In job analysis, we must gather information on all of these types of job activities, or job dimensions, in order to make job-related decisions in the area of, for example, performance appraisal.

Job performance also involves a statement of the level of performance required. For example, how many calls per week should a salesperson make, how many subassemblies should a mechanic prepare per day, or how congenial should a bank teller be toward customers? Obviously, deciding on these performance levels is often difficult as jobs become less routine and programmable.

Job performance is not necessarily static, and this may cause problems in job analysis. Performance levels change over time and are different across job holders. New trainees and those in the lower job grades within a job group or classification would not be expected to perform at the same level as senior job holders. Job analyses must reflect these dynamic aspects of job performance.[3]

The Scope of Job Analysis and Job Descriptions.   A job analysis may contain the job title, activities performed, procedures used, the physical environment of the job, the social environment of the job, and other conditions of employment. Eventually, after the job is analyzed, experience and education levels are specified and supervision performed and received are added to the analysis in order to make it a complete job description. Other possible factors to include in a job description are training times, physical health, and personal interests required. The job description is also useful as a basis for decisions in personnel administration, as it is more detailed than the job analysis. Thus, we would want to include not only the output or effectiveness indices of a job (e.g., sales volume expected), but also what the workers do on the job to attain those outputs. Here, we must emphasize behaviors or activities that are known to separate successful from unsuccessful performers. These can be used to determine job specifications, the characteristics to look for in hiring people for the job. Also, from job descriptions (comprehensive statements about the nature of the job) job classifications (the grouping of similar jobs) can be developed. Job classifications can be used for job evaluation—i.e., the determination of the financial worth of the job.

Methods of Job Analysis.   There are several ways to gather information about jobs. We can interview people performing the job, we can observe people performing the job, we can examine the work environment and equipment used, we can study previous job descriptions and other job information, or we can use a structured job analysis questionnaire. All of these methods have considerable merit and can be used in combination.

Four specific techniques to gather job information will be noted from the many available.[4] These

---

[2] J. P. Campbell et al., *Managerial Behavior, Performance, and Effectiveness* (New York: McGraw-Hill, 1970).

[3] C. E. Schneier, "Content Validity: The Necessity of a Behavioral Job Description," *The Personnel Administrator* 21, no. 2 (February 1976): 38–44.

[4] For a detailed investigation of job analysis, see Ernest J. McCormick, "Job and Task Analysis," in M. D. Dunnette, ed., *Handbook of Industrial and Organizational Psychology* (Chicago: Rand McNally, 1976).

are the functional job language technique,[5] the critical incidents technique,[6] the job element technique,[7] and the Position Analysis Questionnaire (PAQ).[8]

The functional job language technique is a qualitative way to derive job information by interviewing job incumbents and asking them to fill out forms describing what they do on the job. The emphasis here is on identifying worker activities. (We will use a variant of this method in this exercise.) The *U.S. Dictionary of Occupational Titles* (DOT), published by the federal government, is a large volume of information about over 20,000 jobs. For each job, a coded system enables analysts to describe its "functions." These functions can be viewed as the degree of complexity required by the job in terms of working with data, people, and things. The DOT is thus an excellent place to begin when conducting a job analysis.

The critical incident technique requires job incumbents to be interviewed in order to ascertain what activities they perform which are critical to effective or ineffective performance. Rather than identifying all relevant worker functions, as is done in the functional job language technique, only those critical to effective performance are identified. This technique often works well in the design of performance-appraisal systems, especially the behavioral expectation scales (BES) discussed in Exercise 5.

The job element technique is a quantitative procedure used to question job "experts" about the important worker activities. Each expert is to respond to four questions about an element to determine its importance in the job to be done. It should be noted that job elements are usually human qualities or traits and not behaviors.

The fourth method of job analysis, the PAQ, is a standard questionnaire which can be used to build a profile of any job and rank it relative to others on such broad categories as interpersonal activity or job situation and context. The PAQ is a statistically derived instrument resulting from several years of research into the nature of work.

Any of these techniques can help a job analyst specify the behaviors or activities which encompass a particular job. Once this information is gathered, performance, education, training, and experience levels or requirements can be developed. Together with the information about actual worker activities, this additional information comprises the job description and job specification.

What Are the Uses of a Job Description?[9]   As noted above, the information contained in a job description can be used as a basis for the essential decisions made in personnel administration. To the extent that the description is job related (i.e., oriented toward worker behavior on the job), decisions about what selection criteria are relevant can be made. For example, if through a job analysis we find that handling heavy loads is a behavior necessarily performed on the job, we may want either to ask job applicants about their strength and physical health or test it directly by having them lift something.

Job descriptions also help to tell us what our training programs should emphasize—what skills, abilities, and knowledge are needed to perform the tasks spelled out in the job description. Job dimensions can be weighted as to their importance and performance can be evaluated by any one of a number of appraisal techniques (see Exercise 4). The job description can be used in wage and salary administration as the level of difficulty and the contribution to organization goals of each job activity are ascertained and attached to monetary rewards (see Exercise 17).

Job Analysis and the Law.[10]   Several recent pieces of legislation concerning equal employment opportunity and discrimination in employment (e.g., the Civil Rights Act of 1964—see Exercise 17) have certain provisions that impact upon job-analysis techniques. Basically, these laws state that an organization must show that the requirements they are establishing for selection of workers are related to the job the workers

[5] Manpower Administration, U.S. Dept. of Labor, *Handbook for Analyzing Jobs* (Washington, D.C.: Superintendent of Documents, 1972), stock no. 2900–0131. See also *Guide to Writing Class Specifications*, IPPD, USCSC, Region VIII, March 1974.

[6] John C. Flanagan, "The Critical Incident Technique," *Psychological Bulletin* 51, no. 4 (July 1954).

[7] Ernest S. Primoff, "How to Prepare and Conduct Job-Element Examinations," U.S. Civil Service Commission Project No. 6B531A January, 1973. See also Ernest S. Primoff, "The Development of Processes for Indirect or Synthetic Validity: IV. Empirical Validation of the J-Coefficient. A Symposium," *Personnel Psychology* 12 (1959): 413–418.

[8] Ernest J. McCormick, Paul R. Jeanneret, and Robert C. Mecham, "A Study of Job Characteristics and Job Dimensions as Based on the Position Analysis Questionnaire (PAQ)," *Journal of Applied Psychology* 54, no. 4 (August 1972): 347–368.

[9] C. E. Schneier, "Content Validity: The Necessity of a Behavioral Job Description," *The Personnel Administrator* 21, no. 2 (February 1976): 38–44.

[10] This discussion is taken largely from Schneier, "Content Validity: The Necessity of a Behavioral Job Description"; see also Exercises 10 and 18 and *For Further Reading* for additional discussions of the impact of recent discrimination legislation on personnel practices.

will perform. That is, when selecting a job candidate, requiring a high-school diploma is permitted only if the organization can show that persons possessing a high-school diploma perform successfully on the job in question and those without one do not perform successfully. Other requirements, such as experience, knowledge, and skill levels, are treated similarly, as is appraisal of performance which is not job related.

In order to accurately determine job requirements, the job itself must be analyzed carefully in order to identify exactly what the job calls for in terms of human capability. In many cases statistical procedures used to demonstrate the relationship between, for example, a high-school diploma and job performance cannot be used effectively, perhaps because there are too few workers in the same job to ensure statistical validity. Here, an organization might be able to argue that the high-school diploma is necessary because a *thorough job analysis* was performed which indicated that knowledge possessed by those with a high-school diploma is required on the job. Likewise, a thorough job analysis might be used as the rationale for why a certain number of years of job experience can be required.

Certainly, the impact of legislation on job analysis is a complicated matter beyond the scope of this discussion. However, a thorough job analysis is typically the foundation not only for several subsequent personnel programs, as noted above, but also for an organization's attempts to comply with discrimination in employment legislation. A solid foundation formed by a thorough job analysis can pay dividends in all phases of personnel programs.

PROCEDURE

Overview. A variation of the functional job language technique is used to conduct a job analysis and write job descriptions. A few participants are chosen and their jobs are used in the analysis. They are interviewed, data regarding their jobs is collected and analyzed, and a job description is written.

PART A

STEP 1: Divide into small groups and designate one person from each group as the individual whose job will be analyzed. (If no one in the group holds a job, use one of the suggested jobs in Form 6 for the analysis.)

STEP 2: Form 1 gives examples of job items or activities, for several types of jobs. If the job to be analyzed falls into one of these groups, the examples help to show what

behaviors may be typical for the job group. These behaviors are called "items" in the functional job language technique for analyzing jobs.[11]

PART B

STEP 3: Those whose jobs are to be analyzed should fill out Form 3, noting the instructions (Form 2).

TIME: About 35 minutes, Parts A and B.

PART C

STEP 4: Other members of each group should read over the job holder's completed Position Classification Questionnaire, then interview the job holder and fill out a Position Audit Form (Form 4) as the interview is conducted (see Appendix). Be sure to identify the major job items and duties for the job you are analyzing.

TIME: About 45 minutes.

PART D

STEP 5: Next, job analysts will discuss their completed Position Audit Forms, show them to job holders for any additions, and then develop the final Job Description (Form 5). The process of gathering information, interviewing job incumbents, discussing job information, and eventually isolating job items that appear in the job description is similar to the functional job language technique. The terms on the final description represent the "functions" or activities of the job incumbent.

TIME: About 50 minutes.

APPENDIX: GUIDELINES FOR CONDUCTING JOB ANALYSES[12]

Conducting an On-Site Job Analysis. The general procedure of job analysis follows several steps. The first is for the analyst to become familiar with the technologies of the jobs and characteristics of the

---

[11] In practice, it is most desirable for each organization to generate job items for each and every job. The lists in Form 1 can be helpful in attempting to derive items. However, they should never be used as a substitute for each organization's best attempts to derive its own job items.

[12] Adapted from Department of Labor, *Handbook for Analyzing Jobs* (Washington, D.C.: U.S. Government Printing Office, 1972).

organization to be studied. Information for these purposes may be obtained from:

1. Books, periodicals, and other literature on technical or related subjects available in libraries.
2. Catalogs, flow charts, organizational charts, and process descriptions already prepared by the establishment.
3. Technical literature on processes and job descriptions prepared by trade associations, trade unions, and professional societies.
4. Pamphlets, books, and job descriptions prepared by federal, state, and municipal government departments which have interests in the occupational area—e.g., health, agriculture, labor, or commerce.

By planning in advance for the job-analysis study, the analyst will be able to talk intelligently to management, supervisors, and workers in a language common to all. This background information will also help the analyst to observe and evaluate job tasks and processes objectively without loss of time.

Whenever possible, arrangements should be made so that the following are available to the analyst prior to the actual analysis of jobs: (1) an orientation tour of the establishment; (2) introductions to department heads and supervisors with whom he or she will deal during the study; and (3) a list of job titles, together with an indication of the number of men and women employed in each job.

The orientation tour is highly desirable for the analyst to obtain an overall picture of operations, to become familiar with the general processes, and to observe the flow of work within the establishment. During the tour the analyst will usually be introduced to the foreman or heads of the departments where the analyses are to be made. The analyst should take this opportunity to explain briefly the major objective of the study.

The analyst should request information regarding departmentalization, the titles of jobs in the various departments, and the number of workers employed in each job. This information will be used for the preparation of the staffing schedule and to make initial determinations as to processes and jobs involved within the scope of the study.

Good job analysis involves observing workers performing their jobs and interviewing workers, supervisors, and others who have information pertinent to the job. It is the most desirable method for job-analysis purposes because it (a) involves firsthand observation by the analyst; (b) enables the analyst to evaluate the interview data and to sift essential from nonessential facts in terms of that observation; and (c) permits the worker to demonstrate various functions of the job rather than describing the job orally or in writing.

The analyst uses the observation-interview method in two ways:

1. Observes the worker on the job performing a complete work cycle before asking any questions. During the observation, he or she takes notes of all the job activities, including those not fully understood. When the analyst is satisfied that as much information as possible has been accumulated from observation, he or she talks with workers or supervisors, or both, to supplement notes.
2. Observes and interviews simultaneously. While watching, the analyst talks with workers about what is being done and asks questions about what he or she is observing, as well as about conditions under which the job is being performed. Here, too, the analyst should take notes in order to record all the data pertinent to the job and its environment.

The interview process is subjective—a conversational interaction between individuals. Therefore, the analyst must be more than a recording device. The amount and objectivity of information received depends on how much is contributed to the situation. The analyst's contribution is one of understanding and adjusting to the worker and his or her job.

A good background preparation will enable the analyst to obtain facts quickly, accurately, and comprehensively. He or she must be able to establish friendly relations on short notice, extract all pertinent information, and yet be sufficiently detached to be objective and free of bias.

The analyst must develop skill in combining note taking with the conversational aspect of the interview, and must be able to write intelligible notes while engaged in conversation or to intersperse writing with fluent conversation. Often in deference to the analyst, the worker will stop talking while notes are being made. The analyst should make it clear whether he or she wishes the conversation continued or not in these circumstances.

Some workers object to a record being made of what they say. The analyst must decide how much the interview may be affected by this attitude and modify his or her practices accordingly. A small looseleaf book, such as a stenographer's notebook, is best suited for recording notes while observing and interviewing.

Suggestions for Effective Note Taking

1. Notes should be complete, legible, and contain data necessary for the preparation of the job-analysis schedule.
2. Notes should be organized logically, according to job tasks and the categories of information required for a complete analysis.
3. Notes should include only the facts about the the job with emphasis on the work performed and worker traits involved. Use only words, phrases, and sentences that impart necessary information.

(Obviously, on-site observations are difficult in a classroom setting, but may be arranged if a student is working nearby.)

FOR FURTHER READING

Arvey, R. D., and M. E. Begalla. "Analyzing the Homemaker Job Using the Position Analysis Questionnaire (PAQ)." *Journal of Applied Psychology* 60, no. 4 (1975): 513–517. (II–R)

Berenson, C., and H. O. Ruhnke. "Job Descriptions: How to Write and Use Them." *Personnel Journal* 48 (1969). (I)

Brumbeck, G. B. "Consolidating Job Descriptions, Performance Appraisals, and Manpower Reports." *Personnel Journal* 50 (1971): 604–610. (I)

Campbell, J. P., M. D. Dunnette, E. E. Lawler, and C. Weick. *Managerial Behavior, Performance, and Effectiveness.* New York: McGraw-Hill, 1970, Chapters 4 and 5. (II)

Caruth, D. L. "The Trouble with Work Measurement Is . . . ." *Michigan Business Review* 24, no. 1 (January 1972): 7–15. (I)

Davis, L. E., and J. C. Taylor, eds. *The Design of Jobs.* Baltimore, Md.: Penguin, 1972. (II)

Dunnette, M. D. "A Note on *the* Criterion." *Journal of Applied Psychology* 47 (1963): 251–254. (II)

Fine, S. A. *Functional Job Analysis: A Desk Aid.* Kalamazoo, Mich.: W. E. Upjohn Institute, 1973. (II)

Fine, S. A. "Matching Job Requirements and Worker Qualifications." *Personnel,* May–June 1958, pp. 52–58. (I)

Fine, S. A. "Functional Job Analysis: An Approach to a Technology for Manpower Planning." *Personnel Journal* 53, no. 1 (November 1974): 813–818. (I)

Gehm, J. W. "Job Descriptions—A New Handle on an Old Tool." *Personnel Journal* 49, no. 2 (December 1970): 954–983. (I)

Ghiselli, E. E. "Dimensional Problems of Criteria." *Journal of Applied Psychology* 40 (1956): 1–4. (II)

Hackman, J. R., and E. E. Lawler. "Employee Reactions to Job Characteristics." *Journal of Applied Psychology* 55 (1971): 268–286. (II–R)

Henderson, R. I. "Job Descriptions—Critical Documents, Versatile Tools." *Supervisory Management,* Part I (December 1975), Part II (December 1975), Part III (January 1976), Part IV (February 1976). (I)

Inn, A., and C. L. Hulin. "Three Sources of Variance, Static Dimensionality, Dynamic Dimensionality, and Individual Dimensionality." *Organizational Behavior and Human Performance* 8 (1972): 53–83. (II–R)

Jenkins, G. D. et al. "Standardized Observations: An Approach to Measuring the Nature of Jobs." *Journal of Applied Psychology* 60 (1975): 171–181. (II–R)

McCormick, E. J. "Job and Task Analysis." In M. D. Dunnette, ed., *Handbook of Industrial and Organizational Psychology.* Chicago: Rand McNally, 1976.

McCormick, E. J., and J. Tiffin. *Industrial Psychology.* 6th ed. Englewood Cliffs, N.J.: Prentice-Hall, 1974, Chapter 3. (I)

Pinto, P. R., and C. C. Pinder. "A Cluster Analytic Approach to the Study of Organizations." *Organizational Behavior and Human Performance* 8 (1972): 408–422. (II–R)

Prien, E. P., and W. W. Ronan. "Job Analysis: A Review of Research Findings." *Personnel Psychology* 74 (1971): 371–396. (II)

Primoff, E. S. "The J-Coefficient Approach to Jobs and Tests." *Personnel Administration* (1957): 34–40. (I)

Rakich, J. S. "Job Descriptions: Key Element in the Personnel Subsystem." *Personnel Journal* 51, no. 1 (January 1972): 42–45+. (I)

Reuter, V. G. "Work Measurement Practices." *California Management Review* 14, no. 1 (Fall 1971): 24–30. (I–R)

Schneier, C. E. "Content Validity: The Necessity of a Behavioral Job Analysis." *The Personnel Administrator* 21, no. 2 (February 1976): 38–44. (I)

Seashore, S. E., S. P. Indik, and B. S. Georgeopolous. "Relationships among Criteria of Job Performance." *Journal of Applied Psychology* 44 (1960): 195–202. (II–R)

Shartle, C. L. *Occupational Information. Its Development and Application.* 3d ed. Englewood Cliffs, N.J.: Prentice-Hall, 1959. (I)

Thompson, J. W. Functional Job Descriptions. *Personnel Journal* 30, no. 10 (March 1952): 380–388. (I)

Walsch, W. J. "Writing Job Descriptions: How and Why." *Supervisory Management* 17, no. 2 (February 1972): 2–8. (I)

Weitz, J. "Criteria for Criteria." *American Psychologist* 16 (1961): 228–231. (II)

Wernimont, P. F., and J. P. Campbell. "Signs, Samples, and Criteria." *Journal of Applied Psychology* 52 (1968): 372–376. (II)

U.S. Department of Labor, Manpower Administration. *Task Analysis Inventories.* Washington, D.C.: U.S. Government Printing Office, 1973. (I)

U.S. Department of Labor. *Dictionary of Occupational Titles.* 3d ed. Washington, D.C.: U.S. Government Printing Office. (I)

PART A

Form 1 Sample Job Items, Criteria, or Job Requirements

Sample job items for machine operators and first-line personnel:

1. Knowledge of _____ (specify equipment, machinery, structure or components)
2. Knowledge of preventive maintenance
3. Knowledge of electrical equipment
4. Knowledge of equipment assembly, installation, and repair, etc.
5. Operation of motor vehicles
6. Threading (chasing) on lathe
7. Loading, unloading, and feeding machines
8. Knowledge of cutting sheetmetal
9. Knowledge of using gas torch for cutting, etc.
10. Knowledge of painting metal
11. Knowledge of riveting
12. Knowledge of welding
13. Knowledge of forging and forge-welding
14. Work practices (includes keeping things neat, clean, and in order)
15. Ability to instruct
16. Use of measuring instruments (mechanical, electrical, electronic, as appropriate to line of work)
17. Use of test equipment (electronics)
18. Ability to plan and organize the work
19. Ability to interpret instructions, specifications, etc.
20. Ability to read electronic diagrams and schematics
21. Ability to use reference materials and manuals
22. Ability to follow directions in a shop
23. Ability to use carpenter's tools
24. Dexterity and safety
25. Ability to drive safely (motor vehicles)
26. Dexterity and eye-hand coordination
27. Reliability and dependability as a _____ (specify title of job)
28. Troubleshooting (mechanical)
29. Ability to work with others
30. Ability to work as a member of a team
31. Ability to meet deadline dates under pressure
32. Ingenuity (ability to suggest and apply new methods)
33. Ability to keep records and make reports

General job items for office personnel:

1. Ability to apply procedures
2. Ability to determine procedures for handling unique problems
3. Ability to plan and organize work
4. Ability to work independently without immediate supervision
5. Ability to check long technical reports for conformance with given principles of style and format
6. Judgment
7. Cooperative with others
8. Ability to learn new procedures
9. Ability to explain new procedures
10. Ability to help people find things in files
11. Preparing correspondence to explain material being sent in answering requests, following forms
12. Ability to work under pressure
13. Ability to meet short deadlines
14. Ability to order supplies, seeing in advance what is likely to be needed
15. Initiating telephone correspondence to answer questions or explain material being sent
16. Ability to do numerical work in budgeting and planning
17. Ability to do editorial checking for grammar
18. Ability to do editorial checking for punctuation
19. Ability to do editorial checking for spelling
20. Ability to plan coordination of work of several others, in terms of needs of particular task
21. Reliability and dependability

22. Ability to maintain security of confidential materials, in a room where visitors are permitted
23. Willingness to do the same detail over and over
24. Accurate typing (speed not required), cross-outs permitted
25. Accurate and rapid typing
26. Ability to interpret written instructions and regulations
27. Ability to prepare reports
28. Ability to set priorities on work
29. Ability to express oneself orally
30. Memory for procedures
31. Memory for directions
32. Practical knowledge of material and equipment used in office operation
33. Speed and accuracy of alphabetizing
34. Filing accuracy
35. Speed of simple tasks (like folding papers, or stuffing and sealing envelopes)
36. Ability to use business machines (specify which ones)
37. Tact in dealing with angry people

Expanded descriptions of general job items for managerial/supervisory personnel

1. *Training and preparing employees to work:*   The ability to teach, train, and explain to employees thoroughly and clearly the correct methods, work and sequences, changes in methods of work, etc. Make sure they understand by questioning them. Develop skills of workers.

2. *Placing and utilizing manpower:*   The ability to assign work according to abilities, so employees can work most effectively. This involves fitting the right person to the right job; matching individual interests and abilities with the job; knowing how employees feel about their assignments; being aware of employees' ambitions; and recognizing each person's individual abilities when planning assignments.

3. *Giving explicit or general directions:*   The ability to select and give either detailed information to each employee about what is to be done and exactly how it is to be done, or to set up general goals and then encourage employees to do the work in the way they think best.

4. *Checking on work progress:*   The ability to know the daily developments and progress of work; to keep informed about details of each employee's progress; to see that orders are being carried out; to correct and assist employees; to make certain that work is up to standard; and to know promptly when something goes wrong.

5. *Setting levels of effort and achievement:*   The ability to set deadlines; to encourage employees to participate in setting deadlines; to motivate individuals to get and maintain high production; to establish standards of job performance; to encourage effective performance and an atmosphere conducive to good work.

6. *Helping individual workers with job-related problems:*   The ability to help employees with their work problems; to give personal attention to individuals who have difficulty adjusting to the job; to help employees improve their job performance by explaining their mistakes to them.

7. *Giving workers feedback on their job performance:*   The ability to give employees effective feedback on both good and poor performance, recognizing good performance personally and, if possible, when other employees are present; to constructively criticize poor performance privately; to give reasons for the criticism, keeping employees informed on all aspects of the job situation, including progress.

8. *Giving information to employees:*   Keeping workers fully informed about things of general interest; holding meetings to discuss work activities and problems of all types, organizational direction and policies, current work schedules, employee suggestions, and general work problems. Encourage workers to talk and to think through their own opinions.

9. *Getting information from employees and acting on it:*   Receiving employees' suggestions relating to their work as well as ideas for new work methods; asking for suggestions to improve production; acting upon suggestions that have merit; encouraging employees to express ideas and opinions on job improvement; listening to points of view on job matters.

10. *Establishing an appropriate work atmosphere:*   Finding a balance between being a strict, business-like disciplinarian type of leader and being a friendly type.

11. *Getting support and services from outside the unit:*   The ability to get needed equipment and see that employees have required work materials; to coordinate with other supervisors when group action is needed to solve a problem; and to get the full cooperation of other units.

12. *Acting as a buffer between workers and management:*   The ability to clearly explain management to workers and workers to management; to define organizational goals and policies for employees; to defend, explain, and clarify these goals when they are not understood or are criticized by employees; to pass on employees' views to management; to stand up for employees as a group and as individuals.

13. *Helping employees with personal problems:* Looking out for the personal welfare of subordinates, including helping employees solve personal problems; listening when employees ask for advice; settling conflicts between employees; and doing personal favors for them.

14. *Interpersonal relationships:* The ability to talk to, understand, empathize with, work with, and be tolerant of citizens, fellow workers, and visitors.

15. *Dependability/reliability:* The ability to be counted on to perform all duties or assignments whether or not supervision is present.

16. *Organizational ability:* The ability to establish priorities and organize group activities into a plan of action that maximizes use of available resources and minimizes expenditures of time and energy.

17. *Adaptability:* The ability to adjust to ideas and activities in order to cope with varying situations.

18. *Application of management principles and practices:* The ability to apply to any given situation the management knowledge and skills which result in meeting the total needs of the organization and citizens.

19. *Initiative:* The ability to see the need for action and then to act appropriately.

20. *Leadership:* The ability to accept responsibility, to make decisions, to delegate responsibility (where appropriate), and to motivate people toward a coordinated effort.

21. *Teaching ability:* The ability to explain and impart knowledge in an understandable manner and to ensure that it has the intended effect or response.

22. *Professionalism:* The ability to conduct oneself in a manner that will be a credit to the profession.

PART B

Form 2 Classification Questionnaire Instructions for Job Incumbent

The following guides have been developed to assist you in completing Form 3.

1. *Define your job.*   State briefly what is done by the unit in which you work. Explain how your job fits in with others in the organization, and make clear the purpose of your position. This should be as brief and concise as possible.

2. *List your different kinds of duties.*   Describe each briefly, but in enough detail to give a clear understanding of your work. Start with the primary duties of your position. Then estimate the percentage of time for each.

3. *If you have any responsibility for the work of others, explain the nature and extent of your supervision and guidance of their work.*   This includes supervision over those who report to you and their subordinates, and it also includes indirect responsibility. State by kinds of jobs the employees for whom you are responsible and to what extent.

4. *Explain the scope and effect of your work.*   State how and to what extent your actions, recommendations, and decisions affect your organization, your clients, or the public. Explain the consequences of possible mistakes or errors in judgment. Describe how you influence the quality of work produced by others. Explain the extent of your authority to speak or act for your organization. Describe the effects of your work on: (1) policy, procedure, and organization; and (2) use of people, material, equipment, and funds.

5. *Describe the supervision and guidance you receive.*   State what supervision and help you receive before, during, and after performance of your assignments from your supervisor, others, written guides, or practices. Describe any other guides for doing your work, such as regulations, procedures, practices, manuals, and standards, and describe how directly they affect your work.

6. *State the nature and extent of the mental demands of your position.*   They may include any or all of the following:
   a) initiative—taking action without specific instruction;
   b) originality—the creativeness or inventiveness demanded by the work;
   c) judgment—the selection of the best course of action;
   d) any other significant mental demand.

7. *What are the knowledges, skills, and abilities required.*   State any knowledges, skills, and abilities actually required by the job. For instance, include special manual skills, physical abilities, and aptitudes required. Identify the tasks concerned in each case and describe how and why such requirements are necessary.

8. *State the nature and purpose of the contacts you have in your work with persons other than your supervisors or subordinates.*   Tell whether your work contacts are to exchange information, to make explanations, to persuade others, or to take part in group action.

9. *List anything else that affects your position.*   Specify any job conditions or other considerations not covered elsewhere in your position description which affect the responsibility or difficulty of your work.

Name _____   Group Number _____

Date _____   Class Section _____   Hour _____   Score _____

PART B

Form 3 Position Classification Questionnaire For Job Incumbent

_____
Name of employee

_____   _____
Department name   _Position number (if applicable)_

_____   _____
Organization name   _Current position title_

Information on this form will be used to help classify and/or set the pay for your job. Please be as clear and accurate as possible.

Describe below, in sufficient detail including time spent, the work of the position, listing the different duties performed. (If more space is needed, please use additional sheets.)

Percent time spent: _Duties or work performed:_

Job definition:

Nature and extent of mental demands made:

Nature of contacts with others besides workers and supervisor:

Supervision exercised in this position (list names and job titles):

Name and title of immediate supervisor/superior:

Special requirements:

		Incidental or important	Percent of position's work time
Typing	_____	_____	_____
Shorthand	_____	_____	_____
Weapons (specify)	_____	_____	_____
Vehicles (specify)	_____	_____	_____

Machinery (list):

_____	_____	_____
_____	_____	_____
_____	_____	_____

Other (specify):

_____   _____   _____
_____   _____   _____
_____   _____   _____
_____   _____   _____
_____   _____   _____
_____

Other relevant information:

_____

I certify that I have read the above instructions and that entries are correct to the best of my ability.

_____   _____
Employee signature   Date

To be completed by job analyst:
Name _____
Title _____
Date _____

Reviewed by: _____
Name _____
Title _____
Date _____

Training
Deal w/people
Actual duties performed
Job environment
Does he supervise
Communication Required
Product or service produced.
Lateral coordination
Procedures - T.O.'s - manuals (specific guidance) - Emergency?
Standards - clearances, safety, etc.
Are you supervised.
Is job dynamic.

Name _____ Group Number _____

Date _____ Class Section _____ Hour _____ Score _____

PART C

Form 4 Position Audit Form for Job Analysts

GENERAL DATA

1. Organization: _____

2. Date: _____

3. Present job title: _____

4. Name of job incumbent: _____

5. Audited by: _____

ORGANIZATION RELATIONSHIPS

9. Employees supervised—Title	11. Organization of department (sketch an organization chart for the incumbent's part of the organization)
_____	
_____	
_____	
_____	
_____	
_____	
_____	
Total No. supervised: _____	
10. Supervision received:	
_____	
_____	
_____	
_____	

12. Equipment operated:	13. Departmental title:

DUTIES OF THE POSITION

14. _____

_____

_____

_____

_____

_____

_____

_____

_____

_____

_____

_____

_____

_____

_____
_____
_____
_____
_____
_____
_____
_____
_____
_____
_____
_____
_____
_____
_____

QUALIFICATIONS REQUIRED BY THE POSITION

15. Education	16. Experience
17. License requirements	18. Other (specify):

PART D

Form 6 Sample Jobs to Be Analyzed

MANAGER

Responsible for the efficient management of a business. Coordinates the operation of production, distribution, sales departments, and marketing. Determines administrative policies and executes through subordinate managers. Supervises about thirty-six persons.

PROGRESSIVE ASSEMBLER AND FITTER

Works on an assembly line making complex equipment, such as appliances or automobiles. Fastens one or more parts into a larger assembly by means of bolting, riveting, soldering, filing, lining up, or fitting the parts together. Passes assembly to next station on a conveyor system. This work may involve the use of electric or pneumatic drills, screwdrivers, wrenches, or riveting machines.

STENOGRAPHER

Takes dictation in shorthand for correspondence, reports, and other matters and transcribes dictated material, writing it in longhand or using a typewriter. May need to know technical language and jargon used in a particular profession. May perform a variety of related clerical duties such as filing, typing, answering the phone, etc. May take dictation on a stenotype machine or may transcribe information from a sound-producing record.

Name _____ Group Number _____

Date _____ Class Section _____ Hour _____ Score _____

ASSESSMENT OF LEARNING IN PERSONNEL ADMINISTRATION
EXERCISE 3

1. Try to state the purpose of this exercise in one concise sentence.

2. Specifically what did you learn from this exercise (i.e., skills, abilities, and knowledge)?

3. How might your learning influence your role and your duties as a personnel administrator?

4. What common problems are likely to be encountered as a job analyst interviews job incumbents?

5. Why is it a good idea to ask the incumbent and his or her supervisor about job duties?

6. Additional questions given by your implementor:

Section 3
Identifying, Observing, and Appraising Performance in Organizations

Section 3 contains a set of exercises that explain the process of measuring performance levels of workers. This process, typically called performance appraisal, occurs in every organization, regardless of size or type. Workers' performance is continually evaluated, whether it be informally through the judgments of others in the organization or formally through a rating scale.

Before a person's performance can be judged, job behavior itself must be identified and evaluated as to the degree of performance (for example, from excellent to unacceptable) the behavior illustrates. The requirements a job makes in terms of workers' behavior is best assessed from a job analysis. Thus, the development of performance-appraisal systems is a logical outgrowth of job analysis, as the analysis pinpoints what duties, responsibilities, and behaviors are required. These aspects of the job can be used as a basis for rating people. If a job analysis indicates that the major duty of a job is record keeping, record keeping becomes a performance criterion. After such a criterion is identified, the level of record keeping—evaluated as poor, good, average, etc.—must be decided. Once job performance is identified and evaluated, selection of people can begin, for there now exists a process for appraising the performance of those people selected based on job requirements, not on any one individual's job performance.

In this view, performance objectives and standards are seen as an extension of job analysis, or as another phase of gathering job information. Three exercises are included in Section 3 to describe how this job information is translated into performance-appraisal forms, or formats, used to rate people. Exercise 4 presents the general issues in performance appraisal and the advantages and disadvantages of various formats, while Exercises 5 and 6 allow you to design two popular appraisal systems, Behaviorally-Anchored Rating Scales (BARS) and Management by Objectives (MBO).

Exercise 4

APPRAISING JOB PERFORMANCE: GENERAL METHODS

PREVIEW

The subject of this exercise is the problem of appraising performance in organizations. Performance appraisal or evaluation is vital to every organization, as results are used for promotion decisions, wage and salary administration, and many other crucial decisions. Performance-appraisal formats, or forms, are developed for the jobs analyzed in Exercise 2 and various common performance-appraisal formats are compared as to their advantages and disadvantages. Among them are global and dimensionalized scales. Small-group discussions are held in order to familiarize participants with the ways performance is judged, in order to distinguish between good, average, and poor performance.

OBJECTIVES

1. To gain an understanding of the general methods and uses of performance appraisals.
2. To become aware of the difficulty in identifying, observing, and measuring job performance.
3. To gain experience in determining what criteria or job dimensions are appropriate in appraising performance.
4. To build skill in designing different types of performance-appraisal formats.

PREMEETING PREPARATION

Read the entire exercise.

INTRODUCTION

Identifying, Observing, and Appraising Job Performance

Performance appraisal (PA) is one of the most problematic areas in personnel administration. No matter whether the organization is large or small, business, government, or educational, the performance of its members must be evaluated in order to make decisions on wage and salary levels, on promotion, on termination, on training needs, and on many other important programs. Some PA's are quite informal, perhaps an occasional pat on the back and a few encouraging words by one's superior. Often, however, PA is a very formal process, relying on detailed written forms to supply information.

PA has six basic objectives: (1) validating selection techniques; (2) identifying promotion potential; (3) measurement accuracy as a PA; (4) feedback and employee development; (5) assessing training needs; and (6) allocation of organizational rewards.[1] Thus, the decision for management is not *whether* to appraise performance, but rather *how* to do so. The vital questions personnel administration must help answer are how often to appraise, what methods to

---

[1] L. L. Cummings and D. P. Schwab, *Performance in Organizations* (Glenview, Ill.: Scott Foresman, 1973).

use, which raters to use, and what to do with the results of the appraisal.

A first and perhaps most important decision in PA must come when management decides what to measure—what it will base the PA on. As illustrated in the previous exercise, performance is an elusive concept. Essentially, it is evaluated behavior or results. But which behaviors or results ought to be evaluated? In addition, should personality, appearance, or attitudes be evaluated?

PA and the Law.   Organizations often rely on three types of measures of performance: (1) personal traits—for example, initiative or leadership ability; (2) job performance behaviors; and (3) job results—i.e., profit levels, sales volume, number of units rejected, etc. These performance criteria provide standards against which workers' performance can be compared. The frequency of the use of these formats is shown in Table 1.

Table 1. The Use of Varying PA Formats

	Manufacturing	*Non-manufacturing*	*State governments*
Traits	61	65	80
Behaviors	64	65	80
Results	81	87	26

Adapted from W. H. Holley and H. S. Feild, "Performance Appraisal and the Law," *Labor Law Journal*, July 1975, p. 430.

While any criteria that help account for observed differences in performance are useful, certain legal requirements now make it necessary for organizations to demonstrate that their criteria are actually related to job performance. In a recent court case (*Albermanle Paper Co.* v. *Moody*) the Supreme Court found that the company attempted to validate a test using ratings based on subjective and vague factors as criteria. Further, the company did not comply with the *EEOC Guidelines* (see Exercises 10 and 18) by not basing the performance ratings on job analysis. The Court ruled that the employer could no longer use the test, and was required to pay the plaintiffs back pay and their attorneys fees. Thus, using appearance as a criteria may be disallowed if the organization cannot establish a clear relationship between a certain type of appearance and successful job performance. In addition, as discussed in Exercise 10, organizations must show that their PA's are reliable and reasonably accurate in order to use them as evidence of job success itself.[2]

[2] See W. H. Holley and H. S. Feild, "Performance Appraisal and the Law", *Labor Law Journal* 26 (July 1975): 423–430; and Exercises 10 and 18.

Various legal requirements and guidelines regarding equal employment opportunity (see also Exercise 18) are now beginning to affect performance-appraisal practices significantly. Thus, a thorough, accurate PA form and well-trained raters are becoming a necessity rather than a luxury for most larger organizations. The expenditure of time, effort, and money on PA is returned to an organization in numerous ways, such as through compliance with the law, identification of worker skill and ability deficiencies, rational promotion and merit raise decisions, etc. However, the question for an organization becomes one of choosing from amongst the many varieties of PA formats. The major types of formats are discussed below.

Thus, it is becoming more apparent that PA should rely heavily on job relatedness, not only to make the PA more objective, but to comply with the law. Of course, defining the relevant job behaviors to be evaluated, as well as job outcomes or results, is quite difficult and time consuming. As we move up the organizational hierarchy to less routine jobs, identifying and measuring performance is more difficult. However, a sound PA program, coupled with a detailed job analysis, can make this task less of a burden.

Types of PA Formats.   There are several general approaches to PA. Following are some examples:

1. *Comparative techniques*—the ratee is ranked against others in the same department or job class.

2. *Absolute standards*—the ratee is rated against standards determined by company policy and written on the forms. This group includes "qualitative" techniques such as critical incidents[3], and "quantitative" techniques, such as behaviorally anchored rating scales[4] (BARS, see also Exercise 5).

3. *Goal setting*—the ratee is rated according to the degree to which they attain predetermined job goals (see Exercise 6).

4. *Direct indices*—the ratee is rated on the basis of such data as absenteeism, productivity, tardiness, etc.[5]

[3] J. C. Flanagan, "The Critical Incident Technique," *Psychological Bulletin* 51 (1954): 327–358.
[4] P. C. Smith and L. M. Kendall, "Retranslation of Expectations: An Approach to the Construction of Unambiguous Anchors for Rating Scales," *Journal of Applied Psychology* 47 (1963): 149–55.
[5] L. L. Cummings and D. P. Schwab, *Performance in Organizations* (Glenview, Ill.: Scott Foresman, 1973).

Each of these methods has distinct advantages and disadvantages and the best results are probably obtained by matching the characteristics of each technique with the specific goals of a PA program and the characteristics of the organization involved. For example, if only one ratee is doing a certain type of job, comparative techniques would not be appropriate. If desired job behaviors have been identified, weighted, and communicated to ratees, some type of quantitative absolute standard technique may be useful. Often techniques are used in combination. It is not unusual to combine MBO with certain indices of effectiveness to obtain an overall PA. The objective is to obtain as much job-relevant information as possible on which to base the PA.

In addition to the general approaches listed above, there are several specific techniques which appear to be popular in practice. These include trait, global, dimensionalized, and behaviorally anchored (BARS) rating scales, and management-by-objectives. Sample traits used on a scale are shown in Figure 1. Basically, the trait scale uses individual characteristics to evaluate an employee. A global format is an overall evaluation of an employee without using specific traits or dimensions of the job. A dimensionalized scale uses several job aspects or functions to evaluate an employee. BARS uses specific behaviors or several dimensions and MBO uses job results or employee contributions for evaluation purposes. In this exercise, you will design dimensionalized scales. In Exercises 5 and 6, you will design PA formats using BARS and MBO. A comparison of the various formats with respect to how well we believe they meet the previously mentioned objectives of PA is shown in Table 2.

The Ratees in a PA Program. Some research has found that most effective PA programs allow for ratee participation in the development of the PA criteria and provide for feeding back ratings to ratees.[6] This participation helps to gain ratee commitment to the goals of the program and helps them to become aware of raters' problems. Participation also would help to communicate desired levels of performance— just what has to be done to receive a good PA—to ratees.

The Raters in a PA Program. The raters have a difficult task. They must observe and recall performance, they must try to fill out complex forms objectively, and they must justify their ratings to ratees. We can reduce their burden by training them in the use of the particular format we employ and by alerting them to the common types of rater biases and errors (discussed below).

Because performance must be observed over long periods of time (e.g., six months) in a PA program, good raters often make anecdotal records of performance, being careful to include positive and negative incidents. Several raters can be used to get a more

---

[6] R. J. Burke and D. S. Wilcox, "Characteristics of Effective Employee Performance Review and Development Interviews," *Personnel Psychology* 22 (1969): 291–305.

---

1. **Initiative**—Self-starting action; assuming responsibility; self-reliance; independently recognizing unassigned requirements and recommending action.

2. **Adaptability**—Shifting readily to other tasks or assignments; transfering and applying skills and knowledge to changes in the job.

3. **Judgment**—Choosing the best way to accomplish work; deciding when and from whom to seek advice; choosing best alternatives in decision making.

4. **Cooperativeness**—Teamwork, willing acceptance of authorized orders or instructions and willing assistance to coworkers in the interest of meeting group objectives.

5. **Dependability**—Availability when needed; punctuality; ability to work effectively without close supervision.

6. **Creativity**—Contributing new or different ideas; developing new procedures.

7. **Leadership**—Inspiring teamwork and productivity; delegating responsibility; maintaining discipline; utilizing others effectively.

8. **Following through on assignments**—Pursuing work to conclusion; coordinating various tasks involved in getting a job done; meeting deadlines.

9. **Problem solving**—Defining and analyzing problems; using all necessary means to solve problems; resourcefulness; ability to improvise.

Fig. 1. Sample Traits Used on a Trait Scale

Table 2. Potential Advantages and Disadvantages of PA Methods: Relative Ability of Performance-Appraisal Methods to Attain Objectives.*

Performance-appraisal objectives	Personal-trait scales (not behaviorally anchored)	Global scale (adjective or numerically anchored)	Dimensionalized rating scales (not behaviorally anchored)	Behaviorally anchored rating scales (BARS)	Management-by-objectives (MBO)
Validation of Selection Techniques Requires: Job relatedness, comprehensive list of dimensions tapping behavioral domain of the job; and/or Systematic job analysis to derive criteria; and/or Assessment or inter-rater reliability; and/or Professional, objective administration of format; and/or Daily continual observation of ratee performance by raters.	Poor	Poor	Fair	Good to Very Good	Fair to Good
Identifying Promotion Potential Requires: Job-related criteria; and/or Job dimensions dealing with ability to assume increasingly difficult assignments built into form; and/or Ability to rank ratees comparatively; and/or Measurement of contribution to organization/department objectives; and/or Assessment of ratee's career aspirations and long-range goals.	Fair to Good (Varies)	Poor to Fair	Fair to Good (Varies)	Fair to Good (Varies)	Good to Very Good
Measurement Accuracy Requires: Elimination of rater response set errors (e.g., leniency, restriction of range, halo); and/or Agreement with other performance measures not on the format (e.g., direct indices, such as salary, number of promotions); and/or Reliability across multiple raters; and/or Flexibility to reflect changes in job or environment; and/or Job-related criteria; and/or Commitment of raters to observe ratee performance frequently and complete format seriously; and/or The use of similar standards across raters.	Poor to Fair	Poor	Fair to Good	Good to Very Good	Good to Very Good

Table 2. (*Continued*)

Performance-appraisal objectives	Personal-trait scales (*not behaviorally anchored*)	Global scale (*adjective or numerically anchored*)	Dimensionalized rating scales (*not behaviorally anchored*)	Behaviorally anchored rating scales (*BARS*)	Management-by-objectives (*MBO*)
Feedback Development Requires: Specific, behavioral terminology on the format; and/or Setting behavioral targets for ratees to work toward; and/or Participation of raters and ratees in development; and/or Job relatedness, problem-solving performance review which ends with a plan for performance improvement; and/or Reduction of ambiguity/anxiety of ratees regarding job performance required and expected by raters/organization.	Poor	Very Poor	Fair	Excellent	Good to Very Good
Assessing Training Needs Requires: Specifying deficiencies in behavioral terms; and/or Contains all relevant job dimensions; and/or Specifying performance deficiencies in very specific behavioral terms; and/or Eliminating motivation/attitude and environmental conditions as causes of inadequate performance.	Poor to Fair	Very Poor	Fair	Excellent	Fair to Good
Rewards Allocation Requires: Ability to rank order ratees or results in quantifiable performance score; and/or Facilitates a variance or spread of scores to discriminate between good, bad, fair, etc. ratees; and/or Measures contributions to organization/department objectives; and/or Accuracy and credibility with employees.	Poor to Fair	Very Poor to Poor	Fair	Very Good to Excellent	Very Good to Excellent

* Each method's ability to attain the objectives would, of course, depend on several issues particular to each rating situation, such as rater biases, number of raters available, care taken to develop the format, reward structure, etc.

complete opinion of performance. Possible raters include the job incumbent, peers, subordinates, supervisors one and two levels above the ratee, and persons external to the organization brought in to rate performance. As long as potential raters have direct knowledge about a ratee's performance, they may be useful.

Giving Feedback to Ratees about Their Performance. Justifying a PA is perhaps the most difficult problem for raters. They may receive little help from the form, especially if it is a general or global rating. Ratees want to know specifically what parts of their performance need improvement and what parts were satisfactory. Only then can the second objective of PA be attained, that of improving performance. In addition, raters may be unsure of their ratings and/or may have based them on inadequate observation or non–job-related factors, such as personality or appearance. These ratings may be difficult to justify to ratees.

Ratees often feel threatened by PA and become defensive in the appraisal interview. N. R. F. Maier has suggested a "problem solving" approach to the appraisal interview, rather than a "tell and sell" approach.[7] In the former, the rater tries to find the cause of poor performance and develop ways to remove these blocks, perhaps by training programs. The whole process is one of supportive confrontation, coaching and discussion of problems, rather than strictly evaluating. Large-scale studies at General Electric have shown that criticism in the interview has a negative effect on performance, while mutual goal setting has a positive effect on future performance and reduces anxiety and defensive behavior in the appraisal interview.[8]

These suggestions can be helpful, but telling people how they are doing, especially when they are doing poorly, is still a difficult and anxiety-producing process for most raters and ratees. However, ratees want to know where they stand and what they must do to improve their performance. Thus, feedback is vital to them.

Problems in PA. Beside the difficult nature of judging others in general, some particular problems in the PA process can lessen its effectiveness. Raters often make certain types of errors in their ratings. They may

rate all ratees too high (leniency error), or they may not discriminate sufficiently across ratees, but instead "bunch up" PA scores by giving everyone a similar rating (central tendency error). They may base their rating on one key trait or aspect of job performance, rather than rating all of the important aspects of performance separately (halo error). For example, because a ratee is often tardy, he is rated low overall, even if performance at work is good.

Another problem of PA programs is lack of agreement between raters and ratees on the standards for good performance. Many ratees may not know what is required of them. Often, they may not know what the important aspects of job performance are and/or what the desired level of performance is on these dimensions of their job. This ambiguity may come from the lack of any organizational policy in this area, or the lack of communication of this policy to raters or ratees.

These problems in PA require careful consideration by the personnel administrators. The first step is often a thorough job analysis. No matter what PA format is used, the critical elements of performance to be rated—or the job *items*—must be identified. Only then can we make useful *ratings*, or evaluations of employee performance.

PROCEDURE

Overview. Various performance-appraisal techniques, or formats, are compared in order to learn their relative advantages and disadvantages. Appraisal criteria are identified from job descriptions developed in Exercise 2, or from new jobs. Various appraisal formats are then used to evaluate the job holders, and methods of measuring performance are discussed.

PART A

STEP 1: Form into the same small groups used in Exercise 3. Using the final job descriptions written by your group in Exercise 3 (or any of the sample descriptions provided as Form 1 in this exercise), develop first a preliminary and then a final set of Job Dimensions to be used as performance-appraisal criteria for the job you are working on. Examples are provided for the job of police dispatcher in Form 2. The job description for this job appears in Form 1. Remember that the list of dimensions you develop should include those aspects of the job which would be used to rate the job holder.

TIME: About 25 minutes.

---

[7] N. R. F. Maier, "Three Types of Appraisal Interview," *Personnel*, March–April 1958, pp. 27–40.

[8] See, e.g., H. H. Meyer et al., "Split Roles in Performance Appraisal," *Harvard Business Review* 4361 (January–February 1965): 123–129.

PART B

STEP 2:   Next, each group is to study the various types of appraisal forms or formats, offered as Forms 3–8. Some of these formats (Forms 4–6) have been developed to continue with the example of the police dispatcher job. In your group discussions, try to pinpoint the specific differences and similarities between the formats, how each might alleviate or contribute to common rater errors in performance appraisal, which one(s) a ratee might prefer, and why the format might be preferred by ratees. Develop specific responses to these issues.

STEP 3:   Next, pick two of these formats and use them as models for two different PA formats appropriate for the jobs your group analyzed in Exercise 2. Develop your own formats on a separate sheet. After you have done this, discuss how useful and effective each of these formats would be for the job. Show the formats to the job holder and ask for his or her comments. Also ask him or her to sketch out the performance appraisal actually used on the job, if a formal appraisal is used, and why it is better or worse than the formats the group has developed.

TIME: About 55 minutes.

PART C

STEP 4:   Using Form 9, list the dimensions of the job your group is working on and try to decide specifically what *behaviors and standards* would evidence high and low performance on the dimension. For example, in the police dispatcher's job, *how would you decide whether the job holder was operating equipment properly?* You could set a maximum of errors or breakage in order to receive a high evaluation, you could observe performance over time, you could ask peers for their opinion, and so on. Use Form 9 to decide how performance would be evaluated—how a rater would decide whether a good, fair, or poor rating should be given on the dimension. Ask the job holder how performance is actually determined on the job. How can you improve upon these methods?

TIME: About 30 minutes.

FOR FURTHER READING

Barrett, R. S. *Performance Rating.* Chicago: Science Research Associates, 1966. (II)

Bigoness, William J. "Effects of Applicant's Sex, Race, and Performance Ratings: Some Additional Findings." *Journal of Applied Psychology* 61, no. 1 1976: 80–84. (II–R)

Burke, R. J., and D. S. Wilcox. "Characteristics of Effective Employee Performance Review and Development Interviews." *Personnel Psychology* 22 (1969): 291–305. (II–R)

Cuilford, J. P. *Psychometric Methods.* New York: McGraw-Hill, 1954. (II)

Cummings, L. L. "A Field Experimental Study of the Effects of Two Performance Appraisal Systems." *Personnel Psychology* 26 (1973): 489–502. (II–R)

Cummings, L. L., and D. P. Schwab. *Performance in Organizations: Determinants and Appraisal.* Glenview, Ill.: Scott Foresman, 1973. (II)

Davies, C., and A. Francis. "The Many Dimensions of Performance Measurement: There Is More to Performance than Profits or Growth." *Organizational Dynamics* 3, no. 3 (Winter 1975): 51–65. (I)

Flanagan, J. C. "A New Approach to Evaluating Personnel." *Personnel* 26 (1949): 35–42. (I)

Friedman, Barry A., and Edwin T. Cornelius, III. "Effect of Rater Participation in Scale Construction of the Psychometric Characteristics of Two Rating Scale Formats." *Journal of Applied Psychology* 61, no. 2 1976: 210–216. (II–R)

Holley, W. H., and H. S. Feild. "Performance Appraisal and the Law." *Labor Law Journal* 27 (July 1975): 423–430. (I)

Kavanagh, M. J. "The Content Issue in Performance Appraisal: A Review." *Personnel Psychology* 24 (1971): 653–668. (II)

Korman, A. "The Prediction of Managerial Performance: A Review." *Personnel Psychology* 21 (1968): 295–322. (II)

Lopez, F. M. *Evaluating Employee Performance.* Public Personnel Association, 1968. (I)

London, M., and J. R. Paplawski. "Effects of Information on Stereotype Development in Performance Appraisal and Interview Contexts." *Journal of Applied Psychology* 61, no. 2 (1976): 199–205. (II–R)

Maier, M. R. F. *The Appraisal Interview.* New York: Wiley, 1958. (I)

Mayfield, E. C. "Management Selection: Buddy nominations Revisited." *Personnel Psychology* 23 (1970): 377–391. (II–R)

McGregor, D. "An Uneasy Look at Performance Appraisal." *Harvard Business Review*, 1957, pp. 89–94. (I)

Meyer, H. E. "The Science of Telling Executives How They're Doing." *Fortune* 89, no. 1 (January 1974): 102–106+. (I)

Meyer, H. H., E. Kay, and J. R. P. French. "Split Roles in Performance Appraisal." *Harvard Business Review* 43 (1965): 123–129. (II–R)

Miner, J. B. "Management Appraisal: A Capsule Review and Current References." *Business Horizons* 11, no. 5 (1968): 83–96. (I)

Miner, J. B. "Bridging the Gulf in Organizational Performance." *Harvard Business Review* 46 (1968): 102–110. (I)

Polster, H., and H. S. Rosen. "Use of Statistical Analysis in Performance Review." *Personnel Journal* 53, no. 7 (July 1974): 498–506+. (II)

Rieder, G. A. "Performance Review—A Mixed Bag." *Harvard Business Review* 51, no. 4 (July–August 1973): 61–67. (I)

Schaffer, R. H. "Demand Better Results—and Get Them." *Harvard Business Review* 52, no. 6 (November–December 1974): 91–98. (I)

Schneier, C. E., and R. W. Beatty. "Performance Appraisal in Organizations: An Empirical Study of the Effects of Raters' Level in the Hierarchy." *Proceedings of the Thirteenth Eastern Academy of Management Meetings*, Washington, D.C., 1976. (II–R)

Schneier, C. E., and R. W. Beatty. "Toward a Cognitive Theory of the Performance Appraisal (PA) Process: A Field Investigation of the Effects of Matching Rater Cognitive Structure with Cognitive Requirements of PA Formats." Paper delivered at the National Meetings of the Academy of Management, Kansas City, 1976. (II–R)

Shigher, E. A. "A Systems Look at Performance Appraisal." *Personnel Journal* 54, no. 2 (February 1975): 114–117. (I)

Smith, P. C. "Behaviors, Results, and Organizational Effectiveness: The Problem of Criteria." In M. Dunnette, ed., *Handbook for Industrial Psychology*, 1975. (II)

The Bureau of National Affairs, Inc. *Management Performance Appraisal Programs*. PPF Survey No. 104. Washington, D.C.: The Bureau of National Affairs, Inc., January 1974. (I–R)

Thompson, D. W. "Performance Reviews: Management Tools or Management Excuse." *Personnel Journal* 48 (1969): 957–961. (I)

Thompson, P. H., and G. W. Dalton. "Performance Appraisal: Managers Beware." *Harvard Business Review* 48, no. 1 (1970): 149–157. (I)

Williams, M. R. *Performance Appraisal in Management*. New York: Crane Russak, 1972. (I)

Whisler, T. L., and S. F. Harper, eds. *Performance Appraisal*. New York: Holt, Rinehart and Winston, 1962. (II)

PART A

Form 1 Sample Job Descriptions

DESCRIPTION 1: SECRETARY I

DESCRIPTION OF WORK:

General Statement of Duties: Performs a variety of secretarial and clerical work requiring some exercise of independent judgment.

Supervision Received: Works under general supervision of a technical or administrative superior.

Supervision Exercised: Exercises supervision over clerical personnel as assigned.

EXAMPLES OF DUTIES: (Any one position may not include all of the duties listed nor do the listed examples include all the duties that may be found in positions of this class.)

Types correspondence, reports, forms and other items requiring some independence of judgment as to content, accuracy, and completeness.

Takes dictation as required. Transcribes to draft or final copy as appropriate.

Takes and transcribes minutes or notes at hearings, conferences, or meetings.

Receives telephone and personal callers, handling any questions or matters of a less-technical or routine nature and directing others to the appropriate staff members. Assists visitors in filling out forms and applications.

Screens incoming correspondence and refers to appropriate staff members with relevant attachments or notes for their instruction or disposition.

Establishes and/or maintains filing systems, control records, and indexes, using some independence of judgment.

Schedules appointments, makes reservations, arranges conferences and meetings.

Composes routine correspondence and refers to appropriate staff members with relevant attachments or notes for their instruction or disposition.

Operates a variety of office equipment.

MINIMUM QUALIFICATIONS:

Required Knowledges, Skills, and Abilities: Considerable knowledge of grammar, spelling and punctuation. Working knowledge of modern office practices and procedures. Skill in the taking and transcribing of dictation and in the operation of a typewriter. Ability to perform a variety of secretarial work requiring some exercise of independent judgment. Ability to make simple mathematical computations. Ability to follow written and oral instructions. Ability to communicate effectively verbally and in writing. Ability to establish and maintain effective working relationships with employees, other agencies and the public.

Education: High-school graduation or equivalent.

Experience: Two years of increasingly responsible experience in general clerical office work.

　　　OR

Any equivalent combination of education and experience.

DESCRIPTION 2: PUBLIC UTILITIES PLANT SUPERVISOR

DESCRIPTION OF WORK:

General Statement of Duties: Performs supervisory and technical work in the operation of a water or waste-water plant.

Supervision Received: Works under general supervision of an administrative superior.

Supervision Exercised: Exercises supervision over operations and related personnel.

EXAMPLES OF DUTIES: (Any one position may not include all of the duties listed nor do the listed examples include all duties that may be found in positions of this class.)

Supervises operation of a facility system including automatic and automated programmed controls, large-scale pumping devices, chemical flash mixers, various filtration systems, chemical feeders, clarifying installations, settling basins, and related equipment.

Directs crews of operational personnel performing a variety of tasks necessary for the efficient and effective operation of a treatment facility.

Assesses maintenance and repair requirements, schedules work to be done by plant personnel, assists in the letting of bids for contracted work.

Develops methods and procedures to assure proper operations, determines operating schedules and assists in supervising the installation of new equipment; advises higher management and consulting engineers regarding plant improvement and expansion projects.

Maintains and develops operating records and coordinates activities with other sections, departments, and the public.

Performs related work as required.

MINIMUM QUALIFICATIONS:

Required Knowledges, Skills, and Abilities : Thorough knowledge of the methods and techniques of water or waste-water plant operations. Thorough knowledge of all phases of treatment techniques. Considerable knowledge of the principles of plant engineering. Ability to read and interpret engineering plans and specifications. Ability to plan and coordinate a comprehensive work program. Ability to communicate effectively verbally and in writing. Ability to supervise, train, and motivate subordinates. Ability to establish and maintain effective working relationships with employees and the public.

Education: High-school graduation or equivalent.

Experience: Five years of progressively responsible experience in a water or waste-water plant, including two years of supervisory or complex technical experience in plant operations.

   OR

Any equivalent combination of education and experience.

Necessary Special Requirements: Must possess a Class C or higher Water or Waste Water Plant Operator's Certificate from the state.

DESCRIPTION 3: MAINTENANCE TECHNICIAN I

DESCRIPTION OF WORK:

General Statement of Duties: Receives training in and performs a variety of unskilled and semiskilled work in the maintenance of city streets and street drainage structures.

Supervision Received: Works under the close supervision of a technical superior.

Supervision Exercised: None

EXAMPLES OF DUTIES:

Develops methods and procedures to assure proper operations, determines operating schedules and assists in supervising the installation of new equipment; advises higher management and consulting engineers regarding plant improvement and expansion projects.

Maintains and develops operating records and coordinates activities with other sections, departments, and the public.

Performs related work as required.

MINIMUM QUALIFICATIONS:

Required Knowledges, Skills, and Abilities: Thorough knowledge of the methods and techniques of water or waste-water plant operations. Thorough knowledge of all phases of treatment techniques. Considerable knowledge of the principles of plant engineering. Ability to read and interpret engineering plans and specifications. Ability to plan and coordinate a comprehensive work program. Ability to communicate effectively verbally and in writing. Ability to supervise, train, and motivate subordinates. Ability to establish and maintain effective working relationships with employees and the public.

Education: High-school graduation or equivalent.

Experience: Five years of progressively responsible experience in a water or waste-water plant, including two years of supervisory or complex technical experience in plant operations.

OR

Any equivalent combination of education and experience.

Necessary Special Requirements: Must possess a Class C or higher Water or Waste-Water Plant Operator's Certificate from the state.

DESCRIPTION 4:   CHIEF POLICE DISPATCHER

DESCRIPTION OF WORK:

General Statement of Duties: Performs supervisory and technical work in the use of communication equipment in the City Police Department.

Supervision Received: Works under the general supervision of an administrative superior.

Supervision Exercised: Exercises supervision over dispatching personnel.

EXAMPLES OF DUTIES: (Any one position may not include all of the duties listed nor do the listed examples include all duties that may be found in positions of this class.)

Supervises and coordinates the work of a dispatching staff; directs and participates in the overall operation of police support services, including record keeping and communication activities.

Trains all newly hired personnel in the operation of communications equipment and in proper recording and filing procedures; acts as head of the reserve dispatchers.

Prepares work schedules for all shifts; approves dispatcher compensation time; performs various personnel functions as necessary.

Answers incoming calls. Determines urgency and nature of complaint and its location. If call necessitates police action, fills out complaint card with necessary information. Dispatches patrol cars and emergency vehicles and equipment as necessary.

Receives requests from officers on call and provides follow-up services to officers requesting additional information, services, or personnel; operates teletype computer as necessary.

Maintains radio log of communications, location of personnel and equipment; keeps necessary records, files, reports; maintains and checks communication equipment for proper operation.

May assist in other department operations by performing a variety of secretarial duties.

Performs matron duties when necessary.

Performs related work as required.

MINIMUM QUALIFICATIONS:

Required Knowledges, Skills, and Abilities: Working knowledge of the methods and procedures of police communications. Working knowledge of police communications equipment. Working knowledge of modern office practices and procedures. Some knowledge of the FCC regulations and applicable laws and ordinances. Some knowledge of the geography of the city. Ability to understand and operate a variety of radio communications equipment. Ability to think clearly and act quickly and calmly in emergency situations. Ability to perform work requiring good hearing, good diction and a clear voice. Ability to understand and follow complex oral and written instructions. Ability to establish and maintain effective working relationships with police officers, other agencies, and the public.

Education: High-school graduation or equivalent.

Experience: One year of experience as or in a position equivalent to Police Dispatcher I.

OR

Any equivalent combination of education and experience.

PART A

Form 2

PRELIMINARY JOB DIMENSIONS FOR SAMPLE JOB OF POLICE DISPATCHER

1. Maintains and checks all dispatching equipment for proper operation.
2. Receives citizen complaints and gathers pertinent information related to complaint.
3. Decides from information gathered whether or not to dispatch patrol unit.
4. Dispatches emergency equipment to appropriate site.
5. Monitors different law-enforcement agencies and burglar alarms for businesses.
6. Heads up the reserve dispatchers; holds monthly meetings.
7. Responsible for authorizing compensation time.
8. Types specialized reports, licenses, forms, etc.
9. Files specialized reports, folders and other items according to codes.
10. Takes and transcribes dictation.
11. Handles incoming phone calls, answering inquiries or forwarding questions to appropriate staff.
12. Performs public contact work over counter, answering inquiries and directing visitors to appropriate staff.
13. Composes routine correspondence.
14. Checks all materials related to operations for accuracy and completeness.
15. As required, performs matron duties involving searching female suspects and belongings.
16. As required, escorts female suspects or prisoners to jail along with police officer.
17. Supervises dispatching operations and personnel.
18. Orients and trains all newly hired dispatchers and reserves.

FINAL JOB DIMENSIONS FOR SAMPLE JOB OF POLICE DISPATCHER

1. Dispatches emergency equipment.
2. Performs matron duties as required.
3. Performs public-relations contact work.
4. Files reports.
5. Types reports.
6. Operates console and other equipment.
7. Provides technical/legal assistance to officers.
8. Edits and interprets information.
9. Supervises dispatching operations and personnel.
10. Orients and trains all newly hired dispatchers and reserves.

PART B

Form 3 Performance Appraisal Format: Trait Rating Scale

MAGICO	EMPLOYEE PERFORMANCE APPRAISAL			

IDENTIFICATION DATA

NAME OF EMPLOYEE	NO.	DIVISION	EMPLOYEE CLASSIFICATION	CODE

EDUCATION

HIGH SCHOOL DIPLOMA	COLLEGE	DEGREE(S)
☐ YES ☐ NO	YRS.	

PROFESSIONAL & TECHNICAL REGISTRATION

PROFESSIONAL REGISTERED	TYPE OF REGISTRATION	STATES WHICH REGISTERED
☐ YES ☐ NO	☐ EIT ☐ P.E. ☐ LAND SURVEYOR ☐ OTHER:	

EXPERIENCE				ABSENTEEISM			
YEARS EMPLOYED	PREVIOUS	PRESENT ASGN	(SICK)	(CAUSE)	(WITHOUT PAY)	TOTAL	
	YRS. MO.	YRS. MO.	HOURS	HOURS	HOURS	HOURS	

REASON FOR EVALUATION	PERIOD OF REVIEW	
☐ 6 MONTHS REVIEW ☐ ANNUAL REVIEW ☐ OTHER:	FROM	THRU

PERSONAL CHARACTERISTICS		NEEDS IMPROVEMENT				AVERAGE		GOOD		EXCEL.	
ENTHUSIASM: *Excitement brought to the job, eagerness to achieve, desire to excel, pride of accomplishment.*	Reviewing Supervisor	0	1	2	3	4	5	6	7	8	9
	Endorsing Supervisor										
AMBITION: *Desire to succeed and accomplish goals.*	Reviewing Supervisor	0	1	2	3	4	5	6	7	8	9
	Endorsing supervisor										
PERSERVERANCE: *Persistence to achieve positive results, diligence.*	Reviewing Supervisor	0	1	2	3	4	5	6	7	8	9
	Endorsing Supervisor										
INITIATIVE: *Gets things started, desires to achieve, to improve, to seek knowledge, to display innovative thought.*	Reviewing Supervisor	0	1	2	3	4	5	6	7	8	9
	Endorsing Supervisor										
ATTITUDE: *Willingness, disposition, emotional reaction, moods, and temperament.*	Reviewing Supervisor	0	1	2	3	4	5	6	7	8	9
	Endorsing Supervisor										
COOPERATION: *Desire and ability to work with others toward common organizational goal.*	Reviewing Supervisor	0	1	2	3	4	5	6	7	8	9
	Endorsing Supervisor										
HUMAN RELATIONS: *Ability to achieve amiable reactions from peers, supervisors and subordinates.*	Reviewing Supervisor	0	1	2	3	4	5	6	7	8	9
	Endorsing Supervisor										
LEADERSHIP: *Ability to inspire and effectively direct others.*	Reviewing Supervisor	0	1	2	3	4	5	6	7	8	9
	Endorsing Supervisor										
COMPLIANCE WITH COMPANY POLICIES: *Ability to adapt, accept and respect.*	Reviewing Supervisor	0	1	2	3	4	5	6	7	8	9
	Endorsing Supervisor										

PART B

Form 4 Performance Appraisal Format for Sample Job of Police Dispatcher: Global Evaluation

Instructions: This evaluation form asks you to evaluate one of your subordinate's current level of Job Performance. You are requested to think of someone else (doing the same job as the subordinate being evaluated) who you feel is an "average" performer and compare this "average" performer to your subordinate on the scale below. In defining average you might think of some good programmer/analysts and some poor ones and one who is about in the middle. You could then compare your subordinate to the middle or average programmer/analyst. Please place an "X" along the scale to describe what you believe is your subordinate's overall level of performance compared to the "average" performer.

For _____ current level of performance, I would rate him/her:

Unsatis-factory	Well below average	Somewhat below average	A little below average	Average	A little above average	Somewhat above average	Well above average	Extremely successful
1 2	3 4	5 6	7 8	9 10	11 12	13 14	15 16	17 18

←———————————————————————————————————→

Lower evaluation   Higher evaluation

PART B

Form 5 Performance Appraisal Format for Sample Job of Police Dispatcher: Dimensionalized Scale

Job Dimension	Excellent	Very good	Good	Slightly better than average	Average	Slightly less than average	Poor	Very poor	Unacceptable
Dispatches emergency equipment.									
Performs matron duties as required.									
Performs public relations contact work.									
Files reports.									
Types reports.									
Operates console and other equipment.									
Provides technical/legal assistance to officers.									
Edits and interprets information.									
Supervises dispatching operations and personnel.									
Orients and trains all newly hired dispatchers and reserves.									

PART B

Form 6 Performance Appraisal Format for Sample Job of Police Dispatcher: Relative Comparison Performance Appraisal Form (forced distribution)

Job Dimension	Rank Relative to Other Ratees in This Job Class				
	Better than 90% of ratees	Better than 60–80% of ratees	Better than 40–60% of ratees	Better than 20–40% of ratees	Better than 0–10% of ratees
Dispatches emergency equipment.					
Performs matron duties as required.					
Performs public relations work.					
Files reports.					
Types reports.					
Operates console and other equipment.					
Provides technical/legal assistance to officers.					
Edits and interprets information.					
Supervises dispatching operations and personnel.					
Orients and trains all newly hired dispatchers and reserves.					
Overall Performance					

PART B

Form 7 Performance Appraisal Format: Employee Performance and Merit Review by Dimensions

Name _____ Job Class _____

Date Employed _____ Location or Dept. _____

Carefully analyze employee's performance. Study each **factor** and the description of each **degree**. Place an X in the square which most clearly fits the employee's performance. Where necessary, make comments below the factor to explain your evaluation. After completion, discuss review with employee and summarize on back.

Part I—Ability & Application

Initiative (ability to exercise self-reliance and enterprise)	Grasps situation and ☐ goes to work without hesitation	Works independently ☐ often; seldom waits for orders	Usually waits for instruc- ☐ tions; follows others	Does only what is specif- ☐ ically instructed to do
Comments on Initiative:				
Quality of work (accuracy and effectiveness of work; freedom from errors)	Consistently good quali- ☐ ty; errors rare	Usually good quality; few ☐ errors	Passable work if closely ☐ supervised	Frequent errors; cannot ☐ be depended upon to be accurate
Comments on Quality:				
Quantity of work (output of work; performance speed)	Works consistently and ☐ with excellent output	Works consistently with ☐ above average output	Maintains group average ☐ output	Below average output; ☐ slow
Comments on Quantity:				
Job knowledge (technical knowledge of job; ability to apply it)	Knows job thoroughly; ☐ rarely needs help	Knows job well; seldom ☐ needs help	Knows job fairly well; ☐ requires instructions	Little knowledge of job; ☐ requires constant help
Comments on Knowledge:				
Attitude (enthusiasm, coop- erativeness, willingness)	Enthusiastic; outstand- ☐ ing in cooperation; tries new ideas	Responsive; cooperates ☐ well; meets others more than half-way	Usually cooperates; ☐ does not resist new ideas	Uncooperative; resents ☐ new ideas; displays little interest
Comments on Attitude:				
Dependability (willingness to accept responsibility; to follow through)	Outstanding ability to ☐ perform with little super- vision	Willing and able to ac- ☐ cept responsibility; little checking required	Usually follows instruc- ☐ tions; normal follow-up	Refuses or unable to car- ☐ ry responsibility; needs constant follow-up
Comments on Dependability:				
Attendance (reliability to be on the job)	Always can be relied ☐ upon to be at work on time; absent only when real emergency	Usually can be relied ☐ upon to be at work on time; explained ab- sences occur occasion- ally	Comes in late with rea- ☐ sonable excuses; fairly frequent explained ab- sences	Frequent unexplained ☐ lateness and/or ab- sences
Comments on Attendance:				
Leadership (ability to guide, direct others)	Others naturally follow ☐ his example or direction; obtains good results from others	Willingly assumes guid- ☐ ance of others; is fairly well accepted in this role	Is accepted reluctantly ☐ by his group as a guide or example; gets fluc- tuating results	Shows no aptitude or ☐ skill in leadership
Comments on Leadership:				

Part II—Capacity & Ambition for Advancement

Check (√) applicable sections (more than one section may apply):

REGRESSING	NOT SUITED TO JOB	NOT LIKELY TO ADVANCE	PROGRESSING	SATISFACTORY	MAXIMUM PERFORMANCE ON JOB	READY FOR PROMOTION

Review your ratings and comments; then briefly outline what actions you will take or suggest to maintain, to improve, or to correct the behavior and/or output of this employee.

_____

_____

_____

_____

_____

Time set for necessary
improvement to take place: _____

Discuss your rating results with the employee:

Date _____ Signature _____
                                                                    Employee

Employee's reaction to review and suggestions was: (check one)

Appreciation   **Interest**   **Disinterest**   **Resentment**
(Completely willing to   (Will try to   (Satisfied with   (Feels review
strive for improvement) ☐ follow suggestions) ☐   present status) ☐   is imposition) ☐

Other (explain) _____

_____

Conclusions drawn from interview _____

_____

_____

_____

Date _____ Signature _____
                                                                    (Reviewer)

PART B

Form 8 Performance Appraisal Format: Sample Professional Staff Quantitative Appraisal Form

CONFIDENTIAL

Date _____

Period of evaluation _____

Staff member's name _____

Staff member's title _____

Department _____

Instructions: This report is to be completed by the immediate supervisor of each staff member. It will be reviewed and commented on by the immediate superior of the supervisor. The evaluation should be discussed with the staff member to help him or her identify strengths and weaknesses. Please circle the appropriate numbers in each category. Please include a summary comment in the blank space at the end of the form. Use this space to discuss individual's major strengths and weaknesses. Be specific.

Person completing form _____

Signature _____

Date _____

Date of discussion with staff member _____

1. COMPETENCE	0 1	Lacks competence
	2 3	Somewhat competent, shows some strengths
	4 5	Average to high competence
	6 7	Extremely competent

Comment:

2. ORGANIZATIONAL AND ADMINISTRATIVE EFFECTIVENESS	0 1	Poor overall
	2 3	Fair, does routine tasks well
	4 5	Average to good, plans and implements some things quite well
	6 7	Outstanding, plans and implements all tasks and programs very well

Comment:

3. LEADERSHIP	0 1	Abrogates leadership responsibility, does not have respect of subordinates
	2 3	Obtains adequate results from subordinates
	4 5	Motivates others successfully, develops personnel
	6 7	Capable and forceful, inspiring and motivating, develops and evaluates subordinates

Comment:

4. PROFESSIONAL DEVELOPMENT	0 1	Does little or nothing
	2 3	Works to some degree at development
	4 5	Works to a considerable degree at development
	6 7	Works to a very high degree at development and is continually learning and growing in skills

Comment:

5. COOPERATION	0 1	Has difficulty in getting along with others
	2 3	Works fairly well with others; better with a few people
	4 5	Works well with others, which improves effectiveness
	6 7	Works extremely well with all persons and is very effective in a group

Comment:

6. JUDGMENT	0 1	Makes many errors in judgment
	2 3	Judgment sound in routine situations
	4 5	Exercises good judgment and anticipates consequences of actions
	6 7	Exceptional judgment, forecasts decision impacts, is sound and sensible

Comment:

SUMMARY COMMENTS:

Name _____   Group Number _____

Date _____   Class Section _____   Hour _____   Score _____

PART C

Form 9 Worksheet for Developing Ways to Evaluate Performance

Job title _____

Job Dimension	Behavior(s) (or standards) required for:		
	Good performance	Fair performance	Poor performance
1.			
2.			
3.			
4.			
5.			
6.			
7.			
8.			
9.			
10.			

Name _____   Group Number _____

Date _____ Class Section _____ Hour _____ Score _____

ASSESSMENT OF LEARNING IN PERSONNEL ADMINISTRATION
EXERCISE 4

1. Try to state the purpose of this exercise in one concise sentence.

2. Specifically what did you learn from this exercise (i.e., skills, abilities, and knowledge)?

3. How might your learning influence your role and your duties as a personnel administrator?

4. How can you train PA raters to be more accurate?

5. What have you found to be the relationship between PA and job analysis?

6. How would you go about evaluating the effectiveness of a PA system?

7. Additional questions given by your implementor:

Exercise 5

DESIGNING BEHAVIORALLY ANCHORED RATING SCALES: A PERFORMANCE-APPRAISAL SYSTEM BUILT AROUND RATEE JOB BEHAVIOR

PREVIEW

One performance-appraisal (PA) format is gaining in popularity due to its unique characteristics. This system, called Behaviorally Anchored Rating Scales (BARS) or Behavioral Expectation Scales, is an important advance beyond the traditional PA formats discussed in Exercise 4. BARS, as the name implies, are based on actual ratee behavior. As BARS are developed, ratee behaviors are identified, defined, and evaluated as to the level of performance (e.g., good, poor, etc.) they represent. Because this type of system provides a large amount of job-relevant information to raters and ratees alike, BARS can facilitate accurate appraisals and improve job performance as well.

However, BARS are a complex and time-consuming PA system. In this exercise, materials are provided to perform all of the steps required to develop a set of BARS. The advantages and disadvantages of this system are pointed out.

INTRODUCTION

Behaviorally Anchored Rating Scales

One performance-appraisal (PA) technique that many believe to be the most useful currently available is Behaviorally Anchored Rating Scales (BARS). BARS have been credited with success because they have been found to achieve the major objectives of PA, namely, accurate measurement of job performance and improvement of job performance through feedback to ratees.

OBJECTIVES

1. To become familiar with the characteristics of BARS and to become aware of the advantages and limitations of BARS as a tool for measuring and improving job performance.
2. To build your skill in developing BARS, such that you are able to perform all of the steps required to obtain a final, useful performance-appraisal system. Specific skills include identifying job dimensions from job-analysis information and deriving behavioral job anchors.
3. To understand the implications for personnel programs of using a behaviorally based performance system, versus one that does not rely on job behavior as the criterion for appraising people in organizations.

PREMEETING ASSIGNMENT

Read the entire exercise carefully. Be sure you understand the *Procedure* before you begin.

What Are BARS? BARS[1] are a PA format in which the rater is provided with statements of standards against which to evaluate the performance of ratees.

---

[1] For an excellent discussion of the rationale and procedure for BARS, see P. C. Smith and L. M. Kendall, "Retranslation of Expectations: An Approach to the Construction of Unambiguous Anchors for Rating Scales," *Journal of Applied Psychology* 47 (1963): 149–155.

These standards are placed on the scales in BARS, one scale developed for each important broad performance area, or job dimension. The dimensions can be identified by several methods, including those often used to analyze jobs (see Exercise 3). When BARS are developed, small-group discussions are held with potential raters and ratees in order to identify the important aspects of the job which should be evaluated in PA.

Each job dimension identified in these group discussions eventually becomes one of the behaviorally anchored scales. The scale is presented vertically on a page with "Excellent" or "Very Good" performance at the top of the page and "Unacceptable" or "Very Poor" performance at the bottom of the page. Between these two extreme values are a number of scale points, usually seven or nine in number (an example appears as Form 1 in this exercise). Further, a short statement appears beside each of the scale values. Thus, the numerical scale values are said to be "anchored." These statements, or anchors, are usually rather short in length and are meant to illustrate typical ratee behavior for the particular scale value to which they are attached. If six job dimensions have been identified for a job, six scales will be filled out by the rater for each ratee he or she rates. A rater simply marks the level of performance on the scale at the point at which a behavioral anchor most clearly illustrates the ratee's behavior.

Why are BARS useful?   BARS are useful because of their unique PA characteristics, the first such feature being their behavioral orientation. BARS rely on job behavior, or what people actually do on their jobs. This behavioral emphasis takes into account only those things under control of the individual ratee, not overall measures of effectiveness which may not be related to job behavior (see *Introduction*, Exercise 3).

By attaching behavioral anchors to scales, BARS are able to specify precisely what people must do to receive good, fair, or poor ratings. This is often more useful than simply indicating the job dimensions on which people will be evaluated, as was true of many of the forms in Exercise 4. The specificity of BARS allows raters to give feedback to ratees regarding why they received the ratings they did and precisely what they must do to improve their performance. This type of feedback not only helps make PA less subjective and based more on actual observed behavior, but also helps ratees overcome anxiety associated with the ambiguity of PA.

In addition, BARS allow for ratee and rater participation in their development. In the small-group meetings where the job dimensions and anchors are

developed for BARS, raters and ratees give much thought to their jobs, and the important aspects of job performance are thus made explicit. This awareness can be useful to raters, as they now have a guide to use when observing performance. Ratees would be better able to judge their superiors' expectations. Any ambiguities or conflicts regarding duties, responsibilities, or differences between raters' and ratees' ideas of desired performance could be cleared up in the discussion sessions. Finally, the participation of the ultimate users in BARS' design and the retention of actual language used by the job holders help to assure rater and ratee commitment to the PA technique.

Because BARS is a quantitative technique, appraisal scores can be related to current wage and salary structure to determine what behaviors are being highly rewarded with monetary rewards. Ranges of scores on BARS could be tied to different levels of merit raises. Certain job dimensions could be singled out, given high weights relative to other dimensions, and used for bonus administration, etc.

Several "spin-off"[2] effects of BARS make them useful for several personnel programs. BARS can be used to identify the behavioral criteria on which to make selection decisions and design selection tests. BARS can also help to specify behavioral training objectives (see Exercise 12). Eventually, the broad content of training courses would be the job dimensions in BARS and the specific behaviors to be learned in each content area could be derived from the behavioral anchors. Motivation techniques may benefit from BARS, as certain behaviors are identified which could be areas of poor performance for the organization. These could be pinpointed and linked to rewards to help improve performance.

BARS is a rather recent PA technique. Although it shows promise, it is used by only a small portion of organizations and the research available to date is not conclusive regarding the ability of BARS to eliminate certain types of rater errors.[3] This is due to its newness and perhaps because it is a time-consuming technique to develop, requiring much effort of raters. They must observe actual job behavior closely and make many, often difficult judgments. But BARS' advantages as a PA system seem to be considerable and more organizations are adopting

[2] M. R. Blood, "Spin-Offs from Behavioral Expectation Scale Procedures." *Journal of Applied Psychology* 59 (1974): 513–515.
[3] See D. P. Schwab, H. G. Heneman, and T.A. DeCotiis, "Behaviorally Anchored Rating Scales: A Review of the Literature," *Personnel Psychology* 28 (1975): 549–562. Research is also cited in *For Further Reading*.

them each year. They satisfy the demands of performance evaluation in terms of providing specific feedback to employees, identifying training needs, forming a basis for promotion decisions and wage and salary administration, and helping to develop valid selection criteria.

Some Terminology. The meanings of certain terms used in the previous discussion and in the exercise should be clarified at this point. *Job dimensions* are those broad content areas of job performance which describe what duties, skills, responsibilities, or activities are performed. In BARS, each scale has as its title a job dimension, derived from some type of job-analysis technique. *Anchors* are specific statements that illustrate actual job behavior, or worker activity. These anchors are attached to each scale value in each scale of BARS and are the standard against which raters evaluate ratee behavior. Remember the distinction between these anchors, which describe *behavior*, and *performance*, which is measured or evaluated behavior. In BARS, we concentrate (a) on the behaviors essential for success in a particular job as described in the anchors, and (b) on the performance as an evaluation or measurement of an individual on the behaviors specified. We do not directly measure *effectiveness*, or contribution to organization goals with BARS. Effectiveness measures are summary indices of performance which often contain some factors not within the direct control of the person we are rating. Examples would be cost overruns, profit, or productivity (see Exercise 6).

Is a Separate BARS System Needed for Each Job in an Organization? The procedures advocated here to implement BARS are designed to be based on the needs of the specific job. Thus, effective BARS performance-evaluation systems would often require extensive participation of the job incumbent in their design. Cooperation is critical if the performance evaluations are to be "situation specific." In other words, the greater generality that is obtained by making performance evaluations fit wider and wider ranges of jobs, the more the people in those jobs are measured abstractly and not specifically. Thus, we lose specific job relatedness of the performance-appraisal criteria as we attempt to make performance evaluations fit several groups of jobs, unless, of course, they are quite similar. Obviously, greater generality detracts from the usefulness of a performance evaluation for the purposes of employee feedback, identifying training needs, making promotion decisions, wage and salary decisions, and selection validation. If we

are going to reduce rater errors and subjectivity when evaluating an employee's performance, attempts must be made to make performance evaluations as specific and as job related as possible. Obviously, systems can be devised which are generally applicable, but the errors created by general applicability, although meeting short-run needs, can only open the door to criticism, dissatisfaction, and possible litigation, as the criteria may not be valid. The BARS system endeavors to minimize rater errors, subsequent rater and ratee criticisms and dissatisfaction, as well as litigation, by being job specific. But job relatedness can only be achieved if serious commitment on the part of the organization is obtained, for BARS require an in-depth analysis of job content, a time-consuming process.

Toward a Dynamic PA System. PA formats, including BARS, are static in nature. That is, they cannot change over time. However, job performance, job environments, and job holders are all dynamic in nature—they do change over time. For example, assume that a PA system was developed in January and certain performance standards were set to be used to evaluate job performance of ratees at the end of the current appraisal period (i.e., July). During the six-month appraisal period new equipment or technology may be introduced to make the job easier, duties and responsibilities may be added or deleted from the job, and/or the job holder's ability may improve due to experience. Any of these occurrences could make the static performance standards and the PA format based on them obsolete.

In order to prevent this problem, PA formats must constantly be updated, revised, and redesigned in light of the dynamic nature of jobs and worker abilities. BARS are no exception. However, because each scale in BARS is developed separately, and often placed on a separate sheet of paper, the format can be updated by simply removing or adding scales representing job dimensions or by changing the degree of performance each behavioral anchor represents. For example, for a seasoned veteran job holder, the behaviors typically evaluated as excellent performance for less experienced incumbents might be evaluated only as good performance. As a person's ability changes over time, we might have reason to increase expectations regarding performance. The important point is that BARS can be revised and updated to reflect changes in performance, job environment, etc. No PA system can be effective unless it reflects current organizational and performance characteristics.

PROCEDURE

Overview. In this exercise, you first study a set of sample behavioral anchors. You will then practice determining to which job dimension each of a set of sample anchors belongs, as well as deciding what scale value each anchor should have. Practice in identifying job dimensions and anchors from a sample job analysis is provided next. These anchors are "retranslated" back to their original items and scale values are determined for each anchor. Finally, the remaining job dimensions for the sample job are weighted and the appropriate anchors are attached to the scales to produce a final set of BARS for the sample job.

PART A

STEP 1: *Becoming familiar with behavioral anchors.* Read over the examples in Forms 1 and 2 to become familiar with what behavioral anchors are and how they are written for each of the seven or nine levels of performance, from "Excellent" to "Unacceptable" or "Very Poor." Form 1 contains job dimensions from a chemical equipment operator's job and Form 2 contains anchors for the job of police dispatcher. Notice how the anchors in the forms contain language actually used on the job and refer to specific behaviors.

PART B

STEP 2: *Retranslating and scaling anchors.* In order to decide under which job dimension an anchor best fits, all of the anchors written for a job are put on a list in random order and several people with knowledge of the job then indicate which job dimension they feel the anchor was originally meant to illustrate. Thus the anchors are "retranslated" back to the original set of dimensions. If high agreement is reached among those performing this step as to what dimension an anchor best illustrates, the anchor can be placed on that job dimension scale in the final BARS. If people do not agree as to which dimension an anchor belongs, it is probably ambiguous and should be discarded. Further, if after all of the anchors are retranslated, one or a few original job dimensions have not been used (i.e., few or no anchors have been retranslated to them), it may mean that these dimensions were too broad or ambiguous and they should be discarded or combined into other dimen-

sions. If 60 percent or more of the group agree on the placement of an anchor, it should be retained.

Next, each anchor is given a scale value of 1 through 7. These values indicate the degree of performance the anchor illustrates. The values can be averaged among all those participating and the mean is a good approximation of the group's feeling as to where the anchor should be on the scale.[4]

Form 3 provides an experience in retranslating behavioral anchors to job dimensions and weighting a set of anchors for the job of a grocery clerk, a job familiar to most people. The job of grocery clerk has been described as composed of the following dimensions:[5]

1. Knowledge and judgment of checkstand work;

2. Organizational ability of checkstand work;

3. Skill in human relations;

4. Skill in the operation of a register;

5. Skill in bagging; and

6. Skill in monetary transactions.

For each of these dimensions, a set of behavioral anchors has been written by job supervisors and job incumbents. These range from behaviors that are representative of "Extremely good" job performance to "Extremely poor" job performance. Sixteen of these behavioral anchors are listed in Form 3 for the two grocery-clerk job dimensions of "knowledge and judgment in checkstand work" and "Organizational ability of checkstand work." You are asked to specify to which of the two dimensions each anchor belongs and the level of performance (from "Extremely good" to "Extremely poor") that each anchor represents. Once this is done by everyone, a chalk board or flip chart can be used to record everyone's assignment of anchors to job dimensions and their anchor

---

[4] Standard deviations can also be computed for the anchors, with large standard deviations indicating poor agreement among people. Anchors with standard deviations of greater than 1.75 could be discarded.

[5] L. Fogli, C. L. Hulin, and M. R. Blood, "Development of First-Level Behavioral Job Criteria," *Journal of Applied Psychology* 55 (1971): 3–8. Used by permission of author and American Psychological Association.

weights. The degree of agreement can then be checked and a final scale constructed for both dimensions of the grocery-clerk job, using the mean weight given to anchors by the group.

TIME: About one hour, Parts A and B, if *Procedure* read before beginning.

PART C

STEP 3: *Developing job dimensions and behavioral anchors from job analyses.* Now that you have been introduced to the BARS procedure, you are ready to develop a set of BARS. Here you are to derive a set of job dimensions and anchors from a typical job-analysis form. In an organization developing BARS, job descriptions like Form 4 could be used as a starting point for the development of behavioral anchors and dimensions. Of course, small-group discussions with incumbents and their supervisors, or any of the job-analysis techniques noted in Exercise 3, would help to generate information about jobs. Typically, small-group discussions are used in BARS programs to obtain job information in order to help generate commitment to the program.

Once the information about jobs is gathered, job dimensions must be derived. They should comprise a complete list of the important aspects of the job. Then several supervisors and job incumbents would be asked to write anchors for each job dimension illustrative of various degrees of performance. These anchors will eventually appear on the final BARS form after retranslation (see Step 2 above). Form into small groups (seven to ten members) and use Form 4, a job description of a maintenance worker (or the job descriptions written in Exercise 3), to develop a set of job dimensions. If you use jobs already analyzed in a previous exercise, you should already have the list of job dimensions. Put each job dimension on the top of a sheet in Form 5. Then write at least twenty-one behavioral anchors, one for each of the seven levels of performance on Form 5. Make sure *each* group member writes a set of anchors for *each* job dimension.

STEP 4: *Retranslating and scaling anchors.* Now you are ready to retranslate and scale the anchors written for the job in order to develop the final BARS form. This procedure is done the same way as Step 2 above. First, list all of the anchors generated by your group in random order on Form 6. Then, individually fill in a job dimension and a scale value (1 through 7) for *each* anchor. Finally, calculate the percentage of agreement amongst the group as to the job dimension to which each anchor belongs. Then calculate the mean weights for each anchor given by the group.

TIME: Time required will depend on the size of your group, the job chosen, etc. (Try to complete the paperwork and computations outside of class.)

PART D

STEP 5: *The final BARS form.* After percentages of agreement and means are calculated in Step 4 above, discard those anchors that have low agreement as to job dimension. Discard job dimensions for which no anchors seem to belong. Then attach the remaining anchors for each dimension to the proper scale value on the final BARS forms (Form 7).[6] You will have one scale for each job dimension. Next, use Form 8 to weight the job dimensions, using percentage weights. The weights could be used to derive a weighted PA score (i.e., the score [1–7] on each dimension times the weight of the dimension, summed across all dimensions). Such scores could then be linked to merit raises or used to compare ratees for promotion decisions.

The dimension weights could be written on each job dimension scale. The set of scales, one scale for each job dimension, each with their behavioral anchors, makes up the final performance-appraisal format called BARS.

TIME: The total time for Steps 3, 4, and 5 should be about two hours.

---

[6] *Special instructions for attaching anchors to scales*: After you have retranslated and weighted the anchors, you may find that some dimensions do not have seven acceptable anchors. Here you can leave a few scale values void of anchors or write ones specifically for these scale points. Further, after anchor means are calculated, you can attach anchors to the exact point on the scale which reflects their mean (e.g., an anchor with a mean of 6.75 would be placed 3/4 of the way between "Very good performance" and "Excellent performance" on Form 7). Or you can round the mean to the nearest whole number and attach the anchor at the line which denotes that scale number (e.g., the anchor with a mean of 6.75 would be attached at the line for scale value 7, "Excellent performance").

FOR FURTHER READING

Bernardin, J. J., M. B. LaShells, P. C. Smith, and K. M. Alvares. "Behavioral Expectation Scales: Effects of Developmental Procedures and Formats." *Journal of Applied Psychology* 61: (1967): 75–79. (II–R)

Blood, M. R. "Spin-Offs from Behavioral Expectation Scale Procedures." *Journal of Applied Psychology* 59 (1974): 513–515. (II–R)

Borman, W. C. "The Rating of Individuals in Organizations: An Alternate Approach." *Organizational Behavior and Human Performance* 12 (1974): 105–124. (II–R)

Borman, W. C., and M. D. Dunnette. "Behavior Based Versus Trait-Oriented Performance Ratings: An Empirical Study." *Journal of Applied Psychology* 60 (1975): 561–565. (II–R)

Borman, W. C., and W. R. Vallon. "A View of What Can Happen When Behavioral Expectation Scales Are Developed in One Setting and Used in Another." *Journal of Applied Psychology* 59 (1974): 197–201. (II–R)

Burnaska, R. F., and T. D. Hollmann. "An Empirical Comparison of the Relative Effects of Rater Response Biases on Three Rating Scale Formats." *Journal of Applied Psychology* 59 (1974): 307–312. (II–R)

Campbell, J. P., M. D. Dunnette, E. E. Lawler, and K. E. Weick. *Managerial Behavior, Performance, and Effectiveness.* New York: McGraw-Hill, 1970, pp. 119–125. (II)

Campbell, J. P., M. D. Dunnette, R. D. Arvey, and L. N. Hellervick. "The Development of Behaviorally Based Rating Scales." *Journal of Applied Psychology* 57 (1973): 15–22. (II–R)

Cummings, L., and D. Schwab. *Performance in Organizations.* Glenview, Ill.: Scott Foresman, 1973, pp. 91–92. (I)

Dickinson, T. L., and T. E. Tice. "A Multitrait-Multimethod Analysis of Scales Developed by Retranslation." *Organizational Behavior and Human Performance* 9 (1973): 421–438. (II–R)

Fogli, L., C. L. Hulin, and M. R. Blood. "Development of First-Level Behavioral Job Criteria." *Journal of Applied Psychology* 55 (1971): 3–8. (II–R)

Friedman, B. A., and E. T. Cornelius. "Effect of Rater Participation in Scale Construction on the Psychometric Characteristics of Two Rating Scale Formats." *Journal of Applied Psychology* 61 (1976): 210–216. (II–R)

Harari, O., and S. Zedeck. "Development of Behaviorally Anchored Rating Scales for the Evaluation of Faculty Teaching." *Journal of Applied Psychology* 58 (1973): 261–265. (II–R)

Landy, F. J., and R. M. Guion. "Development of Scales for the Measurement of Work Motivation." *Organizational Behavior and Human Performance* 5 (1970): 93–103. (II–R)

Schwab, D. P., H. Heneman, and T. DeCotiis. "Behaviorally Anchored Rating Scales: A Review of the Literature." *Personnel Psychology* 28 (1975): 549–562.

Smith, P. C., and L. M. Kendall. "Retranslating of Expectations: An Approach to the Construction of Unambiguous Anchors for Rating Scales." *Journal of Applied Psychology* 47 (1963): 149–155. (II–R)

Smith, P. C. "Behaviors, Results, and Organizational Effectiveness: The Problem of Criteria." In M. D. Dunnette, ed, *Handbook of Industrial and Organizational Psychology.* Chicago: Rand McNally, 1976. (II)

Williams, W. E., and D. A. Seiler. "Relationships between Measures of Effort and Job Performance." *Journal of Applied Psychology* 57 (1973): 49–54. (II–R)

Zedeck, S., and H. T. Baker. "Nursing Performance as Measured by Behavioral Expectation Scales: A Multitrait-Multirater Analysis." *Organizational Behavior and Human Performance* 7 (1972): 457–466. (II–R)

Zedeck, S., and M. R. Blood. *Foundations of Behavioral Science Research in Organizations.* Monterey, Cal: Brooks/Cole, 1974. (I)

Zedeck, S., N. Imparato, M. Krausz, and T. Oleno. "Development of Behaviorally Anchored Rating Scales as a Function of Organizational Level." *Journal of Applied Psychology* 59 (1974): 249–252. (II–R)

Zedeck, S., R. Jacobs, and D. Kafry. "Behavioral Expectations: Development of Parallel Forms and Analysis of Scale Assumptions." *Journal of Applied Psychology* 61 (1976): 112–115. (II–R)

PART A

Form 1 Sample BARS Format—Job: Chemical Equipment Operator; Dimension: Verbal Communication

7 ☐ This operator could be expected to:
check verbal instructions against written procedures; always check to make sure he or she heard others correctly; brief replacements quickly and accurately, giving only relevant information.

6 ☐ This operator could be expected to:
inform superiors immediately if problems arise; listen to others carefully and ask questions if he or she does not understand; give information, instructions, etc. in a calm, clear voice.

5 ☐ This operator could be expected to:
always inform others of his or her location in the plant; avoid discussing non–work-related subjects when relating plant status to others; inform others of all delays that took place on the shift.

4 ☐ This operator could be expected to:
give others detailed account of what needs to be done, but not to establish priorities; mumble when speaking to others; not face the person communicating with him or her and act disinterested.

3 ☐ This operator could be expected to:
fail to relate all necessary details to those relieving him or her at break or shift change; not seek information and only offer it when asked; guess at status of pots when relaying information; not check to be sure he or she has heard others correctly, but rely on what he or she thought the person said; leave out information about his or her own errors when talking to others.

2 ☐ This operator could be expected to:
never ask for help if unsure of something or if errors are made; refuse to listen to others; continually yell at others and use abusive language.

1 ☐ This operator could be expected to:
not answer when called; refuse to brief replacements; give person relieving him or her inaccurate information deliberately.

PART A

Form 2 Examples of Behavioral Anchors for Various Degrees of Performance on Job Dimensions of Police Dispatcher (see Exercise 4)

Instructions: On this sheet please write as many specific, brief *behavioral* incidents as you can think of which illustrate the seven degrees of performance on this form. Remember, these are *behaviors*—things people actually do or do not do which lead to good, fair, etc. performance; attitudes or feelings are not in question.

Job dimension: Dispatching emergency equipment.

Excellent performance: Information is clearly communicated and sites are always accurate when given to officers. In the event the ambulance doesn't know directions to a particular location, the dispatcher responds quickly and accurately gives directions. Always gathers relevant information and dispatches emergency equipment to appropriate site. Gathers and relays all vital information to hospital of patient status from ambulance. Relays all relevant information to patrol unit accurately, concisely, clearly, and quickly. Knows which vital questions to ask caller and relays accurate information to patrol car. This person can be expected to always correctly use appropriate department codes and languages in radio and phone conversations. Calmly relates information—able to decide when some codes are not enough.

Very good performance: Can always be expected to give clear, distinct information to officers. Information is always accurate and understandable when responding to officers. Responds to emergency situation in a calm, collected manner, never losing control of the situation. Advises other departments of ambulance running through their city. Always advises other units of emergency equipment that is running hot and gives accurate locations and direction of traffic. Able to distinguish priorities. Keeps self informed on any changes made in the codes.

Good performance: Usually both the message and sites specified are accurate. Takes what information possible over phone and relays to officer.

Fair performance: Information is usually accurate and well understood. This employee can be expected to make a sound evaluation of information gathered and dispatch patrol car only when necessary. Sends patrol car immediately to scene after receiving call if patrol car is available. This person can be expected to know all the appropriate codes and languages, but on occasion will forget the right code or language to use.

Poor performance: Sometimes is difficult to understand, but always gives accurate sites. Generally reacts calmly in difficult situations, but may on occasion become upset and nervous affecting job performance. Can be expected to dispatch patrol unit always regardless of the nature and importance of the information gathered. This person will occasionally substitute one code or language for another, causing some confusion, but immediately corrects the same as soon as an error is detected.

Very poor performance: Is always clearly understood, but occasionally fails to give appropriate sites. Occasionally mixes up information and, as a result, emergency equipment is delayed in arrival. Responds in a nervous manner in emergency situations and has a difficult time disguising lack of control. During periods of peak workload, this employee can be expected to occasionally forget to dispatch patrol car when one is needed. Has tendency to give erroneous and confusing information to the dispatched officer.

Unacceptable performance: Fails to dispatch emergency equipment in an immediate and efficient manner. Neglects to relay relevant information to patrol unit. Relays information to patrol unit in a garbled and stuttered fashion. Fails to observe proper FCC regulations in performing dispatch duties.

Name _____   Group Number _____

Date _____   Class Section _____   Hour _____   Score _____

PART B

Form 3 Retranslating and Scaling Behavioral Anchors for the Job of Grocery Clerk

If the behavioral anchors numbered 1–16 seem to best fit in the job dimension "Knowledge and Judgment of Checkstand Work," put a one (1) in the first column on this form ("Job Dimension"). If the behavioral anchors for a grocery clerk's job listed here appear to best represent the job dimension of "Organizational Ability of Checkstand Work," put a two (2) in the first column. In the second column, "Anchor Weight," indicate the level of job performance such anchor illustrates using the following scale:

1 = Extremely good performance
2 = Good performance
3 = Slightly good performance
4 = Neither good nor poor performance
5 = Slightly poor performance
6 = Poor performance
7 = Extremely poor performance

Behavioral Anchor	Job Dimension	Anchor Weight
1. This checker would organize the order when checking it out by placing all soft goods like bread, cake, etc. to one side of the counter and all meats, produce, frozen foods to the other side, thereby leaving the center of the counter for canned foods, boxed goods, etc.		
2. By knowing the price of items, this checker would be expected to look for mismarked and unmarked items.		
3. When in doubt, this checker would ask the other clerk if the item is taxable.		
4. This checker can be expected to verify, with another checker, a discrepancy between the shelf and the marked price before ringing up that item.		
5. This checker can be expected to lay milk and by-product cartons on their sides on the countertop.		
6. Thic checker may be expected to put wet merchandise on the top of the counter.		
7. You can expect this checker to grab more than one item at a time from the cart to the counter.		
8. You can expect this checker to know the various sizes of cans (e.g., no. 303, no. $2\frac{1}{2}$).		

Behavioral Anchor	Job Dimension	Anchor Weight
9. After bagging the order and while the customer is still writing a check, you can expect this checker to proceed to the next order if it is a small order.		
10. You could expect this checker to ask the customer the price of an item that he or she does not know.		
11. You can expect this checker to be aware of items that constantly fluctuate in price.		
12. When operating the quick check—the lights are flashing—this checker can be expected to check out a customer with 15 items.		
13. This checker can be expected to damage fragile merchandise like soft goods, eggs, and lightbulbs on the countertop.		
14. When checking, this checker would separate strawberries, bananas, cookies, cakes, and breads, etc.		
15. In order to take a break, this checker can be expected to close off the checkstand with people in line.		
16. In the daily course of personal relationships, this checker may be expected to linger in long conversations with a customer or another checker.		

PART C

Form 4 Sample Job Description from which to Derive Behavioral Anchors and Job Dimensions

Job Title: Maintenance, vehicle, and machine operator.

Job function: Perform a variety of duties—truck driver, warehouseman, disintegrator operator. Haul trash and outdated records. Maintain control of warehouse inventories.

Reports to: Chief engineer.

Department: Administration department, general-services division.

Qualifications—general: Have chauffeur's license. Be capable of operating a machine per instructions. Good physical condition.

Experience: General experience in machine operation and vehicle operation, light truck preferred.

Machines and equipment used: One-ton truck, disintegrator, two-wheelers and four-wheelers, and various hand tools.

Responsibility for cash and negotiable instruments: None.

Personal contacts: Some contact with other bank personnel. Some contact with delivery personnel.

Job details: Perform duties according to a regular schedule including the following: Select and load trash and records, haul to warehouse, and disintegrate all trash specified. Coordinate with refuse company to provide empty containers. Maintain inventory records of items in warehouse. Transfer of records for auditors. Receive incoming stocks and supplies, verify amounts, and sign receiving ticket. Store items as specified. Deliver as requested. Responsible for proper housekeeping of warehouse and outside areas. Maintain security of warehouse while open; locking and checking all doors when closing. May perform any other maintenance duties as is required under the direction of the Engineering Section. May perform any other duties as directed, within his or her capabilities. Responsible for proper maintenance and repairs of vehicle and machinery.

Name _____ Group Number _____

Date _____ Class Section _____ Hour _____ Score _____

PART C

Form 5 Behavioral Anchor Sheet

Job title:

Job dimension:

Behavioral Anchor Statements:

Instructions: On this sheet please provide three or more behavioral anchor statements for each performance level. You will complete one "Behavioral Anchor Sheet" for *each* job dimension for the job.

1. Excellent performance:

2. Very good performance:

3. Good performance:

4. Fair or average performance:

5. Poor performance:

6. Very poor performance:

7. Unacceptable performance:

Name _____ Group Number _____

Date _____ Class Section _____ Hour _____ Score _____

PART C

Form 5 Behavioral Anchor Sheet

Job title:

Job dimension:

Behavioral Anchor Statements:

Instructions: On this sheet please provide three or more behavioral anchor statements for each performance level. You will complete one "Behavioral Anchor Sheet" for *each* job dimension for the job.

1. Excellent performance:

2. Very good performance:

3. Good performance:

4. Fair or average performance:

5. Poor performance:

6. Very poor performance:

7. Unacceptable performance:

Name _____ Group Number _____

Date _____ Class Section _____ Hour _____ Score _____

PART C

Form 5 Behavioral Anchor Sheet

Job title:

Job dimension:

Behavioral Anchor Statements:

Instructions: On this sheet please provide three or more behavioral anchor statements for each performance level. You will complete one "Behavioral Anchor Sheet" for *each* job dimension for the job.

1. Excellent performance:

2. Very good performance:

3. Good performance:

4. Fair or average performance:

5. Poor performance:

6. Very poor performance:

7. Unacceptable performance:

Name _____ Group Number _____

Date _____ Class Section _____ Hour _____ Score _____

PART C
Form 5 Behavioral Anchor Sheet

Job title:

Job dimension:

Behavioral Anchor Statements:

Instructions: On this sheet please provide three or more behavioral anchor statements for each performance level. You will complete one "Behavioral Anchor Sheet" for *each* job dimension for the job.

1. Excellent performance:

2. Very good performance:

3. Good performance:

4. Fair or average performance:

5. Poor performance:

6. Very poor performance:

7. Unacceptable performance:

Name _____   Group Number _____

Date _____   Class Section _____   Hour _____   Score _____

PART C

Form 5 Behavioral Anchor Sheet

Job title:

Job dimension:

Behavioral Anchor Statements:

Instructions: On this sheet please provide three or more behavioral anchor statements for each performance level. You will complete one "Behavioral Anchor Sheet" for *each* job dimension for the job.

1. Excellent performance:

2. Very good performance:

3. Good performance:

4. Fair or average performance:

5. Poor performance:

6. Very poor performance:

7. Unacceptable performance:

Name _____ Group Number _____

Date _____ Class Section _____ Hour _____ Score _____

PART C

Form 5 Behavioral Anchor Sheet

Job title:

Job dimension:

Behavioral Anchor Statements:

Instructions: On this sheet please provide three or more behavioral anchor statements for each performance level. You will complete one "Behavioral Anchor Sheet" for *each* job dimension for the job.

1. Excellent performance:

2. Very good performance:

3. Good performance:

4. Fair or average performance:

5. Poor performance:

6. Very poor performance:

7. Unacceptable performance:

Name _____ Group Number _____

Date _____ Class Section _____ Hour _____ Score _____

PART C

Form 5 Behavioral Anchor Sheet

Job title:

Job dimension:

Behavioral Anchor Statements:

Instructions: On this sheet please provide three or more behavioral anchor statements for each performance level. You will complete one "Behavioral Anchor Sheet" for *each* job dimension for the job.

1. Excellent performance:

2. Very good performance:

3. Good performance:

4. Fair or average performance:

5. Poor performance:

6. Very poor performance:

7. Unacceptable performance:

Name _____   Group Number _____

Date _____   Class Section _____   Hour _____   Score _____

PART C

Form 5 Behavioral Anchor Sheet

Job title:

Job dimension:

Behavioral Anchor Statements:

Instructions: On this sheet please provide three or more behavioral anchor statements for each performance level. You will complete one "Behavioral Anchor Sheet" for *each* job dimension for the job.

1. Excellent performance:

2. Very good performance:

3. Good performance:

4. Fair or average performance:

5. Poor performance:

6. Very poor performance:

7. Unacceptable performance:

Name _____ Group Number _____

Date _____ Class Section _____ Hour _____ Score _____

PART C

Form 6 Worksheet for Retranslating Behavioral Anchors*

Anchor number and/or abbreviation	Job dimension	Anchor scale value (1 to 7)
1.		
2.		
3.		
4.		
5.		
6.		
7.		
8.		
9.		
10.		
11.		
12.		
13.		
14.		
15.		
16.		
17.		
18.		
19.		
20.		
21.		
22.		
23.		
24.		
25.		
26.		
27.		
28.		
29.		
30.		
31.		
32.		
33.		
34.		
35.		
36.		
37.		
38.		
39.		
40.		
41.		
42.		
43.		
44.		
45.		
46.		
47.		
48.		

PART C

Form 6 *(Continued)*

Anchor number and/or abbreviation	Job dimension	Anchor scale value (1 to 7)
49.		
50.		
51.		
52.		
53.		
54.		
55.		
56.		
57.		
58.		
59.		
60.		
61.		
62.		
63.		
64.		
65.		
66.		
67.		
68.		
69.		
70.		
71.		
72.		
73.		
74.		
75.		
76.		
77.		
78.		
79.		
80.		
81.		
82.		
83.		
84.		
85.		
86.		
87.		
88.		
89.		
90.		
91.		
92.		
93.		
94.		
95.		
96.		
97.		
98.		
99.		
100.		

* Each person in your group will need to fill out a sheet like this one; use additional sheets if necessary.

Name _____ Group Number _____

Date _____ Class Section _____ Hour _____ Score _____

PART D

Form 7 Final Behaviorally Anchored Rating Scale

Job Title: _____

Job Dimension: _____

1. Excellent
   performance:

2. Very good
   performance:

3. Good performance:

4. Fair or
   average performance:

5. Poor performance:

6. Very poor
   performance:

7. Unacceptable
   performance:

Name _____   Group Number _____

Date _____   Class Section _____   Hour _____   Score _____

PART D

Form 7 Final Behaviorally Anchored Rating Scale

Job Title: _____

Job Dimension: _____

1. Excellent
   performance:

2. Very good
   performance:

3. Good performance:

4. Fair or
   average performance:

5. Poor performance:

6. Very poor
   performance:

7. Unacceptable
   performance:

Name _____   Group Number _____

Date _____ Class Section _____ Hour _____ Score _____

PART D

Form 7 Final Behaviorally Anchored Rating Scale

Job Title: _____

Job Dimension: _____

1. Excellent
   performance:

2. Very good
   performance:

3. Good performance:

4. Fair or
   average performance:

5. Poor performance:

6. Very poor
   performance:

7. Unacceptable
   performance:

Name _____   Group Number _____

Date _____   Class Section _____   Hour _____   Score _____

PART D

Form 7 Final Behaviorally Anchored Rating Scale

Job Title: _____

Job Dimension: _____

1. Excellent
   performance:

2. Very good
   performance:

3. Good performance:

4. Fair or
   average performance:

5. Poor performance:

6. Very poor
   performance:

7. Unacceptable
   performance:

Name _____   Group Number _____

Date _____   Class Section _____   Hour _____   Score _____

PART D

Form 7 Final Behaviorally Anchored Rating Scale

Job Title: _____

Job Dimension: _____

1. Excellent
   performance:

2. Very good
   performance:

3. Good performance:

4. Fair or
   average performance:

5. Poor performance:

6. Very poor
   performance:

7. Unacceptable
   performance:

Name _____   Group Number _____

Date _____   Class Section _____   Hour _____   Score _____

PART D

Form 7 Final Behaviorally Anchored Rating Scale

Job Title: _____

Job Dimension: _____

1. Excellent
   performance:

2. Very good
   performance:

3. Good performance:

4. Fair or
   average performance:

5. Poor performance:

6. Very poor
   performance:

7. Unacceptable
   performance:

Name _____ Group Number _____

Date _____ Class Section _____ Hour _____ Score _____

PART D

Form 7 Final Behaviorally Anchored Rating Scale

Job Title: _____

Job Dimension: _____

1. Excellent
   performance:

2. Very good
   performance:

3. Good performance:

4. Fair or
   average performance:

5. Poor performance:

6. Very poor
   performance:

7. Unacceptable
   performance:

Name _____   Group Number _____

Date _____   Class Section _____   Hour _____   Score _____

PART D

Form 7 Final Behaviorally Anchored Rating Scale

Job Title: _____

Job Dimension: _____

1. Excellent
   performance:

2. Very good
   performance:

3. Good performance:

4. Fair or
   average performance:

5. Poor performance:

6. Very poor
   performance:

7. Unacceptable
   performance:

Name _____   Group Number _____

Date _____   Class Section _____   Hour _____   Score _____

PART D

Form 8 Job Dimension Weights

Job Dimension	Weight (in percent)
1.	
2.	
3.	
4.	
5.	
6.	
7.	
8.	
9.	
10.	
(Total = 100%)	

Name _____ Group Number _____

Date _____ Class Section _____ Hour _____ Score _____

ASSESSMENT OF LEARNING IN PERSONNEL ADMINISTRATION
EXERCISE 5

1. Try to state the purpose of this exercise in one concise sentence.

2. Specifically what did you learn from this exercise (i.e., skills, abilities, and knowledge)?

3. How might your learning influence your role and your duties as a personnel administrator?

4. What characteristics of jobs, organizations, etc. should be considered before a decision to implement BARS is made?

5. How could a BARS PA system be evaluated as to its cost effectiveness?

6. Additional questions given by your implementor:

Exercise 6

DESIGNING AND IMPLEMENTING A MANAGEMENT-BY-OBJECTIVES (MBO) PROGRAM: MEASURING EMPLOYEE CONTRIBUTIONS

PREVIEW

One widely used performance-appraisal technique is Management-By-Objectives (MBO). MBO has been used effectively in many types of organizations and is based on setting objectives or goals and evaluating people based on the degree to which they attain the objectives. MBO is not only used as a performance-appraisal system, but also as a basic management-planning and control tool. It helps to focus effort of people on important organizational goals and emphasizes results of their efforts and their contributions to organizational success. In this exercise MBO is discussed and you are able to assess your own understanding of MBO via a quiz. You also design an MBO program and conduct and evaluate a performance-review session.

INTRODUCTION

Management-By-Objectives

Management-By-Objectives (MBO) is a management technique and process whereby *objectives* or goals may be established for: (1) the organization; (2) each department; (3) each manager within each department; and (4) each employee who works in an area where the establishment of objectives would be practical and valuable. MBO is not a measure of employee behavior, but is an attempt to measure employee *effectiveness*, or contribution to organizational success and goal attainment.

OBJECTIVES

1. To become familiar with the advantages of MBO as a performance-appraisal and a general planning-and-control technique.
2. To become familiar with the actual design and implementation process of MBO, including an appreciation for problems typically encountered and the type of forms used in MBO.
3. To gain skill in conducting an MBO performance-review session and in giving people feedback about their performance.

PREMEETING ASSIGNMENT

Read the entire exercise.

Establishing objectives usually consists of having the key people affected by the objectives meet to agree on the major objectives for a given time period (e.g., one year), develop plans for how and when the objectives will be accomplished, and decide on the criteria for determining if the objectives have been met. Once objectives have been established, progress reviews are made regularly until the end of the period for which the objectives were established. At that time the people who established the objectives at each level in the organization meet to evaluate actual results and then agree on the objectives for the next period.

The most important tool a manager has in setting and achieving forward-looking goals is people, and to achieve results with this tool he or she must be able, first, to instill in workers a sense of commitment and desire to contribute to organizational goals; second, control and coordinate the efforts of workers toward goal accomplishment; and third, help subordinates to improve their ability to make ever greater contributions to the organization. Often the personnel department plays a vital role in this process by helping managers understand and implement MBO and reviewing employees' progress in appraisal interviews or review sessions.

MBO: Some History. The MBO approach, in the sense that it requires managers to set specific objectives to be achieved in the future and encourages them to continually ask what more can be done, is offered as a partial answer to the question of maintaining organizational vitality and creativity. Management-By-Objectives was introduced first by Peter Drucker in 1954. As a management approach, it has been further developed by many management practitioners and theoreticians, among them Douglas McGregor, George Odiorne, and John Humble. Essentially MBO is a process or system in which a superior and subordinates sit down and jointly set specific objectives to be accomplished within a set time frame and for which the subordinate is then held directly responsible.

All organizations exist for a purpose, whether it be, for example, to make steel products or to educate others. To achieve that purpose top management sets goals and objectives that are common to the whole organization. In organizations not using MBO, most planning and objective setting to achieve these common organizational goals is directed from the top down. Plans and objectives are passed from one managerial level to another and subordinates are told both what to do and what their responsibilities are. The MBO approach injects an element of negotiation and dialogue into this process. The superior may bring specific goals and measures for his or her subordinate to a meeting with this subordinate, who also brings specific objectives and measures which he or she sees as appropriate or as contributing to better accomplishment of the job. Together they develop a group of specific goals, measures of achievement, and time frames. The subordinate commits himself or herself to the accomplishment of those goals and is then held responsible for them within some tolerance limits. The manager and subordinate may have occasional progress reviews and reevaluation meetings,

but at the end of the set period of time the subordinate is judged on the results achieved. He or she may be rewarded for success by salary, praise, or promotion. If objectives were not met, the employee may receive additional training or be transferred to a job that will give needed training or supervision. Whatever the outcome, it will be based on accomplishment of the goals people had some part in setting and were hopefully committed to achieving.

Varieties of MBO. In practice, this MBO approach of necessity varies widely, especially in regard to how formalized and structured it is in a given organization and to what degree subordinates are allowed to set their own goals. In some organizations MBO is a very formal management system with precise scheduling of performance reviews, formal evaluation techniques, and specific formats in which objectives and measures must be presented for review and discussion. In other organizations it may be so informal as to be described simply as the process of getting together and deciding what we've done and what we're going to do in the future. However, in most organizations using MBO it takes the form of formal objective-setting and appraisal meetings held on a regular basis, often quarterly, semiannually, or annually.

Even more variable than the degree of formality and structure in MBO is the degree to which subordinates are allowed to set their own goals. In this regard the kind of work that an organization does plays a large part in determining how much and on what level a subordinate will be allowed to participate in formulating his or her own goals. In some organizations subordinates are almost told what they need to do and simply asked if they will commit themselves to achieve this goal, while in others they are given a great latitude and room for innovation.

The MBO Process. Regardless of the type of organization, however, the MBO process usually consists of three steps:

1. Mutual goal setting;
2. Freedom for the subordinate to perform;
3. Reviewing performance.

These steps are detailed as follows:

Step 1: Setting Objectives. Individual managers determine what specific outcomes they plan to produce as a result of their efforts. They also carefully plan how these results will be produced, but the emphasis is on the *result*. The objectives are stated as precisely as possible. For most organizations, this means in quantitative terms whenever feasible. Finding the right measure to use for an objective has proven to be as hard as finding the right objective in the first place. Organizations have also discovered that they must ensure that the objectives of one manager merge, rather than conflict, with those of other managers who may share in the accomplishment of some larger organizational goal. Providing for this "interlock" of objectives both vertically and horizontally has also proved difficult. While individual managers initiate the process of setting objectives, the proposals they originate are reviewed by their supervisors to ensure that subordinate goals are in support of the goals of higher levels in the organization and that, ultimately, the organizational objectives will be achieved. This has meant, in most organizations, that information about the view of the future from the top has had to be transmitted downward in the organization, so that individual managers have a meaningful context within which to formulate their goals. Organizations have developed a variety of means for achieving this two-way flow of information and objectives, including committee meetings, conferences, and memoranda.

Step 2: Working toward the Goals: Action Planning. Organizations often report pleasant surprises at the genuine commitment employees bring to their work in an MBO system. Achieving the objectives they have helped to develop seems really to matter to managers. Subordinates are typically given latitude regarding how they will meet objectives. While specific behaviors are seldom spelled out as they would be in a BARS system (see Exercise 5), the subordinate must still behave within limits set by resources available, law, or ethics.[1]

Step 3: Reviewing Performance. Objectives not only serve to point effort in the right direction, they serve in measuring progress as well. This review of progress is the performance appraisal aspect of MBO. It takes the form of normal managerial controls which attempt to measure effectiveness, but may facilitate greater effectiveness because of clearer goals and more detailed advanced planning concerning how to achieve them. While the types of objectives may be changed as a result of these reviews, most organizations do so reluctantly and only if it is clearly necessary. On the other hand, the levels of objective accomplishment may be mediated depending on extraneous factors, or those external to the organization (e.g., interest rates or general product demand). Thus, performance must be evaluated with this in mind.

MBO: What Can Go Wrong.   While the basic MBO process seems simple enough, there are several problems associated with the actual implementation of MBO which can prevent it from being an effective PA process. Because many organizations have attempted MBO and/or are currently using it, the problems that manifest themselves in implementation are reasonably well known and have been catalogued in several published articles.[2] A brief listing and explanation of the more common problems follows:

1. Overemphasis on objectives (ends) at the expense of specifying how these objectives are to be attained (means). This can lead to ambiguity; lack of recognition for effort, creativity, and motivation; and a "results at any price philosophy" that may be harmful to an organization in the long run

2. Too much paperwork reduces commitment and overloads managers.

3. Lack of commitment from top management often makes MBO just another fad.

4. Lack of proper training and knowledge in goal-setting, MBO philosophy and methods, and in holding review sessions can deter MBO efforts.

5. No genuine participation by superior and subordinate in goal setting due to personality, supervisory style, or status differences precludes subordinates from seeing any real effort on the part of managers to include them and thus their commitment is lost.

6. Failure to recognize that many aspects of performance are group efforts and that MBO for a single worker may hurt group cohesiveness unless the entire group shares in rewards from goal attainment. Likewise, failure to meet one's goals in MBO may be due to the performance of others on whose work one depends.

7. Relying only on performance goals reduces incentive to improve certain skills and ability. Training goals, staff and self-development goals, etc. are helpful.

8. Goal-setting difficulty, especially for higher-level, unprogrammed positions can thwart MBO. Data on job performance and discussions with others familiar with job performance may help.

---

[1] See C. E. Schneier and R. W. Beatty, "The Action Planning Phase in MBO: Using Behaviorally-Anchored Rating Scales," *Management by Objectives*, 1977, in press.

[2] See, e.g., Schneier and Beatty, "The Action Planning Phase in MBO"; A. P. Raia, *Managing by Objectives* (Glenview, Ill.: Scott Foresman, 1974), Chap. 9; H. Levinson, "Management by Whose Objectives?", *Harvard Business Review*, July–August 1970, A8, pp. 125–134; B. D. Jamieson, "Behavioral Problems with Management by Objectives," *Academy of Management Journal* 16 (1973): 496–505.

In summary, MBO has been an effective PA system in several organizations. However, attention must be paid to details. Advance planning and education are required, an assessment of an organization's willingness to accept MBO is necessary, and continual evaluation, analysis, and redesign can help improve MBO effectiveness.

Research has generally supported the effectiveness of MBO efforts to improve performance.[3] Various problems have been noted with such research, one of which is that when an organization adopts MBO, it typically makes other changes in policy, planning, and control techniques, and/or in supervisory practices as well. It is therefore difficult to isolate MBO from these other changes as direct causes of any subsequent improvement in organizational effectiveness.

MBO and Behaviorally Anchored Rating Scales (BARS). MBO is a system that specifies the desired results or *ends* for a task, department, or organization. However, there may be a need to specify the *means* or methods available and desired to attain these results. That is, while MBO derives much of its motivational ability by providing for the delegation of discretion and authority to people in order that they may carry out their objectives, it may permit too much freedom for some and not specify methods of goal attainment in enough detail for others.

Experienced job incumbents may know of several methods for goal attainment. With no formal guidelines available to define those accepted methods, however, incumbents may be so anxious to attain their objectives that they adopt a "results at any price" philosophy. Thus, they might go beyond the bounds of ethics (or the law) to meet their sales quota, lower their costs, increase their profit, win an election, or develop a new product, service, or program. Inexperienced incumbents, on the other hand, may need to have methods for goal attainment specified due to their lack of experience or their interest in attempting to find more-effective approaches to goal attainment.

Behaviorally anchored rating scales (BARS, see Exercise 5) can be very helpful in this regard, as they enable incumbents to become aware of the types of behaviors thought to be instrumental for goal attainment. The behavioral anchors used in BARS pinpoint desired performance. They thus can be used to give ratees ideas on how to obtain objectives and can cue ratees as to the judgment the organization has made on the utility or ethics of certain behaviors.

For example, an objective in MBO may be to increase the effectiveness of one's communications with subordinates. It is to be measured by increases in satisfaction scores obtained from questionnaires submitted to subordinates. If a BARS system were implemented for the job in question before MBO is attempted, the anchors on the BARS for the dimension called Communications Skills could inform a job incumbent that effective communications would come about through such behaviors as the solicitation of subordinates' views, holding frequent, regularly scheduled departmental meetings, and/or developing a system of memoranda sent to all staff members. These behaviors would be the anchors which indicate desired performance on the BARS form for the Communications Skill dimension. The BARS would tell job incumbents *how* to attain their objectives in behavioral terms,[4] while an MBO system would help decide what the objectives should be.

MBO and BARS can thus be seen as very compatible performance-appraisal systems with BARS a useful prerequisite to implementing an MBO program.

PROCEDURE

Overview. MBO is a process of evaluating performance which focuses on the individual's effectiveness or contributions to the organization and not their behavior or evaluations of behavior. Thus, MBO attempts to determine what people at work are to contribute and measures this in terms of quantity, quality, cost, timeliness of output, etc. In this exercise you are given an opportunity to measure contributions to effectiveness.

First, a checklist is used to review your understanding of MBO concepts. Examples of MBO information and a few typical MBO forms are presented next. A task follows in which various measures of effectiveness, or indices, are linked to appropriate methods of measuring these effectiveness indices. An MBO form is then developed for a familiar job. Fi-

---

[3] For a review of MBO research, see G. P. Latham and G. A. Yukl, "A Review of Research on the Application of Goal Setting in Organizations," *Academy of Management Journal* 18 (1975): 824–843. Since much of the effectiveness of MBO can be traced to the effect of goal setting on performance, Edwin Locke's theory of goal setting, and its related body of supporting research, is also a relevant aspect of the MBO literature. Locke's theory is explained in E. A. Locke, "Toward a Theory of Task Motivation and Incentives," *Organizational Behavior and Human Performance* 3 (1968): 157–189. Research on the theory is reviewed in the Latham and Yukl article cited in this note.

[4] See Schneier and Beatty, "The Action Planning Phase MBO . . ."; and Exercise 5.

nally, an MBO performance review session is conducted and evaluated.

PART A

STEP 1: Form 1 provides a brief review of your understanding of MBO. Complete the form and review your answers with those given by the implementor or discuss them in small groups.

TIME: 15 minutes.

PART B

STEP 2: In Forms 2 and 3 there are two examples of forms used in MBO programs. These contain job *objectives*, along with the *methods* used to assess performance on these objectives. Study these forms so that you are familiar with the type of objectives used in MBO and how they are assessed. Also provided are a few blank MBO forms (Forms 4 and 5) which serve as examples to further familiarize you with the MBO process and paperwork. Study these carefully, as they can be used as models for the MBO forms you develop later in the exercise.

TIME: About 15 minutes.

STEP 3: Form 6 consists of a brief exercise which will help you to make the distinction between "objectives" and the "methods of measuring" these objectives. You are requested to review the measures of objective accomplishment in Form 6. This list consists of quantity, quality, cost, timeliness dimensions, and other dimensions that may be useful in attempting to implement an MBO program. They describe the broad categories to which the specific effectiveness measures, or results, in the right column of Form 6 might belong. You are to take the "what is measured" items (A through J) and assign them to each of the "specific outcomes" items by placing the appropriate letter(s) to the left of each outcome. Obviously, several of the items on the right column may need more than one letter; thus, you may use several letters for a specific outcome.

Once you have completed Form 6, review it with the implementor or others in your group to determine if you understand that the MBO approach is an attempt both to determine *what* is to be done on the job (objectives or specific outcomes) *and* to provide some *means*

of measuring what level of accomplishment was achieved.

TIME: About 30 minutes.

PART C

STEP 4: After you understand the concepts in Form 6, you are ready to design an MBO program for a job with which you have some familiarity. Form into groups of not more than six people and choose one member whose job will be used for the MBO system. The remaining group members will interview the job holder and construct an MBO form. Any type of job may be used. You may want to use the job the group has used in the past (Exercises 3, 4, or 5). If you do not use a job one of the group members now holds or has held in the past, use one of the jobs for which job descriptions are given in Exercises 3, 15, or 17. Fill out Form 7 first. It is a worksheet to be used as you decide upon goals or objectives. The objectives used in Form 7 should be set *jointly* by the job holder and the interviewers. In completing Form 7, be certain that you have listed *objectives, not methods* in the objectives column. For example, scheduling is often placed in the objective column, but it is really a method for accomplishing an objective, as better scheduling will lead to reduced costs, complaints, or maintenance. Generally, many items, such as planning or organizing, are methods not objectives and should be treated as such. After you have completed Form 7, devise your own MBO form, including objectives, actions planned, etc. This form should be placed on a separate sheet of paper and will be used below. Use Forms 2–5 as examples of how your MBO form might look. You will need two copies of your MBO form for Step 5.

TIME: About 40 minutes.

PART D

STEP 5: The last step in the exercise is the Performance Review process. One of the group members who helped design the MBO form developed above in Step 4 and who also has the most knowledge about the job should role-play the part of the supervisor who will conduct the performance review. The person who supplied the information for the form (i.e., the person who holds the job) will role-play the part of the ratee in the review. If jobs were chosen which do not belong to any of the group members, any member who has some knowledge of the job chosen can act as the ratee.

Two separate reviews will be held. First, the rater and ratee should assume that the ratee had only fair performance. That is, he or she did not meet all of the objectives and/or did not meet them at the level of performance specified. One copy of the MBO form designed for the job in Step 4 above can be filled out to reflect this degree of performance. Then the review is held and the remaining group members act as observers and complete Form 8. They each answer each question and mark their answers in the answer row designed for the "fair performance" review. The rater's job, of course, would be to discuss the ratee's performance: its pros and cons, its relation to set goals, reasons for poor performance, and what can be done to improve performance. The ratee's job would be to respond in a way he or she feels appropriate, given fair performance.

The second performance review is conducted in the same manner; however, this time the assumption is that the ratee's performance has been very good. The MBO form can be filled out to reflect this level of performance and the review proceeds with the rater giving the feedback and the ratee responding. Again, remaining group members complete Form 8, but this time mark their answers in the answer row designated for the "very good performance" review.

When both reviews are complete the observers can each compare their observations on Form 8 and discuss them with the rater and ratee. What patterns emerged in the two reviews? What were the major differences and similarities? Which was most constructive for the ratee? The group could also critique the performances of the rater and ratee. Was a "problem-solving" focus or a "criticism" focus used?

TIME: About 7 minutes per review and about 20 minutes for discussion.

FOR FURTHER READING

Beck, A. C., and E. D. Hillman. "OD to MBO or MBO to OD: Does It Make a Difference?" *Personnel Journal* 51 (1972): 827–834. (I)

Bryan, J. F., and E. A. Locke. "Goal Setting as a Means of Increasing Motivation." *Journal of Applied Psychology* 51 (1967): 274–277. (II–R)

Carroll, S. J., and H. L. Tosi. "The Relationship of Characteristics of the Viewed Process as Moderated by Personality and Situation Factors to the Success of Management by Objectives Approach." *Proceedings, Academy of Management National Meeting,* 1969. (II–R)

Carroll, S. J., and H. L. Tosi. *Management by Objectives: Application and Research.* New York: MacMillan, 1973. (I)

Drucker, Peter. *The Practice of Management.* New York: Harper, 1954. (I)

French, W. L., and R. W. Hollmann. "Management by Objectives: Team Approach." *California Management Review* 17 (Spring 1975): 13–22. (I)

Humble, J. W. *Management by Objectives.* London: Industrial Education and Research Foundation, 1967. (I)

Humble, J. W. *Improving Business Results.* London: McGraw-Hill, 1968. (I)

Humble, J. W. *Management by Objectives in Action.* London: McGraw-Hill, 1970. (I)

Ivancevich, J. M. "A Longitudinal Assessment of MBO." *Administrative Science Quarterly* 17 (1972): 126–138. (II–R)

Ivancevich, J. M. "Changes in Performance in a Management by Objectives Program." *Administrative Science Quarterly* 19 (1974): 563–574. (II–R)

Ivancevich, J. M., J. H. Donnelly, and H. L. Lyon. "A Study of the Impact of Management by Objectives on Perceived Need Satisfaction." *Personnel Psychology* 23 (1970): 139–151. (II–R)

Jamieson, B. D. "Behavioral Problems with Management by Objectives." *Academy of Management Journal* 16, no. 3 (1973): 496–505. (II)

Latham, G. P., and G. A. Yukl. "A Review of Research on the Application of Goal-Setting in Organizations." *Academy of Management Journal* 18 (1975): 824–845. (II)

Latham, G. P., and G. A. Yukl. "Effects of Assigned and Participation Goal-Setting on Performance and Job Satisfaction." *Journal of Applied Psychology* 61 (1976): 199–205. (II–R)

Levinson, J. "Management by Whose Objectives?" *Harvard Business Review* 48 (July–August 1970): 125–134. (I)

Locke, E. A. "Toward a Theory of Task Motivation and Incentives." *Organizational Behaviors and Human Performance* 3 (1968): 157–189. (II)

Locke, E. A. "Performance Goals as Determinants of Level of Performance and Boredom." *Journal of Applied Psychology* 51 (1957): 120–130. (II–R)

Mager, R. F. *Preparing Objectives for Programmed Instruction.* San Francisco: Fearon, 1962. (I)

MBO Symposium. *Training and Development Journal* 26, no. 4 (April 1972): 2–23. (I)

McGregor, Douglas. "An Uneasy Look at Performance Appraisal." *Harvard Business Review* 35 (1957): 80–94. (I)

McGregor, Douglas. *The Human Side of Enterprise.* New York: McGraw-Hill, 1960. (I)

McGregor, Douglas. *Leadership and Motivation.* Cambridge: The MIT Press, 1966. (I)

Odiorne, G. S. *Management by Objectives.* New York: Pitman, 1964. (I)

Odiorne, G. S. *Training by Objectives: Economic Approach to Management Training.* New York: MacMillan, 1970. (I)

Odiorne, G. S. *Personnel Administration by Objectives.* Homewood, Ill.: Irwin, 1971. (I)

"Public Sector MBO." (Special feature.) *Public Personnel Management* 5 (March–April 1976): 83–102 (3 articles). (I)

Raia, A. P. "Goal Setting and Self Control." *Journal of Management Studies* 2 (1965): 34–53. (I)

Raia, A. P. *Managing by Objectives.* Glenview, Illinois: Scott Foresman, 1972. (I)

Reddin, W. J. *Managerial Effectiveness.* London: McGraw-Hill, 1971. (I)

Schleh, E. C. *Management by Results.* New York: McGraw-Hill, 1961. (I)

Schneier, C. E., and R. W. Beatty. "Making Action Plans Work in MBO: The Use of Behaviorally Anchored Rating Scales." *Management by Objectives*, 1977, in press. (I)

Stedary, A. C. *Budget Control and Cost Behavior.* Englewood Cliffs, New Jersey: Prentice Hall, 1960. (I)

Steers, R. M. "Factors Affecting Job Attitudes in a Goal-Setting Environment." *Academy of Management Journal* 19 (1976): 6–16. (II–R)

Tosi, H. L., and S. J. Carroll. "Managerial Reaction to Management by Objectives." *Academy of Management Journal* 11 (1968): 415–425. (II–R)

Wickens, J. S. "Management by Objectives: An Appraisal." *Journal of Management Studies* 5 (1968): 365–370. (I)

Wikstrom, W. S. *Managing by and with Objectives. Studies in Personnel Policy, No. 212.* New York: Conference Board, 1968. (I)

Name _____   Group Number _____

Date _____   Class Section _____   Hour _____   Score _____

PART A

Form 1 MBO Review List

1. Which of the following are the *major* focuses of MBO?
    ____ results (or output)
    ____ employee on-the-job activities
    ____ the goal-setting process
    ____ the performance review process
    ____ advising employees how to do their job
    ____ leaving people alone to do their job

2. Which of the following terms may typically be used to measure MBO *results*?
    ____ timeliness/dependability   ____ lost time
    ____ quality   ____ training
    ____ cost reduction   ____ maintenance
    ____ innovations   ____ employee satisfaction
    ____ profit realization   ____ technical accomplishments
    ____ quantity   ____ employee turnover

3. What factors can we assume to be responsible for motivating people to perform well through an MBO system?
    ____ mutual goal setting
    ____ freedom to perform
    ____ feedback on performance
    ____ annual review procedures
    ____ changes in job content

PART B

Form 2 Sample Job Objectives and Methods of Measurement

Job Objectives of a Paper Deliverer

Objectives	Measures			Time frame	Methods
	Measure	Present level	Desired level		
1. Deliver papers	quantity	90% 1½ hrs. after received	95% 1½ hrs. after received	2 mos.	Bike, car, walk
	quality	4 complaints per 1000	1 complaint per 1000	1 mo.	Dry and porched—Accurate
	cost	1.00 (25¢ per complaint)	0.25	1 mo.	collections
2. Sales	quantity	1 new customer per month	2 new customers per month maintain for one year	6 mos.	Make more calls
	quality				Good service
3. Profit	quantity	75¢ per customer per month	1.00 per customer per month	2 mos.	Reduce costs
	cost	3.25 per month	3.00 per month	2 mos.	Control expenses (i.e., runner bands, plastic sleeves, delinquent accounts)
4. Collections	quantity	90% of customers pay in one week of month end	95% of customers paid in one week of month end	1 mo.	Make more follow-ups, use the telephone, use stamped envelopes
5. Paying for papers	cost	5% delinquency charge	2% delinquency charge	2 mos.	Develop working capital, increase payment of accounts receiveable

PART B

Form 3 Sample Managerial Job Objectives

Sam Speedy
_____
Prepared by manager   Date

Harry Slow
_____
Reviewed by supervisor   Date

General manager
_____
Position title

Production
_____
Position title

Progress reviews

1st _____
2nd _____
3rd _____

Date

Major job objectives	% WT	Measures of results	Std. of perf.	Results		Dates	
				Target	Actual	Target	Actual
1. Product delivery (May be broken down by products)	25%	a. Percent of on-schedule delivery	94%	Increase to 98%		8/31	
		b. Number of customer complaints as a % of monthly purchase orders	4%	Decrease to 3%		9/30	
2. Product quality (May be broken down by products)	30%	a. Percent of rejects per total monthly volume	6%	Decrease to 4%		7/31	
		b. Ratio of factory repair time to total production hours/month.	7%	Decrease to 4%		9/31	
		c. Number of units service free during warranty period	73%	Increase to 86%		10/31	
3. Operating efficiency	25%	a. Cost per unit of output per month	$35.75/ unit	Reduce to $35.50/unit		2/1	
		b. Equipment utilization time as a % of monthly available hours	86%	Increase to 95%		11/15	
4. Other key objectives	20%						

PART B

Form 4 A Goal-Setting-Program Form

Level of objective (check the appropriate one)

1. Organizational	____
2. Departmental	____
3. Divisional	____
4. Managerial employee or individual	____

Type of objective (check the appropriate ones)

1. Routine responsibilities	____
2. Problem solving	____
3. Innovative	____
4. Personal or organizational development	____
5. Other	____

	1	2	3	4
R A N K	*Objectives* (What must I/we accomplish in order for the organization to function?)	*How will the attainment of objectives be measured?* (How will I/we know when the objective is accomplished?)	*Time frame for goal*	*Plan for obtaining the objective* (What must be done to accomplish the objective?)
		Quantity measure: Quality measure: Cost measure: Other measures (please describe):		

PART B

Form 5 Performance Plan and Review

Employee name: _____ Position title: _____ Appraisal period: _____

Department _____ Date _____ Reviewed by _____

PERFORMANCE PLAN

1 List responsibilities (*Key words to describe the major elements of this employee's job.*)	2 List performance objectives and/or results to be achieved (*A more specific statement of the employee's key responsibilities and/or goals he can reasonably be expected to achieve in the coming period.*)	3 Determine relative importance (*Rank order*)	PERFORMANCE REVIEW 6 Note actual achievements, comment on performance
	FOR ADDITIONAL COMMENTS USE REVERSE SIDE		FOR ADDITIONAL COMMENTS USE REVERSE SIDE

4 Long-range goals	Work goals beyond this appraisal period and/or career goals.	Supervisor's comments
5 What help is required from your supervisor or others to achieve goals for this appraisal period and/or long range goals?		Supervisor's comments

Name _____   Group Number _____

Date _____ Class Section _____ Hour _____ Score _____

PART B

Form 6 MBO Measurement

Instructions: Place one or more of the letters A through J beside each of the items in the right hand column.

What is measured (in MBO)

A. Quantity
B. Quality
C. Cost control
D. Timeliness/dependability
E. Training
F. Sales volume
G. Maintenance
H. Employee satisfaction
I. Profit
J. Technical Accomplishments

Specific outcomes or results used as measures (ways of measuring)

_____ Type A units sold
_____ Transfers due to unsatisfactory performance
_____ Training programs
_____ Minority persons hired
_____ Warranty claims
_____ Items entered in a ledger
_____ Days off the job
_____ Mileage per replacement vehicle
_____ Turnover
_____ Sales
_____ Tools replaced
_____ Reduction in expenses from previous period
_____ Extent of contribution and amount of innovation in the project (i.e., highly creative ideas)
_____ Rejects
_____ Pedestrain-vehicle accidents
_____ Visits to the first-aid room
_____ Cost of material used in training
_____ Reports completed by X date
_____ Community complaints received
_____ Maintenance budget plus or minus
_____ Grievances received
_____ Profit by product line
_____ Mileage per replacement tire
_____ Potential contribution to total sales and profits
_____ Returned goods
_____ Research projects completed on time and within budget
_____ Traffic accidents
_____ The rate at which individuals advance
_____ Transfers at employee's request
_____ Employees ready for assignment
_____ Units constructed
_____ Days tardy
_____ Earnings on commissions
_____ Length of service
_____ EEOC complaints received
_____ Units produced
_____ Claims received and processed
_____ Complaints from employees
_____ Containers filled to capacity
_____ Discharges
_____ Plus or minus budget

_____ Dollars of savings realized from project
_____ Burglaries
_____ Errors in filing
_____ Housing units occupied
_____ Cost of each research project against budget
_____ Damaged units shipped
_____ Value of new cost-reducing procedures
_____ Days sick
_____ Percentage of profits to sales
_____ Garbage cans emptied
_____ Contributions and suggestions made via the suggestion program
_____ Ratio of maintenance cost to production cost
_____ Calls per day
_____ Penetration of the market
_____ Number of repairs on warranty
_____ Time to reach expected results
_____ Length of frequency of unauthorized visits
_____ Injury accidents
_____ Type L units sold
_____ Letters typed
_____ Minority persons trained
_____ Cost of maintenance per machine
_____ Number of promotable persons
_____ Number of new units sold vs. old
_____ Successful completion of a course
_____ Number of crimes against persons
_____ Number of disgruntled customers
_____ Results of a morale or attitude survey
_____ Cost of spoiled work
_____ Calls answered
_____ Quits
_____ Return of invested capital
_____ Gallons used per vehicle
_____ Amount of downtime
_____ Complaints per 1000
_____ New customers per month
_____ Customers maintained for one year
_____ Customers paid by end of month
_____ Delinquency charges
_____ Percent of on-schedule delivery
_____ Number of customer complaints as a % of monthly purchase orders
_____ Percent of rejects per total monthly volume
_____ Ratio of factory repair time to total production hours/month
_____ Number of units service free during warranty period
_____ Cost per unit of output per month
_____ Equipment utilization time as a percent of monthly available hours

Name _____   Group Number _____

Date _____ Class Section _____ Hour _____ Score _____

PART C

Form 7 Management by Objectives Worksheet for Joint Goal Setting

Job Title: _____

Objectives (What?)	Levels of Accomplishment (How measured?)			Time Frame (When?)	Methods used to Meet Objectives (How?)
	Type of measure	Present level	Desired level		
1.					
2.					
3.					
4.					
5.					
6.					
7.					
8.					
9.					
10.					

Name _____ Group Number _____

Date _____ Class Section _____ Hour _____ Score _____

PART D

Form 8 Evaluation of MBO Performance Review Session

Record your opinions about the conduct of each MBO review session below:

Criteria	Review agenda*	Level of performance (please circle) ←Not at all→←Average→←Very much→
1. Did the ratee clearly understand the objectives? Did they agree with them?	F:	0 1 2 3 4 5 6 7 8 9 10
	VG:	0 1 2 3 4 5 6 7 8 9 10
2. Was the rater willing to give the subordinate the freedom to perform the job and seem interested in having them do it their own way?	F:	0 1 2 3 4 5 6 7 8 9 10
	VG:	0 1 2 3 4 5 6 7 8 9 10
3. Did the rater stick to the MBO items and not wander into new items or personal characteristics?	F:	0 1 2 3 4 5 6 7 8 9 10
	VG:	0 1 2 3 4 5 6 7 8 9 10
4. Was the rater very supportive of the ratee?	F:	0 1 2 3 4 5 6 7 8 9 10
	VG:	0 1 2 3 4 5 6 7 8 9 10
5. Did the rater listen and clearly understand what the ratee was saying?	F:	0 1 2 3 4 5 6 7 8 9 10
	VG:	0 1 2 3 4 5 6 7 8 9 10
6. Did the ratee leave feeling he or she had been fairly reviewed?	F:	0 1 2 3 4 5 6 7 8 9 10
	VG:	0 1 2 3 4 5 6 7 8 9 10
7. Did the rater become defensive?	F:	10 9 8 7 6 5 4 3 2 1 0
	VG:	10 9 8 7 6 5 4 3 2 1 0
8. Did the ratee become defensive?	F:	10 9 8 7 6 5 4 3 2 1 0
	VG:	10 9 8 7 6 5 4 3 2 1 0
9. Overall, was the review effective in helping improve performance?	F:	0 1 2 3 4 5 6 7 8 9 10
	VG:	0 1 2 3 4 5 6 7 8 9 10

* F = Review session based on ratee having fair performance.
  VG = Review session based on ratee having very good performance.

Name _____ Group Number _____

Date _____ Class Section _____ Hour _____ Score _____

ASSESSMENT OF LEARNING IN PERSONNEL ADMINISTRATION
EXERCISE 6

1. Try to state the purpose of this exercise in one concise sentence.

2. Specifically what did you learn from this exercise (i.e., skills, abilities, and knowledge)?

3. How might your learning influence your role and your duties as a personnel administrator?

4. What are the major strengths and weaknesses of MBO as a performance appraisal system?

5. How would you go about convincing line managers that MBO was necessary?

6. How could an MBO system be evaluated in a cost-benefit analysis?

7. Additional questions given by your implementor:

Section 4
Human-Resource
Selection and Staffing

After the groundwork for a human-resource program has been laid through planning and forecasting of future needs, job analyses, and performance definition and appraisal (see Sections 2 and 3), the procurement process can begin. Selection of people to fill various positions, due to attrition, succession, and expansion, is of obvious importance to an organization, particularly in a dynamic and mobile post-industrial society in which organizations and people change rapidly. However, selection can be much more efficient if a clear statement of human-resource needs, job duties and responsibilities, and desired performance are developed first. That is, the selection system can only be as effective as the foundation on which it is built. Only after we have, for example, thoroughly analyzed a job and decided what requirements successful job performance demands in terms of human knowledge, ability, skill, personal characteristics, and experience, can we hope to find the best person to fill that job.

Selection is thus a matching problem—to find the best person for a job, given constraints of time, money, and the supply and characteristics of available human resources. Further, selection is decision making under uncertainty. We can never be sure a person is "right" for a job until after he or she performs it for some time, but we do not have the luxury of such hindsight in organizations. Therefore, we must attempt to predict future job performance from past and present information. As in any risky decision, we would attempt to reduce the degree of uncertainty and the consequences of error—or increase our odds of winning—by gathering as much relevant information as is practical on which to base the decision.

Several types of information we gather in the human-resource selection and staffing process and certain techniques have proven to be effective in predicting future performance. In this section, the following four different techniques, each concentrating on a different type of information, are presented: (1) biographical data (Exercise 7); (2) interviewing (Exercise 8); (3) work sampling and simulation (Exercise 9); and (4) testing (Exercise 10). Each of these techniques has certain advantages and disadvantages as selection devices, and they are best employed in combination rather than singly, as each facilitates the gathering of a different type of information. When all of the information gathered from the various techniques is combined, the odds on making an incorrect selection decision can be reduced. However, gathering such information is not without cost in terms of organizational resources. Those making the selection decision must be convinced that the cost involved in gathering each additional piece of information is outweighed by the benefit of using it in selection decision making. The basic selection validation procedure is illustrated in Fig. 1.

The four exercises in Section 4 explain the major selection techniques and enable you to design them in order to better understand their objectives and operation.

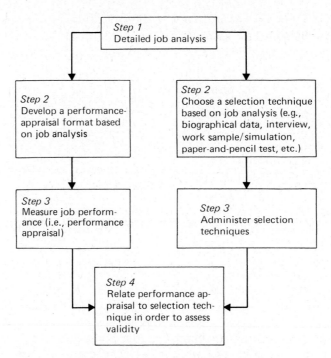

Fig. 1.   The Basic Selection Validation Procedure

Exercise 7

BIOGRAPHICAL DATA AS A PREDICTOR OF JOB SUCCESS

PREVIEW

Numerous organizations use an applicant's organizational memberships, previous work experiences, education, and other biographical information to help make their selection decisions. The assumption behind this practice is that certain bits of biographical data are good predictors of job success. That is, those whose backgrounds contain these items will eventually perform well on the job. This exercise examines both the assumption that biographical data predicts job performance, as well as typical personnel practices dealing with the use of biographical data as a selection strategy. The predictive accuracy of various types of biographical data are discussed, resumes are evaluated, and job application blanks are developed and assessed as to their validity in this exercise.

OBJECTIVES

1. To become familiar with current personnel practices regarding the use of biographical data in selection decisions.
2. To become familiar with the advantages and disadvantages of using biographical data to help make selection decisions.
3. To develop skill in evaluating resumes and references, and in drafting application blanks.
4. To begin to develop skill in assessing the validity of biographical data in selection procedures.

PREMEETING ASSIGNMENT

Read the *Introduction* and *Procedure* only. Do not read through any of the forms with the exception of Form 1, until told to do so by your implementor.

INTRODUCTION

Using Biographical Data to Make Selection Decisions

Application blanks and an applicant's personal resume appear to be used nearly as widely as interviewing to help make selection decisions in organizations. Obviously, the greatest relevance of the application blank is for selecting people from outside the organization, as biographical data for people currently inside an organization would typically be on record already. Recently, attention in personnel administration has been refocused on the application blank as a predictor of future job success. Systematic scoring and weighting techniques have been developed and, in some cases, long biographical-data forms resemble personality or interest tests in content. But most application forms still include questions about age, education, marital status, experience, and references.

Uses of Biographical Data. Biographical data has typically been used to aid in the selection process in the following ways:

Biographical data Aids selection process in following ways :

1. To facilitate an initial screening out of applicants who are obviously not qualified for the job;
2. To furnish background data useful in planning an upcoming selection interview with the applicant;
3. To obtain names of references that may be contacted for additional information about the applicant's work experience and general character; and
4. To collect information for administration of personnel programs (i.e., social security number, number of dependents, etc.).

"Hard" versus "Soft" Items.[1]   Many have advocated that only an individual's previous experiences that are directly and easily verifiable should be classified as biographical items, since many other items are "fakable." Examples of verifiable items are "rank in high school graduating class" or "prior jobs with inclusive dates." These items can be checked with other records.

Verifiable items are called "hard" items, while those that are not verifiable are called "soft" items. The latter are often expressed in abstract value judgments rather than realistic behavior. An example of a soft item would be "What high school subject did enjoy most?" There is, of course no reasonable way to check the truthfulness of such an item. An applicant could indicate any subject he or she thinks the organization is looking for.

While an enlarged classification of biographical items (i.e., hard *and* soft) obviously expands the amount of personal information collected, a more constrained classification may reduce the tendency towards fictionalization. Items that are historical and verifiable may result in a narrow, but representative, set of data about the individual, while an enlarged classification may be quite unrepresentative. For example, even when applicants tend to respond honestly, items calling for conjecture, interpretation, and supposition may have enough ambiguity to enable an individual to respond in a way that is either an exaggeration or a misrepresentation of the facts.

Despite these shortcomings of biographical data, they seem to have accuracy in predicting job performance. One explanation is that the weighted or scorable application blank (one in which each question is given a numerical weight)[2] is representative of an individual's history, while other predictors, especially the unstructured selection interview, may be but a caricature based on the perceptions of an interviewer. The most effective scorable application blank also should contain only "relevant" items—that is, only those directly related to job performance. Further, the scorable application blank may work because it escapes the fallacy of attempting to predict future job performance by measuring general items, such as overall ability or formal education as opposed to more specific, quantifiable items, such as specific job skills.

Developing Biographical-Data Items.   Several suggestions could be valuable as aids in developing biographical-data questions. Questions should be concise; they should be expressed such that responses can be given in numbers; and options given to respondents in a question should contain *all* reasonable alternatives, or if this is not possible, then an "escape" option (i.e., "other") should be provided. Further, questions should convey a neutral or pleasant connotation to the respondent and should not be threatening.

Biographical Data as a Predictor of Job Success.   The application blank itself can be used as a predictor of future job performance in two ways. First, in scored application forms each item of information on the form is examined to determine if it is actually predictive of some aspect of job performance, such as tenure or quality and quantity of work output. Items that actually discriminate between successful and unsuccessful employees (i.e., a strong positive correlation exists between those whose performance is high and those who respond in a certain way to an item) are usually scored quantitatively. In other words, each item is assigned a weight or score and the score is awarded if the item is answered in the way the organization thinks most appropriate. All of the scores awarded are then summed so that a numerical total score can be used as a basis for making selection decisions—in the same manner as scores of aptitude tests are used. For example, for some jobs a certain cutoff or minimum score might be decided on. The application blanks are scored and those job applicants scoring above the cutoff score are hired or sent to the next step in the selection process, while those scoring below the cutoff are eliminated.[3]

---

[1] Many of the ideas discussed here were adapted from J. J. Asher, "The Biographical Item: Can It be Improved?" *Personnel Psychology* 25 (1972).

[2] See, e.g., G. W. England, *Development and Use of Weighted Application Blanks* (University of Minnesota: Industrial Relations Center, 1971).

[3] A scored application form is validated by procedures similar to those employed in the validation of tests (see Exercise 10 and England, 1971). The discussion of weighted application blanks and validation of biographical items above is meant only as a brief introduction to a complex process. Detailed discussions can be found in England, 1971.

Application blanks are also used to predict job success, as judgments based on the applicant's total personal history are used in situations where the applicant cannot be interviewed. Thus, selection decisions are sometimes based primarily on personal-history data.

Reference Checks. Typically, applicants are asked to furnish a few names of references on an application blank. These are often past employers or supervisors, teachers or professors, or friends and associates. Sometimes, an application blank will specify the inclusion of one professional or academic reference and a personal one. These persons may then be contacted in order to provide additional information about an applicant's background, work experience, or character and integrity. In addition, they are used to verify certain statements made on an application blank.

Some jobs require applicants to ask references to submit a letter of recommendation or fill out a form giving their opinion of the applicant. Others simply require an applicant to furnish names of references. In either case, the use of references can be useful only if the references are honest in their evaluation and if the organization actually makes the reference check.

Many people tend to exaggerate when writing references as they do not wish to say negative things about someone or fear the applicant will be penalized if they give anything but the most favorable judgment. Further, references may provide a biased view of the applicant, as an applicant would only use references who he or she felt would give favorable responses.

Despite these problems, references can be useful in providing data for selection decisions. Their credibility and hence their utility can be increased if they are contacted by phone instead of in writing, if they have bothered to write an unsolicited personal letter rather than filling out a recommendation form, and if certain methods of asking questions are used which can reduce leniency in responses. One such method is a forced-choice format in which the reference must read through several groups of statements and mark only those in each group representative of the applicant.[4]

The Law and Biographical Data. Equal employment opportunity laws and various guidelines of federal agencies restrict the types of information that can be asked on application blanks in certain situations. For example, it may not be legal to ask if a person has ever been arrested, but only if they have ever been convicted of a crime. All arrests do not lead to convictions and there is typically a higher percentage of minority-group persons arrested than nonminorities—thus, the question can be discriminatory.[5] All biographical-data-collection devices must be checked for compliance with the various laws and guidelines (see Table 2, Exercise 18).

In addition, certain other laws, such as the Fair Credit Reporting Act of 1970, restrict and control the gathering of additional specific types of information. The Fair Credit Reporting Act requires that if credit-rating organizations are used to furnish information about an applicant, the applicant is entitled to disclosure and must be notified in writing that the information is being sought. Such organizations gather information about indebtedness, character, alcohol and drug use, etc. This information can be useful in selection decisions, but should be gathered only with the knowledge of the applicant and restricted to those types of information shown to have a direct impact on job performance. The abuses possible from gathering such personal information are obvious.

A Note on Recruitment. Recruitment of human resources refers to an organization's positive efforts to seek out qualified job applicants. Of course, the degree of recruitment activity depends on several factors. Among these are the human-resource requirements of the organization, characteristics of the job, the labor supply, geographic location of the organization relative to the labor supply, general economic conditions and unemployment rates, ability to staff positions from internal human resources (i.e., people who are already members of the organization), and affirmative action plans (see Exercise 18). Typically, an organization will actively recruit or seek job applicants in order to increase the numbers of women and minorities in their labor pool (affirmative action plans); to find a person with particular skills, ability, etc.; or to improve the mix and diversity of their work force to enable it to solve future problems and implement future plans.

Several external sources of human resources can be tapped. These include: advertising in newspapers, professional publications; educational organizations; public and private employment agencies; professional organizations; and labor unions. Each of these offers unique advantages and can prove to be a valuable

---

[4] See A. N. Nash and S. J. Carroll, "A Hard Look at the Reference Check," *Business Horizons* 13, no. 5 (1970): 43–49.

[5] See R. L. Minter, "Human Rights and Pre-employment Inquiries," *Personnel Journal* 51 (1972): 431–433. The laws on equal employment opportunity affecting selection are discussed in Exercise 18.

source of personnel. For example, the placement office of a university is a source of younger, typically inexperienced people with specialized education, which makes them appropriate for entry-level managerial and administrative positions. Employment agencies charge employers (and/or job seekers) a fee for their service, but may be able to locate someone to fill a job that requires unusual education and experience. Unions sometimes are able to control supply, especially skilled and craft labor, through apprenticeship programs and agreements with employers. In the construction industry, for example, the union will furnish the organization with the entire skilled labor pool and funnel workers to organizations through their own recruiting and placement process. This can be very economical to an employer.

Any recruiting efforts, or lack of them, provide publicity for an organization. As part of the overall selection and staffing process, this publicity can be positive or negative, useful in making better selection decisions or not useful. In recruiting activities, therefore, an organization must be cognizant of the utility of recruiting or selection decisions, as well as the effects such activity might have on the people already employed and the general public. Finally, recruiting efforts must be subjected to a rigorous cost/benefit analysis. In certain occupations, geographical areas, and industries, little recruiting is necessary, perhaps due to general economic conditions and the supply of labor. The costs and benefits can be economic as well as intangible, such as goodwill. Both need to be considered as recruitment activities are planned and implemented.

PROCEDURE

Overview. First, the many types of data that are possible to collect via an application blank are reviewed; then, sample resumes are presented for a job of administrative officer. You will evaluate these resumes and choose the best candidate for the job based on the information in the resumes. Completed application blanks for the same job are then compared to the resumes. Finally, you will develop an application blank for a job based on information gathered in a job analysis.

PART A

STEP 1: Break into small groups. Form 1 provides a set of sixteen statements, along with eight pairs of adjectives which each describe a type of information that can be obtained from an application blank. First, each person in the group will determine which of the two adjectives in each number (1–8) is best described by each of the sixteen statements. Next, each person chooses which adjectives in the list appearing at the end of Form 1 provide the type of information most useful for predicting job success via an application blank. Be sure to discuss your responses with the other group members and try to reach consensus on this group task.

TIME: About 20 minutes.

PART B

STEP 2: Forms 2, 3, and 4 contain resumes of three applicants for the job of an administrative officer. The officer reports to the president of a manufacturing firm which employs 200 people. See the job description, Form 5. Information about the organization is given in Form 6. Rank the applicants in the order you believe represents their probable success with the company. Then, compare your choices with other members of your group and answer the following questions:

a) Why did you assign this order? Can you justify your decisions?

b) What questions would you like to ask each candidate in an interview and what additional information would you like about each candidate in order to improve your decision making?

TIME: About 25 minutes.

PART C

STEP 3: Forms 7, 8, and 9 contain completed job-application blanks for the three candidates in Step 2 above. Read over these applications carefully and then answer the following questions in your group discussion:

a) What are the benefits of the completed application blanks over merely using resumes in making selection decisions?

b) What do you notice now about the applicants that you missed previously when you read only the resumes?

c) Did the use of the application blank provide answers to any of the questions you may have developed in question b of Step 2 above?

d) What is your ranking of the three candidates now? If it has changed, why has it?

TIME: About 25 minutes.

PART D

STEP 4: The last task in this exercise is to develop a job-application blank to gather biographical data based on job-analysis information. Form 8 contains the job description for the job of administrative officer. From this information you are asked first to determine a set of criteria to be used in selecting among candidates for this job. That is, what would be the qualifications, education, etc., you would look for when selecting a person for the job? Then you are asked to:

a) Design an application blank that captures the selection criteria your group has developed. Be sure the items (questions) are presented with enough alternatives to cover the possible responses to them. You may use Form 7 as a model for your application blanks, but develop your own on a separate sheet of paper.

b) Determine a scoring or weighting system for evaluating the application blank. Go through all of the items and give each a weight that reflects its relative importance as a predictor of future job success. Decide how each item should be answered in order for the applicant to receive, for example, all of the points assigned to the item, half the points, etc. Then develop a cutoff score which would be the minimum total score an applicant could get and still be considered for the job.

c) Complete your new application blank for each of the three candidates, using their resumes and the application blanks in Forms 2–4 and 7–9 as the basis for the information required. Then score the application blank according to the scoring system you devised in (b) above.

d) Select the new administrative officer based on the new application blank. Was it the same person as your group had chosen in Step 3 above?

e) Prepare a brief rationale for your choice such that you could defend it to the unsuccessful applicants and to other parties.

f) What information do you still not have about the applicants that you feel is necessary for making a good selection decision? How would you ascertain this information?

TIME: About two and one-half hours.

FOR FURTHER READING

Ash, P., and L. P. Krocker. "Personnel Selection, Classification, and Placement." *Annual Review of Psychology* 26 (1975): 481–507. (II)

Asher, J. J. "The Biographical Item: Can It Be Improved?" *Personnel Psychology* 25 (1972): 251–269. (II–R)

Beason, G. M., and J. A. Belt. "Verifying Job Applicants' Backgrounds." *Personnel Administrator* 19 (1974): 29–32. (I)

Browning, R. C. "Validity of Reference Ratings from Previous Employers." *Personnel Psychology* 21 (1968): 389–393. (II–R)

Clark, E. "Holding Government Accountable: The Amended Freedom of Information Act," *Yale Law Journal* 84 (March 1975): 741–769. (II)

Clarke, J. R. "Landing that Right Executive Job." *Management Review* 69 (August 1975): 31–36. (I)

Davies, G. K. "Needed: A National Job Matching Network." *Harvard Business Review* 47, no. 5 (1969): 63–72. (I)

Dornon, J. M. *Identification of Long-Tenure Hourly Factory Workers Using a Weighted Application Blank.* (Experimental Publication System Ms. No. 276–2.) Washington, D.C.: American Psychological Association, 1970. (II–R)

England, G. W. *Development and Use of Weighted Application Blanks.* Minneapolis: University of Minnesota, Industrial Relations Center, 1971. (I)

Fleishman, E. A., and J. Berniger. "One Way to Reduce Office Turnover." *Personnel* 37 (1960): 63–69. (I)

Goldstein, I. L. "The Application Blank: How Honest Are the Responses?" *Journal of Applied Psychology* 55 (1971): 491–492. (II–R)

Guion, R. M. "Recruiting, Selection, and Job Placement." In M. D. Dunnette, ed., *Handbook of Industrial and Organizational Psychology.* Chicago: Rand McNally, 1976. (II)

Hawk, R. *The Recruitment Function.* New York: Amacom, 1967. (I)

Henry, E. R. *Research Conference on the Use of Autobiographical Data as Psychological Predictors.* Greensboro, N. C.: The Richardson Foundation, 1965. (II–R)

Kavanaugh, M. J., and D. Y. York. "Biographical Correlates of Middle Managers' Performance." *Personnel Psychology* 25 (1972): 319–332. (II–R)

Kessler, C. C., and G. J. Gibbs. "Getting the Most from Application Blanks and References. *Personnel* 52 (Jan.–Feb. 1975): 53–62. (I)

Lee, R., and J. M. Booth. "A Utility Analysis of a Weighted Application Blank Designed to Predict

Turnover for Clerical Employees." *Journal of Applied Psychology* 59 (1974): 516–518. (II–R)

Lopresto, R. "Recruitment Sources and Techniques." In J. Famidaro, ed., *Handbook of Modern Personnel Administration.* New York: McGraw-Hill, 1972. (I)

Lunnenborg, C. A. "Biographic Variables in Differential vs. Absolute Prediction." *Journal of Educational and Psychological Measurement* 5 (1968): 207–210. (II–R)

Maslin, H. L. "How to Avoid Discrimination in Your Help-Wanted Ads." *Supervisory Management* 21 (February 1976): 2–5. (I)

McClelland, J. N., and F. Rhodes. "Prediction of Job Success for Hospital Aides and Orderlies from MMPI Scores and Personal History Data." *Journal of Applied Psychology* 53 (1969): 49–54. (II–R)

Minter, R. L. "Human Rights Laws and Preemployment Inquiries." *Personnel Journal* 51 (June 1972): 431–433. (I)

Morrison, R. R., W. A. Owens, J. R. Glennon, and L. E. Albright. "Factored Life History Antecedents of Industrial Research Performance." *Journal of Applied Psychology* 46 (1962): 281–284. (II–R)

Mosel, J. N., and R. R. Wade. "A Weighted Application Blank for Reduction of Turnover in Department Store Sales Clerks." *Personnel Psychology* 4 (1951): 177–184). (II–R)

Nash, A. J., and S. J. Carroll. "A Hard Look at the Reference Check." *Business Horizons* 13, no. 5 (1970): 43–49. (I).

Nevo, B. "Using Biographical Information to Predict Success of Men and Women in the Army." *Journal of Applied Psychology* 61 (1976): 106–108. (II–R)

Novack, S. R. "Developing an Effective Application Blank." *Personnel Journal* 49 (May 1970): 419–423. (I)

Owens, W. A. "Background Data." In M. D. Dunnette, ed., *Handbook of Industrial and Organizational Psychology.* Chicago: Rand McNally, 1976. (II)

Owens, W. A., J. R. Glennon, and L. W. Albright. "American Psychological Association Scientific Affairs Committee, Division 14." *A Catalog of Life History Items.* Greensboro, N.C.: The Richardson Foundation, 1966. (I)

Owens, W. A., and E. R. Henry. *Biographical Data in Industrial Psychology: A Review and Evaluation.* Greensboro, N.C.: Richardson Foundation, 1966. (II)

Rosenbaum, R. W. "Predictability of Employee Theft Using Weighted Application Blanks." *Journal of Applied Psychology* 61 (1976): 94–98. (II–R)

Rosenfeld, C. "Job Seeking Methods Used by American Workers." *Monthly Labor Review* 98 (August 1975): 39–42. (I–R)

Scott, R. D., and R. W. Johnson. "Use of the Weighted Application Blank in Selecting Unskilled Employees." *Journal of Applied Psychology* 51 (1967): 393–395. (II–R)

Schuh, A. J. "Application Blank Items and Intelligence as Predictors of Turnover." *Personnel Psychology* 20 (1967): 59–63. (II–R)

Sweet, D. H. *The Job Hunter's Manual.* Reading, Mass.: Addison-Wesley, 1975. (I)

Tanofsky, R., R. R. Shepps, and P. J. O'Neill. "Pattern Analysis of Biographical Predictors of Success as an Insurance Salesman." *Journal of Applied Psychology* 53 (1969): 136–139. (II–R)

Tucker, M. F., V. B. Cline, and J. R. Schmitt. "Prediction of Creativity and Other Performance Measures from Biographical Information among Pharmaceutical Scientists." *Journal of Applied Psychology* 51 (1967): 131–138. (II–R)

Wanous, J. P. "Tell It Like It Is at Realistic Job Previews." *Personnel* 52 (July–August 1975): 50–60. (I)

Webb, S. C. "The Comparative Validity of Two Biographical Inventory Keys." *Journal of Applied Psychology* 44 (1960): 177–183. (II–R)

Wessel, M. R. *Freedom's Edge: The Computer Threat to Society.* Reading, Mass.: Addison-Wesley, 1974. (I)

Name _Gary L. Shores_   Group Number _____

Date _____ Class Section _____ Hour _____ Score _____

PART A

Form 1 Categories of Biographical Data

A. Circle the word that best describes each statement below.

1a. (Verifiable)—Unverifiable

    How many full-time jobs have you had in the past five years?

1b. Verifiable—(Unverifiable)

    What aspect of your last full-time job did you find most interesting?

2a. (Historical)—Futuristic

    List your three best subjects in high school.

2b. Historical—(Futuristic)

    Do you intend to further your education?

3a. (Actual behavior)—Hypothetical behavior

    Did you ever build a model airplane that flew?

3b. Actual behavior—(Hypothetical behavior)

    If you had the training, do you think you would enjoy building innovative model airplanes for a toy manufacturer?

4a. (Memory)—Conjecture

    Before you were twelve years old, did you ever try to perform chemistry experiments at home?

4b. Memory—(Conjecture)

    If your father had been a chemist, do you think you would have performed chemistry experiments at home before you were twelve years old?

5a. (Factual)—Interpretive

    Do you repair mechanical things around your home, such as appliances?

5b. Factual—(Interpretive)

    If you had the training, how would you estimate your performance as an appliance repairperson?

6a. (Specific)—General

    As a child, did you collect stamps?

6b. Specific—(General)

    As a child, were you an avid collector of things?

7a. (Actual response)—Response tendency

    Which of the following types of cameras do you own?

7b. Actual response—(Response tendency)

    In buying a new camera, would you most likely purchase one with automatic features.

8a. (External event)—Internal event

Did you ever have private tutoring lessons in any school subject?

8b. External event—(Internal event)

How important did you view homework when you were in high school?

B. Which of the following words seem to describe the best type of data to collect on an application blank? Why?

✓ Verifiable	___ Memory	___ General
___ Unverifiable	✓ Conjecture	✓ Actual response
___ Historical	✓ Factual	___ Response tendency
✓ Futuristic	___ Interpretive	___ External event
✓ Actual behavior	✓ Specific	✓ Internal event
___ Hypothetical behavior		

PART B

Form 2 Resume No. 1

Merle Wonder
9680 Willow
Bigville, USA

JOB OBJECTIVE

Position in Administration Heading a Major Department

EDUCATION

1962-1965:   Harding College, Harding, Vermont
              Majors: Music History and Literature; Voice
              Degree: B. Mus., June 1966, cum laude   G.P.A.: 3.75
              Honors: Independent Study Honors in Music History & Literature
              Member: Omega Alpha National Scholastic Honorary Fraternity

1973-1974:   University of the West, Western, Arizona
              Major: Business Administration; Emphasis: Organizational Behavior
              Degree: M.B.A. June, 1974   G.P.A. 3.95
              Member: Who's Who Among Students in American Universities & Colleges

Other: While employed at New York University (1971-1972), completed two
              graduate courses in guidance and counseling.
              While employed at the University of Missouri (1972-1973), completed
              six graduate fundamentals courses in business administration in
              preparation for M.B.A. program.

EMPLOYMENT

2/72-8/73:   Planters International, Columbia, Missouri
              Administrative Assistant to Head of Budget Department

8/71-1/72:   New York University, New York, New York
              Administrative Assistant to Director of Planning and Director
              of Exhibitions

9/70-2/71:   Heckl and Dunover, 355 Madison Avenue, New York, N.Y.
              Assistant to Sales Manager, Upbeat Books Division

10/66-9/70:   G. Whiz, Inc. 76 Third Avenue, New York, N. Y.
              Assistant to Head of Performance Department in Record Compilation

12/65-10/66: Peter A. Flop & Co., Inc., 101 Grand Street, New York, N. Y.
              Record Clerk

Prior: Please see amplification.

PERSONAL

Born: 2/3/42 in Minneapolis, Minnesota   Height: 5'8"; wt.: 135 lbs.
Health: Good; no physical limitations   Marital Status: married; no children
Residence: Rents apartment; willing to relocate
Finances: Good order; no debt encumbrance
Hobbies: Music, creative writing, travel, swimming, hiking

EDUCATION

Graduate courses in business administration and guidance and counseling completed include the following:

Management and Organization
Administrative Theory and Practice
Organizational Behavior
Labor Relations
Personnel Management
Behavior of Task Groups
Administrative Controls
Business Policy

Accounting
Financial Accounting
Managerial Accounting

Methods
Business Statistics
Introduction to Management Science
Business Research

Marketing
Fundamentals of Marketing
Consumer Behavior

Business Law
Fundamentals of Business Law

Finance
Fundamentals of Finance

Economics
Fundamentals of Economics
Business and Economic Analysis
Business and Its Environment

Guidance and Counseling
Principles and Practices of Counseling
Tests and Measurements

EMPLOYMENT HIGHLIGHTS

2/72-8/73:
PLANTERS INTERNATIONAL

Employed as Director of Budget Department. Duties and responsibilities included:

Monitoring departmental budgets and grants and initiating budget changes; researching and preparing annual reports; preparing weekly, monthly and quarterly payroll forms; supervising secretarial and office personnel and delegating assignments; handling and coordinating administrative matters for 25 employees and research assistants; ordering and procuring equipment and supplies; managing department in manager's absence; arranging conferences, and meetings.

Reason for leaving: To return to school on a full-time basis to get my M.B.A.

8/71-1/72:
NEW YORK UNIVERSITY

Employed as Administrative Assistant to Director of Planning and Director of Exhibitions. Duties and responsibilities included:

Reading and interpreting mail and reports and advising employer as to appropriate action; initiating and following up various matters by telephone; writing own correspondence; scheduling and arranging art exhibitions on campus; coordinating art department; scheduling courses, helping draft course proposals, and preparing teaching schedules for art department; preparing press releases and publicity material for art department and exhibitions; advising students; creating new forms and initiating new procedures; organizing and maintaining a complex filing system; delegating tasks to junior secretary and student assistants; keeping employer informed of relevant campus matters; ordering office equipment and supplies for art department, exhibitions department, and libraries.

Reason for leaving: Moving to Columbia, Missouri

9/70-2/71:
HECKL AND DUNOVER (book publishing company)

Employed as Assistant to Sales Manager, Upbeat Books Division. Duties and responsibilities included:

Writing own correspondence and memos; making travel arrangements; reorganizing and maintaining filing system; keeping sales records; ordering and sending books; coordinating about 100 salesmen and keeping personnel records; utilizing computer printouts; preparing kits for new salesmen.

Reason for leaving: Injury to elbow.

10/66-9/70:
G. WHIZ, INC.

Employed as Assistant to Head of Performance Department. Duties and responsibilities included:

Preparing reports, promotional material involving research and compilation; duties involved much public contact, both in person and on telephone; making many decisions on own; much high pressure work involving deadlines. Writing own correspondence; handling telephone and written orders; handling all routine Performance Department matters.

Reason for leaving: No opportunity for advancement

12/65-10/66:
PETER A. FLOP & CO., INC. (construction materials distributing company)

Employed as Record clerk in Personnel Department. Duties and responsibilities included:

Processing invoices; keeping personnel records; interviewing applicants for screening; administering aptitude tests to applicants. Typing correspondence, forms, reports; various clerical duties.

Reason for leaving: To accept better position.

Prior Employment:

Part-time and summer employment during school and college years included receptionist (Franklin-Hall, Harding College); cashier (Globe Theater, Green, Nebraska); and stock work, clerical duties, and some sales work (Green Shoe Company, Green, Nebraska).

REFERENCES

Available on request.

PART B

Form 3 Resume No. 2

Gaylord Golden   2825 E. Closer Dr.
Born: February 18, 1937   Phoenix, Arizona
Married: Three children

I. Educational Background   GPA

      BA-United College, Schenectady, New York   1959   2.31
        -University of Maine, Portland, Maine   1966   3.0
      MBA-University of Colorado   1971   3.58

II. Engineering

     The first two years of undergraduate work were in the mechanical engineering
     program. This program included two years of physics, one year of chemistry, the
     basic courses from ME, CE, and EE as well as English and German.

     At the end of sophomore year, transferred into the Industrial Administration
     program. Utilizing engineering credits and majoring in economics.

III. Mathematics and Quantitative Courses

        Analytical Geometry and Algebra   United College
        Differential Calculus   United College
        Integral Calculus   United College
        Business Statistics   United College
        Quantitative Methods II (chi Square, ANOVA) University of Colorado
        Business Decision Theory (in progress)   University of Colorado
        Computer Programming (Fortran IV)   University of Colorado
        General Math Review (Algebra and Calculus)   University of Colorado
        Persons in Society   University of Colorado
        Introduction to Management Science   University of Colorado

IV. Accounting and Finance

        Principles of Accounting I and II   United College
        Using Accounting Information   University of Colorado
        Corporation Finance   United College
        Public Finance   United College
        Financial Administration   University of Colorado

V. Economics

        Elementary Economics I and II   United College
        Development of Economic Thought
           (Price and Income Theory)   United College
        Money and Banking   United College
        Economics of Transportation   United College

VI. Management

        Problems of Business and Industry   United College
        Human Relations   University of Colorado

	University of Colorado
Administrative Problems	University of Colorado
Business Problems	University of Colorado
Public Administrative Systems	University of Colorado
Administrative Policies	University of Maine
Persons in Society	University of Colorado
Social Psychology	University of Colorado

VII. Marketing

Marketing Concepts and Issues	University of Colorado
Marketing Policies	University of Colorado
Global Marketing Problem	University of Colorado

VIII. Other

Advanced Business Law	University of Colorado

IX. Experience - *denotes a basic background in electronics + working w/engineers.*

Chief Mountain Community College (enrollment 4,000)   Nov. 1970 to present
Assistant to the President and Member of Marketing Department.
Duties: Administrative officer to oversee internal operation of entire college including budgets, promotions and personnel procedures. Instructor in Retail Merchandising Program.
Courses Taught: Principles of Management, Personnel Management, Retailing, Basic Marketing, Salesmanship, Cooperative Work Experience.

Other Activities: Involved in program design and development; conducted an Institutional Research and Development Program; member of the Community College Curriculum Committee.

Sweetwell, Inc. Residential Div.   Jan. 1967 to Oct. 1970
Product: Residential temperature controls and accessories. Gas valves, thermostats, limit switches, electronic aircleaners, combustion safeguard equipment, zone valves.
Position and Duties: Sales Engineer. Responsible for selling all division products and promotional programs to dealers and wholesalers. Also, heavily involved with technical training of dealer service personnel. A major portion of effort was devoted to resolving constant channel conflicts.
Customers: Heating, plumbing and air conditioning wholesalers and their associated dealers and service organizations. Also, called on OEMS and "quasi" OEMS (Wards, other chains). Occasionally called on architects, mechanical engineers, city engineers, inspectors, building owners and utilities.

Territory: Portions of Western Colorado, and Montana.

Volume: Approximately 450,000 per year

Reasons for change: Left to begin work on MBA and to enter the education field.

L.D. Jones Systems and Metering Division   May 1966 to Nov. 1967

Product: Meters and valves for the petroleum and petrochemical industry. Also, service station pumps and other marketing equipment.

Position and duties: District Sales Manager. Working with customers on technical application of meters and valves, contacting major oil companies to sell pumps, working with local representatives and distributors on sales problems. Finding and evaluating service representatives.

Customers: Production engineers, project engineers, PA's terminal superintendents, Major oil companies, pipelines, jobbers and chemical companies.

Territory: Rocky Mountain States

Volume: Approximately $100,000.

Reason for change: This division is eliminating direct sales force.

Hedena Electrical Agencies   April 1962 to May 1966

Product: Capacitors, Resistors, Semiconductors, Integrated circuits.

Position and duties: 8/65-6/66 Sales Account Manager at main plant. Handled all customer problems, e.g. order processing, quoting, expediting, engineering liason. Processed approximately $5 million/year. 6/62-8/65 Sales Engineer in Houston office. Sold all company products in territory. Included technical application work, attaining account control and liason with the factory.

Contacts: Component and Project engineers, buyers and PA's

Territory: Texas, Kansas, New Mexico

Volume: Approximately $85,000. Helped achieve 35% increase in '65.

Accomplishments: Obtained largest order ever taken in territory ($9,000).

Reason for change: Limited future in the inside sales position.

Circle Fast Corp., Cinch Division   May 1959 to April 1962

Products: Electrical connectors, ignition systems, specialized capacitors.

Position and duties: Applications Engineer. Handled inside and outside sales work. Sold concept, pushed design thru engineering, costing, manufacturing. Worked on sales and advertising programs.

Customers: OEM manufacturers of electronics equipment.

Contacts: Component and Project Engineers, buyers.

Territory: No specific assignment-where demand required.

Reason for change: Greater opportunity with Hedena Electrical Agencies.

PART B

Form 4 Resume No. 3

CHARLOTTE PYLE

Health: Excellent
Interests: Tennis, swimming, reading, photography

Home   Office

2121 S. Broadway   Two West Exposition Place
Muncie, Indiana   Muncie, Indiana

Professional Experience

Skyline Management Corp., Muncie, Indiana

1971-present   Vice President and Member of the
                                        Board of Directors

1966-1971   Senior Consulting Associate

Skyline Management Corp. is a research, consulting, and executive development company
devoted primarily to retailers, wholesalers, and manufacturers with distribution, marketing and administrative problems. The firm also provides consulting services to
Skyline Data Systems. The latter is a subsidiary of Towncorp and a major supplier of
on-line computer services in the field of distribution. In the aggregate, these companies employ over 150 professional associates, most of whom have advanced degrees in a
variety of fields, including economics, accounting, finance, quantitative business analysis, management, and marketing. Background materials on Skyline Management and the
company's annual reports are available upon request.

Directed or provided major support for over 80 industry studies on the changing structure
and economics of distribution. These studies covered emerging developments in virtually
all lines of retail and wholesale trade.

Designed and/or participated in over 30 management development programs sponsored by
individual companies or trade associations. All programs were based on a substantial
amount of corporate and industry research, and most of the programs involved specialized
seminars for senior and middle management executives.

Served as a featured speaker at over 30 national conferences. Each presentation was
based on the findings of original or ongoing research.

The following activities are illustrative of the types of assignments completed during
this time period.

- Authored a major research report on the applicability of quantitative marketing
  concepts to retailing and the implications of the hypermarket for manufacturers,
  wholesalers, and retailers.

- Conducted management audits of several companies to determine their capability
  to meet long-run company objectives. The firms analyzed include two of the
  largest discount department store firms and one of the largest department store
  firms in the United States and several of the largest retailing organizations
  in Europe.

- Developed step-by-step profit planning and management by objectives systems for numerous firms and trade associations. Clients in this area include firms in wholesale and retail distribution in the United States and Canada.

- Prepared a detailed market potential analysis for a leading drygoods wholesaler. This study evaluated sales potential on a county-by-county basis utilizing multiple regression analysis techniques.

- Developed systems for determining the profitability of individual merchandise items, suppliers, and customers for a leading wholesaler trade association.

- Assisted several major retailing corporations in developing long-run budgeting programs. These analyses were based on a detailed understanding of the company's strengths and reactions and related factors.

Education

MBA (1966) -- University of Wisconsin

- Ford Foundation Fellowship
- NCR Thesis   Grant
- Teaching Associate

BA (1964) -- University of Indiana - Ft. Wayne -- Graduated with honors/earned 100 percent of undergraduate expenses.

PART B

Form 5 Job Description

ADMINISTRATIVE OFFICER'S JOB—Palms Pacific Corporation, Inc.

DESCRIPTION OF WORK:

General Statement of Duties: Supervises and coordinates responsible administrative work of a complex nature involving program responsibility; does related work as required.

Supervision Received: Receives policy guidance from an administrative superior or board members.

Supervision Exercised: Plans, organizes, develops, coordinates, and directs a staff of administrative and clerical personnel. Total at all levels exceeds twenty.

EXAMPLE OF DUTIES: (Any one position may not include all of the duties listed, nor do the listed examples include all tasks that may be found in positions.)

Administers, coordinates, and directs a complex administrative management program involving program responsibility for a department or equivalent; organizes and directs the work of personnel in day-to-day operation, and conducts long-range planning.

Establishes working methods and procedures and develops departmental procedures and policies related to administrative functions.

Directs major staff services, including budget, training, record keeping, and personnel and general administrative services. Develops supporting data and presents budget estimates and requests.

Directs or performs studies on efficiency, work flow, procedures, work standards, and research and planning.

Develops and compiles comprehensive reports.

Develops and implements immediate and long-range plans for administrative areas of the organization.

Performs related work as required.

REQUIRED KNOWLEDGE, SKILLS, AND ABILITIES:

Extensive and broad knowledge of complex administrative management programs. Skill and ability in administering, planning, and directing personnel in day-to-day programs appropriate to the position to be filled. Ability to interpret and apply laws, rules, regulations, and industry practices. Ability to relate with and coordinate department activities with employees, other departments, and the general public.

QUALIFICATIONS FOR APPOINTMENT:

Education: Graduation from a college or university with major course work in public or business administration or related field.

Experience: Six years progressively responsible experience in a supervisory, technical, or professional area related to management or administration; familiarity with computer software very helpful.

   OR

Any equivalent combination of education and experience.

PART B

Form 6 The Palms Pacific Corporation, Inc.

Palms Pacific Corporation (PPC) is a small organization whose primary objectives are the following: to manufacture specialized electronics equipment, including meters, scopes, scanners, etc.; to manufacture certain medical/electronic products, such as "heart pacers" (devices implanted into a person's chest cavity through surgery in order to help stimulate and regulate their heartbeat); to engage in research and development in the electronics field; and to provide technical assistance in a consulting capacity to other organizations, including government and educational clients. PPC is located in a large West Coast city in the United States. It is only ten years old and has grown rapidly since its founding by an electrical engineer, a heart specialist, a former designer of computer hardware, and a lawyer. These four founders still own over eighty percent of the stock in this closed corporation, although not in equal shares.

PPC had about two million dollars in gross sales last year, brought in another $750,000 from government contracts, and about $300,000 from consulting contracts. PPC has finally gotten to the point where the four principals noted above no longer take part in day-to-day operations. Their expertise is better spent on planning and strategy making, on securing new business and clients, and on consulting activities. They hired an administrative vice president a year ago to oversee the operations, but soon realized that this person was overburdened as well. They thus decided to look for an administrative officer who would be responsible for the clerical and some technical aspects of the operations, while the administrative vice president, to whom the officer would report, would still oversee the major functional areas. The four principals of PPC are actually board members, but still do take part in some operating-level decisions in their area of expertise (see organization chart, Figure 1).

The administrative vice president is a 45-year-old white male who has a bachelor's degree from a major California university in management. He had had twenty years of administrative experience and was considered a "good catch" by the directors of PPC. He is a native of the West Coast, married, no children, and an avid environmentalist. He takes pride in his frequent returns to his alma mater and other schools to take courses, attend seminars and workshops, etc., in order to learn of new techniques in budgeting, training, motivation, leadership, and interpersonal relations. He is knowledgeable and competent and has the respect of those who work with and for him. His leadership style is quite structured and authoritarian and he finds it difficult to delegate work without checking it over closely.

The administrative officer would be in charge of such activities as government-contract administration, personnel record keeping, training and development, state and federal government relations, wage and salary administration, and coordinating efforts of the scientific/technical and manufacturing personnel. Report writing, planning, and policymaking are additional duties. Selection and staffing are currently handled by each individual division of PPC, as are performance appraisal, wage and salary administration, and motivation programs. There is currently no union in PPC. Most of its employees are professionals in law, medicine, management, or engineering. Operating-level persons are highly skilled.

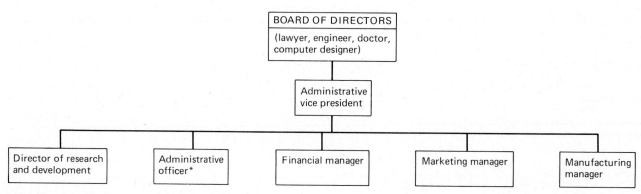

*Position being sought by three applicants in Exercise 7.

Fig. 1. Organization Chart for Palms Pacific Corporation (top management levels only; doctor is current president and board chairman)

PART C

Form 7 Application 1 for Job of Administrative Assistant

<table>
<tr><td colspan="2">FOR OFFICE USE ONLY</td></tr>
<tr><td>Possible Work Locations</td><td>Possible Positions</td></tr>
<tr><td></td><td></td></tr>
</table>

APPLICATION FOR EMPLOYMENT

(PLEASE PRINT PLAINLY)

<table>
<tr><td colspan="2">FOR OFFICE USE ONLY</td></tr>
<tr><td>Work Location_____</td><td>Rate_____</td></tr>
<tr><td>Position_____</td><td>Date_____</td></tr>
</table>

To Applicant: We deeply appreciate your interest in our organization and assure you that we are sincerely interested in your qualifications. A clear understanding of your background and work history will aid us in placing you in the position that best meets your qualifications and may assist us in possible future upgrading.

Very Neat completed form

PERSONAL   Date: _June 18_

Name _Wonder_ _M._ Social Security No. _821-34-6063_
   Last   First Initial   Middle Initial

Present address _9680 Willow_ _Bigville_ _USA_ Telephone No. _482-3668_
   No.   Street   City   State   Zip

How long have you lived at above address? _one year_

Previous address _616_ _31st_ _New York_ _N.Y._ How long did you live there? _5 mo._
   No.   Street   City   State   Zip

To Applicant: READ THIS INTRODUCTION CAREFULLY BEFORE ANSWERING ANY QUESTIONS IN THIS BLOCKED-OFF AREA. The Civil Rights Act of 1964 prohibits discrimination in employment practice because of race, color, religion, sex or national origin. P.L. 90-202 prohibits discrimination on the basis of age with respect to individuals who are at least 40 but less than 65 years of age. The laws of some States also prohibit some or all of the above types of discrimination.
   DO NOT ANSWER ANY QUESTION CONTAINED IN THIS BLOCKED-OFF AREA UNLESS THE EMPLOYER HAS CHECKED THE BOX NEXT TO THE QUESTION, thereby indicating that the requested information is needed for a bona fide occupational qualification, national security laws, or other legally permissible reasons.

[X] Are you over the age of twenty-one? _yes_ If no, hire is subject to verification that you are of minimum legal age.

[X] Sex: M _x_ F _____ [X] Height: _5_ ft. _8_ in. [X] Weight: _142_ lbs.

[X] Marital Status: Single _____ Engaged _____ Married _xx_ Separated _____ Divorced _____ Widowed _____

[X] Date of Marriage _1971_ [X] Number of dependents including yourself _1_ [X] Are you a citizen of the U.S.A.? _yes_

[X] What is your present Selective Service classification? _1-Y_

[X] Indicate dates you attended school: *Delete all educ. items*

Elementary _1948 - 1956_ High School _1956 - 1960_ College _1962 - 1966_
   From   To   From   To   From   To

Other (Specify type of school) _M.B.A. Graduate Degree in Business Administration_ _1973 - 1974_
   From   To

Have you ever been denied bond? If yes, explain.
[X] Have you ever been bonded? _no_ If yes, on what jobs?

Employer may list other bona fide occupational questions on lines below:

[ ] _____
[ ] _____

What method of transportation will you use to get to work? _Drive_

Rate of pay. Salary Required

Position(s) applied for _Administrative Officer_ Rate of pay expected $ _300_ per week

Include
Would you work Full-Time _yes_ Part-Time _____ Specify days and hours if part-time _____

Were you previously employed by us? _____ If yes, when? _____

List any friends or relatives working for us _none_
   Name(s)

If your application is considered favorably, on what date will you be available for work? _July_ 19___

Are there any other experiences, skills, or qualifications which you feel would especially fit you for work with the Company? _____
   I feel my extensive administrative experience uniquely qualifies me for the
   position of an administrative assistant.

Outside Activities
Professional association - fraternal clubs, etc.

Do you have any physical defects which preclude you from performing certain kinds of work? __none__   If yes, describe such defects and specific work limitations. _____

Have you been convicted of a crime in the past ten years, excluding misdemeanors and summary offenses? __no__   If yes, describe in full _____

Have you had a major illness in the past 5 years? _____ If yes, describe _____

Have you received compensation for injuries? __yes__ If yes, describe __injury to elbow__ _____

RECORD OF EDUCATION

School	Name and Address of School	Course of Study	Check Last Year Completed				Did You Graduate?	List Diploma or Degree
High Elementary	Lincoln Elementary / Minneapolis, Minn.	✕	5	6	7	8	[X] Yes / [ ] No	✕
College High	Dungan High School / Minnespolis, Minn.	music	1	2	3	4	[X] Yes / [ ] No	Diploma
College	Harding College / Harding, Vermont	music	1	2	3	4	[X] Yes / [ ] No	B.Mus.
Other (Specify)	University of the West / Western, Arizona	Business Administration	1	2	3	4	[X] Yes / [ ] No	M.B.A.

MILITARY SERVICE RECORD

Were you in U.S. Armed Forces?   Yes _____ No __XX__ If yes, what Branch? _____

Dates of duty: From _____ To _____ Rank at discharge _____
Month   Day   Year   Month   Day   Year

List duties in the Service including special training _____

Have you taken any training under the G.I. Bill of Rights? _____ If yes, what training did you take? _____

PERSONAL REFERENCES (Not Former Employers or Relatives)

Name and Occupation	Address	Phone Number
Sam Dow	Minneapolis	461-3822
Helen Sapp	Minneapolis	436-4916
Doris Paulsen	New York	834-9006

Cut-off ~~30~~ | 30 | 5 | 5 | - 70.

4084

Position held

Describe the work you did

List below all present and past employment, beginning with your most recent

	Name and Address of Company and Type of Business	From Mo.	Yr.	To Mo.	Yr.	Describe in detail the work you did	Weekly Starting Salary	Weekly Last Salary	Reason for Leaving	Name of Supervisor
I	Planters Int'l Columbia, Mo.	2	72	8	73	Administrative Assistant	225	225	to get MBA	Phyllis Dorn

	Name and Address of Company and Type of Business	From Mo.	Yr.	To Mo.	Yr.	Describe in detail the work you did	Weekly Starting Salary	Weekly Last Salary	Reason for Leaving	Name of Supervisor
II	New York University New York	8	71	1	72	Administrative Assistant	183	209	moving	Helen Gurgle

	Name and Address of Company and Type of Business	From Mo.	Yr.	To Mo.	Yr.	Describe in detail the work you did	Weekly Starting Salary	Weekly Last Salary	Reason for Leaving	Name of Supervisor
III	Heckl & Dunover New York	9	70	2	71	Assistant to Sales Manager	126	143	Injury to elbow	J. Paul Hadnsom

	Name and Address of Company and Type of Business	From Mo.	Yr.	To Mo.	Yr.	Describe in detail the work you did	Weekly Starting Salary	Weekly Last Salary	Reason for Leaving	Name of Supervisor
IV	G. Whiz, Inc. New York	10	66	9	70	Assistant to Head of Performance Dept.	113	141	no opportunity	Dan Block

	Name and Address of Company and Type of Business	From Mo.	Yr.	To Mo.	Yr.	Describe in detail the work you did	Weekly Starting Salary	Weekly Last Salary	Reason for Leaving	Name of Supervisor
V	Peter A. Flop & Co. New York	12	65	10	66	Glorified record clerk	86	94	to obtain better position	Laurence R. Dunn

May we contact the employers listed above? __yes__ If not, indicate by No. which one(s) you do not wish us to contact _____

The facts set forth above in my application for employment are true and complete. I understand that if employed, false statements on this application shall be considered sufficient cause for dismissal. You are hereby authorized to make any investigation of my personal history and financial and credit record through any investigative or credit agencies or bureaus of your choice.*

Merle Wonder

—3—   Signature of Applicant

*To Employer: The requirements of the Fair Credit Reporting Act may be applicable if a credit report on the applicant is obtained and considered.

PART C

Form 8 Application 2 for Job of Administrative Assistant

FOR OFFICE USE ONLY	
Possible Work Locations	Possible Positions

APPLICATION FOR EMPLOYMENT

(PLEASE PRINT PLAINLY)

FOR OFFICE USE ONLY	
Work Location _____	Rate _____
Position _____	Date _____

To Applicant: We deeply appreciate your interest in our organization and assure you that we are sincerely interested in your qualifications. A clear understanding of your background and work history will aid us in placing you in the position that best meets your qualifications and may assist us in possible future upgrading.

PERSONAL   Date: June 1

Name Golden   G   Social Security No. 322-10-0003
      Last   First Initial   Middle Initial

Present address 2825 Closer Dr.   Minute   U.S.A.   Telephone No. 632-4242
                No.   Street   City   State   Zip

How long have you lived at above address? 4 years

Previous address 123   Main   Yuma   Co.   How long did you live there? 3 yrs.
                 No.   Street   City   State   Zip

To Applicant: READ THIS INTRODUCTION CAREFULLY BEFORE ANSWERING ANY QUESTIONS IN THIS BLOCKED-OFF AREA. The Civil Rights Act of 1964 prohibits discrimination in employment practice because of race, color, religion, sex or national origin. P.L. 90-202 prohibits discrimination on the basis of age with respect to individuals who are at least 40 but less than 65 years of age. The laws of some States also prohibit some or all of the above types of discrimination.
DO NOT ANSWER ANY QUESTION CONTAINED IN THIS BLOCKED-OFF AREA UNLESS THE EMPLOYER HAS CHECKED THE BOX NEXT TO THE QUESTION, thereby indicating that the requested information is needed for a bona fide occupational qualification, national security laws, or other legally permissible reasons.

☒ Are you over the age of twenty-one? ___yes___ If no, hire is subject to verification that you are of minimum legal age.

☒ Sex: M __M__ F _____   ☒ Height: __6__ ft. __4__ In.   ☒ Weight: _185_ lbs.

☒ Marital Status: Single _____ Engaged _____ Married __XX__ Separated _____ Divorced _____ Widowed _____

☒ Date of Marriage _1963_ ☐ Number of dependents including yourself _4_ ☒ Are you a citizen of the U.S.A.? _yes_

☒ What is your present Selective Service classification? _2-D_

☒ Indicate dates you attended school:

Elementary _1945_   _1951_ High School _1951_   _1955_ College _1955_   _1959_
           From   To   From   To   From   To

Other (Specify type of school) _____
                                                                        From   To

☒ Have you ever been bonded? _no_ If yes, on what jobs? _____

Employer may list other bona fide occupational questions on lines below:

☐ _____

☐ _____

What method of transportation will you use to get to work? ___Drive___

Position(s) applied for Administrative Officer _____ Rate of pay expected $ _350_ per week

Would you work Full-Time _yes_ Part-Time _____ Specify days and hours if part-time _____

Were you previously employed by us? _no_ If yes, when? _____

List any friends or relatives working for us ___no___
                                                          Name(s)

If your application is considered favorably, on what date will you be available for work? _August_   _1_   19___

Are there any other experiences, skills, or qualifications which you feel would especially fit you for work with the Company? _____

All of my work experience and education appears directly related to the job of the

Administrative Officer

Do you have any physical defects which preclude you from performing certain kinds of work? __no__   If yes, describe such defects

and specific work limitations. _____

Have you been convicted of a crime in the past ten years, excluding misdemeanors and summary offenses? __no__   If yes, describe

in full _____

Have you had a major illness in the past 5 years? __no__ __ If yes, describe _____

Have you received compensation for injuries? __no__ __ If yes, describe _____

RECORD OF EDUCATION

School	Name and Address of School	Course of Study	Check Last Year Completed				Did You Graduate?	List Diploma or Degree
Elementary	Linwood Elementary South Bend, Indiana	✕	5	6	7	(8)	☒ Yes ☐ No	✕
High	Jefferson High School South Bend, Indiana	Sciences	1	2	3	(4)	☒ Yes ☐ No	Diploma
College	United College Schenectady, New York	Industrial Administration	1	2	3	(4)	☒ Yes ☐ No	B.A.
Other (Specify)	University of Maine Portland, Maine University of Colorado	Business Administration	1	(2)	3	4	☒ Yes ☐ No	MBA

MILITARY SERVICE RECORD

Were you in U.S. Armed Forces? Yes _____ No __no__ If yes, what Branch? _____

Dates of duty: From _____ To _____ Rank at discharge _____
       Month   Day   Year   Month   Day   Year

List duties in the Service including special training _____

Have you taken any training under the G.I. Bill of Rights? _____ If yes, what training did you take? _____

PERSONAL REFERENCES (Not Former Employers or Relatives)

Name and Occupation	Address	Phone Number
Helen Hope	South Bend, Indiana	443-2821
Paul Bean	Schenectady, N.Y.	211-0348
Horace West	Yuma, Colorado	866-4328

List below all present and past employment, beginning with your most recent

	Name and Address of Company and Type of Business	From Mo.	From Yr.	To Mo.	To Yr.	Describe in detail the work you did	Weekly Starting Salary	Weekly Last Salary	Reason for Leaving	Name of Supervisor
I	Chief College Eduction Phoenix, Arizona	11	70	pres.		Instructing in Business Administration Courses and Adminis. Officer	275	340	want to return to industry	Hank Low, President

	Name and Address of Company and Type of Business	From Mo.	From Yr.	To Mo.	To Yr.	Describe in detail the work you did	Weekly Starting Salary	Weekly Last Salary	Reason for Leaving	Name of Supervisor
II	Sweetwell Thermostatic Controls Phoenix, Arizona	1	67	10	70	Sales Engineer	230	460 (with bonus)	wanted to try college teaching	Ray Bones President

	Name and Address of Company and Type of Business	From Mo.	From Yr.	To Mo.	To Yr.	Describe in detail the work you did	Weekly Starting Salary	Weekly Last Salary	Reason for Leaving	Name of Supervisor
III	L.D. Jones Petroleum Meters & Valves Peublo, Colorado	5	66	11	67	District Sales Manager	200	265	to take better opportunity	Dan I. Davis

	Name and Address of Company and Type of Business	From Mo.	From Yr.	To Mo.	To Yr.	Describe in detail the work you did	Weekly Starting Salary	Weekly Last Salary	Reason for Leaving	Name of Supervisor
IV	Hedena Electrical Capacitors, etc. Dallas, Texas	4	62	5	66	Sales Account Manager	160	218	for better opportunity	William H. Rue

	Name and Address of Company and Type of Business	From Mo.	From Yr.	To Mo.	To Yr.	Describe in detail the work you did	Weekly Starting Salary	Weekly Last Salary	Reason for Leaving	Name of Supervisor
V	Circle Fast Cor. Electrical Connectors Ft. Worth, Texas	5	59	4	62	Applications Engineer	130	156	to get a better job	Edward Hanson

May we contact the employers listed above? __yes__ If not, indicate by No. which one(s) you do not wish us to contact _____

The facts set forth above in my application for employment are true and complete. I understand that if employed, false statements on this application shall be considered sufficient cause for dismissal. *You are hereby authorized to make any investigation of my personal history and financial and credit record through any investigative or credit agencies or bureaus of your choice.*

Gaylord Golden

—3—   Signature of Applicant

*To Employer: The requirements of the Fair Credit Reporting Act may be applicable if a credit report on the applicant is obtained and considered.

PART C

Form 9 Application 3 for Job of Administrative Assistant

FOR OFFICE USE ONLY	
Possible Work Locations	Possible Positions

APPLICATION FOR EMPLOYMENT

(PLEASE PRINT PLAINLY)

FOR OFFICE USE ONLY	
Work Location _____	Rate _____
Position _____	Date _____

To Applicant: We deeply appreciate your interest in our organization and assure you that we are sincerely interested in your qualifications. A clear understanding of your background and work history will aid us in placing you in the position that best meets your qualifications and may assist us in possible future upgrading.

PERSONAL   Date: May   16

Name ___Pyle_____ C. _____   Social Security No. 388-42-6066
     Last   First Initial   Middle Initial

Present address ___2121 S. Broadway___ Muncie___ Indiana___   Telephone No. 322-0367
     No.   Street   City   State   Zip

How long have you lived at above address? ___three years___

Previous address ___1414 South Continental___ Muncie, Indiana___ How long did you live there? __3 yr__
     No.   Street   City   State   Zip

To Applicant: READ THIS INTRODUCTION CAREFULLY BEFORE ANSWERING ANY QUESTIONS IN THIS BLOCKED-OFF AREA. The Civil Rights Act of 1964 prohibits discrimination in employment practice because of race, color, religion, sex or national origin. P.L. 90-202 prohibits discrimination on the basis of age with respect to individuals who are at least 40 but less than 65 years of age. The laws of some States also prohibit some or all of the above types of discrimination.
    DO NOT ANSWER ANY QUESTION CONTAINED IN THIS BLOCKED OFF AREA UNLESS THE EMPLOYER HAS CHECKED THE BOX NEXT TO THE QUESTION, thereby indicating that the requested information is needed for a bona fide occupational qualification, national security laws, or other legally permissible reasons.

☒ Are you over the age of twenty-one? _____ If no, hire is subject to verification that you are of minimum legal age.

☒ Sex: M _____ F _____   ☒ Height: _____ ft. _____ in.   ☒ Weight: _____ lbs.

☒ Marital Status: Single _____ Engaged _____ Married _____ Separated _____ Divorced _____ Widowed _____

☒ Date of Marriage _____   ☒ Number of dependents including yourself _____   ☒ Are you a citizen of the U.S.A.? __yes__

☒ What is your present Selective Service classification? _____

☒ Indicate dates you attended school:

Elementary _____   High School _____   College ___1961 – 1966___
   From   To   From   To   From   To

Other (Specify type of school) _____
                                     From   To

☒ Have you ever been bonded? __no__ If yes, on what jobs? _____

Employer may list other bona fide occupational questions on lines below:

☐ _____

☐ _____

What method of transportation will you use to get to work? ___Bus___

Position(s) applied for ___Administrative Officer___   Rate of pay expected $ _280 to start_ per week

Would you work Full-Time __xx__ Part-Time _____ Specify days and hours if part-time _____

Were you previously employed by us? __no__ If yes, when? _____

List any friends or relatives working for us ___none___
                                        Name(s)

If your application is considered favorably, on what date will you be available for work? ___June 30___ 19___

Are there any other experiences, skills, or qualifications which you feel would especially fit you for work with the Company? _____
   ___This job looks as if it was made for me! It seems a most logical step in my___
   ___professional development.___

(Turn to Next Page)

Do you have any physical defects which preclude you from performing certain kinds of work? ___none___ If yes, describe such defects

and specific work limitations. _____

Have you been convicted of a crime in the past ten years, excluding misdemeanors and summary offenses? ___no___ If yes, describe

in full _____

Have you had a major illness in the past 5 years? ___no___ If yes, describe _____

Have you received compensation for injuries? ___no___ If yes, describe _____

RECORD OF EDUCATION

School	Name and Address of School	Course of Study	Check Last Year Completed				Did You Graduate?	List Diploma or Degree
Elementary	Pure Grade School Houston, Texas	✕	5	6	7	⑧	☒ Yes ☐ No	✕
High	Lafayette Central Hobart, Indiana		1	2	3	④	☒ Yes ☐ No	Diploma
College	University of Indiana Ft. Wayne, Indiana		1	2	3	④	☒ Yes ☐ No	BA
Other (Specify)	University of Wisconsin		①	2	3	4	☒ Yes ☐ No	MBA

MILITARY SERVICE RECORD

Were you in U.S. Armed Forces?   Yes _____   No ___no___   If yes, what Branch? _____

Dates of duty: From _____ To _____ Rank at discharge _____
                     Month   Day   Year   Month   Day   Year

List duties in the Service including special training _____

_____

Have you taken any training under the G.I. Bill of Rights? _____ If yes, what training did you take? _____

PERSONAL REFERENCES (Not Former Employers or Relatives)

Name and Occupation	Address	Phone Number
David L. Good	Muncie, Indiana	442-4046
Harold E. Luba	Muncie, Indiana	442-4046
Frank Curtis	Hobart, Indiana	863-6023

List below all present and past employment, beginning with your most recent

	Name and Address of Company and Type of Business	From Mo.	Yr.	To Mo.	Yr.	Describe in detail the work you did	Weekly Starting Salary	Weekly Last Salary	Reason for Leaving	Name of Supervisor
I	Skyline Management Corp. Research and Consulting Firm Muncie, Indiana	6	66	present		Vice President	160	300 (with options)	I want to move into a purely administrative position in preparation for top management of a major corporation.	David L. Good, President
II	Name and Address of Company and Type of Business					Describe in detail the work you did	Weekly Starting Salary	Weekly Last Salary	Reason for Leaving	Name of Supervisor
III	Name and Address of Company and Type of Business					Describe in detail the work you did	Weekly Starting Salary	Weekly Last Salary	Reason for Leaving	Name of Supervisor
IV	Name and Address of Company and Type of Business					Describe in detail the work you did	Weekly Starting Salary	Weekly Last Salary	Reason for Leaving	Name of Supervisor
V	Name and Address of Company and Type of Business					Describe in detail the work you did	Weekly Starting Salary	Weekly Last Salary	Reason for Leaving	Name of Supervisor

May we contact the employers listed above? __yes__ If not, indicate by No. which one(s) you do not wish us to contact _____

The facts set forth above in my application for employment are true and complete. I understand that if employed, false statements on this application shall be considered sufficient cause for dismissal. You are hereby authorized to make any investigation of my personal history and financial and credit record through any investigative or credit agencies or bureaus of your choice.*

Charlotte Pyle

—3—   Signature of Applicant

*To Employer: The requirements of the Fair Credit Reporting Act may be applicable if a credit report on the applicant is obtained and considered.

Biographical data stage is a screen before interview.

Does B.D. indicate job success?

Should have job analysis before you & appraisal criteria
when making selection (1st step) - not evaluation of resumes.
Everything that is verifiable should be included in interview.

* Data should discriminate between successful & unsuccessful
performance on the job.

Companies tend to stick to safe items on form.

Validity must be assessed.

Name _____   Group Number _____

Date _____   Class Section _____   Hour _____   Score _____

ASSESSMENT OF LEARNING IN PERSONNEL ADMINISTRATION
EXERCISE 7

1. Try to state the purpose of this exercise in one concise sentence.

2. Specifically what did you learn from this exercise (i.e., skills, abilities, and knowledge)?

3. How might your learning influence your role and your duties as a personnel administrator?

4. What type of data is available from an application blank that is not typically available from personal resume's?

5. What advantages do weighted, or scorable application blanks have over traditional ones?

6. Additional questions given by your implementor:

Exercise 8

INTERVIEWING AS A PREDICTOR OF JOB SUCCESS

PREVIEW

In this exercise a pervasive selection technique, the interview, is explored. Although the selection interview is used very widely, it can easily become a very subjective and biased selection tool. Not only are interviewers able to inject their own personal prejudices into the selection decision process via the interview, but they may not be furnished with relevant questions that can differentiate between successful and unsuccessful job holders. This exercise is designed to acquaint you with the interview process and to build your skills in conducting interviews. Applicants are interviewed in role-playing episodes and a group selects a most qualified from among three candidates. A structured or patterned employment interview is also designed from job-analysis information.

INTRODUCTION

The Interviewing Process

A Key Selection Device. There is every indication that the interview continues to be used almost universally as a selection device. Some time ago Scott et al.[1] reported that 98.4 percent of a sample of 852 companies used the interview in their selection process. This, of course, does not tell us how important a part of the process the interview is, but the fact that 93.9 percent of the companies in the Scott et al. study said they never hired anyone without an interview suggests that it is indeed a critical phase in the selec-

[1] W. D. Scott, R. C. Clothier, and W. R. Spriegel, *Personnel Management*, 6th ed. (New York: McGraw-Hill, 1961).

OBJECTIVES

1. To become aware of the uses of the interview as a device to predict future job success.
2. To become aware of the types of information that can be gathered from the interview, the limitations and typical errors in the interviewing process, and ways to improve the effectiveness of the interview.
3. To build skills in interviewing for selection purposes and in designing structured forms to record interviewer comments.

PREMEETING ASSIGNMENT

Read the entire exercise.

tion process. There is little reason to believe the importance and pervasiveness of the interview has changed in the years since the Scott study.

Robert Martin, in an article entitled "Confessions of An Interviewer," made the following remarks:

Most of the corporate recruiters with whom I've had contact are decent, well-intentioned people. But I've yet to meet anyone, including myself, who knows what he (or she) is doing. Many interviewers seem to have absolute faith in their omniscience, but I suspect that their "Perceptiveness" is based more upon preconceived untested assumptions than upon objectively derived data.[2]

Further, Dunnette and Bass sum up the interviewing process by stating that:

> The personnel interview continues to be the most widely used method for selecting employees, despite the fact that it is a costly, inefficient, and usually invalid procedure. It is often used to the exclusion of far more thoroughly researched and validated procedures. Even when the interview is used in conjunction with other procedures, it is almost always treated as the final hurdle in the selection process. In fact, other selection methods (e.g., psychological tests) are often regarded simply as supplements to the interview.[3]

At this point a reasonable conclusion would seem to be that the interview remains the key selection instrument for most firms, but quite an imperfect one. The popularity of the interview continues and its importance has not suffered from the increased use of tests and other selection devices. Insistence on selecting people on the basis of interviews can best be explained by reference to the needs of the interviewer to talk to a candidate face-to-face, rather than on the grounds of its demonstrated efficacy as a selection device to predict subsequent job performance.

Validity Problems.   Regrettably, there is not an abundance of research on the interview. This is particularly disconcerting in light of the great importance placed on interviewing and because of the probability that the proposed government *Uniform Selection Guidelines* referring to nondiscriminatory hiring practices may insist on the validation of the interview procedure. In fact, Section 10 of the present Official Federal Contract Compliance (OFCC) guidelines on validation of employment tests states:

> Selection techniques other than tests may also be improperly used so as to have the effect of discriminating against minority groups. Such techniques include, but are not restricted to, unscored interviews, unscored application forms, and records of educational and work history.[4]

This citation indicates that the selection interview and other unscored procedures (i.e., those whose interpretation is not quantifiable and hence overly subjective) may require validation (often meaning the evidence of a statistical relationship between the selection interview responses and subsequent job performance—see Exercise 10) if such techniques result in different rates of rejection between, for example, certain ethnic groups.

In attempts to tighten up the interviewing process many forms have been developed to record results quantitatively. Forms in use by interviewers to record their perceptions vary considerably from those weighting just a few items, like grades and means of support while at college, to long biographical data forms administered in addition to the regular application form. The trend is toward increased use of these instruments, but it is difficult to tell how far their use will go.

The interview has a long and controversial history. Reviewers of the literature often conclude that the empirical studies offer few firm conclusions.[5] They frequently caution against putting much faith in the validity of an interview as a selection device, primarily due to interviewer bias and to the inability of many of the questions typically asked to predict job success.[6]

Most information-getting interviews essentially involve measurement. The interview agenda can usefully be regarded as a measurement device, and the interviewer as a measurer of the interviewee. However, in this case, there are no sophisticated instruments, such as the microscope used in chemistry, to add accuracy to this measurement situation. Thus, because humans are quite subjective in their judgments, errors exist. Errors include perceptual biases and stereotypes, erroneous and misunderstood com-

[2] R. A. Martin, "Confessions of an Interviewer," *MBA*, January 1975, p. 8.

[3] M. D. Dunnette, and B. M. Bass, "Behavioral Scientists and Personnel Management," *Industrial Relations* 2, no. 3 (1963): 115–130.

[4] Office of the Federal Contract Compliance Employee Testing and Other Selection Devices, *Federal Register* 36, no. 77 (1971): 7532–7535.

[5] E. C. Mayfield, "The Selection Interview—A Re-Evaluation of Published Research," *Personnel Psychology* 17 (1964): 239–260; R. Wagner, "The Employment Interview, A Critical Summary," *Personnel Psychology* 2 (1949): 17–46; N. Schmitt, "Social and Situational Determinants of Interview Decisions: Implications for the Employment Interview," *Personnel Psychology* 29 (1976): 79–101.

[6] Dunnette and Bass, "Behavioral Scientists and Personnel Management."; L. W. Porter, "Personnel Management," *Annual Review of Psychology* 17 (1966): 405; S. B. Sells, "Personnel Management," *Annual Review of Psychology* 15 (1964): 404; E. K. Taylor, and E. C. Nevis, "Personnel Selection," *Annual Review of Psychology* 12 (1961): 393; E. C. Webster, *Decision-Making in the Employment Interview* (Montreal, Quebec: Industrial Relations Centre, McGill University, 1964); and Schmitt, "Social and Situational Determinants of Interview Decisions."

munication, personality conflicts between interviewer and interviewee, and measurements made on variables perhaps not relevant to job success, such as appearance or sex.

Effective Interviewing. As mentioned earlier, the interview is often a misused selection technique, partly because it can be used with little or no advance preparation. It is becoming evident that good interviewing requires more thought and structure than it commonly receives. In analyzing the role of the interview in employee selection, a number of principles can be stated:

1. The primary purpose of the interview is the prediction of the applicant's success on the job. Therefore, the effectiveness of the interview should be assessed by measuring the extent to which it accurately predicts job performance.

2. Preemployment interviews that are described as guided, patterned, or structured (e.g., a specific set of predetermined questions are asked) usually give the most consistent results across interviews.

3. The interview should not emphasize the evaluation of dimensions of applicant behavior that can be measured more accurately by other selection techniques less susceptible to bias or less costly.

4. Through the interview the prediction of social and motivational aspects of job performance may be assessed, in addition to biographical data.[7]

Hakel[8] has provided a basic checklist for interviewing as shown in Table 1. The table outlines basic skills and specific suggestions for interviewers which facilitate an effective interview.

In some instances it may be desirable to construct a form for interviewers to use in order to record their evaluations of the interviewee. This would help achieve interviewer agreement as each interviewer would have the same standards of judgment. The form, of course, should be tailored to the specific needs of the organization. The following procedures for constructing interview recording forms are recommended:

1. Job dimensions should be carefully defined and made relatively specific to facilitate interviewer reliability.
2. Interviewer judgments should be made to reflect their predictions of an interviewee's actual job performance (performance evaluation procedures

---

[7] See H. O. Osborn, and W. R. Manese, *How to Install and Validate Selection Techniques* (Houston: American Petroleum Institute, 1971).
[8] Personal communication, April 1976.

Table 1. Basic Interviewing Skills*

I. *Planning the Interview.* Examination of the application blank, the job requirements, and also mapping out areas to be covered in the interview, planning and organizing questions pertinent to these areas. Insuring that the interview will be held in an optimal environment, free from interruption.

II. *Getting Information.* Use of appropriate questioning techniques to elicit relevant information in the same sequence over all interviewees. Probing incomplete answers and problem areas while maintaining an atmosphere of trust. Structuring the interview. Comprehensive questions and follow-up comments.

III. *Giving Information.* Effectiveness in communicating appropriate and accurate information about the company and available jobs for which the applicant would qualify, and in answering the applicant's questions. Closing the interview.

IV. *Personal Impact.* The total effect the interviewer has on the applicant, both as an individual and as a representative of the organization. This includes the applicant's first impression of the interviewer, given to the applicant through the interviewer's tone of voice, eye contact, personal appearance and grooming, postures and gestures, as well as the interviewer's impact throughout the interview.

V. *Responding to the Applicant.* Concern for the applicant's feelings while maintaining control over the interview. Reacting appropriately to the applicant's comments, questions, and nonverbal behaviors. Convey a feeling of interest in the applicant, encourage an atmosphere of warmth and trust, and make use of encouragement and praise.

VI. *Information Processing.* Gathering, integrating, and analyzing interview information, culminating in a final placement decision. Identifying personal characteristics and judging them in the context of the job requirements. Skill in assimilating, remembering, and integrating all information relevant to the final evaluation.

---

* Contributed by Milton D. Hakel, Department of Psychology, Ohio State University.

used in Exercises 4, 5, and 6 can be used to gather appraisal criteria).

3. The form should be evaluated using specific methods for validity and reliability (see Exercise 10).

Because it is generally agreed that the interview can tap social and motivational factors, it may be possible for perceptive interviewers to predict such factors on the basis of the interview, in addition to the job dimensions relative to the applicant's work experience, abilities, knowledge, and skills. However, such social and motivational factors may be questioned for job relatedness, as these would seldom emerge from any type of job analysis. Therefore, an interview may be limited to explorations of an applicant's education and specific vocational training—questions that could indicate possession of knowledge and skills required by the job. In most cases, preemployment tests measuring basic abilities and basic job skills will better indicate potential to learn and to understand the operations required by the job than the interview. An explanation of specific experience and training in relation to job position requirements may supplement test information, but must be job related. In fact, as with all selection techniques, interview questions must be job related. The interview, however, is far more likely than most selection tools to use non–job-related factors in making selection decisions, and the interviewer must be alert to the dangers of overstepping legal bounds.

Keeping the above caveats about job relatedness and the dangers of subjective, perceptually determined evaluations in mind, social and motivational factors may still be worthy of consideration. The following types of social and motivational factors are often used to help predict future job success in an interview:

Social & Motivational Factors:

1. Does this applicant appear to be dependable? Will he or she demonstrate and maintain good work habits and attendance records and require a minimum of supervision? Experience indicates that many individuals who have ability and aptitude still do not seem able to maintain good work habits. This latter factor is frequently labeled poor "motivation" (see Exercise 16).

2. Will this individual assume responsibility for the job to be done? Will he or she take the initiative where appropriate and seek assistance when it is needed? While this factor is related closely to the preceding one, it has the added dimensions of leadership, judgment, and understanding.

3. Will this applicant be willing and able to work with others? Will he or she accept and understand the need for coordination and communication? Here the emphasis on interpersonal relations is in maintaining work flow rather than personality.

4. Will this applicant be sincerely interested in the job and its possibilities? Will he or she be motivated by and obtain personal satisfaction from the job? Here the emphasis is on the "fit" between the interests of the applicant and the position requirements of the job.

5. Will the applicant be a relatively adaptable employee, one who does not lose his or her head in emergencies? A common complaint of supervisors is the fact that some individuals go to pieces when the routine is disturbed.

6. Are the goals and aspirations of this applicant consonant with the available opportunities? Turnover among nonprofessionals was relatively unheard of a few years ago. Today each individual seems to have a personal timetable of accomplishments.

7. Is the manner and appearance of this applicant consistent with job requirements? Manner and appearance are important for some types of jobs, and they should be considered in the light of job requirements.

8. Considering the applicant's qualifications as a whole in relation to job requirements, will this applicant's overall work performance be satisfactory?

Interviewer Accuracy and Reliability. It is recommended that interviewers' judgments be recorded in the form of predictions of the applicant's job performance. Predictions should be made with respect to such aspects of job performance as interpersonal relations and motivation to work. These aspects of an applicant's suitability are difficult to obtain with other selection devices and thus the interview can be especially useful in providing input in these areas.

To help make the interview more "objective," the interviewer should write an applicant evaluation report and should also be required to select applicants in such a way that those selected will be judged to have varying degrees of predicted job success on the various dimensions. To validate interviewer predictions, it is necessary to have such variations among those actually hired, for the variations enable the interviewer's predictions to be related to subsequent measures of actual job performance. If the interviewer's predictions of high success, for example, are consistently confirmed by actual job-performance evaluations, the predictive ability of the interviewer is evidenced to be high.

The reliability of interviewer judgments can also be measured by the degree of agreement between the judgments of two or more independent interviewers who have interviewed the same applicants. Interviewer reliability can be faulty for several reasons: (a) the recording form may be ambiguous or otherwise faulty, making it difficult to obtain agreement between independent interviewers (a remedy is, of course, to revise the form); and (b) interviewers may have varying frames of reference for making predictions about job performance (the remedy may be interviewer training).

It is usually possible to distinguish between these sources of unreliability by analyzing the nature of the disagreement among interviewers. Of course, both factors noted above may be present. In checking reliability between two or more interviewers, the following procedures are recommended:

1. Each interviewer should independently interview and rate the same sample of applicants. An adequate sample would be at least thirty applicants, preferably more.
2. The mean rating assigned by each interviewer and the standard deviation[9] of these ratings should be calculated for each job dimension.
3. The product-moment correlation coefficient[10] between the ratings assigned by two interviewers should be calculated for each dimension. In general, if the correlation coefficient is less than 0.60 there is cause for concern about the degree of agreement between the two interviewers.

Figure 1 depicts the information-processing procedure typically used by interviewers as they make their evaluation of an interviewee. Each small box represents a specific type of information. For example, skill in communicating verbally, previous experience, and education would be types of information available about a job candidate. The interviewer also uses information describing successful job holders (e.g.,

---

[9] See *Appendix*, Exercise 10.
[10] *Ibid.*

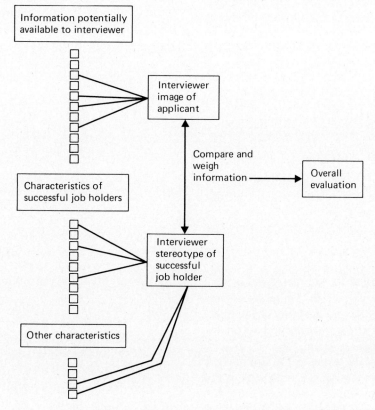

Fig. 1. Interviewer Information-Processing Model (Contributed by Milton D. Hakel, Department of Psychology, Ohio State University.)

very knowledgeable in technical matters, considerable previous supervisory experience, etc.) and "other" information (e.g., current plans regarding expansion). Some information from each category is used to form the interviewer's image of the interviewee and his or her perception or stereotype of the "ideal" job holder. Comparing these two types of information, interviewers make an evaluation. The evaluation could be erroneous if any of the information or perceptions used to form it are incorrect or biased. As Fig. 1 shows, the process is necessarily subjective, as individual judgment and perception play such an important role.

Training in the techniques of interviewing involves methods of establishing rapport with an interviewee, lines of questioning, and means to achieve thorough coverage of an applicant's background. Training in these areas can be accomplished by recording practice interviews or role plays of interviews on audio- or videotape. Tape playback affords an objective analysis of interviewer technique. Training to predict applicant job performance is best conducted by having two interviewers independently interview and rate the same applicant. The ratings and the evidence utilized in making the resulting predictions are then examined and discussed after the interviewee has performed on the job and job success can be measured.

PROCEDURE

Overview.   First, an interviewer's report (rating) form is assessed as to its applicability for recording interviewer's observations for the job of personnel technician III. Next, an improved interviewer report form is designed for the job. Finally, an interview procedure is developed for the job of administrative officer in Exercise 7. Candidates are interviewed by groups after they develop interviewer report forms and a set of questions and final selection decisions are compared.

PART A

STEP 1: You are to review the job description for a personnel technician III (Form 1) and discuss in small groups the applicability of the interviewer rating forms (Forms 2 and 3) for evaluating candidates for this job. These are forms interviewers use to record their evaluation of an interviewee both during and after the session. Assess whether or not you feel the forms help the interviewer to be more objective and gain more information and describe why you feel the way you do.

TIME: About 35 minutes.

PART B

STEP 2: Break into small groups and design an interviewer rating form specifically designed for the job of a personnel technician III (Form 1). It should cover all of the important questions you would ask of an applicant for the personnel technician job and it should be quantifiable. That is, a total interviewee score should be able to be derived from the form. Incorporate the improvements over Forms 2 and 3 you noted above into this form.

TIME: About 35 minutes.

PART C

STEP 3: Divide into small groups and design an interviewing procedure (i.e., interviewer report form and specific questions to ask interviewees) for the job of the administrative officer of Palms Pacific Corporation (refer back to the organization description, job description, resumes, application blank, etc., for this job in Exercise 7). Those persons playing the roles of Charlotte, Gaylord, and Merle should not be involved in this activity as they are ratees. The interviewing procedure should adhere to the following criteria:

a) It should focus on that information not obtained on the biographical data sheets or application blanks presented in Exercise 7, but which is relevant to the job.

b) It should attempt to tap social and motivational factors deemed important for job success (see *Introduction* to this exercise).

c) It should be quantifiable, i.e., the interviewer report form should be able to be scored in order to check the form's reliability and validity.

STEP 4: Each group is then to interview all three persons playing the roles of Merle Wonder, Gaylord Golden, and Charlotte Pyle for the job of administrative officer. (They have been chosen for the last exercise or will be chosen from the larger group by the implementor.) Once all three applicants have been interviewed by each group, the choices of all groups are to be revealed and compared.

TIME: About one hour.

FOR FURTHER READING

Andler, E. C. "Preplanned Question Areas for Efficient Interviewing." *Personnel Journal 55* (January 1976):8–10. (I)

Carlson, R. E. "Selection Interview Decisions: The Effect of Interviewer Experience, Relative Quota Situation, and Applicant Sample on Interviewer Decisions." *Personnel Psychology* 20 (1967): 259–280. (II–R)

Carlson, R. E., and E. C. Mayfield. "Evaluating Interview and Employment Application Data." *Personnel Psychology* 20 (1967): 221–460. (II)

Drake, J. D. *Interviewing for Managers.* New York: Amacom, 1972. (I)

Dunnette, M. A., and B. M. Bass. "Behavioral Scientists and Personnel Management." *Industrial Relations* 2 (1963): 115–130. (I)

Fear, R. A. *The Evaluation Interview.* 2d ed. New York: McGraw-Hill, 1973. (I)

Gordon, R. L. *Interviewing.* Rev. ed. Homewood, Ill.: Dorsey, 1975. (I)

Greller, M. M. "Subordinate Participation and Reactions to the Appraisal Interview." *Journal of Applied Psychology* 60 (1975): 544–549. (II–R)

Guion, R. M. "Recruiting, Selection, and Job Placement." In M. D. Dunnette (ed.), *Handbook of Industrial and Organizational Psychology.* Chicago: Rand McNally, 1976. (II)

Hall, E. T. *The Silent Language.* Grenwich, Conn.: Fawcet. 1959. (I)

Hakel, M. D. "Similarity of Post-Interview Trait Rating Intercorrelations as a Contributor to Interrater Agreement in a Structured Employment Interview." *Journal of Applied Psychology* 55 (1971): 443–448. (II–R)

Hakel, M. D., and M. D. Dunnette. "Interpersonal Perception in the Employment Interview: A Report of the 1965 Cattell Award Winners." *The Industrial Psychologist* 5 (1968): 30–38. (II–R)

Heneman, H. G. et al. "Interviewer Validity as a Function of Interview Structure, Biographical Data and Interviewee Order." *Journal of Applied Psychology* 60 (1975): 748–753. (II–R)

Kahn, R. L., and C. F. Cannell. *The Dynamics of Interviewing.* New York: Wiley, 1958. (I)

Kleinke, C. L. *First Impressions.* Englewood Cliffs, New Jersey: Prentice-Hall, 1975. (I)

Landy, F. J. "The Validity of the Interview in Police Officer Selection." *Journal of Applied Psychology* 61 (1976): 193–198. (II–R)

London, M., and J. R. Poplawski. "Effects of Information on Stereo-Type Development in Performance Appraisal and Interview Contexts." *Journal of Applied Psychology* 61 (1976): 199–205. (II–R)

Lopez, F. M. *Personnel Interviewing,* 2d ed. New York: McGraw-Hill, 1975. (I)

Mayfield, E. C. "The Selection Interview—A Re-Evaluation of Published Research." *Personnel Psychology* 17 (1964): 239–260. (II)

Mayfield, E. C., and R. E. Carlson. "Selection Interview Decisions: First Results from a Long-Term Research Project." *Personnel Psychology* 19 (1966): 41–53. (II–R)

Osborn, H. O., and W. R. Manese. *How to Install and Validate Selection Techniques.* Houston: American Petroleum Institute, 1971. (I)

Odiorne, G. S., and A. S. Hann. *Effective College Recruiting.* Ann Arbor: Bureau of Industrial Relations, University of Michigan, 1961. (I)

Schmitt, N. "Social and Situational Determinants of Interview Decisions: Implications for the Employment Interview." *Personnel Psychology* 29 (1976): 79–102. (II)

Schmitt, N., and B. W. Coyle. "Applicant Decisions in the Employment Interview." *Journal of Applied Psychology* 61 (1976): 184–192. (II–R)

Schwab, D. P. "Why Interview? A Critique." *Personnel Journal* 48 (1969): 126–129. (I)

Serafini, C. R. "Interviewer Listening." *Personnel Journal* 54 (1975): 398–399+. (I)

Solberg, P. A. "Unprogrammed Decision Making." *Industrial Management Review* 8 (1967): 19–30. (I)

Sydiaha, D. "Bales' Interaction Process Analysis of Personnel Selection Interviews." *Journal of Applied Psychology* 45 (1961): 393–401. (II–R)

Ulrich, L., and D. Trumbo. "The Selection Interview since 1949." *Psychological Bulletin* 63 (1965): 100–116. (II)

Vroom, V. H. "Organizational Choice: A Study of Pre- and Post-decision Processes." *Organizational Behavior and Human Performance* 1 (1966): 212–225. (II–R)

Wagner, R. "The Employment Interview: A Critical Summary." *Personnel Psychology* 2 (1949): 17–46. (II)

Webster, E. C. *Decision-Making in the Employment Interview.* Montreal, Quebec: Industrial Relations Center, McGill University, 1964. (I)

Weiner, Y., and M. Schneiderman. "Use of Job Information as a Criterion in Employment Decisions of Interviewers." *Journal of Applied Psychology* 59 (1974): 699–704. (II–R)

Wright, A. O. "Summary of Research on the Selection Interview since 1964." *Personnel Psychology* 22 (1964): 391–413. (II)

PART A

Form 1 Job Description

PERSONNEL TECHNICIAN III

DESCRIPTION OF WORK:

General Statement of Duties: Performs complex technical work in recruitment, examination, classification, wage and salary administration, training, and other functions of a personnel program.

Supervision Received: Works under general supervision of an administrative or technical superior.

Supervision Exercised: Exercises supervision over assigned personnel.

EXAMPLES OF DUTIES: (Any one position may not include all of the duties listed, nor do the listed examples include all tasks which may be found in positions of this class.)

Conducts position audits on departmental and classwide basis and recommends human-resource allocations; interviews employees, supervisors, and department heads; observes work performed; studies department organization and work assignments; and reviews other factors affecting classification and class relationships. Reviews, analyzes, and recommends class-specification revisions and drafts new class specifications.

Assists in obtaining, assembling, and computing wage and salary data; collects pay data through personal interviews with private and public employers; determines comparability of job duties and responsibilities between community and city positions. Collects, tabulates, and computes wage and salary data collected on national pay surveys.

Analyzes personnel requisitions. Conducts recruitment; drafts promotional and employment announcements and composes classified advertising. Interviews and advises applicants of job opportunities. Reviews experience, education, test scores, and other factors regarding eligibles with appointing authorities.

Selects and recommends standardized aptitude, intelligence, achievement, performance, and other tests; determines cutoff scores. Selects, revises and constructs test items and prepares tests; develops rating patterns. Evaluates experience and education of applicants; interviews, evaluates, and certifies eligibles. Organizes oral panel interviews.

Performs related work as assigned.

QUALIFICATIONS FOR APPOINTMENT:

Knowledges, Skills, and Abilities: Considerable knowledge of the principles of personnel administration, including working knowledge of examination processes and job-evaluation methods and techniques. Some knowledge of statistics and ability to make statistical computations. Ability to organize and present effective oral and written reports. Ability to establish and maintain effective working relationships with employees, department heads, officials, and the general public.

Education: Graduation from a four-year college with major course work in business administration, public administration, public administration, or related fields.

Experience: Three years experience in technical personnel work involving recruitment, examination, classification, pay administration, training or other personnel functions at the professional level.

OR

Any equivalent combination of education and experience.

PART A

Form 2 Interviewer Report Form

Job Title:	Candidate's Name:		Date:

Rating factors Consider all factors in relation to the position for which the examination is being given.	*Rating* Mark your tentative rating in pencil by checking the appropriate boxes. Mark your final rating in ink after all candidates have been interviewed.											
	Below acceptable level						*Accept-able*	*Good*	*Outstanding*			
	10	20	30	40	50	60	70	80	90	100	*WT*	*SCORE*
1. Appearance, physical condition												
2. Ability to communicate ideas												
3. Ability to understand and respond to questions												
4. Attitude, manner, interest and willingness to work and learn												
5. Knowledges, skills, and abilities required by job specification												
6.												
7.												
8.												

Examiner's signature _____

PART A

Form 3 Interviewer Report Form*

Candidate for: _____ Interviewer: _____

Name of applicant: _____ Date: _____

Please record your conclusions noting the extent to which the applicant possesses or will probably demonstrate the qualities listed below. The specific items under each category are intended to direct your attention to the kinds of evidence you may need to consider. Check the relevant items.

1. *Cooperation*—Will applicant get along with others and work as member of team?

Overall rating on this item

Lowest	Low	Below average	Average	Above average	High	Highest
☐	☐	☐	☐	☐	☐	☐

Check below those items applicable.
☐ Evidence of previous friction with supervisors, peers, subordinates.
☐ Preference for solitary work assignments.
☐ Tendency to be a "loner" in social activities.
☐ Evidence of involvement in community, religious, and/or athletic activities.
☐ Openness and candidness in the interview.
☐ Evidence of excessive reactions to criticisms.

2. *Need for achievement*—Are the goals and aspirations of this applicant consistent with available opportunities?

Overall rating on this item

Lowest	Low	Below average	Average	Above average	High	Highest
☐	☐	☐	☐	☐	☐	☐

Check below those items applicable
☐ Level of abilities and qualifications consistent with available opportunities.
☐ Level of ambition consistent with available opportunities in the company.
☐ Is easily discouraged by obstacles and setbacks.

3. *Job satisfaction*—Will applicant be involved in and derive personal satisfaction from job?

Overall rating on this item

Lowest	Low	Below average	Average	Above average	High	Highest
☐	☐	☐	☐	☐	☐	☐

Check below those items applicable.
☐ Has participated in job-related activities (clubs, societies, etc.)
☐ Has taken advantage of company-sponsored opportunities to develop skills related to job.
☐ Evidence of success in school or work situations.
☐ Hobbies, interests, and personal goals are in line with job activities.

4. *Rewards needed*—Does applicant give evidence that he or she will find the rewards offered by the organization in terms of financial rewards and supervisory recognition compatible with the opportunities provided by the company?

Overall rating on this item

Lowest	Low	Below average	Average	Above average	High	Highest
☐	☐	☐	☐	☐	☐	☐

Check below those items applicable.
☐ Needs too much constant recognition by others.
☐ Seems to get much satisfaction from the job itself.
☐ Will soon demand more in financial rewards than we are in a position to offer.

5. *Work experience*—Does applicant's work history indicate the ability to learn and understand the operations required?
Overall rating on this item

Lowest	Low	Below average	Average	Above average	High	Highest
☐	☐	☐	☐	☐	☐	☐

Check below those items applicable.
☐ Has experience in performing similar tasks.
☐ Evidence of job failure due to lack of ability.
☐ Has knowledge of tools, equipment, and work procedures.
☐ Evidence of job progression.
☐ Assignment to special projects or task forces.

6. *Responsibility and initiative*—Will applicant exercise judgment in getting the job done, taking initiative where appropriate and seeking assistance when needed?
Overall rating on this item

Lowest	Low	Below average	Average	Above average	High	Highest
☐	☐	☐	☐	☐	☐	☐

Check below those items applicable.
☐ Evidence of capacity for independent thought and action to meet work standards.
☐ Evidence of ability to assume leadership role when required.
☐ Instances of seeking easy way out to meet work deadlines.
☐ Tendency to blame others for work delays and interruptions.
☐ Evidence of sticking it out till the job is done.

7. *Manner and appearance*—Will others react favorably to applicant?
Overall rating on this item

Lowest	Low	Below average	Average	Above average	High	Highest
☐	☐	☐	☐	☐	☐	☐

Check below those items applicable.
☐ Over-all appearance favorable.
☐ Shows interpersonal tact.
☐ Adequate level of self-confidence.
☐ Has ability to present and communicate ideas.
☐ Is sensitive to the needs of others.

8. *Composure*—Will applicant maintain composure under pressure, keeping head in emergencies?
Overall rating on this item

Lowest	Low	Below average	Average	Above average	High	Highest
☐	☐	☐	☐	☐	☐	☐

Check below those items applicable.
☐ Evidence of ability to adjust to changes in work environment (work interruptions, machine failure, other disruptions of routine schedule).
☐ Evidence of reacting impulsively in emergencies.
☐ Evidence that the quality of his or her work suffers in emergencies.
☐ Evidence of ability to adjust to changes in work procedures.

9. *Dependability*—Will applicant have a good attendance record and maintain good work habits?
Overall rating on this item

Lowest	Low	Below average	Average	Above average	High	Highest
☐	☐	☐	☐	☐	☐	☐

Check below those items applicable.
☐ Attendance record: times sick, late or otherwise absent from work.
☐ Evidence of reprimands for poor work performance.
☐ Safety record: evidence of responsibility for or involvement in accidents or work interruptions.
☐ Evidence of good work habits.

10. *Training*—Does applicant's experience give him or her an edge over other applicants?

Overall rating on this item

Lowest	Low	Below average	Average	Above average	High	Highest
☐	☐	☐	☐	☐	☐	☐

Check below those items applicable.

☐ Adequate level of educational attainment.
☐ Evidence of relevant on-the-job training.
☐ Evidence of relevant vocational school training.
☐ Has participated in workshops, continuing-education classes.
☐ Evidence of self-initiated skill development (e.g., correspondence school, programmed instruction, etc.).

Should applicant be hired for the job stated? Yes _____ No _____

If yes, state reason. _____
_____
_____

If no, state reason. _____
_____
_____

COMMENTS: _____
_____
_____
_____
_____
_____

* Adapted from H. G. Osborn and W. R. Manese, *How to Install and Validate Employee Selection Techniques.* (Washington, D.C.: American Petroleum Institute, 1971).

Name _____ Group Number _____

Date _____ Class Section _____ Hour _____ Score _____

ASSESSMENT OF LEARNING IN PERSONNEL ADMINISTRATION

EXERCISE 8

1. Try to state the purpose of this exercise in one concise sentence.

2. Specifically what did you learn from this exercise (i.e., skills, abilities, and knowledge)?

3. How might your learning influence your role and your duties as a personnel administrator?

4. What are your own strengths and weaknesses as an interviewer or interviewee?

5. What type of information about job applicants can be obtained from an interview which cannot be obtained via application blanks and reference checks?

6. How would you evaluate the effectiveness of an interview program? Could you subject such a program to a cost/benefit analysis?

7. Should a line manager who would be an interviewee's superior conduct final-selection interviews, should the personnel specialists conduct them, or should both be involved? Under what conditions might each of these three strategies be effective?

8. Additional questions given by your implementor:

Exercise 9 ✓

WORK SAMPLING AND SIMULATION AS PREDICTORS OF JOB SUCCESS

PREVIEW

There has been a trend in personnel administration toward devising selection techniques that allow job applicants to perform activities during selection which closely parallel those they will actually perform on the job. The assumption is, of course, that the best predictor of job performance is job performance itself, rather than previous education, test scores, or interview data. These devices are called "situational" tests when used as selection tools, because they present applicants with situations similar to those actually found on the job. Their performance in these situations is assumed to represent their performance in the actual job situation. Two types of techniques have been used in this regard. In the first, work sampling, prospective applicants are asked to perform a sample activity of the job to gauge their ability to perform the entire job. The second technique, simulation, utilizes activities designed to simulate actual job performance. For example, a role-playing activity would give selection specialists an idea of how an applicant would act in a supervisory role. In this exercise, you design a work sample and participate in two common types of simulations, an in-basket test and a leaderless group discussion.

OBJECTIVES

1. To become familiar with work sampling and simulation as selection devices and with their advantages over more traditional selection tools (e.g., interviews and biographical data).
2. To gain skill in designing a work sample that could be used to aid in selection decisions.
3. To learn how assessment centers are designed and implemented and to build skill as assessors and assessees in an assessment center.
4. To receive feedback on your own potential for success in administrative positions and task groups as you participate as an assessee in an in-basket test and a leaderless group discussion.

PREMEETING ASSIGNMENT

Read the entire exercise, except procedure and forms of Parts C and D until asked to do so, paying particular attention to the parts of the *Procedure* you are asked to read.

INTRODUCTION

Assessing Future Job Behavior at the Time of Selection

Beyond the measuring of historical information (biographical data) and responses to verbal questions (interviewing) as selection techniques, there have recently been attempts to measure behavior similar to that observed on the job. Obviously, if we can measure an applicant's behavior in situations that are very close to those actually found on the job, we can perhaps obtain indications of ability and skill levels far better than inferences about ability and skill levels obtained from biographical data, interviews, or even psychological testing.[1]

Work Sampling.   The first of the methods designed to approximate job content closely, work sampling (see also Fig. 4, Exercise 10), should provide a good measure of an applicant's suitability for a job, for it requires applicants to perform actual segments of the job before a final hiring decision is made. Wernimont and Campbell have proposed such a procedure and advocate what they refer to as the "behavioral consistency" of such a technique.[2] They believe that the behavioral consistency approach to selection (i.e., allowing candidates to evidence behaviors actually required on the job and/or inferring future job behavior from past job behavior or present behavior on a work sample) would have several immediate advantages, such as diminishing the problem of faking and reducing charges of discrimination and invasion of privacy which often accompany testing.

Campion[3] studied the job of an auto mechanic with work sampling. He developed a work sample for a few aspects of the mechanic's job by having subjects actually perform some of the typical tasks performed by mechanics and then observing and scoring their performance. This scoring was done via a scale for each task which gave a certain number of points for each response subjects made. For example, when prospective mechanics were asked to measure radial misalignment, they received ten points if they used a dial indicator, three points if they used a straightedge, one point if they relied only on "feel," and zero points if they used any other method. A similar scoring procedure was developed for several other automobile mechanic tasks (e.g., installing pulleys and gears, etc.).

When performance on work samples was compared with that on paper-and-pencil tests, the mechanics' performance on the work-sample measure was in all instances significantly and positively related to supervisory evaluations of their actual subsequent performance on the job. However, none of the rela-

tionships between actual job performance and the paper-and-pencil tests reached statistical significance. Successful performance on the work sample was more accurately able to predict subsequent successful performance on the job than were traditional ability tests.

Thus, it seems that personnel selection could often be improved by a strategy that used a behavioral consistency assumption. Of course, some additional factors, such as a candidate's anxiety level during the sample performance or lack of ability to perform the sample in the case of new workers, would have to be considered when work sampling was used as a selection device.

Simulations—Assessment Centers.   The second type of measure of actual job behavior is simulation, the most popular type being the assessment center (described below). This measure differs from work sampling in that it uses a simulation of job content rather than a sample of actual job content. The technique has gained considerable acceptance in recent years, especially for predicting success in managerial jobs.

The assessment-center concept evolved around the time of World War II to evaluate candidates for assignments in America's intelligence organization, the Office of Strategic Services (OSS). Assessees experienced a series of interviews, tests, and performance simulations designed to reveal whether they possessed the qualities for intelligence work. The candidates were examined not only for mental ability and motivation, but for physical stamina, emotional stability, resistance to stress, and other characteristics. To this end they were sent over obstacle courses, attacked in "stress" interviews, and observed when they were falsely told that they had "flunked out." The program was designed to reveal every asset and weakness they possessed which could affect their subsequent job performance.

This assessment center was staffed by psychologists and psychiatrists under the direction of Dr. Henry A. Murray of Harvard University. Murray's pioneering work in the 1930s had paved the way for evaluations of human characteristics and potential. Murray felt it necessary to observe candidates for several days and to put them through elaborate individual and group performance situations, based on the conviction that ordinary interviews and standard paper-and-pencil psychological tests were insufficient to assess potential for successful job performance.

A large number of organizations are now using simulations in determining management potential. Studies indicate that assessment centers are often superior to other techniques in identifying manage-

---

[1] See R. M. Guion, "Open A New Window: Validities and Values in Psychological Measurement," *American Psychologist* 29 (1974): 287–296.

[2] P. F. Wernimont, and J. P. Campbell, "Signs and Samples, and Criteria," *Journal of Applied Psychology* 52 (1968): 372–376.

[3] J. E. Campion, "Work Sampling for Personnel Selection," *Journal of Applied Psychology* 56 (1972): 40–44.

ment potential.[4] They are used at all levels of management, from the first level of supervision to top corporate management. Organizations using centers may be found in every major industry, in government, and in almost all the industrialized nations of the world.

Proponents of assessment centers argue that they are more accurate in measuring potential for job success than traditional tests because they sample actual behavior, not what the applicant *says* he or she would do. For years, managers have observed that applicants can often talk a better story than they can perform. The assessment center checks on actual performance. The assessment-center method appears to provide validities (i.e., correlations of assessment-center performance with actual job performance) above those normally associated with tests or panel interviews. Reviews of published validity studies of the assessment-center process have recently been published.[5]

The most-publicized and largest research study on the assessment center is AT&T's Management Progress Study. Results of assessments of several groups of managers were retained for research purposes only and not released to the assessees or their superiors so as to preclude influencing subsequent promotion decisions regarding the assessees. The researchers administered an assessment center to 422 male employees of Bell Telephone companies beginning in 1956 and waited eight years before obtaining information on the assessees' success. Comparisons made in 1965 of the management level attained by people assessed several years earlier demonstrated that of the total number who reached middle management, 78 percent were correctly predicted to do so by the assessment staff. Among those who had not progressed further than first-level management within ten years, 95 percent were predicted not to do so by the assessors. Later communications indicate that similar accuracy was achieved after a longer time from original assessment to subsequent performance.[6]

From the studies to date, overall ratings of potential or performance from assessment-center procedures generally have shown impressive predictive

power in determining future job success. Unfortunately, the use of the ratings in decision making about assessees' careers somewhat inhibits total acceptance of some findings. A "self-fulfilling prophecy" is argued (i.e., those branded as successful in assessment centers may attain success because of the label and not competence). Nevertheless, predictive accuracy has been demonstrated in a few studies.[7]

Assessment Center Design. The first stage in developing an assessment center is thorough job analysis to determine major job elements and define dimensions to be measured in the assessment center. A list of dimensions for a managerial job is not a list of the characteristics of a perfect manager. Rather, the job analysis defines areas about which the assessment should be concerned—areas that should be evaluated in making a selection decision. Very few are expected to be rated high on all of the dimensions.

The dimensions used thus depend on the job, as the objective is to simulate job content. The dimensions listed below are examples. Notice that some of these may not be found through a job analysis (e.g., energy) and others are felt necessary for successful performance in almost any job (e.g., high level of motivation). Generalizing from managerial dimensions selected in assessment centers, the following seem to be important dimensions of managerial work in addition to knowledge, abilities, and specific skills:

1. Energy
2. Organizing and planning*
3. Use of delegation*
4. Overall potential
5. Oral and written communications skills*
6. Behavior flexibility
7. Controlling*
8. Decision making*
9. Human relations competence*
10. Initiative
11. Self-direction
12. Analytical ability*
13. Resistance to stress
14. Originality
15. Leadership*
16. Perception of threshold social cues*
17. Personal impact

Obviously, many of these dimensions may not be said to be job-relevant, an important consideration when contemplating using assessment centers for selection procedures (also see Exercises 3 and 10 for discussions regarding legal restrictions placed on job

[4] See J. R. Huck, "Assessment Centers: A Review of the External and Internal Validities," *Personnel Psychology* (Summer 1973): 191–212.
[5] Ibid. See also, A. Howard, "An Assessment of Assessment Centers," *Academy of Management Journal* 17 (1974): 115–134.
[6] D. W. Bray et al., *Formative Years in Business: A Long Term AT&T Study of Managerial Lives* (New York: Wiley, 1974); see also, A. Howard, "An Assessment of Assessment Centers," *Academy of Management Journal* 17 (1974): 115–134.
[7] Ibid.

analyses and selection tests or techniques). Therefore, designing the assessment dimensions around actual job content may not only be good practice, but also safe practice in that it may reduce the probability of violating equal opportunity laws or guidelines. When using assessment centers as a selection method, it may be helpful to consult the list above. The dimensions of managerial jobs which may be more closely tied to the content of managerial jobs are indicated with an asterisk (*).

Types of Assessments. Common types of simulations of job content used in assessment centers include:

In-baskets: This is the most frequently used technique and is usually considered the most important. The most relevant simulations are developed from actual "in-basket items" in the organization. The candidate is usually faced with an accumulation of memos, reports, notes of incoming telephone calls, letters, and other materials typically collected in the in-basket of the job incumbent. The candidate is asked to dispose of these materials in the most appropriate manner by writing letters, notes, delegating, self-reminders, agenda for meetings, etc. Often the in-basket is followed by a questionnaire or an interview by an assessor, in which the candidate is asked to justify decisions, actions, or nonactions. Ratings of performance may be subjective evaluations or highly standardized checklists.

Leaderless group discussions: The participants in leaderless group discussions are usually given a discussion question and instructed to arrive at a group decision. No one in the group is designated as its leader. Topics often include promotion decisions, disciplinary actions, or production expansion problems. Participants may be given a particular point of view to defend, although they know the group must eventually come to a mutually agreeable decision. Dimensions that can be revealed in the leaderless group discussion include interpersonal skills, acceptance by a group, individual influence, and leadership.

Management games: Management games usually require participants to solve problems, either cooperatively or competitively. Stock-market tasks, manufacturing exercises, merger negotiations, or acquisitions are common. Games often use a computer to simulate the consequences of decisions. The games may bring out leadership and organizational abilities or interpersonal skills. Some games also permit observations

under stress, especially when conditions suddenly change or when competition stiffens. The games are often used as a "warm-up" exercise in assessment centers.

Presentation: Assessees are often given time to make an oral presentation on a management topic or theme. Presentations are typically short (5–10 minutes). Assessors observe oral communications skills, persuasiveness, poise, and reaction to the stress of making a group presentation.

Supplementary Data Used in the Assessment Center

Tests: All types of paper-and-pencil tests of mental ability, personality, interests, and achievement (e.g., reading, arithmetic, general knowledge) are often used as supplements to the above. The tests are generally standardized instruments, although organizations have developed their own. Some are more objective tests while others are more projective (e.g., candidates respond to different stimuli, such as pictures). Seldom do organizations select the same tests, as jobs vary within and between organizations.

Interviews: Most assessment centers have at least one interview with the assessee. Current interests and motivation, as well as general background and comments on past performance are assessed. The type of interview varies in terms of structure, standardization of interpretation, and the general climate in which it is conducted.

Other assessments: Often written exercises, such as autobiographical essays or personal-history questionnaires, are completed before entering the center. Creative writing assignments may also be required of assessees.

The Assessment Center Procedure. The general procedure begins with an analysis of the job to be performed, as noted above. Next is the selection of the simulations most appropriate, then the training of assessors, conduct of the simulations, and finally the evaluation report of each assessee is written.

The training of assessors usually focuses on interviewing, managing the in-basket exercises, and observing behavior. Almost all of the assessment-center simulations call for some combination of these skills. Assessors are often managers two or more levels above the level being assessed. A typical assessment center will have four to six assessors in anywhere from a 4:1 to 1:1 ratio to assessees. The assessors may be psychologists, members of management, or both.

Assessors become familiar with the exercises by

participating themselves, watching videotapes, or observing actual assessee performances as nonvoting (trained) members of an assessment team. The job dimensions to be assessed are defined and assessors are given practice and instruction in how to recognize varying degrees of performance on them. Assessor training varies widely in duration, from brief orientations to two or three weeks of intensive training. Companies highly interested in training managers in appraisal techniques may change assessors frequently, while those most interested in producing a stable selection program or in saving money on training, such as AT&T, may make changes less often.

Perhaps the most critical aspect of using the assessment center method is the evaluation report. Usually, a large body of data for each assessee is ultimately reduced to a few reported test scores and booklets containing judgments and comments. A formal written report summarizing the assessment findings and recommendations is needed (see Form 5 of this exercise) in order to summarize the data.

Peer and self-ratings and rank orderings of assessees may also be part of the evaluation process. But assessors typically write reports, skill by skill, exercise by exercise, and candidate by candidate. The reports are read aloud in a final evaluation meeting where each assessee is rated by every assessor on each dimension. Meaningful differences of opinion are discussed and either resolved or noted. Final reports are usually written in a narrative style, relating remarks to specific behaviors and specifying the candidate's strengths, weaknesses, and developmental needs.

Feedback of results to candidates is handled differently in various organizations according to the original objectives of the program. Those highly concerned with management development emphasize the directions in which the candidate should move in the future. Others concerned with training may stop in the middle of the assessment program and offer feedback and discussion of particular exercises. Oral feedback is much more frequent than written. Line management or assessment-center personnel may provide feedback either automatically or on request only.

The assessment-center concept is important as a selection device because of its close relationship to actual job performance and its accuracy in measuring potential and predicting future job success. However, it is as yet a comparatively new selection tool and much research is required. Further, it is a complex and costly selection device, requiring considerable planning and expertise.

PROCEDURE

Overview. First, you are asked to design a work sample that could be used as a selection aid. Next, you will actually conduct an assessment center. A sample report made by assessors is provided to acquaint you with the evaluations made in assessment centers. In-basket and leaderless-group-discussion simulations are used to assess the three candidates for the job of administrative officer.

PART A

STEP 1: Forms 1 and 2 contain two job descriptions, one for the job of heavy-duty mechanic and one for the job of clerk typist III. Form into groups of four or five and design a work-sampling procedure for one of the jobs. That is, develop activities similar to those actually performed on the job which prospective job applicants could be asked to perform in order to assess their suitability for the job. Your work sample should include a method for scoring or evaluating applicants. Use the examples of work samples for a mechanic's job given in the *Introduction* to this exercise as a guide. Why would the sample offer better data about an applicant than an application blank or interview?

TIME: About 35 minutes.

PART B

STEP 2: This part contains instructions for *assessees* and *assessors* for an assessment center containing an in-basket exercise and a leaderless group discussion (LGD). Read only the appropriate instructions below, depending on whether you were chosen to be an assessor or an assessee.

Instructions for assessees. If you were chosen to play the role of an *assessee*, reacquaint yourself with the job of administrative officer of Palms Pacific Corp. (see the job description in Exercise 7 reprinted as Form 3 of this exercise; also see the organizations description, appropriate resume, and application for your role in Exercise 7). The implementor may give you additional instructions for your role. Use all of this information as a jumping-off point for your behavior in the in-basket exercise and leaderless group discussion (LGD) simulations in which you will participate. Others will form into small groups and assess the three applicants' (who will be joined by three other people for the LGD) performance and potential for success in the job. The instructions for the in-basket and LGD are given in Parts C and D at the end of this exercise. Do *not* read these until you are instructed to do so. You will be given a time limit for each of these activities.

Instructions for assessors. Below is an outline of the assessment-center procedure. Your group of assessors will be assessing three candidates for the job of administrative officer for Palms Pacific Corp., used in Exercises 7 and 8.

A. Form into small groups. Review both the job description for administrative officer (first appearing in Exercise 7 and reproduced as Form 3 here) and the other information about the job first given in Exercise 7. Then develop a set of job dimensions for the job which should be assessed in an assessment center. You may have such lists from previous exercises which can be amended, if necessary, and used here. Be sure to weight your dimensions in order of importance for success on the job.

Two simulation activities are used here, an in-basket and a leaderless group discussion (LGD). Half of your group will be assessors for each simulation and will assess a group of candidates for the job, write three assessor reports, and choose the best candidate for the job. Each assessor should read through both simulations, including the instructions, very carefully. These situations simulate realistic administrative problems. They yield insights into performance dimensions common to many management positions. The situations are ones that might be expected regardless of organizational type. The assessees must determine many courses of action, such as planning meetings, gathering reports, and delegating. Suitability for the job would be determined by performance in these simulations, coupled with other selection tools.

Although the in-basket and LGD yield many insights, an interview with the assessee, when conducted as soon as possible after the simulation is completed, is also quite valuable. This interview can probe into the reasons for each action taken, perceptions, values, etc. and thus provide more information on which to base the selection decision.

The in-basket situation and LGD may yield information on the following job dimensions:

Written communication	Analytical ability
Creativity	Planning, organizing, controlling
Stress tolerance	Use of delegation
Work standards	Problem analysis
Sensitivity	Judgment
Risk taking	Decision making
Initiative	Tenacity
Level of aspiration	Leadership
Interpersonal skill	Acceptance by a group
	Influence

The interview may add information on the above dimensions, but also permits assessment on the following dimensions:

Impact	Tenacity
Initiative	Flexibility
Oral communication skill	Independence
	Leadership

B. In order to conduct a valid assessment, compare the job dimensions you identify as relevant from the job description of administrative officer with those listed above. You are given an Assessor's Report Form (Form 4) which can be used to help you decide how to judge the assessees' performance in the simulations. Place a mark by all of the relevant dimensions you have identified, both from the job description and the lists given in Step A above, on Form 4. Add any dimensions not on the form you feel are relevant. These become the dimensions on which you will evaluate assessees. Try to define each dimension and cite an example of assessee behavior which would illustrate performance on that dimension.

TIME: About 45 minutes.

C. Once you have identified the relevant dimensions on which to assess candidates for the job of administrative officer and noted them on Form 4, you are ready to begin the assessment. Three people who have assumed the roles of the three job applicants (Merle Wonder, Gaylord Golden, and Charlotte Pyle) in Exercises 7 and 8 will play the roles of assessees. These assessees will each be given the in-basket exercise (Part C) and participate in a leaderless-group-discussion situation (Part D). They will be assessed by each group of assessors on each dimension noted on Form 4. Check whether the dimension was assessed via the in-basket or the role play on Form 4 as you fill it out. Now divide your group in half so one half can concentrate on assessing in the in-basket and the other half in the group discussion. Three more persons will join the three job applicants for the job of administrative officer in order to form a group of six assessees. Together these six people will form a discussion group and complete the LGD exercise in Part D.

TIME: About 15 minutes.

PARTS C AND D

STEP 3: Administer first the in-basket and then the group discussion to the assessees. Instructions and time limits for both simulations are given in Parts C and D at the end of this exercise. Be sure to time the assessees as they perform these tasks and observe them very closely.

The in-basket exercise cannot be scored until it is completed. Therefore, since the assessor groups have already been split into those who have primary responsibility for scoring the in-basket and those who have primary responsibility for scoring the LGD, the in-basket should be conducted first so that it can be scored while the LGD is conducted. Be sure to fill out Form 4 while your part of the assessor group reads the in-basket results. (You will have to share the in-basket results with other assessor groups, as only one set of in-basket results are available for each of the three assessees.)

Observe and record assessee behavior on the in-basket and LGD (see the forms for specific instructions). Score behavior in the simulations is as follows: Assess each person on dimensions selected using the scale below. Report your rating on the right-hand side of Form 4.

5—very much of the dimension was demonstrated (excellent)

4—a considerable amount of the dimension was demonstrated (above average)

3—some of the dimension was demonstrated (average)

2—a little of the dimension was demonstrated (below average)

1—very little was demonstrated or not at all (poor)

0—there was no opportunity for the dimension to be demonstrated

After the two simulations are finished, prepare and conduct an interview with assessees to obtain additional relevant information, if you feel it necessary. You may want to score the in-basket before holding these interviews. Be sure to revise the scores on the Assessor's Report Form after the interview to reflect the additional information.

TIME: The in-basket requires 45 minutes and the LGD requires 30 minutes. Postexercise interviews would, of course, require additional time.

STEP 4: The in-basket should now be scored and the LGD completed and scored. Each assessor team is to have the team members who had primary responsibility for scoring performance in the in-basket discuss assessee's performance on the in-basket, while the team members who observed and scored the discussion group are to discuss the performance on the LGD. The entire group should then reach agreement on each assessee's performance and compose the Assessor's Overall Report, or "Management Report," for each of the three assessees. A sample report is included as Form 5 of this exercise. See also Part III E of Form 4 for additional instructions.

TIME: About one hour to two hours.

FOR FURTHER READING

Asher, J. J., and J. A. Scarrino. "Realistic Work Sample Tests: A Review." *Personnel Psychology* 27 (1974): 519–533. (II)

"Assessment Centers." *Public Personnel Management* 3, no. 5 (September–October 1974), symposium of three articles. (I)

Bray, D. W., R. J. Campbell, and D. L. Grant. *Formative Years in Business: A Long-Term AT&T Study of Managerial Lives.* New York: Wiley, 1974. (I–R)

Bray, D. W., and R. J. Campbell. "Selection of Salesmen by means of an Assessment Center." *Journal of Applied Psychology* 52 (1968): 36–41. (II–R)

Bray, D. W., and J. L. Moses. "Personnel Selection." *Annual Review of Psychology* 23 (1972): 545–576. (II)

Bray, D. W., and D. L. Grant. "The Assessment Center in the Measurement of Potential for

Business Management." *Psychological Monographs* 80 (1966). (II–R)

Brown, D. D., and E. E. Ghiselli. "The Relationship between the Predictive Power of Aptitude Tests for Trainability and for Job Proficiency." *Journal of Applied Psychology* 36 (1952): 370–377. (II–R)

Byham, E. C. "Assessment Center for Spotting Future Managers." *Harvard Business Review* 48, no. 4 (1970): 150–160+i. (I)

Byham, W. C. "The Assessment Center as an Aid in Management Development." *Training and Development Journal* (December 1971): 10–22. (I)

Campbell, R. J., and D. W. Bray. "Assessment Centers: An Aid in Management Selection. *Personnel Administration* 30, no. 2 (1967): 6–13. (I)

Campion, J. E. "Work Sampling for Personnel Selection." *Journal of Applied Psychology* 56 (1972): 40–44. (II–R)

Catalog of Assessment and Development Exercises. Pittsburgh: Development Dimensions, 1975. (I)

Cohen, B. M. "What the Supervisor Should Know about Assessment Centers." *Supervisory Management* 20 (June 1974): 30–34. (I)

Cowan, J., and M. Kurtz. "Internal Assessment Center: An Organization Development Approach to Selecting Supervisors." *Public Personnel Management* 5 (January–February 1976): 15–23. (II)

Dodd, W. E., A. O. Kraut, and S. H. Simonetti. "Selected Annotated Bibliography on Identification and Assessment of Management Talent." *Professional Psychology* 3 (1972): 193–199. (I)

Dunnette, M. D. *Personnel Selection and Placement.* Belmont, Calif.: Wadsworth, 1966. (I)

Finkle, R. B. "Managerial Assessment Centers." In M. D. Dunnette, ed., *Handbook of Industrial and Organizational Psychology.* Chicago: Rand McNally, 1976. (II)

Finkle, R. D., and W. S. Jones. *Assessing Corporate Talent.* New York: Wiley, 1970. (I)

Flanagan, J. C. "Some Considerations in the Development of Situational Tests." *Personnel Psychology* 7 (1954): 461–464. (II)

Fleishman, E. A. "Individual Differences and Motor Learning." In R. M. Gagne, ed., *Learning and Individual Differences.* Columbus, Ohio: Merrill, 1967. (II)

Frederikson, M. "Validation of a Simulation Technique." *Organizational Behavior and Human Performance* 1 (1966): 87–109. (II–R)

Frederikson, M., O. Jensen, A. Beaton, and B. Bloxom. *Prediction of Organizational Behavior* (New York: Pergamon, 1972). (II)

Grant, D. L., W. Kathovsky, and D. W. Bray. "Contributions of Projective Techniques to Assessment of Management Potential." *Journal of Applied Psychology* 55 (1967): 226–232. (II–R)

Hamner, W. C. et al. "Race and Sex as Determinants of Ratings by Potential Employers in a Simulated Work-Sampling Task." *Journal of Applied Psychology* 59 (1974): 705–711. (II–R)

Hinrichs, J. R. "Comparison of "Real Life" Assessments of Management Potential with Situation Exercises, Paper and Pencil Ability Tests, and Personality Inventories," *Journal of Applied Psychology* 53 (1969): 425–432. (II–R)

Hinrichs, J. R., and S. Haanpera. "Reliability of Measurement in Situational Exercises: An Assessment of the Assessment Center Method." *Personnel Psychology* 29 (1976): 31–40. (II)

Howard, A. "An Assessment of Assessment Centers." *Academy of Management Journal* 17 (1974): 115–134. (I)

Huck, J. R., and D. W. Bray. "Management Assessment Center Evaluations and Subsequent Job Performance of White and Black Females." *Personnel Psychology* 29 (1976): 13–30. (II–R)

Huck, J. R. "Assessment Centers: A Review of the External and Internal Validities." *Personnel Psychology* 26 (1973): 191–212. (II)

Jaffee, C. L. *Effective Management Selection: An Analysis of Behavior by Simulation Techniques.* Reading, Mass.: Addison-Wesley, 1971. (I)

Jaffee, C. L., J. Bender, and C. Calvert. "The Assessment Center Technique: A Validation Study." *Management of Personnel Quarterly* (Fall 1970): 9–14. (I–R)

Korman, A. L. "The Prediction of Managerial Performance. A Review." *Personnel Psychology* 21 (1968): 295–322. (II)

Kraut, A. I., and G. J. Scott. "Validation of an Operational Management Assessment Program." *Journal of Applied Psychology* 56 (1972): 124–1129. (II–R)

Mackinnon, D. W. *How Assessment Centers Got Started in the United States.* Pittsburgh: Development Dimensions Press, 1974. (I)

MacKinnon, D. W. *An Overview of Assessment Centers* (Technical Report No. 1). Greensboro, N.C.: Center for Creative Leadership, 1975. (I)

Meyer, H. H. "The Validity of the In-basket Test as a Measure of Managerial Performance." *Personnel Psychology* 23 (1970): 297–307. (II–R)

Mitchel, J. O. "Assessment Center Validity: A Longitudinal Study." *Journal of Applied Psychology* 60 (1975): 573–579. (II–R)

Moses, J. L. "Assessment Center Performance and Management Progress." *Studies in Personnel Psychology* 4 (1972): 7–12. (I)

Moses, J. L., and V. R. Boehm. "Relationship of Assessment Center Performance to Management Progress of Women." *Journal of Applied Psychology* 60 (1975): 527–529. (II)

Moses, J. "The Development of an Assessment Center for the Early Identification of Supervisory Potential." *Personnel Psychology* 26 (1973): 569–580. (II–R)

Moses, J. L., and W. C. Byham, eds. *Applying the Assessment Center Method.* New York: Pergamon, 1976. (I)

OSS Staff. *The Assessment of Men.* New York: Rinehart, 1948. (I)

Tracy, W. "The Empty In-Basket Trick." *Personnel Journal* 52 (1973): 36–40. (I)

Wollowick, H., and W. McNamara. "Relationship of the Components of an Assessment Center to Management Success." *Journal of Applied Psychology* 53 (1969): 348–352. (II–R)

Zoll, A. A. *Dynamic Management Education.* 2d ed. Reading, Mass.: Addison-Wesley, 1969. (I)

PART A

Form 1 Job Description

HEAVY-DUTY MECHANIC

DESCRIPTION OF WORK:

General Statement of Duties: Performs skilled work in the repair and maintenance of automotive and heavy-duty equipment.

Supervision Received: Works under the supervision of a foreman.

Supervision Exercised: None.

EXAMPLE OF DUTIES: (Any one position may not include all of the duties listed nor do the listed examples include all tasks that may be found in positions of this class.)

Overhauls, repairs, and maintains cars, trucks, earth moving, road-construction, and heavy-duty equipment.

Performs major repairs on gasoline, semi-diesel, and diesel engines; transmissions; differentials; drive units; brakes; suspension systems, chassis; front and rear ends; cooling systems, fuel systems; instruments; electrical systems; hydraulic systems; and accessory power equipment. Rebuilds engines, carburetors, ignition systems, and radiators.

Performs general tune-up, using testing machines.

Performs emergency road service.

Performs welding as required.

Performs related work as required.

REQUIRED KNOWLEDGES, SKILLS, AND ABILITIES:

Considerable knowledge of the standard practices, methods, materials, and tools used in the automotive mechanic trade. Working knowledge of the hazards and safety precautions peculiar to the trade. Working knowledge of the design, operation, and repair of light- and heavy-duty gasoline and diesel equipment, hydraulic systems, and accessory power equipment. Skill in the use of mechanics tools, materials, welding equipment, and testing equipment. Ability to diagnose mechanical defects and determine parts and adjustments necessary to put equipment into proper operating condition. Ability to follow written and oral instructions. Ability to establish and maintain effective working relationships with employees and the public.

QUALIFICATIONS FOR APPOINTMENT:

Education: Eighth-grade completion or equivalent.

Experience: Four years experience in the repair and maintenance of automotive equipment, including one year on heavy-duty and construction equipment.

              OR

Any equivalent combination of education and experience.

PART A

Form 2 Job Description

CLERK TYPIST III

DESCRIPTION OF WORK:

General Statement of Duties: Performs a variety of clerical and typing work requiring the exercise of some independent judgment.

Supervision Received: Works under general supervision of a clerical or technical superior.

Supervision Exercised: Exercises supervision over personnel as assigned, or full supervision incidental to the other duties.

EXAMPLES OF DUTIES: (Any one position may not include all of the duties listed nor do the listed examples include all tasks that may be found in positions of this class.)

Types correspondence, reports, and other office forms requiring some independence of judgment as to content, accuracy, and completeness.

Reviews correspondence and reports, determines what information is to be cross-filed and/or included in other files or reports in order that a ready and complete history or file is available; determines routing and filing.

Compiles, computes, and tabulates data for reports requiring judgment as to content.

Locates source material, edits, and coordinates material for inclusion into research-and-development reports, recognizing variations and verifies completeness of report.

Furnishes the public with information and advice in areas where the public is generally uninformed (such as auto theft, and where time is of the essence), which requires a working knowledge of both agency policies and procedures and applicable laws.

Determines and collects amount of fees, where some degree of personal judgment is involved in the decision, issues receipts, keeps records of transactions.

Performs related work as required.

REQUIRED KNOWLEDGES, SKILLS, AND ABILITIES:

Considerable knowledge of grammar, spelling, and punctuation. Working knowledge of office practices and procedures. Skill in operating a typewriter. Ability to follow written or oral instructions. Ability to make mathematical computations. Ability to establish and maintain effective working relationships with employees, the public, and other agencies.

QUALIFICATIONS FOR APPOINTMENT:

Education: High-school graduation or equivalent.

Experience: Two years experience in general clerical work involving typing.

   OR

Any equivalent combination of education and experience.

PART B

Form 3 Job Description

ADMINISTRATIVE OFFICER'S JOB—PALMS PACIFIC CORPORATION, INC.

DESCRIPTION OF WORK:

General Statement of Duties: Supervises and coordinates responsible administrative work of a complex nature involving program responsibility; does related work as required.

Supervision Received: Receives policy guidance from an administrative superior or board members.

Supervision Exercised: Plans, organizes, develops, coordinates, and directs a staff of administrative and clerical personnel.   Total at all levels exceeds twenty.

EXAMPLE OF DUTIES: (Any one position may not include all of the duties listed, nor do the listed examples include all tasks that may be found in positions.)

Administers, coordinates, and directs a complex administrative management program involving program responsibility for a department or equivalent; organizes and directs the work of personnel in day-to-day operation, and conducts long-range planning.

Establishes working methods and procedures and develops departmental procedures and policies related to administrative functions.

Directs major staff services, including budget, training, record keeping, and personnel and general administrative services.   Develops supporting data and presents budget estimates and requests.

Directs or performs studies on efficiency, work flow, procedures, work standards, and research and planning.

Develops and compiles comprehensive reports.

Develops and implements immediate and long-range plans for administrative areas of the organization.

Performs related work as required.

REQUIRED KNOWLEDGES, SKILLS, AND ABILITIES:

Extensive and broad knowledge of complex administrative management programs.   Skill and ability in administering, planning, and directing personnel in day-to-day programs appropriate to the position to be filled.   Ability to interpret and apply laws, rules, regulations, and industry practices.   Ability to relate with and coordinate department activities with employees, other departments, and the general public.

QUALIFICATIONS FOR APPOINTMENT:

Education: Graduation from a college or university with major course work in public or business administration or related field.

Experience: Six years progressively responsible experience in a supervisory, technical, or professional area related to management or administration; computer familiarity with computer software very helpful.

　　　　OR

Any equivalent combination of education and experience.

Name _____   Group Number _____

Date _____ Class Section _____ Hour _____ Score _____

PART B
Form 4

Assessor's name _____   Date _____

Job title _____   Group no. _____

PART I

Instructions: Select job dimensions from the glossary of dimensions at the end of this form that you believe are relevant performance criteria for the job of administrative officer; provide an example of behavior which would illustrate each dimension selected (as indicated in the example below). Indicate from which simulation(s) the performance on the dimension being rated originated (i.e., In-basket, LDG, or both). Score on a scale of 0–5 for each of the assessees against each dimension. Make additional copies of this section as required.

Scale

5—extremely favorable behavior on the dimension was demonstrated   (Excellent)
4—considerable favorable behavior on the dimension was demonstrated   (Above Average)
3—some favorable behavior on the dimension was demonstrated   (Average)
2—a little favorable behavior on the dimension was demonstrated   (Below Average)
1—very little favorable behavior on the dimension was demonstrated   (Poor)
0—no behavior on the dimension was demonstrated

Relevant dimension	Simulation assessed	Assessees' performance rating	
EXAMPLE: *Impact:* Example: On first meeting rest of the assessee group, how he/she handles getting-to-know-them procedures, establishes rapport and respect, etc.	In-Basket ____ LGD X Both ____	No. 1 ____ No. 4 4 No. 2 ____ No. 5 3 No. 3 ____ No. 6 1	
1. _____ Example:	In-Basket ____ LGD ____ Both ____	No. 1 ____ No. 4 ____ No. 2 ____ No. 5 ____ No. 3 ____ No. 6 ____	
2. _____ Example:	In-Basket ____ LGD ____ Both ____	No. 1 ____ No. 4 ____ No. 2 ____ No. 5 ____ No. 3 ____ No. 6 ____	
3. _____ Example:	In-Basket ____ LGD ____ Both ____	No. 1 ____ No. 4 ____ No. 2 ____ No. 5 ____ No. 3 ____ No. 6 ____	
4. _____ Example:	In-Basket ____ LGD ____ Both ____	No. 1 ____ No. 4 ____ No. 2 ____ No. 5 ____ No. 3 ____ No. 6 ____	

5. _____
   Example:

   In-Basket _____   No. 1 _____   No. 4 _____
   LGD   _____   No. 2 _____   No. 5 _____
   Both   _____   No. 3 _____   No. 6 _____

6. _____
   Example:

   In-Basket _____   No. 1 _____   No. 4 _____
   LGD   _____   No. 2 _____   No. 5 _____
   Both   _____   No. 3 _____   No. 6 _____

7. _____
   Example:

   In-Basket _____   No. 1 _____   No. 4 _____
   LGD   _____   No. 2 _____   No. 5 _____
   Both   _____   No. 3 _____   No. 6 _____

8. _____
   Example:

   In-Basket _____   No. 1 _____   No. 4 _____
   LGD   _____   No. 2 _____   No. 5 _____
   Both   _____   No. 3 _____   No. 6 _____

9. _____
   Example:

   In-Basket _____   No. 1 _____   No. 4 _____
   LGD   _____   No. 2 _____   No. 5 _____
   Both   _____   No. 3 _____   No. 6 _____

10. _____
    Example:

    In-Basket _____   No. 1 _____   No. 4 _____
    LGD   _____   No. 2 _____   No. 5 _____
    Both   _____   No. 3 _____   No. 6 _____

PART II

Dimensions not included in the Glossary of Dimensions, but considered relevant:

Relevant dimension	*Simulation assessed*	*Assessees'* *performance rating*	

1. _____
   Example:

   In-Basket _____   No. 1 _____   No. 4 _____
   LGD   _____   No. 2 _____   No. 5 _____
   Both   _____   No. 3 _____   No. 6 _____

2. _____
   Example:

   In-Basket _____   No. 1 _____   No. 4 _____
   LGD   _____   No. 2 _____   No. 5 _____
   Both   _____   No. 3 _____   No. 6 _____

3. _____   In-Basket ____   No. 1 ____   No. 4 ____
   Example: LGD   ____   No. 2 ____   No. 5 ____
                             Both   ____   No. 3 ____   No. 6 ____

4. _____   In-Basket ____   No. 1 ____   No. 4 ____
   Example: LGD   ____   No. 2 ____   No. 5 ____
                             Both   ____   No. 3 ____   No. 6 ____

5. _____   In-Basket ____   No. 1 ____   No. 4 ____
   Example: LGD   ____   No. 2 ____   No. 5 ____
                             Both   ____   No. 3 ____   No. 6 ____

6. _____   In-Basket ____   No. 1 ____   No. 4 ____
   Example: LGD   ____   No. 2 ____   No. 5 ____
                             Both   ____   No. 3 ____   No. 6 ____

7. _____   In-Basket ____   No. 1 ____   No. 4 ____
   Example: LGD   ____   No. 2 ____   No. 5 ____
                             Both   ____   No. 3 ____   No. 6 ____

PART III

A. One sentence summary description of performance for each assessee.

No. 1 _____

No. 2 _____

No. 3 _____

No. 4 _____

No. 5 _____

No. 6 _____

B. Provide an assessment of method of organizing situation, setting priorities, and use of background data and calendar for each assessee, based on in-basket.

No. 1 _____

No. 2 _____

No. 3 _____

No. 4 _____

No. 5 _____

No. 6 _____

C. Briefly note below each assessee's leadership ability and ability in interpersonal situations, as evidenced by the LGD and a postsimulation interview, if held.

No. 1 _____

No. 2 _____

No. 3 _____

No. 4 _____

No. 5 _____

No. 6 _____

D. Brief summary of major strengths and weaknesses for each assessee.

No. 1 _____

No. 2 _____

No. 3 _____

No. 4 _____

No. 5 _____

No. 6 _____

E. Write a management report for each assessee (see the sample report, Form 5). Be sure the report includes an evaluation of performance both on the In-basket and the LGD. Refer back to your comments on this form to write the report. Include the following in the report for each assessee:

1. Participant's name and name of types of simulations.
2. Summary description of performance (Part III A).
3. Evaluation of organizing ability, ability to set priorities, etc., from In-Basket (Part III B).
4. Leadership and interpersonal ability from LGD (Part III C).
5. Behaviors by dimensions (a brief note for each, some may be combined) (Parts I and II).
6. Summary of major strengths and weaknesses (Part III D).

Proofread your report for clarity, organization, conciseness, and coherence.

GLOSSARY OF DIMENSIONS

Analytical ability
Ability to oversee complex nuances in decision-making situations.

Controlling
Appreciation of needs for standards and maintenance of feedback from processes.

Creativity
Ability to come up with imaginative solutions in business situations.

Decision making
Readiness to make decisions or to render judgment.

Energy
Ability to be self-starting and to achieve a high activity level.

Flexibility
Ability to modify behavioral style and management approach to reach a goal.

Impact
Ability to create a good first impression, to command attention and respect, to show an air of confidence, and to achieve personal recognition.

Independence
Action based on own convictions rather than a desire to please others.

Initiative
Active efforts to influence events rather than passive acceptance.

Judgment
Ability to reach logical conclusions based on the evidence at hand.

Leadership
The skill of motivating and integrating the interests of a group to resolve job-related problems.

Level of aspiration
Doing the best of which one is capable.

Oral communication
Effectiveness of expression in individual or group situations.

Planning
Effectiveness in forecasting and proceduralizing own activities and those of a group.

Problem analysis
Effectiveness in seeking out pertinent data and determining the source of the problem.

Risktaking
Extent to which calculated risks are taken, based on sound judgment.

Sensitivity
Skill in perceiving and reacting to the needs of others.

Stress tolerance
Stability of performance under pressure and opposition.

Tenacity
Willingness to stay with a problem until completed.

Use of delegation
Ability to effectively use subordinates and to understand where a decision can best be made.

Work standards
The desire to do a good job for its own sake.

Written communication
Ability to express ideas clearly in writing, in good grammatical form.

PART B

Form 5 Sample Assessment Center Management Report

Assessee: Joel Harris   Date: October 12

On October 12 Joel Harris attended the Assessment Center

Harris's overall performance in the Assessment Center was average or below average on most exercises. He showed strengths in energy and initiative.

Observers see him as having some potential for a middle-manager position but as requiring a great deal of development. The odds of his actually being a middle manager were seen as slim.

In the background interview, Harris was extremely open in discussing his problems and hopes in detail. He came across as a loyal, hardworking, highly-motivated person who has a strong desire to do a good job, but he is weak in creativity, initiative, independence, and leadership skills. He appeared to be tenacious and have a high stress tolerance but to be weak in problem analysis. He struck the assessors as being overwhelmed by his job where his efforts are not bearing the fruit he would like. He may well fear for his job given the Division's performance. Delegation seemed weak as was subordinate development. He feels the only way to train is to teach by example. Sensing poor morale, he doesn't know how to improve it.

Harris participated energetically in the exercises and appeared to be intent on doing well. In the group discussion exercises, he showed initiative in starting the group on its task and providing initial organization. His oral communications were somewhat hampered by his use of slang, but in general he spoke in a clear, articulate, fluent manner. His voice was low in volume. On the negative side, he tended to be repetitive in speech and have a great need to summarize and then resummarize. He did not seem overly stressed.

Unfortunately Harris's impact on exercise groups was fleeting. Others quickly took control with usually only a minor fight from Harris. Peer and self-ratings indicate he was never recognized as the group leader. His overall contribution was usually in the middle. His principal difficulty in group exercises came from his inability to convince the group. Rather than pursue an argument until he won, he would too quickly give in.

Harris's financial analysis presentation in the LGD was excellent, but he had several flaws in his analysis. His presentation in the group discussion was weak, and he was unable to convince the group. He was an effective secretary for the group.

Questioning in the "Research Budget" fact-finding exercise was not well-organized but effective. He appeared to find decision-making difficult, but once the decision was made, he stuck to his idea. Slightly nervous, he was not stressed by the resource person.

Writing seemed to be a weak area. Harris's financial presentation was hard to read and disorganized. Similar observations were made about his creative writing assignment, and his in-basket.

In the in-basket exercise, he did quite poorly, failing to organize material or set priorities. He did not handle all the material and on several occasions displayed poor judgment.

STRENGTHS:

Work standards: Tried hard in every exercise; works very hard on job; does not want to personally settle for less than the best. Was disappointed by own performance as indicated by his self-evaluation.
Intelligence: Fast reader, catches on fast.
Corporate Thinking: A company man, very loyal.
Integrity: Will not compromise convictions, e.g., copy machine discussion.
Energy: Active in all exercises.
Stress Tolerance: Except for management game, showed little stress.
Interest in Self-Development: Welcomes help; worked his way through college, willing to move. While interest seemed very high, there was some doubt about strength of drive for self-development.
Level of Aspiration: Seems to be unhappy without winning or doing the best possible.

WEAKNESSES:
Creativity: Not seen in approach to current job or in exercises - nothing shown in creative writing exercise.
Leadership: After an initial positive impact, he could not influence group.
Independence: In present job, seems to do what his boss wants; same attitude expressed in in-basket where he tended to delegate up and to follow "what boss wants."
Use of Delegation: Average in in-basket. He reports he does mail that should be done by subordinates.
Problem Analysis: Didn't understand "conglomerate"; didn't see many of the major problems in in-basket; background interview indicates a lack of problem definition in job; did not see all facets of Pretzel Company problem.
Financial Analytical Ability: Below average on financial problems, e.g., missed opportunity to change product mix.
Range of Interest: Seems to be restricted to marketing.
Flexibility: Seemed to approach every case and every situation the same way (was flexible in accepting ideas of others).
Temper: When did not get his way in compensation committee discussion, he became an obstruction to the leader's efforts.

MIXED FINDINGS:
Impact: Good first impression - after that would not stand out in a crowd.
Oral Communication Skill: Fluent, somewhat articulate, talks too much but doesn't sell.
Oral Presentation Skill: Formal presentations good, e.g., financial presentation; informal poor, e.g., group discussion situations. Seems to depend on preparation.
Written Communication Skill: English ability adequate, very hard to read writing.
Salesmanship: Except for the formal financial presentation, showed little salesmanship; in the "Compensation Committee" exercise he tried for too much money, didn't convince peers; in group situations could not sell under opposition.
Sensitivity: Assessors described him variously as sensitive, very sensitive, too sensitive and insensitive during the center. There was a general feeling that he might be soft, e.g., his delay in firing one of his subordinates he admitted should have been fired sooner. Yet he seemed less sensitive to people problems in in-basket cases than to needs of individuals in discussion groups, where on several occasions he showed good sensitivity and understanding.
Tenacity: When ego is involved or he feels there is an ethical problem, Harris can be very tenacious, e.g., fighting for doing right by customer regarding the photocopier. On the other hand, he did not follow up on points in group discussions.
Management Style: Expressed concern for "subordinate training" but assessors wondered how effective he is; tends to delegate up -- lets people "over-lead" him. Realizes need to be more "tough-minded," but does not take action to change.
Planning & Organizing: Attempted to organize most groups but did not attempt to maintain organization. In-basket organization of work and priorities poor.

<u>Management Control</u>: Interview indicated some weaknesses in this area: felt Harris would have a tendency to overcontrol too far down, but in in-basket he did an above average job of controlling, using due dates, etc.
<u>Judgment</u>: Showed good judgment in marketing-related problems; weak in judgment in other areas.

While Harris did poorly in many areas, it was felt that he is definitely trainable. He was seen as needing a lot of support and guidance and a supportive, understanding, "fatherly" supervisor, but one that would force him to make decisions. It was felt he would develop best in a highly structured job with slowly increasing planning and organizing responsibility as his skills develop. An assignment in Illinois as a product manager might be good.

Some priority development challenges: -management through others
                                          -problem analysis
                                          -organization
                                          -administrative skills

Harris should be easy to communicate with regarding his assessment. He is extremely open and was accurate in his self-appraisals. A potential difficulty may be his insecurity causing him to view "help" as a threat.

PART C

In-Basket Exercise

ANALYZING SITUATIONS AND TAKING ACTION

Instructions. This exercise is called an in-basket because the materials are correspondence waiting on your desk for your attention and action. This is a means of capturing your responses to issues, problems, and opportunities with which you are confronted in a managerial situation. After you have spent *45 minutes* responding to the ten items and stated *exactly* how you would handle *each* one on the bottom of the items, you may be interviewed by the assessor team, at which time you will have an opportunity to further explain your decisions and actions.

Situation. Assume you are the executive officer of a manufacturing company that employs about 2000 people. You report directly to the president and founder of the company. The organization primarily manufactures relatively standard electronics components, but still must have technical people on board for routine product updating and the design of new products. The business has now begun to prosper and last year sales topped four million dollars and earned a return on investment of 11.2 percent. Your employees will be described below and an organization chart of the company is also enclosed.

For the first three days of this week you were attending a management development conference and your duties were assigned to Mr. Rogers, but he had an emergency appendectomy. The work was then given to Mr. Sloane, but his father suffered a heart attack and he flew home. You were called three hours ago and arrived five minutes ago. The time is 1:15 on Wednesday (3/6). The ten items in this packet are on your desk waiting for your attention. Ms. Pitts is not at her desk.

Assignment. Go through the entire packet of in-basket items making decisions and taking any appropriate action you feel is necessary. Write down *exactly* what you would do on each item. If some items are to be handled later, decide what you would do then. Your sequence of handling the items is important, so note how you would prioritize them.

Reminder. You are the next to the top person in the organization, you have been gone, and there are only two working days remaining in this week for all of the production units. Don't forget to *write down* your responses to each item itself.

Description of Some Key Employees.
Gladys Pitts: Executive secretary; 38 years old. A widow, quite aware of company communication lines and procedures. She is putting her son through college.

Buster Rogers: Administrative assistant; 58 years old. An old friend of "Hap" Seer. He was given his present job based on "Hap's" strong insistence. Although he has not always met your expectations, he has been a valuable source of information and knows most of the company's employees well.

Fred Sloane: Production manager; 57 years old. Another long-time company employee who began to work for "Hap" when he was testing the first component in his garage.

Harold "Hap" Seer: President; 54 years old. Owner and principal stockholder of the company. He is also the designer of the company's biggest selling product, although most of the design work is now left to others as he primarily interfaces with clients and the local community.

Jack Thompson: Head of New Product Development; 33 years old. Very bright and a good team leader.

Tom Vaughn: Purchasing manager; 41 years old. Always thought to be a "nervous nellie," overreacts in many situations.

Note: Other lower-level employees may be named in the items that follow.

ORGANIZATION CHART

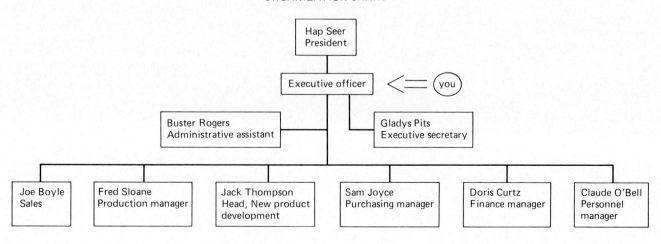

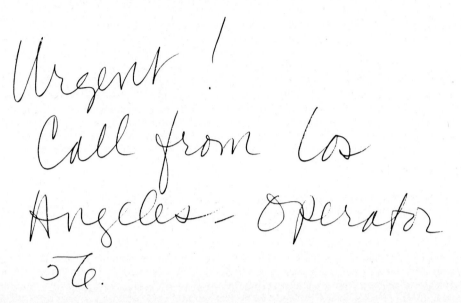

Urgent !
Call from Los
Angeles — Operator
56.

Assessee name:
What, if any, action would you take? (Both a major client and your mother live in Los Angeles.)

To: Boss

From: Gladys

Time: 1:00 (3/6)

Ms. Flakey (clerk in Finance Dept.) is in the Woman's Lounge,
claiming to be sick. She wants your permission to go home.

Assessee name:
What, if any, action would you take?

From: *Hap Sein*

To: *Executive Officer*

Time: *9:45 (3/6)*

See me immediately!

Assessee name:
What, if any, action would you take?

To: Executive Officer

From: Personnel Manager

Got word Jack Thompson has been interviewing for other jobs.
We can't lose him. Will you talk to him?

Assessee name:
What, if any, action would you take?

Executive Officer
Capacitor Plant
City

Dear_____

    As we agreed last month, you are to address the group next Friday on "Management Leadership in Times of Economic Cutbacks." Because the talk is next week we need your Outline by Friday to get it to our members.

As Always,

Paul
President

Assessee name:
What, if any, action would you take?

To: Executive Officer

From: Boyle

Just wanted to let you know that my idea of inviting some of the big contractors out for a drink is really paying off. Ralph Victor, Henry Aris, and Pete Hiskin were here last month. And Pete placed a nice order on the spot!

That crab Doris won't pay for the booze, though. She says that it isn't a legitimate business expense. Will you set her straight?

Joe

Assessee name:
What, if any, action would you take?

To: Executive Officer

From: Doris

        Something must be done about teaching Hanson and Williams about credit risks. They tried to get me to approve a new account order from General Instruments for $110,900. I would not approve it. They argued with me even after I showed them the company owed six firms a total of $115,000 in past-due notes.

        Also, something must be done about the wild parties that go on around here on Saturdays. Monday morning there were cigar and cigarette butts all over the back room and even a whisky bottle!

        I am not to be expected to work in a place where such things are tolerated.

Assessee name:
What, if any, action would you take?

To: Executive Officer

From: Buster

    I thought you ought to know that Fred told me the other day a man came into the plant pretending to be a customer. I say "pretending" because he left after a half hour without buying anything. But he did talk quite a bit to Mr. White and Mr. Hyde out in the plant.
    I think that he is an organizer for the Union.
    I thought you would like to know. Maybe we should review our plant security?

B⸺

Assessee name:
What, if any, action would you take?

TO: Executive Officer

From: Fred

    Someone has been stealing building materials over the weekend. I first noticed this three weeks ago when I helped a fellow load some last Saturday. On Monday, the pile was much smaller. The next Saturday I took a count and wrote it down. Sure enough, on Monday there were 25 less. They got away with 30 the next weekend.

    If you okay it, here's what I propose to do. I will come back to the yard late Saturday afternoon with a shotgun and some of my pals from the police department (who will be off duty) and stand watch. Then if we have "visitors," they will have a big surprise.

    Is this all right with you?

Fred

Assessee name:
What, if any, action would you take?

To: Executive Officer

From: Doris

> Do you want these sent to Mr. Seer? What explanation
> should be included?

<u>Results</u>

SALES DATA

1.	Current sales/sales last year	87.8%
2.	Sales percentages:	
	Lumber & building materials	60.4%
	Hardware, tools, home & garden	15.3%
	Paint & painting supplies	8.0%
	Remodeling contracts	16.2%
3.	New sales per full employee	$7,500.00
4.	Net sales/average net worth	1.9
5.	Net sales/average net working capital	2.5

OPERATING DATA

Net sales divided into:

6.	Net cost of materials sold	72.9%
7.	Gross wages excluding management's	15.6%
8.	Depreciation expense	1.8%
9.	Auto and truck expense	1.0%
10.	Advertising expense	1.2%
11.	Bad debts less recoveries	2.8%

FINANCIAL STATISTICS

12.	Current ratio	1.8
13.	Inventory turnover (on cost)	2.1
14.	Accounts-receivable turnover	4.9
15.	Long-term debts/total assets	12.0%
16.	Net worth/total assets	38.1%

REPORTED PROFITABILITY (before taxes)

17.	As percent of net sales	3.8%
18.	As percent of tangible assets	4.4%
19.	As percent of net worth	7.2%

Assessee name:
What, if any, action would you take?

PART D

Leaderless Group Discussion: Bonus Allocation Problem

There are six people required for this problem. Each of you is a representative to the Bonus Allocation Committee of an organization. A total of forty employees have been recommended for bonuses by their supervisors. For this purpose, the company has allocated $50,000. Today you are to make decisions on six of these people. About twenty-eight of the forty workers have already been allocated their bonuses and you have allocated about $38,500 of the $50,000 for them.

The date is November 1, 1976. Your assignment during the committee meeting is to help the committee make the most equitable use of the available funds. You have *30 minutes* to do this task. Remember that five other people will be working with you and the group must decide on an exact bonus figure (or zero bonus) for each of the six workers about whom you have data sheets (data sheets follow). The sheets discuss the reasons behind the supervisors' nominations for the bonuses and contain some data from the worker's personnel file to assist you in this group decision.

TO: Bonus Allocation Committee

FROM: Wilson Harvey

SUBJECT: Bonus for Sam Dulle

DATE: 10/30/76

The position of head custodian has traditionally been underestimated in our firm, but last month, based on recommendations of consultants, it was elevated to a higher level of compensation. I personally feel that Sam's contributions also have been underestimated for many years. His quiet, unassuming manner might be the reason that he is not noticed, but his work clearly speaks for itself.

   We have a flawless custodial staff that has a low turnover rate and few union grievances. Sam has developed this group and it has functioned nearly perfectly since its inception.

   Because Sam was at the top of his previous job class, he was overlooked for a salary increase last time around (6/15/76). In light of his new job class, relation to range, survey data, and performance, I highly recommend a <u>substantial</u> increase for Sam.

PERSONNEL FILE ON ___Sam Dulle___

Job Title...Head Custodian

 1. Date of employment..................................6/15/59

 2. Starting salary.....................................$4,000

 3. Education...High-school diploma

 4. Experience in job class.............................27 years

 5. Age...51

 6. Number in family....................................7

 7. Date of next merit review...........................6/15/77

 8. Last increase.......................................$250 (12/1/75)

 9. Present salary......................................$12,000

10. Salary comparison with employer's council survey*...Lowest quartile

*This recent survey consisted of twenty local organizations.

TO: Budget Allocation Committee

FROM: Swede Hagen, Manager

SUBJECT: Harry Slack's Bonus

DATE   10/18/76

I am recommending a special increase for Harry at this time to recognize increased responsibilities in the company's research center in the last six months. Harry was a "bargain" when we hired him a few years ago. He had worked as a research analyst in the Coast Guard and our offer was noticeably higher than his service pay, so Harry accepted this offer on the spot. The data shows that he is underpaid for the job, while his duties have reflected a heavier workload and increased responsibilities. The nearest qualified applicant for a similar job is asking $18,000.

   Harry has demonstrated total competence in his job, which he performs much better than some of my longer-service analysts.

PERSONNEL FILE ON_____Harry Slack_____

Job Title..Research Analyst

 1. Date of employment...3/18/73

 2. Starting salary..$8,500

 3. Education...B.S.

 4. Experience in job class...................................4 years

 5. Age..27 years

 6. Number in family...2

 7. Date of next merit review................................3/18/77

 8. Last increase..$575 (3/15/76)

 9. Present salary...$13,750

10. Salary comparison with employer's council survey...................Lowest fifth

TO: Bonus Allocation Committee

FROM: Fel A. T. Eldora, Manager Corporate Data Analysis

SUBJECT: Bonus for Flo Fanstop

DATE: 10/31/76

Flo's contributions have exceeded expectations such that she has now completed three projects several months before deadline. Despite her age (28) and limited experience, her academic tools and analytical approach to problems are far better than I have witnessed in years. She has not only received critical praise from her team members, but has received several lucrative offers from competitive firms.

Flo receives about the same compensation as two associates with more seniority with the company (with less potential and education), but her productivity is second to none.

She has also shown definite leadership potential. At this time, we cannot offer her an advanced supervisory position that would meet her need for more autonomy and status, but I feel she is already qualified. (I am hoping to offer her a promotion within a year.)

In the meantime, I believe we can recognize her value with a handsome special increase that would indicate our pleasure with her performance and offset the substantially higher salary ($24,000) and status (Systems Manager) offered to her by competitors.

PERSONNEL FILE ON_____Flo Fanstop_____

Job Title...Computer Systems Analyst

 1. Date of employment......................................7/11/71

 2. Starting salary...$20,100

 3. Education..Ph.D.

 4. Experience in job class...............................4 years

 5. Age...28

 6. Number in family..1

 7. Date of next merit review.............................7/11/77

 8. Last increase..$350 (3/15/76)

 9. Present salary...$21,500

10. Salary comparison with employer's council survey.........50th percentile

TO: Bonus Allocation Committee

FROM: Maggie Hard, Head Accounts Manager

SUBJECT: Special Increase/ R. W. Good

DATE   10/27/76

Bud did not receive a merit increase in August principally because he is near the maximum of his job class, a most unfair ceiling. He is the only "manager" who is not in the next higher grade (range $17,500 - $25,100). His position is to be reclassified but I don't know when. I don't think we should downgrade positions in the middle-management range when they are as important as this one. I'm sure Bud's patience is becoming shorter because of his "second-class citizen" standing. In fact, he may be already looking for another job.

I recommended an increase at the last bonus time because (1) the cost-of-living rate of increase has been 11 percent in this area; (2) his performance has been more than satisfactory; (3) he came in early from his vacation to finish a priority project when his assistant was hospitalized. The president sent him a letter of commendation for the materials he prepared for the stockholders' meeting. In addition, his staff has increased from two to five.

PERSONNEL FILE ON_____R. W. Good_____

Job title..Head of Accounts Payable

 1. Date of employment.......................................8/4/63

 2. Starting salary...$8,250

 3. Education...Diploma

 4. Experience in job class.................................15 years

 5. Age...43

 6. Number in family..4

 7. Date of next merit review...............................8/4/77

 8. Last increase...$1000 (1/1/76)

 9. Present salary..$19,375

10. Salary comparison with employer's council survey.........80th percentile

TO: Bonus Allocation Committee

FROM: Larry Snyder, VP for Personnel and Public Relations

SUBJECT: Bonus for A.M. Jones, Personnel Administrator

DATE: 10/18/76

A.M. was very unhappy with the size of the salary increase awarded last time, which was a smaller percentage than he had been getting. I feel it is imperative that we at least match it now. Normally I would oppose this type of action (as my record shows), if it were only for the reason of being contrary to corporate policy. However, A.M. has matured in his job so rapidly that he truly deserves a larger raise than he was given. In addition, his rapport with our two most important departments is unmatched by anyone on our staff. In fact, one has recently advised me that his relationship with A.M. was the only reason his department is willing to attempt our job-enrichment program.

  Purely for financial reasons, A.M. is prepared to accept an offer of $19,000 from another firm, but told me he will remain with us if we grant him a good increase. We desperately need him, at least until I can develop a potential replacement to gain the confidence of our most important departments (which should take about 12-18 months).

PERSONNEL FILE ON_____A. M. Jones_____

Job title..Personnel Administrator

 1. Date of employment...................................5/12/67

 2. Starting salary......................................$9,500

 3. Education..LLB

 4. Experience in job class.............................11 years

 5. Age...38

 6. Number in family....................................3

 7. Date of next merit review...........................5/12/77

 8. Last increase.......................................$850 (3/15/76)

 9. Present salary......................................$17,250

10. Salary comparison with employer's council survey..........50th percentile

TO: Bonus Team

FROM: Sally Headdy

SUBJECT: Delores Hopes' Bonus
          Supervisor of Technical Writing

DATE: 10/31/76

Delores was granted a three-month paid leave of absence to complete her master's thesis. When she returned in December, I submitted a recommendation for a merit salary increase for which she was scheduled, according to normal company policy. At that time management decided to defer her increase for six months, since her "time on the job" was three months short of other staff members for the year, who were also eligible and indeed received increases, and also since she had been on paid leave. As I stated before, I cannot agree with a company policy that encourages an employee to seek academic attainment, but penalizes her financially when she does so. Delores's loyalty to the firm and her work are no problem in terms of her leaving us, but I feel it is only fair that she receive her "normal" increase at this time, retroactive to its regularly scheduled date.

   She should also receive an additional increase in recognition of her academic attainment. It should be noted that her recent academic development, plus extensive experience, make her rather marketable, should she choose to "shop around." In fact, awareness of her skills may be increasing as she just received a government award for her work on the "Red Herring" Project.

PERSONNEL FILE ON_____Delores Hopes_____

Job title..Supervisor of Technical Writing

 1. Date of employment..................................12/12/69

 2. Starting salary.....................................$4,650

 3. Education...M.S.

 4. Experience in job class............................17 years

 5. Age..41

 6. Number in family...................................1

 7. Date of next merit review..........................6/12/77

 8. Last increase.......................................$750 6/15/76

 9. Present salary......................................$12,850

10. Salary comparison with employer's council survey...40th percentile

Name _____   Group Number _____

Date _____ Class Section _____ Hour _____ Score _____

ASSESSMENT OF LEARNING IN PERSONNEL ADMINISTRATION
EXERCISE 9

1. Try to state the purpose of this exercise in one concise sentence.

2. Specifically what did you learn from this exercise (i.e., skills, abilities, and knowledge)?

3. How might your learning influence your role and your duties as a personnel administrator?

4. What job and organizational characteristics would seem to signal the use of assessment centers for selection in addition to interviews and biographical data?

5. How can objectivity of assessors be improved?

6. Should assessors be managers in the same departments or functional areas as assessees? Why or why not?

7. How could you evaluate the effectiveness of a work sampling or simulation selection device?

8. Additional questions given by your implementor:

Exercise 10

TESTING PERSONNEL AND VALIDATING SELECTION PROCEDURES*

PREVIEW

This exercise is designed to facilitate understanding psychological testing as a selection device and the use of statistics to analyze test results to make effective selection decisions. Thus, the *interpretation of test results*, rather than test construction or design, is the focus of the exercise.

Two of the most important concepts in selection are validity and reliability. The former term has been noted briefly in previous exercises and defined as the relationship between a predictor, or selection device (such as an applicant's response to an interview question) and job performance. Reliability has been defined as consistency of a measure over time or across raters (such as many raters' agreement on one person's performance appraisal). However, validity and reliability are much broader concepts which serve as the basis for much of the personnel administrator's work in the area of personnel selection. This exercise explores these concepts in more depth.

INTRODUCTION

Basic Issues in Personnel Testing

When discussing personnel testing, we generally are referring to the use of paper-and-pencil methods of assessing individuals for employment. However, testing can also mean the use of any method (even an informal interview) for collecting information used in making selection decisions. Thus, although in this exercise we will be focusing primarily on psychological paper-and-pencil tests, the methodology of reliability and validity—which will be discussed—can be applied

OBJECTIVES

1. To become aware of the advantages and disadvantages of the use of tests as personnel selection devices.
2. To gain an understanding of the importance of validity and reliability in personnel selection.
3. To build skill in applying basic statistics that enable validity and reliability to be assessed.

PREMEETING PREPARATION

Read the entire exercise. The *Introduction* should be read very carefully. Review elementary regression and correlation computations, as well as the measures of central tendency (i.e., standard deviation and mean) which are used in these computations. See the *Appendix* to this exercise for such a discussion.[1]

to all of the selection techniques treated in Exercises 7, 8, and 9.

---

* The advice and assistance of James R. Beatty (School of Business, San Diego State University) are gratefully acknowledged.
[1] Most statistics textbooks would also contain a discussion of basic regression, correlation, and measures of central tendency.

Two Perspectives on Testing. In looking at the issues involved in personnel testing and selection, two perspectives must be kept in mind. The first perspective concerns the accurate use of all procedures available when an organization is seeking to substantiate the validity of a selection procedure. This may be referred to as the "ideal" practice and should be consistent with the statements various professional groups have made in this regard. These include the combined pronouncements of the American Psychological Association (APA), the American Educational Research Association, and the National Council on Measurement in Education on ethics and the use of tests, and APA Division 14's (Industrial and Organizational Psychology) statement on validation and personnel selection procedures.[2] The profession of psychology, through these groups, can be viewed as seeking the "best" methodology possible.

The second perspective concerning testing seeks "fairness," or the elimination of discriminatory hiring practices. This perspective will be referred to as the "legal" status of tests which emerges from various government pronouncements and court cases.[3] A set of minimum standards to be used as guides in the design of selection procedures will eventually come from the courts and legislatures. Although these two perspectives on testing may be viewed somewhat differently in terms of their objectives, they are not necessarily inconsistent with each other in actual practice. The differences are largely in the degree to which selection procedures should be assessed as to validity, etc. (i.e., the exhaustiveness to which the method of selection is examined). In this exercise, both perspectives will be discussed. Obviously, it would be very difficult to discuss one without the other, as what the first states in the ideal sense, the second amends for the practical sense. A glossary of terminology pertaining to psychological and legal jargon is presented in Exercise 18.

Validity.[4] The ability of an instrument (e.g., a test, a questionnaire, an interview, etc.) to actually measure

the quality or characteristic it was originally intended to measure is called validity. Unfortunately, validity is rather difficult to pin down precisely because it may vary depending on the method used. Therefore, it is necessary to predetermine standards that can be used as guidelines for ascertaining the absence or presence of validity evidence. Since there is no one definite measure of validity, it is important to evaluate all the available measures. If all such evaluations of validity point in one direction—either the presence of or lack of validity—then the decision may not be difficult. If, on the other hand, the results from different assessments vary, it becomes more difficult to determine the degree of validity actually present from the evidence. Also, there is always the problem of making a wrong decision as a result of chance or random error, despite the precautions taken.

Two Basic Empirical, or Data-Based, Validity Models. In order to assess whether or not a measure, say a certain test, is actually measuring what it was orginally intended to measure, several sets of procedures are currently in use. These procedures are called validity models or strategies and can be based on actual statistical data or on judgment. Faced with the problem of actually measuring validity, personnel administrators or others may choose one of the models discussed below, relying on statistical techniques to guide their assessment of validity.

Of the two models noted briefly here, the most basic and preferred model is the *predictive validity* model shown in Fig. 1. In using this model, one would attempt to show that results of a test (or some other selection tool) would accurately predict actual job success. Here, a test's results are called a *predictor* and the actual job success, the *criterion*, or that which we are attempting to relate the predictor to. In a predictive validity study (Fig. 1), we would try to assess the realtionship between a test (predictor) and job success (the criterion) by analyzing the job (t_1), designing an appropriate test and methods of performance-appraisal (t_2), and then administering the test to a group of job applicants (t_3), but not using their test scores as a basis for selection decisions. We could perhaps select on the basis of another "predictor," like high-school grades, or simply hire everyone until the positions are filled (t_4). Then we would evaluate the newly hired applicants' performance, perhaps by using some measure of effectiveness, such as number of cost overruns during a period, or by some type of performance-appraisal system, perhaps using supervisory ratings. After the performance measure is used to evaluate the recently hired applicants (t_5) who have had time to perform their jobs, the

[2] *Principles for the Validation and Use of Personnel Selection Procedures* (Washington, D.C.: American Psychological Association, 1975); and *Standards for Educational and Psychological Tests*, (Washington, D.C.: American Psychological Association, 1975).

[3] The discussion of the legal aspects (i.e., the second perspective) will focus on validation based on job relatedness and not the statistical procedures for the determination of discrimination (called adverse impact). Discrimination or adverse impact is the target of discussion in Exercise 13.

[4] The following discussions are meant only to introduce the topics. More rigorous discussions can be obtained in several entries in the *For Further Reading* section of this exercise.

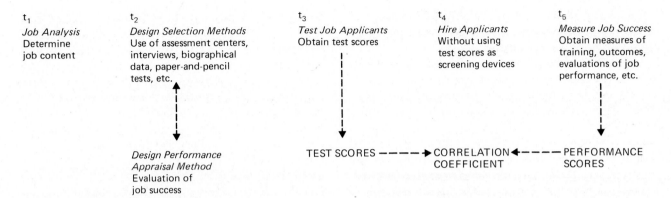

Fig. 1.   The Predictive Validation Model

results of the test administered at t_3 are related to the performance of the group at t_5 by means of a correlation coefficient. The correlation coefficient is a simple statistical measure of association between two groups of paired numbers (see *Appendix*). If the coefficient indicates that those who did well on the test also later did well on the job, then we could assume that a high score on the test would *predict* later job success. Further, we might infer that the results of the study described above indicate validity of the test, because it seemed to measure or predict what it was intended to measure—job success.

Although a predictive validity study as described above is sound in a scientific and statistical sense, it is sometimes difficult in a practical sense. For example, a reasonably large sample of workers (about thirty or so) would be required in order to make firm conclusions from the statistical analysis. In addition, predictive validity studies take some time as we must wait until a sufficient period of time has passed before performance can be ascertained (i.e., t_4 to t_5). Finally, we cannot use the test we may have developed or purchased (both at considerable cost) to make selec-

tion decisions for the *initial* applicants because we must hire them first in order to assess the test's validity. We could use the test scores as a rationale for selection of *future* applicants, however, if the predictive validity of the test was shown.

Due to these problems, a second validity strategy, *concurrent validity* (Fig. 2), is sometimes used. Here current employees rather than new hires are used as the sample on which to base the validity study. As Fig. 2 indicates, some type of test (or other selection technique) for which the validity must be assessed is developed and performance-appraisal methods are also developed, if they are not already in existence (t_1). Then the test (the predictor) is given to the sample of workers on the job and their performance is appraised (t_2). The statistical association between the predictor (test score) and the criterion (job performance) is shown again by the simple correlation coefficient. As in predictive validity, if high test scores are associated with high job performance, the test can be assumed to be valid, provided certain precautions were taken, such as randomly selecting the sample, use of a large enough sample, proper testing environment, an ac-

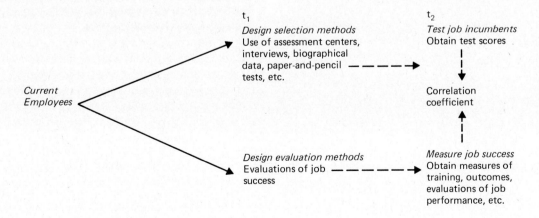

Fig. 2.   The Concurrent Validation Model

curate performance measure, etc. If the test predicts high performance for people currently on the job, it may be used to select new workers.

The study is called a concurrent study because test scores and performance scores can be obtained concurrently (t_2) for a group of current job holders. Thus, this method can be quicker than predictive validity and enables the organization to use the predictor on all future hirees. Thus no future employees would be hired without using their test scores, as in predictive validity. Of course, we run the risk of measuring a group of current employees who may already have high test scores as they are the remainder of a larger group previously screened by some other selection method when they were hired. In addition, they may have learned, or developed, while on the job and could thus get high test scores. When we use the same test on a group of applicants, they may get lower scores simply because they have not yet been able to learn what the original sample was able to while on the job, rather than because they would not be good future performers.

Concurrent validity studies readily illustrate another problem of validity which may also be found with predictive studies. This is the restriction-of-range problem. Figure 3 shows a plot of a relationship between selection test scores and performance-appraisal scores when persons are hired irrespective of scores on the selection test. Notice that the scores are divided into four quadrants by "minimum performance" scores of about 60 and a "cutting score" on the selection instrument of about 150. Of the total of thirty

scores, twenty-two are "hits" because they indicate that twelve of the people who pass the cutting score also perform well (true positives). Ten persons also did not perform well or exceed the cutting score (true negatives). However 26.6 percent of the scores (eight of thirty) are misses because these people either passed the cutting score, but did not perform well (false positives) or did not pass the cutting score, but exceeded the minimum performance standard. This last quadrant, false negatives, is often the concern when using traditional tests to select minionity employees (i.e., excluding employees who could do the job because of a culturally biased test). The restriction-of-range problem is created when the cutting score is used without first using the full range of potential employees to do the job. Thus, in Fig. 3, only the fifteen candidates who passed the cutting score would be employed and thus included in the calculation of the correlation coefficient. Because of this restriction in range, the correlation coefficient would be depressed. Such a finding often calls for an explanation of "differential validity" in which different selection methods may be required for different segments of the applicant population. Each of these tests must then be validated for the appropriate applicant groups. However it may be found that using well-designed selection techniques eliminates the need for differential-validity measures.[5]

Nonempirical, or Logical, Validity Models. The second major strategy for validation are rational (or logical) methods. These methods are permissible under the official guidelines used by the federal government[6] when empirical validation is not feasible, largely because of small sample sizes. These methods concern what is called *content validity* and require a thorough knowledge of job demands based on a careful job analysis.

Content validity refers to the extent to which a test actually measures some aspect of the job itself, or has content similar to job content. As the content of the test approaches the content of the job, performance on the test would approach performance on the job. Of course, in selection, the more closely a selection test or predictor calls for performance which is similar to actual job performance, the better we would be able to predict job performance from test performance. The selection techniques discussed in Exercise 9, work

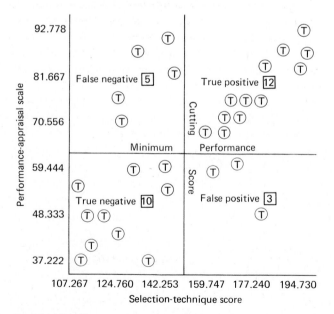

Fig. 3.   **Restriction of Range and Other Validity Problems**

[5] V. B. Bohem, "Negro-White Differences in Validity of Employment and Training Selection Procedures," *Journal of Applied Psychology* 56 (1972): 33–39.
[6] Guidelines have been issued by the Office of Federal Contract Compliance (OFCC) and the Equal Employment Opportunity Commission (EEOC).

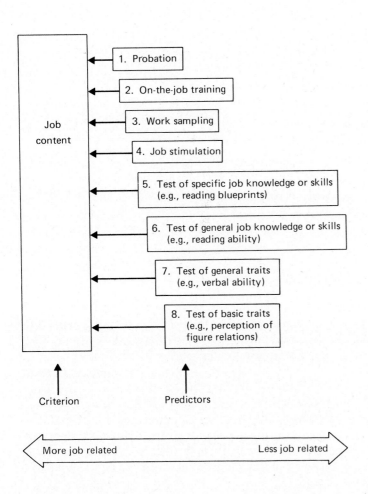

Fig. 4.   **Selection Procedures and Their Relation to Job Content** (Adapted from R. M. Guion, "Open a New Window: Validities and Values in Psychological Measurement," *Am. Psych.* 29, May 1974, p. 291.)

sampling and simulation, were designed to be content valid because, in the case of the former, a sample of actual job content is used as the test. In the latter, actual job content is simulated.

Figure 4 shows how closely various selection techniques approximate actual job content. Of course, the closest selection technique to actual job content would be performing the job itself before final hiring, as in a probation period. The furthest type of predictor from actual job content would be a test of general traits, such as perception of figural relations.

In content validation, inferences about the usefulness of the test or predictor must be made by assessing how the test is constructed and whether it actually taps the behavioral content or domain of the job. Content validity is thus established by a systematic observation of job content via a very thorough job analysis (see Exercise 3). Then selection devices are designed which actually assess or sample knowledge, skills, and behaviors required for job success. For example, typing tests are content-valid measures to use in hiring stenographers, because stenographers type. The same can be said for a shorthand test. When both are used together, we obtain more complete sampling of job content than when each is used alone. The more completely we tap the entire behavioral set or "domain" of the job, the more content valid the selection process would be. Note that no statistical procedures are used in content validity; only expert judgment that the predictor taps the content of the job is really necessary here, as well as a thorough job analysis.

Two additional types of validity should also be mentioned because they are suggested by the *APA Division 14 Principles for the Validation and Use of Selection Procedures.* These are construct and synthetic validity. Construct validity is the degree to which a formally articulated concept of a trait (e.g., perceptual speed, spatial ability, empathy) may be measured by a test and related to job performance. This is difficult to do and requires more than a single criterion-related study. Synthetic validity is where the validity may be inferred from prior research relating predictors to specific relevant criterion elements.

Content and construct validity are applicable in many situations. Excluding these methods would

Table 1. Allocation of Variance in Different Estimates of Reliability

Reliability procedure	Sources of variance						
	I Lasting general characteristics	II A Lasting specific characteristics (specific to whole test)	II B Lasting specific characteristics (specific to particular test items)	III Temporary general characteristics	IV A Temporary specific characteristics (specific to whole test)	IV B Temporary specific characteristics (specific to particular test items)	V Variance not otherwise accounted for (chance)
Immediate test-retest	S*	S	S	S	S	E	E
Delayed test-retest	S	S	S	E	E	E	E
Immediate alternate form	S	S	E†	S	S	E	E
Delayed alternate form	S	S	E	E	E	E	E
Split-half	S	S	E	S	S	S	E

* S = systematic variance.
† E = error variance.
Source: Adapted from R. M. Guion, *Personnel Testing* (New York: McGraw-Hill, 1965), p. 39.

seriously handicap organizations with few employees in a job class—for example, in the selection of astronauts, where they have proved most effective. Such organizations cannot use elegant empirical validation designs which are dependent on large sample sizes. Fortunately, Title VII of the 1964 Civil Rights Act, as interpreted by the *EEOC Guidelines*, allows these methods where predictive and concurrent validation strategies are not technically feasible.

Reliability. Reliability of a measure refers to its trustworthiness, or its stability or consistency. The reliability coefficient (a simple correlation coefficient or a computational formula based on it) indicates how consistent the scores obtained on a measure are. A high reliability coefficient would indicate that the obtained score on a measure (any predictor, including tests, interview responses, etc.) is a stable and trustworthy indication of the person's performance on the measure and is not likely to be due to chance or some other unidentifiable variable.

Three basic types of reliability are used in psychological testing. The first is called the *test-retest* method and is expressed as the correlation between the scores from two different administrations of the same test to the same people. The administrations should be fairly close together so as not to allow learning or maturation to influence the scores too heavily. This method would result in an index of stability.

The second type of reliability estimate is the *alternate forms* method. Here two different forms of the same test can be developed by drawing two different random samples of questions from a larger population of questions, all of which were designed to

measure the same thing. This method may be a little more useful than test-retest because the same items do not appear on both tests.

The third type of reliability, the *split-half* method, assesses the internal consistency of a measure. Here, for example, a test would be split into odd and even items or questions and a correlation coefficient computed for the two sets of scores. If all of the test items were measuring a similar idea or concept, we would expect the relationship between the two halves to be high.

Table 1 shows the sources of variance with alternative methods of estimating reliability. The two types of variance are systematic and error. Systematic variance arises when the characteristics of an individual are repeatedly measured. This increases the correlation coefficient. Error variance occurs when there exist different levels of performance on a test (inconsistency). This lowers the correlation coefficient.

Test Construction. Tests are constructed by sampling job content, whether a predictive, concurrent, content, or other validity study is to be used. This is true for both the predictor and the criterion. Any "test" must be constructed from samples of job content that must be performed; from specific items, such as job knowledge or skills; or from constructs, such as leadership, dexterity, spatial ability, etc. Obviously, the further from actual job samples, the greater the inferences that serve as hypotheses to be tested in terms of job relatedness. In any case, a test must represent a sample of actual job content randomly selected and presented in such a way that the test can differentiate high performers from low performers (i.e., varying level of difficulty of test questions) on the dimensions measured by the test and can be clearly related to job performance. The example used in Exercise 9 (the selection of an auto mechanic) which asks questions about installing pulleys and belts, disassembling gear boxes, aligning a motor, and pressing a bushing illustrates a sampling of job content in the construction of a test. The items within any test should also be checked for reliability and validity by conducting an item analysis to determine if the test actually discriminates in the way intended. For example, will applicants in the top half of the test-score distribution also tend to have a certain question "right" and applicants in the bottom half tend to get the question "wrong?" If this occurs, the item has favorable discriminating power and contributes to the overall reliability and validity of the test.[7] The statistical techniques used to determine usable items in test construction are chi square (χ^2) and point biserial correlation.

Practical Usefulness of Tests. A critical question that is often unanswered, yet is a major issue in validation process, is: How high must a correlation be for it to be useful in predicting success?

> Tests with a coefficient of validity less than 0.50 are practically useless, except in distinguishing between extreme cases, since at that value of r the forecasting efficiency is only 13.4 percent.[8]

This statement, paraphrased from a statistical text, can be found in many other texts as well. Relatively few validity coefficients, however, especially in personnel studies, exceed 0.50.[9] In fact, the 0.30 level may become the accepted standard of practical significance, based on the decision in a recent court case.[10] The following statement is from footnote 13 of the First Circuit decision, which was appealed and cited by the District Court in that case:

> The objective portion of the study produced several correlations which were statistically signifi-

cant (likely to occur by chance in fewer than five of one hundred similar cases) and practically significant (correlation of +0.3 or higher, thus explaining 9% or more of the observed variation). Of the seven statistically significant correlations, four were not practically significant....

Because the higher court cited the lower court's opinion regarding 0.30 being the level of correlation necessary to establish the *practical* utility of a test, it may become an accepted standard.

Why are tests being used even though they generally fall into this "practically useless" class? Is it because of ignorance on the part of test users? Not at all. The "index of forecasting efficiency,"[11] as formulated in statistics texts, is concerned with a precision of prediction much finer than that required in most practical situations. As a measure of the real practical utility of a test, the effectiveness index may be grossly misleading.[12]

The difference between the two concepts of *practical utility* and the *statistical index of efficiency* can be seen more clearly if we consider the predictions, in two different situations, of how far people can broad jump. If the occasion is an athletic contest, we might want to predict just how many feet and inches each person will cover by giving some sort of a test, let's say of strength in their legs. The average difference between our estimated distances based on the test results and the actual jumps will serve as a crude indicator of our test's index of forecasting efficiency—the better (i.e., the more valid) the basis on which we make our predictions, the smaller this average difference will become. But, suppose we move from the athletic contest to a situation in which practical values are more important, say one in which it is necessary to leap across a brook. Those who fail by a fraction of an inch to make the jump will get their feet just as wet as will those who miss by six inches. And those who just clear it will be as successful in staying dry as those who sail over with a few feet to spare. Now the "efficiency" of our predictive test of leg strength does not lie in how close we can predict the exact length of a person's jump, as in the athletic contest, but in the confidence with which our predictive test permits us to say, "Of people who score above a certain point, nine out of ten will make the jump, but of those whose scores are below a certain point, only three out of ten will get across."

---

[7] Statistical tables are available to show how large a correlation coefficient must be, given a certain sample size, in order to have various degrees of certainty (e.g., one error out of 20 trials or $p < 0.05$) that the relationship obtained was not due to chance (see *Appendix*).

[8] J. P. Guilford, *Psychometric Methods* (New York: McGraw-Hill, 1936, p. 364). The index of forecasting efficiency = $100(1 - \sqrt{1 - r^2})$ where r is the validity coefficient, the correlation between the predictor and the criterion. When the number of cases is small, a correction term $(\frac{N-1}{N-2})$ is inserted under the square root sign.

[9] The correlation coefficient's range is +1.00 to −1.00.

[10] *N.A.A.C.P., Inc.* v. *Beecher*, U.S. District Court, Dist. of Mass., Feb. 1974.

[11] J. P. Guilford, "Reliability and Validity of Measures,"

[12] Many of the following comments are reproduced with permission from the Psychological Corporation's *Test Service Bulletins*, nos. 43 and 45.

Of course, the absolute dichotomy (those who make it across the stream versus those who did not) is as extreme in its way as the pinpoint precision estimate is at the other extreme. That is, in trying to predict job performance from tests (or any predictors), we do not attempt to pinpoint performance exactly, as we did in the athletic contest, nor do we often assume that there are only two categories, success and failure, as we did in the jump across the brook. But typically, in selection, we are attempting to guess in which of a few general categories of success (i.e., high, middle, low) our job candidates will eventually fall. Thus, the real situation is much more like the brook jump than the athletic contest; therefore cruder approximations and *practical* significance become important. We thus typically do not attempt to predict specific success levels from test scores; rather, we try to predict with some validity the percentages of people above or below a certain score that will subsequently be high, or middle, or low performers.

Percent of improvement over chance, as used with the index of forecasting efficiency, refers to the narrowing of a zone of error around a predicted score. When the validity coefficient (or correlation coefficient) is zero (i.e., no relationship is indicated between a test score and job performance), knowledge of the test score does not permit us to predict an individual's score on the criterion with any accuracy at all. The best guess we can make with respect to any individual, regardless of how s/he scored on such a test, is that they will be average on the criterion. Here, the band of error (the standard error of estimate) is as large as the spread (the standard deviation) of the ratings on the criterion (job performance) for the entire group (see *Appendix*). As the correlation between the test scores and the criterion ratings increases, our precision in predicting ratings of individuals on the criterion also increases. We may predict with some degree of confidence, for example, that a person who scores in the top quarter of the test will be rated in the top quarter on the criterion as well. Of course, some of our predictions will be in error (i.e., some of those whose scores are in the top quarter on the test will be rated in the second quarter on performance, a smaller number in the third quarter, and a few may even be rated in the lowest quarter). The larger the validity coefficient, the fewer misplaced persons there will be; furthermore, the smaller will be the amount of displacement. In other words, if the validity coefficient is very high (i.e., close to $+1.00$), we may expect most of those who score in the top quarter on the test to be rated in the top quarter on performance as well, a very few to be rated in the second quarter, and fewer still (or perhaps none at all) to be rated in the third or fourth quarters. This is because the relationship between the two sets of scores is so nearly perfect as to almost appear in ascending or descending order. The person with the fifth highest predictor score may have the sixth highest criterion score. Therefore, if we take the top fourth of the predictor scores, we may get very close to the top fourth of the criterion scores as well.

Accuracy and the Standard Error of the Estimate. The number of persons for whom statistically calculated predictions are wrong, and the amount by which estimates are in error, are reflected in the standard error of estimate. When validity is perfect, the standard error of estimate is zero; when validity is reduced, the standard error of estimate increases. The degree to which the standard error of estimate is reduced concerns an improvement over a chance occurrence of a prediction. In this sense, large validity coefficients (i.e., correlation coefficients—r's) are necessary; it takes a very large r to cut the standard error of estimate enough to get, for example, a 50 percent improvement in the probability that a prediction was due to a real association between a predictor and a criterion and was not due to chance.

What permits us to use tests effectively even though their validity coefficients are considerably lower than we would like? First there is the matter of precision. The standard error of the estimate refers to the amount of error around predictions of precise, specific rankings of each individual on the criterion. In most practical work, such precision is unnecessary. We do not ordinarily need to predict that John Jones will be the nineteenth best performer of a group of twenty-five engineering apprentices. We are far more likely to be concerned with whether or not Jones will be one of the satisfactory apprentices. For these purposes, whether Jones is nineteenth or twenty-third is of little consequence; we can, however, make a confident prediction that he may or may not succeed, even though there may be a large standard error of estimate applicable to the specific rank our formula predicts.

A related factor working in our favor in the practical use of tests is that, as the above explanations note, predictions are most accurately made at the extremes—and it is the extremes that are of greatest interest to us. Few organizations fire as many as half of those they hire. More often, the failures are the bottom 10 percent, 20 percent, or possibly 30 percent, the extremes. In organizational selection, a test of "moderate" validity can be efficient in quickly screening out the "clearly ineligible" from the "clearly eligible." There will remain an indifferent zone of test scores for persons in the "eligible" range; for them,

Table 2. Percent of Successful Individuals in Each Decile on Test Score

Standing on the test		When the total percent of failures is 20%, and				When the total percent of failures is 30%, and				When the total percent of failures is 50%, and			
Percentile	Decile	$r = 0.30$	$r = 0.40$	$r = 0.50$	$r = 0.60$	$r = 0.30$	$r = 0.40$	$r = 0.50$	$r = 0.60$	$r = 0.30$	$r = 0.40$	$r = 0.50$	$r = 0.60$
90–99th	10	92%	95%	97%	99%	86%	91%	94%	97%	71%	78%	84%	90%
80–89th	9	89	91	94	97	81	85	89	92	63	68	73	78
70–79th	8	86	89	91	94	78	81	84	88	59	62	65	69
60–69th	7	84	86	88	91	75	77	80	83	55	57	59	61
50–59th	6	82	84	85	87	72	74	75	77	52	52	53	54
40–49th	5	80	81	82	83	70	70	70	71	48	48	47	46
30–39th	4	78	77	77	78	67	66	65	64	45	43	41	39
20–29th	3	75	73	72	71	63	61	59	56	42	38	35	31
10–19th	2	71	68	64	61	59	55	50	45	37	33	28	22
1–9th	1	63	56	49	40	50	43	35	27	29	23	16	10

Source: The Psychological Corporation, *Test Service Bulletin* 45, p. 11. Reprinted by permission.

other considerations than paper-and-pencil test scores may determine whether they should be hired. These could include scores on biographical data items, interviews, work samples or simulation, although the statistical progresses remain the same for all scored selection procedures.

Formal tables are available which can be used to estimate expectancies when the validity coefficient is of a given size and the percent of on-the-job successes and failures is known. Table 2 has been constructed from these formal tables to illustrate the usefulness of coefficients of various magnitudes.

The first part of Table 2 is based on a failure rate of 20 percent. It shows the percent of individuals at different levels on a predictor or test who are successful performers (in marks earned, or dollar sales, or merit rating, or number of widgets assembled, or whatever we are trying to predict) when the validity coefficient is 0.30, 0.40, 0.50, or 0.60. The columns at the left show the decile rank on the test. Individuals with percentile ranks of 90 to 99 are in the tenth decile or top 10 percent, those with percentile ranks from 80 to 89 are in the next (ninth decile), etc. The first decile includes the individuals between the first and ninth percentiles on the test—the 10 percent who scored lowest. In the third column from the left is shown the percent of persons in each decile who may be expected to succeed when the validity coefficient (r) is 0.30. The next column to the right presents similar expectancy information when $r = 0.40$, the next column is for $r = 0.50$, and the last column for a validity coefficient of 0.60.

What does this table tell us? Assume a selection test is given and a correlation of 0.30 is found between scores on the test and success in the first year of work. Ninety-two percent of those who score in the top 10 percent of the group on the test may be expected to

succeed, while only 63 percent in the bottom decile (10 percent) can expect to survive the first year. If the validity coefficient is 0.40, ninety-five percent in the top decile may be expected to survive; of the lowest-scoring applicants, 56 percent are likely to survive. The survival rate when $r = 0.60$ is almost perfect (99 percent) for the top group; it is only 40 percent for the lowest scorers. Notice how the amount of error, or discriminating ability of the test, decreases as the validity coefficient increases, as was explained above. As the validity coefficient approaches evidence of a perfect relationship (i.e., +1.00), between the test scorer and performance, the percentage of people who score very highest on the test and who will succeed on the job goes up while the percentage of people who score lowest on the test and will succeed on the job goes down. That is, the higher validity coefficient has a lower error associated with it and is evidence that the test scores are better able to discriminate between successful and unsuccessful performers.

The last two sections of Table 2 present similar information for validity coefficients of 0.30, 0.40, 0.50, and 0.60 when failure rates are 30 percent and 50 percent. The last column at the right shows, for example, that if only 50 percent of a total group is successful and the validity coefficient is 0.60, the top scoring individuals will have a survival rate of 90 percent; of those in the bottom decile on the test, only one out of ten is likely to succeed.

It is interesting to compare the figures in the column headed $r + 0.50$ (when failures total 20 percent) with the quotation stated above regarding the low practical utility of tests with validity coefficients of less than 0.50 which thus have forecasting efficiency of only 13.4 percent. The "only 13.4 percent" sort of statement may be (and often has been) misinterpreted as indicating that the test can tell us little. Actually,

	Our estimate of chances of success without test information (failure rate = 20%)	Our estimate of chances of success with knowledge of test scores (r = 0.50; failure rate = 20%)
Person in 10th decile	4 to 1 (80%/20%)	32 to 1 (97%/3%)
Person in 7th decile	4 to 1 (80%/20%)	7 to 1 (88%/12%)
Person in 1st decile	4 to 1 (80%/20%)	1 to 1 (49%/51%)

the test with an r of 0.50 has improved our picture dramatically. Without it, we could say only that for every person the odds are four chances to one they will succeed because 20 percent is the total percent of failures. With the test of $r = 0.50$, we can sort the candidates into groups and say that some have distinctly better prospects for success than others. If three people score, respectively, in the tenth, the seventh, and the lowest deciles, we can give odds on their success, as shown in Table 2 and above.

What are the practical implications of these facts? Most apparent is the potential utility of validity coefficients of 0.60, 0.50, 0.40, and even 0.30; the information they provide is far from useless. For personnel people in organizations, data such as these provide information with respect to the selection ratios or the percentage of successful applicants to the total hired. The number hired or assessed to assure a certain minimum number of successes later can be estimated.

As do all other statistics, standard errors of estimate and validity coefficients require full understanding. Our errors of estimate may always be greater than we would like. The precision of our estimates may be less than perfect and we shall aim constantly to increase that precision. At the same time, if a test will increase appreciably our ability to predict performance (even though broadly), we can still use it—with caution, but with an appreciation for the additional information it supplies. Finally, statistics are *not* a substitute for thinking. A rating or a grade represents a judgment; a test score is a statement of accomplishment on a specified set of tasks. Regardless of how high or how low a coefficient of correlation may be, the following issues always demand consideration:

1. how the judgments were determined;
2. the nature of the test and its relation to the job; and
3. the behaviors, skills, and abilities of the particular group of individuals being studied.

The validity (or correlation) coefficient has been likened to a three-legged stool. One leg is the predictor (frequently a test), another is the criterion (ratings of job performance), and the third is the population on which the coefficient is obtained (grade level, job, family, sex, spread of ability, etc.). One who uses a three-legged stool without ascertaining that all three legs warrant confidence is very likely to be floored!

Personnel Testing and the Law. Recent legislation in the area of equal employment opportunity and discrimination in employment have probably had as great an effect on personnel testing as any personnel program. The general impact of these laws on personnel is noted in various exercises, most notably Exercise 18. Regarding personnel testing, however, the *Myart* v. *Motorola* case, which involved the charge of discrimination against a black job applicant on the basis of intelligence, pointed out the possible misuse of personnel testing.

Along with several other important factors, such as the racial tension and violence in this country during the 1960s, the disposition of Congress and the administration, and the general social climate, the above-mentioned case helped to spurn the passage of the Civil Rights Act of 1964. This act protected employers' rights to use tests, but not to discriminate with them on the basis of race, color, relgion, sex, or national origin. As a result of this law, guidelines issued by federal agencies (e.g., Equal Employment Opportunity Commission [EEOC] and Office of Federal Contract Compliance [OFCC]), and court cases, several standards regarding testing have been set. Certainly many more will be developed through precedent and others changed.

Most of these standards deal with validity, explained above to mean the relation of a test's content to job content or the ability of a test to predict job performance. The laws state that tests are illegal which discriminate on the basis of race, etc., rather than on the basis of ability or merit. A problem is that, due to past differences in opportunity and education, certain groups of people may score low on certain types of tests which are related to job performance—thus these applicants would be kept out of certain jobs (see Fig. 3). In these cases validity data may be required for each such group and often lower cutoff scores are used for certain groups.

The Equal Employment Opportunity Commission (EEOC) specifically advocates the following types of procedures to help avoid discrimination:

1. A total personnel assessment system that is non-discriminatory within the spirit of the law and places special emphasis on the following:
   a) careful *job analysis* to define skill requirements
   b) special efforts in *recruiting minorities*
   c) *screening and interviewing* related to job requirements
   d) *tests* selected on the basis of specific job-related criteria
   e) comparison of test performance versus *job performance*
   f) *retesting*
   g) tests should be *validated for minorities*.

2. *Objective administration of tests.* It is essential that tests be administered by personnel who are skilled not only in technical details, but also in establishing proper conditions for test taking. Members of disadvantaged groups tend to be particularly sensitive in test situations and those giving tests should be aware of this and be able to alleviate a certain amount of anxiety.[13]

Besides the *Myart* v. *Motorola* case, the United States Supreme Court has heard three major cases. Two of these have affirmed the use of the *EEOC Guidelines* (*Griggs* v. *Duke Power* and *Albermarle* v. *Moody*) for both predictor and criterion variables. A more recent case (*Washington, D.C.* v. *Davis*) indicated that empirical validity may not be required if a text appears to be job related (although the test in question did correlate significantly with training success as a criterion).

The controversies surrounding employment testing are certainly continuing and impact on an organization's selection processes greatly. Affirmative action programs—explicit attempts to hire certain groups (Exercise 18)—as well as special training programs are extremely helpful. The most effective procedures for compliance with the laws regarding testing, however, are rigorous validation practices to insure that each test is predictive of job performance in a certain job and for a certain group of job applicants.

Summary. In this *Introduction* we have attempted to present the basic issues regarding validity and reliability of personnel-selection tests. It is obvious that even the most basic explanation must involve the use

[13] Equal Employment Opportunity Commission, *Guidelines on Employment Testing Procedures*, August 24, 1966, pp. 3–4. United States Government Printing Office, 1967, 0–302–505(403).

of some statistical terms and concepts, for much of the definition of validity is formulated in these terms.

The selection techniques used by an organization, including psychological test scores, interview responses, etc., in order to form a rationale for selection decisions must be validated in some way, not only due to legal requirements, but also due to the needs of the organization to have a clear picture of the relationship of responses from selection techniques to actual job performance and the accuracy of its techniques to predict subsequent performance. Only then can rational cost/benefit analyses be conducted as to the "worth" of each selection device or, for example, the logic of allocating resources to develop a certain test. The effectiveness of any predictor is measured, in the final analysis, by its predictive accuracy as compared to other competing predictors, or to using none at all. For some jobs and some applicant populations, a very accurate predictor would not seem economical to develop. For example, for some entry-level, unskilled jobs, very gross predictors, such as physical ability, might be sufficient and resources would be better allocated to training and motivation programs in order to assure successful performance once hired. But in selecting a vice-president of finance or a chief of neurosurgery, sophisticated and more costly selection devices would seem warranted. We typically would attempt to select the best vice-president of finance from among all candidates and then assume he or she has the ability to succeed without formal training. But we might select those people among candidates for a stock clerk job with the minimum qualifications and then train them to perform successfully on the job.

The key issues in any discussion regarding validity and testing are the predictors (i.e., test scores, interview responses, biographical items, etc.) and their relation to the criteria (i.e., job success as measured by performance-appraisal formats, profit, sales, number of accidents, etc.) via a validity coefficient (i.e., a correlation coefficient of range -1.00 to $+1.00$). Validity can be calculated using empirical data in the predictive and concurrent models explained above, or by expert judgment in the content-validity model. Reliability of a selection device refers not only to its ability to produce consistent results over time, but also to its ability to predict accurately. Accurate prediction, of course, is a relative concept which depends on many factors, such as the nature and size of the sample of applicants, the cost and nature of the predictor(s), the size of the validity coefficient, the nature and importance of the job, the degree to which we can accurately define and identify job success, and other factors of a judgmental nature. Thus, as was noted above, the statistical techniques briefly reviewed here are seen merely as tools that may help us to improve our predictive ability in personnel selection, point out weaknesses in our predictors, and help us make practical decisions regarding the number of job applicants to assess.

As Fig. 4 depicts, regardless of any statistical analysis at all, we would, of course, be more confident that our predictor is useful the closer its content approaches the actual job content. Thus the predictors near the top of Fig. 4 would, from a practical viewpoint, seem to be very useful because performance on them is so close to performance on the job. Of course, developing job-content-related predictors is sometimes difficult (i.e., for very technical jobs requiring specific skills not possessed by most applicants) and costly, and the other predictors, such as general traits and abilities, are also important determinants of job success.

The selection strategy thus typically reduces to the process of gathering as much relevant, job-related information as possible regarding a job applicant, while considering the cost of developing each additional selection device or predictor, its predictive accuracy, the nature and importance of the job itself, and the relative costs of a sophisticated training versus selection program.

It should be repeated that the selection strategies outlined here, the validity and reliability considerations, and the statistical concepts all also apply to interviews, biographical items, work sampling, simulations, and other predictors or selection devices, as well as to psychological tests, as shown in the figure on page 176. Finally, the *Introduction* of this exercise has concentrated not only on psychological (e.g., pencil-and-paper) tests in its discussions of validity and accuracy, but has concentrated on test-score interpretation rather than test design. The latter, of course, is also a very important issue and must be dealt with as questions for tests are developed from job-analysis data in order to be job-related, and hence relevant and credible, as well as predictive of subsequent job success.

Finally, we close this section on employee selection by stating three basic reasons for doing the best selection job possible. First, we believe it is right and fair to all who may apply for a position in an organization. Second, the organization will benefit in terms of productivity by having the most-capable employees (and, ultimately, consumers will benefit also). Third, by not giving proper attention to selection decisions, an organization opens itself to costly litigation.

PROCEDURE

Overview.   In Part A, you calculate the reliability of tests using sample data provided. In Part B, you assess the validity of a test. Several questions are asked in each part for discussion. The statistical computations to be used in this exercise are explained in the *Appendix* or on the forms themselves.

PART A

STEP 1:   Form 1 contains the test results of a tailor-made test given to a group of machinists. The scores have been divided into odd and even results. You are to apply the split-half method of test reliability to the data and present a brief report on whether or not the test is reliable enough to use as a selection tool. (Hint: assess the probability that your resulting reliability was due to chance.) Place your answers on Form 1.

STEP 2:   There is also a formula to be used with the split-half method that would indicate the number of questions that should be added to a test in order to give a desired level of reliability (see Form 1). You are to calculate the desired number of questions needed on a test to give a reliability of 0.90 and place your answer on Form 1.

TIME: About 35 minutes.

PART B

STEP 3:   After reliability coefficients of tests have been calculated, the tester is often interested in the standard error of measurement (SEM). Because there is always some error involved in testing (i.e., from poor questions, poor conditions, characteristics of the test taker's effort, etc.), we know that the test score a person gets may not be their "true" score—their score if the test, the conditions, etc. were perfect. We often want to know how far away the obtained test score might be from this "true" score and what probability we could assign to the event of the true score being within a certain range around the obtained score. The SEM is a number, based on the variance (σ^2) and the reliability (r) of a test, which gives us the interval around the obtained score in which a "true" score might lie. Because we assume that the errors in a testing situation are randomly distributed throughout the range of test scores, we use the standard normal curve[14] to obtain the probabilities that a "true" score is in an interval defined by the SEM around an obtained score. Since 67 percent of the normal curve lies under plus or minus *one* standard deviation from the mean, we could be 67 percent confident that any true score is within ± 1 SEM from an obtained score. Likewise, we would be 95 percent confident for the interval of ± 2 SEM from an obtained score and 99 percent for the interval of ± 3 SEM from an obtained score.

Form 2 contains the formula for computing the SEM. Using the reliability estimate you obtained in Step 1 above, compute the SEM for the test given to machinists. Then answer the rest of the questions on Form 2 relating to SEM and reliability of tests.

TIME: About 40 minutes.

PART C

STEP 4: Using Form 3 you are to validate a test and critique the validation procedure you are using. Machinists' supervisors have appraised them on a performance-appraisal scale ranging from 0 (lowest performance) to 100 (highest performance). The results of the performance evaluation and scores on a selection test for a group of machinists appear as Form 3. Using this sample data and the information in the *Introduction* and *Appendix*, do the following and place your answers on Form 3:

a) Compute a correlation coefficient for this data;

b) Evaluate the coefficient as to its "appropriateness" or significance and prepare a very brief report that could be used to support or reject the validity of the test for selection purposes;

c) Compute a regression equation for the data, then compute the lowest performance score you would expect with a test score of 128 (at the $p < 0.05$ probability level). Finally, compute the highest performance score you would expect with a test score of 164 (at $p < 0.05$).

TIME: About 60 minutes.

---

[14] See any introductory statistics text for an explanation of the normal curve.

FOR FURTHER READING[15]

American Psychological Association and American Educational Research Association, National Council on Measurement in Education. *Standards for Educational and Psychological Tests.* Washington, D.C.: The American Psychological Association, 1975. (II)

American Psychological Association, *Principles for the Validation and Use of Personnel Selection Procedures.* Washington D.C.: The American Psychological Association, 1975.

Anastasi, A. *Psychological Testing.* 3d ed. New York: Macmillan, 1968. (II)

Ash, D., and L. P. Kroeker. "Personnel Selection, Classification and Placement." *Annual Review of Psychology* 26 (1975): 481–501. (II)

Barrett, R. S. "Gray Areas in Black and White Testing." *Harvard Business Review* 46 (January–February 1968): 92–95. (I)

Bartlett, C. J., and B. S. O'Leary. "A Differential Prediction Model to Moderate the Effects of Heterogeneous Groups in Personnel Selection and Classification." *Personnel Psychology* 22 (1969): 1–17. (II–R)

Bray, D. W., and J. L. Moses. "Personnel Selection." *Annual Review of Psychology* 23 (1972): 545–576. (II)

Buros, O. K., ed. *The Seventh Mental Measurements Yearbook.* Highland Park, New Jersey: Gryphon, 1972. (II)

Byham, W. C., and M. E. Spitzer. *The Law and Personnel Testing.* New York: Amacom, 1971. (I)

Campbell, D. T., and D. W. Fiske. "Convergent and Discriminant Validation by the Multitrait-Multimethod Matrix." *Psychological Bulletin* 56 (1959): 81–105. (II)

Civil Rights Act of 1964, Title VII. (II)

Cronbach, L. J., and G. C. Gleser. *Psychological Tests and Personnel Decisions.* Urbana: University of Illinois Press, 1965. (II)

Cronbach, L. J., and P. E. Meehl. "Construct Validity in Psychological Tests." *Psychological Bulletin* 52 (1955): 281–302. (II–R)

Dick, W., and N. Hagerty. *Topics in Measurement: Reliability and Validity.* New York: McGraw-Hill, 1971. (I)

Dunnette, M. D. "A Modified Model for Test Validation and Selection Research." *Journal of Applied Psychology* 47 (1963): 317–323. (II)

---

[15] See also, *For Further Reading*, Exercise 13.

Equal Employment Opportunity Commission. "Guidelines on Employment Selection Procedures." *Federal Register* 35 (1970): 48–52. (I)

England, G. W., and D. G. Patterson. "Selection and Placement: The Past Ten Years." In H. G. Heneman, L. L. Brown, M. K. Chandler, A. Kahn, H. S. Parnes and G. P. Schultz, eds., *Employment Relations Research.* New York: Harper, 1950, pp. 43–72. (I)

Fincher, C. "Differential Validity and Test Bias." *Personnel Psychology* 28 (1975): 481–500. (II–R)

Fincher, C. "Personnel Testing and the Law." *American Psychologist* 28 (1973): 489–497. (II)

French, W. "Psychological Testing: Some Problems and Solutions." *Personnel Administration* (March–April 1966): 19–24. (I)

Gael, S., D. L. Grant, and R. J. Ritche. "Employment Test Validation for Minority and Nonminority Clerks with Work Sample Criteria." *Journal of Applied Psychology* 60 (1975): 420–426. (II–R)

Ghiselli, E. E. "The Validity of Occupational Aptitude Tests." New York: Wiley, 1966. (II–R)

Gorham, W. A. "Who does the Government Listen To?" Paper presented at the Eighty-Third Annual Convention of the American Psychological Association, 1975. (I)

Gross, A. L., and S. Wen-Lerey. "Defining "Fair" or "Unbiased" Selection Models: A Question of Utilities." *Journal of Applied Psychology* 60, no. 3 (1975): 345–351. (II–R)

Guilford, J. P. "Reliability and Validity of Measures." In J. P. Guilford, *"Psychometric Methods."* New York: McGraw-Hill, 1954, Chap. 14. (II–R)

Guion, R. M. "Open a New Window: Validities, and Values in Psychological Measurement." *American Psychologist* 29 (1974): 287–296. (II)

Guion, R. M. *Personnel Testing.* New York: McGraw-Hill, 1965. (II)

Guion, R. M. "Synthetic Validity in a Small Company: A Demonstration." *Personnel Psychology* 18 (1965): 49–63. (II–R)

Hess, L. R. "Synthetic Validity: A Means of Meeting EEOC Test Validation Requirements." *Training and Development Journal* 27, no. 2 (1973): 48–52. (II–R)

International Personnel Management Association. *Catalogue of Personnel Tests.* Chicago: IPMA, 1975. (I)

Koenig, P. "They Just Changed the Rules on How To Get Ahead. Field Report on Psychological Testing and Job Applicants." *Psychology Today* 8 (June 1974): 87–96+. (I)

Kulhovy, R. W. "Personnel Testing: Validating Selection Instruments." *Personnel* 48 (September–October 1971): 20–24. (I)

Lawshe, C. H., and M. J. Balma. *Principles of Personnel Testing.* New York: McGraw-Hill, 1966. (II)

McNemar, A. "On So-Called Test Bias." *American Psychologist* 30 (1975): 848–851. (II)

Mobley, W. H. "Meeting Government Guidelines on Testing and Selection." *Personnel Administrator* 19, no. 8 (1974): 42–48. (I)

Naylor, J. C., and L. C. Shine. "A Table for Determining the Increase in Mean Criterion Score Obtained by Using a Selection Device." *Journal of Industrial Psychology* 3 (1965): 33–42. (II)

O'Conner, E. J., K. N. Wexley, and R. A. Alexander. "Single-Group Validity: Fact or Fallacy." *JAP* 60, no. 3 (1975): 352–355. (II–R)

O'Leary, L. R. "Fair Employment, Sound Psychometric Practice, and Reality." *American Psychologist* 28 (1973): 147–150. (II)

Osburn, H. G., and W. R. Manese. *How to Install and Validate Employee Selection Techniques.* Washington, D.C.: American Petroleum Institute, 1971. (I)

Punke, H. H. "The Relevance and Broadening Use of Personal Testing." *Labor Law Journal* 25 (March 1974): 173–187. (I)

Rawls, J. E., and D. J. Rawls. "Recent Trends in Management Selection." *Personnel Journal* 53, no. 2 (1974): 104–109. (I)

Robertson, D. E. "Employment Testing and Discrimination." *Personnel Journal* 54, no. 1 (1975): 18–21+. (I)

Sandman, B., and F. Urban. "Formal Testing and the Law." *Labor Law Review*, January 1976. (I)

Schneier, C. E. "Content Validity: The Necessity of a Behavioral Job Description." *Personnel Administrator* 21 (February 1976): 38–44. (I)

Schwartz, D. J. "Federal Government Intervention in Psychological Testing: Is It Here?" Paper presented at 83rd APA Convention, 1975. (II)

Thyne, J. M. *Principles of Examining.* New York: Wiley, 1974. (II)

U.S. Equal Employment Opportunity Commission Guidelines. Washington, D.C.: U.S. Government Printing Office, 1970. (II)

Wallace, S. R. "How High the Validity." *Personnel Psychology* 27 (1974): 397–407. (II)

Walsh, R. J., and L. R. Hess. "The Small Company, EEOC, and Test Validation Alternatives: Do You Know Your Options?" *Personnel Journal* 53, no. 11 (1974): 840–845. (I)

Whyte, W. H. *The Organization Man.* New York: Simon and Schuster, 1956. (I)

Wiener, J., and M. L. Schneiderman. "Use of Job Information as a Criterion in Employment Decisions of Interviewers." *Journal of Applied Psychology* 59 (1974): 699–704. (II–R)

Name _____   Group Number _____

Date _____   Class Section _____   Hour _____   Score _____

PART A

Form 1 Sample Data for Split-Half Reliability Computation

Employee	Odd scores	Even scores
A	90	80
B	85	65
C	84	80
D	83	75
E	81	75
F	95	60
G	92	80
H	94	70
I	93	90
J	98	90
K	97	95
L	97	90
M	60	60
N	66	50
O	68	60
P	70	68
Q	74	70
R	74	36
S	81	75
T	81	80

Split-Half Reliability Formula:

1. First calculate the correlation between the scores on each odd and even item by using the correlation coefficient (*r*) (see *Appendix*).

2. Then put the obtained *r* in the following formula, called the Spearman-Brown formula, which corrects for the size of each of the sets of items being only 1/2 as large as the original test. Since the forty-item total test does not have a reliability double that of the two twenty-item tests (measured by the *r* obtained in Step 1 above), the special Spearman-Brown formula must be used to correct for this fact. The general Spearman-Brown formula for the reliability of a test *n* times as long as a given test is:

$$r_{SB} = \frac{nr_0}{1 + (n - 1)r_0}$$

where r_{SB} = Spearman-Brown, split-half reliability of the original test;

n = ratio of the length of the original test to the length of the tests used to calculate original reliability; and

r_0 = original reliability calculated from two test halves.

Name _____ Group Number _____

Date _____ Class Section _____ Hour _____ Score _____

PART B

Form 2 The Standard Error of Measurement (SEM) and Test Reliability

The computing formula for the SEM of a test is:

$$\text{SEM} = \sigma_0 \sqrt{1 - r},$$

where: σ_0 = standard deviation of a set of scores (square root of variance)

r = reliability estimate

Using both the odd and even test scores of Form 1, calculate the σ_0 then put the Spearman-Brown reliability coefficient r_{SB} and the σ_0 in the formula above to get the SEM.

Computation of the SEM:

Formula for computing the number of test items necessary for a specified level of reliability:

$$N = \frac{R_D (1 - r_{SB})}{r_{SB}(1 - r_D)}$$

where N = total number of questions (items) required (must be multiplied times the present number of items);

r_{SB} = Spearman-Brown split-half reliability; and

r_D = desired reliability level.

Answer the following questions:

1. The Spearman-Brown split-half reliability = _____.

2. The rationale for reliability of test is as follows:

3. The number of test items necessary in order to obtain a reliability of 0.90 = _____.

Answer the following questions:

1. The SEM is _____.
2. For an obtained test score of 98, one could be 67% confident that the "true" score lies between _____ and _____.
3. For an obtained test score of 70, one could be 95% confident that the "true" score lies between _____ and _____.
4. What general factors would seem to influence the reliability of a test?

_____

_____

_____

_____

_____

Name _____   Group Number _____

Date _____   Class Section _____   Hour _____   Score _____

PART C

Form 3 Sample Data for Analysis of the Validity of a Test

Employees	Test scores	Performance rating
A	170	75
B	150	52
C	164	50
D	158	60
E	156	75
F	155	70
G	172	80
H	164	75
I	183	85
J	188	82
K	192	90
L	187	80
M	120	50
N	116	50
O	128	60
P	138	40
Q	144	70
R	110	55
S	156	60
T	161	70

Answer the following questions.

1. The correlation coefficient (or validity coefficient) is: _____.

2. A statement on significance of the coefficient is as follows:

3. The Regression equation is: _____ .

4. The standard error of the estimate is: _____.

5. The cut-off score to insure minimal performance level at 80 is: _____.

EXERCISE 10 APPENDIX

Learning to Use Statistics in Personnel Decision Making*

A basic understanding of a few statistical procedures and concepts enables a personnel administrator to answer any of the following important questions:

1. From what sources are better applicants obtained for specific jobs?

2. Which questions on application blanks are most sensitive in discriminating between good and poor performance; short or long tenure?

3. How well do interview ratings distinguish between high and low job performers?

4. Will the elimination or addition of any particular aspect or phase of the selection process subtract or add significantly to selective effectiveness?

5. How reliable are "tailor-made" tests? How can their reliability be increased?

6. How valid are these tailor-made tests?

7. Do standardized tests enable more valid prediction of job success than tailor-made tests; than subjective judgment?

8. Will maximum and minimum cutoff test scores contribute to more effective job placement?

9. What human-resource needs are required for different levels of production?

10. What personnel data are most sensitive in the forecasting of turnover, low productivity, short tenure?

11. What is the effect of additional training increments on learning curves? On productivity? On job tenure?

12. Are wages internally equitable? How does the company wage curve compare to the community wage curve?

13. Are we paying our managerial and professional personnel in accordance with community salaries based on similar criteria?

14. What is the degree of overlap between the factors on the company-performance or job-evaluation plans?

15. Is a particular policy paying off in terms of improved employee performance?

---

* The statistical materials are adapted with permission from Ceanne Mitchell, Billy Watson, and Otis Lipstreu, *Simplified Statistics* (Boulder, Colorado: Pruett Press, 1964). The critical review of James R. Beatty (School of Business, San Diego State University) is gratefully acknowledged.

Correct answers to these types of questions are not only often required by law, but also provide the rationale for an efficient selection system. Thus the time necessary to learn a few statistical concepts can have very large payoffs. This *Appendix* was prepared to provide a brief introductory overview of the most widely used statistical concepts in personnel selection.

A. Some Definitions and Guidelines for Using Statistics in Personnel Selection

1. When one desires to know the average of any group of items, the *arithmetic mean* can be applied.

2. If, however, one desires to know the *middle* value of a group of items, the *median* is used. (When a group of items contains extreme values at the low or high parts of the distribution, the median is a more meaningful measure than the arithmetic mean for the distribution of items.)

3. The *standard deviation* (*SD*) is used to determine the degree of *dispersion* of values about a mean. Sixty-eight percent of the items will fall within one standard deviation above and below the mean of a group of items when the items within the group approximate a normal distribution. Two standard deviations above and below the mean will include approximately 95 percent of the items; and three standard deviations on either side of the mean will include over 99 percent of the items in the distribution.

4. The *standard error of the mean* (*SEM*) can be used when one is testing the adequacy or representativeness of a sample, since it indicates how far the *sample arithmetic mean* can be (not *is*) away from the *true mean* of the entire population. Hence, it, like all standard error statistics, is a quality control statistic similar to the standard deviation in that one standard error above and below any statistic involves a predictive range of 68 percent; two above and below, 95 percent; and three above and below, 99 percent.

5. The *standard error of the difference* is used to indicate how far the *difference* between *sample means* can be away from the *true difference* between two population means. Hence, it, too, performs a quality-control function.

6. When one wishes to determine whether or not the observed difference between means, percentages, or proportions is due to *chance* or systematic cause, the *t* test is a most useful technique if the sample size is below 25 to 30.

7. To determine the degree of relationship existing between two paired variables—a *correlation*—a product moment coefficient is used. Its range is +1.00 (perfect positive association) to −1.00 (perfect negative correlation). Zero indicates no statistical association.

8. Just as standard error formulas for other statistics have been used for quality-control purposes, so is the *standard error of estimate* (*SEE*) used to determine how far a predicted point *can be* away from the true estimated point for the entire population.

9. The *regression equation* and/or *line* is used to facilitate the prediction of an unknown point or value within one group of items from a particular known point or value within another set of items.

B. *Statistical Formulas*

1. To find the *arithmetic mean of ungrouped information*, which may or may not be arrayed, you:
   a) Add all of the individual items.
   b) Divide the total by the number of individual items.

   These steps are briefly expressed using the symbols below:

   $$AM = \frac{\sum X}{N};$$

   where

   AM = Arithmetic Mean
   $\sum$ = Sum of
   X = Items or test scores, etc.
   N = Total number of items

2. To find the *arithmetic mean* (*AM*) *of grouped data*:
   a) Determine the midpoint of each class interval.
   b) Multiply the midpoint of each class interval by the frequency for that specific class interval.
   c) Add all the products found in Step b.
   d) Divide the total by the number of individual items.

   These steps are expressed by the following formula:

   $$AM = \frac{\sum(f \cdot MP)}{N};$$

   where:

   AM = Arithmetic Mean
   $\sum$ = Sum of
   f = Frequency (number of items in each class interval)
   $\cdot$ = Multiply
   MP = Midpoint of class interval
   N = Total number of items

3. To find the *standard deviation* (*SD*) *of ungrouped data*:
   a) Calculate the arithmetic mean.
   b) Find the difference between each individual item and the AM. (It does not matter whether the difference is a positive or negative value, since the differences are squared in the next step.)
   c) Square each of the differences obtained.
   d) Add these squared values and find their average.
   e) Extract the square root of the resulting number.

   The formula for the standard deviation of ungrouped information is:

   $$SD = \sqrt{\frac{\sum D^2}{N}};$$

   where:

   SD = Standard deviation
   $\sum$ = Sum of
   D^2 = Individual differences squared
   N = Total number of items
   $\sqrt{}$ = Square root sign

4. To calculate the standard deviation (SD) from a frequency distribution:
   a) Find the arithmetic mean.
   b) Find the difference between the midpoint of each class interval and the AM. (It is assumed that the midpoint will represent the average difference of each individual item in the class interval from the AM.)
   c) Square each of the differences obtained.
   d) Multiply the squared results by the frequency for that class interval.
   e) Add the numbers obtained in Step d, and then find the average.
   f) Extract the square root of the average.

   The formula for the standard deviation of grouped data is:

   $$SD = \sqrt{\frac{\sum f(D^2)}{N}};$$

   where:

   SD = Standard deviation
   $\sum$ = Sum of
   f = Frequency of occurrence
   D^2 = Differences squared
   N = Total number of items
   $\sqrt{}$ = Square root sign

5. To find the *standard error of the mean (SEM)*:

Divide the standard deviation of the distribution by the square root of the number of items in the sample.

The formula for the standard error of the mean is:

$$\text{SEM} = \frac{\text{SD}}{\sqrt{N}};$$

where:

$\text{SEM} = $ Standard error of the mean

$\text{SD} = $ Standard deviation

$N = $ Total number of items in the sample

$\sqrt{\ } = $ Square root sign

6. To compute the standard error of the difference (SED):

a) Find the standard error of the mean for each group.
b) Square each standard error of the mean.
c) Add the squared results of Step b.
d) Extract the square root of the resulting number.

Putting these steps into a formula, we have:

$$\text{SED} = \sqrt{\text{SEM}_1{}^2 + \text{SEM}_2{}^2};$$

where:

$\text{SED} = $ Standard error of the difference

$\text{SEM}_1{}^2 = $ Standard error of the mean of group 1 squared

$\text{SEM}_2{}^2 = $ Standard error of the mean of group 2 squared

7. The formula for the *t* test is:

$$(1)\ t = \frac{\text{AM}_1 - \text{AM}_2}{\text{SED}}$$
$$= \frac{D}{\text{SED}};$$
$$(2)\ t = \frac{D}{\text{SED}};$$

Note: For samples of approximately 30 or over, the *t* distribution approaches the *z* distribution.

where:

$t = $ Value of t

$\text{AM}_1 = $ Arithmetic mean of group 1

$\text{AM}_2 = $ Arithmetic mean of group 2

$D = $ Difference between the two arithmetic means

$\text{SED} = $ Standard error of the difference

8. To calculate a *median* (Md) from grouped information:

a) Determine the position of the median value by dividing the total number of items by 2. This will tell you in which class interval the median value will be found.
b) Then, use the following formula:

$$\text{Md} = L + \frac{n_1}{n_2}(i);$$

where:

$\text{Md} = $ Median

$L = $ Lower limit of class interval containing the median value

$n_1 = $ Number of items which must be covered in the median class in order to reach the median item

$n_2 = $ Number of items in the median class itself or the frequency

$i = $ Width of the median class

9. The definitional formula for *Pearson Product Moment Correlation (r)* is:

$$r = \frac{\sum_{i=1}^{n}(X_i - \bar{X})(Y_i - \bar{Y})}{\sqrt{\sum_{i=1}^{n}(X_i - \bar{X})^2 \sum_{i=1}^{n}(Y_i - \bar{Y})^2}}.$$

A computational formula is:

$$r = \frac{N\sum XY - (\sum X)(\sum Y)}{\sqrt{[N\sum X^2 - (\sum X)^2][N\sum Y^2 - (\sum Y)^2]}}.$$

If SD's are computed, a formula is:

$$r = \frac{\frac{\sum XY}{N} - \bar{X}\bar{Y}}{\text{SD}_X \text{SD}_Y};$$

where:

$X = $ Independent variable values

$Y = $ Dependent variable values

$\sum = $ Sum of

$N = $ Total number of items for which there are a pair of scores

$\text{SD}_Y = $ Standard deviation Y variable

$\text{SD}_X = $ Standard deviation X variable

10. The basic formula for calculating the *regression line* is:

$$Y_p = a + b \cdot X;$$

where:

Y_p = A point on the regression line (the "criterion")

a = A measure of the height of the line when $X = 0$

b = The measure of the slope of the line (the coefficient of regression)

X = The known value (the "predictor")

Computational formulae are:

$$b = \frac{N\sum XY - (\sum X)(\sum Y)}{N\sum X^2 - (\sum X)^2};$$

$$a = Y - b_{\bar{x}}.$$

Many of you will recognize $Y_p = a + bX$ as the algebraic formula for computing a simple straight line. In order to locate the line on a graph, the values of a and b must be calculated. The discovery of these values then makes it possible to find either the height of the line or the predicted Y value merely by inserting the appropriate X value in the equation. Since the formula contains two unknown values, a and b, it is technically known as a simultaneous equation. As such, its solution lies in two steps; for the value of either a or b must be found before the remaining value can be calculated.

Thus, we can also begin by finding the value for b by using SD's. This formula for b is:

$$b_{YX} = r\frac{SD_Y}{SD_X}$$

where:

b_{YX} = The value of b for the regression of Y on X

r = The coefficient of correlation

SD_Y = The standard deviation of the Y variable

SD_X = The standard deviation of the X variable

The formula for a is:

$$a_{YX} = AM_Y - b \cdot AM_X$$

where:

a_{YX} = The value of a for the regression of Y on X

AM_Y = The arithmetic mean of the Y variable

b = The b_{YX} value calculated just above

11. The *standard error of the estimate* (SEE) is an estimate of the standard deviation of a set of Y's (criteria) which are conditional on a set of X's (predictors). To calculate the SEE, we assume the SD of all the single Y distributions are the same and then compute this SD based on all the scores in the entire distribution. The formulae are as follows:

$$SEE = SD_X\sqrt{1 - (r)^2}$$ (for predicting Y variables, or criteria from known X variables, or predictors);

$$SEE = SD_Y\sqrt{1 - (r)^2}$$ (for predicting X variables, or predictors from known Y variables, or criteria).

The SEE value allows us to set confidence intervals around a regression line. For example, given any X value, we could predict the corresponding Y value on the basis of the computed regression line. Since we assume that around any such *obtained* Y variable (signified by Y') the *actual* Y values will lie in a normal distribution, the SEE is an estimate of the SD of the original estimate of Y derived from the regression equation. Our estimates of Y' can thus be made within certain limits defined by the value of the SEE and the probability level we choose, indicating our risk of error. If we have chosen the 0.05 level, any estimate of Y' will be within ± 1.96 times the value of SEE from the Y' value obtained from the original regression equation. (This is, of course, because for a normal distribution 0.95 [i.e., $1.00 - 0.05$] of the values lie between plus and minus 1.96 SD's from the population mean—here the obtained regression line.) The SEE allows us to compute *actual* maximum and minimum values, at specified probability levels, from *obtained* values for predictors (or criteria) in a regression requation. This is important since the obtained value from a regression equation is always an *estimate* and we might want to know within what range around the estimate the true value would lie (at different probability levels).

C. Statistical Tables

Table of t Values[a,b]

Degrees of freedom N[c]	Probability Values		
	0.10	0.05	0.01
15	1.75	2.13	2.95
16	1.75	2.12	2.92
17	1.74	2.11	2.90
18	1.73	2.10	2.88
19	1.73	2.09	2.86
20	1.72	2.09	2.84
21	1.72	2.08	2.83
22	1.72	2.07	2.82
23	1.71	2.07	2.81
24	1.71	2.06	2.80
25	1.71	2.06	2.79
26	1.71	2.06	2.78
27	1.70	2.05	2.77
28	1.70	2.05	2.76
29	1.70	2.04	2.76
30	1.70	2.04	2.75
35	1.69	2.03	2.72
40	1.68	2.02	2.71
45	1.68	2.02	2.69
50	1.68	2.01	2.68
60	1.67	2.00	2.66
70	1.67	2.00	2.65
80	1.66	1.99	2.64
90	1.66	1.99	2.63
100	1.66	1.98	2.63
125	1.66	1.98	2.62

[a] Same as critical ratio.
[b] Derived from R.A. Fisher's *Statistical Methods for Research Workers*.
[c] $DF = N_1 - 1 + N_2 - 1$.
Note: This is a two-tail test. For directional probability (one-tail), divide the probability value by 2. Above 50 degrees of freedom this table becomes a z table.

Table of r Values (two variables)

Number of items N	Probability Values*	
	0.05	0.01
10	0.63	0.75
15	0.51	0.63
20	0.44	0.57
25	0.39	0.51
30	0.36	0.46
35	0.33	0.43
40	0.31	0.40
45	0.29	0.38
50	0.28	0.29
75	0.23	0.29
100	0.19	0.25
200	0.15	0.18

* r values listed are statistically significant for the appropriate N and confidence level.

Table of Squares and Square Roots of the Numbers from 1 to 100

Number	Square	Square root	Number	Square	Square root	Number	Square	Square root
1	1	1.000	41	16 81	6.403	81	65 61	9.000
2	4	1.414	42	17 64	6.481	82	67 24	9.055
3	9	1.732	43	18 49	6.557	83	68 89	9.110
4	16	2.000	44	19 36	6.633	84	70 56	9.165
5	25	2.236	45	20 25	6.708	85	72 25	9.220
6	36	2.449	46	21 16	6.782	86	73 96	9.274
7	49	2.646	47	22 09	6.856	87	75 69	9.327
8	64	2.828	48	23 04	6.928	88	77 44	9.381
9	81	3.000	49	24 01	7.000	89	79 21	9.434
10	1 00	3.162	50	25 00	7.071	90	81 00	9.487
11	1 21	3.317	51	26 01	7.141	91	82 81	9.539
12	1 44	3.464	52	27 04	7.211	92	84 64	9.592
13	1 69	3.606	53	28 09	7.280	93	86 49	9.644
14	1 96	3.742	54	29 16	7.348	94	88 36	9.695
15	2 25	3.873	55	30 25	7.416	95	90 25	9.747
16	2 56	4.000	56	31 36	7.483	96	92 16	9.798
17	2 89	4.123	57	32 49	7.550	97	94 09	9.849
18	3 24	4.243	58	33 64	7.616	98	96 04	9.899
19	3 61	4.359	59	34 81	7.681	99	98 01	9.950
20	4 00	4.472	60	36 00	7.746	100	1 00 00	10.000
21	4 41	4.583	61	37 21	7.810			
22	4 84	4.690	62	38 44	7.874			
23	5 29	4.796	63	39 69	7.937			
24	5 76	4.899	64	40 96	8.000			
25	6 25	5.000	65	42 25	8.062			
26	6 76	5.099	66	43 56	8.124			
27	7 29	5.196	67	44 89	8.185			
28	7 84	5.292	68	46 24	8.246			
29	8 41	5.385	69	47 61	8.307			
30	9 00	5.477	70	49 00	8.367			
31	9 61	5.568	71	50 41	8.426			
32	10 24	5.657	72	51 84	8.485			
33	10 89	5.745	73	53 29	8.544			
34	11 56	5.831	74	54 76	8.602			
35	12 25	5.916	75	56 25	8.660			
36	12 96	6.000	76	57 76	8.718			
37	13 69	6.083	77	59 29	8.775			
38	14 44	6.164	78	60 84	8.832			
39	15 21	6.245	79	62 41	8.888			
40	16 00	6.245	80	64 00	8.944			

Name _____ Group Number _____

Date _____ Class Section _____ Hour _____ Score _____

ASSESSMENT OF LEARNING IN PERSONNEL ADMINISTRATION
EXERCISE 10

1. Try to state the purpose of this exercise in one concise sentence.

2. Specifically what did you learn from this exercise (i.e., skills, abilities, and knowledge)?

3. How might your learning influence your role and your duties as a personnel administrator?

4. What is the difference between statistical and practical significance?

5. Why are reliability and validity such important concepts in personnel administration?

6. How could you evaluate an organization's personnel testing program from a legal perspective? From a cost/benefit perspective? What would be the relationship between these two types of evaluations?

7. Additional questions supplied by your implementor:

Section 5
Building Human-Resource Skills:
Training and Development

Once individuals are on the jobs, know what is expected of them (performance appraisal), and have been chosen with *basic* skills and abilities to do the job (selection), their performance may not be satisfactory. Training is one method of improving performance, as is motivation (see Section 6). The purpose of training is to provide or upgrade skills to improve performance, and a diagnosis should be conducted to determine if training is needed to resolve present, or avoid future, performance criticisms.

Training and development, like selection, is an activity made necessary because of the dynamic nature of the environment in which organizations exist, as well as by the changes that occur in its human resources. Both the organization and its members must develop new skills over time to remain viable.

Often, training is required immediately after selection, as a selection strategy may have required that applicants be hired and then trained on the job. Perhaps the training-after-hiring decision was made from an economic standpoint. That is, it was thought to be more economical to train after hiring than to commit funds to selection in order to find those applicants who did not require training. Perhaps such applicants would command too high a wage or salary; perhaps they simply did not exist in the labor market.

An organization may also initiate training in order to add skills, abilities, and knowledge to workers, which may be required as technology changes, as a job's scope changes, or as products or services the organization offers change. Perhaps a worker's performance is deficient and remedial training is called for to improve present job performance. Training is also used to improve future job performance as

workers are prepared, or "groomed" for promotions. This latter situation is often referred to as the development process—an individual or organization's efforts to upgrade skills, ability, or knowledge in order to facilitate the individual's personal growth in any one of a number of areas. Of course, from the organization's standpoint, it is counting on this investment in employee development to be returned in terms of the person's ability to make greater contributions to the organization in the future.

Training is defined most basically as learning; as such, a criterion for effective training is often behavioral change. Whether the organization initiates a skill-development program for entry-level workers operating a punch press or a two-week sensitivity-training session for its top managers as part of an Organization Development (OD) program, behavior change is an ultimate objective. In the former case it could be an increased frequency of punched parts, while in the latter it could be a higher percentage of correct strategic planning decisions.

Training and development are further viewed as a sequential three-phase process. First, training needs must be assessed in order to ascertain whether training would be an effective strategy for the problem at hand (e.g., poor performance, a need for people to fill new positions, etc.). Diagnoses are used to decide who needs training, who would benefit most from training, and what type of training is required (Exercise 11). Second, training-program objectives are established, hopefully in behavioral terms, training-program content is decided on, training methods are chosen and/or designed, and the programs are implemented (Exercise 12). Finally, training programs must be evaluated as to their effectiveness. Here, the vital question becomes: Did job behavior change as a result of the training and/or development program, and was training implemented at the least possible cost? (Exercise 13). While this question is often a difficult and costly one to answer, it is necessary, for it provides the data used to redesign programs or to argue for their continued use.

Exercise 11

ASSESSING TRAINING AND DEVELOPMENT NEEDS

PREVIEW

In order for an organization to grow and remain viable in light of changing conditions in its environment, its human resources must adapt to that dynamic environment by continually adding new skills, knowledge, and abilities to their repertoire. In addition, the organization must maintain an internal pool of human resources capable of moving into higher-level positions. It is through training and development programs that the personnel department is able to help upgrade and add to the existing competence level of an organization's labor pool. However, before any training and development program is begun, a thorough assessment of training needs is required. Here the needs of the organization in terms of human resources are made explicit and the current skill and ability levels of people are measured against these needs. Specific deficiencies found would signify not only *who* needs training, but also exactly what *type* of training is required. These training needs could then be incorporated into a training-program design. In this exercise, data is furnished to enable you to learn how training needs are assessed and to begin to build skill in this vital aspect of the training and development process.

OBJECTIVES

1. To become familiar with the process and purposes of assessing training needs.
2. To build skill in diagnosing workers' deficiencies amenable to training and in making decisions as to who should receive training.

PREMEETING ASSIGNMENT

Read the entire exercise.

INTRODUCTION

Assessing Training and Development Needs: What Information is Required?

Organization, Job, and Person Analyses. If we have defined desired performance in a job and a worker does not perform at the desired level, a possible remedy for the situation may be training. That is, if the person has the basic ability and willingness to do a job well, but has not yet acquired the specific skills necessary, training may be required. Before a training program is designed, several vital tasks must be carried out. First, an analysis of the organization's objectives must be conducted in order to determine its short- and long-run goals and needs. These goals can then be translated into the performance and skill levels of human resources required in order to meet them. Second, a job analysis (see Exercise 3) is conducted to determine the tasks required to meet goals and the salient dimensions of the tasks. Third, current performance levels of workers must be measured by using some type of performance-appraisal technique (see Exercises 4, 5, and 6) in order to pinpoint any deviance from standards and to identify precise areas of performance deficiency. Once these performance measures are made, any deficiencies uncovered are used as the rationale for designing specific training programs to overcome the deficiencies.

Unfortunately, many training programs seem doomed to fail because trainers are more interested in conducting the training program itself than in first assessing the needs of their organizations and the workers. Educators and trainers in organizations often seem to be seduced by such techniques as programed instruction or sensitivity training. Because of sophisticated equipment, fads, or other inducements, trainers are often willing to use techniques before they have determined the needs of their organization and whether the techniques will meet those needs. Thus, a thorough assessment of both the needs of the organization and current levels of performance would be required *before* a training program's content or training method is decided. Only after the specific deficiencies have been uncovered should funds be committed to training.

Crucial Training Decisions and Alternatives. Often, the primary concern of the personnel department is not with assessing the organization to determine goals and objectives, but rather with measuring current performance levels in order to identify deficiencies amenable to training. Through appropriate observation, supervisors' evaluations, and diagnostic testing, we can determine whether performance is substandard and hence if training is needed, whether current employees are capable of benefitting from training, and the specific areas in which they may require training. Also, we need to determine whether current employees with substandard performance can improve their performance through training, or if they should be transferred or terminated to make room for those who can do the job without training. This type of decision involves the weighing of monetary, personal, union contractual, and other considerations. But there are alternatives to training that should always be considered. We must consider: (a) whether changes in job design (see Exercise 15) may bring employee performance up to standard; (b) if new equipment or processes may be a solution; (c) if incentive programs are needed because employees are able, but not *willing* to perform well (see Exercises 16 and 17); (d) if transfer, demotion, layoff, termination, or some other form of discipline (e.g., a pay cut) is required; or (e) if training itself is the best course of action.

Job-knowledge tests, work samples, diagnostic psychological tests, performance-appraisal reports,

union contract provisions, and workers' employment histories provide the kind of information needed to make these decisions. Of course, an assessment of the job and physical environment are also required. For example, one study has shown how tests could accurately identify potential fast and slow workers within one week after beginning work.[1] Thus, those predicted to perform below standard could be trained *before* their poor performance became detrimental to productivity. But perhaps more importantly, through this type of diagnostic work, the organization identified those new workers for whom training was not necessary and thus saved much in training time and cost.

Another actual example of the importance and utility of training needs assessment involved workers using precision measuring instruments.[2] These workers were all sent to a specially designed diagnostic center where their proficiencies in the use of a set of these instruments was measured via work samples (see Exercise 9). Following their assessment, only those workers lacking required skills were sent to training and even these received training only in those particular areas in which they were deficient. Thus, training dollars went to those specific areas where they would be of the most value.

Assessing the Training Needs of New Workers. An instructional or training program must be based on the characteristics of the group to be trained. If the program is intended for those persons already on the job, data from a job analysis, the specification of critical job dimensions, and performance appraisals provide required information. However, if the target population is a new group of employees, performance appraisals would not be available. Thus, it is difficult to assess the performance deficiencies amenable to training of an incoming group of employees. Potential solutions might consist of administering work samples and/or simulations, such as the type discussed in Exercise 9, to hirees, examining employees who have recently been hired for similar jobs, or consulting with organizations that have recently hired similar trainees. The latter procedure must be performed carefully, because small differences between organizations can radically change the makeup of the entering population. Thus, two corporations with the same characteristics, but in differing locales or

[1] See W. McGehee, "Cutting Training Waste," *Personnel Psychology* 1(1948):331–340.
[2] Lawshe, C. H., Jr., R. A. Bolda, and R. L. Brune, "Studies in Management Training Evaluation: I. Scaling Responses to Human Relations Training Cases," *Journal of Applied Psychology* 42(1958):396–398.

with different reputations, may draw significantly different employees with dissimilar training needs.

But assessment of training needs of new hirees can still be made by allowing them to perform on the job for a short period of time and then assessing deficiencies, and/or by inferring from selection data regarding their need for training. For example, amount of previous experience and formal education might indicate that, if hired, a new worker would require some training. Of course, the remedy in these cases could also be one of better selection. An organization might decide that rather than hire people who seem minimally qualified, assess their training needs, and train them soon after hiring, they should improve selection procedures in order to attempt to select persons who do not require training. This latter strategy is adopted in selection for upper-level organizational positions more often than in lower-level positions. We would thus probably expect to select a vice-president who does not require much formal training, but to select clerks or maintenance persons who do. A further consideration in regard to selection versus training strategies obviously includes the supply of qualified labor in the geographical area in which an organization can attract persons.

An analysis of specific training needs is critical—training-program objectives, design, methods, cost, and time frame depend on such an assessment. If organizations are to expect a quick return on their training expenditures, they must know who they are training and why they are being trained. A careful assessment of training needs, backed by a thorough job analysis and performance-appraisal system, provide such information.

PROCEDURE

Overview. You are asked to review both a training program and eight workers' performance records. Assumptions about training needs and a set of selection criteria for trainees entering a training program are then developed. Next, the candidates are assessed as to their potential to benefit from the training program and the candidates who are thought to benefit most from the training program are identified.

PART A

STEP 1: Divide into small groups. Review the outline of the "Success in Middle Management" training program (Form 1), as well as the information about the middle-management position given in Form 2. Then, using Form 3, write down both the assumptions you make about what successful job performance is and those skills needed by persons in order to be successful in the middle-management job. For example, does the middle manager need to write many reports? If so, an assumption you would make would be that report writing is a prerequisite for successful performance.

STEP 2: Next, determine a set of selection criteria for prospective trainees which would help you decide who should be trained. For example, one such criterion could be that anyone with three years or less of experience could not be considered for training. Put your list of criteria on Form 3. You will probably want to look over the information about the job given in Form 2, the training program outline (Form 1), and the information about prospective trainees (Forms 4–11) before you develop the criteria.

TIME: About 40 minutes.

PART B

STEP 3: In Forms 4–11 you are given fact sheets on eight employees who have been recommended by their superior for training for the middle-management position described in Form 2. Consider each of these candidates and make decisions as to whether or not each should attend the training program described in Form 1. The two week program (trainees fly home for the weekend) will cost $550 per week, plus expenses, or a total of about $1,850 per person. The budget will permit only *three* of the eight persons to attend at this time.

The training program is being conducted by a well-known management group (Training Specialists, Inc.) in a resort/retreat setting. There will be extensive use of many types of techniques, including an assessment center. Each participant will also receive a review of his or her performance from the training-program committee. Your organization has used the program in the past and the participants have been most enthusiastic about it. In fact, the "rumor mill" indicates that entry into this program is almost a sure step to the top.

Make a decision as to whether or not to send each of the eight candidates to the training program and provide the reasons for your decisions on Forms 4–11. Assume you will have to present your reasons to each of the eight candidates and to their superiors in a meeting to be scheduled later. Your written rationale (using the bottom of each candidate's fact sheet as a worksheet for your decision making) will also be placed in the candidate's personnel file. Use your assumptions and selection criteria from Form 3 as you make the decisions. Note what additional information, if any, you would require before making this decision, but make the decision on the basis of the information presented. Remember that only three people can attend the program. Choose an alternate in case one of the candidates cannot attend due to illness, family matters, etc. Recommend a different type of training for those candidates whom you feel could benefit from training, but not from the program described here. After you have made your decisions, fill out Form 12 completely by indicating each chosen candidate's name, a rationale for the choice, any alternate type of training needed, and any additional information you would have liked to have had in order to facilitate your diagnosis of training needs.

TIME: About 50 minutes.

FOR FURTHER READING

Argyris, C. *Intervention Theory and Method.* Reading, Mass.: Addison-Wesley, 1970. (II)

Bass, B. M., and J. A. Vaughan. *Training in Industry: The Management of Learning.* Belmont, Cal.: Wadsworth, 1966, Chap. 6. (II)

Beatty, R. W. "Personnel Systems and Human Performance." *Personnel Journal* 52 (1973): 307–312. (I)

Bennis, W. G. *Nature of Organization Development.* Reading, Mass.: Addison-Wesley, 1969. (I)

Berg, I. *Education and Jobs: The Great Training Robbery.* New York: Praeger, 1970. (I)

Blake, R. R., and J. S. Mouton. *Corporate Excellence through Grid Organization Development.* Houston: Gulf, 1964. (I)

Brown, F. B., and K. R. Wedel. *Assessing Training Needs.* Washington D.C.: Washington National Training and Development Service Press, 1974. (I)

Cantalanollo, R. F., and D. L. Kirkpatrick. "Evaluating Training Programs—The State of the Art." *Training and Development Journal* 20, no. 8 (1966): 38–44. (I)

Fordyce, J. K., and R. Weil. *Managing with People.* Reading, Mass.: Addison-Wesley, 1971. (I)

French, W., and C. Bell. *Organizational Development.* Englewood, Cliffs, New Jersey: Prentice-Hall, 1973. (I)

Gallegos, R. C., and J. G. Phelan. "Using Behavioral Objectives in Industrial Training." *Training and Development Journal* 28, no. 4 (April 1974): 42–48. (I)

Gill, T. W. "The Training Forecast: How to Make It—How to Use It." *Training in Business and Industry* 3, no. 11 (1966): 34–35+. (I)

Gordon, M. E. "Planning Training Activity." *Training and Development Journal* 27, no. 1 (1973): 3–6. (I)

Hautaluoma, J. E., and J. F. Gavin. "Effects of Organizational Diagnosis and Intervention on Blue-Collar 'Blues'." *Journal of Applied Behavioral Science* 11 (1975): 475–496. (II)

Johnson, R. B. "Determining Training Needs." In R. L. Craig and L. R. Bittel, eds., *Training and Development Handbook.* New York: McGraw-Hill, 1967, Chap. 2. (I)

Lester, R. I. "Training Research: Identification of Training Needs." *Personnel Journal* 52, no. 3 (1973): 180–183. (I)

Levinson, H. et al. *Diagnosing Organizations.* Cambridge, Mass.: Harvard University Press, 1972. (II)

Lynton, R. P., and U. Pareek. *Training for Development.* Homewood, Ill.: Irwin, 1967. (I)

Mager, R. *Preparing Objectives for Programmed Instruction.* San Francisco: Fearon, 1962. (I)

Margulies, N., and J. Wallace. *Organizational Change.* Glenview, Ill.: Scott Foresman, 1973. (I)

McGehee, W., and P. W. Thayer. *Training in Business and Industry.* New York: Wiley, 1961. (I)

Morgan, C. P., C. E. Schneier, and R. W. Beatty. "Diagnosing Organizations: New Fad or New Technology in Management Consulting?" *Proceedings of the Thirty-Fourth Annual Meeting of the Academy of Management,* Seattle, 1974 (abstract). (II)

O'Reilly, A. "What Value Is Job Analysis in Training?" *Personnel Review* (Great Britain) 2, no. 3 (1973): 50–60. (I)

Page, D. "Identifying the Costs and Benefits of Training." *Personnel Practice Bulletin* (Australia) 28, no. 3 (September 1972): 222–234. (I)

Rose, H. C. "A Plan for Training Evaluation." *Training and Development Journal* 22, no. 5 (1968): 38–51. (I)

Tracey, W. R. *Designing Training and Development Systems.* New York: American Management Association, 1971. (I)

U.S. Civil Service Commission. *Assessing and Reporting Training Needs and Progress.* Personnel Methods Series No. 3, December 1961, pp. 6–28. Washington: U.S. Government Printing Office, 1961. (I)

Warren, M. W. *Training for Results.* Reading, Mass.: Addison-Wesley, 1969. (I)

Wheeler, E. A. "Economic Considerations for Industrial Training." *Training and Development Journal* 21, no. 1 (1969): 14–19. (I)

PART A

Form 1 Training Program Outline for the Course Offered by Training Specialists, Inc. Entitled "Success in Middle Management: An Intensive Training Program for Managers"

PROGRAM OUTLINE

I. *Management Techniques*
- **The Art of Management**
  What is Management?
  Roles of a Manager

- **Planning and Organizing Your Work**
  Planning
      Setting objectives
      Developing a strategy
  Organization
      Principles of organization
      Line vs. staff
      Formal vs. informal

- **Managing Your Time and Delegating Your Work**
  Time
      Cost of poor time management
      Guidelines for good time management
  Delegation
      Factors causing delegation problems
      How to make delegation work

- **Standards of Performance**
  Definition of Standards
  Types of Standards
      Positive
      Negative

- **Performance Appraisal—An Aid to Control**
  Key Questions which Require Answers
  Tools and Techniques of Effective Appraisal

- **The Making of a Decision**

- **Motivation and the Human Side of Management**
  Understanding Human Behavior
  Developing Employee Attitudes
  Motivational Needs of Today's Employees

- **Elements of Effective Communications**
  Written vs. Verbal
  Barriers to Effective Communication

- **How to Further Yourself as a Manager**
  Developing Self-Direction
  Is There a Formula?

- **Union Management Relations**

II. *Special Topics in Operations Analysis*
- **Production Scheduling**
- **Production Standards and Quotas**
- **Establishing a General Maintenance Policy**
- **Inventory Control**
- **Inspection Systems**
- **The Occupational Safety and Health Act (OSHA)**

PART A

Form 2 Middle-Management Position Information

This job is one in a medium-sized publishing and printing organization. There are about thirty (upper) middle managers typically supervising about fifty people each and reporting to vice presidents. They are often plant or division managers. The managers are almost exclusively concerned with the administrative, technical, and manufacturing aspects of the organization. The journalists, writers, editors, and salespersons are separated administratively from these managers. It is a very responsible job, typically one most managers in the organization aspire to, and commands a good salary and excellent benefits, including stock options. These positions are the training ground for those few who reach top management. The middle managers prepare budgets, hire and fire subordinates, supervise other managers, including professional people, and develop new administrative or operating procedures and/or new products. They also develop policies and plans and see to it that the plans are implemented.

Since many of the departments, divisions, or plants operate as "profit centers," these managers would be responsible for profit and cost of their units and for making most strategic decisions regarding production scheduling and standards. A few different unions (e.g., typesetters) are represented, but their contracts with the company are settled centrally, not on a plant-by-plant or divisional basis.

The managers have varied backgrounds and amount of experience. The organization sometimes promotes those young people who show great promise to this position quite early in their careers. However, for those who fail to reach top management positions after being promoted, there is a good chance of "early retirement." Turnover is also high in these positions and they are considered to be quite stress-producing. They typically mean relocation, often in small towns or cities. The move back to corporate headquarters, if it is made, of course involves another relocation to a major East Coast city.

Name _____ Group Number _____

Date _____ Class Section _____ Hour _____ Score _____

PART A

Form 3 Assumptions and Criteria for Selection to the "Success in Middle Management Program"

1. *Basic Assumptions about Training Needs and Job Performance.* List below some specific skills, abilities, and/or knowledge you are assuming to be required in order to be successful at the job described in Form 2. This list will better enable you to assess potential candidates' readiness for training.

   1.

   2.

   3.

   4.

   5.

   6.

   7.

   8.

   9.

   10.

2. *Criteria for Selection to Training Program.* List below specific qualifications you feel candidates to be selected for the course must possess. These may include previous work experience, education, past performance, personal qualities, etc.

   1.

   2.

   3.

   4.

   5.

   6.

   7.

   8.

   9.

   10.

PART B

Form 4 Fact Sheets for Prospective Trainees

Worker No. 1

Name: Sam Horn

Present job: Credit manager and assistant to finance director

Number of subordinates: 6

Years in present job: 2

Years in managerial position: 3

Years with the organization: 5

Age: 38

Education: B.A. in finance

Performance evaluation: Overall given a "very good" (5th level of five steps).
Rated high in planning, flexibility, motivating others, and
oral communication

Test scores (based on company norms): High in "initiating structure": (LOQ)*.
Medium to high in "consideration": (LOQ)*.
Very high in intelligence.

Assessment center report: Excellent in budgeting, planning, organization, and coordination.
Low on creativity, leadership and delegation.

Aspiration level: Wants to be president of the company.

Decision: _____ send _____ not send

Reasons:

Alternative type of training recommended:

Other information desired:

---

* Note: The LOQ (Leadership Opinion Questionnaire) is a widely used instrument to measure leadership style. Initiating structure refers to the degree to which a leader feels it important to structure work and tasks for subordinates and consideration refers to the degree to which a leader feels it is important to show warmth, empathy, or support for subordinates.

PART B

Form 5 Fact Sheets for Prospective Trainees

Worker No. 2

Name: Joyce Juice

Present job: Assistant personnel director

Number of subordinates: 51

Years in present job: 4

Years in managerial position: 8

Years with the organization: 15

Age: 39

Education: Business College plus 92 university hours, still working on
    degree in business management.

Performance evaluation: 94 of 100
    High in interpersonal skills, motivation of others, problem solving;
    Lowest on coordination and organization.

Test scores: (based on company norms) Typing:105 wpm
    Intelligence:upper 1/3
    Consideration:top 10%
    Initiating structure:lowest 25%

Assessment center report: None available (was ill, has been rescheduled).

Aspiration level: Has decided she wants to go as far as she can.

Decision: ____ send   ____ not send

Reasons:

Alternative type of training recommended:

Other information desired:

PART B

Form 6 Fact Sheets for Prospective Trainees

Worker No. 3

Name: Jack Hoerner

Present job: Assistant director of wage, salary, benefit, and incentive
    system administration

Number of subordinates: 17

Years in present job: 5

Years in managerial position: 5

Years with the organization: 15

Age: 46

Education: High school, plus evening accounting courses (about 21 hours)

Performance evaluation: "Above average"
    Lowest rating in interpersonal skills, delegating, and risk taking.
    High on accuracy and control in meeting schedules.

Test scores: (based on company norms) Average on intelligence.
    High on initiating structure.
    Low on consideration.

Assessment center report: Declined to attend the last two times he was asked.
    Reason given: did not have time, his job kept him too busy.

Aspiration level: Wants to move up in the accounting section. Feels he
    is ready to move. Says he will definitely attend the next assess-
    ment center.

Decision: ____ send ____ not send

Reasons:

Alternative type of training recommended:

Other information desired:

PART B

Form 7 Fact Sheets for Prospective Trainees

Worker No. 4

Name: Edgar Everlasting

Present job: Sales manager, Western United States

Number of subordinates: 18

Years in present job: 5

Years in managerial position: 15

Years with the organization: 30 (all in sales)

Age: 56

Education: B.A. in industrial engineering

Performance evaluation: His salespersons have increased volume markedly
   in the last four years; subordinates report him as "good to work with."

Test scores: (based on company norms) High in intelligence.

Assessment center report: Never asked to attend by superiors.

Aspiration level: Wants to move as fast as he can in the years he has
   left with the company. Has a son who is ready for college.

_____

Decision: ____ send   ____ not send

Reasons:

Alternative type of training recommended:

Other information desired:

PART B

Form 8 Fact Sheets for Prospective Trainees

Worker No. 5

Name: Lawrence A. Rabia

Present job: Production manager; assistant plant manager

Number of subordinates: 32

Years in present job: 3

Years in managerial position: 4

Years with the organization: 5

Age: 28

Education: M.B.A. in management science

Performance evaluation: High on scheduling, organizing material requests,
   efficiency and timeliness.
   Low on interpersonal skills, team work, delegation, oral communication.
   Has had severe absenteeism and turnover among subordinates.

Test scores: (based on company norms) <u>Very</u> high in intelligence.
   <u>Very</u> high on initiating structure.
   Medium in consideration.
   <u>Very</u> high need for achievement.

Assessment center report: Excellent in planning and organization.
   Low in sensitivity, oral communication, flexibility.

Aspiration level: Wants to go to the top, fast!

Decision: ____ send   ____ not send

Reasons:

Alternative type of training recommended:

Other information desired:

PART B

Form 9 Fact Sheets for Prospective Trainees

Worker No. 6

Name: Alice Reddy

Present job: Assistant chief corporate council

Number of subordinates: 16

Years in present job: 4

Years in managerial position: 5

Years with the organization: 5

Age: 34

Education: J.D.; masters degree in tax law

Performance evaluation: Very good in most catagories.
   High in organization, communication, and flexibility.
   Average in planning.
   Average in judgment.
   Low in stress tolerance.

Test scores: (based on company norms) High in need for achievement.
   High in intelligence.
   High in consideration.
   Average in initiating structure.

Assessment center report: Excellent in sensitivity, stress tolerance, flexibility,
   creativity.
   Average in planning and organization.

Aspiration level: Wants to assume positions of considerable authority;
   <u>very</u> career oriented and professional.

Decision: ____ send   ____ not send

Reasons:

Alternative type of training recommended:

Other information desired:

PART B

Form 10 Fact Sheets for Prospective Trainees

Worker No. 7

Name: Helen O'Cool

Present job: Advertising manager; chief of layout and product design

Number of subordinates: 13

Years in present job: 2

Years in managerial position: 3

Years with the organization: 8

Age: 36

Education: B.A., advertising; M.F.A., drawing; M.B.A., marketing

Performance evaluation: Very good on creativity, planning, organization, communication.
    Average in delegation.
    Low on budgeting, team work.

Test scores: (based on company norms) High in intelligence.
    High in initiating structure.
    Low in consideration.

Assessment center report: High in risk taking, planning, and organization.
    Average to low in flexibility, stress tolerance, problem analysis,
    sensitivity.

Aspiration level: She feels she is long past consideration for promotion; quite
    dissatisfied with her progress to date.

Decision: ____ send   ____ not send

Reasons:

Alternative type of training recommended:

Other information desired:

PART B

Form 11 Fact Sheets for Prospective Trainees

Worker No. 8

Name: Hercule P. Rowe

Present job: Assistant to Vice President of Manufacturing

Number of subordinates: 22

Years in present job: 5

Years in managerial position: 9

Years with the organization: 12

Age: 33

Education: B.A. in English; M.B.A. in management science.

Performance evaluation: High in interpersonal skills, working with others, communication, flexibility, delegation.
Average in planning and organization.
Low in control and budgeting.

Test scores: (based on company norms) High in consideration.
High in initiating structure.
Above average in intelligence.

Assessment center report: Excellent in sensitivity and creativity.
High in flexibility, energy, risk taking, decision making, independence.
Average in planning and organization.

Aspiration level: Wants to make V.P. in five years.

Decision: _____ send   _____ not send

Reasons:

Alternative type of training recommended:

Other information desired:

Name _____ Group Number _____

Date _____ Class Section _____ Hour _____ Score _____

PART B

Form 12 Summary of Training Needs Assessment

Worker	Chosen to attend training	Not chosen to attend training	Concise rationale for choice to send or not send	Alternate training required or recommended for candidate	Further information designed to facilitate diagnosis of training needs
1. Sam Horn					
2. Joyce Juice					
3. Jack Hoerner					
4. Edgar Everlasting					
5. Lawrence A. Rabia					
6. Alice Reddy					
7. Helen O'Cool					
8. Hercule P. Rowe					

Name _____ Group Number _____

Date _____ Class Section _____ Hour _____ Score _____

ASSESSMENT OF LEARNING IN PERSONNEL ADMINISTRATION
EXERCISE 11

1. Try to state the purpose of this exercise in one concise sentence.

2. Specifically what did you learn from this exercise (i.e., skills, abilities, and knowledge)?

3. How might your learning influence your role and your duties as a personnel administrator?

4. What skills, abilities, and knowledge must one possess in order to be successful at assessment of training needs?

5. What would the major differences be between assessing training needs at entry-level, versus managerial-level, jobs?

6. How are job analyses, performance appraisal, and human-resource planning related to assessment of training needs?

7. Additional questions given by your implementor:

Exercise 12

DESIGNING AND IMPLEMENTING TRAINING AND DEVELOPMENT PROGRAMS

PREVIEW

Once training needs have been assessed, those responsible for training still have many important decisions to make. Among these are the methods to be used in training (e.g., lecture, on-the-job coaching, etc.) the length of the program, who the trainers shall be and how they will be trained, and whether training will take place in the organization or at an external site. These decisions can all be grouped under the category of training program design and implementation considerations. In this exercise various methods used to train people in organizations are explored. An introduction to training-program procedures, methods, and objectives is given, and practice in writing behavioral training objectives is provided. Two simple tasks are used to demonstrate the relative effectiveness of two different training methods. A complete training program for disadvantaged and/or entry-level workers is designed.

OBJECTIVES

1. To increase your awareness of the many types of training methods and their relative strengths and weaknesses.
2. To learn how to identify and write behavioral training objectives and specific target training behaviors.
3. To build skill in training and/or teaching others and evaluating their learning.
4. To build skill in designing effective training programs for entry-level jobs.

PREMEETING ASSIGNMENT

Read the *Introduction* to the exercise and the *Procedure*. Do *not* read beyond Form 3 until told to do so by the implementor.

INTRODUCTION

Training and Development Program Design and Training Method Considerations

Why Training Is Important. Training, defined most basically, is simply a program to facilitate learning in organizations. While many training programs in organizations may not appear to be similar to classrooms or schools where we assume learning traditionally takes place, their basic objective is the same: to teach or to transmit information, to build skills and abilities, and to change behavior.

Training has become an even more important organization activity in the last few decades. One reason is that the many advances in technology have greatly influenced the work people do in organizations. Because more jobs have become automated and specialized and because very sophisticated machinery is now often used, workers must possess very specific knowledge and abilities to perform their jobs. Further, as organizations become more complex, jobs become more specialized at all organizational levels. Also, as organizations become more interested in providing a career orientation for their members, skills, ability, and knowledge must be added periodically to members' repertoires through formal training programs to enable individuals to assume higher-level positions as their careers advance. Training and development are vital due to the consequences of age and obsolescence. Rapid changes in technology cause current skills to be outdated and advances in age can lead to obsolescence unless skills are continually updated through development programs. Finally, to achieve success in many jobs, experience alone is no longer sufficient. As organizations develop their own unique procedures and work processes, employees often must be retrained to perform the same job in a new organization that they held in a previous one. This fact, coupled with the high degree of mobility in much of the labor market, makes training increasingly important.

Training versus Selection. As noted in Exercise 11, in many cases organizations have a choice between providing training to adequately prepare an employee for a position after hiring or to hire a person who already possesses the skill or ability to perform well. In the latter case, initial training may not be necessary. The choice is thus often between selection and training. Each endeavor has obvious costs and many considerations enter into the organization's decision. Among these considerations would be the type of job in question, the composition of the available labor market, and the relative sophistication and effectiveness of existing training and selection programs. Typically, organizations select many entry-level employees with rudimentary selection systems and then train them with inhouse training programs to prepare them for employment. But as we proceed up the hierarchy to higher levels, sophisticated selection systems are more common and initial formal training less common.

Training as Learning. Organizations do use some training at most job levels to add to or improve members' skills and abilities. Often programs are quite formal and structured, such as entry-level skill training, training for clerical positions, or management training for new college graduates. At other times training is quite unstructured, meant to help participants become aware of their own behavior and its impact on others in groups.[1] If training is essen-

tially learning, even the most informal learning processes—such as a colleague informing someone of the whereabouts of the cafeteria or which secretary not to use for dictation—are essentially training. Discovering new work methods through one's own mistakes or self-study programs could also be considered training. As organizations and job content change and as people aspire to move ahead in organizations, exposing oneself to the proper experience (and people) and adding skills, abilities, and knowledge are important training considerations in anyone's career plans.

Behavioral Objectives. Learning can be defined as "a relatively permanent change in behavior that occurs as a result of practice or experience."[2] The emphasis on *behavioral change* is the vital aspect of this definition. In formal organizational training programs, we are interested in facilitating behavioral change—changing poor performance to good performance or adding certain behaviors and perhaps removing others. The key question to ask when considering what a training program's content should be is: What should the trainee be able to *do* upon completion of the program? Thus, training-program designers must set *behavioral objectives* for their programs. These objectives would specify what trainees would be able to do if training were successful.

Behavioral objectives help planners focus on the end result of training: behavioral change. Even though the aim of many programs is to transmit information to the trainees (e.g., by lectures and reading programs), the ultimate purpose of even this training is to change trainee behavior on the job as a result of the exposure to new information. Of course, at higher levels of organizations, the exact changes in behavior desired of trainees may be difficult to pinpoint, as jobs are unprogrammed and thus identification of desired job behaviors is difficult and time consuming. For example, we may not always be sure exactly what behaviors we would like managers to change as a result of a seminar on human-relations training. Analysis can produce specific behavioral objectives, even at this level (e.g., increase "helping" behaviors or decrease "authoritarian" behaviors).

Transfer of Training. If behavioral objectives are set prior to training and if these objectives are similar to those behaviors actually performed on the job, transfer of learning from training environment to job environment is more easily facilitated. Of course,

[1] See, for example, R. T. Golembiewski and A. Blumberg, eds., *Sensitivity Training and the Laboratory Approach* (Ithaca, Ill.: Peacock, 1970).

[2] B. M. Bass and A. A. Vaughan, *Training in Industry: The Management of Learning* (Belmont, Cal.: Wadsworth, 1966), p. 8.

learning is transferred most readily by designing a training program that teaches behaviors identical to those required in the job—that is, if report writing is required on the job, training would attempt to build skill in report writing. Transfer is also facilitated by training for understanding of principles; after training, these principles can be applied to actual job situations.

Transfer is further aided if what is learned in training is reinforced on the job. For example, if workers had just finished a training program that taught them how to be more assertive and offered suggestions on how to perform their jobs better, they may not be able to transfer this learning to the job if their supervisor dictates job procedure and allows no deviance. Clearly, what was learned in training will not be reinforced on the job; new behaviors cannot realistically be transferred. In these cases, training efforts obviously are very inefficient and indicate an improper assessment. That is, the supervisor may be the one who needs training!

Training and Learning Theory. Because training is essentially learning, much learning research and theory is relevant for those designing training programs. Learning theory and research has much to offer trainers regarding the following aspects of learning: (1) the structure of the training environment, (2) the role of the teacher/trainer, (3) the influence of the individual characteristics of the trainee on learning, (4) basic human learning processes, (5) reinforcement and punishment, (6) retention and transfer of learning, and (7) the role of practice in learning.[3] Trainers can become familiar with this research as they develop training course designs and incorporate recommendations based on its findings.

Some of the specific learning principles or concepts which are important considerations in training are:

1. *Practice:* Practice in training is simply performing the training tasks after learning in order to improve proficiency. Practice should be taken seriously by trainees and inducements to motivate trainees may improve the benefits of practice. Practice should typically be distributed over periods of time, rather than be "massed" at one time and should include requiring trainees to make responses to stimuli other than those encountered in training, so as to "generalize" their learning.

2. *Feedback:* Feedback, or the knowledge of results of one's effort, is vital in training. Feedback can be positive or negative, but trainees need to know where they stand and whether or not they are on the right track. Tests, programmed learning, evaluations of trainees by trainers, and observing one's own performance (i.e., by videotape) provide feedback.[4]

3. *Reinforcement:* In operant learning theory, reinforcement is the change in one's environment, or a consequence of behavior, which strengthens the probability of the future occurrence of the behavior that produced the reinforcer. For example, if performing a new task correctly (behavior) produces verbal praise from a trainer, the correct performance may be associated with the (pleasant) outcome and perhaps occur in the future, if the verbal praise was rewarding to the person receiving it. Among the many outcomes of behavior occurring in organizations are recognition, money, verbal praise, grades, prizes, and successful completion of the training itself.[5]

4. *Shaping behavior:* Behavior shaping refers to the selective reinforcement of successively approximate performances of a target behavior until the target is duplicated. For example, if a certain task is to be learned, it can be broken into small component behaviors. Each of these is reinforced when it is observed as the trainees come closer and closer to the total completion of the task, until they are finally able to complete the task. In this way, behaviors not previously in one's repertoire can be added to existing behaviors.[6]

Obviously, many other relevant issues in learning are also vital to training. Among these are punishment, schedules of reinforcement, verbalization of learning, testing, retention and transfer, and the role of the learning environment. The point for trainers and personnel administrators designing training programs is that training *is* learning. Thus, what we know about how people learn should be incorporated into training programs. As a start, training programs could be designed which rely on positive reinforcement, allow for practice at proper intervals, break complex tasks into smaller components used as inter-

[3] See C. E. Schneier, "Training and Development Programs: What Learning Theory and Research Have to Offer," *Personnel Journal* 53 (1974): 288–293, 300.

[4] See C. P. Latham and J. J. Baldes, "The Practical Significance of Locks's Theory of Goal Setting," *Journal of Applied Psychology* 60 (1975): 122–124.

[5] See Exercise 16 for a more thorough discussion of reinforcement.

[6] C. E. Schneier, "Behavior Modification in Management: A Review and Critique," *Academy of Management Journal* 17 (1974): 528–548.

mediate learning goals, assess and facilitate trainee interest and motivation, and so on.

Training Methods. Many methods can be employed in training programs to facilitate learning. At the managerial level, these have been grouped into information-processing methods, simulation methods, and on-the-job methods.[7] Each category contains several specific methods, including the following:

Information-Processing
lecture
conference
t-group
laboratory training
observation
closed-circuit TV
programmed instruction
correspondence courses
motion pictures
reading lists

Simulation
cases
incidents
role playing
business games
in-baskets

On-the-Job
job rotation
committee assignments or Junior Boards
on-the-job coaching
feedback from performance appraisal
apprenticeships

Obviously, some methods are more time consuming, costly, and appropriate for certain jobs than others. Therefore, how does a training-program designer choose a training method from this large list?

Some of the factors that signal the use of one method over others are the training objectives, trainee characteristics, trainer skill, cost, time, and nature of the job. In addition, the type of learning that will take place (e.g., concept learning, rule learning, problem-solving) would determine the type of method to be chosen. Clearly, a sensitivity-training group or a week-long conference may not be appropriate for a group of unskilled laborers learning simple mainte-nance jobs—on-the-job coaching may be applicable here. Job rotation, in which some time is spent learning several jobs, could be useful for the young management trainee. Programmed instruction has

been found quite effective for learning a complex set of rules or procedures.[8]

Each of the three general types of training methods listed above has advantages as well as limitations. For example, on-the-job methods are usually inexpensive, as they require no special personnel equipment or space. They are also practical, offer flexibility and control to the organization, and allow for practice. Off-the-job methods eliminate the pressures and restrictions of the work environment. However, transfer of learning is often difficult to assess with these methods.

The Training-Program Designer's Task. The trainers or training-program designers thus have a large task. They must first assess training needs, then formulate behavioral objectives for the training program. Next, they must consider such operating constraints as time, space, and physical and human resources. Their selection of a training method would depend on such factors as the nature of trainer, trainees, and the job. Personnel administrators must also decide, in conjunction with others close to the job, the relative amount of organizational time, energy, and money that should be given to training as opposed to selection. Here other variables, such as labor-market composition, must be taken into account. Administrators must determine when to train—before the job begins, early in the job, periodically as additional skills are needed, and/or at promotion decision time? Clearly, with a task as multifaceted as this, no easy answers or guidelines can be realistically offered. Careful thought, analysis, and learning from experience is required.

Training-program design is influenced by personnel programs in addition to training. Designing training hinges on accurate job analyses to pinpoint job performance, on human-resource planning estimates to assess future human-resource needs, on selection systems to funnel qualified hirees into training programs, and/or on motivation programs that enable employees to see career opportunities in the organization and thus acquire skills and abilities necessary for promotion. In turn, training influences other personnel programs as well. For example, a successful and practical training program removes some pressure from recruitment and selection.

PROCEDURE

Overview. First, you will practice identifying behavioral training objectives and specific target training

[7] J. P. Campbell, M. D. Dunnette, E. E. Lawler, and K. Weick, *Management Behavior, Performance, and Effectiveness* (New York: McGraw-Hill, 1970), Chap. 10.

[8] See S. J. Carroll, F. T. Paine, and J. J. Ivancevich. "The Relative Effectiveness of Training Methods: Expert Opinion and Research." *Personnel Psychology* 25 (1972): 495–509.

objectives for a few common jobs. Next, simple tasks are used to compare the effectiveness of two different training methods: lecture and on-the-job coaching. Finally, you are asked to design a training program for disadvantaged and/or entry-level workers in a manufacturing company.

PART A

STEP 1: Think about the five jobs listed on Form 1 and how you could train someone to perform them. In the second column of the form write at least three *general* behavioral training objectives for each job. These are duties or activities job incumbents are required to perform which may require training. They are the end result of a training program—what the trainee should be able to *do* when finished with training. An example for the job of bank teller could be "to operate the computerized savings-account balance system." In column three of Form 1, list at least three *specific* target training behaviors for each objective you write in column two. These are specific behaviors that you would watch for to give you evidence that the general objectives are being attained. An example for the general objective listed above could be "copies savings-account number correctly from customer's I.D. card."

TIME: About 30 minutes.

PART B

STEP 2: Here you will form into groups of about 6–8 members and compare two methods of training for two simple tasks. First, complete Form 2, which asks for general and specific behavioral objectives for two tasks: tying a necktie and using the Kuder-Richardson formula for reliability. Also, specify how you would assess trainee learning on these tasks (e.g., a quiz, by observation, etc.) in column 3 of Form 2.

STEP 3: After you have filled in Form 2, pick four members of your group to act as trainees and then ask them to leave the room or area. You will teach two of them how to do *each* task by the "on-the-job coaching method." That is, explain to them how to do the tasks according to the objectives you have specified. Show them each step, allow them to perform the step, and critique them, working closely (preferably on a one-to-one basis) with them until they have learned the task. Teach the other two trainees how to perform the same

two tasks by the "lecture" method. That is, write out a set of instructions which trainees read and which explains how to perform each task (tying a tie and using the Kuder-Richardson formula [K–R]) in detail. Use Form 3 to prepare your "lectures." Then present the lecture to ratees and allow them to perform the tasks. An explanation of the second training task (using the Kuder-Richardson formula) is provided (for *trainers* only) in Form 4. Trainees should be able to use the formula to compute the reliability of a test after training. Trainers may have to supply additional numerical examples for trainees to use the KR formula.

TIME: About 70 minutes.

STEP 4: Now allow trainees to perform the tasks while you observe them. Record your observations on Form 5. Be sure to score them on accuracy, speed, and/or any other criteria you feel relevant. After trainees are evaluated and the evaluations have been recorded on Form 5, answer the questions at the bottom of Form 5 in your small groups. Trainers can compare and contrast the two methods used to train group members.

TIME: About 30 minutes.

PART C

STEP 5: In Part C you are asked to design a training program for culturally disadvantaged and/or entry-level workers. Read the information given in Form 6 carefully and plan your training program by using the guidelines provided. Discuss the questions raised on Form 6 *before* you decide on the details of the program. Try to design an efficient and practical program for the trainees and the organization involved. Be prepared to present your program to the larger group.

TIME: One or more hours.

FOR FURTHER READING

Aldefer, C. "Change Processes in Organizations." In M. D. Dunnette, ed., *Handbook of Industrial and Organizational Psychology*. Chicago: Rand McNally, 1976. (II)

Argyris, C. *Intervention Theory and Method*. Reading, Mass.: Addison-Wesley, 1970. (II)

Bass, B. M., and J. A. Vaughan. *Training in Industry: The Management of Learning.* Belmont, Cal.: Wadsworth, 1966. (I)

Beatty, R. W. "Personnel Systems and Human Performance." *Personnel Journal* 52 (1973): 307–312. (I)

Beatty, R. W., and C. E. Schneier. "Training the Hard-Core Unemployed through Positive Reinforcement." *Human Resource Management* 11, no. 4 (Winter 1972): 11–17. (I)

Beer, M. "The Technology of Organization Development." In M. D. Dunnette, ed., *Handbook of Industrial and Organizational Psychology.* Chicago: Rand McNally, 1976. (II)

Belbin, R. M. *Training Methods for Older Workers.* Paris: Organization for Economic Cooperation and Development, 1965. (I)

Bennis, W. G. *Nature of Organization Development.* Reading, Mass.: Addison-Wesley, 1969. (I)

Berg, I. *Education and Jobs: The Great Training Robbery.* New York: Praeger, 1970. (I)

Blake, R. R., and J. S. Mouton. *Corporate Excellence through Grid Organization Development.* Houston: Gulf, 1964. (I)

Blavis, A. S. "Some Training Factors Related to Procedural Performance." *Journal of Applied Psychology* 58 (1973): 214–218. (II–R)

Broadwell, M. M. *The Supervisor and On-the-Job Training.* Reading, Mass.: Addison-Wesley, 1969. (I)

Bugelski, B. R. *The Psychology of Teaching.* 2d. ed. Indianapolis: Bobbs-Merrill, 1971. (I)

Burris, R. W. "Human Learning." In M. D. Dunnette, ed., *Handbook of Industrial and Organizational Psychology.* Chicago: Rand McNally, 1976. (II)

Byers, K. T., ed. *Employee Training and Development in the Public Sector.* Rev. ed. Chicago: International Personnel Management Association, 1974. (I)

Campbell, J. P. "Personnel Training and Development." *Annual Review of Psychology* 22 (1971): 565–602. (II)

Campbell, J., M. Dunnette, E. Lawler, and C. Weick. *Managerial Behavior, Performance and Effectiveness.* New York: McGraw-Hill, 1970. (II)

Carroll, S. J., F. T. Paine, and J. J. Ivancevich. "The Relative Effectiveness of Training Methods: Expert Opinion and Research." *Personnel Psychology* 25 (1972): 495–509. (II–R)

Craig, R. L., and L. R. Bittel, eds. *Training and Development Handbook.* New York: McGraw-Hill, 1967. (I)

Dubin, R., ed. *Professional Obsolescence.* Lexington, Mass.: Heath, 1972. (I)

Duet, C. P., and J. W. Newfield. "Sources of Information for the Development of Training Programs." *Personnel Journal* 54 (1975): 162–164+. (I)

Engel, H. M. *Handbook of Creative Learning Exercises.* Houston: Gulf, 1973. (I)

Farr, J. L., B. S. O'Leary, and C. J. Bartlett. "Effect of Work Sample Tests upon Self-Selection and Turnover of Job Applicants." *Journal of Applied Psychology* 58 (1973): 283–285. (II–R)

Fordyce, J. K., and R. Weil. *Managing with People.* Reading, Mass.: Addison-Wesley, 1971. (I)

French, W., and C. Bell. *Organizational Development.* Englewood, Cliffs, New Jersey: Prentice-Hall, 1973. (I)

Gagne, R. M. "Military Training and Principles of Learning." *American Psychologist* 17 (1962): 83–91. (II)

Gagne, R. M. *Learning and Individual Differences.* Columbus: Merill, 1967. (II)

Gallegos, R. C., and J. G. Phelan. "Using Behavioral Objectives in Industrial Training." *Training and Development Journal* 28, no. 4 (April 1974): 42–48. (I)

Goldstein, A. P., and M. Sorcher. *Changing Supervisor Behavior.* New York: Pergamon, 1974. (I)

Golembiewski, R. T., and A. Blumberg, eds. *Sensitivity Training and the Laboratory Approach.* Itasca, Ill.: Peacock, 1970. (I)

Gomersall, E. R., and M. S. Myers. "Breakthrough in On-the-Job Training." *Harvard Business Review* 44, no. 4 (1966): 62–72. (I)

Goldstein, I. L. *Training: Program Development and Design.* Monterey, Cal.: Brooks/Cole, 1974. (I)

Goodman, P. S., P. Salipante, and H. Paransky. "Hiring, Training, and Retraining the Hard-Core Unemployed: A Selected Review." *Journal of Applied Psychology* 58 (1973): 23–33. (II)

Gordon, M. E., and S. L. Cohen. "Training Behavior as a Predictor of Trainability." *Personnel Psychology* 26 (1973): 261–272. (II–R)

Hall, D. T. "Potential for Career Growth." *Personnel Administration* 34 (May–June 1971): 18–30. (I)

Hand, H. H., and J. W. Slocum. "A Longitudinal Study of the Effects of a Human Relations Training Program on Managerial Effectiveness." *Journal of Applied Psychology* 56 (1972): 412–417. (II–R)

Hinrichs, J. R. "Personnel Training." In M. D. Dunnette, ed., *Handbook of Industrial and Organiza-*

tional Psychology. Chicago: Rand McNally, 1976. (II)

Hughes, J. L. *Programmed Instruction for Schools and Industry.* Chicago: Science Research Associates, 1962. (I)

Huse, E. F. *Organizational Development and Change.* St. Paul: West, 1975. (I)

Kegan, D. L. "Organizational Development: Description, Issues, and Some Research Results." *Academy of Management Journal* 14 (1971): 453–464. (II–R)

Kellogg, M. S. *Career Management.* New York: Amacom, 1972. (I)

Levitan, S. A., and G. L. Mangum. *Federal Training and Work Programs in the Sixties.* Ann Arbor, Mich.: Institute of Labor and Industrial Relations, University of Michigan., 1969. (I)

Lynton, R. P., and U. Pareek. *Training for Development.* Homewood, Ill.: Irwin, 1967. (I)

Lysaught, J. P., and C. M. Williams. *A Guide to Programmed Instruction.* New York: Wiley, 1963. (I)

Mager, R. *Preparing Objectives for Programmed Instruction.* San Francisco: Fearon, 1962. (I)

Margulies, M., and J. Wallace. *Organizational Change.* Glenview, Ill.: Scott Foresman, 1973. (I)

McGehee, W., and P. W. Thayer. *Training in Business and Industry.* New York: Wiley, 1961. (I)

Moment, D. "Career Development." *Personnel Administration* 30 (July–August 1967): 6–11. (I)

Nash, A. N., J. P. Muczyk, and F. L. Veltoni. "The Relative Practical Effectiveness of Programmed Instruction." *Personnel Psychology* 24 (1971): 397–418. (I–R)

Neary, H. J. "The BLS Pilot Survey of Training in Industry." *Monthly Labor Review* 97 (February 1974): 26–32. (I)

Odiorne, C. S. *Training by Objectives.* New York: MacMillan, 1970. (I)

Pheiffer, J. W., and J. E. Jones, eds. *Structured Exercises for Group Facilitators.* Vols. 1–4. Iowa City, Iowa: University Associates Press, 1974. (I)

Pinto, P. R. et. al. *Career Planning and Career Management: Perspectives of the Individual and the Organization* (Industrial Relations Center Bulletin 62). Minneapolis: University of Minnesota, 1975. (I)

Raphael, M. A. "Work Previews Can Reduce Turnover and Improve Performance." *Personnel Journal* 54 (1975): 97–98. (I)

Robbins, J. C. "Training the Professional Communicator: The Case Study Method." *Journal of Business Communication* 12 (Spring 1975): 37–45. (I)

Rummler, G. A., J. P. Yaney, and A. W. Schrader, eds. *Managing the Instructional Programming Effort.* Ann Arbor, Mich.: Bureau of Industrial Relations, 1967. (I)

Saliparnte, P., and P. Goodman. "Training, Counseling, and Retention of the Hard-Core Unemployed." *Journal of Applied Psychology* 61 (1976): 1–11. (II–R)

Schneier, C. E. "Training and Development Programs: What Learning Theory and Research Have to Offer." *Personnel Journal* 53 (1974): 288–293,300. (I)

Schein, E. H. "The First Job Dilemma." *Psychology Today* 1 (March 1968): 27–37. (I)

Silverman, R. E. "Learning Theory Applied to Training." In C. P. Otto and O. Glaser, eds., *The Management of Training.* Reading, Mass.: Addison-Wesley, 1970. (I)

Skinner, B. F. *The Technology of Teaching.* New York: Appleton-Century-Crofts, 1968. (II)

Slocum, W. *Occupational Careers.* 2d. ed. Chicago: Aldine, 1974. (I)

Tracey, W. R. *Designing Training and Development Systems.* New York: American Management Association, 1971. (I)

Triandis, H., J. Feldman, D. Weldon, and W. Harvey. "Ecosystems Distrust and the Hard-to-Employ." *Journal of Applied Psychology* 60 (1975): 303–307. (II–R)

U.S. National Technical Information Service. *Management Games; A Bibliography with Abstracts.* Springfield, Virginia: NTIS, 1975. (I)

Vanderpert, A. E. "The Transfer of Training: Some Organizational Variables." *Journal of European Training* 2 (1973): 251–263. (I)

Warren, M. W. *Training for Results.* Reading, Mass.: Addison-Wesley, 1969. (I)

Whyte, W. H. *The Organization Man.* New York: Simon and Schuster, 1956. (I)

Zeira, Y. "An Evaluation of a Planned Change Effort through Top Management Training." *Industrial Relations Journal* 6 (1975): 42–52. (I–R)

Zoll, A. *Dynamic Management Education.* 2d. ed. Reading, Mass.: Addison-Wesley, 1969. (I)

Name _____   Group Number _____

Date _____   Class Section _____   Hour _____   Score _____

PART A

Form 1 Identifying General Behavioral Training Objectives and Specific Target Training Behaviors

Job title 1	General behavioral training objectives 2	Specific target training behaviors 3
1. Bank teller	1.	1. 2. 3.
	2.	1. 2. 3.
	3.	1. 2. 3.
2. Sales clerk	1.	1. 2. 3.
	2.	1. 2. 3.
	3.	1. 2. 3.
3. Librarian	1.	1. 2. 3.
	2.	1. 2. 3.
	3.	1. 2. 3.
4. Plant manager	1.	1. 2. 3.
	2.	1. 2. 3.
	3.	1. 2. 3.
5. Punch press operator	1.	1. 2. 3.
	2.	1. 2. 3.
	3.	1. 2. 3.

Place information for any additional job titles given by your implementor on reverse.

Name _____   Group Number _____

Date _____   Class Section _____   Hour _____   Score _____

PART B

Form 2 Comparison of Training Methods

General behavioral training objective 1	Specific target training behaviors 2	How will trainee learning be assessed on each target training behavior? 3
Training task 1: Tying a tie		
Tying a knot in a necktie.	1.	
	2.	
	3.	
*Training Task 2: Using the Kuder-Richardson 20 (K−R 20) formula for test reliability**		
Learning the K¬R 20 formula and using it to assess the reliability of tests.	1.	
	2.	
	3.	

* See Form 4 for an explanation of the K−R 20.

PART B

Form 3 Worksheet for Lectures

Write your "lectures" for Training Task 1 (Tying a tie) and Training Task 2 (Using the Kuder-Richardson 20 formula for reliability) on the reverse side and/or on additional sheets if necessary.

PART B

Form 4 (for trainers only) The Kuder-Richardson Formula 20 (K−R 20) for Estimating Test Reliability[1]

The reliability of a test refers to its consistency or repeatability. Responses to questions should form a similar pattern across test takers or over time. This would lead to the inference that the test was measuring something stable over time or throughout all of its questions. Several methods are available for assessing reliability,[2] but one common method is split-half reliability. Reliability scores are obtained by correlating two sets of scores on one administration of a test in order to assess the relationship of scores on one portion of the test to those on another portion. The reliability coefficient is thus a correlation coefficient with range of $+1$ (perfect positive relationship), to 0 (no relationship), to -1 (perfect negative relationship). After the test is split in half, scores on one "half" are compared to the other. The first half versus the last half, or odd-numbered items or questions versus even-numbered questions, can be used as the two "halves." Obviously, items of a test can be split in many other ways to complete split-half reliability (e.g., first and third versus second and fourth quarters, etc.). But for each such split, a different correlation coefficient for the two sets of scores could be obtained as different questions or items are used. Therefore, which one is the best estimate of reliability?

Kuder and Richardson have developed a computational procedure that is equivalent to assessing the average of all possible split-half reliability coefficients that could be computed for a given test. This formula is easy to use and gives an excellent estimate of reliability, as it accounts for all possible splits and thus reduces the chances of obtaining a biased reliability coefficient due to one particular pattern of questions used in one split.

The formula, typically referred to as the K−R 20, is as follows:

$$r_{KR} = \left(\frac{k}{k-1}\right)\left(\frac{\sigma_0^2 - \sum p_i q_i}{\sigma_0^2}\right).$$

The meanings of the symbols are:

k = number of items in the test;
p_i = proportion of students responding correctly to item i;
$q_i = 1 - p$ (the proportion of students responding incorrectly);
σ_0^2 = the test variance;
$\sum p_i q_i$ = sum of p times q for all test items.

The term $k(k - 1)$ is a correction factor permitting r to equal 1.0. The term $p_i q_i$ is actually the difficulty of item i multiplied by 1 minus the difficulty of the item. To get $\sum p_i q_i$, all of the $p_i q_i$ for each item must be summed. The assumptions of the K−R 20 are that items can be scored either right or wrong and that the total score on the test is the sum of the scores on each item. Thus, on items where partial credit is given, the K−R 20 is not applicable.

Example: Below is a table showing the responses of five students on each item of a six-item test. A "O" indicates that the incorrect response was given and a "1" indicates that a correct response was given.

	Item						
Student	1	2	3	4	5	6	Total no. correct responses per student (X)
1	1	0	0	1	1	1	4
2	1	0	1	1	1	1	5
3	0	0	1	1	0	1	3
4	1	0	1	0	0	0	2
5	1	1	0	1	1	1	5
							19

The K–R reliability estimate for this test is computed below.

		Item						
		1	2	3	4	5	6	
Total number of correct responses per item		4	1	3	4	3	4	$\bar{X}$ = Mean correct responses per student, 3.8
Proportion of correct responses per item	(p)	0.8	0.2	0.6	0.8	0.6	0.8	σ_0^{2*} = 1.36 (variance)
Proportion of incorrect responses per item	(q)	0.2	0.8	0.4	0.2	0.4	0.2	$\imath_{KR} = \left(\dfrac{6}{5}\right)\left(\dfrac{1.36 - 1.12}{1.36}\right)$
pq		0.16	0.16	0.24	0.16	0.24	0.16	$\imath_{KR}$ = 0.212 = KR20 reliability coefficient
$\sum pq$	1.12							

* Variance $= \dfrac{\sum (X - \bar{X})^2}{N}$

[1] Adapted from W. Dick and N. Hagerty, *Topics in Measurement, Reliability and Validity* (New York: McGraw-Hill, 1971), pp. 23–24, 31–33.
[2] See Exercise 10 and R. Guion, *Personnel Testing* (New York: McGraw-Hill, 1965); W. Dick and N. Hagerty, *Topics in Measurement, Reliability and Validity*; and J. Guilford, *Psychometric Methods* (New York: McGraw-Hill, 1954).

Name _____   Group Number _____

Date _____ Class Section _____ Hour _____ Score _____

PART B

Form 5 Evaluation of Trainee Learning

Criteria for evaluation of trainee learning		Task	
		No. 1 (Tying tie)	No. 2 (K–R 20)

Method 1 (Lecture)

Speed	Trainee 1		
	Trainee 2		
Accuracy	Trainee 1		
	Trainee 2		
Other:	Trainee 1		
	Trainee 2		

Method 2 (Coaching)

Speed	Trainee 1		
	Trainee 2		
Accuracy	Trainee 1		
	Trainee 2		
Other:	Trainee 1		
	Trainee 2		

After the training programs have been designed and trainees have used them and have been evaluated, discuss the following issues and briefly summarize your discussions:

1. Which method led to attainment of the criteria speed for each task? Under which method for each task were trainees most accurate?

2. How did the ratees feel about learning under each of the methods? Which method did they prefer? Why?

3. What are the advantages and disadvantages of each method?

4. For what type of training task would each of the methods seem to be most appropriate?

5. What training method would be most effective for each of these tasks? Why?

PART C

Form 6 Designing a Training Program for the Disadvantaged and/or Entry-Level Worker

The Edward Bedframe Company is a medium-sized manufacturer of bedframes located in a large Midwestern city. It is a family-owned business run by the original founder, his son, and his son-in-law, each of whom bring a different type of expertise to the organization. Through a combination of excellent salesmanship and customer service, administrative and legal acumen, and a rigorously controlled, sophisticated production system, Edward Bedframe has been able to make increasing inroads into the bedframe market traditionally split among the few giant companies that dominate the industry. Annual gross volume is over seven million dollars and the company's profit margin is considerably above the industry's average.

One of the largest bedframe manufacturers is located in the same metropolitan area as Edward. It recently decided to implement a huge community welfare program, including the donation of a plot of land for a park, a wing for the local hospital, and the establishment of a Chair in Management at the business school of the nearby state university. Many have said such expenditures are merely returns for the favorable tax position the company receives from the community. Nevertheless, these programs are of obvious benefit and generate favorable publicity.

Edward's management team, feeling some pressure from local leaders to follow the other company's lead, decided to help the local citizens, not merely the few who could attend the state university, by initiating a program to hire and train local workers for entry-level positions in the company. Such an idea was welcomed by the community and its leaders, not to mention the national and local union, who seemed to sense a potential increase in membership.

Edward Bedframe is going to hire forty workers for entry-level jobs in the company. These workers will not all have finished high school and will be all ages. To qualify for the training program, they must have been unemployed for the past six months or more and have no marketable job skills. Because Edward Bedframe is located in a high unemployment area, this program is both economically and socially useful to the community, as well as the company.

The company will hire the workers for entry-level operating jobs on any one of a number of machines currently used to produce the bedframes. These include punch presses, riveting machines, drill presses, and machines for boxing frames. The budget for the training program is $17,000, including salaries for trainees. A two-week time limit has been set to train the forty workers. The starting wage at Edward Bedframe, according to the union agreement, is $3.90/hr.

Design a training program for the forty new workers. The training program should include the following:

1. general behavioral training objectives;
2. specific target training objectives;
3. a method for assessing trainee learning;
4. a training methodology (i.e., lecture, coaching, programmed learning, etc.);
5. special equipment or spatial arrangements required;
6. a budget of expenses;
7. a training program timetable;
8. requirements for trainers; and
9. a small bonus or reward system for trainees.

In designing your training program, you may want to consider the following issues:

1. What changes in organization policy, procedures, etc., if any, will have to be made for these particular trainees?
2. Is the training program going to emphasize only skills for job-related activities, or will general skills (e.g., arithmetic or reading) be included?
3. How will disciplinary problems be handled? (Remember: there is a union.)
4. Will training take place off-job, on-job, or both?
5. Will any type of employee orientation program be included in the training design?
6. Will any training of trainers or supervisors be required?

Name _____ Group Number _____

Date _____ Class Section _____ Hour _____ Score _____

ASSESSMENT OF LEARNING IN PERSONNEL ADMINISTRATION
EXERCISE 12

1. Try to state the purpose of this exercise in one concise sentence.

2. Specifically what did you learn from this exercise (i.e., skills, abilities, and knowledge)?

3. How might your learning influence your role and your duties as a personnel administrator?

4. What training/learning method(s) do you learn best under? Why?

5. Why is behavior change such an important objective of training and development programs?

6. Additional questions given by your implementor:

Exercise 13

EVALUATING THE EFFECTIVENESS OF TRAINING AND DEVELOPMENT PROGRAMS

PREVIEW

As with all personnel programs, training and development programs should be evaluated as to their effectiveness. Because large sums of money are spent on training and development, because it is a time-consuming activity, and because training often has specific objectives, it seems reasonable to inquire whether or not the money and the time have been used wisely and whether or not the objectives have been met. Very often this is accomplished most easily by asking the question: Was there any change in behavior in the desired direction after training? Often, however, this question is not asked or the answer is obscured by faulty measurement, inappropriate type of questions, and/or lack of data obtained before training against which to compare that obtained after training.

In this exercise, the importance of systematically and rigorously evaluating the effectiveness of training and development programs is discussed. Several activities are designed to enable you to decide on the criteria to use in your evaluation and to develop the evaluation instruments needed to gather appropriate data.

OBJECTIVES

1. To become aware of the importance of the evaluation of training-and-development-program effectiveness as a vital process in the administration of programs.
2. To become familiar with the types of data required from various parties in order to evaluate a training program rigorously.
3. To become familiar with the more common types of experimental designs that can be used to systematically assess differences in groups of trainees before and after training and/or differences between groups who have received training and those who have not.
4. To begin to build skill in designing instruments to gather the data needed in training-program evaluation.

PREMEETING ASSIGNMENT

Read the entire exercise. Review Exercises 5 and 6, as well as the *Appendix* to Exercise 10 covering *t*-tests for differences between means, or a statistics text on the same topic.

INTRODUCTION

A Rationale, a Method, and Criteria for Training-and-Development-Program Evaluation

The evaluation of training and development programs is a complex task. Basically, this task involves determining what, if anything, the training program actually accomplished. The task is difficult because many aspects of the training situation (i.e., content, duration, etc.), as well as individual characteristics of trainers and trainees, can influence the outcomes of programs. Evaluators thus must design an assessment procedure that is sensitive to such differences. They must determine training goals, which include a complex array of possible changes in knowledge and behavior after training. Further, evaluators must define these goals very specifically and explain their interrelationships before training can be evaluated with confidence.

Surprisingly, few organizations seriously attempt to evaluate their training programs. This is often because of the difficulty in measuring job performance itself in order to assess whether performance was enhanced by training. Given the expense of training programs, the scant amount of research devoted to evaluating the impact of training is astonishing. A major question at this point is how long organizations will follow a policy that often can be characterized as spending millions for training but not one penny for training evaluation.

A Rationale for Evaluation. Often evaluation is deferred because training programs are designed with little or no thought as to how they will subsequently be evaluated. The prescribed training techniques of a program are *assumed* to be capable of moving the trainee toward the stated training objectives, but we never know what a particular program actually accomplished without evaluation. Often, if evaluation is attempted, the criterion of training-program accomplishment is merely a statement by the trainees indicating whether they *think* they have learned something, or whether the trainees' superiors *think* the trainees learned something. Only occasionally is the criterion how much trainees *actually* learned, (i.e., changes in behavior). Evaluation of training should be as carefully planned and executed as the training program itself, for careful evaluation is the only means we have for assessing the value of such programs and determining the nature of the necessary changes in order to make future programs more effective.

Evaluation Criteria. It has been suggested that evaluation procedures consider the following four levels of criteria: reaction, learning, behavior, and results.[1] *Reaction* is defined as what the trainees thought of the particular program—i.e., their opinions. It does not include a measure of the learning that takes place. Following are some guidelines for gauging participant reaction to a training program:

[1] D. L. Kirkpatrick, "Techniques for Evaluating Training Programs," *Journal of American Society of Training Directors* 13 (1959): 3–9.

1. Design a questionnaire based on information directly related to program design and methods. The questionnaire should be validated by carefully standardized procedures to be certain that the responses actually reflect the opinions of the participants.
2. Design the instrument so that the responses can be tabulated and quantified easily (e.g., by using an answer sheet for responses).
3. To obtain more honest opinions, provide for the anonymity of the participants.
4. Provide space for opinions about items that are not covered in the questionnaire. This procedure often leads to the collection of important information that is useful in the subsequent redesign of the questionnaire (e.g., a space for "other comments or reactions to the program").
5. Pretest the questionnaire on a sample of participants to determine its completeness, the time necessary for completion, and participant reactions to the questions themselves.

The reaction of the majority of participants is often a critical factor in the continuance of training programs; decisions should not turn on the comments of only a few very satisfied or disgruntled participants who choose to be vocal. Receptivity to a program (i.e., positive reactions) provides a good atmosphere for learning; it does not, however, necessarily *cause* high levels of learning.

In *learning*, the second aspect of training to be evaluated, the training analyst is concerned with measuring principles, facts, techniques, and attitudes that were specified as training objectives. The measures must be objective and quantifiable indicators of the learning that has taken place in the training program. There are many different measures of learning, including paper-and-pencil tests and learning curves. The original training objectives help to determine the choice of the most appropriate measure. Of course, it is best if learning is assessed both before and after training in order to determine changes.

Behavior measures refer to actual job performance. Just as favorable reaction does not necessarily mean that learning will occur in the training program, superior training performance (i.e., learning) does not always result in similar behavior in the job setting. The measurement of learning does not always accurately represent performance on the job and should not be substituted for studies of on-the-job behavior without first determining that a strong relationship exists between the two. Behavior on the job is often measured with such performance-appraisal techniques as behaviorally anchored rating scales

(BARS) (see Exercise 5). Again, before-and-after training measures of performance levels should be taken to see whether or not learning from training has transferred to job performance.

The fourth criterion for training effectiveness, the *results* of a training program, refers to a program's impact on organizational objectives. Some of the results that could be examined include costs, turnover, absenteeism, grievances, and morale. This data is easily gathered by examining company records, both finanical and personnel. Hopefully, all of the previous three criteria would affect results. That is, if we design a training program that people felt was useful, that they learned something from, and that improved their own individual job performance, we would hope organizational performance would improve also.

Although great disparities show up in the kinds of training evaluation reported in the literature and in the degree of scientific rigor with which evaluation is performed, general agreement seems to exist concerning the following principles:

1. Evaluation should be planned at the same time as the training program and should constitute an integral part of the total program from beginning to end.
2. Evaluation should be carried out at several levels and at several times.[2]
3. Evaluation should follow the most rigorous experimental design possible.

Conducting Research on Training-Program Effectiveness.   There are many possible experimental designs

[2] B. M. Bass and J. A. Vaughan, *Training in Industry: The Management of Learning* (Belmont, California: Wadsworth, 1968), Chap. 8.

or ways in which trainees (a) are grouped, (b) are administered training programs and evaluation questionnaires, and (c) are compared to other groups (see Fig. 1). Most such designs, however, are of the "after-only" variety. That is, the trainee's reactions, learning, or behavior are observed or measured only after their exposure to training. It is thus impossible to tell whether, for example, knowledge was developed as a result of training or existed before training. A slight improvement over this single-measure method is a comparable measure of a matched "control" group, a group that does not receive training. This latter design can be further improved if evaluation includes both "before and after" measures of the experimental (i.e., training) group and a matched control group. The use of two or more control groups permits even more sophistication in design and allows isolation of possible events occurring simultaneously with training (i.e., maturational processes and the initial measurement itself) from training effects. The utility of the basic experimental designs can be compared in Fig. 1.

In Design A no control group is used and each subject serves as their own control. The difference between the before and after measures would indicate change due to training. However, as there is no control group, we may have noticed change simply due to maturation, or learning on the job over time, or increased motivation.

To avoid this, Design B employs a control group. Neither group is measured before training, but if the subjects in the two groups are randomly assigned, and a fairly large number of people are in each group (e.g., thirty or more), we can be reasonably confident that if the after measure for the experimental group

Fig. 1. Sample Training Designs

	Design A: "Before" and "After" with no control group	Design B: "After" only with one control group		Design C: "Before-After" with one control group	
		Experimental group	Control group	Experimental group	Control group
"Before" training measurement taken:	Yes (X_1)	No	No	Yes (X_1)	Yes (Y_1)
Training given:	Yes	Yes	No	Yes	No
"After" training measurement taken:	Yes (X_2)	Yes (X_2)	Yes (Y_2)	Yes (X_2)	Yes (Y_2)
Change due to training assumed by measuring difference (D) between:	$D = X_2 - X_1$	$D = X_2 - Y_2$		$D_1 = X_2 - X_1$ $D_2 = X_2 - Y_2$ (if $X_1 = Y_1$)	

Source: Adapted from B. Bass and J. Vaughan, *Training in Industry* (Belmont, Cal.: Wadsworth, 1968), p. 146.

is significantly greater than that of the control group (i.e., $X_2 > Y_2$), training has had an effect. Of course, we still do not know whether learning, knowledge, etc. increased for either group from before to after the training without a before measure.

Thus, a still more rigorous design is Design C, which uses both a before and after measure and a control group. If we randomly assign people to each of the groups and note that they are at about the same level before training (i.e., $X_1 = Y_1$), then differences in the experimental group over the control group after training would indicate that training had an effect (i.e., $X_2 > Y_2$). We would also hope that the change between the before and after measures for the experimental group is large (i.e., $X_2 > X_1$), indicating change due to training for the experimental group. More sophisticated designs are available which account for such factors as changes due to the measuring itself, and these allow us to be even more confident that results are due to training.[3] However, the more sophisticated the design, the more costly evaluation becomes. Design C in Fig. 1 should be used as a minimally rigorous design when possible.

The Training Subsystem. The entire training process, or subsystem of the larger personnel system, can be represented as a systematic program to assess

---

[3] See D. Campbell and J. Stanley, *Experimental and Quasi-experimental Designs for Research* (Chicago: Rand McNally, 1967); and B. Bass and J. Vaughan, *Training in Industry* (Belmont, California: Wadsworth, 1968).

training needs (Exercise 11), design and implement training programs (Exercise 12), and finally evaluate training effectiveness (Exercise 13). This entire process can be represented in a schematic, such as the one in Fig. 2.

In Fig. 2, it is obvious that all aspects of training are sequentially related. In addition, the development of criterion measures—that is, the criteria on which trainees and the program itself will be assessed—comes early in the sequential process. The feedback loops suggest that after trainees have graduated from the program and have been assessed on the criteria, training content, methods, and/or materials may have to be changed to reflect new requirements of trainees or inadequacies of the existing program. This re-design after evaluation enables training programs not only to remain relevant to the needs of trainees, but also to remain flexible enough to accommodate changes in jobs.

PROCEDURE

Overview. In this exercise, you build skill in designing instruments to assess the four criteria that can be used in evaluating training programs: reactions, learning, performance, and results. Techniques discussed in Exercises 5 and 6 on performance appraisal are utilized.

PART A

STEP 1: You are to break into groups of about four to six members and determine how you would

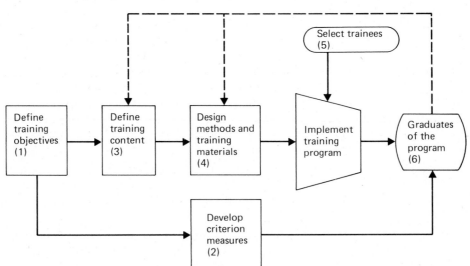

Fig. 2. The Training Subsystem (Adapted from G. A. Eckstrand, "Current Status of the Technology of Training," *AMRL Document Technical Report 64–86*, Sept. 1964, p. 3; see also, R. W. Beatty, "Personnel Systems and Human Performance," *Personal Journal* 52 (1973): 307–312.)

measure an individual's *reactions* to the middle-management training program described in Exercise 11. You are to design a questionnaire to measure these reactions (Form 1). Give careful thought to precisely how you would define the term "reactions." Make sure the questions are clearly worded and allow for proper response alternatives. Remember that reactions include opinions and attitudes about various aspects of the program.

TIME: About 30 minutes.

PART B

STEP 2: In Part B each group is to design a questionnaire to evaluate *learning* that might have taken place in the middle-management training program presented in Exercise 11. First, devise questions that would provide data on what *knowledge* the trainees gained. They might have gained knowledge in the areas noted in the training-program outline, such as communications, etc. What questions could you ask in a pencil-and-paper test to assess this knowledge? Tell how you would score the answers to these questions—in order to do this, you must, of course, formulate your own answers to the questions.

Next, discuss how you would actually measure the *change in learning* of the trainees which resulted from the program by comparing, for example, their answers to your questions before and after training (see Fig. 1, *Introduction*) and/or using a control group. What statistic(s) would you use to measure this type of change and how could you be assured that any change you detect is not merely due to chance (refer to *Appendix*, Exercise 10). Finally, how would you determine if any change that did occur, even if you felt it was not due to chance, *was* due to the training program itself? Answer these questions as a group and write your answers in the spaces provided on Form 2.

TIME: About 50 minutes.

PART C

STEP 3: Here you evaluate behavioral change as a result of training. You are to choose among the skills being taught in the training program in Exercise 11 and design one Behaviorally Anchored Rating Scale (BARS) to measure behavior on this skill. Use Form 3 for your BARS. You may want to refer to Exercise 5 (you can simply write in a set of anchors without performing the retranslation procedure). BARS, as you remember, was argued to be an excellent performance-appraisal system, as it was developed to measure *behavior*. If we measure behavior change as a result of training, we can use this behavior to rate performance change indicated by the various degrees of performance illustrated by each anchor on the BARS scale.

TIME: About 35 minutes.

PART D

STEP 4: Using Form 4, you are to evaluate the *results* of a training program by first identifying key results for the middle-management job described in Exercise 11 and then indicating how you would measure these results. The results can either be on an individual or an organizational level. Identifying and measuring results is the basic process in Management by Objectives (MBO) and you may want to refer to Exercise 6 to refresh your memory of MBO. Remember also that results are measures of effectiveness, such as profit margin, as distinct from behaviors measured by BARS.

TIME: About 30 minutes.

PART E

STEP 5: Form 5 contains data from an experimental and a control group which have been used in a "JIT Plus" (Job Instruction Training) program that you, as personnel administrator, have developed and implemented. The JIT Plus training program was used for twenty-five randomly selected new employees of the fifty currently holding assembler I jobs. You have randomly selected an equal number of the remaining assemblers (i.e., twenty-five) who have completed the regular JIT training program as a control group and you are now in a position to compare the JIT with the JIT-Plus in a cost/benefit analysis. Your group is to do the following:

a) Evaluate the experimental JIT-Plus program by assessing production changes one year after the training and determine whether or not the JIT-Plus approach makes enough difference to warrant its extra costs. If a difference was observed, was it due to change in learning?

b) Prepare a brief report on the statistical analyses you used and recommendations relative to instituting one of the training programs for all new assemblers I, based on the results of your analysis.

(The *Appendix* to Exercise 10 may help with the statistical analysis.)

TIME: About 35 minutes.

FOR FURTHER READING

Andrews, K. R. "Reaction to University Development Program." *Harvard Business Review* 3, no. 39 (1961): 116–134. (I)

Anderson, S. B. et al. *Encyclopedia of Educational Evaluation.* San Francisco: Jossey Bass, 1975. (I)

Bass, B. M., and J. A. Vaughan. *Training in Industry: The Management of Learning.* Belmont, California: Wadsworth, 1966. (I)

Blasco, J. A., and H. M. Trice. *The Assessment of Change in Training and Therapy.* New York: McGraw-Hill, 1969. (I)

Biel, W. C. "Training Programs and Devices." In R. M. Gagne, ed., *Psychological Principles in Systems Development.* New York: Holt, Rinehart and Winston, 1962. (I)

Bowles, W. J. "The Mismanagement of Supervisory Training." *Personnel* 38 (1961): 50–57. (I)

Buchanan, P. C. "Evaluating the Results of Supervisory Training." *Personnel* 33, no. 4 (1957): 362–370. (I)

Campbell, D. "Considering the Case against Experimental Evaluations of Social Innovations." *Administrative Science Quarterly* 15, no. 1 (1970): 110–113. (II)

Campbell, D. T., and J. Stanley. *Experimental and Quasiexperimental Designs for Research.* Chicago: Rand McNally, 1966. (II)

Catalenello, R., and D. Kirkpatrick. "Evaluating Training Programs—the State of the Art." *Training and Development Journal* 23, no. 5 (1968): 2–9. (I)

Cook, T. D., and D. T. Campbell. "The Design and Conduct of Quasi-Experiments and True Experiments in Field Settings." In M. D. Dunnette, ed., *Handbook of Industrial and Organizational Psychology.* Chicago: Rand McNally, 1976. (II)

Fleishman, E. A. "Leadership Climate, Human Relations Training and Supervisory Behavior." *Personnel Psychology* 6 (1953): 205–222. (II–R)

Form, W. H., and A. L. Form. "Unanticipated Results of a Foreman Training Program." *Personnel Journal* 32 (1953): 207–212. (I)

Goldstein, J. L. *Training Program Development and Evaluation.* Monterey, California: Brooks/Cole, 1974. (I)

Hamblin, A. C. *Evaluation and Control of Training.* New York: McGraw-Hill, 1974. (I)

Haire, M. "Some Problems of Industrial Training." *Journal Social Issues* 4 (1948): 41–47. (I)

Hughes, J. L. "The Effectiveness of Programmed Instruction: Experimental Findings." In S. Marfulies and L. D. Eigen, ed., *Applied Programmed Instruction.* New York: Wiley, 1962. (II)

King, B. T., and I. L. Jacis. "Comparison of the Effectiveness of Improvised versus Non-Improvised Role Playing in Producing Opinion Changes." *Journal of Human Relations* 9 (1956): 177–187. (II–R)

Kirkpatrick, D. L. "Techniques for Evaluating Training Programs." *Journal of American Society of Training Directors* 13 (1959): 3–9, 21–26. (I)

Kohn, W., and T. Parker. "Some Guidelines for Evaluating Management Development Seminars." *Training and Development Journal* 23, no. 7 (1968): 18–22. (I)

Lawshe, C. H., Jr., R. A. Bolda, and R. L. Brune. "Studies in Management Training Evaluation: I. Scaling Responses to Human Relations Training Cases." *Journal of Applied Psychology* 43 (1959): 287–292. (II–R)

Lawshe, C. H., Jr., R. A. Bolda, and R. L. Brune. "Studies in Management Training Evaluation: II. The Effects of Exposures to Role Playing." *Journal of Applied Psychology* 43 (1959): 287–292. (II–R)

McKenney, J. L. "An Evaluation of a Business Game in an MBA Curriculum." *Journal Business* 35, no. 3 (1962): 278–286. (I–R)

MacKinney, A. C. "Progressive Levels in the Evaluation of Training Programs." *Personnel* 34 (1957): 72–77. (I)

Martin, H. O. "The Assessment of Training." *Personnel Management* (Great Britain) 39 (1957): 88–93. (I)

Morse, N., and E. Reimer. "The Experimental Change of a Major Organizational Variable." *Journal of Abnormal Social Psychology* 52 (1956): 120–129. (II–R)

Nixon, G. *People, Evaluation, and Achievement.* Houston: Gulf, 1973. (I)

Oberg, E. "Top Management Assesses University Executive Programs." *Business Topics* 2, no. 2 (1963): 7–27. (I)

Odiorne, G. S. "The Need for an Economic Approach to Training." *Journal of the American Society of Training Directors* 18, no. 3 (1964): 3–12. (I)

Randall, L. K. "Evaluation: A Training Dilemma." *Journal of American Society of Training Directors* 19, no. 1 (1965): 35–42. (I)

Selltiz, C., M. Jahoda, M. Deutsch, and S. W. Cook. *Research Methods in Social Relations.* New York: Holt, Rinehart and Winston, 1962. (II)

Viteles, M. S. "Human Relations and the Humanities in the Education of Business Leaders: Evaluation of a Program of Humanistic Studies for Executives." *Personnel Psychology* 12 (1959): 1–28. (II–R)

Wholey, J. S. et al. *Federal Evaluation Policy.* Washington, D.C.: The Urban Institute, 1970. (I)

Woodward, N. "The Economic Evaluation of Supervisor Training." *Journal of European Training* 4 (1975): 134–141. (I)

Name _____ Group Number _____

Date _____ Class Section _____ Hour _____ Score _____

PART A

Form 1 Evaluating Reactions to the "Success in Middle Management" Training Program (See Exercise 11)

A Reactions Questionnaire

Questions:

1.

2.

3.

4.

5.

6.

7.

8.

9.

10.

11.

12.

13.

14.

15.

Name _____ Group Number _____

Date _____ Class Section _____ Hour _____ Score _____

PART B

Form 2 Evaluating Learning in the "Success in Middle Management Training Program" (See Exercise 11)

I. List several sample questions (along with their answers) that could be used in a pencil-and-paper test to evaluate what knowledge trainees have gained as a result of the training.

Question:

1.

   Answer:

2.

   Answer:

3.

   Answer:

4.

   Answer:

5.

   Answer:

6.

   Answer:

7.

   Answer:

8.

   Answer:

II. Develop a design that will allow you to indicate whether or not the training program actually led to changes in knowledge (see Fig. 1, Exercise 13). Explain the statistics you would use to decide whether or not your answer was due to change (see *Appendix* to Exercise 10 or a statistics text).

Name _____ Group Number _____

Date _____ Class Section _____ Hour _____ Score _____

PART C

Form 3 Evaluating Behavior Change in the "Success in Middle-Management" Training Program (see Exercise 11) with BARS (see Exercise 5).

Middle-management skill chosen _____

Performance or skill level   *Behavioral description or anchors:*

Excellent	7
Very good	6
Good	5
Average	4
Fair	3
Poor	2
Unacceptable	1

Name _____ Group Number _____

Date _____ Class Section _____ Hour _____ Score _____

PART D

Form 4 Evaluating Results of the "Success in Middle Management" Training Program (see Exercise 11) with MBO (see Exercise 6).

Key result area to be measured (e.g., quantity, cost, etc.)	Measure used to assess key result area (e.g., profit margin, etc.)
1.	
2.	
3.	
4.	
5.	
6.	
7.	
8.	

PART E

Form 5 Assessing the Worth of a Training Program via a Cost/Benefit Analysis

Using the data presented below concerning an experimental training program (JIT Plus) and the traditional program (JIT) for persons holding the job of assembler I, calculate which program is economically most beneficial to the organization during a *one-year* period. (*Note:* the data presented were collected *after six months*.)

	JIT Plus program (experimental—E)	JIT program (control—C)
Sample size (N)	$N_E = 25$	$N_C = 25$
Average no. of units produced before training for entire group of trainees (per day)	$\bar{X}_{E1} = 47$	$\bar{X}_{C1} = 47$
Average no. of units produced before training for entire group of trainees (per day)	$\bar{X}_{E2} = 52$	$\bar{Y}_{C2} = 50$
Cost of training program (per trainee)	$150.00	$100.00

Additional information: The total profit from units produced in a six-month period is $50.00 per trainee. The average tenure for each assembler I is one year. The *t*-statistic computed for the difference between the mean production of the experimental and training groups is 1.77. (Refer to *Appendix*, Exercise 10 or any statistics text for explanation of *t* statistic and appropriate tables.) The basic difference in cost per trainee between the two programs is due to additional instructional equipment necessary in the JIT-Plus program. However, training times are quite short and equal for the two programs. The same number and type of trainers are required for each program.

Name _____   Group Number _____

Date _____   Class Section _____   Hour _____   Score _____

ASSESSMENT OF LEARNING IN PERSONNEL ADMINISTRATION
EXERCISE 13

1. Try to state the purpose of this exercise in one concise sentence.

2. Specifically what did you learn from this exercise (i.e., skills, abilities, and knowledge)?

3. How might your learning influence your role and your duties as a personnel administrator?

4. What skills and knowledge are required in order to evaluate training and development programs effectively?

5. When during training and development program design and implementation should evaluation be considered? Why?

6. What problems might you encounter as you attempt to develop behavioral criteria for management development programs?

7. Additional questions given by your implementor:

Section 6
Maintaining and Improving Commitment, Performance, and Productivity

An effective human-resource-management system does not end with the selection and training of people. Once these procurement and development functions are completed, human resources must be utilized to their fullest capacity toward the mutual benefit of the organization and the individual. Here, the role of personnel administrators, directors of human resources, and their staffs of specialists is to conduct research in order to ascertain the degree of commitment, satisfaction, and performance of their human resources. Deficiencies in these areas can thereby be pinpointed and programs aimed at improvement initiated. However, even when no glaring deficiencies are uncovered through investigation and diagnosis, programs must be developed to maintain current levels of performance and commitment.

Section 6 begins with Exercise 14, which demonstrates the uses of an effective research and diagnostic test, the Job Descriptive Index (JDI). The JDI has been used extensively due to its brevity, yet comprehensiveness, and its validity. The data obtained from an instrument such as the JDI would form the rationale for developing specific programs aimed at maintaining and improving commitment and performance.

While innumerable such programs are in use, many seem to be based on such "intrinsic" rewards as challenge, variety, autonomy, and recognition available from the work itself. Thus, Exercise 15 describes these job-enrichment programs and provides activities designed to build skill in their design and implementation. Other motivation or incentive programs improve performance through "extrinsic" rewards—those often tangible rewards dispensed by the organization or others external to the person receiving the rewards. The use of such extrinsic rewards as money, verbal praise, feedback, time off from work, etc., is discussed in Exercise 16. Their utility is explained by their ability to modify behavior as they are systematically dispensed and withdrawn in the work environment.

Programs designed to make the most effective use of that pervasive extrinsic organizational reward—money—are discussed in detail in Exercise 17, "Job Evaluation and Wage and Salary Administration." This exercise begins with job-evaluation techniques used to rank jobs in order of value or worth. Subsequent to such a ranking, different wage or salary levels can be attached to each job type in a rational manner in order to develop an entire wage and salary system.

Exercise 14

JOB SATISFACTION: ITS MEANING AND ITS MEASUREMENT

PREVIEW

In this exercise the causes and consequences of positive and negative feelings or attitudes about one's work are discussed. Negative feelings toward a job, often broadly called job dissatisfaction, have been linked to subsequent poor performance and productivity of workers, in addition to poor mental health. Thus, the assessment of the extent of job dissatisfaction in organizations could be an important first step in improving organizational performance. The exercise provides experiences that build skill in assessing and alleviating job dissatisfaction. A widely used and validated questionnaire, the Job Descriptive Index (JDI), is explained as a technique to measure job satisfaction.

OBJECTIVES

1. To become aware of the possible causes, consequences, and remedies for job dissatisfaction.
2. To build skill in diagnosing those particular aspects of jobs which might lead to dissatisfaction.
3. To build skill in designing and using instruments to assess the degree of job satisfaction-dissatisfaction within an organization and in interpreting their results.

PREMEETING ASSIGNMENT

Read the entire exercise.

INTRODUCTION

Job Satisfaction as an Indicator of Performance Problems

There has been much publicity lately regarding worker discontent in America.[1] It seems that "blue collar blues" and "white collar woes" have become familiar phrases, not only in the media and among academics, but among the work force itself. Many workers are generally dissatisfied with their jobs—with the boring, routine work they do. They feel they are mere "cogs in a wheel," unable to see the impact of their labor on society. Absenteeism, high turnover, strikes, sabotage, and generally poor productivity are cited as evidence of widespread worker discontent.

The task for the personnel administrator and his or her staff is first to define specifically the extent of this type of discontent, and then to assess whether or not it is a problem in the organization. If workers are dissatisfied and deleterious consequences for both themselves and the organization can be pinpointed, remedies must be devised. These remedies are typically within the responsibilities assigned to the personnel function in an organization.

What Is Job Satisfaction (JS)? After a thorough analysis of the concept of JS, Edwin Locke offered the following definition: "Job satisfaction is the pleasurable emotional state resulting from the appraisal of

---

[1] One of the most publicized documents is *Work in America* (Cambridge, Mass.: MIT, 1973) prepared by a special task force for the Secretary of Health, Education and Welfare.

one's job as achieving or facilitating one's job values."[2] Thus JS is an emotional concept, a feeling—not a behavior or activity. Research has shown that this feeling is related to behavioral outcomes that are counterproductive when it is negative (i.e., job dissatisfaction or JD).[3] Most importantly, a negative feeling towards one's job is a symptom, a cue that something is wrong. It may simply be disenchantment with one's own lot in life, or it may be psychological frustration resulting from a feeling of uselessness because one's job offers no challenge.

Causes of Job Dissatisfaction (JD). Many theories as to the nature and causes of job dissatisfaction have been advanced.[4] Negative feelings can arise from lack of variety, autonomy, or challenge. They may be traced to the inability of one's work to offer a chance for promotion and recognition, or to the fact that workers are unable to see the impact of their work. Those aspects of jobs which deal with job *content* are called "motivators" by Frederick Herzberg,[5] an advocate of job enrichment (see Exercise 15) as a way of redesigning jobs to add satisfaction and improve performance, the absence of motivators leads to JD only if workers *want* and *need* challenge, autonomy, etc., from their job. Some workers may be dissatisfied with environmental aspects of their jobs, such as relations with their supervisors and co-workers, pay, fringe benefits, and working conditions (called "hygiene" factors by Herzberg), in addition to content factors or motivators. Thus, any one of a number of aspects of one's job could lead to discontent, depending of course on each worker's own needs, experience, and expectations.

Expectations and JS. The emotional feelings we have defined as JS are perceptually determined by each individual. A certain level of pay is perhaps not dissatisfying until it is *perceived* to be too low by the worker. People decide on the degree to which their jobs are satisfying by comparing them with their own expectations, and aspects of jobs which fall short can cause discontent.

But how are these expectations set? Often people compare their perceptions of what a job offers to their perceptions of what "significant" others' jobs offer. Significant others are those people or groups a person might use as points of comparison, such as family, classmates, co-workers, or friends. If a worker's subjective evaluation or perception of his or her ratio of inputs (e.g., effort) to output (e.g., pay) is lower than, for example, a brother-in-law's or a similarly employed friend's, he or she is very likely to feel shortchanged and dissatisfied. In other words, discrepancies between what people feel they *should* receive—based on their past experience, on comparisons with significant others, and/or on what they feel they need—and what they *are* receiving, can generate dissatisfaction.

It should be noted, however, that these expectations and comparisons are subjective, and often biased or even erroneous. For example, if a worker makes $13,000 per year and perceives that a neighbor makes $15,000 per year working at a similar job, the worker may be dissatisfied and hence reduce his or her effort on the job. It makes no difference if the neighbor *actually* only makes $13,000 or if the neighbor must also work evenings—what counts is the worker's *perception* of the neighbor's situation. Since we are often dealing with individual perceptions when discussing JS, the many possible causes and consequences of JD are difficult to pin down.

Consequences of JD. When someone *feels* that one or more aspects of their job are inadequate and other aspects of the job do not make up for these inadequacies, they may resort to any number of actions. They can seek another job, thereby causing the organization to select and train a replacement, often a costly process. They can come to work late or stay away the entire day, thus causing higher costs and slower production due to incomplete work crews, etc. Or, the dissatisfied worker may come to work, but withdraw psychologically—i.e., not concentrate, do no more than absolutely necessary, and have no interest or initiative. As a result, machines requiring maintenance go unattended, possible problems do not get reported to superiors, or accidents occur due to carelessness. Workers can also actively engage in behavior to either "get back" at the company (e.g., sabotage) or inject challenge into an unchallenging job by trying to see how little work they can do without getting caught. Finally, discontent can be harmful to the worker's own mental health, for it can lead to feelings of depression, inadequacy, and powerlessness.

Generally, the research evidence indicates that

[2] E. A. Locke, "What is Job Satisfaction," *Organizational Behavior and Human Performance* 4 (1969): 316. The conceptual development and research instruments for job satisfaction were initially developed by P. C. Smith and her associates. See P. C. Smith, L. M. Kendall, and C. L. Hulin, *The Measurement of Satisfaction in Work and Retirement: A Strategy for the Study of Attitudes* (Chicago: Rand McNally, 1969).

[3] See L. Porter and R. M. Steers, "Organizational, Work, and Personal Factors in Employee Turnover and Satisfaction," *Psychological Bulletin* 50 (1973): 151–176.

[4] J. P. Wanous and E. E. Lawler, "Measurement and Meaning of Job Satisfaction," *Journal of Applied Psychology* 36 (1972): 95–105.

[5] See F. Herzberg, "One More Time: How Do You Motivate Workers?" *Harvard Business Review* 46 (1968): 53–62 and Exercise 15.

a lack of job satisfaction may not result in lowered productivity, but instead manifest itself in increased production costs, such as turnover, absenteeism, tardiness, sabotage, raw-materials waste, and lower production quality. Therefore, a plant with a high level of worker dissatisfaction may not have lower productivity, but most likely will have higher production costs.[6]

Any of these consequences are not only costly financially, but also are costly in terms of wasting human resources. If people are not utilized to their capacity, both they and the organization suffer. Because these consequences of JD can be so grave, the assessment of and remedy of JD is an important task of the personnel administrator.

Remedies for JD.   Before remedies can be developed, the extent of dissatisfaction must be carefully determined. Questionnaires, observation, interviews, and assessment of company records can help to provide this type of information. The personnel administrator must tap attitudes, expectations, and discrepancies between what workers get and what they feel they deserve. This can be a time-consuming and costly activity, and distorted data are a danger. However, several questionnaires, scales, and other pencil-and-paper instruments have been designed and used for these purposes.[7] Of course, they must be tailored to the needs of each organization.

Once the extent and degree of dissatisfaction, the specific nature of the discontent (e.g., regarding pay, promotions, etc.), and the seriousness of the consequences have all been determined, a decision can be made as to whether or not anything should be done, and if so, what.

Remedies obviously depend on the specific nature of discontent. For example, if job content is a cause of dissatisfaction, Job Enrichment (JE) or job redesign may be required (see Exercise 15). If jobs and roles are ambiguous and lacking in structure, Management by Objectives (MBO) may be called for (see Exercise 6). If workers feel they do not have the required skills to perform their jobs adequately or to get promotions, training may be signaled (see Exercises 11, 12, and 13). If workers are dissatisfied with pay and extrinsic rewards, new motivational programs could be implemented (see Exercises 16 and 17). Changes in working conditions and fringe benefits, such as four-day weeks,

flexible working hours, time off with pay for good performance, modernization of facilities, offering prizes and bonuses, and even playing music and adding bright colors and art work to plants are all possible programs to improve JS.[8]

But for the personnel administrator and concerned others, the decision is not merely determining how innovative one can be in devising remedies, which may merely be fads. The task is to first assess the extent and specific nature of dissatisfaction; second, to identify and evaluate the seriousness of its consequencies; third, to decide whether or not anything should be done to remedy problems; and fourth, to design specific remedies and assess both their cost and their probable benefit. Rushing to change jobs or other aspects of work without determining the extent and nature of the problem is a primary reason for the failure of some of the remedies to job dissatisfaction listed above.

PROCEDURE

Overview.   Jobs are assessed to identify possible job characteristics leading to JD. Then, a questionnaire is designed to assess the level of JS within an organization. Data on the JS of members of an organization are provided, the extent of dissatisfaction is thereby assessed, and possible remedies are proposed. Finally, you are to detail the steps you, as a personnel administrator or personnel staff member, would take to increase JS.

PART A

STEP 1:   Choose at least one type of job listed on the top of Form 1 and determine what you believe are the major aspects of the job, its content, its environment, etc., or those "variables" influencing JS/JD in that job (column 1). Also determine why these areas are important (column 2) and what could be done to enhance satisfaction in each (column 3). For example, one "variable" may be "the chance for participation in decision making," an important factor because it leads to a feeling of worth and autonomy, which might make one feel positive (satisfied) about the job. Thus, to improve participation in decision making, and hence improve satisfaction, you could hold open meetings or request employee input regarding organizational decisions.

TIME: About 35 minutes.

---

[6] E. E. Lawler, *Motivation in Work Organizations* (Monterey, Cal.: Brooks/Cole, 1973).

[7] The Institute of Social Research of the University of Michigan has been a leader in the development and compilation of these instruments. Catalogues and specific instruments appear in *For Further Reading.*

[8] See *For Further Reading* for case studies of these various techniques.

PART B

STEP 2: Using Form 2 you are to design a survey questionnaire or instrument to collect information on the level of JS in an entire organization. Begin by determining the variables influenced by organization-wide policies and programs affecting several types of jobs (e.g., pay, work load, supervision, etc.) that you wish to measure. Then design questions that would provide information on the level of satisfaction on the variables. Also present ideas about possible alternatives to improve satisfaction on each dimension. Be sure to indicate a set of possible responses to be used by respondents for each question. For example, possible responses to the question, "How satisfied are you with your recent pay raise?" could be "Extremely satisfied," "Satisfied," "Neutral," etc. Numerical values could also be attached to responses in order to assess the level of dissatisfaction quantitatively. Several of the sources in the *For Further Reading* section offer ideas on how to set up the questions and response alternatives, as well as possible remedies to JD.

TIME: About 50 minutes; additional time is required if external sources are to be used for suggestions.

PART C

STEP 3: In Form 3 you are given a sample set of data, the result of a job-satisfaction survey in an organization. The instrument used to gather the data was the Job Descriptive Index (JDI) (Form 4), a very useful JS measuring tool.[9] Review both the JDI itself and the sample scores provided and determine what the consequences of JD might be and what specific action you would take for each of the types of jobs listed (based on the JDI scores) to improve satisfaction in those cases where you feel action is necessary. Record this information on Form 5. For example, for production workers the average JDI score for "satisfaction with supervision" is 26.24. Since the norm or average response on this scale for

men is 41.10, the 26.24 obtained would indicate very low satisfaction. On Form 5, you would thus indicate low satisfaction on supervision for production workers in column 2; you would indicate what negative consequences this could have (column 3); and what steps could be taken to remedy the low satisfaction (column 4).

TIME: About 60 minutes.

FOR FURTHER READING

Allen, A. D. "The Topeka System—Beating the Blue Collar Blues." *Personnel Administrator* 19, no. 1 (1974): 49–52. (I)

Bouchard, T. J. "Field Research Methods: Interviewing, Questionnaires, Participant Observation, Systematic Observation, Unobtrusive Measures." In M. D. Dunnette, ed., *Handbook of Industrial and Organizational Psychology*. Chicago: Rand McNally, 1976. (II)

Brayfield, A. H., and W. H. Crockett. "Employee Attitudes and Employee Performance." *Psychological Bulletin* 52 (1955): 396–424. (II)

Cherns, A. "Perspectives on the Quality of Working Life." *Journal of Occupational Psychology* 40 (1975): 155–167. (II)

Deci, E. L. "Work—Who Does Not Like It and Why." *Psychology Today* 5 (1972): 57–84+. (I)

Dunnette, M. D., ed. *Work and Nonwork in the Year 2001*. Monterey, Cal.: Brooks/Cole, 1973. (I)

Fairfield, R. P., ed. *Humanizing the Workplace*. Buffalo: Prometheus, 1974. (I)

Garson, B. *All the Livelong Day: The Meaning and Demeaning of Routine Work*. Garden City, N.J.: Doubleday, 1975. (I)

Greene, C. N. "The Satisfaction-Performance Controversy." *Business Horizons* 15 (1972): 31–42. (I)

Hackman, J. R., and G. R. Oldham. "Development of the Job Diagnostic Survey." *Journal of Applied Psychology* 60 (1975): 159–170. (II–R)

Herzberg, F. "The Wise Old Turk." *Harvard Business Review* 52 (1974): 70–80. (I)

Hulin, C. L., and M. R. Blood. "Job Enlargement, Individual Differences and Worker Responses." *Psychological Bulletin* 69 (1968): 41–55. (II)

Hulin, C. L., and P. C. Smith. "A Linear Model of Job Satisfaction." *Journal of Applied Psychology* 49 (1965): 209–216. (II–R)

Hunt, J. W., and P. N. Saul. "The Relationship of Age, Tenure, and Job Satisfaction in Males and Females." *Academy of Management Journal* 18 (1975): 690–702. (II–R)

---

[9] Each of the five subscales of the JDI is given a different score. Within each subscale, each positive item marked "Y" (see Form 4) receives three points, each item marked "?" receives one point, and each item marked "N" receives zero points. Negative items are scored in the opposite manner (i.e., Y = 0 points, ? = 1 point, N = 3 points). Points are summed for all items within a subscale to compute the JDI for the subscale.

Kahn, R. L. "The Work Module—A Tonic for Lunch-pail Lassitude." *Psychology Today* 6 (1973): 35–39+. (I)

Keller, R. T. "Role Conflict and Ambiguity: Correlates with Job Satisfaction and Values." *Personnel Psychology* 28 (1975): 57–64. (I)

Lawler, E. E. "Should the Quality of Work Life Be Legislated?" *Personnel Administrator* 21, no.1 (January 1976): 17–21. (I)

Locke, E. A. "What Is Job Satisfaction?" *Organizational Behavior and Human Performance* 5 (1970): 484–500. (II)

Locke, E. A. "The Nature and Causes of Job Satisfaction." In M. D. Dunnette, ed., *Handbook of Industrial and Organizational Psychology.* Chicago: Rand McNally, 1976. (II)

Mayo, Elton. *The Social Problems of an Industrial Civilization.* Cambridge, Mass.: Harvard University Press, 1945. (I)

McGrath, J. E. "Stress and Behavior in Organizations." In M. D. Dunnette, ed., *Handbook of Industrial and Organizational Psychology.* Chicago: Rand McNally, 1976. (II)

Paine, F. T., and M. J. Gannon. "Job Attitudes of Supervisors and Managers." *Personnel Psychology* 26 (1973): 521–530. (II–R)

Porter, L. W., and K. H. Roberts. "Communication in Organizations." In M. D. Dunnette, ed., *Handbook of Industrial and Organizational Psychology.* Chicago: Rand McNally, 1976. (II)

Porter, L. W., and R. M. Steers. "Organizational, Work, and Personal Factors in Employee Turnover and Satisfaction." *Psychological Bulletin* 50 (1973): 151–176. (II)

Pritchard, R. D., and B. W. Karasick. "The Effects of Organizational Climate on Managerial Job Performance and Job Satisfaction." *Organizational Behavior and Human Performance* 9 (1973): 126–146. (II–R)

Quinn, R. P., and L. J. Shepard. *The 1972–73 Quality of Employment Survey.* Ann Arbor, Mich.: Survey Research Center, 1974. (I–R)

Robinson, J. P., R. Athanasiou, and K. B. Head. *Measures of Occupational Attitudes and Occupational Characteristics.* Ann Arbor, Mich.: Survey Research Center, 1973. (II)

Seeman, M. "On the Meaning of Alienation." *American Sociological Review* 24 (1959): 783–791. (I)

Sims, H. P., and A. D. Szilagyi. "Leader Reward Behavior and Subordinate Satisfaction and Performance." *Organizational Behavior and Human Performance* 14 (1975): 426–438. (II–R)

Skinner, W. "The Anachronistic Factory." *Harvard Business Review* 49 (1971): 61–70. (I)

Smith, P. C., L. M. Kendall, and C. L. Hulin. *The Measurement of Satisfaction in Work and Retirement: A Strategy for the Study of Attitudes.* Chicago: Rand McNally, 1969. (II–R)

Special Task Force to the Secretary of Health, Education, and Welfare and W. E. Upjohn Institute. *Work in America.* Cambridge, Mass.: MIT, 1973. (I)

Stone, E. F., and L. W. Porter. "Job Characteristics and Job Attitudes: A Multivariate Study." *Journal of Applied Psychology* 60 (1975): 57–64. (II–R)

Taylor, J. C., and P. R. Shaver. *Measures of Social Psychological Attitudes.* Ann Arbor, Mich.: Survey Research Center, 1973. (II)

Terkel, S. *Working.* New York: Pantheon, 1974. (I)

"The Job Blahs: Who Wants to Work." *Newsweek,* 26 March 1973, pp. 79–82, 84, 89. (I)

U.S. Department of Labor. *Job Satisfaction: Is There a Trend?* Washington, D.C.: U.S. Government Printing Office, 1974. (I)

U.S. National Technical Information Service (NTIS). *Job Satisfaction: A Bibliography with Abstracts.* Springfield, Va.: NTIS, 1975. (I)

Wanous, J. P., and E. C. Lawler. "Measurement and Meaning of Job Satisfaction." *Journal of Applied Psychology* 56 (1972): 95–105. (II)

Weaver, C. N. "Correlates of Job Satisfaction: Some Evidence from the National Surveys." *Academy of Management Journal* 17 (1974): 373–375. (I–R)

Wernimont, P. F. "A Systems View of Job Satisfaction." *Journal of Applied Psychology* 56 (1972): 173–176. (II)

Williams, L. K., J. W. Seybolt, and C. C. Pinder. "On Administering Questionnaires in Organizational Settings." *Personnel Psychology* 28 (1975): 93–103. (II)

Wool, H. "What's Wrong with Work in America? A Review Essay." *Monthly Labor Review* 96, no. 3 (1973): 38–44. (I)

Zimbardo, P. *Influencing Attitudes and Changing Behavior.* Reading, Mass.: Addison-Wesley, 1969. (I)

Name _____   Group Number _____

Date _____ Class Section _____ Hour _____   Score _____

PART A

Form 1 Diagnosing Determinants of Satisfaction-Dissatisfaction in Various Job Types

Type of job (check one or more)

_____ machine operator

_____ clerical worker

_____ executive

_____ sales staff

_____ research and development scientist

_____ other (please specify)

List the major "variables" related to worker job satisfaction for the job checked above. 1	List reasons for the importance of this variable. 2	What could be done to enhance worker satisfaction on this variable? 3
1.		
2.		
3.		
4.		
5.		

Type of job (check one or more)

_____ machine operator   _____ sales staff
_____ clerical worker   _____ research and development scientist
_____ executive   _____ other (please specify)

List the major "variables" related to worker job satisfaction for the job checked above. 1	List reasons for the importance of this variable. 2	What could be done to enhance worker satisfaction on this variable? 3
6.		
7.		
8.		
9.		
10.		

Name _____   Group Number _____

Date _____ Class Section _____ Hour _____ Score _____

PART B

Form 2 Organizational Survey Questionnaire for Job Satisfaction and Dissatisfaction

Dimension 1 _____

    A. Questions (to measure level of satisfaction):

       1.

       2.

    B. Alternatives (to improve level of satisfaction, if desired):

       1.

       2.

Dimension 2 _____

    A. Questions:

       1.

       2.

    B. Alternatives:

       1.

       2.

Dimension 3 _____

    A. Questions:

       1.

       2.

    B. Alternatives:

       1.

       2.

Dimension 4 _____

    A. Questions:
       1.

       2.

    B. Alternatives:
       1.

       2.

Dimension 5 _____

    A. Questions:
       1.

       2.

    B. Alternatives:
       1.

       2.

Dimension 6 _____

    A. Questions:
       1.

       2.

    B. Alternatives:
       1.

       2.

PART C

Form 3 Sample Results of the JDI for an Organization by Department and JDI Norms for Males and Females

I. Sample results for an organization (hypothetical data).

Subscale of the JDI*	Management			Production workers			Clerical workers			Sales staff			Research and development			Finance department		
	N (Sample size)	$\bar{X}$ (Mean)	SD† (Std. deviation)	N	$\bar{X}$	SD	N	$\bar{X}$	SD	N	$\bar{X}$	SD	N	$\bar{X}$	SD	N	$\bar{X}$	SD
Work	118	51.43	6.23	189	31.68	5.43	58	43.28	4.88	12	51.38	4.66	14	52.57	7.61	23	19.44	4.37
Pay	143	23.24	10.06	189	20.28	3.66	58	16.23	5.67	13	25.46	1.32	14	23.11	6.61	23	16.87	3.24
Promotions	117	18.36	5.24	168	24.37	4.28	58	20.47	3.21	13	23.62	4.33	14	18.88	3.32	23	11.43	3.97
Supervision	126	30.37	10.28	187	26.24	18.11	58	42.43	6.74	13	35.57	6.72	14	35.61	4.67	23	30.88	4.68
Co-workers	118	26.32	11.46	189	46.23	11.36	58	46.29	9.53	13	40.25	7.36	14	38.23	11.29	23	36.24	3.61

II. Male and female norms for the JDI based on large, diverse samples (hypothetical data).

Subscale of the JDI*	Males			Females		
	N	$\bar{X}$	SD	N	$\bar{X}$	SD
Work	2150	35.56	11.53	2077	34.68	8.87
Pay	1997	17.90	15.92	1876	19.60	16.62
Promotions	3153	21.64	16.76	3026	20.31	17.83
Supervision	1952	40.87	11.85	1771	42.82	10.36
Co-workers	1947	44.44	9.63	1631	45.90	8.47

* Maximum possible scores are work—54; pay—27; promotions—27; supervision—54; and co-workers—54.
† SD refers to the degree to which scores are scattered about the mean. Hence, low SD figures indicate little scatter about the mean, an indication of agreement amongst the sample.

PART C

Form 4

**THE
JOB
DESCRIPTIVE
INDEX**

Code Number _____

Company _____

City _____

Think of your present work. What is it like most of the time? In the blank beside each word given below, write

_Y_ for "Yes" if it describes your work

_N_ for "No" if it does NOT describe it

_?_ if you cannot decide

WORK ON PRESENT JOB

_____ Fascinating

_____ Routine

_____ Satisfying

_____ Boring

_____ Good

_____ Creative

_____ Respected

_____ Hot

_____ Pleasant

_____ Useful

_____ Tiresome

_____ Healthful

_____ Challenging

_____ On your feet

_____ Frustrating

_____ Simple

_____ Endless

_____ Gives sense of accomplishment

Think of the pay you get now. How well does each of the following words describe your present pay? In the blank beside each word, put

_y_ if it describes your pay

_N_ if it does NOT describe it

_?_ if you cannot decide

PRESENT PAY

____ Income adequate for normal expenses

____ Satisfactory profit sharing

____ Barely live on income

____ Bad

____ Income provides luxuries

____ Insecure

____ Less than I deserve

____ Highly paid

____ Underpaid

Think of the kind of supervision that you get on your job. How well does each of the following words describe this supervision? In the blank beside each word below, put

_y_ if it describes the supervision you get on your job

_N_ if it does NOT describe it

_?_ if you cannot decide

SUPERVISION ON PRESENT JOB

____ Asks my advice

____ Hard to please

____ Impolite

____ Praises good work

____ Tactful

____ Influential

____ Up-to-date

____ Doesn't supervise enough

____ Quick tempered

____ Tells me where I stand

____ Annoying

____ Stubborn

____ Knows job well

____ Bad

____ Intelligent

____ Leaves me on my own

____ Around when needed

____ Lazy

Think of the opportunities for promotion that you have now. How well does each of the following words describe these? In the blank beside each word put

_y_ for "Yes" if it describes your opportunities for promotion

_N_ for "No" if it does NOT describe them

_?_ if you cannot decide

OPPORTUNITIES FOR PROMOTION

____ Good opportunities for promotion

____ Opportunity somewhat limited

____ Promotion on ability

____ Dead-end job

____ Good chance for promotion

____ Unfair promotion policy

____ Infrequent promotions

____ Regular promotions

____ Fairly good chance for promotion

Think of the majority of the people that you work with now or the people you meet in connection with your work. How well does each of the following words describe these people? In the blank beside each word below, put

_y_ if it describes the people you work with

_N_ if it does NOT describe them

_?_ if you cannot decide

PEOPLE ON YOUR PRESENT JOB

____ Stimulating

Boring

____ Slow

____ Ambitious

____ Stupid

____ Responsible

____ Fast

____ Intelligent

____ Easy to make enemies

____ Talk too much

____ Smart

____ Lazy

____ Unpleasant

____ No privacy

____ Active

____ Narrow interests

____ Loyal

____ Hard to meet

Name _____ Group Number _____

Date _____ Class Section _____ Hour _____ Score _____

PART C

Form 5 Record Form for Identifying Areas of Job Dissatisfaction and Planning Courses of Action

Job group (Refer to Form 3) 1	Particular area(s) of highest job dissatisfaction (i.e., work, pay, etc.) 2	Possible negative or deleterious consequences to the organization and/or worker if dissatisfaction persists 3	Specific possible steps to be taken to remedy the situation 4
Management	1.	a. b.	a. b. c.
	2.	a. b.	a. b. c.
	3.	a. b.	a. b. c.
Production workers	1.	a. b.	a. b. c.
	2.	a. b.	a. b. c.
	3.	a. b.	a. b. c.

Job group 1	Particular area(s) of highest job dissatisfaction (i.e., work, pay, etc.) 2	Possible negative or deleterious consequences to the organization and/or worker if dissatisfaction persists 3	Specific possible steps to be taken to remedy the situation 4
Clerical workers	1.	a. b.	a. b. c.
	2.	a. b.	a. b. c.
	3.	a. b.	a. b. c.
Sales staff	1.	a. b.	a. b. c.
	2.	a. b.	a. b. c.
	3.	a. b.	a. b. c.

Job group 1	Particular area(s) of highest job dissatisfaction (i.e., work, pay, etc.) 2	Possible negative or deleterious consequences to the organization and/or worker if dissatisfaction persists 3	Specific possible steps to be taken to remedy the situation 4
Research and development	1.	a. b.	a. b. c.
	2.	a. b.	a. b. c.
	3.	a. b.	a. b. c.
Finance department	1.	a. b.	a. b. c.
	2.	a. b.	a. b. c.

Name _____ Group Number _____

Date _____ Class Section _____ Hour _____ Score _____

ASSESSMENT OF LEARNING IN PERSONNEL ADMINISTRATION

EXERCISE 14

1. Try to state the purpose of this exercise in one concise sentence.

2. Specifically what did you learn from this exercise (i.e., skills, abilities, and knowledge)?

3. How might your learning influence your role and your duties as a personnel administrator?

4. Do you feel job dissatisfaction is a major organizational problem in this country? Why or why not?

5. Could you translate job satisfaction scores on the JDI to actual dollar amounts representing various costs to an organization? What type of cost data would you need to do this?

6. Assume there is very high job dissatisfaction amongst janitorial workers in a hospital. What are some of the specific, possible consequences for the organization, its patients, and the rest of its staff?

7. Additional questions given by your implementor:

Exercise 15

DESIGNING AND IMPLEMENTING JOB ENRICHMENT PROGRAMS

OVERVIEW

Many times problems of poor performance cannot be remedied by training. In these cases, workers have the skill and ability to perform well but may be *unwilling* to do so. The reasons are many and complex. Several techniques have been developed to "motivate" workers or to induce them to choose those behaviors that lead to successful performance. One such technique to improve worker performance and satisfaction is Job Enrichment (JE). In JE, the *content* of jobs is changed in order to provide such rewards as recognition, challenge, and autonomy to workers. These types of rewards are referred to as "intrinsic" rewards, because they are mediated by the person doing the work (i.e., he or she feels pride). The work itself, rather than what is gained by doing the work (e.g., money), is rewarding. JE is a technique designed to improve performance and productivity by offering intrinsic awards. The *Introduction* to the exercise explains JE and its assumptions and discusses the implementation of JE programs. You are asked to assess jobs as to their applicability for JE and to role play in a situation in which a JE program is being considered.

OBJECTIVES

1. To introduce the motivational strategy of JE, improving performance through intrinsic rewards, and its theoretical basis.
2. To build skill in identifying both job and situational characteristics which could lead to effective or ineffective JE programs.
3. To build skill in JE program design and implementation.

PREMEETING ASSIGNMENT

Read the entire exercise, except for Part D. Do not read this part until instructed to do so by your implementor.

INTRODUCTION

Job Enrichment as a Motivation Technique

As noted in Exercise 14, well-publicized surveys[1] of blue-collar and white-collar workers suggest that they are basically dissatisfied with their jobs: they view their jobs as "dead-ends" and feel no pride in their work. Several reasons can be suggested to account for these feelings. The high degree of specialization in industry has fractionalized tasks and precludes workers from seeing the relationship of their work to the whole. Also, workers' expectations regarding what they want from work are more demanding. In addition, educational levels of the work force have risen steadily, and this increase may lead people to expect more from their jobs than merely the receipt

---

[1] The HEW Special Task Force Report called *Work in America* (Boston, Mass.: MIT Press, 1973).

of economic rewards. They may desire to develop their own skills and abilities and grow emotionally and intellectually.

Frederick Herzberg's Work. A management response to this situation of dissatisfaction has been to change the *content* of work from dull, routine, and unchallenging jobs to ones that offer challenge and a chance for growth and recognition. Frederick Herzberg[2] has developed a theory that views the job situation as offering both *hygiene* factors to workers, which relate to the job context or environment (i.e., pay, supervision, interpersonal relations, security, etc.) and *motivator* factors, which concern the job content (i.e., growth, recognition, challenge, autonomy, etc.). In Herzberg's thesis, job satisfaction and, hence, desired job performance can only come from the motivators—hygiene factors cause job dissatisfaction when they are absent, but do not lead to job satisfaction when they are present. Only by changing jobs to include motivators can we motivate workers. In other words, the absence of dissatisfaction (i.e., hygiene factors are present) does not necessarily ensure the presence of job satisfaction. Motivators must be built into the job for job satisfaction, and Herzberg sees satisfaction as a prerequisite to successful performance.

Herzberg's ideas are based on certain assumptions about work and workers. One assumption is that workers require and expect to be satisfied *on* the job, through meaningful work (i.e., enriched with motivators), rather than *off* the job. Hygiene factors, if they motivate people at all, only do so in the short run; motivators are needed for long-run commitment and good performance. Herzberg also assumes that as motivators are provided for workers, their desire for costly hygiene factors will decrease.[3]

Vertical Job Loading. The management strategy that follows from these ideas is to redesign jobs to provide motivators—in short, to "enrich" jobs. Job enrichment (JE) has been attempted in some organizations by increasing the degree of worker autonomy, achievement, and so on. This is usually accomplished by *vertical* job loading. For example, an assembler's job would be increased in a *vertical* fashion by allowing the assembler to perform the

tasks necessary to produce an entire subassembly, rather than merely making one small addition to a half-completed subassembly. The job is thus loaded vertically to encompass tasks that previously preceded and succeeded the task, rather than simply adding tasks at the same level (job enlargement or horizontal job loading). The worker now feels more of a sense of accomplishment and may feel increased pride as a result of the change. By building in intrinsic rewards, the job has been enriched.

The objective in JE is to motivate workers by the work itself—by providing work that is interesting and challenging, rather than motivating by means of larger and larger hygiene factors (such as money) as inducements to perform monotonous jobs.

Applicability of JE. Thus, JE would seem most appropriate for dull, routine jobs—jobs where there is considerable worker dissatisfaction, absenteeism, turnover, or sabotage.[4] JE would be best applied where a measure of productivity is available or where desired performance has been specified such that any improvement in work output as a result of JE can be identified. JE is also effective in jobs where the cost of hygiene factors is very high. Finally, a JE program would be most beneficial for those jobs that have a significant impact on overall organization goal attainment. It is in these jobs that poor attitudes, lack of motivation, and poor performance are obviously most problematic and costly.

Implementing JE. A typical JE program should be carefully planned and coupled with specific organizational needs.[5] Perhaps one of the most common failures of JE programs is selecting a job to be enriched which does not fit the profile suggested above. Another problem is failing to account for the workers' sociological and psychological make-up—their values, cultural background, age, and personal needs. For example, rural workers, as opposed to those with urban backgrounds, may desire more interesting work with more variety and autonomy due to their previous employment history (e.g., as self-employed farmers). Younger workers may have higher job expectations than older workers and, particularly if

[2] See F. Herzberg, *Work and the Nature of Man* (Cleveland: World, 1966); or F. Herzberg, "One More Time: How Do You Motivate Workers?" *Harvard Business Review* 46, no. 1 (1968): 53–62.
[3] F. Herzberg, "One More Time: How Do You Motivate Workers?" *Harvard Business Review* 46, no. 1 (1968): 53–62.

[4] R. W. Beatty and C. E. Schneier, "A Case for Positive Reinforcement," *Business Horizons* 18, no. 2 (1975): 71–78.
[5] J. R. Hackman and his colleagues have been developing an extremely useful procedure which explains those aspects of jobs leading to poor performance and offers a diagnostic system that facilitates the identification of specific problems that could be amenable to JE programs. See, e.g., J. R. Hackman et al., "A New Strategy for Job Enrichment," *California Management Review* 17 (Summer 1975): 57–71.

they do not have families to support, may value money and job security less than autonomy and challenge at work. These individual and group disparities could spell the difference between success and failure of a JE program.

Although JE is a complex system which exists in many varieties in actual practice,[6] typical steps in the implementation procedure can be summarized as follows:

1. Select an appropriate job—one in which there is now poor performance and in which successful performance is crucial to organizational or departmental goal attainment. The job must be amenable to JE by having potential for content change.
2. Assess worker attitudes, values, and expectations regarding work.
3. Determine measures of performance in order to note any changes after JE and direction of the changes.
4. Identify changes in job content which would be required to enrich the job, as well as changes in discretion or amount of "say" the worker has.
5. Make sure the changes are feasible and practical, and represent vertical, rather than horizontal, job loading.
6. Implement the job-content changes and enlist the cooperation of job holders and supervisors by allowing them to participate in program design.
7. Assess the effects of the program over time to note changes in actual performance.

Is JE a Cure-All?   JE is not the remedy to all motivation problems. Its effectiveness is limited by assumptions that are not universally applicable, by practical considerations, and by the fact that relatively few organizations have used JE and, therefore, a large amount of data is not yet available regarding its effectiveness. For individuals interested in obtaining rewards (i.e., money) that enable them to satisfy any needs they might have for autonomy and challenge *off* the job, JE would not seem appropriate—these workers want simply to be paid. Further, some jobs cannot be enriched feasibly— the economic costs of changes required in equipment and work flow may be great enough to offset the potential gains of JE.[7] Until more data is available

on the merits of JE, some organizations may be reluctant to try it. A review of the literature,[8] although now some years old, concluded that the case for JE had been overstated. Not enough conclusive data were available and the positive results seemed to apply only to certain segments of the labor force.

Despite limitations, JE remains potentially an extremely useful strategy for motivation problems, as it enables workers to perform challenging jobs that provide variety, autonomy, and a chance for personal growth and achievement. If workers can be motivated "through the work itself," rather than by other types of rewards, certain long-run motivation problems can possibly be alleviated. Behind the JE programs lies the assumption, noted by Herzberg, that if people are not utilized to their fullest capacity in their jobs, motivation problems will eventually surface.

PROCEDURE

Overview.   Your basic understanding of the factors that enrich jobs is reviewed in Part A. Aspects of the work situation which would lead to effective or ineffective JE efforts are reviewed in Part B. In Part C, jobs are analyzed as to their potential for being enriched through a JE program, and in Part D, a JE program is discussed by workers in a role-playing situation.

PART A

STEP 1:   Frederick Herzberg has distinguished those factors that, when built into a job, would enrich it, from those that would not. The former are called *motivator* factors and the latter *hygiene* factors. Review the list of motivators and hygiene factors (Form 1) and identify them as such. Break into small groups to discuss the following questions: What do the factors in each of the two groups have in common? How are they dissimilar?

TIME: About 15 minutes.

PART B

STEP 2:   Because job enrichment, or vertical job loading, is a method designed to build motivators into jobs, it is typically used to implement Herzberg's theory. But certain considerations are important in this process

---

[6] For examples of JE programs in organizations, see W. Reif, D. Ferrazzi, and R. Evans, "Job Enrichment: Who Uses It and Why," *Business Horizons* 17, no. 1 (1974): 71–78.

[7] S. A. Levitan and W. B. Johnson, "Job Redesign, Reform, Enrichment—Exploring the Limitations," *Monthly Labor Review* 96 (1973): 36–41.

[8] C. L. Hulin and M. R. Blood, "Job Enlargement, Individual Differences, and Worker Happiness," *Psychological Bulletin* 69 (1968): 41–55. More recent reviews and discussions are found in *For Further Reading*.

of job redesign. Listed in Form 2 are considerations regarding the job, the people involved, and particular aspects of an organization. Below each consideration briefly note whether or not it would facilitate or deter a job-enrichment program's effectiveness and why. In your small groups, discuss what the items in each of the two categories (i.e., deterrents and facilitators) have in common.

TIME: About 25 minutes.

PART C

STEP 3: Certain jobs are more amenable to vertical job loading or job enrichment than others. Before a job-enrichment program is begun, the job to be enriched should be assessed as to the applicability of job enrichment. A questionnaire (Form 3) and tally sheet (Form 4) are provided, which enable you to evaluate or "score" various jobs according to their potential for job enrichment. Remember: usually those jobs most amenable to job enrichment are dull, repetitive, and narrow, and are characterized by poor performance, high turnover, and/or absenteeism. Also, performance in such jobs is critical to organizational success, and high set-up costs for sophisticated machinery or high fixed costs in work flow might outweigh positive motivation considerations and preclude an economical change to JE. After reading each of the job descriptions provided in Forms 5–9, score each of the jobs with the questionnaire. A job with high potential for job enrichment will receive an average score of 4.0–5.0; jobs of low potential will receive scores of 1.0–2.0. "Potential" refers to the probability of positive return in terms of performance for the investment in a job-enrichment program. What do the jobs with high potential have in common? What do the jobs with low potential have in common?

TIME: About 40 minutes.

PART D

STEP 4: In order to implement a job-enrichment program and observe the process of changing job content, a role-playing situation is provided (Form 10). Each member of a small group takes part in the role play. There are six workers and one or more observers. Do

not read any of the roles until your implementor has told you to do so.

One person assumes the role of Janice Jaguar, the manager, and another assumes the role of Lem Hooper, the personnel director. There are roles for four workers, and one or more observers is also used. Each person reads *only* their own role instructions and the general instructions to the role play. Then the roles are enacted in a group discussion involving the workers and their supervisor. Observers record their observations on the form provided (Form 11). Observers should read their instructions carefully before they fill out the form. After this group discussion, Janice briefly meets alone with Clem to relay the decision made by the group and the final decision as to any change is made between Janice and Clem.

After your group has completed the role play, discuss the solution you reached in light of what you now know about job enrichment. Discuss the observers' comments and the feedback given to the person who played the role of the manager. Was your group's solution job enrichment? Who in the group was satisfied? Why?

TIME: About 35 minutes for role plays and 20 minutes for discussion.

FOR FURTHER READING

Allen, A. D. "The Topeka System—Beating the Blue Collar Blues." *Personnel Administrator* 19, no. 1 (1974): 49–52. (I)

Beatty, R. W., and C. E. Schneier. "A Case for Positive Reinforcement." *Business Horizons* 18, no. 2 (April 1975): 71–78. (I)

Beck, R. "Can the Production Line Be Humanized?" *MSU Business Topics* 22 (Autumn 1974): 27–36. (I)

Campbell, J. P. "Motivation Theory in Industrial and Organizational Psychology." In M. D. Dunnette, ed., *Handbook of Industrial and Organizational Psychology.* Chicago: Rand McNally, 1976. (II)

Cooper, R. "Task Characteristics and Intrinsic Motivation." *Human Relations* 26 (1973): 387–413. (II–R)

Davis, L. E. "Job Design and Productivity: A New Approach." *Personnel* 33 (1957): 418–429. (I)

Davis, L. E., and J. C. Taylor, eds. *Design of Jobs*. Baltimore: Penguin, 1972. (II–R)

Dyer, L., and D. F. Parker. "Classifying Outcomes in Work Motivation Research: An Examination of the Intrinsic-Extrinsic Dichotomy." *Journal of Applied Psychology* 60 (1975): 455–458. (II–R)

Ford, R. N. *Motivation through the Work Itself*. New York: American Management Association, 1969. (I)

Ford, R. N. "Job Enrichment Lessons at AT&T. *Harvard Business Review* 51, no. 1 (1973): 96–106. (I)

Frank, L. L., and J. R. Hackman. "A Failure of Job Enrichment: The Case of the Change That Wasn't." *Journal of Applied Behavioral Science* 11 (October–December 1975): 413–436. (II–R)

Gibson, C. H. "Volvo Increases Productivity through Job Enrichment." *California Management Review* 15, no. 4 (Summer 1973): 64–66. (I)

Hackman, J. R. "Group Influences on Individuals." In M. D. Dunnette, ed., *Handbook of Industrial and Organizational Psychology*. Chicago: Rand McNally, 1976. (II)

Hackman, J. R. et al. "A New Strategy for Job Enrichment." *California Management Review* 17 (Summer 1975): 57–71. (I)

Hackman, J. R., and E. E. Lawler. "Employee Reactions to Job Characteristics." *Journal of Applied Psychology Monograph* 55 (1971): 259–286. (II–R)

Herzberg, F. "One More Time: How Do You Motivate Workers?" *Harvard Business Review* 46, no. 1 (1968): 53–62. (I)

Herzberg, F. "New Perspectives on the Will to Work." *Personnel Administrator* 19 (July–August 1974): 21–25. (I)

Herzberg, F. et al. *The Motivation to Work*. New York: Wiley, 1959. (I)

Herzberg, F. "Motivation-Hygiene Profiles." *Organization Dynamics* 3, no. 2 (Fall 1974): 18–29. (I)

Herzberg, F. *Work and the Nature of Man*. Cleveland: World, 1966. (I)

House, R. J., and L. A. Wigdor. "Herzberg's Dual-Factor Theory of Job Satisfaction and Motivation: A Review of the Evidence and a Criticism." *Personnel Psychology* 20 (1967): 369–389. (II)

Hulin, C. L., and M. R. Blood. "Job Enlargement, Individual Differences, and Worker Responses." *Psychological Bulletin* 69 (1968): 41–55. (II)

Kahn, R. L. "The Work Module—A Tonic for Lunchpail Lassitude." *Psychology Today* 5 (February 1973): 35–39. (I)

Lawler, E. E., J. R. Hackman, and S. Kaufman. "Effects of Job Redesign: A Field Experiment." *Journal of Applied Social Psychology* 3 (1973): 49–62. (II–R)

Levitan, S. A., and W. B. Johnson. "Job Redesign, Reform, and Enrichment: Exploring the Limitations." *Monthly Labor Review* 96 (July 1973): 35–41. (I)

Locke, E. A. "Toward a Theory of Task Motivation and Incentives." *Organizational Behavior and Human Performance* 3 (1968): 157–189. (II)

Maher, J. R. *New Perspectives in Job Enrichment*. New York: Van Nostrand, 1971. (I)

Miner, J. B., and J. F. Brewer. "The Management of Ineffective Performance." In M. D. Dunnette, ed., *Handbook of Industrial and Organizational Psychology*. Chicago: Rand McNally, 1976. (II)

Morgan, C. P., and R. W. Beatty. "Organizational Considerations in Applying Job Enrichment." *Colorado Business Review* 47, no. 9 (September 1974): 2–4. (I)

Myers, M. S. "Every Employee a Manager." *California Management Review* 10, no. 3 (Spring 1968): 9–20. (I)

Reif, W. E., and P. P. Schoderbek. "Job Enlargement: Antidote to Apathy." *Management of Personnel Quarterly* 5, no. 1 (Spring 1966): 16–23. (I)

Reif, W., D. Ferazzi, and R. Evans. "Job Enrichment: Who Uses It and Why." *Business Horizons* 17, no. 1 (1974): 71–78. (I)

Roche, W., J., and N. L. MacKinnon. "Motivating People with Meaningful Work." *Harvard Business Review* 48, no. 3 (May–June 1970): 97–110. (I)

Sandler, B. E. "Eclecticism at Work—Approaches to Job Design." *American Psychologist* (October 1974): 767–773. (II)

Schappe, R. H. "Twenty-Two Arguments against Job Enrichment." *Personnel Journal* 53, no. 2 (1974): 116–123. (I)

Sirota, D., and A. D. Wolfson. "Pragmatic Approach to People Problems." *Harvard Business Review* 51, no. 1 (1973): 120–128. (I)

"The Job Blahs: Who Wants to Work?" *Newsweek*, 26 March 1973, pp. 79–90. (I)

Vroom, V. H. "Leadership." In M. D. Dunnette, ed., *Handbook of Industrial and Organizational Psychology*. Chicago: Rand McNally, 1976. (II)

Walters, R. W., and Associates, Inc. *Job Enrichment for Results: Strategies for Successful Implementation*. Reading, Mass. : Addison-Wesley, 1975. (I)

"Wanted: Ways to Make the Job Less Dull." *Business Week*, 12 May 1973, pp. 147–148. (I)

Whitsett, D. A. "Where Are Your Unenriched Jobs?" *Harvard Business Review* 51, no. 1 (January–February 1975): 74–80. (I)

Whitsett, D. A., and E. K. Winslow. "An Analysis of Studies Critical of the Motivation-Hygiene Theory." *Personnel Psychology* 20 (1967): 391–415. (II)

Name _____ Group Number _____

Date _____ Class Section _____ Hour _____ Score _____

PART A

Form 1 Identifying Motivators and Hygiene Factors for Job Enrichment

I. Which of the following items are Frederick Herzberg's* motivators? Please place an M beside the items he would call motivators, and an H beside the items he would call hygiene factors.

____ 1. Personal life outside the job
____ 2. The possibility of growth
____ 3. Interpersonal relations with subordinates
____ 4. Recognition
____ 5. The organization's policy and administration
____ 6. Achievement
____ 7. Interpersonal relations with supervisor
____ 8. The work itself
____ 9. Supervision
____ 10. Responsibility
____ 11. Status
____ 12. Advancements, promotions
____ 13. Job security
____ 14. Work conditions
____ 15. Salary
____ 16. Interpersonal relations with peers

II. How are the motivators similar to each other and different from the hygiene factors?

---

* See *Introduction* to this exercise and/or F. Herzberg, "One More Time: How Do You Motivate Workers?" *Harvard Business Review* 46, no. 1 (1968): 53–62.

Name _____ Group Number _____

Date _____ Class Section _____ Hour _____ Score _____

PART B

Form 2 Considerations in Implementing Job Enrichment

Below each of the following items indicate whether it would seem to facilitate or deter the job enrichment implementation process, the effectiveness of a job enrichment program, and why. In small groups discuss what those items you decided as being facilitators have in common. What do the rest of the items have in common?

1. People in the organization seem to value hard work and involvement.

   _____
   _____

2. Initial meetings on JE are not held with top management before JE is implemented.

   _____
   _____

3. Workers have urban, as opposed to rural, backgrounds.

   _____
   _____

4. Workers generally have low skill levels.

   _____
   _____

5. There is a high degree of formality and inflexibility of organizational structure, policies, and processes.

   _____
   _____

6. There is low confidence in JE among line managers.

   _____
   _____

7. People seem presently satisfied with their jobs, based on recent surveys.

   _____
   _____

8. JE techniques used in another organization are borrowed and used "as is."

   _____
   _____

9. There is high interaction among co-workers in many departments.

   _____
   _____

10. There is a strong union which traditionally has favored and emphasized large salary increases at the bargaining table.

    _____
    _____

11. JE is introduced to managers through their regular management training programs.

    _____
    _____

12. Large sums have recently been invested for a highly automated plant and equipment.

    _____
    _____

13. Performance levels have never been measured rigorously.

    _____
    _____

14. Top management believes in the potential of JE, but feels that intelligent line managers can learn JE on their own and implement it when (and if) they see fit.

_____

_____

15. A new JE program is begun in jobs which are only marginally important to organizational success.

_____

_____

16. Meetings with workers and supervisors are held to come up with ideas that tend to make the relation between an employee and his or her work more meaningful.

_____

_____

PART C

Form 3 Job Enrichment Potential Questionnaire*

Instructions: Answer each of these questions for each of the jobs in Forms 5–9 and place the number of your answer (one through five) in the appropriate column of Form 4.

1. How much autonomy would typically be present on the job?

1	2	3	4	5
A great deal				Very little

2. Does the job involve a whole and identifiable piece of work with a beginning and an end?

1	2	3	4	5
Doing whole piece of work				Job is only tiny part of whole

3. How much variety, or the chance to do different things, is there on the job?

1	2	3	4	5
A great deal				Very little

4. In general, how significant or important is the job to the larger society; how much does it affect others' lives?

1	2	3	4	5
A great deal				Very little

5. To what extent would supervisors and/or co-workers be able and willing to let the incumbent know how well he or she is doing?

1	2	3	4	5
A great deal				Very little

6. Would the work itself, or actually doing the job, let the person in the job know how well he or she is doing?

1	2	3	4	5
A great deal				Very little

7. Does the job offer challenge?

1	2	3	4	5
A great deal				Very little

8. Does the job enable a person to be creative and imaginative, to use their own initiative?

1	2	3	4	5
A great deal				Very little

9. Does the job typically offer the chance to develop new skills and to advance in the organization and/or career?

1	2	3	4	5
A great deal				Very little

10. Does the job offer the chance to work closely with others and develop relationships with co-workers?

1	2	3	4	5
A great deal				Very little

11. Can a person gain recognition outside the organization from this job?

1	2	3	4	5
A great deal				Very little

12. Are there alternate methods to performing the job; is there flexibility in job performance?

1	2	3	4	5
A great deal				Very little

---

* Adapted loosely from J. R. Hackman and G. R. Oldham, "The Job Diagnostic Survey: An Instrument for the Diagnosis of Jobs and the Evaluation of Job Redesign Projects," Technical Report No. 4, Department of Administrative Sciences, Yale University, May 1974.

Name _____ Group Number _____

Date _____ Class Section _____ Hour _____ Score _____

PART C

Form 4 Job Enrichment Potential Tally Sheet

Question No.	Job Titles				
1					
2					
3					
4					
5					
6					
7					
8					
9					
10					
11					
12					
Job enrichment potential (Total score ÷ 12 = average) — total					
average					

Which jobs would seem to be ready for a JE program?

PART C

Form 5 Job Description

EQUIPMENT OPERATOR I

DESCRIPTION OF WORK:

General Statement of Duties: Performs semiskilled work in the operation of light automotive or specialized equipment without final responsibility for assigned equipment.

Supervision Received: Works under supervision of technical administrator supervisor.

Supervision Exercised: None

DISTINGUISHING FEATURES: Positions assigned to Equipment Operator classes are distinguished by duties that involve utilizing mechanized equipment. Equipment Operator classes are further distinguished by having responsibility for the piece of equipment assigned. Positions assigned to City Services Worker classes are distinguished by duties that involve utilizing manual skills, although some equipment utilized by Equipment Operators may be used on an incidental basis to accomplish specific tasks.

EXAMPLES OF DUTIES: (Any one position may not include all of the duties listed, nor do the listed examples include all tasks that may be found in positions of this class.)

Operates ancillary equipment under the direction of a higher-level Equipment Operator.

Operates sewer jet equipment, locates and cleans manholes by utilizing pumps, generator, compressors, jackhammers, etc.

Operates automotive equipment such as jeeps, station wagons, passenger cars, pick-up trucks, flat beds, panel trucks and stake trucks, utility trucks, material and crew transport trucks, sign trucks, small ladder trucks, and similar equipment.

Operates farm-type tractors, including agricultural attachments.

Loads or assists in loading and unloading truck. Distributes load evenly over bed of truck. Performs general labor duties on the jobs to which equipment is assigned.

Services equipment with gas, oil, and water; reports mechanical defects.

Performs related work as required.

REQUIRED KNOWLEDGES, SKILLS, AND ABILITIES: Considerable knowledge of city and state traffic laws. Working knowledge of city street systems. Working knowledge of safety rules and regulations. Some knowledge of methods and materials used in servicing light automotive equipment. Skill in the operation of light automotive equipment. Ability to recognize and report abnormal operating functions on the equipment. Ability to perform arduous work with a full range of body movements. Ability to follow written and oral instructions. Ability to establish and maintain effective working relationships with other employees and the general public.

QUALIFICATIONS FOR APPOINTMENT:

Education: Eighth-grade completion or equivalent.

Experience: One year's experience in the operation of light automotive equipment.

   OR

Any equivalent combination of education and experience.

Necessary Special Requirements: Possession of a valid chauffeur's license issued by the state.

PART C

Form 6 Job Description

JOB TITLE:	Security trader
JOB FUNCTION:	To purchase and sell all types of securities, including, but not limited to, the following: Treasury bonds and notes, issues of governmental agencies, municipal bonds, corporate bonds, preferred and common stocks. Also would deal in certificates of deposit and commercial paper.
REPORTS TO:	Head of Investment Division
DEPARTMENT:	Trust
QUALIFICATIONS—GENERAL:	Needs college undergraduate degree or equivalent.
EXPERIENCE:	Would be helpful, but not necessary.
MACHINES AND EQUIPMENT USED:	Calculators, quote machines, telephones
RESPONSIBILITY FOR CASH AND NEGOTIABLE INSTRUMENTS:	Handles receipt and delivery of large blocks of securities at times. Deals in large amounts of negotiable securities.
PERSONAL CONTACTS:	Personal contacts are frequent with both trust customers and commercial customers as well as contacts with correspondent banks, country banks, and corporations.
JOB DETAILS:	Opens and supervises accounts for individuals, using authorization of the manager of the Investment Division. Purchases and sells securities arranging for time and place of settlement, nature of payment and other matters. Follows up on incomplete transactions. Most of this work is done by long-distance phone calls, usually to New York City, but also to Chicago, San Francisco, and other money centers. May perform other related duties within capabilities as may be requested by supervisor.

PART C

Form 7 Job Description

JOB TITLE:	Credit clerk
JOB FUNCTION:	Follow financial statements on commercial loan customers and maintenance of related index system.
REPORTS TO:	Lead credit clerk, Credit Division
DEPARTMENT:	Banking Department—Credit Division
QUALIFICATIONS—GENERAL:	High-school education or equivalent. Skill in typing required. Knowledge of accounting desirable.
EXPERIENCE:	Two or three months on-the-job training necessary.
MACHINES AND EQUIPMENT USED:	Typewriter Ditto reproduction machine
RESPONSIBILITY FOR NEGOTIABLE ITEMS:	None
PERSONAL CONTACTS:	Frequent contact with lending officers in person and by telephone.
JOB DETAILS:	Assists Lead Credit Clerk in maintainence of current balance sheets and profit & loss statements on all commercial loan customers by following statements on an annual basis, by way of monthly index file and perpetual follow-up system. Responsible for transfer of all commercial loan data to diary sheets in credit files on both secured and unsecured loans. Reviews file input data sent to Credit Division from commercial loan officers to determine significance as it relates to review by others. Assists in preparation and processing of outdated file material to be transferred to record room for storage. Assists in maintainence of alphabetic index for credit files. Will serve as backup to file clerk (see file clerk—Credit Division). May perform other duties within capabilities as requested by supervisor.

PART C

Form 8 Job Description

ENGINEERING AIDE I

DESCRIPTION OF WORK:

General Statement of Duties: Performs routine subprofessional engineering work.

Supervision Received: Works under close supervision of a technical superior.

Supervision Exercised: None

EXAMPLE OF DUTIES: (Any one position may not include all of the duties listed, nor do the listed examples include all tasks that may be found in positions of this class.)

Acts as roadman, flagman, or rear chainman on a survey crew.

Uses line staff to indicate a point or places staff where directed.   Uses level rod and adjusts and reads target in obtaining existing elevations, or in establishing elevations.

Drives hubs and stakes to indicate points and grades.   Digs and searches for survey monuments.

Cuts and removes brush and undergrowth from instrumentman's line of sight.   Cleans and cares for surveying instruments and tools.

Does routine tracing and simple drafting, such as plotting profiles and cross-sections.   Makes simple mathematical computations.   Performs a variety of office engineering tasks.

Performs the duties of head chainman and instrumentman as a part of in-service training.

Assists in the collection of samples and testing of construction materials.

Performs related work as required.

REQUIRED KNOWLEDGES, SKILLS, AND ABILITIES: Some knowledge of high-school mathematics, including algebra and trigonometry.   Ability to make simple mathematical computations rapidly and accurately.   Ability to follow oral and written instructions.   Ability to do strenuous physical work.   Ability to establish and maintain effective working relationships with other employees and the public.

QUALIFICATIONS FOR APPOINTMENT:

Education: High-school graduation or equivalent, including courses in algebra and trigonometry.

Experience: Six months experience in construction or related fields.

   OR

Any equivalent combination of education and experience.

PART C

Form 9 Job Description

MAINTENANCE MECHANIC I

DESCRIPTION OF WORK:

General Statement of Duties: Performs skilled and semiskilled maintenance and repair work involving a variety of trade skills.

Supervision Received: Works under supervision of a foreman.

Supervision Exercised: None.

EXAMPLE OF DUTIES: (Any one position may not include all of the duties listed, nor do the listed examples include all tasks that may be found in positions of this class.)

Performs carpentry, painting, plumbing, electrical, and other maintenance work in the repair of buildings, equipment, and related activities.

Operates equipment for snow removal and maintenance of the runways.

Assists in overhauling, cleaning, repairing and adjusting pumps, water and waste water treatment plant machinery, and related equipment.

Replaces and services equipment parts such as radiators, generators, distributors, motor mounts, engines and clutches. Rebuilds and repairs minor damage to body frames.

Performs related work as required.

REQUIRED KNOWLEDGES, SKILLS, AND ABILITIES: Considerable knowledge of the hazards and safety precautions of the construction and mechanical trades. Working knowledge of the standard practices, methods, materials, and tools of several trades. Skill in the use of tools, materials, and equipment of at least one trade, and in the use of the most common tools in several trades. Ability to learn a variety of mechanical and building maintenance skills. Ability to establish and maintain effective working relationships with employees and the public.

QUALIFICATIONS FOR APPOINTMENT:

Education: Eighth-grade completion or equivalent.

Experience: Two years experience in maintenance and repair work, including experience in equipment operation.

     OR

Any equivalent combination of education and experience.

PART D

Form 10 Implementing Job Enrichment: A Role Play*

GENERAL INSTRUCTIONS FOR ALL

You work in a group that does a few different tasks. Janice Jaguar is the manager of several of these groups, including the one with which we are concerned. Doris, Hal, Laverne, and Bruce make up your particular group. The operation is divided into four jobs in which quality is very important. The four jobs are rather simple and each group member is familiar with all of the operations. Three of the operations involve simple physical and machinery work, but the fourth is an assembler/inspector operation. The person doing this job, because of the chance to critique others' work and assemble the entire product, has more responsibility and variety than the others. Some workers would like to exchange jobs or positions frequently, but have not done so because the methods engineers have been studying the jobs in order to find the fastest times for each. Presently, several of you will be asked to role play one of the following: the personnel director (Clem), one of the work group members (Doris, Hal, Laverne, or Bruce), or the manager (Janice). In some instances, one or more observers will be present in the group. Role descriptions follow for all persons who are named above. Janice, Clem, and the observers read all roles and observers complete Form 11. Work-group members should read only their own roles.

   In role playing, you can begin with your written role and then expand it by making up things consistent with yourself and the role you have been asked to play.

   The group's task is to decide whether or not they want a job enrichment program for the jobs they hold; if so, what the tasks would be; and, if not, why not. With the help of Janice, the group will arrive at a decision regarding what, if anything, they would like to change about their work.

ROLE FOR PERSONNEL ADMINISTRATOR

Clem Hooper, Personnel administrator

You have asked Janice Jaguar to hold a meeting with her work group to go over the jobs members perform, considering both the potential for job enrichment, as well as the results of a time and motion study. You have discussed the potential of job enrichment with Janice Jaguar and administered the Job Enrichment Potential Questionnaire for the job under consideration. You strongly favor the JE approach, as you have documented recent decreases in quality and rising absenteeism and tardiness. You may sit in on the meeting and observe or serve as a resource person, but you have told Janice that the decision rests with her and her group, provided performance can be improved. However, you believe Janice is sold on the JE ideas you have suggested. After the group meeting, you meet separately with Janice and together decide what, if any, changes will be made based upon the group's decision.

ROLES FOR WORK GROUP MEMBERS

1. Janice Jaguar, Supervisor (48 years old)

You are the manager who supervises the work of about twenty people. Most of the jobs are piece-rate jobs, and some of the employees work in teams and are paid on a team piece-rate basis. In one of the teams, Doris, Hal, Laverne, and Bruce work together. Each one of them does a different operation each day. W. F. Taylorly, the methods engineer, studied conditions in your section, timed Doris, Hal, Laverne, and Bruce on each of the operations, and came up with the following facts:

TIME PER OPERATION

	Operation 1	Operation 2	Operation 3	Operation 4 (assembler/inspector)	Total
Doris	16 min.	14 min.	19 min.	26 min.	75 min.
Hal	20 min.	10 min.	14 min.	36 min.	80 min.
Laverne	27 min.	10 min.	20 min.	29 min.	86 min.
Bruce	17 min.	13 min.	18 min.	20 min.	68 min.
				Average =	77.25 min.

   Taylorly had observed that with the group rotating, an average time for all four operations would be a total of 77.25 minutes per complete unit. If, however, Doris worked only on the first operation, Laverne worked only of the second, Hal worked only on the third, and Bruce worked only on the fourth, the time for all four operations would only be 60 minutes. Thus, in an eight-hour work day, the group, by Taylorly's figures, could complete twenty-four units per day. (This is the present maximum because the fastest assembler, Bruce can complete three units per hour.) Operations 1, 2, and 3 are pretty much the same. They involve working on one small part of a product. The fourth operation is that of

---

* Loosely Adapted from N. R. F. Maier, *Psychology* in *Industrial Organizations*, 4th ed. (Boston: Houghton Mifflin, 1973), pp. 294–299.

assembler/inspector who inspects for defects and puts the entire subassembly together. Evaluating the others' work in this way and putting together the entire product can make the assembler/inspector feel like he or she has some autonomy and prestige, but at present this person receives no more money because the members of the group rotate and get paid on a *group* piece-rate system.

A quality problem exists as rejects have increased from 2 percent to 6 percent and the results of administering the Job Enrichment Potential Questionnaires (Form 3) gave the operation an average score of 4.1 for the series of four jobs. You also know absenteeism and turnover are on the rise and are concerned about this increase. Job Enrichment makes pretty good sense to you, so you have decided to take up the problem with the group. You feel they should go along with any proposed change if it will resolve the problems you face, and you will thus try to convince them of the importance of trying to change their work design. You must then convey their decision to Clem Hopper, the person to whom you report. You and he will make the final decisions. You are concerned that the group's decision fulfills your and Clem's need to improve performance and try out JE, the technique you both feel has merit.

2. Bruce (23 years old)

You are the fastest of a crew that works on an assembly job. Each of you has an operation you do fastest and you are best at the assembler/inspector operation. Even though the job has some variety, it really isn't so hot; you don't earn any more money at it, yet work a little harder sometimes.

You would like to do the whole job (all four operations) instead of just parts of it, as you are bored to death and you know your quality may be slipping. In fact, you really don't care too much any more about the people on the job and are considering leaving to find a more interesting job. You have been tardy several times lately and have missed more days of work than you feel good about. But if you did the entire job yourself, you wouldn't be bored and your pay would be higher, too, because you could do the tasks faster!

3. Laverne (38 years old)

You work with Doris, Hal, and Bruce on a job and get paid on a team piece-rate basis. The four of you work very well together and make a pretty good wage. Doris, Hal, and Bruce like to make a little more than you think is necessary, but you go along with them and work as hard as you can so as to keep the production up where they want it. They are good people; in fact, they often help you out if you fall behind, so you feel it is only fair to try to go along with the pace they set.

You like the No. 2 position the best because it is easiest, but when you get the No. 3 position, you can't keep up and you feel Janice, the manager, is watching you. Sometimes Doris, Hal, and Bruce slow down and then Janice seems satisfied. You would like to get and *keep* the No. 2 job. In fact, if you don't get it, you may soon leave to find a job with less pressure.

Lately a "methods man" has been hanging around watching you and your job. You wonder what he is up to. Can't they leave people alone who are doing all right?

4. Doris (26 years old)

You are one of four workers in a group. Laverne, Hal, and Bruce are your teammates and you enjoy working with them. You get paid on a team basis and you are making wages that are entirely satisfactory. Laverne isn't quite as fast as Hal and you, but when you feel she is holding things up too much, each of you sneak in and help her out.

Except for operation No. 4, which you only get to do occasionally, the work is very monotonous. The saving thing is that you can talk when Janice, your supervisor, is not watching. In this way, you get your mind off the job. You are best on the No. 1 position, so in that spot you often turn out some extra work and can sometimes make the job easier for Laverne.

You have been on this job for two years and have never run out of work. Apparently your group can make pretty good pay without running yourselves out of a job. Lately, however, the company has had some of its experts hanging around. It looks like the company is trying to work out some "speed-up" methods. If they make these jobs any more simple, you won't be able to stand the monotony. Janice, your manager, is an OK person who seldom has criticized your team's work. However, you find you have trouble making it to work on time every morning because the job is basically uneventful and routine.

5. Hal (27 years old)

You work with Doris, Laverne, and Bruce on a job that requires four separate operations. Each of you works on a different operation every day. But you have helped out others and that is satisfactory to you because you get paid on a team piece-rate basis. You could actually earn more if Laverne were a faster worker, but she is a swell person and you would rather have her in the group than someone else who might do a little bit more.

As you think about all four positions you find them about equally desirable. Operation No. 4 is better as there is more variety. But they are all pretty simple and routine. The monotony doesn't bother you much because you can talk, daydream, and change your pace. By working slow for a while and then fast, you can sort of set your pace to music you hum to yourself. You like the idea of changing jobs, and even though Laverne is slow on some positions, changing has its good points; it breaks up the monotony a little.

Lately some type of expert has been hanging around. He stands some distance away with a chart in his hand. The company could get more for its money if it put some of those guys to work. You say to yourself, "I'd like to see one of these guys try to tell me how to do this job. I'd sure give him an earful."

If Janice, your manager, doesn't get him out of here pretty soon, you're going to tell him what you think of her dragging in spies.

Name _____   Group Number _____

Date _____   Class Section _____   Hour _____   Score _____

PART D

Form 11 Instructions for Observers of the Job Enrichment Implementation Efforts

Your job is to observe the method used by Janice in handling a problem with the group. Pay special attention to the following:

a) Method of presenting problems: Does she criticize, suggest a remedy, request their help on a problem, or use some other approach?

b) Initial reaction of members: Do group members feel criticized or do they try to help?

c) Handling of discussion by Janice: Does she listen or argue? Does she try to persuade? Does she use threats? Or does she let the group decide?

d) Forms of resistance expressed by the group: Which members express fear, hostility, satisfaction with present method, etc.?

e) Pick out what you think is the best thing that Janice did.

Fill out the following questionnaire as you observe the group discussion.

QUESTIONNAIRE FOR OBSERVERS OF JOB ENRICHMENT IMPLEMENTATION EFFORTS

I. The group discussion

1. Observe the manager's attitude toward change during the discussion.

   a) Was he or she partial to the new method?

Unsupportive attitude	0	5	10	Supportive attitude
	/ / / / / / / / / /			

   neutral

   b) Did he or she seem mainly interested in more production or in improving the job *and* its satisfaction for the group?

Production only	0	5	10	Production and satisfaction
	/ / / / / / / / / /			

   neutral

   c) To what extent was the manager considerate of the objections raised by the group?

Inconsiderate of objections	0	5	10	Considerate of objections
	/ / / / / / / / / /			

   neutral

   d) What effect did the manager's remarks have on the progress of the discussion?

Inhibited progress	0	5	10	Aided progress
	/ / / / / / / / / /			

   neutral

2. Make notes on characteristic aspects of the discussion.

   a) Did arguments develop? If so, who was involved?

   b) Was any group member unusually stubborn and/or defensive? Who and why?

   Name   *Reason*

   1. _____   _____
   2. _____   _____
   3. _____   _____
   4. _____   _____

c) Were any of the group members inhibited? Who and why?

Name   *Reason*

1. _____   _____
2. _____   _____
3. _____   _____
4. _____   _____

d) Did the group members listen to each other?

Listened   0   5   10   Listened
poorly   / / / / / / / / / / well
neutral

e) List below the main points of differences between group members.

1. _____
2. _____
3. _____
4. _____
5. _____

II. *Evidences of problem-resolving behavior*

a) What was agreed on, if anything?

1. _____
2. _____
3. _____
4. _____

b) In what respects was the manager willing to compromise?

Low willingness to   0   5   10   High willingness to
compromise by manager   / / / / / / / / / / compromise by manager
neutral

c) What did the manager do to help or hinder a mutually acceptable work method for the benefit of the organization and its employees?

Helping behavior(s)   *Hindering behavior(s)*

1. _____   1. _____
2. _____   2. _____
3. _____   3. _____
4. _____   4. _____

III. *The discussion between the manager and the personnel administrator*

Record your overall reactions to the discussion between Janice and Clem. Was Janice ashamed of the group's decision? Did she distort the actual conclusion reached by the group when she and Clem discussed it? What was the outcome of this discussion among supervisors?

_____
_____
_____
_____
_____
_____
_____

Name _____   Group Number _____

Date _____ Class Section _____ Hour _____ Score _____

ASSESSMENT OF LEARNING IN PERSONNEL ADMINISTRATION
EXERCISE 15

1. Try to state the purpose of this exercise in one concise sentence.

2. Specifically what did you learn from this exercise (i.e., skills, abilities, and knowledge)?

3. How might your learning influence your role and your duties as a personnel administrator?

4. How would you evaluate the effectiveness of a JE program?

5. How can the specialists in personnel or human-resources management interface with line managers to accomplish a JE program's objectives? (Be specific.)

6. Additional questions given by your implementor:

Exercise 16

IMPROVING PERFORMANCE THROUGH POSITIVE REINFORCEMENT

PREVIEW

As a motivation tool, JE operates on the premise that performance can be improved by offering workers intrinsic rewards. Intrinsic rewards come from the the activity or work itself and are dispensed by oneself (e.g., a feeling of pride or autonomy as a result of enriched job content). However, there is much to suggest that performance can also be improved by offering extrinsic rewards to people. These rewards, such as money, come from external sources (the supervisor or the organization) and are gained as a result of attempting or completing a task or job. In this exercise the systematic utilization of extrinsic rewards, such as money, is developed as a possible remedy for the problem of motivating workers and managers. Techniques from basic operant principles, such as the use of positive reinforcement, can point to some deficiencies in traditional organizational motivation programs. These operant techniques differ from other motivational programs (e.g., JE) in that they concentrate on changing observable behavior and the environment rather than attitudes, satisfaction, or other vague psy-

chological concepts. After the basic concepts of the operant learning model are introduced, organizational practices are critiqued from an operant perspective and a motivation program emphasizing positive reinforcement is designed.

OBJECTIVES

1. To provide feedback to participants regarding their understanding of behavior modification and operant concepts.
2. To develop skill in assessing motivation programs' effectiveness from an operant perspective.
3. To develop skill in designing motivation programs that emphasize the use of positive reinforcement.

PREMEETING ASSIGNMENT

Read the entire exercise and supplementary material on operant conditioning/behavior modification, if necessary. (References cited in *For Further Reading* can provide background material in addition to the *Introduction*.)

INTRODUCTION

Behavior Modification and Positive Reinforcement (PR)

Behavior modification is the general term applied to the systematic conditioning of behavior in order to change or modify it by managing the environment. This environmental management involves the offering of rewards and punishments for desired and undesired behavior. The strategy is derived from the operant learning model, which simply posits that *behavior is a*

function of its consequences.[1] Consequences are those

---

[1] See, e.g., A. Bandura, *Principles of Behavior Modification* (New York: Holt, 1969); R. Ulrich et al., *Control of Human Behavior*, vols. 1 and 2 (Glenview, Ill.: Scott Foresman, 1970); B. F. Skinner, *The Technology of Teaching* (Appleton-Century-Crofts, 1968).

changes in the environment which elicit reward or punishment. Although B. F. Skinner is usually given credit for the development of these ideas, most of the actual applications of the operant model for humans have been through thousands of behavior-modification programs and experiments in mental institutions, schools, and correctional institutions.[2]

Recently, however, the use of operant principles to help change behaviors of working adults in organizations has received much attention. In addition to papers expressing the views of those who advocate the potential use of these ideas in work organizations, there are also reports of actual applications that have been well-received by employees and management and have saved some organizations considerable amounts of money, while leading to increased productivity.[3]

What is Behavior Modification?   The key to the operant approach lies in the relationship between behavior and its consequences—that is, the outcomes brought about by a particular behavior. The outcomes may be perceived as positive, such as monetary rewards, or negative, such as a disciplinary layoff. If these consequences *increase* the probability that the behavior producing them will occur in the future, the consequences are called *positive reinforcers*. For example, a positive reinforcer—a bonus for punctuality—when dispensed after the behavior it is meant to reinforce—arriving at work on time—would increase the probability that arriving on time will occur in the future. A *negative reinforcer*, such as a disciplinary layoff for tardiness, also may *increase* the probability of a future behavior, punctuality, for punctuality would remove the layoff from a worker's job environment.

These reinforcers, both positive and negative, seem to be most effective if linked closely in time to the behaviors they are meant to control. They are thus said to be *contingent* on these behaviors. This contingency relationship is useful for organizations simply because if people observe through experience that the receipt of a reward, say a promotion, is contingent on their good performance, their behavior may be changed such that they choose those behaviors that lead to the reward more often. If the reward (i.e.,

promotion) is not contingent on good performance, but on seniority, good performance will not be the only way to get the reward and employees may not perform well. Rather, they may choose simply to keep their jobs and build seniority while performing at minimally acceptable levels.

Punishment also influences behavior. Unlike reinforcement, punishment *decreases* the probability of the future occurrence of the behavior on which it is made contingent. For example, if tardiness is punished by layoff, tardiness may decrease in the future, because punctuality means the punishment will not appear. But the *desired* behavior, punctuality, may not be *increased* in all cases. Not getting caught or having a co-worker punch your time clock would also cause punishment not to be given. Thus, while punishment can decrease the probability of the occurrence of one undesired behavior, there is no assurance that the desired behavior will be built in. Therefore, punishment may be most effective if it is coupled with positive reinforcement to help assure that desired behaviors recur. Simply put, workers benefit not only from knowing what they did wrong to receive punishment, but also from knowing what they can do correctly to receive positive reinforcement.

Schedules of Reinforcement.   Reinforcement and punishment can be dispensed on any one of a number of schedules. *Continuous schedules* reward and/or punish after every desired behavior is observed—for example, receiving a compliment every time you exceed your sales quota. *Fixed-interval schedules* dispense reinforcement after a certain fixed period of time. If pay were contingent on performance rather than attendance, these interval schedules would be like the weekly or monthly paycheck common in work organizations. *Fixed-ratio schedules* allow for reinforcement (or punishment) after a certain fixed number of behaviors are observed, say, if you are docked a day's pay after each three unexcused absences.

Intermittent or *variable-ratio schedules* also dispense reinforcement or punishment after a number of behaviors, but the number changes, is unknown to the person being reinforced, and is not fixed as in fixed-ratio schedules. For example, a supervisor may give you an afternoon off (perhaps this is a positive reinforcer) after one excellent report is turned in, then not until after three reports are turned in, then after two, etc. The number of behaviors (i.e., completion of good reports) required to receive the reward varies over time and because you do not know which behavior will bring the reward, you may be motivated to continue the desired behaviors, as the next one *may* be the one that brings the reward. A slot machine and

---

[2] See, e.g., Ulrich et al., *Control of Human Behavior.*

[3] See C. E. Schneier, "Behavior Modification in Management: A Review and a Critique," *Academy of Management Journal* 17 (1974): 528–548; specific applications include W. Nord, "Improving Attendance through Rewards," *Personnel Administration* 34, no. 4 (1971): 41–47; and E. Pedalino and V. Gamboa, "Behavior Modification and Absenteeism: Intervention in One Industrial Setting," *Journal of Applied Psychology* 59 (1974): 694–698. See also *For Further Reading.*

other gambling devices work on the same principle of variable-ratio schedules. That is, because the next "play" may be a winner, we are highly motivated to insert the money and pull the arm "one more time." In some studies, variable-ratio schedules have been found to sustain required behavior over longer periods of time than other schedules.[4]

PR as a Motivation Strategy. For organizations, the operant learning model and various behavior-modification concepts explained above may offer a different approach to motivation problems. Punishment and threat of punishment often have deleterious side effects, such as building negative emotional feelings toward the punishing agent. When used alone, punishment may fail to build in or shape desired behaviors, even if it distinguishes undesired ones. Therefore, positive reinforcement may be a more effective way to change behavior at work. Some consequences of behavior, such as monetary rewards, verbal praise, promotion, or recognition, may be positive reinforcers and should be relied on as heavily as are punishers. Further, variable-ratio schedules of reinforcement may be quite useful in sustaining desired behavior, as opposed to the more-often-used interval schedules. Reinforcement can be useful to workers if it is given in specific behavioral terms; this enables feedback to focus on behavioral deficiencies that can be amended. A behaviorally based performance-appraisal system, such as BARS (see Exercise 5) would facilitate this type of feedback.

In general, motivation, incentive, and pay systems in many organizations would be judged deficient from an operant perspective simply because they do not allow for a contingent relationship between performance and reinforcement. In many cases, rewards are contingent on *undesired* behavior (such as performing poorly and not getting caught), or positive reinforcement *and* punishment may be the consequence of the same behavior. For example, high performance is rewarded by the supervisor, but punished by the work group as peers intimidate the "rate-buster." In addition, the operant perspective refers to antecedents or cues that set the stage for behavior and the consequences of that behavior. These antecedents concern the individual reinforcement history and experience of each worker; thus, the operant model would predict for example, that a given reinforcement may be perceived as positive by some and negative by others. The use of certain consequences would need to be individually determined in some instances to help assure that the consequences are perceived in the way intended by the organization.

Implementing PR in Work Organizations. Although some obvious potential gains can be derived from a PR program in organizations, implementation requires careful planning and often poses problems. First, desired behavior must be identified in a very specific manner in order to know what to make reinforcement contingent on. However, in higher-level positions, desired performance is difficult to pin down. What *exactly* does the executive do? Certainly a comprehensive job analysis (see Exercise 3) may help.

Second, a list of available reinforcers must be developed. Money is a reinforcer for many people, but perhaps not for all. Verbal praise, participation in decision making, fringe benefits, promotion, the chance to do unusual and exciting tasks, time off, bigger offices, organization-wide recognition, and bonuses are all possible reinforcers. Discretion must be given to supervisors such that they can offer reinforcers for desired performance, and these reinforcers must be shown to be effective in changing the behavior of the particular worker involved. Assessment of a worker's reinforcement preferences is often difficult; therefore, general reinforcers such as money are frequently used.

Third, the receipt of the reinforcers in a PR program must be made contingent on evidence of desired performance—the behavior identified in the first step above, rather than attendance or seniority alone. Behavior must be observed and recorded and provisions must be made to reinforce this behavior, perhaps through promotions, bonuses, or verbal praise. Above all, the worker must "see" the relationship between reinforcement and performance. If seniority, attitude, appearance, or nepotism lead to rewards (i.e., are reinforced by the organization) and *not* performance, workers will strive for these instead of performance. Thus, the contingent relationship between rewards and performance is destroyed.

Finally, rewards are most useful if they are linked closely to the performance they are meant to reinforce. If employees receive a compliment six weeks after they exceeded the sales quota, the compliment's effect as a reinforcer is weakened considerably according to the operant model.

---

[4] See G. Yukl et al., "Effectiveness of Pay Incentives under Variable Ratio and Continuous Reinforcement Schedules," *Journal of Applied Psychology* 56 (1972): 19–23. An interesting analysis of the issue of schedules of reinforcement is offered by C. J. Berger, L. C. Cummings, and H. G. Heneman, "Expectancy Theory and Operant Conditioning Predictions of Performance under Variable Ratio and Continuous Schedules of Reinforcement," *Organizational Behavior and Human Performance* 14 (1975): 227–243.

While PR has been extremely successful in some organizations,[5] systematic PR programs have been attempted in very few work organizations to date. The practical problems noted above, as well as philosophical issues (i.e., behavior modification is seen merely as worker manipulation by some[6]), may be deterrents to successful applications. But as long as organizations are controlling workers' environments and are offering rewards and punishment to workers, they are controlling their behavior, or certainly attempting to do so. However, many rewards systems are covert and rely on threat and punishment rather than positive reinforcement. An analysis of these efforts from an operant perspective may point out some deficiencies and the systematic use of PR may improve employee motivation by making rewards contingent on desired performance. In addition, PR programs open up the appraisal process and allow people to know where they stand regarding performance and performance standards.

PROCEDURE

Overview. In this exercise, you will review your understanding of PR concepts by completing Part A. Then two types of motivational programs are assessed from an operant viewpoint. Finally, you are required to design a motivation program for traveling salespersons using PR. The training program designed in Exercise 12 is redesigned according to operant techniques.

PART A

STEP 1: Two questionnaires (Form 1) are presented to enable you to check your understanding of operant concepts and PR. Answer the questions and review any errors you have made after the implementor notes correct responses. Be sure you have operant concepts clearly in mind before you continue with the exercise.

TIME: About 25 minutes.

---

[5] See, e.g., "At Emery Air Freight: Positive Reinforcement Boosts Performance," *Organizational Dynamics* 1 (Winter 1973): 41–50.

[6] Criticisms of the operant approach applied to management and work organizations, and its research base, are found in F. Fry, "Operant Conditioning and O. B. Mod: Of Mice and Men," *Personnel* 51 (July–August 1974): 17–24; T. C. Mawhinney, "Operant Terms and Concepts in the Description of Individual Work Behavior: Some Problems of Interpretation, Application, and Evaluation," *Journal of Applied Psychology* 60 (1975): 704–712; W. F. Whyte, "Skinnerian Theory in Organizations," *Psychology Today* 5, no. 11 (1972): 66–68+.

PART B

STEP 2: Form into groups of four to six persons and read the two situations presented in Forms 2, 3, and 4. Two motivational programs are described. Assess these programs from an operant standpoint by answering all of the questions on Form 2, by completely filling in Form 3, and by answering all of the questions in Form 4. Discuss the questions at the end of the descriptive material for each program in your small groups. Reach consensus on the answers.

TIME: About 55 minutes.

PART C

STEP 3: Design a PR motivation program for traveling salespersons. Pertinent facts are given in Form 5. The program should be practical and use operant concepts correctly. Sketch out the program orally and have someone in the group outline it in writing, briefly noting and describing all major steps in sequence.

TIME: About one to one-and-one-half hours.

PART D

STEP 4: Form 6 asks you to redesign the training program you developed in Exercise 12 from an operant standpoint. If you have not yet designed this program, design the training program now relying on PR principles and concepts. Outline the program as you did the motivation program in Part C above.

TIME: About one to one-and-one-half hours.

FOR FURTHER READING

Aldis, Owen. "Of Pigeons and Men." *Harvard Business Review* 39, no. 4 (1961): 59–63. (I)

"At Emery Air Freight: Positive Reinforcement Boosts Performance." *Organizational Dynamics* 1 (Winter 1973): 41–59. (I)

Bandura, Albert. *Principles of Behavior Modification* (New York: Holt, 1969). (II)

Beatty, R. W., and C. E. Schneier. "A Case for Positive Reinforcement." *Business Horizons* 18, no. 2 (April 1975): 57–66. (I)

Beatty, R. W., and C. E. Schneier. "Training the Hard Core Unemployed through Positive Reinforcement." *Human Resources Management* 4 (Winter 1972): 10–17. (I)

Berger, C. J., L. L. Cummings, and H. G. Heneman.

"Expectancy Theory and Operant Conditioning Predictions of Performance under Variable Ratio and Continuous Schedules of Reinforcement." *Organizational Behavior and Human Performance* 14 (1975): 227–243. (II–R)

Brethower, D. M. *Behavioral Analysis in Business and Industry: A Total Performance System.* Kalamazoo, Mich.: Behaviordelia, 1972. (I)

Campbell, J. P. "Motivation Theory in Industrial and Organizational Psychology." In M.D. Dunette, ed., *Handbook of Industrial and Organizational Psychology.* Chicago: Rand McNally, 1976. (II)

Cherrington, D. J., and J. O. Cherrington. "Participation, Performance, and Appraisal." *Business Horizons* 17, no. 6 (1974): 35–44. (I)

Deci, E. L. "The Effects of Contingent and Noncontingent Rewards and Controls on Intrinsic Motivation." *Organizational Behavior and Human Performance* 8 (1972): 217–229. (II–R)

Deci, E. L. "The Hidden Costs of Rewards." *Organizational Dynamics* 4, no. 3 (1976): 61–72. (I)

Farris, G. F. "Chickens, Eggs, and Productivity in Organizations. *Organizational Dynamics* 3 (1975): 2–15. (I)

Ferster, C. B., and M. C. Perrott. *Behavior Principles* (New York: Meredith, 1968). (I)

Goldstein, A. P., and M. Sorcher. *Changing Supervisor Behavior,* (New York: Pergamon, 1974). (I)

Hamner, W. C. "Current Methods of Worker Motivation in Organizations: The Importance of Climate, Structural, and Performance Consequences." In W. C. Hamner and F. L. Schnmidt, eds., *Contemporary Problems in Personnel.* Chicago: St. Clair, 1974. (I)

Hamner, W. C., and E. P. Hamner. "Behavior Modification on the Bottom Line." *Organizational Dynamics* 4, no. 4 (1976): 3–21. (I)

Heiman, G. W. "A Note on Operant Conditioning Principles Extrapolated to the Theory of Management," *Organizational Behavior and Human Performance* 13 (1975): 165–170. (II)

Jablonsky, S. F., and D. C. DeVries. "Operant Conditioning Principles Extrapolated to the Theory of Management." *Organizational Behavior and Human Performance* 7 (1972): 340–358. (II)

Kerr, S. "On the Folly of Rewarding A, while Hoping for B." *Academy of Management Journal* 6 (1975): 768–783. (I)

Kim, J. S., and W. C. Hamner. "Effect of Performance Feedback and Goal Setting on Productivity and Satisfaction in an Organizational Setting. *Journal of Applied Psychology* 61 (1976): 48–57. (II–R)

Latham, G. P. "The Effect of Various Schedules of Reinforcement on the Productivity of Tree Planters." Paper delivered at the Annual Convention of the American Psychological Association, New Orleans, 1974. (II–R)

Lawler, E. E. *Pay and Organizational Effectiveness.* New York: McGraw-Hill, 1971. (II)

Luthans, F., and R. Krietner. *Organizational Behavior Modification.* Glenview, Ill: Scott Foresman, 1975. (I)

Luthans, F., and D. D. White, Jr. "Behavior Modification: Application to Manpower Management." *Personnel Administration* 34, no. 4 (July–August 1971): 41–47. (I)

Markin, R. J., and C. M. Lillis. "Sales Managers Get What They Expect." *Business Horizons* 17, no. 3 (June 1975): 51–58. (I)

Miner, J. B., and J. F. Berwer. "The Management of Ineffective Performance." In M. D. Dunnette, ed., *Handbook of Industrial and Organizational Psychology.* Chicago: Rand McNally, 1976. (II)

Mawhinney, T. C. "Operant Terms and Concepts in the Description of Individual Work Behavior: Some Problems of Interpretation, Application, and Evaluation." *Journal of Applied Psychology* 60 (1975): 704–712. (II)

McClelland, D. C. "Money as a Motivator: Some Research Highlights." In T. T. Herbert, ed., *Organizational Behavior: Readings and Cases.* New York: Macmillan, 1976. (I)

Meyer, H. H. "The Pay for Performance Dilemma." *Organizational Dynamics* 3 (Winter 1975): 39–50. (I)

Morasky, R. L. "Self-Shaping Training Systems and Flexible-Model Behavior, i.e., Sales Interviewing." *Educational Technology* 11, no. 5 (1971): 57–59. (I)

Nord, W. "Improving Attendance through Rewards." *Personnel Administration* 33, no. 6 (1970): 37–41. (I)

Nord, W. "Beyond the Teaching Machine: The Neglected Area of Operant Conditioning in the Theory and Practice of Management." *Organizational Behavior and Human Performance* 4 (1969): 375–401. (II)

Notz, W. W. "Work Motivation and the Negative Effects of Extrinsic Rewards." *American Psychologist* 30 (1975): 884–891. (II)

Pedalino, E., and V. Gamboa. "Behavior Modification and Absenteeism: Intervention in One Industrial Setting." *Journal of Applied Psychology* 59 (1974): 694–698. (II–R)

Porter, L. W. "Turning Work into Nonwork: The Rewarding Environment." In M. D. Dunnette, ed., *Work and Non-Work in the Year 2001.* Monterey, Cal.: Brooks/Cole, 1973. (I)

Reynolds, G. S. *A Primer of Operant Conditioning.* Glenview, Ill.: Scott Foresman, 1968. (I)

Rotundi, T. "Behavior Modification on the Job. *Supervisory Management* 21, no. 2 (February 1976): 22–28. (I)

Schneier, C. E. "Behavior Modification in Management: A Review and Critique. *Academy of Management Journal* 17 (1974): 528–548. (I)

Schneier, C. E. "Behavior Modification: Training the Hard-Core Unemployed." *Personnel* 50, no. 3 (1973): 65–69. (I)

Skinner, B. F. *Beyond Freedom and Dignity.* New York: Knopf, 1971. (I)

Ulrich, R., T. Stachnik, and J. Mawbry, eds. *Control of Human Behavior*, vols. 1, 2. Glencoe, Ill.: Scott Foresman, 1970. (II–R)

"Where Skinner's Theories Work." *Business Week,* 2 December 1972, pp. 64–65. (I)

Whyte, W. F. "Skinnerian Theory in Organizations." *Psychology Today* 5, no. 11 (1972): 66, 68+. (I)

Wiard, H. "Why Manage Behavior? A Case for Positive Reinforcement." *Human Resource Management* 1, no. 2 (1972): 15–20. (I)

Yukl, G., K. Wexley, and J. E. Seymour. "Effectiveness of Pay Incentives under Variable Ratio and Continuous Reinforcement Schedules." *Journal of Applied Psychology* 56, no. 1 (1972): 19–23. (II–R)

Name _____ Group Number _____

Date _____ Class Section _____ Hour _____ Score _____

PART A

Form 1 Receiving Feedback on Your Understanding of PR

A. Please check either True or False for the following statements.

		True	False
1.	Behavior-modification principles have been derived from thousands of experiments.	____	____
2.	Behavior-modification applications in industrial organizations afford managers with quantitative data about behavior.	____	____
3.	It is worthwhile to reward even small improvements in performance because the reward often encourages more improvement.	____	____
4.	Behavior modification requires great financial risk, it is impossible to demonstrate behavior change in a small, inexpensive program.	____	____
5.	Operant conditioning does manipulate people. But we are constantly, often unconsciously, manipulating others, especially in organizations. Using operant conditioning can make desired behavior more explicit in organizations and therefore allows workers to know where they stand.	____	____
6.	A difference between behavior modification and other techniques of performance improvement is that it doesn't rely on the analysis of the attitudes of the employees.	____	____
7.	Reinforcers are defined as the consequences of behavior which strengthen or weaken behavior when presented.	____	____
8.	Without specific measurements, it is impossible to determine the success or failure of any performance-improvement program.	____	____
9.	Managers should be aware of the basic principles of behavior modification if they are given authority to present or withdraw reinforcers.	____	____
10.	Offering positive reinforcers for certain behaviors is a means of encouraging desired behavior.	____	____
11.	Feedback from an operant perspective is information that quickly and accurately reflects to an employee a quantitative record of his or her performance.	____	____
12.	Most managers are very aware of the effects of contingencies of reinforcement and apply them properly.	____	____
13.	The use of reinforcement systems assumes that some employees may want more from their jobs than intrinsic satisfaction or rewards alone.	____	____
14.	Both positive and negative reinforcement can strengthen desired work behaviors.	____	____
15.	Compensation systems can reinforce undesirable as well as desirable employee behavior.	____	____
16.	The frequency of scheduling reinforcement has little impact on the frequency of desired behavior demonstrated on the job.	____	____
17.	Training courses are always good solutions to performance problems.	____	____
18.	Performance problems should be defined in terms of observed behavior, not the behavior the employee is likely to demonstrate.	____	____
19.	If an employee's work output was accomplished correctly yesterday but incorrectly today, it is clear evidence that the employee lacks knowledge of the job and a training program is necessary.	____	____
20.	Punishment alone will always increase the occurrence of desired work behavior and decrease the occurrence of undesired behavior.	____	____

21. With positive reinforcement, only desired work behavior should be reinforced.   ___ ___

22. Punishment can be efficient in eliminating undesired behavior.   ___ ___

23. Desired behavior tends to remain longer after the use of fixed reinforcement schedules than variable reinforcement schedules.   ___ ___

B. For this set of statements, please indicate conditions that would be desirable and those that would be undesirable for the effective use of operant-conditioning/positive-reinforcement programs in work organizations.

	Desirable	Undesirable
1. Employees can gauge their own progress relative to set, quantifiable standards.	D	U
2. The organization makes explicit the consequences to the worker for doing or not doing the job correctly.	D	U
3. The organization focuses on the process of how goals are achieved, or on the behaviors used to attain goals.	D	U
4. The organization does not determine the cost of performance deficiencies in dollar terms.	D	U
5. The organization trains supervisors to analyze performance problems and measure their frequency.	D	U
6. Supervisors, or a third party, alone make the measurement of a subordinate's behavior.	D	U
7. The organization evaluates programs based on change in on-the-job behavior.	D	U
8. No feedback is given the employee about performance; or feedback goes only to the manager or supervisor.	D	U
9. Measurement of effectiveness is based on attitudes of trainees, numbers of people asking to attend future sessions, classes, or pencil-and-paper tests given in the classroom setting.	D	U
10. PR programs are undertaken with no quantitative measurement of current performance levels.	D	U
11. Feedback is given to people often and as the work progresses, leading to self-correction.	D	U
12. Trainees show they can apply learning successfully before the line manager (e.g., the instructor) leaves the training environment.	D	U
13. Feedback, such as, "Here is what you did well in relation to a goal . . . ," is given.	D	U
14. Feedback to workers continues permanently on all items of performance.	D	U
15. Feedback is given on a random sampling basis, only on certain items or on certain days.	D	U
16. Feedback is expressed numerically for workers.	D	U
17. Feedback is obtained by the worker after the work is completed, delayed by days or weeks.	D	U
18. Performance goals are not established, or they are not communicated across organizational levels.	D	U
19. Feedback is obtained by workers themselves.	D	U
20. Performance feedback is given to the worker, to supervisors, to managers, and to top executives (in some cases).	D	U
21. Feedback, such as, "Here is what you did wrong," is given.	D	U
22. The organization does not estimate the total probable cost of PR solutions or compare this cost with the cost of the performance deficiency, or it works only on relatively small problems.	D	U

Name _____   Group Number _____

Date _____ Class Section _____ Hour _____ Score _____

PART B

Form 2 Behavior Modification Case Study I

Analyze changes in the following work situation due to a change in reward structure and determine why the changes occurred. After calculating the costs on Form 3, fill in the blanks below.

SITUATION

A large discount retail chain store was having considerable difficulty with its salaried salespeople. Absenteeism as well as tardiness continued to increase. After using several disciplinary methods which were ineffective, the company decided to try two types of positive-reinforcement procedures in a desperate attempt to lower the cost of absenteeism and tardiness. The first program was for employees in the stores in the Western Region of the organization. All employees who were neither absent nor late for one month received $5.00 worth of trading stamps which could be used in exchange for merchandise in the store. In the stores in the Eastern Region, it was decided that all employees who were on time and did not miss a day of work for a month would have their names included in a drawing. Three winners of the drawing were selected at random each month and each received a portable color television (if they were previous winners they could receive merchandise comparable in value, i.e., $400). The results of the programs are listed below. After reviewing the results, please answer the questions that follow.

	Western Region	Eastern Region
Number of employees	415	382
Total annual absenteeism percentage before the program	12%	11.5%
Annual paid* absenteeism before the program (as a percentage of total number of days absent)	4%	3.75%
Annual absenteeism percentage after program	4.5%	2%
Annual paid* absenteeism after the program (as a percentage of total number of days absent)	3.5%	1.5%
Annual cost of absenteeism before the program* (see Form 3)	_____	_____
Annual cost of absenteeism after the program* (see Form 3)	_____	_____
Approximate direct costs of the program*	$24,000	$14,400
Net saving from PR programs (cost reduction less direct program cost)	_____	_____

_____

* The cost figures make the following assumptions:
1. Employees receive fringe benefits (medical and life insurance, social security, unemployment tax, etc.) equaling 30% of total wages, which must typically be paid if absent due to union contractual agreements.
2. Absent employees must be replaced with part-time workers to staff the departments and the check-outs in the discount operation (which already attempts to keep the number of employees to a minimum). The part-time workers can be procured easily and do not receive benefits.
3. The cost figures are exclusive of any drop in sales due to late employees or due to using replacement, as opposed to experienced, salespersons.

Name _____   Group Number _____

Date _____ Class Section _____ Hour _____ Score _____

PART B

Form 3 A Cost/Benefit Analysis of Positive Reinforcement Motivation Programs

Instructions: Using the information on Form 2, as well as the hints provided in the first row of this table, complete the table and enter the appropriate figures on Form 2. Then answer the discussion questions which follow.

	Before programs		After programs	
	Western Division	*Eastern Division*	*Western Division*	*Eastern Division*
Annual days of absenteeism	(415 employees × 240 work days/yr. × 12% absenteeism) =	(382 employees × 240 work days/yr. × 11.5% absenteeism) =	(415 × 240 × 4.5%) =	382 × 240 × 2% =
Annual days of paid absenteeism				
Annual days of unpaid absenteeism				
Annual cost of paid absences @ $63/day ($30 = salary, $9 = fringes, $24 = substitute employees)				
Annual cost of unpaid absences @ $33/day ($24 = substitutes' salary, $9 = fringes for regular employees)				
Total annual cost of absenteeism (paid and unpaid)				
Total *daily* cost of absenteeism (paid and unpaid)				

(continued)

DISCUSSION QUESTIONS (to be answered after Form 3 is completed)

1. What type of scheduling is being used for each region?

2. Which schedule is more effective? Why?

3. What problems, if any, might you anticipate from the implementation of this procedure? What could be done to resolve any problems you anticipate?

4. Why is one region's program more costly than the other's and also has a higher absenteeism rate? Explain this below using behavior-modification concepts and principles.

Name _____   Group Number _____

Date _____ Class Section _____ Hour _____ Score _____

PART B

Form 4 Behavior Modification Case Study II

The following is a discussion* of one attempt to increase productivity in a job that could not be enriched (i.e., made more interesting or made to offer more challenge and autonomy; see Exercise 15). Read the paragraph below and answer the questions.

In a recent study involving people who plant trees for a large tree-harvesting organization, bonuses were given to planters for planting bags of seedlings. Most of the planters were older women from southern and rural areas with strong moral and religious backgrounds and norms. The first crew of planters was told that, in addition to their regular base pay, they would receive a $2.00 bonus contingent on planting each entire bag of trees. The second crew was told that they would receive their base pay and a $4.00 bonus contingent on planting each bag of trees and correctly guessing the outcome of a coin toss. The third crew was told they would receive their base pay and an $8.00 bonus contingent on planting each bag of trees and correctly guessing the outcome of two coin tosses. A fourth crew, isolated geographically from the first three, was used as a control group and was paid only hourly base wages.

DISCUSSION QUESTIONS

1. What type of scheduling of reinforcement was used with each of the four crews?

2. Based only on information about behavior modification and the scheduling of reinforcement, what do you predict as the outcome of relative productivity of tree-planting crews?

3. What individual characteristics, problems, or obstacles might influence the outcomes of these crews such that they might not meet the expectations predicted in question 2?

4. Over the long run, would you expect the salaries of the crew members to differ? If so, how?

_____

*Adapted (roughly) from G. P. Latham, "The Effect of Various Schedules of Reinforcement on the Productivity of Tree Planters," paper delivered at the Annual Convention of the American Psychological Association, New Orleans, 1974.

PART C

Form 5 Designing a PR Motivation Program

Using the facts given below, design a PR motivation program for the traveling salespersons of Leon and Sons Company. Specify reinforcers, punishment, schedules of reinforcement, performance-reward contingencies, etc., and outline your procedure for implementing the program.   Be sure to state any assumptions you have made.

1. The program is to be designed for a group of thirty salespersons who sell housewares to retail outlets. They work for Leon and Sons, a medium-sized midwestern housewares wholesaler. The housewares consist of glassware, kitchen gadgets, home-improvement products, etc. In fact, Leon and Sons sells so many different products, its catalogue must be carried into stores in several sections by its salespersons.

2. Each salesperson has a territory consisting of about 850 square miles, and often crosses state lines. The salespersons sell to large retail and discount chain stores, as well as to small independent stores. Stores are located in cities, in small towns, and in suburbs of large cities.

3. The territories for each salesperson are unequal regarding sales volume, which ranges from $20,000 to $40,000 per month for each. Territories were either originally assigned on the basis of seniority and past performance or were "built up" into high-producing areas by salesperson's own efforts.

4. There is fairly high turnover amongst the salespersons of the twelve territories that have been averaging between only $10,000 and $20,000 volume per month. Management feels these twelve territories are currently undersold and that a $25,000–$30,000 volume per month is possible, adjusted for seasonal sales, current levels of unemployment, etc.

5. Salespersons all receive commission at the rate of 7% on gross sales, plus a set amount for monthly expenses. Neither commission rate nor allowance for expenses vary across salespersons.

6. No bonuses or other monies are currently available (i.e., overtime, etc.), but a pension fund, life-insurance program, credit union, and health-insurance plan are all offered to salespersons. The pension and life-insurance benefits depend on the size of earnings, however.

7. One week vacation with pay is given after one year of service, two weeks after three years, three weeks after six years, and one additional week after each additional ten years of service. The average length of service for the twelve salespersons in territories with sales volume of $20,000 to $40,000 is 10.8 years and for the remaining eighteen salespersons is 1.4 years.

8. The newer salespersons have complained that their territories contain few large discount chain stores, which limits their sales volume and causes them to spend much time driving to service the many small stores. They state that they sometimes must drive for four hours to write an order of $500 (a commission of only $35.00), while some territories have central buying offices for a chain of stores. In four to six hours a salesperson can write an order for $20,000 for these stores (at a commission of $1400).

9. The companies whose lines are carried often offer trips, merchandise, and cash to salespersons who break certain sales quotas set by these manufacturers, but these seem to go only to salespersons in certain territories with the big stores.

10. There is considerable competition in the housewares wholesaling industry in the area and each retail outlet is often serviced by three or four other housewares wholesalers in addition to Leon and Sons. Further, because many of the products are not necessities, economic slumps and high unemployment in the industrialized Midwest affect sales.

11. Leon and Sons has grown considerably in the last decade. It has added nine salespersons to make the current total of thirty. It has added two new warehouses, a computerized inventory-control system, and has been able to keep many prices below competitors due to volume buying and the lower warehouse costs stemming from automation. The company office and its warehouses are located outside a smaller city where land is relatively inexpensive. However, the city is centrally located, so shipping costs to most customers are minimized. Being a family-owned business, Leon and Sons typically maintains a policy of returning profits to the organization for capital improvements. Further, because Mr. Leon, the owner, has developed an excellent reputation with manufacturers for honesty and excellent salesmanship, he has been able to acquire many of the most popular brands of merchandise for his salespersons to carry. In addition, Leon and Sons' new salespersons are typically trained and introduced to new accounts by Mr. Leon himself, which adds a personal touch many customers, especially the smaller ones, appreciate.

12. At present, there is one sales manager, Roger "Smiley" O'Malley. He is a long-time employee of Leon and Sons and was the second salesperson hired many years ago. He has been sales manager for three years and gives considerable latitude to the sales force regarding the number of calls they make, how they spend their time, etc.

His primary duties are to hire and fire salespersons, to assign territories, and to settle disputes or complaints arising from salespersons interaction with clients. He feels that selling is an art: "You either have it or you don't!" he is often heard to say. He does not, therefore, feel training programs or seminars are useful.

Smiley O'Malley has periodic sales meetings to introduce new products and is openly quite friendly at these meetings with a few of the more senior salespersons, whom he also sees socially. In fact, the decision to design a motivation program was made by Mr. Leon in light of the high turnover amongst younger salespersons. Obviously, neither Smiley O'Malley nor several of the more senior salespersons feel it is necessary.

PART D

Form 6 Designing an Operant Training Program

Reread Form 6 in Exercise 12. You are asked to design a training program for entry-level and/or minority workers.

A. If you have already designed this program, do the following:

1. Assess the program from an operant perspective (i.e., the use of reinforcers, punishment, schedules of reinforcement, performance-reward contingencies).

2. Redesign the program such that operant principles and PR are explicitly used to facilitate learning.

B. If you have not already designed this program, design it as a PR training program, using the principles of the operant model as your basis for the design.

Refer back to Form 6 in Exercise 12 and note the suggested questions to answer as you design the training program.

Name _____   Group Number _____

Date _____ Class Section _____ Hour _____ Score _____

ASSESSMENT OF LEARNING IN PERSONNEL ADMINISTRATION
EXERCISE 16

1. Try to state the purpose of this exercise in one concise sentence.

2. Specifically what did you learn from this exercise (i.e., skills, abilities, and knowledge)?

3. How might your learning influence your role and your duties as a personnel administrator?

4. What skills, abilities, and knowledge would a person responsible for implementing extrinsic-rewards programs be required to possess?

5. How could an organization's motivation programs be evaluated as to their ability to improve performance or productivity?

6. Would intrinsic-rewards motivation programs be compatible with those that emphasize extrinsic rewards? What organizational and job characteristics might determine whether these programs could be implemented simultaneously?

7. Additional questions given by your implementor:

Exercise 17

JOB EVALUATION AND WAGE AND SALARY ADMINISTRATION

PREVIEW

This exercise concerns the allocation of money to members or organizations. Its purposes are to demonstrate how money can be effectively used as a reward for performance and to outline the characteristics of the type of system which would be required to effectively administer wages and salaries. In order to make money an effective reinforcer or reward for desired performance, certain determinations must be made. First, desired behavior must be defined and different methods of allocating financial rewards considered in light of organization and individual objectives. Vital data (e.g., wage and salary surveys and individual performance levels) must be gathered and important decisions regarding the relative worth of jobs (i.e., a job evaluation) also need to be made before the level of financial rewards can be tied to each job and each organizational member. This exercise builds skill in data gathering and decision-making tasks required for the development of a rational and equitable wage and salary system. A point system of job evaluation is designed and implemented using data from a municipality. A wage structure for several job classes and individual salary levels are determined in the exercise.

OBJECTIVES

1. To build understanding of the role of money as a reward and motivator of job behavior.
2. To build skill in designing job-evaluation systems and in salary-structure determination.
3. To appreciate the various factors influencing implementation of an effective, equitable salary system in an organization.

PREMEETING ASSIGNMENT

Read the entire exercise.

INTRODUCTION

Considerations in Evaluating Jobs and Attaching Wage or Salary Levels to Them

Many obvious considerations influence an organization's allocation of pay to its members. These include the importance of pay for the organization (as it may comprise a major proportion of total cash outflow), the financial consequences of employee withdrawal (e.g., turnover, absenteeism, and tardiness) due to dissatisfaction with pay, and government regulations regarding pay systems. Another important consideration is the motivational aspect of pay—that is, the use of pay to induce people to perform at certain levels and to retain their commitment to the organization and to desired performance.

Over the last half century the field of management has developed many theories of what makes organizations effective.[1] Most deal with pay administration, but tend to assign pay relatively different degrees of importance and functions. Scientific management, for example, uses pay as the most important reward for employees. More modern management theory, however, sees money as only one of many influences on behavior. The degree to which management regards pay as an important influence on behavior and employee satisfaction often determines, to a great extent, the organization's wage and salary programs.

Satisfaction with Pay. Organizations should be concerned about the level of pay satisfaction as it can lead to strikes, grievances, absenteeism, turnover, and the ineffective use of human assets. Certainly strikes cost organizations money, but grievances, absenteeism, and turnover are also expensive. Organizations are often not aware of how expensive the costs of these factors are and they underestimate their importance. As discussed in Exercise 14, many of these costs are hidden. An example is the cost of having an inexperienced worker doing a job because someone has left the organization. The inexperienced worker's quality and/or quantity of work is likely to be low. Other costs, such as training, recruitment, and clerical requirements, are not always tied to turnover, absenteeism, tardiness, and grievances, but are often a result of these situations.

The consequences of pay dissatisfaction[2] can be more clearly seen in Fig. 1, which shows that pay dissatisfaction may eventually lead to psychological withdrawal, poor physical and mental health, etc. Certainly dissatisfaction with pay can also lead to desired outcomes, such as improved performance and lower absenteeism to earn more money. The preponderance of research evidence, however, indicates that building pay satisfaction is an effective way of managing organizations.

What then determines pay satisfaction? An experienced researcher in this area, Edward Lawler, provides several determinants of pay satisfaction in organizations. Many of these reasons for a person's dissatisfaction with pay are obvious, such as lack of skill or ability to land a higher-paying job. However, people are also dissatisfied with their pay if they

perceive they are being paid too little for their effort or if they perceive others with similar or lower efforts (or job importance) are receiving more than they are. Thus, much of the feeling of satisfaction or dissatisfaction with pay results from people thinking that the pay system is not equitable. Here, perceptions—how people subjectively judge a situation—are most important.[3]

Based on the above discussion, we would assume that having workers satisfied with pay would be an important organizational goal. How, then, is pay satisfaction to be achieved? This difficult and complex task may involve determining rates of pay according to performance level and by having pay perceived as equitable, relative to job accomplishment, to other organizational pay levels, and to other workers in the same jobs in other organizations within the community. Reducing pay secrecy may also be an important factor helpful in raising pay satisfaction. More openness concerning actual pay rates could prevent erroneous perceptions.

Another idea organizations are using more and more often to improve satisfaction with pay, as well as to give workers more discretion over their work situations, is called a "cafeteria" style[4] benefit plan. Here, as in a cafeteria, workers can choose among several types of benefits, merit increases, etc. Table 1 is an example of a such a set of pay and fringe-benefit alternatives.

Table 1. An Example of a "Cafeteria-Style" Benefit System in which Employees Would Be Given a Certain Number of Choices

1. Pension increase of $50.00 *Or* Two extra weeks paid vacation.
2. Dental insurance *Or* three percent pay raise.
3. Ten Fridays off per year with pay *Or* four-day weeks with 9.5 hours per day.
4. Two weeks extra paid vacation *Or* dental insurance.
5. Five days retirement credit each year *Or* one week extra paid vacation.
6. Merchandise at 20 percent off *Or* two-percent pay raise.
7. Three-percent pay raise *Or* eight Fridays off per year with pay.
8. Five day week with 7.5 hours per day *Or* pension increase of $100 per year.
9. Two-percent pay raise *Or* one week extra paid vacation.
10. Free lunches in company lunchroom *Or* merchandise at 5 percent off.

[1] See, e.g., H. L. Tosi and S. J. Carroll, *Management: Contingencies, Structure, and Process* (Chicago: St. Clair, 1976), Chap. 2; M. J. Gannon, *Dimensions of Management: An Integrated Perspective* (Boston: Little Brown, 1977), Chap. 2; A. N. Nash and S. J. Carroll, *The Management of Compensation* (Belmont, Cal.: Wadsworth, 1975), Chap. 3.

[2] Much of the work cited here is adapted from E. E. Lawler, III, *Pay and Organizational Effectiveness: A Psychological View* (New York: McGraw-Hill, 1971).

[3] For a fuller discussion of "equity" theory, see Lawler, *Pay and Organizational Effectiveness: A Psychological View*.

[4] See, e.g., L. M. Baytos, "The Employee Benefit Smorgasbord: Its Potential and Limitations," *Compensation Review* 2 (1970): 16–28.

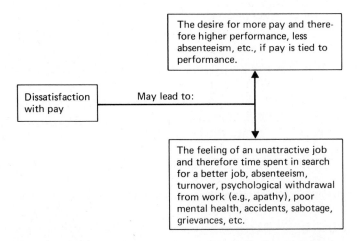

Fig. 1. Some Possible Consequences of Pay Dissatisfaction (Adapted from E. E. Lawler, III, *Pay and Organizational Effectiveness: A Psychological View*, New York, McGraw-Hill, 1971.)

Wage Structure and Job Evaluation. A wage structure is the determination of the "worth" or "value" of each job relative to other jobs within an organization. There are numerous methods for this determination. The objective is to provide equal pay for jobs of equal worth or importance, and an acceptable rational set of differentials between jobs not of equal worth. Thus, the rationale for a wage structure is that jobs are not all equally valuable to an organization and therefore are not compensated the same. For example, some jobs are in high demand and others are in low demand, some have high status and others low, some call for large amounts of responsibility and others little, some are boring and others interesting, some are risky and others safe, some demand a high degree of specialized training or education and others do not.

Labor-market information concerning demand and supply of workers or job openings collected by individual firms is not usually sufficiently detailed to use in deciding a wage structure. Further, the organization's employees may differ in their perceptions of the worth of jobs and in their own preferences as to the kinds of compensation available. Thus, other information is often necessary. This information consists of job and performance evaluations.

Job Evaluation Methods. The four most commonly used methods of job evaluation are: the point method, the factor-comparison method, the classification method, and the ranking method.[5] While these four methods are similar in many respects, a few differences are noted below.

Although the *factor-comparison* method is quite complex, it can be a useful system. Essentially, certain "key" jobs are compared to other jobs on the basis of several factors. The key jobs are assumed to have the correct salary attached to them and thus represent a standard, provided there is agreement that the salaries for these jobs are correct. Indeed, identifying the key jobs is the first step in the system. The key jobs are usually compared to other jobs on the basis of mental demands, skill, working conditions, responsibility, and physical demands. Jobs are ranked from highest to lowest on these factors by evaluators. Then, the existing salary for each key job is divided up into these factors according to their relative importance in the key job. That is, the total amount of money offered is divided into that amount offered for factor A, B, etc., based on their importance. The key jobs are placed on a scale indicating the importance of each factor; other jobs may fall above or below the key job on each factor. Then, additional jobs each are placed on the scale at the proper location. After all of the jobs appear on the scale, salaries are determined by looking at the amount of money (or points convertible to money) beside each of the factors for each job. These amounts are summed to arrive at the salary (or wage) level for each job.

The *classification* method of job evaluation, used often for grading civil-service jobs (i.e., GS ratings), begins with a certain number of predetermined job grades. Jobs are categorized according to their characteristics. For example, ten grades may be established, each defined as to certain characteristics the jobs in it would have. Grade three might include those jobs in which people perform tasks without direct supervision, grade one might contain those jobs

---

[5] See A. Nash and S. Carroll, *The Management of Compensation*, for a more detailed discussion of job evaluation methods.

in which people perform tasks under constant super-vision, etc. Evaluators do not define each factor and then compare jobs on a factor-by-factor basis, as in the factor-comparison method, but define whole grades of jobs. The higher the grade, the more educa-tion, skill, etc. is required. Expert judgment is relied on very heavily here and the chances of bias or in-consistency are reasonably high, but the system is relatively easy to implement.

The *ranking* methods of job evaluation are prob-ably the simplest. Often, job descriptions are ranked from highest to lowest in terms of worth (straight ranking). Entire jobs can be compared or they can be compared on a factor-by-factor basis—the former is usually the case. Without factor-by-factor ranking, the subjective judgments of evaluators may be prob-lematic and disagreement among them is likely to increase. Although the ranking method is quick and therefore inexpensive, it is quite subjective and easily outmoded by changes in jobs.

By far the most popular method of the four major methods for determining the worth of a job is the *point method*. The point method requires evaluators to rate jobs on a factor-by-factor basis, weighting each factor (e.g., use of machinery, complexity of tasks, education, risk, etc.) in terms of its contribution to overall job worth. A scale is used to determine the extent to which each job possesses each factor. Job descriptions are studied to determine the degree to which the factor is required in performing the job. After a set of degrees on each factor has been defined and allocated a number of points, points are allocated to each job depending on the degree to which factors are required and the weight of the factors. Then, a total point score can be assigned to each job in order to compare their relative worth and eventually assign salary levels to them.

This method probably has the best chance of attaining job-evaluation objectives in most organiza-tions. Jobs can be reliably differentiated and the system is simple enough to be explained convincingly to employees. Table 2 demonstrates the use of factors, weights, degrees, and points. This method is ex-plained more fully in the activities that follow this Introduction.

Grades or job classes are also used in a job evaluation. Types of jobs that are similar in content, such as clerical or maintenance jobs, are considered to be within one class. There would typically be different grades or levels within each class also (e.g., clerical worker I, II, and III).[6]

---

[6] A more thorough discussion can be found in Nash and Carroll, *The Management of Compensation*.

Table 2. An Example of the Meaning of Factors, Weights, Degrees, and Points Used in the Point Method of Job Evalua-tion. The Points Alloted to Each Factor are Summed to Arrive at One Point Total for Each Job.

FACTOR: A broad category of job content, qualifications, etc., which can be used to group jobs (e.g., education, training, physical demands). Each broad factor may have several subfactors.

WEIGHT: The relative worth of factors to each other, usually on a scale of 1 to 100 (e.g., education—weight 35; physical demand—weight 55, etc.). The weights do not always sum to 100.

DEGREE: The relative amount of each factor a job possesses. For example, there may be four "degrees" of the factor, education. Degree 4 could be possession of a doctoral degree; degree 3, possession of a master's degree, and so on.

POINTS: The relative worth of each degree is designated in points, with the highest number of points given to the highest degree. For example, degree 4 of education may be worth 40 points, while degree 3 is only worth 20 points, as a doctoral degree is significantly more difficult to attain than a master's degree.

Federal Legislation Concerning Wage and Salary Administration. Wages and salaries are governed quite closely by numerous federal, state, and municipal laws and regulations. As with many of the federal laws affecting organizations, the laws regulating wage and salary administration reflect the mood or climate of the nation at the time of their passage. Such factors as war, depression, and minority-group relations could have a substantial effect on the passage of certain laws. The more important of these federal laws are noted below,[7] along with a few of their key provisions:

1. *Davis-Bacon Act of 1931.* Covers federal con-struction and repair work for contracts in excess of $2,000. Holders of such contracts must pay laborers the prevailing wages of the applicable locality.

2. *Walsh-Healey Public Contracts Act of 1936.* Extends provisions of Davis-Bacon Act beyond federal construction contracts to nonconstruction work exceeding $10,000. Prescribed wages are industry minimums, rather than prevailing wages in localities. Overtime must be paid at one-and-one-half the regular rate, with exceptions. Em-ployers must publicly display minimum wages. Violators are often prohibited from federal con-tracts for three years.

---

[7] This and all other laws have several additional provisions, exceptions, etc; see, e.g., Nash and Carroll, *The Management of Compensation*.

3. *Fair Labor Standards Act of 1930.* Sets minimum wages, maximum hours, overtime rates, and child-labor standards. Has been updated through several amendments. (The 1974 minimum wage for covered workers was $2.00 per hour.) Farm workers are presently excluded, as are retail establishments with less than $250,000 in annual sales.

4. *Discrimination laws of the 1960s.* The Equal Pay Act of 1963, amending the Fair Labor Standards Act, prohibits employers from discriminating in pay rates on the basis of sex. The Age Discrimination in Employment Act of 1967 prohibits discrimination in pay rates on the basis of age (for workers between 40 and 65 in certain types and sizes of organizations). (See also Exercise 18.)

PROCEDURE

Overview. A brief case study is presented in which you are able to identify various wage and salary problems occuring in an organizational setting and suggest solutions. An activity is then included to familiarize you with the terms and essentials of the point method of job evaluation. A job evaluation is conducted for six sample jobs in an organization, salary levels and a salary structure are developed, and individual salary levels are determined based on performance data.

PART A

STEP 1: Read the case in Form 1 and then form into small groups. In your groups, you are to discuss the case and responses to the questions below.

a) What would you recommend to Buster in this situation?

b) How would you go about implementing your recommendations? Be specific in outlining your recommendations and/or action steps. Specifically, you should give attention to (a) the current problems concerning pay for the company, (b) solutions to the problems, and (c) the criteria that might be used to aid the organization in designing a compensation plan.

TIME: About 30 minutes.

PART B

STEP 2: In Part B, you are to use Form 2 to determine the relative importance of each subfactor for successful performance in the three job types listed. Place a 1, 2, or 3 in each job-type column for each subfactor on the left in the form. That is, rank each subfactor separately. If you are in a small group, discuss any disagreements with other group members.

TIME: About 20 minutes.

PART C

STEP 3: Form into groups and assume you are employees of the City of Eastern Shore chosen to represent *all* employees in terms of job level and department function. One of you is from the custodial service, another is a librarian, and another is the assistant city manager. Others represent public works (streets and sanitation), city planning, personnel, and the Parks and Recreation Department. You are to assign these roles to members of your group.

Read the information provided about the small city of Eastern Shore in Form 3. Then, using Form 4, develop a point system of job evaluation for the jobs in Eastern Shore. Indicate all of the definitions and points for each factor, subfactor, and degree. For instance, you might allocate 400 of the 1,000 points to "skill." You might decide that subfactor A = 150, B = 100, C = 50, and D = 100 of these points. Of the 100 points allocated to subfactor B, you might give degree one (perhaps defined as up to one year previous experience) 30 points, degree two (perhaps defined as one-to-three years experience) 40 points. Be sure to write precise definitions in order to separate factors, subfactors, and degrees.

TIME: About 40 minutes

STEP 4: After Form 4 is completed, read and study carefully the six job descriptions appearing in Forms 5–10 for six municipal jobs of Eastern Shore. Then, using Form 11, rate each of the six jobs with the point system you developed on Form 4. Indicate the relative ranking of the six jobs based on their total points. Does your ranking seem logical? If not, you may want to reanalyze the jobs or change the point system. After completion of Form 11, you should have a total number of points allocated for each of the six jobs and can simply order them relative to "worth" from lowest to highest number of points.

TIME: About 40 minutes.

STEP 5: Read and study carefully the Salary Survey (Form 12) for six municipalities in the Northeast United States. Based on this survey, your point-system evaluation, and any other information in the case (Form 3), attach a yearly salary range to each of the six jobs (see Form 13). Plot the yearly salary rates against the point ranges to obtain a salary rate curve and answer the questions in Part II of Form 13.

TIME: About 35 minutes.

PART D

STEP 6: Using the data in Form 14 concerning the present job incumbents in each of the six Eastern Shore jobs, decide on an individual salary for each of the six people. Use all of the data generated so far, in addition to Form 14, to make the decision. Put the recommended salary levels, in an exact dollar amount, on Form 15, along with a brief rationale or comment for each level.

TIME: About 30 minutes.

FOR FURTHER READING

Adams, J. S. "Inequity in Social Exchange." In L. Berkowitz, ed., *Advances in Experimental Social Psychology.* Vol. 2. New York: Academic Press, 1965, pp. 267–299. (II)

Adams, J. S. "Toward an Understanding of Inequity." *Journal of Abnormal and Social Psychology* 56 (1972): 75–94. (II–R)

Andrews, I. R., and M. M. Henry. "Management Attitudes toward Pay." *Industrial Relations* 3 (1963): 29–39. (I–R)

Baytos, L. M. "The Employee Benefit Smorgasbord: Its Potential and Limitations." *Compensation Review* 2 (1970): 16–28. (I)

Belcher, D. W. *Wage and Salary Administration.* Englewood Cliffs, New Jersey: Prentice-Hall, 1962. (I)

Bittner, R. H., and E. Rundquist. "The Rank Comparison Rating Method." *Journal of Applied Psychology* 34 (1950): 171–177. (II–R)

Brennan, Charles W. *Wage Administration.* Homewood, Ill.: Irwin, 1963. (I)

Charles, A. W. "Installing Single-Factor Job Evaluation." *The Compensation Review* 3 (1971): 9–21. (I)

Chazen, C. "Compensation Plans: Bottom Line Results." *Management Review* 64 (November 1975): 19–25. (I)

Cook, A. H. "Equal Pay: Where Is It?" *Industrial Relations* 14 (1975): 158–177. (I)

Dunn, J. D., and F. M. Rachel. *Wage and Salary Administration: Total Compensation Systems.* New York: McGraw-Hill, 1971. (I)

Eckstein, O., and T. W. Wilson. "The Determination of Money Wages in American Industry." *Quarterly Journal of Economics* 26 (1962): 379–414. (II–R)

Epperson, L. L. "The Dynamics of Factor Comparison/Point Evaluation." *Public Personnel Management* 4, no. 1 (1975): 38–48. (I)

Feldstein, M. S. "Unemployment Insurance: Time for Reform." *Harvard Business Review* 53 (March–April 1975): 51–61. (I)

Foegen, J. H. "Far Out Fringe Benefits." *Personnel* 44 (1967): 65–71. (I)

Foegen, J. H. "Is It Time to Clip the Fringes?" *Personnel* 49 (1972): 36–42. (I)

Foster, K. E., G. F. Wajda, and T. R. Lawson. "Global Plan for Salary Administration." *Harvard Business Review* 39 (1961): 62–66. (I)

Giles, B. A., and G. V. Barrett. "The Utility of Merit Increases." *Journal of Applied Psychology* 55 (1971): 103–109. (II–R)

Goodman, P. J. "The Effect of Perceived Inequity on Salary Allocation Decisions." *Journal of Applied Psychology* 60 (1975): 372–375. (II–R)

Gordon, T. J., and R. E. LeBlew. "Employe Benefits, 1970–1985." *Harvard Business Review* 48 (1970): 94. (I)

Henderson, R. I. *Compensation Management.* Reston, Virginia: Reston, 1976. (I)

Heneman, H. G., III. "Impact of Performance on Managerial Pay Levels and Pay Changes." *Journal of Applied Psychology* 58 (1973): 128–130. (II–R)

Hinrichs, J. R. "Correlates of Employee Evaluations of Pay Increases." *Journal of Applied Psychology* 53 (1969): 481–489. (II–R)

Hulme, R. D., and R. J. Bevan. "The Blue Collar Worker Goes on Salary." *Harvard Business Review* 53 (March–April 1975): 104–112. (I)

Jacques, E. *Equitable Payment.* New York: Wiley, 1961. (I)

Kline, S. M., and J. R. Maher. "Education Level and Satisfaction with Pay." *Personnel Psychology* 19 (1966): 195–208. (II–R)

Lanham, Elizabeth. *Administration of Wages.* New York: Harper & Row, 1963. (I)

Lanham, E. *Job Evaluation.* New York: McGraw-Hill, 1955. (I)

Lawler, E. E. *Pay and Organizational Effectiveness.* New York: McGraw-Hill, 1971. (II)

Lawler, E. E., III. "How Much Money Do Executives Want?" *Transaction* 4 (1967): 23–29. (I)

Lawler, E. E. "The Mythology of Management Compensation." *California Management Review* 9 (1966): 11–22. (I)

Lawler, E. E., III. "Compensating the New-Life-Style Worker." *Personnel* 48 (1971): 19–25. (I)

Lawler, E. E. "Secrecy about Management Compensation: Are There Hidden Costs?" *Organizational Behavior and Human Performance* 2 (1967): 182–189. (II–R)

Lawler, E., and J. R. Hackman. "Corporate Profits and Employee Satisfaction: Must They Be in Conflict?" *California Management Review* 14 (1971): 46–55. (I)

Lawler, E., and E. Levin. "Union Officers' Perceptions of Members' Pay Preferences." *Industrial and Labor Relations Review* 21 (1968): 509–517. (II–R)

Lawsche, C. H., Jr., and R. F. Wilson. "Studies in Job Evaluation: VI. The Reliability of Two-Point Rating Systems." *Journal of Applied Psychology* 31 (1947): 355–365. (II–R)

Lesieur, F. G., ed. *The Scanlon Plan: A Frontier in Labor Management Cooperation*. New York: Wiley, 1958. (I)

Lester, R. A. "Pay Differentials by Size of Establishment." *Industrial Relations* 7 (1967): 57–67. (I)

Livernash, E. R. *Concepts in Wage Determination*. New York: McGraw-Hill, 1957. (I)

Livernash, E. R. *Wages and Benefits. A Review of Industrial Relations Research* 1 (1970): 79–144. (I)

Livis, B. *Job Evaluation: A Critical Review*. New York: Wiley, 1975. (I)

Locke, E. A. "What Is Job Satisfaction? *Organizational Behavior and Human Performance* 4 (1969): 309–336. (II)

Louden, J. Keith, and J. Wayne Deegan. *Wage Incentives*. New York: Wiley, 1959. (I)

Lovejoy, Lawrence C. *Wage and Salary Administration*. New York: Ronald Press, 1959. (I)

Lytle, C. W. *Job Evaluation Methods*. New York: Ronald Press, 1954. (I)

Marriott, R. *Incentive Wage Systems*. London: Staples Press, 1968. (I)

Miller, L. K., and R. L. Hamblin. "Interdependence, Differential Rewarding, and Productivity." *American Sociological Review* 28 (1963): 768–777. (II–R)

Miner, M. G. "Pay Policies: Secret or Open? And Why?" *Personnel Journal* 54 (1974): 110–115. (I)

Munson, F. "Four Fallacies for Wage and Salary Administration." *Personnel* 40 (1963): 57–64. (I)

Nealey, S. M., and J. G. Goodale. "Worker Preferences among Time-Off Benefits and Pay." *Journal of Applied Psychology* 51 (1967): 357–361. (II–R)

Norrgard, D. L. "The Public Pay Plan: Some New Approaches." *Public Personnel Review* 32 (1971): 91–95. (II–R)

Otis, J. L., and R. H. Leukart. *Job Evaluation*. 2d ed. Englewood Cliffs, New Jersey: Prentice-Hall, 1954. (I)

Ozame, R. *Wages in Practice and Theory*. Madison, Wisconsin: The University of Wisconsin Press, 1968. (II)

Patchen, M. *The Choice of Wage Comparisons*. Englewood Cliffs, New Jersey: Prentice-Hall, 1969. (I)

Penzer, W. M. "Educational Level and Satisfaction with Pay: An Attempted Replication." *Personnel Psychology* 22 (1969): 185–199. (II–R)

Pritchard, R. D., M. D. Dunnette, and D. O. Jorgenson. "Effects of Perceptions of Equity and Inequity on Worker Performance and Satisfaction." *Journal of Applied Psychology* 56 (1972): 75–94. (II–R)

Reggio, V. A. "How to Set Fair Salaries at Branch Locations." *Personnel Journal* 50 (1971): 626–629. (I)

Scheible, P. L. "Changes in Employee Compensation, 1966 to 1972." *Monthly Labor Review* 98 (March 1975): 10–16. (I)

Schuster, J. R. "Another Look at Compensation Preferences." *Industrial Management Review* 10 (1969): 1–18. (I)

Schuster, J. R. "Executive Compensation—in the Eyes of the Beholder." *Business Horizons* 17 (1974): 79–86. (I)

Schuster, J. R., and J. A. Colletti. "Pay Secrecy: Who Is For and Against It?" *Academy of Management Journal* 16 (1973): 35–40. (I–R)

Sibson, Robert E. *Wages and Salaries—A Handbook for Line Managers*. New York: American Management Association, Inc., 1967. (I)

Wernimont, P. F., and S. Fitzpatrick. "The Meaning of Money." *Journal of Applied Psychology* 56 (1972): 218–226. (I)

Whyte, W. F. et al. *Money and Motivation*. New York: Harper, 1955. (I)

Winton, D. C., and C. R. Sutherland. "A Performance-Based Approach to Determining Executive Incentive Bonus Awards." *Compensation Review* 18 (1976): 14–26. (I)

Yoder, Dale, H. G. Heneman, Jr., John G. Turnbull, and G. Harold Stone. *Handbook of Personnel Management and Labor Relations*. New York: McGraw-Hill, Inc., 1958. (I)

Yukl, G., K. N. Wexley, and J. D. Seymore. "Effectiveness of Pay Incentives under Variable Ratio and Continuous Reinforcement Schedules." *Journal of Applied Psychology* 56 (1972): 19–23. (II–R)

Zedek, S., and P. C. Smith. "A Psycho-Physical Determination of Equitable Payment: A Methodological Study." *Journal of Applied Psychology* 52 (1968): 343–347. (II–R)

Zollitsch, H. G., and A. Langsner. *Wage and Salary Administration.* 2d ed. Cincinnati: South-Western, 1970. (I)

PART A

Form 1 Farmhelper Manufacturing Corporation

In 1948, Steven Buster began manufacturing farm equipment. During the following years his business prospered and he added additional products and employees to the business. In the early sixties, the business moved out of the family farm and into a small factory. As the business continued to grow, it was incorporated as the Farmhelper Corporation with Steven Buster as its president. By 1975 the firm had grown to include more than 110 employees located in five modern buildings in the East Arapahoe Industrial Park, located on the edge of a major midwestern city of over one million people. As Mr. Buster saw his firm continue to grow, he began to give some thought to the employees within his organization and their current pay rates. He felt it might be time for a change.

The Organization

Farmhelper is a privately owned corporation with Mr. Buster holding most of the outstanding stock. Of the 110 employees, 60 are blue-collar workers who do piecework; the remaining are supervisors, salesmen, or others in staff roles (e.g., clerks, clerical workers, etc.). Farmhelper is unionized. Most of the blue-collar workers are skilled machinists. A variety of machinery is used in the many processes involved in the production of the products (e.g., stamping, drilling, etc.). Most workers are capable of running all of the machines. The average age of the work force is thirty-three. Physical working conditions are excellent and care is taken to maintain a safe, pleasant working environment. The organization is also very concerned with the employees' safety and Occupational Safety and Health Administration (OSHA) standards are rigidly followed.

Pay System

The pay scale throughout the organization is generally on the low side of industry averages. Most of the blue-collar workers earn between $2.80 and $5.79 an hour. The rates of the managerial workers average 9 percent below the average pay rates for similar jobs in the greater metropolitan area, and those of the unionized workers are average. There also appear to be inequities in pay rates both within and between the organization's six different departments. No formal performance-evaluation system exists and apparently no direct relationship between performance and compensation can be argued in many cases. (The union has seniority provisions in the current contract.) Fringe benefits are few and salary levels are secret. Individuals do not seem to talk about pay or tell each other what they make. This is particularly true of the workers not covered by the union, which has recently been hit by antidiscrimination suits and publicity concerning internal mismanagement and corruption regarding its pension fund. The union is therefore seen by Farmhelper as docile at this time.

Employees appear to have mixed feelings about working at Farmhelper. Mr. Buster is very well liked and some workers seem to have a friendly and informal relationship with him. Many people seem to be highly involved in their jobs and also concerned about the success of the company, but mostly at higher levels in the organization. Satisfaction with pay, however, is generally low and employees are extremely dissatisfied with the way pay is administered in the company. Young workers complain that they earn too much less than older workers with less-important jobs. While workers seem to trust each other and cooperate with each other in the course of their work, trust of the company seems to be low. Turnover is extremely high, about 23 percent a year. Absenteeism is also high, although the situation is not as bad as turnover. This puzzles Mr. Buster because of the relatively high unemployment rate in the city.

Summary

The organization appears to be doing well; growth in sales has continued and financial performance has been excellent during the past few years. In the most recent fiscal year, return on investment before taxes increased seven percent over last year and was highest in Farmhelper's history. Steven Buster is concerned about the future and has become interested in "human relations" in his organization. He has asked you to come in and work with him regarding wage and salary administration, job evaluation, and motivation of workers using pay schemes. He is concerned with both the workers covered by the union contract and those who are not. The union contract expires in four months.

Name _____ Group Number _____

Date _____ Class Section _____ Hour _____ Score _____

PART B

Form 2 The Relative Importance of Common Job Factors to Different Types of Jobs

Rank the importance for job success of each subfactor for each of the three job types. For example, if mental effort is most important for clerical jobs, you would put a 1 in the clerical column, if it is second most important for administrative/ professional jobs, you put a 2 in that column, and so on. Rank all three types of jobs separately for each subfactor.

Job Factors	Job Types		
	Trades and Crafts	Administrative/Professional	Clerical
1. Job skills			
a) Knowledge			
b) Experience			
c) Special training			
2. Effort			
a) Physical			
b) Mental			
3. Responsibility			
a) Latitude/scope			
b) For product output			
c) Control exercised over others			
d) For safety of others			
4. Relationships			
a) With peers			
b) With superiors and subordinates			
5. Other Factors			
a) Working conditions			
b) Hazards and risks			
c) Complexity of work			
d) Security requirements			

PART C

Form 3 The City of Eastern Shore

Eastern Shore is a small (population 60,000) city in the central Atlantic Coast region. It is located about 75 miles from a major metropolitan area of several million people and 20 miles from a city of 125,000. Eastern Shore is basically an industrial city containing several metalworking and precision-equipment manufacturers, only one of which is a large national corporation. There are also several small foundries, a few shoe factories, and a few small electronics companies. Despite its name, Eastern Shore is about 100 miles from the ocean and is not a tourist attraction; however, it is a county seat and the center of a vegetable farming area. There is one small private liberal arts college with an enrollment of 2,500 in the city.

The municipal government of Eastern Shore, like that of so many other very small towns that grew rapidly during the 1950s and 1960s, has suddenly found itself quite large and diversified. Thirty years ago a mayor and a few part-time employees ran the city, but today there are 200 city employees. The city council consists of seven members who, six years ago, hired a city manager to run the day-to-day operations of the city. But, in the last ten years, the population has increased by 35 percent and many additional services had to be provided to the citizenry, which called for skilled workers such as the head librarian, the city engineer, the detectives in the police department, the city auditor, and the fire chief.

The city is divided into several departments, each with a director who reports to the city manager. These directors include recreation, public works, police, fire, library, finance, legal, personnel, and auditing and records. Public works, which includes water and sewer, streets, garbage, etc., is the largest department, with 76 employees. The police department has 20 workers and the fire department has 14. Recreation and the auditing and records departments each have about 30 workers. All full-time city jobs are salaried. The jobs are quite varied and include road crews, garbage collectors, machinery operators, groundskeepers, engineers, policemen, clerks, secretaries, lawyers, administrative assistants, a city planner, etc.

The city manager is forceful and successful in dealing with the city council and over the years has been able to collect taxes and float bond issues to improve municipal services and equipment. Now Eastern Shore has a new and modern library, a new high school (as well as an older one), a new city hall-jail-justice building, and has given its downtown a facelift by widening streets and adding a park and fountains. The city manager has also been able to attract and keep some excellent city employees because of his power over the budget and his innovative, growth-oriented ideas.

The city's employees have, in the past, received fewer and smaller pay increases than industrial workers in the city. The latter are almost all unionized. Their average pay increase per year has been about 7 percent over the last five years, while Eastern Shore employees have averaged only about 4 percent. There seems to be no serious talk of organizing the city workers into a union, however. The city does have pension plans, health insurance, small merit raises, and other benefits for its employees, including paid sick leave. The cost of living is rising very rapidly in the area. The entire 4 percent average salary increase noted above does not match the cost-of-living increase. At present, there is no automatic cost-of-living escalator in the salary system and merit raises have been extremely small when given.

Name _____   Group Number _____

Date _____ Class Section _____ Hour _____ Score _____

PART C

Form 4 The Point System of Job Evaluation

Instructions: Define each *factor*, each *subfactor*, and each *degree* for each subfactor in the block provided. Then indicate the number of points allocated to each factor, subfactor, and each degree in the small boxes. Use a total of 1,000 points. The total number of points in each degree for a subfactor must equal the points alloted to the subfactor, and the total number of points alloted to each subfactor must equal the total given to the factor. The total number of points for all factors equals 1,000.

Job Factor	*Subfactor*	*Degree 1*	*Degree 2*	*Degree 3*
1. Skill	A. Job knowledge			
	B. Experience			
	C. Special training			
	D. Diversity			
2. Effort	A. Physical			
	B. Mental			
3. Responsibility	A. Latitude			
	B. Safety of others			
	C. Work of others			
	D. Material/Product			

Job Factor	Subfactor	Degree 1	Degree 2	Degree 3
4. Relationships	A. With peers			
	B. With superiors and subordinates			
5. Other factors	A. Working conditions			
	B. Hazards and risks			
	C. Complexity of work			
	D. Security requirements			
TOTAL POINTS 1000	1000			

PART C

Form 5 City of Eastern Shore—Job No. 1

SECRETARY III

DESCRIPTION OF WORK:

General Statement of Duties: Performs complete secretarial duties and administrative detail work for the chief elected official or head of a major unit of city government, requiring extensive exercise of independent judgment in the role of "Personal Assistant."

Supervision Received: Works under broad policy guidance or direction of a chief elected official or head of major unit of city government. Would rarely receive supervision by any other party and can be considered to perform duties on a "one-to-one" basis.

Supervision Exercised: Exercises supervision over personnel as assigned, or full supervision incidental to other duties.

EXAMPLES OF DUTIES: (Any one position may not include all of the duties listed, nor do the listed examples include all tasks that may be found in positions of this class.)

Performs complete secretarial duties for the chief elected official or head of a major unit of city government; handles confidential matters concerning major city policy; keeps advised of the current status of the work of the executive; collects information for the use of the executive; determines action necessary in situations arising during absence of superior.

Handles a variety of administrative details, which involves contact with various officials in the public service and in private industry; relieves the department head of administrative detail; relays departmental policies and instructions; arranges meetings; briefs correspondence and miscellaneous data.

Furnishes the public with advice and assistance requiring good knowledge of city. Departments, rules and regulations, and policies.

Takes complex dictation; takes notes of meetings; keeps official records and reports; prepares correspondence. Makes travel arrangements; maintains appointment calendar. Uses dictaphone, typewriter, copier, and other office equipment.

Performs related work as required.

REQUIRED KNOWLEDGES, SKILLS, AND ABILITIES: Extensive knowledge of modern office practices and procedures. Extensive knowledge of grammar, spelling, and punctuation. Thorough skill of the taking and transcribing of dictation and in the operation of a typewriter. Ability to exercise initiative and sound judgment and to react resourcefully under varying conditions. Ability to establish and maintain effective relationships with the public, other agencies, and employees.

QUALIFICATIONS FOR APPOINTMENT:

Education: High-school graduation or equivalent.

Experience: Four years experience in progressively responsible general office work, including one year in a position comparable to Secretary II.

  OR

Any equivalent combination of education and experience.

PART C

Form 6 City of Eastern Shore—Job No. 2

POLICE CHIEF

DESCRIPTION OF WORK:

General Statement of Duties: Performs administrative work in planning, coordinating, and directing the activities of the city police department.

Supervision Received: Works under broad policy guidance and direction of the city manager.

Supervision Exercised: Exercises supervision over all department personnel directly or through subordinate officers.

EXAMPLES OF DUTIES: (The listed examples may not include all duties found in this class.)

In conformance with applicable laws and in accordance with the rules and regulations of the department, develops or revises department operating policies and procedures; has final authority, within given laws, rules, and regulations, on all aspects of the department's activity.

Establishes department organization, including channels of authority, responsibility, and communication; revises department organization as appropriate to maximize efficiency.

Assigns to commanding officers the authority to direct operations and supervise subordinate officers and civilian personnel within their assigned responsibility.

Has overall responsibility for the maintenance of departmental discipline and the conduct and general behavior of officers and civilian employees.

Meets with elected or appointed officials, other law-enforcement agencies, community and business representatives, and the public on all aspects of the department's activities.

Prepares, presents, and controls the departmental budget.

Organizes and participates in programs on police and safety subjects for the public; meets with associations, civic organizations, and related groups.

Researches and prepares new and revised ordinances pertaining to traffic and safety.

Performs related work, as required.

REQUIRED KNOWLEDGES, SKILLS, AND ABILITIES: Extensive knowledge of modern law-enforcement practices, procedures, techniques, and equipment. Thorough knowledge of federal, state, and local laws and ordinances governing departmental activities. Thorough knowledge of the policies, organization, rules, regulations, and procedures common to police department operations. Considerable knowledge of the principles and practices of administration. Ability to organize and coordinate department activities. Ability to communicate effectively—verbally and in writing. Ability to supervise personnel directly or through subordinate officers. Ability to establish and maintain effective working relationships with elected and appointed officials, other law-enforcement agencies, and the public. Ability to meet necessary special requirements.

QUALIFICATIONS FOR APPOINTMENT:

Education: Graduation from a college or university with an associate degree in police science.

Experience: Two years of law-enforcement experience in the rank of captain.

   OR

Any equivalent combination of education and experience.

PART C

Form 7 City of Eastern Shore—Job No. 3

DIRECTOR OF PUBLIC WORKS

DESCRIPTION OF WORK:

General Statement of Duties: Plans, organizes, and supervises the public-works program of the city.

Supervision Received: Works under broad policy guidance and direction of the city manager.

Supervision Exercised: Exercises supervision over public-works personnel directly or through subordinate supervisors.

EXAMPLES OF DUTIES: (The listed examples may not include all duties found in this class.)

Plans, coordinates, and provides overall direction for the various program activities of the department, including engineering, street construction, maintenance and repair; design and construction of public-works structures and facilities; waste-water and water and sewage plant operations.

Develops and revises the department's operating policies and procedures in accordance with applicable laws and the department's rules and regulations; has final authority, within given laws, rules, and regulations, over all aspects of the department's activity.

Establishes department organization, including channels of authority, responsibility, and communication; revises department organization to maximize efficiency.

Assigns to subordinate supervisors the authority to direct operations and supervises personnel within their assigned responsibility.

Meets with city officials, private contractors, and the public on all aspects of the department's work.

Prepares and submits department budget requests and controls the programs from viewpoint of costs.

Prepares and presents operating and special reports as necessary.

Performs related work as required.

REQUIRED KNOWLEDGES, SKILLS, AND ABILITIES: Thorough knowledge of the principles and methods of public-works administration. Thorough knowledge of the principles, methods, materials, and equipment common to public-works and utilities operations. Ability to organize and direct the activities of personnel and equipment. Ability to communicate effectively—both verbally and in writing. Ability to establish and maintain effective working relationships with employees, other agencies, and the public.

QUALIFICATIONS FOR APPOINTMENT:

Education: Graduation from a college or university with a bachelor's degree in civil engineering or a related field.

Experience: Six years of progressively responsible public-works experience, including four years in an administrative or supervisory capacity.

    OR

Any equivalent combination of education and experience.

Necessary Special Requirements: Possession of, or eligibility for within six months after employment, a state professional engineer's license.

PART C

Form 8 City of Eastern Shore—Job No. 4

CLERICAL WORKER II (Accounts Receivable)

DESCRIPTION OF WORK:

General Statement of Duties: Performs a variety of general clerical work requiring some exercise of independent judgment.

Supervision Received: Works under general supervision of a clerical, technical, or administrative superior.

Supervision Exercised: Exercises supervision of clerical personnel as assigned.

EXAMPLES OF DUTIES: (Any one position may not include all of the duties listed, nor do the listed examples include all duties that may be found in positions of this class.)

Processes reports, forms, payments, billings, or other materials; examines for accuracy and completeness; makes additions or resolves discrepancies, consulting with supervisor or other employees as appropriate.

Maintains records, files, and books according to established methods and procedures; compiles and tabulates data for records and reports; keeps books requiring ledger entries.

Accepts fees or payments, issues receipts and notices, and keeps simple records of transactions; makes simple mathematical computations.

Receives telephone and personal callers, handling any questions or matters of a nontechnical or routine nature and directing others to the appropriate staff members.

Operates simple office equipment.

Performs related work as required.

REQUIRED KNOWLEDGES, SKILLS, AND ABILITIES: Working knowledge of modern office practices and procedures. Ability to perform a variety of clerical work requiring some exercise of independent judgment. Ability to follow written and oral instructions. Ability to make simple mathematical computations. Ability to establish and maintain effective working relationships with employees, other agencies, and the public.

MINIMUM QUALIFICATIONS:

Education: High-school graduation or equivalent.

Experience: One year of experience in general clerical work.

OR

Any equivalent combination of education and experience.

PART C

Form 9 City of Eastern Shore—Job No. 5

ASSISTANT LIBRARIAN

DESCRIPTION OF WORK:

General Statement of Duties: Performs supervisory duties relating to coordination of library activities.

Supervision Received: Works under general supervision of an administrative superior.

Supervision Exercised: Exercises supervision over personnel as assigned.

EXAMPLES OF DUTIES: (Any one position may not include all of the duties listed nor do the listed examples include all duties that may be found in positions of this class.)

Acts as assistant to the Library Director; types letters, records, and order forms; supervises library activities in absence of director.

Maintains shelf list file and count; types catalog cards, registration, and I.D. cards; assists library patrons in checking in and out library materials; reserves library materials.

Reserves 16 mm films and insures delivery to library patrons.

Instructs other staff members in proper methods of processing after cataloging; locates reading sources and other library materials, shelving and circulation desk responsibilities.

Operates a variety of office equipment, including the Regiscope and 3-M Reader Printer.

Performs related work as required.

REQUIRED KNOWLEDGES, SKILLS, AND ABILITIES: Considerable knowledge of library principles, methods, materials, and practices. Considerable knowledge of reader interest levels. Ability to assign, supervise, and inspect the work of others. Ability to exercise sound judgment in making decisions. Ability to communicate effectively verbally and in writing. Ability to establish and maintain effective working relationships with other employees and library patrons.

MINIMUM QUALIFICATIONS:

Education: Graduation from a college or university with a Master's degree in library science or a related field.

Experience: Two years of progressively responsible experience in library work.

     OR

Any equivalent combination of education and experience.

PART C

Form 10 City of Eastern Shore—Job No. 6

PUBLIC UTILITIES PLANT OPERATOR II

DESCRIPTION OF WORK:

General Statement of Duties: Performs skilled work in the operation, servicing, and minor maintenance of equipment in a water or waste-water plant on an assigned shift.

Supervision Received: Works under general supervision of technical superior.

Supervision Exercised: Orientation on the job of operator-in-training personnel.

EXAMPLE OF DUTIES: (Any one position may not include all of the duties listed, nor do the listed examples include all tasks that may be found in positions of this class.

Operates plant equipment to control the water flow and maintains proper conditions for treatment of water.

Performs a variety of tasks, such as inspecting and oiling pumps, monitoring chemical feeders, motors, gauges, and valves.

Operates filters, takes water samples to determine that units of the plant are functioning efficiently and the treatment process is maintained.

Makes periodic rounds of plant and pumping stations to check equipment operation and flow meter records.

Assists in orienting and instructing operator-in-training personnel in the duties and responsibilities of plant operations.

Records meter readings and reports plant operations.

May operate truck to carry solid wastes to landfill.

Performs related work as required.

REQUIRED KNOWLEDGES, SKILLS, AND ABILITIES: Considerable knowledge of the operation of motors, pumps, meters, and related equipment of a water or waste water plant. Skill in the operation of mechanical equipment. Ability to make accurate readings, keep records, and make reports. Ability to communicate effectively orally and in writing. General mechanical ability to work effectively and react quickly to situations that develop. Ability to work independently. Ability to instruct and orient other employees. Ability to establish and maintain effective working relationships with other employees and the general public.

QUALIFICATIONS FOR APPOINTMENT:

Education: High-school graduation or equivalent.

Experience: Two years experience in mechanical maintenance or repair work, including one year's experience in a water or waste-water plant.

          OR

Any equivalent combination of education and experience.

Necessary Special Requirements: Must possess a Class I Water and Waste Water Plant Operator's Certificate from the state.

Name _____   Group Number _____

Date _____ Class Section _____ Hour _____ Score _____

PART C

Form 11 Job Evaluation Computation Worksheet for Six Eastern Shore Jobs

Indicate the number of points allocated to each job by entering the proper amount of points (copied from the master point system of Form 4) in each block that applies to each job. Then, total all the points allocated for each job in order to arrive at the relative ranking of the six jobs. (Note: Each job can only be at one degree level—therefore blank blocks will appear for each job.)

Job Factor	Subfactors and Degrees		Jobs					
			No. 1	No. 2	No. 3	No. 4	No. 5	No. 6
1. Skill	A. Job knowledge	Degree 1						
		Degree 2						
		Degree 3						
	B. Experience	Degree 1						
		Degree 2						
		Degree 3						
	C. Special training	Degree 1						
		Degree 2						
		Degree 3						
2. Effort	A. Physical	Degree 1						
		Degree 2						
		Degree 3						
	B. Mental	Degree 1						
		Degree 2						
		Degree 3						
3. Responsibility	A. Latitude	Degree 1						
		Degree 2						
		Degree 3						
	B. Safety of others	Degree 1						
		Degree 2						
		Degree 3						
	C. Work of others	Degree 1						
		Degree 2						
		Degree 3						
	D. Material product	Degree 1						
		Degree 2						
		Degree 3						
4. Relationships	A. With peers	Degree 1						
		Degree 2						
		Degree 3						
	B. With superiors and subordinates	Degree 1						
		Degree 2						
		Degree 3						

Job Factor	Subfactors and Degrees		Jobs					
			No. 1	No. 2	No. 3	No. 4	No. 5	No. 6
5. Other factors	A. Working conditions	Degree 1						
		Degree 2						
		Degree 3						
	B. Hazards	Degree 1						
		Degree 2						
		Degree 3						
	C. Complexity of work	Degree 1						
		Degree 2						
		Degree 3						
	D. Security requirements	Degree 1						
		Degree 2						
		Degree 3						
Total Points Allocated to Each Job								

Final relative ordering of jobs based on the point system:

	Job title	Points
Highest value or worth	_____	_____
↑	_____	_____
	_____	_____
	_____	_____
↓	_____	_____
Lowest value or worth	_____	_____

PART C

Form 12 Salary Survey Data for Six Selected Municipalities in the Northeast United States*

Job title	Municipality	Salary range (per yr.)		Actual paid range (per yr.)		
		maximum	minimum	maximum	minimum	median
Secretaries to city manager	A	10,750	8,500	10,750	8,500	10,000
	B	9,900	7,750	9,000	7,750	8,400
	C	11,000	8,400	10,750	8,900	9,750
	D	9,500	8,000	9,250	8,500	8,750
	E	10,200	7,750	10,200	8,000	8,500
	F	11,250	8,750	11,000	9,000	9,500
Police chief†	A	18,250	13,500	N/A	N/A	18,250
	B	16,500	11,500	N/A	N/A	16,000
	C	18,750	13,500	N/A	N/A	18,000
	D	17,000	14,000	N/A	N/A	17,250
	E	16,000	11,500	N/A	N/A	15,500
	F	17,500	12,500	N/A	N/A	14,500
Director of public works†	A	21,300	16,250	N/A	N/A	18,400
	B	20,250	15,500	N/A	N/A	16,750
	C	20,500	14,500	N/A	N/A	18,500
	D	19,500	14,500	N/A	N/A	17,500
	E	18,000	13,750	N/A	N/A	15,750
	F	19,000	14,000	N/A	N/A	16,000
Accounts-receivable clerks	A	9,500	7,250	9,000	7,500	8,250
	B	9,000	7,500	8,750	7,500	7,750
	C	10,000	7,000	10,000	7,400	8,000
	D	8,750	7,500	8,500	7,750	8,000
	E	8,500	7,750	8,000	7,750	7,750
	F	9,750	7,250	9,500	8,500	9,250
Assistant librarian	A	12,500	9,000	11,000	9,000	10,000
	B	10,750	8,000	9,750	8,000	9,000
	C	10,500	8,000	10,000	8,750	9,250
	D	11,000	9,000	11,000	9,500	10,250
	E	11,500	8,750	11,000	8,750	9,250
	F	12,000	9,750	10,500	9,750	10,250
Public utility plant operators	A	8,750	7,250	8,500	7,250	7,250
	B	9,000	7,000	8,000	7,000	7,500
	C	8,500	7,500	8,500	8,000	8,500
	D	8,750	7,000	7,750	7,000	7,250
	E	8,000	6,500	7,500	6,750	7,000
	F	8,750	6,750	8,000	6,750	7,500

* Illustrative data.

†Since only one person occupies these positions in each municipality, there are no actual paid maximums and minimums. Salary range data was developed historically.

NOTES: Municipalities are all in the same geographical area (Northeastern United States) and all have between 30,000 and 65,000 populations. Municipality B received a 12 percent "across-the-board" pay raise last year, while all others received increases of between 5.5 percent and 9 percent, with the exception of E, which got no increase. Unions exist in C and F. In C, a new contract negotiated last year calls for about an 8.5 percent salary increase over each of the next three years for all workers, while in jurisdiction F, a new contract will be negotiated next year. The salary figure for F indicates a 7 percent raise over last year. All figures represent salary only, not fringe benefits.

Name _____   Group Number _____

Date _____   Class Section _____   Hour _____   Score _____

PART C
Form 13

Part I.   Salary Structure for Six Eastern Shore Jobs

Instructions: Enter the required data for the six Eastern Shore jobs based on your analysis of the salary survey, your point system, and any other relevant data.

Job Title	Appropriate point range for each job (min. to max.)	Appropriate yearly salary range	
		maximum	minimum

Part II: The Relationship of Points to Salary for Six Eastern Shore Jobs

Instructions: Draw a salary rate structure here by plotting the yearly salary against points you have allocated to each of the six jobs, using midpoints of the ranges you indicated in Part I above. There should be six points in the graph which, when connected, form a line or curve that explains the relationship between job salaries and their allocated points from your point system of job evaluation. What type of relationship is indicated? Is it logical? What, if anything, needs to be changed and why? (Place your answers on reverse.)

Yearly salary rate
(midpoint of salary range above,
in thousands of dollars)

0

Points allocated to each of the six jobs (midpoint of point range)

PART D

Form 14 Data from Personnel Records of Eastern Shore Workers Currently Holding the Six Selected Jobs

Job title	Age	Sex	Formal education	Years worked for city	Years at present position	Years of previous experience		Amount of last merit raise (per month)	Overall performance rating (10 point scale)		Supervisor's current assessment of promotability
						General work experience	Specific to current job		Last period	This period	
1. Secretary to city manager	34	F	High school; secretarial school	6	6	10	4	$30	8	9	Promotable now, perhaps in highest applicable position
2. Police chief	55	M	College; police academy	14	8	21	21	$50	10	10	Promotable now, but in highest applicable position
3. Director of public works	37	M	College; master's degree	5	3	12	3	$45	9	10	Promotable now
4. Accounts-receivable clerk	43	F	High school	2	2	8	1	$8	8	7	May be promotable at future date
5. Assistant librarian	24	M	High school	1	1	2	0	0	5	6	Definitely not promotable
6. Public works plant operator	27	F	Some college	2	1	3	0	0	7	8	May be promotable at future date

Name _____ Group Number _____

Date _____ Class Section _____ Hour _____ Score _____

PART D

Form 15 Recommended Salary Levels for Six Current Eastern Shore Workers

	Job title	Recommended yearly salary	Amount of Increase/Decrease	Rationale or comments
1.				
2.				
3.				
4.				
5.				
6.				

Name _____   Group Number _____

Date _____ Class Section _____ Hour _____ Score _____

ASSESSMENT OF LEARNING IN PERSONNEL ADMINISTRATION

EXERCISE 17

1. Try to state the purpose of this exercise in one concise sentence.

2. Specifically what did you learn from this exercise (i.e., skills, abilities, and knowledge)?

3. How might your learning influence your role and your duties as a personnel administrator?

4. How could a wage and salary program be evaluated as to its effectiveness?

5. What problems might you encounter from line managers as you implement a new salary system?

6. Do you feel organizations rely too heavily on money as rewards?   Why?

7. Additional questions given by your implementor:

Section 7
Personnel Administration and Human-Resource Management in the Contemporary Environment

Exercise 1 emphasized the rapidly changing environment in which people in personnel must operate. This external environment affects their work, just as it affects the work of others in organizations, and is a reason the jobs of those in personnel command ever-higher prestige and salaries. The changing nature of the environment also places more demands on those in personnel; thus, complex technical and administrative skills, as well as interpersonal skills, are now required in order to meet these new challenges.

While several aspects of the contemporary environment have been discussed throughout these exercises, two have been mentioned repeatedly: equal-employment-opportunity laws and guidelines, and labor unions. Their impact on the tasks and roles of those in personnel is significant and pervades each specific personnel program discussed in previous exercises. Thus, the final two exercises consider these important issues separately.

Exercise 18 outlines the basic legal issues regarding equal employment opportunity. It contains activities designed to illustrate and simulate the process of determining whether a personnel program violates an EEO law or federal guideline and enables you to build skill in designing and implementing affirmative action plans to increase the participation of women and minorities in an organization.

Exercise 19 considers the impact of unions on personnel programs. Rather than discuss union organizing or labor laws, the exercise attempts to illustrate the actual impact of unionization on personnel and human-resource programs. Most importantly, Exercise 19 points out that unions place certain constraints on personnel programs, as well as afford certain opportunities for improving these programs. The most successful people in personnel seem to be those who recognize and plan for the former and capitalize on and seize the latter.

Exercise 18

ISSUES IN EQUAL EMPLOYMENT OPPORTUNITY AND AFFIRMATIVE ACTION

PREVIEW

If you have completed the exercise on testing (Exercise 10), you should be familiar with basic employee selection procedures which facilitate the selection of the best person to do a specific job. However, another aspect of selection must be addressed—job discrimination. Two important points should be noted at the outset: first, the personnel administrator is typically responsible for identifying any "adverse impact" an organization's selection procedures may have on certain "protected groups" (i.e., minorities and women); and second, even if the selection procedures demonstrate adverse impact, they may not be considered discriminatory *provided* they are shown to be job related. Of course, the exact definition of terms such as job related must be specified, as it is in the exercise, in order to really understand the issue of discrimination in employment. Further, Congress has decided that not only must the past practices causing adverse impact be eliminated, but in many cases organizations must actually initiate practices and programs to compensate for past discrimination. These programs are commonly called affirmative-action programs. These two topics, job discrimination and affirmative action, and their impact on the human-resource function of an organization, are the focus of this exercise.

OBJECTIVES

1. To gain an understanding of the many laws that define and propose to remedy employment discrimination.
2. To build skill in identifying discriminatory personnel practices.
3. To build skills in avoiding discriminatory practices, as well as in planning for specific remedies through affirmative-action programs.

PREMEETING ASSIGNMENT

Read the entire exercise carefully, especially the *Introduction*. (You may also find Exercise 10 a useful review.)

INTRODUCTION

Discrimination in Employment: Definition, Legal Regulation, and the Design and Implementation of Remedies at the Organizational Level*

In 1964 no one knew precisely the extent of racial discrimination in employment practices. But Congress, in creating the Equal Employment Opportunity Commission (EEOC), assumed such practices were widespread. The Commission, composed of five members appointed by the president for five-year terms, confirmed the assumption. It found that in 1966 blacks made up only 2.6 percent of the "white-collar" headquaters staffs of the hundred major New York City-based corporations that ac-

---

* The terms and concepts discussed in this *Introduction* are defined in a glossary of EEO and related legal terms, which is appended to this exercise.

450

counted for nearly 16 percent of the gross national product.

Thus, Title VII of the Civil Rights Act of 1964 (which did not apply to government) barred discrimination in employment.[1] It contained the following passage:

> Nor shall it be unlawful employment practice for an employer to give and act upon the results of any professionally developed ability test provided that such test, its administration, or action upon the results is not designed, intended, or used to discriminate because of race, color, religion, sex, or national ancestry.[2]

The above statement is the essence of the so-called Tower Amendment, which, although it initially appears to be a simple statement, has caused much confusion in the application of selection strategies. The EEOC issued its first *Guidelines on Employment Testing Procedures* in 1966. These were revised in 1970, and reissued as the *EEOC Guidelines on Employee Selection Procedures*. These *Guidelines* applied only to the private sector when issued. They elaborated the EEOC's interpretation of the words "professionally developed test" by referencing the *Standards for Educational and Psychological Tests and Manuals*, published by the American Psychological Association in 1966 for principal use in education and research. The *EEOC Guidelines* of 1970 also define the meaning of the word "test" very broadly (effectively including any nonrandom personnel selection procedure, including interviews and application blanks). The *Guidelines* released in 1970 help define and interpret broad statements in the laws, but confusion and controversy have marked these laws from their inception and the EEOC's history has in turn been influenced by these controversies.

The EEOC's Work Record.   The passage of the Civil Rights Act of 1964 and the creation of the EEOC have had the effect of putting pressure on companies and unions to cease overt discrimination, identify covert discrimination, and open additional job opportunities for all groups. In its first four years, the Commission's investigations of alleged illegal discrimination resulted in the filing of a mere handful—fewer than two dozen—federal suits to stop discrimination by employers or by unions. Most of the suits were against small companies or union locals. It was not until mid-1968 that a suit was brought against the nationwide operations of a large employer.

There are several reasons for the EEOC's slow initial performance. Congress first appropriated about $2 million for the Commission in 1964, but President Johnson did not name the commissioners until well into 1965. The chairman was Franklin D. Roosevelt, Jr. But Roosevelt resigned after a few months to run for political office. So, roughly two years passed before the Commission began. When it did, it found the administrative machinery provided by Congress slow and cumbersome. Initially it could only investigate complaints against private employers, employment agencies, unions, or labor-management apprenticeship programs. Upon finding illegalities, it could only try conciliation and had to recommend to the Justice Department that suits be brought. The EEOC had no authority to hold administrative hearings on its complaints or to ban illegal union or employer discriminatory practices. Authority to hold such proceedings is a basic part of the powers of other regulatory agencies and accounts for the tremendous volume of their work. The EEOC has asked repeatedly for such authority and Congress has refused to grant it, perhaps in part because of the Commission's strong advocacy position compared to other regulatory agencies.

A change came in 1972 when the Act was expanded to include state and local governments and educational institutions. This provided coverage for 11 million and 4.3 million employees, respectively. There was also a change in procedure in that the EEOC no longer viewed discrimination as a single, isolated act, but viewed systematic discrimination that had disparate effects on "protected groups." The major charge to the EEOC was then to eliminate discrimination due to race, color, religion, sex, and national origin in hiring and to upgrade all employee conditions. It was also given the power to sue discriminatory employers.

Of the first 175,000 EEOC cases, 63 percent were found in favor of the complainant and at least 250 suits have been brought against employers. In 1974 alone over 6,000 cases involving women were filed and many traditional hiring requirements, such as height, weight, working hours, childbearing, etc., have been ruled against. Millions of dollars have been paid by organizations for their discriminatory behavior. The most famous of these is probably the AT&T case, in which the company paid several million dollars to various management and nonmanagement groups for discrimination. Part of these payments were in

---

[1] Many of the ideas compiled here were obtained from a paper delivered by Glenn G. McCluny at the IPMS–OMPO Personnel Directors' Seminar, Vail, Colorado, August 28–29, 1975. Reprinted in *Personnel Letter* No. 280, November 1975, pp. 6–8.

[2] Civil Rights Act of 1964, 42 U.S.C., 20008 *et seq*, Title VII.

the form of back pay, wage adjustments, and promotion payments. In another case, nine steel companies (representing 73 percent of the industry's output) and unions paid $31 million in back pay (ranging from $250 to $3000 per person) to members of minority groups and to women. The organizations also established goals and timetables concerning seniority, transfer, earnings, promotions, and test validity to eliminate discrimination in the future.

The *EEOC Guidelines* received little criticism from industry from 1966 to 1970; however, the now famous 1971 *Griggs* v. *Duke Power Co.*[3] case changed all that. In this case the United States Supreme Court said, "The administrative interpretation of the Act by the enforcing authority is entitled to great deference." A more recent case (*Albemarle Paper Co.* v. *Moody*)[4] seems to have affirmed that the *1970 EEOC Guidelines on Employee Selection Program* is "entitled to great deference" as the procedures to be used in selection design.

The *Griggs* case also established that any selection standard found to have an "adverse impact" (defined below) on protected groups must be shown to be demonstrably job related. As people interested in the field of personnel administration, we recognize that selection procedures should be job related. There is, however, controversy over the meaning of the term and how it can be demonstrated. Many feel that the *EEOC Guidelines* are so strict that compliance is impossible. Even the chief psychologist for the EEOC was forced to admit that he had never seen a study that would meet the literal requirements of the *Guidelines*. In fact, the American Psychological Association has replaced its 1966 *Standards* with a comprehensive new 1974 publication (which has not yet been accepted by the EEOC). The older APA *Standards*, meant to be professional ideals, were often misinterpreted and misused as legalistic documents and therefore were radically changed. In the new *Standards* it is stated that "... validity is itself inferred, not measured,"[5] a considerable departure from the strictness implied in the earlier document.

Because employers were receiving conflicting signals from various federal agencies, President Nixon in 1973 established the Equal Employment Opportunity Coordinating Council.[6] The EEOCC, not to be confused with the EEOC, was charged with developing a "uniform set of federal guidelines" on which all federal agencies would agree.

Numerous drafts of the *Uniform Guidelines* have been released. The June 1975 draft was "less favorably" received than any which preceded it. There are two principal snags: (1) general intransigence on the part of some who oppose "uniform" *Guidelines*; and (2) the EEOC continues to be successful in court and perhaps is not eager for change. Many argue that the beginning of government intervention into employee selection began much earlier than the original EEOC *Guidelines*. The case of *Myart* v. *Motorola*[7] in 1963 certainly caught personnel psychologists and businesspersons flatfooted. Many businesses were shocked to learn that employment testing, a generally accepted management prerogative, was being challenged on the grounds of racial discrimination. Several psychologists involved in this case lined up on opposite sides of the issues. Test publishers were fearful that their sales would slacken or even begin to decline.

During the late 1950s and the early 1960s employment testing had achieved a fashionable stature and many were adopting this latest fad in selection techniques. Unfortunately, employment tests were sold or recommended to many employers who had not a single person trained in psychological measurement or test use. Even worse, some sellers of tests rarely followed up to determine the utility of tests in selecting a workforce. Concern for equal-employment-opportunity issues in the application of personnel selection procedures was virtually nonexistent at that time. The forces of the civil rights movement were also becoming evident and, after the Civil Rights Act of 1964, few employers, unions, or employment agencies were prepared to cope with the idea that tests had a discriminatory effect on minorities. In fact, there was typically no evidence of their validity in determining job success. Perhaps even more discomforting was the development of evidence that different racial groups performed equally well on a job even though they performed poorly on a test presumed to predict performance on the job in question. This set of complex environmental situations set the stage for the bulk of the EEO legislation; its major laws are reviewed below.

Major Equal Employment Opportunity (EEO) Legislation and Executive Orders. Four major federal laws are now available for seeking redress for discrimina-

[3] *Griggs* v. *Duke Power Co.*, 401 U.S. 424 (1971).
[4] *Albemarle Paper Co.* v. *Moody*, 95 S. Ct. 2362, 2379 (1975).
[5] *Standards for Educational and Psychological Tests and Manuals* (Washington D.C.: American Psychological Association, 1974).
[6] The Council consists of the U.S. Civil Service Commission, the EEOC, the OFCC, the U.S. Justice Department, the U.S. Department of Labor, and the U.S. Civil Rights Commission.
[7] See H. C. Lockwood, "Testing Minority Applicants for Employment," *Personnel Journal* 44 (1965): 356–360+ and W. L. French, *The Personnel Management Process*, 3d ed. (Boston: Houghton Mifflin, 1974), p. 287.

tion in employment: The Civil Rights Act of 1866; Title VII of the Civil Rights Act of 1964, as amended in 1972; the Age Discrimination in Employment Act of 1967; and the Equal Pay Act of 1963. The Civil Rights Act of 1866 was seen as parallel to the 1964 act. Basically, the 1866 act states that "All persons shall have the same right in every state and territory... as is enjoyed by White citizens...." It has purview over private as well as public acts of discrimination by race. Title VII of the 1964 law generally forbids employment discrimination on the basis of race, color, religion, sex, and national origin, as stated above. The Age Discrimination in Employment Act bans discrimination in employment on the basis of age against persons who are 40–65 years of age. The Equal Pay Act requires that individuals must receive equal pay, regardless of sex, if they perform equal work.

Executive Orders 11246 and 11141 (issued by the executive branch of the government) prohibit employment discrimination by contractors and subcontractors doing business with the federal government. Executive Order 11246 prohibits employment discrimination on the basis of race, color, religion, sex, and national origin. Executive Order 11141 forbids discrimination on the basis of age. The Executive Orders form the terms under which the federal government will award a contract or subcontract. Contractors who want to deal with the government accept the terms voluntarily; if they do not wish to accept the terms, they need not bid on a government contract. Executive Order 11478 prohibits discrimination against federal employees on the basis of race, color, religion, sex, or national origin. Executive Order 11345 specifically prohibits sex as a basis of discrimination. The Executive Orders operate in addition to, not instead of, the federal laws on employment discrimination.

The 1964 Civil Rights Act created the Equal Employment Opportunity Commission (EEOC) to enforce the provisions of its Title VII. The 1972 amendments to Title VII strengthened the authority of the EEOC to eliminate discrimination in employment as discussed above. In addition, the 1964 Civil Rights Act provides that the U.S. Attorney General may intervene to enforce Title VII by bringing civil suit in a federal court. In fact, an attorney who wins a case for the complainant may even receive the legal fees for the government if the complainant cannot pay.

Title VII contains several exceptions. The law does not apply to private membership clubs exempt from taxation. It does not protect members of the Communist Party of the United States or members of communist-action or communist-front groups required to register by the Subversive Activities Control Board. It does not prohibit businesses located on or near Indian reservations from giving employment preference to Indians living on or near the reservations. It does not affect federal or state laws creating special employment rights or preferences for United States veterans. The law does not apply to workers outside the United States. Aliens, like anyone else, are protected from race, sex, religious, and national-origin discrimination. National-origin bias (not hiring a person because of his or her nationality) and alienage bias (not hiring for lack of United States citizenship) are different concepts. The law also does not prohibit employment discrimination if the discriminatory action is in the interest of national security.

Title VII allows exceptions from its bans on discrimination on the basis of religion, sex, or national origin (though not on the basis of race or color) if religion, sex, or national origin is a bona fide occupational qualification (BFOQ). The BFOQ exception is interpreted narrowly by the EEOC. In order to qualify as a BFOQ exception, a particular religion, sex, or national origin must be a requirement for occupation of a job and the requirement must be necessary to the normal operation of a business (e.g., an actress's job can be given to females over males).

The 1972 amendments to Title VII eliminated the exception for educational institutions which was available under the original 1964 Civil Rights Act. Educational institutions, both public and private, are now subject to the Title VII bans on employment discrimination as to the employment of persons to perform work connected with the institutions' educational facilities. However, an exception is still made in the case of educational institutions maintained by a religious corporation or society. This exception applies only to the ban on religious discrimination (not to bans on discrimination on the basis of race, color, sex, or national origin). Before the 1972 amendments, the exception was restricted to the employment of persons working at religious activities. The amendments broadened the exception to cover all secular, as well as religious, activities of the corporation or society.

Title VII of the Civil Rights Act of 1964 and the Equal Employment Opportunity Act of 1972 thus cover the following types or organizations:

- All private employers of fifteen or more persons

- All educational institutions, both public and private

- State and local governments

- Public and private employment agencies

- Labor unions with fifteen or more members

- Joint labor-management committees for apprenticeship and training.

The Age Discrimination in Employment Act of 1967 also allows exceptions from its provisions if the exceptions are based on BFOQs. In order to qualify as a BFOQ exception, a particular age limitation must be required for a job and the requirement must be necessary to the normal operation of a business. The act also provides that the secretary of labor, acting in the public interest, may make specific exceptions from the provisions of the act. Retirement, pension, or insurance plans and seniority systems may qualify for exception under the act if they are established in good faith with no intent to evade the law. Such plans will not excuse the failure to hire any worker because of age.

The Equal Pay Act also contains many exceptions. However, these exceptions hold up only when the Equal Pay Act is the basis used for attacking an employment practice. Equal Pay Act exceptions will not necessarily ward off an attack under Title VII. When both Title VII and the Equal Pay Act apply to an employment situation, Title VII provides that its provisions will be harmonized with the Equal Pay Act to avoid conflicting interpretations of the law. However, Title VII also applies in cases of sex discrimination not covered by the Equal Pay Act.

In addition to the federal laws described above, state and other federal laws may be used as a basis for attacking employment practices. Minorities may bring suit against employers under:

1. the Fourteenth Amendment to the United States Constitution, which forbids the denial of equal protection of the laws;
2. the Civil Rights Act of 1870, which proscribes racial discrimination under the color of state law;
3. the Civil Rights Act of 1871, which addresses the right of persons deprived of rights to sue for redress.

In addition, the states have passed laws dealing with employment discrimination. Title VII invalidates state laws that are inconsistent with any of the purposes or provisions of the federal law. However, Title VII will not provide relief from a duty or liability imposed by state law if the state law does not tolerate what would be unlawful under Title VII. Neither will Title VII invalidate a state law provision which is not inconsistent with the federal law, even though employers are thereby subject to more than one set of laws. The provisions of the Equal Pay law do not excuse noncompliance with any state law establishing higher equal-pay standards than those provided by the federal law. Correspondingly, compliance with a state law will not excuse noncompliance with the Equal Pay Act.

Federal Agencies: Their Enforcement Responsibilities and Powers. The federal agencies involved with Equal Employment Opportunity and their functions are summarized in Table 1. The table includes the legislation or executive order which grants each agency its enforcement power.

The EEOC was established to receive and, on its own initiative, to investigate job-discrimination complaints. Where the Commission finds the charge to be justified, against individuals or against groups, it attempts through conciliation to reach an agreement. Should it fail in its efforts, however, the Commission has the power to go directly into federal court to enforce the law. In addition, interested organizations may also file suits on behalf of individuals or groups who feel that they have been discriminated against by their employers and, in this connection, can claim back pay, damages, and legal fees. Furthermore, an aggrieved individual can also go to court directly to sue an employer for alleged discriminatory practices. The EEOC issues appropriate periodic guidelines to assist companies in making sure that their employment systems are in compliance with the law.

Enforcement powers under the Age Discrimination Act, the Equal Pay Act, and Executive Order 11246 are vested in the Department of Labor. The Wage and Hour Division of the Labor Department is charged with administration of the Equal Pay Act. The secretary of labor is charged with administration and enforcement of the Age Act and Executive Order 11246. Under orders from the secretary, the authority and responsibility for administration and enforcement of the Age Act belong to the Wage and Hour Administrator. The Office of Federal Contract Compliance (OFCC) was created to administer and enforce Executive Order 11246. The director of the OFCC has the authority to carry out the Executive Order and the responsibility for coordinating matters relating to Title VII with the EEOC and the Department of Justice.

Executive Orders 11141 and 11478 direct the heads of government departments and agencies to take appropriate action to publicize the government policy against age discrimination. Acting upon the directive, the General Services Administration (GSA) has issued regulations to implement Executive Order

Table 1. A Review of Employment Discrimination Legislation and Federal Agencies with Enforcement Authority

Federal agency responsible for enforcement	Laws/orders granting authority to the agency	Agency's scope of authority
Equal Employment Opportunity Commission (EEOC)	1964 Civil Rights Act (78 Stat 241), as amended by 1972 EEO Act (86 Stat 103)	Can bring suits against private employers and labor unions with more than 15 employees. Suits must be preceded by efforts at conciliation and must originate in individual complaints—although they may be expanded to pattern and practice suits. All Justice Department authority to bring EEO suits goes to EEOC.
Justice Department, Civil Rights Division	1964 Civil Rights Act, as amended by 1972 EEO Act	Can bring suit where there exists a *prima facie* case of a private employer or labor union with more than 15 employees engaging in a pattern or practice of discrimination. May complete individual complaint suits begun before 1972 Act. Can bring individual as well as pattern and practice suits against agencies of state and local government. (After March 1974, all of this authority was transferred to EEOC.)
Civil Service Commission	1972 EEO Act, ExecOrder 11478 1970 Intergovernmental Personnel Act (84 Stat 1909)	Reviews and approves EEO policies of all federal agencies. Consults with state and local governments to establish and improve merit hiring systems and conducts compliance reviews.
Labor Department, Office of Federal Contract Compliance (OFCC)	ExecOrder 11246, as amended (ExecOrder 11375): Labor Department Revised Order No. 4	Requires all federal contractors with more than $50,000 in contracts to take affirmative action to bring about EEO.
All other federal agencies	ExecOrders 11246 and 11375; Labor Department Revised Order No. 4	Authority delegated by OFCC to review contract compliance. Each agency also is responsible for internal EEO, consistent with Civil Service guidelines.
Equal Employment Opportunity Coordinating Council	1972 EEO Act	Members include representatives from EEOC, Justice, Civil Service, Labor, and the Civil Rights Commission. Responsibility is to coordinate EEO policy for the first four of these agencies.

11141. The GSA will enforce compliance with Executive Order 11141. The Civil Service Commission is charged by the president with the responsibility of providing leadership and guidance in fulfilling the terms of Executive Order 11478. The 1972 amendments to Title VII also give the EEOC the authority to investigate alleged violations of the nondiscrimination provisions of Title VII as they apply to federal employees.

To help employers, labor unions, employment agencies, and joint labor-management committees to obey the law and the Executive Orders on employment discrimination, the various enforcement agencies have issued rules, regulations, and guidelines. The EEOC has issued guidelines on sex discrimination, religious discrimination, national-origin discrimination, and, of course, on testing and selecting employees. The EEOC has also issued a release on prehire inquiries and has issued regulations on reporting and

recordkeeping. The Wage and Hour Division of the Department of Labor has issued regulations on recordkeeping and interpretative bulletins on equal pay for equal work and on age discrimination. The secretary of labor has issued regulations on equal employment opportunity in apprenticeship and training and on the ratio of apprentices to journeymen on federal construction work. The OFCC has issued regulations on the duties of contractors under Executive Order 11246, on affirmative-action programs by government contractors, and on testing and selecting of employees by government contractors. It has also issued sex-discrimination guidelines. The GSA has issued regulations on equal employment opportunity in several areas, including nondefense procurement contracts and nondiscrimination because of age on such contracts. The Civil Service Commission has issued regulations on equal federal employment opportunity (see *For Further Reading*).

Executive Orders Number 11246 and 11375 (and Office of Federal Contract Compliance Revised Orders Number 4 and 14) affect all organizations that hold federal contracts. Adherence to these Executive Orders is administered by the Office of Federal Contract Compliance of the United States Department of Labor. These orders apply specifically to contractors and subcontractors with federal contracts in excess of $50,000, or who employ fifty or more people. The orders, once again, prohibit discrimination in employment, but in addition, *also* require that each organization develop and implement affirmative-action programs (discussed in detail below), regularly audited by an assigned federal compliance agency, to remedy the effects of past discriminatory practices.

Specifically, under these presidential orders, a government contractor is required to furnish a results-oriented written commitment for an affirmative-action program together with specific goals and timetables for their attainment. Most significantly, an organization found not to be in compliance with Revised Order Number 4 (which calls for concrete affirmative-action programs) faces the possibility of cancellation of its government contracts.

Avoiding Job Discrimination and Complying with the Laws. Due to the complexity, ambiguity, and number of laws, guidelines, and Executive Orders regarding discrimination, compliance is not always a simple matter. Further, laws continue to be changed and interpreted by court decisions, often making earlier decisions and practices irrelevant. Obviously, the best way to comply to EEO laws would be to develop a rational, systematic set of personnel programs that are job- and performance-based. Translated into actual personnel practice, however, such a system would vary widely across organizations. It would also require considerable and diverse knowledge, skills, and abilities, as previous exercises in this book have pointed out. Many organizations, often due to their small size or their lack of awareness of the laws, simply do not have the expertise to comply in *every* technical sense at this time. However, a considerable amount can be done to help assure compliance; this actually constitutes nothing more than sound personnel practice.

The EEOC specifically advocates the following types of procedures to help avoid discrimination.

1. A total personnel assessment system that is non-discriminatory within the spirit of the law and places special emphasis on the following:
   a) Careful job analysis to define skill requirements.
   b) Special efforts in recruiting minorities.
   c) Screening and interviewing related to job requirements.
   d) Tests selected on the basis of specific job-related criteria.
   e) Comparison of test performance versus job performance.
   f) Retesting.
   g) Tests which are validated for minorities.

2. Objective administration of tests: It is essential that tests be administered by personnel who are skilled not only in technical details, but also in establishing proper conditions for test taking. Members of disadvantaged groups tend to be particularly sensitive in test situations and those giving tests should be aware of this and be able to alleviate a certain amount of anxiety.[8]

What Is "Adverse Impact"? Rather than trying to determine if an employer's practices were designed or intended to be discriminatory, the courts have looked first at the apparent results of discrimination and, secondly, at the procedures and practices that led to these apparent results. The result of apparent discrimination is generally referred to as "adverse impact" and it can be established in several ways. Adverse impact would be concluded, for example, when there are disproportionate representations of minority and nonminority or sex groups among present employees in different types of jobs. Adverse impact would also be concluded upon finding differential rates of selection or corresponding rejection rates for the various minority and nonminority or sex groups applying for different jobs. The selection rate is defined as the number hired compared to the number of applicants for any protected group.

Differences exist between the Office of Federal Contract Compliance's *Testing and Selection Order* published in 1971 and 1974 and the *EEOC Guidelines*. According to the Office of Federal Contract Compliance, if the selection rate of applicants from a covered or protected group is less than four-fifths

---

[8] As previously noted, the Commission will not recommend any particular test, but adopts the 1966 *Standards for Educational and Psychological Tests and Manuals* (Washington, D.C.: American Psychological Association, 1966), prepared by a joint committee of the American Psychological Association, American Educational Research Association, and National Council on Measurement in Education. The revised (1974) edition of this publication, endorsed by the panel of psychologists consulted by the Commission, was prepared by recognized spokesmen for the profession and establishes standards and technical merits of evaluation procedures. However, as stated above, it has not yet been accepted by the EEOC at this writing.

the rate for the remaining applicants, adverse impact is concluded. For instance, if 90 percent of male applicants are selected and 30 percent of female applicants (a protected group) are selected, adverse impact would be concluded because 30 percent is less than four-fifths of 90 percent. However, if 85 percent of the male applicants are selected and 75 percent of the female applicants are selected, adverse impact would not be concluded. Seventy-five percent is more than four-fifths of 85 percent.

The EEOC test is for statistically significant differences in selection rates; for large numbers of applicants, it can be more sensitive than the OFCC four-fifths rule of thumb. There are statistical tools available for assessing the statistical significance of differences in proportions of percentages.[9] Employers would be well advised to perform these statistical analyses to see if, in fact, the tests (and "nontest" standards such as interviews) being used are disqualifying a statistically significant greater percentage of minorities. If not, the government guidelines do not require submission of evidence of validity.

The legal conclusion of unfair discrimination is based on two conditions being established, one by the charging party and one by the respondent in Title VII cases. If a charging party can establish that an employer's hiring, transfer, promotion, membership, training, referral, or retention practices result in adverse impact on an individual or a class protected by Title VII, the court then places the burden of proof on the respondent employer for evidence that the selection procedure having adverse impact is job-related or is predictive of performance on the job. This is, of course, the demonstration of evidence for validity. A validation study of job-relatedness of any selection procedure found to have adverse impact is the first rebuttal by a Title VII respondent employer to a charge of discrimination. If a respondent cannot convince the court that the selection procedure resulting in adverse impact is job related, then the court may conclude that unfair discrimination has been established. If, on the other hand, the respondent can convince the court that a selection procedure resulting in adverse impact is job related, the fact that adverse impact is found becomes moot, provided the employer can demonstrate that selection procedures having a lesser adverse impact are unavailable for use. One of the ways an employer can demonstrate that such alternative procedures (e.g., different types of tests) having lesser adverse impact are unavailable is to show that when a choice was made between several alternative procedures, all

having validity, the final choice was based on that procedure having the least adverse impact on protected or covered groups. The legal conclusion of disallowed or illegal discrimination thus is based on a showing of adverse impact by a charging party and lack of unacceptable evidence of job relatedness on the part of the respondent employer. Table 2 presents some examples of lawful and unlawful inquiries made in selection. As you can see, many "standard" inquiries *can* be unlawful.

In defining the scope of practices covered by the *EEOC Guidelines*, "the term 'test' is defined as any pencil and paper or performance measure used as a basis for any promotion decision." Also included in the definition of tests are "formal scored quantified or standardized techniques of assessing job suitability including specific qualifying or disqualifying personal history or background requirements, specific educational or work history requirements and scored interviews." Unscored interviews are also covered by the *EEOC Guidelines* if the interview is part of an employer's selection procedure that results in adverse impact on a class of applicants covered by Title VII. Thus, the chance of violating the law can come from any number of practices, such as performance appraisals or interviews, in addition to pencil-and-paper tests themselves. As stressed throughout these exercises, each personnel activity must therefore be designed properly and be job related.

Establishing valid selection practices, as discussed in detail in Exercise 10, is a difficult and often time-consuming activity. It is, however, a necessary one and can be facilitated by the other personnel programs. The two types of criterion-related validity, predictive and concurrent validities (see Exercise 10), would be the type of evidence accepted from an employer by a court if discriminatory practices were charged. In conducting such validation studies, several important guidelines must be followed, such as the use of a large enough sample size and the proper administration of any tests.[10]

Five primary considerations in conducting a criterion-related validation are noted in the *EEOC Guidelines*.

1. The sample of subjects must be representative of the normal or typical candidate group for the job or jobs in question in the local labor market.

2. Tests must be administered and scored under controlled and standardized conditions, with proper safeguards to protect the security of test

[9] See any introductory statistics text and/or relevant references listed in *For Further Reading*, Exercise 10.

[10] See American Psychological Association *Standards, op. cit.* and/or relevant references in *For Further Reading*.

Table 2. General Guidelines to Lawful and Unlawful Employment Practices*

Types of inquiries of job applicants typically made by employers in selection	Lawful practice(s) related to inquiry	Possibly unlawful practice(s) related to inquiry
1. Name	Inquiry as to full name.	Inquiry into any title which indicates race, color, religion, sex, national origin, or ancestry.
2. Address	Inquiry into place and length of current and previous addresses.	Specific inquiry into foreign addresses that would indicate national origin.
3. Sex		Any inquiry that would indicate sex.
4. Religion-creed		a) Any inquiry to indicate or identify denomination or customs. b) May not be told this is a Protestant, Catholic, or Jewish organization. c) Request of a recommendation or reference from someone in clergy.
5. Birthplace or national origin		a) Any inquiry into place of birth. b) Any inquiry into place of birth of parents, grandparents, or spouse. c) Any other inquiry into national origin.
6. Race or color		Any inquiry which would indicate race or color.
7. Citizenship	a) Whether or not a U.S. citizen. b) If not, whether intends to become one. c) If U.S. residence is legal. d) If spouse is citizen. e) Require proof of citizenship after being hired.	a) If native-born or naturalized. b) Proof of citizenship before hiring. c) Whether parents or spouse are native-born or naturalized.
8. Age	a) Request proof of age in form of work permit issued by school authorities. b) Require proof of age by birth certificate after hiring.	Require birth certificate or baptismal record before hiring.
9. Photographs	May be required *after* hiring for identification purposes.	Require photograph *before* hiring.
10. Education	a) Inquiry into what academic, professional, or vocational schools attended. b) Inquiry into language skills, such as reading and writing of foreign languages.	a) Any inquiry asking specifically the nationality, racial, or religious affiliation of a school. b) Inquiry as to what is mother tongue or how foreign-language ability was acquired, unless necessary for job.
11. Relatives	Inquiry into name, relationship, and address of person to be notified in case of emergency.	Any inquiry about a relative which is unlawful (e.g., race or religion inquiries).
12. Organization	a) Inquiry into organization memberships, excluding any organization the name or character of which indicates the race, color, religion, sex, national origin, or ancestry of its members. b) What offices are held, if any.	Inquiry into all clubs and organizations where membership is held.
13. Military service	a) Inquiry into service in U.S. Armed Forces. b) Rank attained. c) Which branch of service. d) Require military discharge certificate after being hired.	a) Inquiry into military service in armed service of any country but United States. b) Request military service records.

Types of inquiries of job applicants typically made by employers in selection	Lawful practice(s) related to inquiry	Possibly unlawful practice(s) related to inquiry
14. Work schedule	Inquiry into willingness to work required work schedule.	Any inquiry into willingness to work any particular religious holiday.
15. Other qualifications	Any question that has a direct reflection (i.e., can be shown to be job related) on the job to be applied for.	Any non–job-related inquiry that may present information permitting unlawful discrimination.
16. References	General personal and work references not relating to race, color, religion, sex, national origin, or ancestry.	Request references specifically from clergymen or any other persons who might reflect race, color, religion, sex, national origin, or ancestry of applicant.

* This table was developed after the general guidelines used by a state government. Exceptions include Bona Fide Occupational Qualifications (BFOQs).

scores and to insure the scores do not enter into any judgments of employee adequacy that are to be used as criterion measures.

3. The work behaviors or other criteria of employee adequacy which the test is intended to predict or identify must be fully described. Such criteria may include measures other than actual work proficiency—such as training time, supervisory ratings, regularity of attendance, and tenure. Whatever criteria are used, they must represent major or critical work behaviors as revealed by careful job analysis. With respect to using standards for higher jobs than the one the person is being selected for, if job progression structures and seniority provisions are so established that new employees will probably, within a reasonable period of time and in a great majority of cases, progress to a higher level, it may be considered that candidates are being evaluated for jobs at that higher level. However, where job progression is not so nearly automatic or the time spent is such that higher-level jobs or employees' potential may be expected to change in significant ways, it shall be considered that candidates are being evaluated for a job at or near the entry level.

4. Supervisory rating techniques should be carefully developed and the ratings should be closely examined for evidence of bias.

5. Differential validity data must be generated and results separately reported for minority and non-minority groups whenever technically feasible.

Evidence of content or construct validity as defined in the *APA Standards* may be utilized where criterion-related validity is not feasible. However, evidence for content or construct validity should be accompanied by sufficient information from a job analysis to demonstrate the relevance of the content in the case of job knowledge or proficiency, or the relevancy of the construct in the case of measures of personality traits or characteristics.[11] According to the *1970 EEOC Guidelines*, "Evidence of content validity alone may be acceptable for well developed tests that consist of suitable samples of the essential knowledge, skills, or behaviors composing the job in question. It must be cautioned that the types of knowledge, skills or behaviors contemplated here do not include those which can be acquired in a brief orientation to the job."

A final note on discriminatory practices: if an organization's selection procedures show no "adverse impact" (i.e., this organization is not discriminatory), there is no legal requirement that they validate selection procedures. Also, the recent case rulings clearly indicate that any procedure an organization uses to select a white male is acceptable.

Affirmative Action. Federal equal-employment-opportunity laws now require noncomplying employers, government contractors, and parties administering apprenticeship programs not only to refrain from deliberate acts of discrimination, but also to take positive steps to assure that current practices are nondiscriminatory and that any continuing effects of past discrimination be erased. Affirmative action, as called for by Executive Orders No. 11246 and 11375, is the method by which the employer, contractor, or

[11] For a discussion of the different types of validity, see Exercises 10 and 18, *For Further Reading*; and C. E. Schneier, "Content Validity: The Necessity of a Behavioral Job Description," *The Personnel Administrator* 21, no. 2 (1976): 38–44.

party administering an apprenticeship program insures that those positive steps have been, are being,
or will be taken to achieve equal employment
opportunity.

Affirmative action was ambiguously defined in
Presidential Executive Order No. 11246 and 11375
in that it "required companies contracting with the
federal government to take affirmative action to
recruit and promote minorities and females," but
the order did not spell out what affirmative action
meant or what obligations such contractors would
have. Revised Order No. 4, issued under President
Nixon, defined contractors' obligations and established how an affirmative-action program should be
developed. Affirmative-action programs are now
being used by the EEOC as a remedy where a complaint has been filed and a pattern or practice of
discrimination has taken place.

Many companies have had an explicit or im-
plicit nondiscrimination policy; so, an affirmative-
action program can be viewed as not a new policy,
but rather as a continuation of an existing one with a
new and stronger emphasis. A company has four
avenues open in developing a nondiscriminatory
policy. The first is *passive nondiscrimination*, or a
willingness in all decisions regarding hiring, promotion, and pay to treat the sexes and races alike.
Second, *pure affirmative action* involves a concerted
effort to expand the pool of applicants, so no one is
excluded because of past or present discrimination.
Third is *affirmative action with preferential hiring*,
which means the company has a large labor pool
and systematically favors women and minority-group
members.[12] The final alternative, *hard quotas*, implies
that a specific number or proportion of minority-
group members must be hired. Quotas, unless imposed by a court, have been found to be illegal.[13]

The government's objective in establishing affirmative action is based on the second alternative, but
the real issue involved probably concerns the affirmative-action programs stated in the third alternative.
In other words, perhaps the best way to ensure that
everything possible is being done to eliminate discrimination is to develop and vigorously implement
an affirmative-action plan (in addition to a job-
related personnel system for all employees). Such a
plan can be a valuable management tool, as well as
a means to comply with the law. Even the process of
developing a plan can be an extraordinarily useful
diagnostic management activity. Such diagnoses include the following: a review to determine if the
organization is employing blacks, Spanish-speaking
Americans, American Indians, women, and members
of other minority groups in quantities that make
sense in terms of the availability of these groups in
the labor supply; an examination to discover if
minority-group members and women are clustered
in lower-level jobs with little opportunity to advance
to better paying positions; and a close scrutiny of
policies, procedures, and practices that may tend to
favor one group over another. All of these analyses
can be helpful to management in improving the organization's ability to get the best qualified people to
serve its clients or customers.

Goals, Timetables, and Quotas. Once the affirmative-
action plan is developed, it can serve as the basic
management guide to action, providing it has enough
specificity to be meaningful. Managers and supervisors at all levels can use it to guide their actions and
measure their progress. The plan should provide for
the establishment of reasonable employment goals for
certain groups (i.e., to increase minority employment
by actively seeking minority members and perhaps
changing recruiting practices), as distinguished from
mandatory *quotas* (i.e., to have 14 percent black managers within one year). It can call for deadlines by
which certain programs (such as special recruiting
programs or training programs) can be initiated or
completed. These goals and timetables are appropriate for problem areas, for they will encourage progress. Areas for affirmative action might be those
organizations, localities, occupations, and grade levels
where minority and female employment does not come
up to reasonable expectations in view of the supply
of qualified minority-group members or women in
the recruiting areas and the availability of job
opportunities.

In large organizations, numerical goals (to be
distinguished from hard quotas) should be developed

---

[12] During the Summer of 1976 federal courts found that certain types of preferential treatment in promotion or selection
given to females over equally qualified males, even if done
under policies of an affirmative-action program, may be illegal.
Thus, "reverse discrimination" has been held to be illegal.
However, these decisions will no doubt be appealed by the
organizations involved and a Supreme Court ruling may be
necessary. The potential illegality of reverse discrimination
leaves organizations in an ambiguous position regarding EEO and stresses the tentative nature of EEO guidelines
and laws and their continually emerging status. The necessity
of both a completely job-related total personnel system, as well
as requiring personnel professionals to keep abreast of latest
developments in EEO, cannot be overstated.
[13] This was determined in a March 23, 1973 agreement among
the Department of Justice, United States Civil Service Commission, Equal Employment Opportunity Commission, and
the Office of Federal Contract Compliances.

at the divisional, departmental, and organizational level—rather than on a broader level—in order to take into account special circumstances. In this way, detailed statistics on minority groups and women will aid in identifying areas where additional affirmative action is required and can be translated into specific action plans for the level or component concerned. To be valid, goals and timetables must be closely aligned with estimated turnover data and anticipated hiring, as well as estimated changes in the total number of positions by job classification for the period covered by the timetable.

Goals can be qualitative as well as quantitative. For example, an organization that has lost a substantial proportion of minority employees through turnover or layoff due to union seniority provisions may find that its climate for employment of minorities is poor. In such a case, new goals might include attempts to improve the attitude of other employees and supervisors toward acceptance of a minority group; to provide more effective orientation and motivation of new employees; to evaluate and improve training operations; or to strengthen grievance and discrimination appeal processes. An affirmative-action plan should establish specific steps leading toward achievement of these goals.

As with other management programs, an affirmative-action program needs periodic evaluation. Evaluation of operations may result in the conclusion that a greater number of minority-group employees should be employed throughout the organization or one of its components. In other situations, the component may have acceptable program results overall, but improvements may be needed in certain locations, divisions, grades, or occupations. Evaluations should lead to new updated goals and target progress dates based on the needs of the program.

Affirmative Action: Illustrative Court Cases. Some important recent EEO cases include the Supreme Court Decision in *Albemarle Paper Co.* v. *Moody*.[14] that back pay can be awarded in an employment testing case, even though no bad faith is established on the part of the employer. Albemarle had failed to meet EEOC's standards for adequate empirical validations which reaffixed the use of the *EEOC Guidelines* (although a reading of the opinions would seem to indicate that the Court is less than totally enamored with the *EEOC Guidelines*).

A second case is that of *Douglas* v. *Hampton*,[15] which involves the U.S. Civil Service Commission. The issue was whether employers must show that *predictive* validation studies (see Exercise 10) are infeasible before they can defend the validity of the test on other grounds. At least for the moment, the existing *EEOC Guidelines* have received another nod from the courts. Further, the EEOC, despite several attempts to revise the *Guidelines*, appears tied to the ones issued in 1970.

Finally, a less well-known case with enormous implications is that of *Brito* v. *Zia*,[16] which was decided two years ago in the Tenth Circuit Court of Appeals. In this case, the court held that the Zia Company's employee performance evaluations, used for lay-off, were, in fact, *tests* under the meaning of *EEOC Guidelines* and were thus subject to emprirical validation as required by EEOC. This decision, of course, brings performance-appraisal practices under the impact of EEO laws as discussed in Exercise 4.

Soon, decisions from the United States Supreme Court on two equal-employment-opportunity cases of major importance to personnel administrators may be forthcoming. One case involves the EEOC's requirement that pregnancy-related disabilities be treated like other sickness and accident disabilities under disability income insurance plans.[17] The other case involves both the use of aptitude testing in employment as a tool for making decisions purely on merit, and the extent, if any, to which training success can be a criterion of test "job relatedness."[18]

Thus, EEO laws are having an increasingly large impact on personnel programs. These programs not only include selection, but also training, wage and salary administration, and performance appraisal, to name a few. The modern personnel administrator and his or her staff must be knowledgeable both in the laws themselves and in the design and implementation of programs to facilitate compliance.

PROCEDURE

Overview. First, you become familiar with EEO issues through a self-quiz and a method of determining "adverse impact." You will then be given completed

---

[14] *Albemarle Paper Co.*, v. *Moody*, 95 S. Ct. 2362, 2379 (1975).

[15] *Douglas* v. *Hampton*, D.C. Circuit Court of Appeals, 512 F. 2d. 976, 1975.
[16] *Brito* v. *Zia Company*, 478 F. 2d 1200 (1973).
[17] *General Electric Co.* v. *Gilbert*, Docket No. 74–1589. This same issue is also presented in *Liberty Mutual Insurance Co.* v. *Wetzel*, Docket No. 74–1245. The Court will decide the two cases together.
[18] *Washington* v. *Davis*, Docket No. 74–1492.

information on an organization's affirmative-action program. You are to evaluate the program and present your evaluation to the organization's managing committee. Finally, you construct affirmative-action programs in increasing levels of sophistication. In one, an in-basket will be used to establish an organization's climate for affirmative-action programs.

PART A

STEP 1: Form 1 provides a series of questions about EEO and affirmative action. You are to place a check in the column you believe is appropriate. Discuss your answers in a small group and then listen to the correct answers given by your implementor.

STEP 2: Form 2 asks you to record your height, sex, and race and determine if "adverse impact" has been witnessed for persons who are members of protected groups under current Office of Federal Contract Compliance (OFCC) guidelines. Assume that the minimum height requirement set by an organization to obtain the job in consideration is five feet, five inches. Fill out the bottom of Form 2, tear it off, and give it to your implementor. He or she will make selections for the job by race and sex and provide you with the results. Use these results to calculate the "qualifying rates" by both sex and race by filling in the blanks on the top of Form 2. Was "adverse impact" observed? If so, what must now be done, given that the first of two steps in demonstrating that job discrimination exists has been completed? (Refer to *Introduction*.)

TIME: About 35 minutes.

PART B

STEP 3: Littleco is an assembly plant in a Southern metropolitan area. Small groups, each representing the personnel department, are to assess the company's affirmative-action proposal (Form 3) and make an oral report to the managing committee of this small organization. Six persons will be chosen to serve as the managing committee and will ask questions of the assessor group(s). Your group may also wish to use Form 4 to assess the current job levels of the minority and women employees of Littleco in your discussion with the committee. In fact, you may wish to show how the affirmative-action program should be advanced by including recommended changes in your job levels in the analysis.

Whether or not your group was chosen to present its evaluation to Littleco's Managing Committee, outline your assessment briefly in writing.

TIME: About 50 minutes for analysis and 15–20 minutes for presentation.

PART C

STEP 4: In this part of the exercise you are to critique and evaluate a city's employee profile. First, read the background information given about the city in Form 5. Small groups are to review the employee profile of the city's workers for Supercity (Form 6) and critique it, much as was done in Step 3 above. Based on your review of the organization's original documents, you are to present your plans to the class and be prepared to defend them.

STEP 5: Based on any discrimination found for women or a minority group, the organization (which receives considerable federal funding) would be asked by the OFCC to develop an affirmative-action program with appropriate goals and timetables. Develop such a program, using Form 7. Again, you are to develop a plan that you believe will gain the acceptance of the OFCC compliance panel. For ease of computation, assume that only the office and clerical minority employees are women. If you assume any growth rates which affect your projections on Form 7, indicate such a rate(s) on the bottom of the form or on a separate sheet. You may want to supplement your calculations on Form 7 with some explanations and statements of your assumptions, which can be put on a separate sheet.

TIME: About two hours.

PART D

STEP 6: This part of the exercise consists of an in-basket and an affirmative-action-forecast activity.

Form into small groups of six persons. One of the group's members will play the role of Al Smiley, the newly hired personnel administrator of the Perfect Tool Corporation. Al Smiley, as well as everyone else in the group, should read the sketch of the Perfect Tool Company given in Form 8. Also reread or review Form 5, which contains information about Supercity, as Perfect Tool is located in Supercity. Al Smiley will then complete the in-basket exercise (Form 9). The following information will be helpful for Al Smiley, as well as the other group members:

Al Smiley was hired as the Perfect Tool Corporation personnel administrator only a few days ago. He has had several years of previous experience in personnel in local organizations and his last job was assistant director of personnel of a manufacturing organization employing about 225 people.

The first few days on the job were spent with introductions and meetings. Smiley still has only a sketchy picture of the organization. He does know, however, that this company moves very fast and there are several changes regarding people, programs, and policy that he will be expected to make quickly. Smiley was sent to an EEO workshop after only three days on the job. Now he is back in the office and has an opportunity to go through his in-basket.

The person playing the role of Al Smiley should read the memos, letters, reports, etc. in Form 9 and respond to each of them on the bottom of each item. This gives him an idea of the climate of Perfect Tool with respect to minority relations and personnel programs in general. Al Smiley and the rest of the group members should note the organization chart for Perfect Tool contained as the first sheet of Form 9.

While Al Smiley is working on the in-basket, which should take no more than 45–50 minutes, the other group members should assume the following roles:

President: I. M. Ready
Administrative assistant: Tom Short
V.P. engineering: Sam Tinker
V.P. marketing: Mar Tini
V.P. finance: Kari Full

Members should familiarize themselves with these roles and the organization by looking through the in-basket items briefly and studying Forms 10, 11, and 12.

TIME: About 50 minutes.

STEP 7: All of the group members should now meet. Their objective is to sketch out an affirmative-action plan for Perfect Tool. Each member playing a role should determine what aspects of the program the person in their position would be concerned with and should adopt the stance he or she might take. No other information about these roles will be given other than that obtained from the in-basket items (Form 9). Al Smiley will participate heavily in this meeting. He is ultimately responsible for the design, implementation, and success of the plan, but relies on the others as he is so new to the organization. He realizes this is his first major task and, based on the in-basket items, forms his opinions of the organization, its officers, and how he can design an affirmative-action plan for Perfect Tool which is effective.

Forms 10, 11, and 12 aid in the development of the plan and should be studied carefully. Forms 10 and 11 provide a profile of all one hundred Perfect Tool workers. The profile contains job type, salary, seniority, and other information. By filling out Form 12, the group can assess Perfect Tool's current situation. The group should then fill out Forms 13–17, which develop a breakdown of Perfect Tool's human resources by race, age, and sex for each of the next five years. (Remember that Perfect Tool's president is committed to a strong affirmative-action program and hired Smiley for that reason, as well as to develop other human-resource programs.) Be sure to fill out the bottom portion of Forms 13–17 as necessary.

Form 18 contains an overall breakdown and summary of the Perfect Tool plan for each of the next five years. The figures are derived from Forms 13–17. After you have filled out all blanks in this form, assess your affirmative-action plan and answer the following questions orally in your group or to hand in to your implementor:

a) Is the plan practical? That is, given Perfect Tool's probable resources and a typical labor supply, could the plan be implemented?

b) Does the plan concentrate more heavily on women or minorities? Why?

c) What aspects of the climate of the organization, as evidenced by the in-basket items and the city and company information, would deter the effective implementation of such a plan? What would facilitate the plan's implementation?

d) How would the following personnel programs be affected by the decision to implement the affirmative-action plan (be specific): selection and staffing; performance appraisal; training and development; wage and salary administration; recruitment; human-resource planning and forecasting.

e) How could the plan be evaluated after each year to assess whether or not it is on target?

TIME: About 2 to 3 hours.

FOR FURTHER READING*

American Psychological Association, Taskforce on Employment and Testing of Minority Groups. "Job Testing and the Disadvantaged." *American Psychologist* 24 (1969): 637–650. (II).

Baughman, E. E. *Black Americans: A Psychological Analysis.* New York: Macmillan, 1971. (II)

Beatty, R. W. "First and Second Level Supervision and the Job Performance of the Hard-Core Unemployed." *Proceedings of the American Psychological Association Annual Meetings,* Washington, D.C., 1971. (II–R)

Beatty, R. W. "Black's as Supervisors: A Study of Training, Job Performance, and Employers' Expectations." *Academy of Management Journal* 16 (1973): 196–206. (II-R)

Beatty, R. W. "Supervisory Behavior Related to Hard-Core Unemployed Job Success over a Two-Year Period." *Journal of Applied Psychology* 57 (1974): 38–42. (II–R)

Beatty, R. W. "A Two-Year Study of the Effect of Basic Education, Job Skill, and Self-Esteem with the Job Success of the Hard-Core Unemployed." *Personnel Psychology* (1975): 165–174. (II–R)

Beatty, R. W., and C. E. Schneier. "Reducing Welfare Roles through Employment: The Changes Required in Society, Organizations, and Individuals." *The Forensic Quarterly* 41, no. 3 (1973): 380–390. (I)

Bell, D. "Bonuses, Quotas, and the Employment of Black Workers." *Journal of Human Resources* 6 (1971): 304–320. (II)

Bem, S. L., and D. J. Bem. "Does Sex-Biased Job Advertising 'Aid and Abet' Sex Discrimination?" *Journal of Applied Psychology* 5 (1973): 6–18. (II–R)

Bloom, L. Z., K. Cobunn, and J. Pearlman. *The New Assertive Woman.* New York: Delacorte, 1975. (I)

Boyle, M. B. "Equal Opportunity for Women is Smart Business." *Harvard Business Review* 51 (May–June 1973): 85–95. (I)

Brummet, R. L., W. C. Pyle, and E. G. Flamholtz. "Human Resource Accounting in Industry." *Personnel Administration* (July–August 1969). (I)

Business Week. "Up the Ladder, Finally." 24 November 1975, pp. 58–68. (I)

Connolly, W. B. *A Practical Guide to Equal Employment Opportunity: Law Principles, and Practices.* Vols. 1 and 2. New York: Law Journal Press, 1975. (I)

Doeringer, P., ed. *Programs to Employ the Disadvantaged.* Englewood Cliffs, N.J.: Prentice-Hall, 1969. (I)

Dowey, L. M. "Women in Labor Unions." *Monthly Labor Review* 94 (1971): 42–48. (I)

Equal Employment Opportunity Commission. *Personnel Testing and Equal Employment Opportunity.* Washington, D.C.: U.S. Government Printing Office, 1970. (I)

Equal Employment Opportunity Court Cases. U.S. Civil Service Commission Bureau of Intergovernmental Personnel Programs. Washington, D.C.: U.S. Government Printing Office, March 1974. (I)

Farr, J. L., B. S. O'Leary, and C. J. Bartlett. "Ethnic Group Membership as a Moderator of Job Performance." *Personnel Psychology* 24 (1971): 604–636. (II–R)

Flippo, E. B. *Principles of Personnel Management.* 4th ed. New York: McGraw-Hill, 1976, Chap. 3. (I)

Goldberg, P. "Are Women Prejudiced against Women?" *Transaction* 5 (1968): 28–31. (I)

Goodman, P. S., H. Paransky and P. Salipante. "Hiring, Training, and Retaining the Hard-Core Unemployed." *Journal of Applied Psychology* 50 (1973): 23–33. (I)

Goodman, P., and P. Salipante. "Organizational Rewards and Retention of the Hard-Core Unemployed." *Journal of Applied Psychology* 61 (1976): 12–21. (II–R)

Goodman, P., P. Salipante, and H. Paransky. "Hiring, Training, and Retaining the Hard-Core Unemployed: A Selected Review." *Journal of Applied Psychology* 58 (1973): 23–33. (II)

Greenman, R. L., and E. J. Schmertz. *Personnel Administration and the Law.* Washington D.C.: Bureau of National Affairs, Inc., 1972. (I)

Heinen, J. S. et al. "Developing the Woman Manager." *Personnel Journal* 54 (1975): 282–286.

Higgins, J. M. "The Complicated Process of Establishing Goals for Equal Employment." *Personnel Journal* 54 (December 1975): 631–637. (I)

---

* Also see *For Further Reading,* Exercise 10.

Hodgson, J. D. "Title 41—Public Contracts and Property Management: Part 60–3—Employee Testing and Other Selection Procedures." *Federal Register* (36F.R. 7532), 1971. (I)

Horgan, N. J. "Upgrading Underqualified Minority Workers." *Personnel* 49 (January–February 1972): 59–64. (I)

Janger, A. *Employing the Disadvantaged: A Company Perspective.* New York: Conference Board, 1972. (I)

Job Discrimination Handbook. Waterford Conn: Bureau of Business Practice, 1974. (I)

Jones, E. H. *Blacks in Business.* New York: Grosset, 1971. (I)

Kilberg, W. J. "Progress and Problems in Equal Employment Opportunity." *Labor Law Journal* 24, no. 10 (October 1973): 651–661. (I)

Levine, M. J. *The Untapped Human Resource: The Urban Negroes and Employment Reality.* Morristown, N.J.: General Learning Press, 1972.

Loring, R., and T. Wells. *Breakthrough: Women in Management.* New York: Van Nostrand, 1972. (I)

McBee, M. L., and K. A. Blake, eds. *The American Woman: Who Will She Be?* Beverly Hills, Cal.: Glencoe, 1974. (I)

Mennerick, L. A. "Organizational Structuring of Sex Roles in a Nonstereotyped Industry." *Administrative Science Quarterly* 20 (1975): 570–586. (II–R)

Montagu, A. *The Natural Superiority of Women.* Rev. ed. New York: Macmillan, 1970. (I)

Nasen, R. W. "The Dilemma of Black Mobility in Management." *Business Horizons* 15, no. 4 (1972): 57–68. (I)

Ornati, O. A., and E. Giblin. "The High Cost of Discrimination." *Business Horizons* 17 (February 1975): 35–40. (I)

Ornati, O. A., and A. Pisano. "Affirmative Action: Why Isn't It Working?" *The Personnel Administrator* 17 (September–October 1972): 50–52. (I)

Osipow, S. H., ed. *Emerging Woman: Career Analysis and Outlooks.* Columbus: Merrill, 1975. (I)

Padfield, H. *Stay Where You Are: A Study of Unemployables in Industry.* Philadelphia: Lippincott, 1973. (I)

"Part 60–3—Employee Testing and Other Selection Procedures." *Federal Register* 39, no. 12 (January 17, 1974). (I)

Pati, G. C., and P. E. Fahey. "Affirmative Action Programs: Its Realities and Challenges." *Law Labor Journal* 24, no. 6 (June 1973).

Pearson, D. W. "OFCC and EEOC Demands—Guidelines to Frustration." *The Personnel Administrator* 18 (November–December 1973): 21–25. (I)

Pendergrass, V. E. et al. "Sex Discrimination Counseling." *American Psychologist* 31 (1976): 36–46. (I)

Perry, L. W. "The Mandate and Impact of Title VII." *Labor Law Journal* 26 (December 1975): 743–749. (I)

"P-H/ASPA Survey: Employee Testing and Selection Procedures—Where Are They Headed?" *Personnel Management: Policies and Practices.* Englewood Cliffs, N.J.: Prentice-Hall, 1975. (I)

Purcell, T. V., and G. F. Cavanagh. "Blacks in the Industrial World: Issues for the Manager." New York: Free Press, 1972. (I)

Rosen, B., and T. H. Jerdee. "Influences of Sex Role Stereotypes on Personnel Decisions." *Journal of Applied Psychology* 59 (1974): 9–14. (II–R)

Rosen, B., and T. H. Jerdee. "Sex Stereotyping in the Executive Suite." *Harvard Business Review* 52 (1974): 45–58. (I)

Salipante, P., and P. Goodman. "Training, Counseling, and Retention of the Hard-Core Unemployed." *Journal of Applied Psychology* 61 (1976): 1–11. (II–R)

Schein, V. E. "Relationships between Sex Role Stereotypes and Requisite Management Characteristics among Female Managers." *Journal of Applied Psychology* 60 (1975): 340–344. (II–R)

Schneier, C. E. "Behavior Modification: Training the Hard-Core Unemployed." *Personnel* 50, no. 3 (1973): 65–69. (I)

Schneier, C. E. "Content Validity: The Necessity of a Behavioral Job Description." *The Personnel Administrator* 21, no. 2 (1976): 38–44. (I)

Seligman, D. "How Equal Opportunity Turned into Employment Quotas." *Fortune* 87, no. 3 (March 1973): 160–168. (I)

Smith, L. "What's It Like for Women Executives?" *Dun's Review* 106 (December 1975): 58–61. (I)

Sowell, T. "Affirmative Action Reconsidered." *Public Interest,* Winter 1976, pp. 47–65. (I)

Sweet, J. A. *Women in the Labor Force.* New York: Seminar, 1973. (I)

Triandis, H. C., and R. S. Malpass. "Studies of Black and White Interaction in Job Settings." *Journal of Applied Social Psychology* 1 (1971): 101–117. (II–R)

U.S. Civil Service Commission. *Equal Employment Opportunity Counseling: A Guidebook.* Rev. ed. (Prepared by office of Federal Equal Employment Opportunity.) Washington, D.C.: U.S. Government Printing Office, 1975. (I)

U.S. Civil Service Commission. *Guidelines for the Development of an Affirmative Action Plan.* (Prepared by Bureau of Intergovernmental Personnel

Programs.) Washington, D.C.: U.S. Government Printing Office, 1975. (I)

U.S. Equal Employment Opportunity Commission. *A Directory of Resources for Affirmative Recruitment.* Washington, D.C.: U.S. Government Printing Office, 1975. (I)

U.S. News and World Report. "The American Woman." 8 December 1975, pp. 54–64+. (I)

Van Dusen, R. A., and E. B. Sheldon. "The Changing Status of American Women." *American Psychologist* 31 (1976): 106–116. (I)

Vetter, L. "Career Counseling for Women." *The Counseling Psychologist* 4 (1973): 54–67. (I)

Waldman, E., and B. J. McEddy. "Where Women Work—An Analysis by Industry and Occupation." *Monthly Labor Review* 97, no. 5 (1974): 3–13. (I–R)

Young, R. A. *Recruiting and Hiring Minority Employees.* New York: AMACOM, 1969. (I)

Zimpel, L., ed. *The Disadvantaged Worker: Readings in Developing Minority Manpower.* Reading, Mass: Addison-Wesley, 1971. (I)

APPENDIX

Glossary of EEO and Legal Terms*

AFFECTED CLASS

Those groups of minorities, females, the elderly, and the disabled who, by virtue of past discrimination, continue to suffer the effects of such discrimination. Affected-class status must be determined by statistical analysis and/or court decision.

AFFIDAVIT

A written declaration of facts made voluntarily under oath. This is made without notice to the opposing party and without the opportunity for cross-examination.

AFFIRMATIVE ACTION

Any activity initiated by an employer which contributes toward the greater utilization of minorities, females, the elderly, and the disabled, including goals established by units and timetables for completion.

---

* A few of the more common legal terms are listed here as an aid to understanding the *Introduction* and activities of the exercise. For more complete coverage, see H. C. Black, *Black's Law Dictionary* (St. Paul: West, 1968).

AFFIRMATIVE ACTION GROUPS

Those persons identified by the federal and state laws and the County Board of Commissioners to be specifically protected from employment discrimination; includes minorities, females, the elderly, and the disabled.

AFFIRMATIVE ACTION PLAN

A document required of government contractors under regulations of the OFCC. The employer is obliged to compare the internal distribution of minorities and females to their incidence in the external labor market and to determine whether or not the employer is at parity with the external labor market. The affirmative action plan is a statement of goals, timetables, and programs indicating how the employer plans to move from his current status of parity.

AMICUS CURIAE

A party not involved in a lawsuit but who has an interest in its outcome and who submits arguments to the court to aid it in making its judgment.

ANSWER

A response by the person who is sued.

BENCH TRIAL

Follows discovery by both parties and is always before a judge in Title VII proceedings and never before a jury.

BFOQ or BOQ

"Bona fide occupational qualification," or a minimum qualification requirement needed as a prerequisite to be hired and succeed on that job. BFOQs, if challenged, must be demonstrated to be valid by the employer. The courts have interpreted BFOQ very narrowly, especially with regard to sex. Each applicant must be treated as an individual in comparing his or her skills to the skills required to perform the job.

BRIEF

In American practice, a paper written by a lawyer to serve as a basis for his or her later oral argument to the court. Its use is largely to inform the court of the lawyer's argument, authorities on questions of law, and desired interpretation of the case.

BURDEN OF PROOF

The responsibility for demonstrating to the requisite degree the truth of one's claim; the affirmative duty of proving or disproving the claim at issue.

BUSINESS NECESSITY

Criteria placed on applicants that are valid and necessary for the effective conduct of the organization objectives and the particular job. The courts have consistently struck down overly stringent criteria that have been shown to have a disparate effect on affirmative-action-category groups.

CAREER LADDER

Composed of jobs requiring related and increasingly more-responsible duties, through which employees advance by experience and in-service training. Career ladders should be equal in quantitative opportunity and salary range for those jobs having high affirmative-action-group utilization compared with those having primarily white male incumbents.

CHARGING PARTY

Person alleging that he or she is aggrieved as the result of an unlawful employment practice.

COMPLIANCE AGENCIES

Organizations established under the OFCC as internal subunits of major government departments or agencies, including, for example, the Atomic Energy Commission; Department of Health, Education and Welfare; or the Department of Labor. They are charged with the administration of Executive Order 11246, Revised Orders No. 4 and No. 14, and with the collection and analysis of EEO Reports and affirmative action plans. Their powers of enforcement include the ability to deny government business to contractors found in violation.

COMPLAINT

The first paper filed by a plaintiff.

COMPLIANCE

Developing legal practices, within the limits of the nondiscrimination laws and their interpretations by the courts. While organizations, through self-analysis and official changes, can remove their exposure to class-action suits through complying with all civil-rights legislation, individual cases of discrimination can be avoided through training, sessions with managers, supervisors, and other employees in the personnel process.

CONCILIATION

A settlement through administrative processes, such as those initiated by EEOC; a means by which a case is settled by resolution of charges without a trial.

CONSENT DECREE

By comparison, the judicial counterpart to conciliation; a formal court document approved by a judge.

DECISION

Result of legal action which generally goes one of two directions—dismissal of charges or injunction.

DEFENDANT

The person(s) or organization(s) being sued.

DEPOSITION

A written declaration of facts made voluntarily out of court but under oath in the presence of the opposing party, who may conduct cross-examination in front of a court reporter.

DISCRIMINATION

The impact or effect of personnel policies, practices, and procedures that result in affirmative-action groups being less-favorably situated in their employment (cannot be the result of BFOQs or valid criteria of "business necessity"). Thus, a conclusion of law based on a demonstration of adverse impact by the plaintiff and failure by a defendant to demonstrate that the practice was job related to the court's satisfaction.

DISCOVERY

The legal term for the investigation phase after a complaint is filed and the defendant has answered.

DISPARATE EFFECT OR DISPARATE IMPACT

The result of an employment policy, practice, or procedure that, in practical application, has less-favorable consequences for an affirmative-action group than for the dominant group.

DISTRIBUTION RATE

(1) The degree (percentages) to which a given protected class is employed in the various job titles, job classes, and other units within the employing organization; and (2) the degree (percentages) to which individuals of a given protected class are involved in various employment transactions (for example, applications for employment, hiring, placement, promotion, separation, etc.).

EEOC

A federal Equal Employment Opportunity Commission which has the power to bring suits, subpoena witnesses, issue guidelines that have the force of law, render decisions, provide technical assistance to employers, provide legal assistance to complainants, etc.

EMPLOYMENT PARITY

When the proportion of affirmative-action groups in the external labor market is equivalent to their proportion in the company work force without reference to classification.

EMPLOYMENT PROCESS

Under Title VII, the employment process includes recruitment, applicant flow, hiring, job placement, compensation, promotion, transfer, termination, shift assignments, geographical and departmental assignments, and all other such activities.

EXPERT WITNESS

An individual qualified by credentials to give opinion testimony. Although this term has to be limited to a specific application, generally, in test validation at least, a master's degree in psychology and experience in the field is required.

EXTERNAL LABOR AREA

The geographic area from which an employer may reasonably be expected to recruit new workers. In a compliance sense, this total labor market has submarkets within it, comprised of persons with the requisite skills, experience, etc., to fill given jobs.

EXTERNAL LABOR MARKET

The civilian work force within a labor area.

GED

General Educational Development—the GED certificate is the high-school equivalency certificate, generally recognized as equal to a high-school diploma for all practical purposes.

GOALS

Good faith quantitative objectives an employer voluntarily sets as the minimum progress that can be achieved within a certain time period through all-out efforts at outreach recruitment, validating selection criteria, creation of trainee positions, career ladders, etc. Setting goals and objectives are considered proper and legal responses to underutilization of minority groups by various federal agencies.

HUMAN-RELATIONS TRAINING

Interpersonal skill development, especially with respect to affirmative-action-group awareness, communication, and compatible attitude development. Techniques may include T-groups, seminars, workshops, role reversal, attitude assessment, etc.

INCIDENCE RATE

A measurement of the degree to which a specific protected class is involved in any of the various steps of the employment process. If, out of a group of eighty black males, twenty are promoted, the incidence rate is 25 percent. As a measure of compliance, the incidence rate is compared with the degree to which the specific protected class is represented in the external labor market.

INJUNCTION

May either require that a certain practice be stopped or that something be done in the future; orders other actions, such as relief, to affected class members.

INTERROGATORIES

Written questions drawn up and served on an opposing party with a prescribed time period to answer. The party must then serve answers to the questions under oath. Sometimes used in the deposition procedure.

JURY TRIAL

More formal than a bench trial; a jury hears the case.

LITIGATION

A judicial controversy; lawsuits.

MAKING WHOLE

Award of back pay employees would have received but for the effects of the unlawful practice.

MANDAMUS

An order issued by a court to a private or municipal corporation; an executive, judicial, or administrative officer; or to an inferior court commanding the performance of a particular act within the responsibility of the latter party.

OBJECTIVES

Similar to goals, a good-faith effort to meet numerical goals through modifications in employment procedures and practice. Goals and objectives are set after careful external and internal labor analysis.

OCCUPATIONAL PARITY

When the proportion of affirmative-action-group employees in all occupational levels is equivalent to their respective availability in the external labor market. Eventually, with the goal of equal educational and training opportunities, employment parity and occupational parity will be equal.

OFCC

Office of Federal Contract Compliance—has set guidelines for all federal contractors with respect to nondiscrimination and affirmative action.

PARITY

The long-term goal of affirmative action, reached when employment and occupational parity are identical.

PARTICIPATION RATE

(1) The percentage of incumbents of a job title, class, department, or other organization unit (including the whole organization) who belong to a given protected class; and (2) the percentage of individuals involved in an employment-process transaction (for example, application for employment, hiring, placement, promotion, separation) who belong to a given protected class.

PERSONNEL POLICIES AND PRACTICES

All rules and operations through which an organization recruits, hires, places, transfers, promotes, and separates employees; administers wages and benefits; and all other terms, conditions, and privileges of employment.

PLAINTIFF

The person who initiates litigation.

PRESENT EFFECTS OF PAST PATTERNS OF DISCRIMINATION

The EEOC and the courts have consistently held that employers are liable for correcting situations in which employees continue to suffer the "present effects of past patterns of discrimination." Simply stated, this can mean that an employee (or group of employees) who should (in the eyes of the Commission and/or the courts) have been promoted three years ago

(whether a complaint had been lodged or not) are still entitled to be "made whole," accomplished through retroactive pay or other means.

PRIMA FACIE

Violation where evidence is shown that an employment practice has an adverse impact affecting an individual as a member of a similarly affected class covered by Title VII. It shifts the burden to the defendant. The elements necessary to support the claim have been presented and unless evidence can be presented to rebut the previous arguments, the claim will be supported. In the EEO area, statistics of underutilization can be sufficient to make a prima facie case for discrimination. It is then the responsibility of the employer to justify those statistics through "business necessity," BFOQs, etc.

PROTECTED CLASS

Legally identified groups that are specifically protected by statute against employment discrimination. Unlike affected-class status, which must be demonstrated, protected-class status is automatically conferred on recognized minority-group members, females, etc., by virtue of the law or other court decisions interpreting the law.

PROBABLE CAUSE

Reasonable on the basis of the evidence but not certain or proved. Before initiating court action, the EEOC makes a determination of *no cause*, *probable cause*, or *cause*. In incidents of probable cause or cause, pretrial negotiations and conciliation generally resolve the issues before the case can get into court.

QUOTAS

Fixed hiring and promotion rates based on race, sex, etc., which must be met at all costs and do not take into consideration the availability, education, or training of the external labor force, of protected class members, or the employer's internal labor situation with respect to projected manpower requirements. Quotas are considered to be last-resort measures available only for the courts to impose when good faith efforts do not exist. Court cases are currently being decided as to their advisability and legality.

REBUT

An answer to an argument, a prima facie case, or a presumption.

RELEVANT LABOR POOL

The total number of incumbent employees who are in position for a specific promotion, or all candidates who could conceivably be considered for a promotion.

REMAND

To send back. For example, if a court of appeals finds further action is necessary in a case or if further testimony is needed to decide the case, it will remand the case to the lower court.

RESPONDENT

That person against whom an administrative charge of discrimination is filed.

SMSA

Standard Metropolitan Statistical Area—the area of employee recruitment against which parity and utilization levels are compared. The SMSA may vary depending on level of job class, availability of applicants, location of work station, etc.

STIPULATION

An agreement between the opposing parties, somewhat akin to a contract, identifying which facts or issues are not disputed. Used as a time-saving device to narrow a case down to the essential matters.

SUBPOENA

An order of the court commanding individuals (or documents) to appear and give testimony. Derived from the Latin *sub* (under) and *poena* (penalty) because failure to appear may be considered contempt of court.

SUMMARY JUDGMENT

Could be issued by the court at the point where there is *no* dispute of material facts.

SYSTEMIC DISCRIMINATION

Equal employment opportunity may be denied as the inevitable consequence of some established business practice, persisting over a period of time, rather than of a specific overt action against an aggrieved party. Such a result of the "system" is systemic discrimination and has been at the root of most Title VII settlements to date. Inadvertent and usually unintentional, the disparate effect produced by systemic discrimina-

tion constitutes a prime area of vulnerability for most businesses.

TIMETABLES

Consecutive time (generally in affirmative action, a timetable covers one year) during which the specific quantitative goals and objectives for that period are to be met and evaluations of progress made before beginning the subsequent timetable with its own specific goals and objectives.

TITLE VII OF THE CIVIL RIGHTS ACT OF 1964 (AS AMENDED BY THE EQUAL EMPLOYMENT OPPORTUNITY ACT OF 1972).

The first legislation to make it an unlawful employment practice to discriminate on the basis of race, color, religion, sex, or national origin. All other federal and state EEO legislation is patterned after or supportive of Title VII.

UNDERUTILIZATION

Term used to describe a lower number of affirmative-action-group employees than parity would predict. Once underutilization is quantitatively established, the burden of proof rests on the employer to demonstrate that the underutilization is the legitimate effect of BFOQ and valid criteria of business necessity (also called underrepresentation).

UTILIZATION ANALYSIS

An audit of the current distribution, participation, compensation, and movements of an organization's employees. The analysis is made by job grade, title, and lines of progression for all sex and race groups, across all units of the organization, for each step of the employment process. Current distribution must be analyzed in terms of relevant external labor markets, and such comparisons must be made at each step of the employment process. A utilization analysis establishes a legal and accurate basis for realistic goal setting.

VALIDITY

The extent to which a test, criterion, or qualification measures the trait (some job performance ability) for which it is being used, rather than some other trait. "Business necessity" considerations are addressed to the usefulness of the test in predicting job performance and the minimum cut-off scores.

Name _____ Group Number _____

Date _____ Class Section _____ Hour _____ Score _____

PART A

Form 1 EEO and Affirmative Action Review Questionnaire

	True	False	Undecided
1. It would be inappropriate for courts to impose goals and timetables on employers engaged in discriminatory practices.			
2. Unions may be held liable for labor contracts that are overtly or covertly discriminatory.			
3. State and local governments were subject to the Civil Rights Act of 1964 before 1972.			
4. If an employer can show an employee profile which demonstrates that the organization does not discriminate, there is no legal requirement that the organization validate its selection procedures.			
5. Goals are determined by analyzing the job classifications within a unit or organization.			
6. Some lawyers may now receive their fee from the government if they win an EEOC case.			
7. A voluntarily developed affirmative-action plan is a management guideline and is not a legal document.			
8. Failure to impose quotas means failure of commitment to EEO.			
9. EEOC is an affirmative-action agency.			
10. Affirmative-action plans are not required of every organization by law, they are only recommended by guidelines.			
11. Criteria for determining job requirements for minorities and women for the same positions should be the same as for white males.			
12. The EEO Act gave the Civil Service Commission enforcement responsibilities for eliminating discrimination in state and local governments.			
13. EEOC is responsible for nondiscrimination and affirmative action among government contractors.			
14. The responsibility for remedying unintentional or covert discrimination practices remains with the employer.			
15. The new EEO Act (1972) prohibits discrimination based on age, race, religion, and sex, and national origin.			
16. Complaints of race or sex discrimination may be filed on the basis of a specific practice or on the basis of systematic discrimination.			
17. Affirmative-action programs are designed to achieve equal employment opportunity only for minorities.			

18. An important distinction can be made between quotas and goals.			
19. It is wise to involve a representative group of employees in the development of affirmative-action programs.			
20. Numerical goals, as well as quotas, are incompatible with merit principles for promotions, etc.			
21. The development of voluntary affirmative-action programs is a protection for employers if a complaint of race or sex discrimination is filed.			
22. Attaining an affirmative-action goal may sometimes require hiring less-qualified persons over better-qualified ones.			

Name _____ Group Number _____

Date _____ Class Section _____ Hour _____ Score _____

PART A

Form 2 Calculations of Adverse Impact

CALCULATIONS FOR SEX

$$\frac{\text{Number of women selected (i.e., height greater than 5'5'')}}{\text{Total number of women}} \times 100 = \_\_\_\_\_\%$$

$$\frac{\text{Number of men selected (i.e., height greater than 5'5'')}}{\text{Total number of men}} \times 100 = \_\_\_\_\_\%$$

$$\frac{\text{Selection rate for women}}{\text{Selection rate for men}} \times 100 = \_\_\_\_\_\%$$

CALCULATION FOR RACE

$$\frac{\text{Number of whites selected (i.e., height greater than 5'5'')}}{\text{Total number of whites}} \times 100 = \_\_\_\_\_\%$$

$$\frac{\text{Number of nonwhites selected (i.e., height greater than 5'5'')}}{\text{Total number of nonwhites}} \times 100 = \_\_\_\_\_\%$$

$$\frac{\text{Selection rates for whites}}{\text{Selection rates for nonwhites}} \times 100 = \_\_\_\_\_\%$$

Complete the questions below, tear off, and give to your instructor.

(tear or cut here)

YOUR HEIGHT _____

YOUR SEX _____

YOUR RACE _____

PART B

Form 3 Affirmative Action Master Plan—Statistics: Littleco, Metro, U.S.A.*

	STANDARD METROPOLITAN STATISTICAL AREA POPULATION DATA (Metro, U.S.A.)		LITTLECO EMPLOYEE PROFILE											
			Current-year employees (see also Form 4)		Each of previous five years[†]									
					1st		2nd		3rd		4th		5th	
Group	Totals	% of total within groups	No.	%	No.	%	No.	%	No.	%	No.	%	No.	%
Total	1,000,000	100	500	100	500	100	500	100	500	100	500	100	500	100
Male	495,000	49.5	350	70	334	67	329	66	306	61	295	59	291	58
Female	505,000	50.5	150	30	166	33	171	34	194	39	205	41	209	42
Minority	(200,000)	20.0	20	4	33	6	46	9.2	68	14	90	18	100	20
Total white	800,000	80	(100)	480	96	460	92	440	88	420	84	400	80	400	80
Male	399,500	49.4	340	71	300	60	280	56	260	52	240	48	240	48
Female	400,500	50.6	140	29	160	32	160	32	160	32	160	32	160	32
Total black	150,000	15	(100)	10	2	20	4	30	6	50	10	70	14	80	16
Male	74,550	49.7	5	50	10	2	15	3	25	5	35	7	40	8
Female	75,450	50.3	5	50	10	2	15	3	25	5	35	7	40	8
Total Indian	10,000	1	(100)	2	0.4	3	0.6	4	0.8	5	1	5	1	5	1
Male	4,900	49.0	1	50	2	0.4	2	0.4	3	0.6	3	0.6	3	0.6
Female	5,100	51.0	1	50	1	0.2	2	0.4	2	0.4	2	0.4	2	0.4
Total Spanish surname	30,000	3	(100)	5	1	6	1.2	7	1.4	9	2	10	2	10	2
Male	14,500	48.3	2	40	3	0.6	3	0.6	4	0.8	5	1	5	1
Female	15,500	51.7	3	60	3	0.6	4	0.8	5	1	5	1	5	1
Total other	10,000	1	(100)	3	0.6	4	0.8	5	1	5	1	5	1	5	1
Male	4,950	49.5	2	67	2	0.4	3	0.6	3	0.6	3	0.6	3	0.6
Female	5,050	50.5	1	33	2	0.4	2	0.4	2	0.4	2	0.4	2	0.4

* Illustrative data, rounded for computational purposes.
[†] Littleco has had a stated policy to keep its total work force at 500 due to little absolute growth. While certain figures vary throughout the year due to attrition, etc., the figures in the table represent those at the current year's end.

PART B

Form 4 Littleco's Employee Profile by Race, Sex, and Job Level for Current Year

Job categories	Job cat. no.	Total employed including minorities	Total males including minorities	Minority males				Total females including minorities	Minority females				Total minorities and women
				Black	American Indian	Spanish surname	Other		Black	American Indian	Spanish surname	Other	
Officials, managers and administrators	1	50	50	0	0	0	0	0	0	0	0	0	0
Professionals	2	10	9	0	0	0	1	1	0	0	0	1	2
Technicians	3	10	10	0	0	0	1	0	0	0	0	0	1
Protective service workers	4	10	10	0	0	1	0	0	0	0	0	0	1
Sales	5	10	10	0	0	0	0	0	0	0	0	0	0
Paraprofessionals	6	5	5	0	0	0	0	0	0	0	0	0	0
Office and clerical	7	50	0	0	0	0	0	50	3	0	0	0	50
Skilled craft workers/craftsmen	8	5	5	0	1	0	0	0	0	0	0	0	1
Operatives (semiskilled)	9	300	204	1	0	0	0	96	0	0	3	0	100
Laborers (unskilled)	10	25	22	1	0	1	0	3	2	1	0	0	5
Service/ maintenance workers	11	25	25	3	0	0	0	0	0	0	0	0	3
TOTALS		500/100%	350/70%	5	1	2	2	150/30%	5	1	3	1	163/32.6%

PART C

Form 5 Background Information for Supercity

Supercity is a large Southern metropolitan area which is the hub of much industrial activity. The city is facing the problems of most cities its size, including a deteriorating tax base and a physically deteriorating central city area. The central city contains most of the minority residents.

Supercity's financial picture is not terribly dismal, however, due to the thriving industrial sections of the city. In addition, two residential areas are composed primarily of middle and upper-middle-class citizens. One is a high-rise apartment area close to downtown and the other is a renovated area of brownstone houses, apartments, rowhouses, etc. Both are growing in population and contribute much to the city, both aesthetically and economically. However, the city itself has enjoyed no population growth in the last two years.

Suburban areas, located outside the city limits, are quite nice and are expanding rapidly. So far, only very few industrial firms have relocated there.

The central city area was renovated recently by several moderate-income housing projects and general urban-renewal work. Parks were enlarged, and streets were widened and repaved. This work, however, has deteriorated significantly in the decade since it was begun.

The government of Supercity is actually quite small in overall size relative to the size of the city. Financial problems have limited expansion somewhat in recent years, but unionized city workers have not disrupted services to any great extent due to strikes. Basically, city workers turn over rapidly. Wage rates are somewhat below those of local industry.

Supercity's government is almost exclusively white in the upper-level positions and the city has been accused by many groups of being hostile to minorities. Although schools are integrated, most contain only children of the poorest families. In the two wealthier residential areas of the city, parents generally send their children to private schools.

The Chamber of Commerce of Supercity, composed largely of industrialists who live in the suburbs, as well as the city government, want Supercity to be known as a more progressive city. They are attempting to attract industry to Supercity and to the suburbs in the area.

PART C

Form 6 Employee Profile of All City Workers,* Supercity Municipal Government

Table 1. Male—Female

Classification	Male	Female	Total
Officials/managers	37	1	38
Professionals	434	6	40
Technicians	862	11	873
Office and clerical	4	872	876
Craftspersons (skilled)	456	0	456
Operatives	541	21	562
Laborers and sanitation workers	2296	1	2297
Totals	4630	912	5542

Table 2. Minority—Nonminority

Classification	White	Minority†				Total
		B	AI	SS	O	
Officials/managers	36	1	0	0	1	38
Professionals	421	3	1	2	13	440
Technicians	866	1	2	2	2	873
Office and clerical	668	155	0	38	15	876
Craftspersons (skilled)	436	12	4	4	0	456
Operatives (semiskilled)	480	44	0	38	0	562
Laborers and sanitation workers	734	1246	0	317	0	2297
Totals	3641	1462	7	401	31	5542

* Does not include police or fire workers.
† B = Black, AI = American Indian, SS = Spanish Surnamed, O = Other
  (primarily Oriental)

Name _____   Group Number _____

Date _____   Class Section _____   Hour _____   Score _____

PART C
Form 7 Affirmative Action Master Plan—Supercity, U.S.A.

STANDARD METROPOLITAN STATISTICAL AREA (Supercity, U.S.A.)			SUPERCITY EMPLOYEE PROFILE OF CITY WORKERS													
			Employee (current year)		Goals for each of next five years										
					1st		2nd		3rd		4th		5th		
Group	Total	% of total within group	Numbers	%	No.	%	No.	%	No.	%	No.	%	No.	%	
TOTAL	1,553,038	100	5542	100											
Male	757,443														
Female	795,595														
Minority	(776,559)														
WHITE	776,439	49.9 (100)	3641												
Male	374,261	48.2													
Female	402,178	51.8													
BLACK	656,384	42.2 (100)	1462												
Male	325,631	49.6													
Female	330,753	50.4													
INDIAN	10,663	0.7 (100)	7												
Male	4,934	46.3													
Female	5,729	53.7													
SPANISH SURNAME	105,956	6.8 (100)	401												
Male	51,203	48.3													
Female	54,753	51.7													
OTHER (primarily Oriental)	3,596	0.2 (100)	31												
Male	1,414	39.3													
Female	2,182	60.7													

TOTALS

PART D

Form 8 Basic Information for the Perfect Tool Corporation

You are Al Smiley, the recently appointed director of personnel for Perfect Tool Corporation, reporting to the president. Your department has primary responsibility for monitoring personnel matters. The company employs 100 people; you have a personal secretary.

Perfect Tool is located in the suburbs of Supercity, a large southern industrial metropolitan hub (see Form 5). Transportation to the suburbs is convenient by bus or car. Perfect Tool is a subcontracting firm which specializes in control devices for a prime military contractor. The company also makes controls for the large industrial boilers. Perfect Tool's products were designed by its founder, who sold the business to the present owner, I. M. Ready, ten years ago. Perfect Tool has had a growth rate of 15 percent and has been in a very healthy financial situation since 1939. The President, I. M. Ready, voluntarily determined to implement an affirmative-action program. He feels if he does not, the OFCC will request a compliance review, which could jeopardize his government contracts. Upon inspection, he recognized he could be penalized in both the Protobar and Hawkeye divisions, since all of their customers are government contractors. The president's sons-in-law head the engineering and finance groups.

Of the one hundred persons employed, eighteen are women, three are black men, seven are males with Spanish surnames, and one is an American Indian male. All others are white males. All whites live near the plant. The minority personnel live in the urban areas of Supercity. All women are in clerical jobs, but there are now women applicants who want to work in the plant. Presently, three women are eligible for promotion. If promoted they would have men working for them. A black and the Chicanos are paid at a commensurate salary. Although they are in effect supervisors, they do not get supervisor's pay. Soon there will be three production job vacancies on different shifts. Also, a new position will be created because of an expanded production schedule.

Most workers seem to feel that women should not work in the plant and believe that Perfect Tool has its "quota" of minorities already. Many feel that minorities want to "take over"; rumor has it that blacks want to move into the neighborhood where the plant is located. In fact, the American Indian wants to move from Supercity so he can be closer to his job. Few blacks apply for jobs as the organization does not use popular minority media for recruiting. There is an overabundance of women applicants.

Each of the company's departments is headed by a manager with employees reporting to him. The president has recently had trouble with the production department. Effective administrative control of the department has been a continuing problem for the past two years. Twenty-five of the employees are professionals. Of that number, most are engineers assigned to various projects. The previous personnel director, Mr. Cy Long, retired after twenty years. Most people felt he lost interest in keeping up with his job after he decided to retire. In fact, he may have lost interest before he retired. The former director favored EEO and philosophically agreed with the president's expressed EEO commitment. However, he did not devote much time to the subject, feeling his organization had no problems in this area.

Supercity considers the Perfect Tool a stable institution. The suburban community, however, has been hostile to minorities, Jews, and Catholics in the past. Schools in Supercity are integrated and Perfect Tool employees' children are bussed to outlying Supercity schools. Suburban schools close to Perfect Tool were closed by the school board. There had been trouble with the local policy in the predominantly black urban areas of Supercity. The local community newspaper devotes much space to Perfect Tool releases and does not print adverse information about the company. The major metropolitan newspaper, the *Supercity Crusader*, will, however, print all of the news, including Perfect Tool's employment problems.

The Chamber of Commerce of Supercity desperately wants to be known as a "progressive" city. It is attempting to create the impression that Supercity, including the surrounding suburban areas, is a good community for industry.

PART D

Form 9 An In-Basket for Al Smiley, New Personnel Administrator of Perfect Tool Corporation

Organization Chart

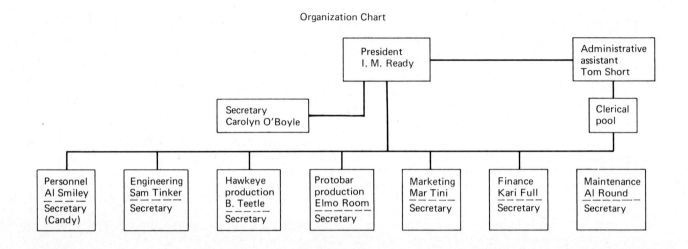

ITEM 1

August 18

TO: Personnel Director

    As you know for some months we have been negotiating with the
skilled trades council to get more minorities into apprentice programs.
Progress has been slow and the council has been extremely reluctant to
change its old ways of doing business.

    Our position, in addition to our well-known statements about EEO,
has been the expansion of this program to better utilize our unemployed
youth.

    One of the union's arguments which we feel must be broken down is
that the available training facilities are being used to capacity.
Unfortunately from our view Perfect Tool Corporation has provided very
limited leadership in this vital area. It is suggested that the departments of Perfect Tool be used as training sites and that the electricians
would be the ideal place to start. You already have electrician
journeymen, so it should be a simple matter to establish an apprentice
program. Minorities in this community are becoming very aggravated over
this problem and a declaration of commitment on your part would help to
cool tempers.

    We would appreciate the opportunity to discuss this matter at your
earliest convenience.

The Urban Group for a Better Community

Supercity

ITEM 2

EEOC Regional Office
18 August

President
Perfect Tool Corporation
Supercity, U.S.A.

Dear Sir:

Our office has received notification from the office of Federal Contract
Compliance that an employee of Perfect Tool Corporation has charged your
company with sex discrimination. They have passed the charge to us because
we have the investigatory powers regarding such charges.

Thus, we request a review of the charges on your premises at your convenience.
At that time, we would prefer to review all of your employment practices.

Your immediate attention to this notification is appreciated. I look forward
to hearing from you.

Sincerely,

Richard Dengrone

District Director
Equal Employment Opportunity
Commission

Cy/ What has happened here? What do you plan to do? IMR

ITEM 3

Mr. Cy Long   8/4
Personnel Director

We've got a problem! You know we picked up an Indian guy, Howard
Eagle Feather, last month. Well, everything was working out fine.
He's already productive--fits in great! <u>But</u> he now tells me he can't
find a house to buy. He wants to bring his wife and kids to the suburbs
but seems like everywhere he goes they take one look at that natural
suntan and he gets the cool treatment!

I've tried to help, but no luck! I'm at the end of my rope. I can't
lose him. You don't know how far I searched to get somebody for that
high wire stuff on the building maintenance crew.

                              <u>HELP</u>

                              Al Friendly

ITEM 4

Smiley - Personnel   Aug 30

     Please look over these two civil engineer's resumes (attached) who
will graduate in June. I've interviewed them and pretty much decided
on #1 because personality-wise I think he'll get along better with the
major Sub-contractor. Old Joe can be pretty salty and we need this job
on schedule. This guy knows some good stories, plus he is an ex-marine.
     To keep to the rules I included a gal who showed up as #2. I even
had to interview her!! She's a real smart kid but she'd turn blue when
old Joe got through with her, besides having to slop around in the mud
out there.
     I don't know why she'd waste her time in engineering school!
Anyway, look at these two and tell me what you think.

                              Sam Tinker

                              Head of Engineering

ITEM 5

TO: Cy Long

FROM: Tom Short, Assistant to President

This is some preliminary information on our engineers needed for
the first section of the President's report on affirmative action
(Due 12/3):

    (1)   In the last two years, eight professionals have been hired--
        all engineers.
        (5 for development--1 Oriental, 1 White)
        (3 for applications--all White)
        Turnover has been 10% in the past few years including
        retirements (mandatory retirement is at 65). Current
        vacancies: 3.

    (2)   There is one black engineer in Maintenance who has been with
        the department 5 1/2 years.

ITEM 6

Director of Personnel   8/2
Perfect Tool Corporation
Supercity, U.S.A.

Dear Sir:

I understand that some of your departments will soon be hiring clerical employees. We would like to bring to your attention our school, the Secretarial Success Institute, which might serve as a recruitment source for you and lower your costs.

We are interested in meeting with you to discuss:

(1) The possibility of placing some of our best graduates with your organization.

(2) The possibility of negotiating an on-the-job training agreement with you for some of our students. We feel that mutual benefits would derive from this which could result in considerable financial savings for you.

You may be aware of the fact that our Institute is set up to serve the needs of this community under a grant from the U.S. Minority Business Enterprises Agency. Our school is accredited by the Accrediting Commission Business Colleges and is approved by the U.S. Veterans Administration training.

We offer quality eduction and have an extensive clerical and secretarial curriculum, based on current technology. Our classes are limited to 10 students so that our experienced teachers can offer intensified individualized instruction. We take pride both in our trainees and in our graduates.

                                        Cordially,

                                        Kelly Mc Gillicutty

                                        Director of Placement
                                        Secretarial Success Institute

ITEM 7

7/16

Mr. Cy Long,

What are we going to do about the retirement party for Hector? We've got to send the notice around sometime in the next couple of weeks but where the heck should we have it? The club would be ideal but Kari Full has some strong feelings about THOSE PEOPLE in OUR club.

I could get messy and remind him that it's supposed to be a public establishment, but----

Or maybe we could forget it and just plan to go to the Cafeteria. Everybody in the office chipped in, so we'll probably have enough left after the gift and stuff to buy meals and maybe hire a band. Let me know what you think? Please hurry on this one.

Gloria Nevercharge

ITEM 8

Human Relations Commission
Supercity, U.S.A.

Dear Commissioner:

At the present time I am a civil engineer in the Engineering Division of Perfect Tool Corporation. I am the only black engineer employed by the company.

The position of Maintenance Manager will be available the first of the month due to the retirement of the incumbent and I intend to apply for that vacancy. However I already know that I will be passed over when the final decision is made and it will be due to race rather than qualifications. This organization could never stand to have a black man in a position with that much authority. I have always given my best to this organization but find that because of my race this is apparently not enough.

Therefore I would like to know the proper procedure for filing a complaint because I intend to carry this matter as far as possible to see that justice is done.

Any information you can provide regarding my rights would be appreciated.

Sincerely,

James "Bo" Witherspoon

cc: Mayor

P.S. By the way, Harry, I really want to pursue this based on our lunch last week.

Al: Bo gave me a copy of this and I thought you should see it. Any comments?

ITEM 9

October 31

Mr. Room

We have been in your Production Department three months now. This is
our second complaint about poor working conditiions which seem to have fallen
on deaf ears so far <u>including yours</u>, just like when we were in the Maintenance
Department.

We are sick and tired of greasing machines, it is dangerous and often
the machines are not completely off. It's only by pure luck that none of us
have been killed so far. We have to supply our own gloves and have no other
protective clothing or equipment.

If there were some whites on here and we weren't all black or Spanish
there'd be some equipment pretty fast. Now this is our last time to tell
you about this. If something doesn't happen within <u>two</u> weeks, we'll take our
case to the highest levels in the city or this State or the Supreme Court
if necessary. We want this corrected <u>now</u>.

Felippe LaBato

Lucius Nomore

Clarence C. Smith

Al: what can I do?
Elmo

ITEM 10

Dear Mr. Smiley: Sept 6

I am Mexican-American and though I read and write English well my accent
gives some trouble when I speak. I just started working here and already my
supervisor (Mrs. Meany) is being very unfair to me. She has suspended me for
three days because she says I was AWOL but I was not. She won't believe me
when I tell her my story but she listens to her white typists when they tell
her all sorts of tales.

She told us to call in when we are sick and do that very early in the
day. Last Tuesday at 8:30 a.m. I called to say I was sick and would not be
in and to tell Ms. Meany. The girl who answered the phone said O.K. and hung
up before I got her name. I was upset because I didn't recognize the voice
and was afraid it might be the new girl from the typing agency we got the day
before. But I figured it would be O.K. and didn't call back because I didn't
want to get her into trouble.

When I went in Wednesday Mrs. Meany asked why didn't I call and I was
considered AWOL, I told her I called but didn't know who I talked to. She
said nobody said nothing to her and she didn't believe me, that I had a three
day suspension and if it happened again I would be fired.

She doesn't treat the white girls this way. When they are late or absent
they don't even get a warning letter and I think she doesn't like me because
I'm Chicano.

I don't feel I did anything wrong and am concerned about this being on
my record. Besides I need the money. I hope you can do something to correct
this terrible situation.

Your employee,

Inez

Inez Vigil

P.S. please don't tell Mrs. Meany I talked to you.

ITEM 11

Retirement is great,
as are the Fiji Islands!
I'm sure you will
enjoy the pleasant
people at Perfect Tool.
They are all a good
group. Good Luck.
Say hello for me.
            Cy Long

Mr. A. Smiley
Personnel Director
Perfect Tool Corp.
Supercity Suburb
U.S.A.

ITEM 12

July 17

Dear Mr. Long

    We, the undersigned Quality Control Technicians, would like to
meet with you to express our concern over the distortion of our duties
and responsibilities over the past year.

    Our duties include testing samples to determine the quality of our
product. This information is recorded and presented to the staff
engineers for evaluation.

    In the past year as the engineering staff has decreased we have
been called upon to make additional evaluations. Though some of us are
qualified by experience to make this judgment we are not being paid at
the professional level--we are still labeled technicians.

    Therefore it would be appreciated if you would review this matter,
for we feel we should be paid for the work or not be required to do it.

    We appreciate that there is a union grievance procedure, but feel
this is a personnel problem that cannot be solved by our department head.

Technicians

S. M. (Al) Berkes

A. Clamp

N. O. Stopper

Gregg Reader

cc: Department Head

P.S. Have you
heard of a
technique called
job analysis? —
my neighbor
mentioned it.
            Al

ITEM 13

Sept. 10

Dear New Boss:

How was your trip? I hope you enjoyed the meetings. I knew you would need the Haskel report first thing tomorrow so I finished what I could except for that narrative that Mr. Long used to do himself. (It will be on your desk with those statistics that Morse asked for.)

When you called I told you that I would not need to be off tomorrow. Well, I started thinking about it and decided to go ahead with that job interview anyway. I talked to them again and they can't offer more salary but they are talking about possibilities of moving up and they want me to take that Secretary's Seminar that I've been wanting to go to. Anyway, I thought I'd just talk to them.

I'll be in at 10:30.

Candy

P.S. I made arrangements for Dodo to cover me until I get in.

ITEM 14

Sept. 4

Personnel Director

We Production workers have been discriminated against regarding opportunity for overtime. The white guys are always given preference everytime to work overtime. Our Supervisor just picks his favorites and nobody else gets a chance. We are going to refuse to work unless the situation is corrected. Mr. Crow, our union rep, is sick today so we are bringing this matter to your attention. We need a meeting to resolve the problem right now!

P.S. How come Round and Room take 3-hour lunches but we have to punch a time clock?
(out at 12:18 and back at 12:48 or we get docked)

PART D

Form 10 Employee Codes for Perfect Tool Personnel Records (see Form 11)

RACE CODE

    B = Black (Negro)
    O = Oriental (Asian American)
   AI = American Indian
SSA = Spanish Surname American (Mexican, Cuban, Spanish, Puerto Rican, Latin)
    W = Caucasian

SALARY LEVEL

1 = 30,000 +
2 = 20–25,000
3 = 18–20,000
4 = 16–18,000
5 = 14–16,000
6 = 12–14,000
7 = 10–12,000
8 = 6–10,000

EDUCATION

D = Doctorate
M = Masters
B = Bachelor
H = High school
G = Grade school

DEPARTMENT CODE

  A = General administration
  M = Marketing
  P = Production
  E = Engineering
PS = Personnel
MT = Maintenance
  F = Finance

JOB CATEGORIES

1 = Officials and managers
2 = Professionals
3 = Technicians
4 = Sales representatives
5 = Office and clerical
6 = Skilled craft workers/craftspersons
7 = Paraprofessionals
8 = Security guards
9 = Operatives
10 = Laborers (unskilled)
11 = Service/maintenance workers

PART D

Form 11 Perfect Tool Personnel Profile

Employee number	Job category	Salary	Department	Seniority (in years)	Education	Sex	Race	Age
1	1	1	A	10	M	M	W	60
2	7	4	F	15	M	M	W	35
3	10	7	E	10	H	M	B	35
4	4	2	M	20	M	M	W	45
5	1	1	A	15	D	F	W	53
6	4	2	P	20	B	M	W	40
7	6	3	F	15	B	M	W	41
8	6	3	E	16	B	M	W	36
9	10	8	P	1	G	F	W	35
10	6	4	P	15	B	M	W	55
11	11	6	F	5	G	M	W	63
12	6	5	P	15	H	M	W	57
13	9	7	MT	10	H	F	W	27
14	5	8	P	5	H	M	W	19
15	11	8	MT	10	H	M	B	30
16	8	5	A	22	B	M	W	41
17	10	6	MT	9	H	F	W	43
18	6	5	P	11	B	M	W	32
19	9	4	P	26	B	M	W	46
20	3	3	E	15	B	M	W	55
21	11	7	P	8	G	F	W	44
22	6	7	E	19	H	M	W	37
23	10	8	MT	16	H	M	SSA	37
24	2	5	A	1	M	M	B	27
25	6	3	F	16	B	M	W	41

Employee number	Job category	Salary	Department	Seniority (in years)	Education	Sex	Race	Age
26	8	6	PA	21	H	M	W	38
27	10	7	MT	7	G	F	SSA	29
28	10	8	MT	7	H	F	W	24
29	9	7	M	5	H	M	W	29
30	10	8	F	15	H	M	B	35
31	6	4	A	19	B	M	W	41
32	6	6	E	27	H	M	W	61
33	5	6	MT	6	H	F	SSA	60
34	7	4	P	3	B	M	W	33
35	3	6	P	7	H	M	W	41
36	4	4	PS	15	B	M	W	35
37	5	8	M	4	H	M	W	26
38	11	8	A	8	H	F	B	47
39	4	7	A	2	H	M	W	45
40	8	4	E	3	B	M	W	58
41	9	7	F	9	H	M	W	29
42	5	8	A	8	H	F	W	18
43	8	6	E	6	B	M	W	26
44	7	8	E	1	H	M	W	21
45	5	6	MT	11	B	M	W	31
46	2	4	M	20	M	M	W	40
47	9	7	P	7	H	M	AI	27
48	6	6	F	19	B	M	W	49
49	7	7	P	9	H	M	SSA	26
50	3	6	P	5	H	M	W	33

Employee number	Job category	Salary	Department	Seniority (in years)	Education	Sex	Race	Age
51	3	5	M	8	B	M	W	28
52	10	7	P	10	H	M	O	45
53	5	6	F	5	H	M	W	37
54	7	4	PS	19	H	M	W	49
55	6	8	F	1	H	M	W	27
56	6	7	MT	5	H	F	W	55
57	3	5	E	2	B	M	W	28
58	11	8	P	9	H	M	SSA	29
59	7	5	PS	11	B	M	W	31
60	5	6	A	3	B	M	W	27
61	9	8	MT	7	H	M	SSA	37
62	6	6	M	9	H	M	W	32
63	9	6	P	23	B	M	W	43
64	6	8	F	1	H	M	W	22
65	8	8	PS	16	H	M	W	46
66	10	7	MT	3	H	F	W	43
67	8	6	E	21	H	M	W	51
68	6	7	E	16	H	M	W	32
69	9	8	A	5	H	M	SSA	29
70	9	8	P	8	H	M	W	27
71	7	4	M	11	B	M	W	47
72	6	5	P	7	B	M	W	35
73	5	7	MT	5	H	F	W	42
74	3	4	P	20	H	M	W	40
75	8	6	PA	21	H	M	W	37

Employee number	Job category	Salary	Department	Seniority (in years)	Education	Sex	Race	Age
76	10	7	MT	3	G	F	W	39
77	6	5	PS	8	B	M	W	48
78	4	5	M	1	B	M	W	21
79	3	3	E	15	M	M	W	45
80	9	6	MT	3	B	F	B	41
81	8	6	PS	16	H	M	W	51
82	10	8	MT	2	H	F	O	37
83	9	6	P	13	H	M	W	43
84	1	2	A	2	M	M	W	32
85	5	4	F	29	H	M	W	65
86	5	8	MT	4	H	F	SSA	63
87	9	6	PS	7	B	M	W	27
88	8	5	E	20	B	M	W	40
89	11	7	F	15	H	M	SSA	35
90	2	3	PS	16	M	M	O	37
91	7	7	M	1	H	M	W	26
92	9	5	E	20	H	M	W	41
93	10	8	MT	3	H	F	W	23
94	11	6	M	9	H	M	W	53
95	11	7	P	5	H	M	O	37
96	7	5	A	2	B	M	W	29
97	11	6	E	9	B	M	W	60
98	1	2	PS	11	D	M	W	41
99	6	7	MT	9	H	M	W	28
100	10	7	F	8	H	M	SSA	31

Name _____   Group Number _____

Date _____   Class Section _____   Hour _____   Score _____

PART D
Form 12

Total Company Breakdown by Race (from Form 11)—Year: Present

Job categories	Professional, executive, managerial (1, 2, 4)	Clerical (5)	Skilled (3, 6, 7)	Semi-Skilled (8, 9, 11)	Unskilled (10)
Race					
White					
Black					
Spanish Surname					
American Indian					
Oriental					
Other					

Total Company Breakdown by Age (from Form 11)

Job categories	Professional, executive, managerial (1, 2, 4)	Clerical (5)	Skilled (3, 6, 7)	Semi-Skilled (8, 9, 11)	Unskilled (10)
Age					
16–25 years					
26–35 years					
36–40 years					
41–45 years					
46 years or older					

Total Company Breakdown by Sex (from Form 11)

Job categories	Professional, executive, managerial (1, 2, 4)	Clerical (5)	Skilled (3, 6, 7)	Semi-Skilled (8, 9, 11)	Unskilled (10)
Sex					
Male					
Female					

Name _____ Group Number _____

Date _____ Class Section _____ Hour _____ Score _____

PART D

Form 13

Total Company Breakdown by Race—Year One

Job categories	Professional, executive, managerial (1, 2, 4)	Clerical (5)	Skilled (3, 6, 7)	Semi-Skilled (8, 9, 11)	Unskilled (10)
Race					
White					
Black					
Spanish Surname					
American Indian					
Oriental					
Other					

Total Company Breakdown by Age

Job categories	Professional, executive, managerial (1, 2, 4)	Clerical (5)	Skilled (3, 6, 7)	Semi-Skilled (8, 9, 11)	Unskilled (10)
Age					
16–25 years					
26–35 years					
36–40 years					
41–45 years					
46 years or older					

Total Company Breakdown by Sex

Job categories	Professional, executive, managerial (1, 2, 4)	Clerical (5)	Skilled (3, 6, 7)	Semi-Skilled (8, 9, 11)	Unskilled (10)
Sex					
Male					
Female					

Assumptions/Explanations/Notes:

Name _____   Group Number _____

Date _____   Class Section _____   Hour _____   Score _____

PART D
Form 14

Total Company Breakdown by Race—Year Two

Job categories	Professional, executive, managerial (1, 2, 4)	Clerical (5)	Skilled (3, 6, 7)	Semi-Skilled (8, 9, 11)	Unskilled (10)
Race					
White					
Black					
Spanish Surname					
American Indian					
Oriental					
Other					

Total Company Breakdown by Age

Job categories	Professional, executive, managerial (1, 2, 4)	Clerical (5)	Skilled (3, 6, 7)	Semi-Skilled (8, 9, 11)	Unskilled (10)
Age					
16–25 years					
26–35 years					
36–40 years					
41–45 years					
46 years or older					

Total Company Breakdown by Sex

Job categories	Professional, executive, managerial (1, 2, 4)	Clerical (5)	Skilled (3, 6, 7)	Semi-Skilled (8, 9, 11)	Unskilled (10)
Sex					
Male					
Female					

Assumptions/Explanations/Notes:

Name _____   Group Number _____

Date _____   Class Section _____   Hour _____   Score _____

PART D
Form 15

Total Company Breakdown by Race—Year Three

Job categories	Professional, executive, managerial (1, 2, 4)	Clerical (5)	Skilled (3, 6, 7)	Semi-Skilled (8, 9, 11)	Unskilled (10)
Race					
White					
Black					
Spanish Surname					
American Indian					
Oriental					
Other					

Total Company Breakdown by Age

Job categories	Professional, executive, managerial (1, 2, 4)	Clerical (5)	Skilled (3, 6, 7)	Semi-Skilled (8, 9, 11)	Unskilled (10)
Age					
16–25 years					
26–35 years					
36–40 years					
41–45 years					
46 years or older					

Total Company Breakdown by Sex

Job categories	Professional, executive, managerial (1, 2, 4)	Clerical (5)	Skilled (3, 6, 7)	Semi-Skilled (8, 9, 11)	Unskilled (10)
Sex					
Male					
Female					

Assumptions/Explanations/Notes:

Name _____   Group Number _____

Date _____   Class Section _____   Hour _____   Score _____

PART D

Form 16

Total Company Breakdown by Race—Year Four

Job categories	Professional, executive, managerial (1, 2, 4)	Clerical (5)	Skilled (3, 6, 7)	Semi-Skilled (8, 9, 11)	Unskilled (10)
Race					
White					
Black					
Spanish Surname					
American Indian					
Oriental					
Other					

Total Company Breakdown by Age

Job categories	Professional, executive, managerial (1, 2, 4)	Clerical (5)	Skilled (3, 6, 7)	Semi-Skilled (8, 9, 11)	Unskilled (10)
Age					
16–25 years					
26–35 years					
36–40 years					
41–45 years					
46 years or older					

Total Company Breakdown by Sex

Job categories	Professional, executive, managerial (1, 2, 4)	Clerical (5)	Skilled (3, 6, 7)	Semi-Skilled (8, 9, 11)	Unskilled (10)
Sex					
Male					
Female					

Assumptions/Explanations/Notes:

Name _____ Group Number _____

Date _____ Class Section _____ Hour _____ Score _____

PART D

Form 17

Total Company Breakdown by Race—Year Five

Job categories	Professional, executive, managerial (1, 2, 4)	Clerical (5)	Skilled (3, 6, 7)	Semi-Skilled (8, 9, 11)	Unskilled (10)
Race					
White					
Black					
Spanish Surname					
American Indian					
Oriental					
Other					

Total Company Breakdown by Age

Job categories	Professional, executive, managerial (1, 2, 4)	Clerical (5)	Skilled (3, 6, 7)	Semi-Skilled (8, 9, 11)	Unskilled (10)
Age					
16–25 years					
26–35 years					
36–40 years					
41–45 years					
46 years or older					

Total Company Breakdown by Sex

Job categories	Professional, executive, managerial (1, 2, 4)	Clerical (5)	Skilled (3, 6, 7)	Semi-Skilled (8, 9, 11)	Unskilled (10)
Sex					
Male					
Female					

Assumptions/Explanations/Notes:

Name _____   Group Number _____

Date _____   Class Section _____   Hour _____   Score _____

PART D

Form 18 Master Plan for Perfect Tool Corporation Affirmative Action Program

	Standard Metropolitan Statistical Area (Supercity)		Perfect Tool Corporation Plan											
					Year in future									
					1		2		3		4		5	
Group	Total in metro area	Percentage of metro area	Total in Perfect Tool currently	Percentage in Perfect Tool currently	No.	%	No.	%	No.	%	No.	%	No.	%
TOTAL	1,553,038	100												
Male	757,443	48.8												
Female	795,595	51.2												
Minority	(776,559)													
WHITE	776,439	49.9												
Male	374,261	48.2												
Female	402,178	51.8												
BLACK	656,384	42.2												
Male	325,631	49.6												
Female	330,753	50.4												
INDIAN	10,663	0.7												
Male	4,934	46.3												
Female	5,729	53.7												
SPANISH SURNAME	105,956	6.8												
Male	51,203	48.3												
Female	54,753	51.7												
OTHER	3,596	0.2												
Male	1,414	39.3												
Female	2,182	60.7												

Assumptions/Explanations/Notes:

Name _____ Group Number _____

Date _____ Class Section _____ Hour _____ Score _____

ASSESSMENT OF LEARNING IN PERSONNEL ADMINISTRATION

EXERCISE 18

1. Try to state the purpose of this exercise in one concise sentence.

2. Specifically what did you learn from this exercise (i.e., skills, abilities, and knowledge)?

3. How might your learning influence your role and your duties as a personnel administrator?

4. What would be the potential benefits for an organization if it successfully developed an affirmative-action program? What would be the potential costs?

5. How could an affirmative-action program be evaluated as to its effectiveness?

6. At what stage(s) should the personnel staff charged with developing an affirmative-action program or complying with EEOC guidelines coordinate its efforts with line managers? How could such coordination be achieved?

7. Precisely what is "adverse impact"?

8. What would be the areas of interdependence between affirmative-action programs and the following human-resource programs: interviewing, testing, assessing training needs, designing training and development programs, human-resource planning, wage and salary administration, motivation programs, and union contractual administration? (Use additional sheets.)

9. Additional questions given by your implementor:

Exercise 19

THE IMPACT OF UNIONS ON PERSONNEL ADMINISTRATION AND HUMAN-RESOURCE MANAGEMENT: CONSTRAINTS AND OPPORTUNITIES

PREVIEW

Labor unions are now a very visible and powerful element in the workings of a postindustrial society such as exists in the United States. They are no longer limited to craft or industrial workers, but now include virtually all types of occupations, including white-collar and professional ones. The internal operations of an organization that has a labor union are often quite different from those of one without a union; virtually every phase of human-resource management is affected directly or indirectly.

Developing human-resource programs when unions are present, as well as direct negotiation with the union as to working conditions, wages, and other aspects of employment, are tasks typically given to the personnel department or the industrial- or employee-relations department of an organization. As illustrated in previous exercises, the personnel administrator and his or her staff are constrained and influenced by the concerns and objectives of different groups, notably government and management. Labor unions must now be added to the list. As was noted in Exercise 1, personnel administrators are often required to walk a fine line in attempting to please each of these three groups simultaneously.

The constraints unions place on human-resource management are often quite obvious, such as promotion and wage and salary decisions that must be made within contract provisions. But a union also can present potential opportunities for cooperation between labor and management which can benefit individuals, organizations, and the personnel department. For example, a union's affirmative-action program can be coordinated with an organization's such that recruitment, selection, training, and placement costs are shared. This exercise explores the constraints and opportunities unions present to personnel administration.

OBJECTIVES

1. To provide an overview of the impact of labor unions on personnel and human-resource program design and implementation.
2. To provide information about major labor laws, labor-relations terminology, and labor concepts—all prerequisites to establishing an effective labor-relations program.
3. To build skill in interpreting union agreement (contract) language and provisions, and in computing the economic cost of certain contractual provisions.
4. To begin to build skills in contract administration by analyzing several grievance situations, and in contract negotiation and bargaining by negotiating several issues of a contract.

PREMEETING PREPARATION

Read the *Introduction, Procedure, Appendixes,* and all forms in Parts A, B, and C. Read only Forms 6–9 and 13 of Part D. Do not read Forms 10, 11, or 12 until you are assigned a role by your implementor. For Form 4 of Part B, you will need a copy of a union contract. Read Form 4 well in advance of the time you plan to fill it out in order to allow sufficient time to obtain a contract from a local or national union office, a library, an acquaintance who is a union member, etc.

INTRODUCTION

Labor Relations: An Introduction to Policy, Practice, and Contract Negotiation and Administration*

When a union represents employees of an organization, personnel-administration decisions and programs are subject to the terms specified in the labor contract, or agreement. Because of this potential constraint, personnel administration becomes more complex in a unionized company. As part of management, personnel cannot act unilaterally when unions exist. It must consult the contract and perhaps union officials first. For example, if a vacancy occurs in a supervisory position, rather than interviewing all existing workers in a department in order to find the most qualified one to take the promotion, the personnel staff must consult the contract. It may specify who the promotion must be given to through its seniority provisions. In addition, if workers are not unionized, various personnel practices affect the potential attraction a union may have for employees. The employees' desire to unionize or not would, of course, depend in part on the type of personnel or human-resource-management decisions currently being made, their scope and their fairness.

Thus, knowledge about unions and skill in dealing with them is essential for all managers, but particularly for those in personnel, as they typically have primary responsibility for direct relations with the union.

The impact of unions on personnel is huge and complex, and stems from the unions' impact on an employer in general. Managerial control over personnel programs and policy is restricted, as is managerial authority. However, as will be later pointed out, the union may present some opportunities for more effective human-resource management along with these constraints. In their efforts to deal with the demands of unions, management, and government simultaneously, wise personnel staffs look for these opportunities and exploit them. The *Introduction* touches upon the union's appeal to workers, the development of labor unions in this country, labor legislation, and labor-contract negotiation and administration. The final section of this review notes how some specific personnel programs are typically affected by labor unions, as well as the positive consequences of unionism for personnel administration.

Given the size and importance of this area and our space limitations, this review must be brief and selective.[1]

Why Workers Join Unions. Unions are formal groups of workers founded to represent workers' interests to management. Given differences in status and resources, as well as for other reasons, workers acting individually cannot be expected to have much influence over managerial decisions, unless, of course, management actively seeks their participation. However, there is strength in numbers. Collectively, workers can have enormous power and influence. When this influence is channeled through recognized and certified labor unions with huge memberships, enormous financial resources, technical expertise, and professional leadership, it often becomes equal to, and sometimes greater than, the influence and power held by management.

Unions offer self-protection to their members from real and perceived exploitation and mistreatment by employers. Through collective action they can improve wages, working conditions, hours, and other aspects of the work environment. Vast gains have been realized in these areas over the years.

Unions also offer workers self-expression.[2] Strikes, grievances, meetings, and other activities offer a relief from the monotony of many jobs. The union brings with it opportunities for action, for developing personal abilities and skills, for recognition, for interpersonal relationships, and for excitement. Anyone who has been involved in a strike or a union organizing campaign may attest to the last item.

The promise of solidarity or togetherness is also a motivation to join unions. A "we-feeling" or cohesion is fostered among people who share the same problems, frustrations, and life circumstances. Besides providing a vent for frustration and an outlet for action, unions pull together people who are largely in similar positions. These shared problems and experiences—the feeling that you are not alone—is important to many.

---

* The legislation and terminology mentioned here are detailed in Appendixes A and B, respectively, of this exercise.

---

[1] Refer to *For Further Reading* for sources containing more information about the issues covered here.
[2] M. S. Myers, *Managing without Unions* (Reading, Mass.: Addison-Wesley, 1976), Chapter 5.

Of course, people join unions for reasons other than self-protection, self-expression, and solidarity. Many join through real or perceived coercion by others; others have little choice due to the control unions have over entry into certain trades; and some join due to social pressure and conformity. In addition, some join primarily for economic benefits, others to become active leaders, and others to gain personal power and position.

The Development of Labor Unions. Unions in one form or another have existed in this country since it was formed over 200 years ago. In the early days of unionism, the unions were largely fraternal organizations. After the country became industrialized, unions began to form to influence employers, but initially they had little impact. Employers could discharge union members at will and uneven financial situations in the late 1800s and early 1900s often forced persons to accept whatever jobs and conditions they were offered. Legally, too, employers had the upper hand, for they could require employees to sign (yellow dog) contracts indicating they would not join unions.

Under the Sherman Anti-Trust Act of 1890 (see *Appendix A*) union efforts to exert pressure on employers were considered illegal conspiracies. This conspiracy doctrine limited union activity severely. Unions during the late 1800s were primarily concerned with social reform and better working conditions, and were often led by people with deep philosophical differences from the free-enterprise, capitalistic business values that prevailed as this country moved rapidly toward industrialization.

The Civil War brought a somewhat relaxed stance toward unions and, after the war, several nationwide associations of various sorts were attempted. The National Labor Union was the first of these, established in Baltimore in 1866, but it had a very brief life. In 1869 the Knights of Labor, including members of craft unions, as well as skilled and unskilled labor, was formed in Philadelphia. The Knights were successful at centralizing unionizing efforts for some years and had over 700,000 members at one time. In 1886 the American Federation of Labor (AFL) was formed; it has since merged (in 1955) with the Congress of Industrial Organizations (CIO). The AFL-CIO is the largest organization of its type and is extremely powerful and visible today in contract negotiation and general political and economic spheres.

In the 1930s, a deep split occurred between craft unions, composed of members of such occupations as typographers, and industrial unions, made up of semiskilled and unskilled workers in industry. A faction of those in the AFL decided unskilled workers should also be unionized, as industrialization made craft workers increasingly less important. After facing stiff initial opposition from within the AFL, since craft unions felt the inclusion of unskilled labor would dilute their earnings and power, this minority group favoring unskilled unionization broke off to form the CIO. Eventually, as craft unions did decline and industrial unionization became increasingly prevalent during the 1940s and 1950s, the AFL and CIO merged.

Today, about one in four workers belongs to a union,[3] and the composition of unions is changing to include white-collar workers. Office and professional workers in government, insurance, finance, trades and services, and educational organizations have viable unions. Service professionals, such as law enforcement workers and fire fighters, are also organized.

Further, unions are concerned with many issues in addition to economic ones—they provide recreational, educational, financial, health, and other services to their members. Unions, in a way, are now big business. They are often very well off financially and, due to pension funds and other assets, control huge sums of money—consequently, their investment decisions affect the entire United States economy. Some are extremely active politically. They work for various candidates at all levels and public endorsement from a large national union's president is a highly prized benefit to politicians. Unions have research branches, sponsor grants and fellowships, and hold various types of meetings, conventions, and workshops. They hire professionals of almost every type, including accountants, economists, lawyers, personnel specialists, librarians, communications experts, psychologists, and others. However, a brief look at United States labor laws and their chronological emergence indicates that the modern-day national union, housed in a high-rise downtown headquarters building staffed by highly trained professionals, is a rather recent phenomenon.

United States Labor Legislation.[4] Unions first posed an understandable threat to the authority and freedom of management. Employers initially responded to unions in this country with strong opposition. While there were no early laws that specifically protected

---

[3] D. Yoder, *Personnel Management and Industrial Relations*, 6th ed. (Englewood Cliffs, N.J.: Prentice-Hall, 1976), Chapter 16.

[4] See also *Appendix A*.

employers and few viable employer associations or groups to counteract unions' power, courts were used to challenge unions quite successfully. Unions were considered conspiracies and injunctions were issued by the courts which prohibited unions and their members from certain activities, such as strikes or picketing. The courts felt such activities damaged employers' private properties and infringed on their rights to operate their businesses.

Employers' associations were eventually developed to counteract unions—some to unify employers' positions and hence their power, others to destroy unions and prevent bargaining. They maintained "blacklists" of union organizers, members, and sympathizers, and employed strike breakers and armed guards to crush strikes and picket lines. Currently, both employers' and unions' tactics are strictly limited and controlled by various "unfair labor practices" issued through legislation (discussed below).

Employers now bargain together with other organizations in an industry to form "master" agreements with a union. They have formed numerous trade and other types of associations, such as the National Association of Manufacturers, which lobby for favorable legislation and conduct advertising and educational campaigns to convey employers' points of view. Employers have, for the most part, recognized the viability and power of unions. They have developed effective bargaining techniques and other strategies, but their posture toward unions still runs from cooperation to open conflict.

No matter what the general posture of any particular employer or union may be toward the other, as a group, both have been very active in influencing United States public policy and legislation relevant to unions. This legislation's development has generally reflected the prevailing attitude in the country toward unions, an attitude that has shifted back and forth from antiunion to prounion to neutrality.[5]

The conspiracy doctrine noted above marks the antiunion period. Under the Sherman Anti-Trust Act of 1890, courts interpreted union activity as conspiracies to restrain trade and, therefore, outlawed them. Until various court cases stemming from the Clayton Act of 1914 were decided, union activity was basically illegal and unions suffered greatly.

The Clayton Act, also meant to curb monopolies and restraint of trade, did severely limit the use of injunctions against labor practices and asserted the

right to strike. The Railway Labor Act of 1926 was the first law to specifically state a favorable United States stand toward collective bargaining. The prounion period, spurred by depression and characteristics of the political climate, had begun.

The Norris-LaGuardia Act of 1932 further helped unions by restricting injunctions and stating that collective-bargaining attempts must be made before disputes can be brought to court. But the National Labor Relations Act (Wagner Act) of 1935 was the key piece of legislation favoring unions. It's impact was monumental: it stated that the policy of the United States was to encourage collective bargaining, defined several employer unfair labor practices that were prohibited, and established the National Labor Relations Board (NLRB) to administrate the act.

From 1935 to 1947 unions grew very rapidly. Strikes, political activity, and the charges by employers that the 1935 Act was too biased in favor of unions, among other factors, led to the passage of the Taft-Hartley Act in 1947. This act represented a shift back to the employer side of the continuum representing United States policy regarding unions. The Taft-Hartley Act specified several union unfair labor practices in an effort to curb union excesses and to rid unions of communist influence. Reporting and disclosure rules were also established for unions to allow public scrutiny of their internal operations.

In 1959, passage of the Landrum-Griffin Act signalled a return to neutrality in United States labor legislation. Both unions and management were given more stringent reporting and disclosure rules. Unions were prohibited from exploiting their members financially and in other respects, and provisions prohibiting secondary boycotts and hot-cargo agreements, as well as provisions to assure union democracy, were written.

While other legislation since 1959 has certainly influenced labor relations, the laws noted above were fundamental. They established the framework of United States labor relations and mirrored the prevailing attitudes toward organized labor as unions were developing. Recent legislation, with the exception of the 1964 and 1972 Equal Employment Opportunity Laws (see Exercise 18), is narrow in scope. Laws deal with specific aspects of human-resource management, such as wages (see Exercise 17), not with overall labor relations.

Collective Bargaining and Labor Contract Negotiations. In the early days of collective bargaining, little real negotiation or discussion took place. Depending on the relative strength of the union and

---

[5] See Yoder, *Personnel Management and Industrial Relations,* for a more detailed account of labor-legislation trends.

management, one notified the other of wage rates and other conditions. If there was a dispute, a strike or lockout often resulted. Today, collective bargaining—the process of negotiation, administration, and interpretation of collective agreements, as well as dispute settlements—is still emerging and changing.

Collective bargaining is actually a form of industrial democracy. Management and union representatives sit down at a table and deliberate, argue, discuss, bargain, haggle, and try to influence each other regarding various aspects of the employment situation. Their eventual agreement is written up as a contract which becomes "industrial law" governing the parties. They must bargain in good faith; that is, they must agree to meet, to continue to meet, to offer proposals and counterproposals, and to try to reach agreement.

In this country, most contracts are negotiated by a single company and a single union, called single-employer bargaining. This bargaining can be for one plant or location of an organization, or for several. Recently, however, multiple-employer bargaining has become more common. Organizations come together to bargain with one or more unions simultaneously. Such bargaining can be set up by labor market (e.g., a city), by geographical region (e.g., the Southwest), or by industry. Single-employer bargaining is common in manufacturing, but if a large organization has several plants organized by the same national union (e.g., GM and United Auto Workers), each local union at each plant will send representatives to a national board which will formulate the major contract proposals. Then, a master agreement will be negotiated with the company and each local may bargain with each individual plant for supplemental provisions.

Multiemployer bargaining is common in construction, lumbering, mining, trucking, textiles, and steel. It has the advantage for the employer of reducing competition from other organizations by limiting advantages they might achieve in separate negotiations—for example, lower wages that would permit them to sell their competing products cheaper. For smaller unions, it is efficient and sometimes beneficial to bargain with several employers at once. However, the consumer may suffer, as multiemployer bargaining may result in higher wages (and therefore prices). When a strike occurs, the whole industry may be shut down and product availability shrinks.

Contract Negotiation. In the early days of contract negotiation, unions demanded certain provisions and management's first response was usually a simple "no"—since they had no idea what the union would propose, they were not prepared to respond with counterproposals. Now, months are often spent preparing for negotiations. Research is conducted on both sides to gather information about industry agreements, trends, how well the current contract is working, financial situations, etc. The costs of possible demands are estimated. Often, unions poll their members to ascertain their desires. Priority issues are decided on and overall strategy is discussed. Besides background data, both sides need to know the laws and procedures established by the National Labor Relations Board and legislation regarding unfair labor practices to assure compliance.

The negotiating teams typically consist of the local union president, a few additional local union officials, perhaps an official from the international union, the labor relations or personnel administrator from the organization, and one or more of his or her staff, as well as sometimes other experts (e.g., lawyers, financial experts, line managers, or executives). The initial meeting is important because a climate is established which usually continues throughout the negotiations. It varies from belligerence and conflict to cooperation. Rules and procedures are agreed on for subsequent sessions; initial proposals may be exchanged; and each side may ask the other to explain the proposals in order to ascertain how important they might be to the proposing side or how well thought out and defensible they might be.

Negotiations are not unlike a good poker game: bluffing tactics, feinted anger, appeals to the press or observers, and very careful divulging of one's "hand" are common strategies. Total candor is seldom seen. Neither side wants the other to know how it will ultimately go or how important each item may really be. Some proposals must be attained, others are desirable but not critical, and others are merely for trading purposes.

As negotiations continue, proposals may be accepted, amended, or withdrawn; counterproposals may be made; and/or compromises may be settled on. The most important issues usually come last. If one party proposes a solution definitely out of the "bargaining zone," or tolerance limit, of the other and the first party does not change the proposal, a deadlock may result.[6] Of course, acceptance, rejection, deadlock, or compromise on any issue is determined

---

[6] For a very interesting discussion of the psychology of negotiations and strategy in bargaining, see R. Stagner and H. Rosen, *Psychological Union-Management Relations* (Belmont, Cal.: Wadsworth, 1965).

by the many characteristics of each individual situation.

Negotiators realize they must secure the approval of their superiors, as well as the rank-and-file members in the case of the union, for any agreements made. Often union members will fail to ratify a contract and it must be renegotiated. Union leaders try to prevent this, as it speaks poorly for their ability to represent their constituents. Therefore, there is little to gain in negotiations by trying to push something through that is unrealistic, unreasonable, will not work, or will not be ratified.

Each side uses several types of pressure to help gain acceptance of their demands. The most powerful weapon for the union is usually the strike, a cessation of work which can force the employer to cease operations. The seriousness of strikes often makes them a last-resort tactic.[7] Picketing involves parading in front of the organization and other locations with banners or posters which signify a dispute is in progress; the objective is to enlist support, publicize the strike, and often to prevent other employees from entering the building. Boycotts prevent union members (and other parties in a secondary boycott) from buying employer products or services. Grievances are also a dispute tactic. They are formal complaints filed with an organization arising out of an individual dispute. The contract typically has provisions for handling these grievances which must be followed.

One of the employer's most effective responses to a union dispute is the lockout, or a refusal to employ the workers during the dispute. Lockouts are sometimes used if violence or damage to property has occurred. However, employers are typically reluctant to use a lockout due to lost revenue and unfavorable public opinion. They usually attempt to continue operations while a dispute or strike is in progress. This keeps their organization earning revenues, sometimes lowers prestige of union leaders, and can gain more favorable provisions as the power of the strike is lessened.

On the other hand, deep-seated bitterness may develop if an organization continues to operate during a strike, and this can lead to problems in future negotiations. Negotiations occur for each contract and some victories may be "hollow" ones if the "losing" side enters the next set of negotiations seeking to make up for lost ground or to "teach the other side a lesson." Retaliation and revenge, which can result from bitter relations, unreasonable de-

mands, violence, destruction of property, or inflexibility on the part of either side, color subsequent negotiations and block cooperation.

If a strike or lockout occurs, sooner or later both sides feel its effects. Unions have only so much money in their "strike funds" and employers can suspend operations only so long before they lose customers or are unable to pay their expenses. When disputes arise which cannot be settled by negotiations, outside third parties are often called in. A conciliator may be used to reestablish communication between the parties and set a climate more favorable to negotiation. A mediator may be used to offer suggestions and proposals. An arbitrator or an umpire may also be called in to actually decide the dispute after hearing both sides. Usually arbitration becomes necessary as contracts are administrated and grievances occur, rather than as they are negotiated. Finally, the government may intervene to settle a dispute, strike, and/or lockout if there is a threat to national security or public welfare.

The Labor Agreement. Several substantive issues or provisions are typically contained in most labor agreements, as well as additional ones particular to the two parties involved. Union security is usually the first substantial area dealt with in the contract, for it concerns the union's right to exist and continue to exist. A contract provision may specify the union has security by stating that all employees must join the union (i.e., a union shop), or must pay a fee to the union but do not have to join (i.e., an agency shop). Unions, of course, are opposed to employees who do not join the union but benefit from the gains it obtains. Most employer groups resent compulsory unionism, however, and feel a union shop grants a union too much power.

A second area covered in the agreement is management rights. Management seeks to obtain agreement that certain areas (e.g., product pricing, accounting methods, directing employees, job content, etc.) are exclusive management rights. Although unions typically concede that the above areas are rightfully in management's domain, the two parties sharply disagree over certain others. Among these latter issues are work standards, discipline, work scheduling, work assignment, and promotions. Unions often do have a say in many of these now.

Wages, the third major area in contracts, includes many specific items, such as wage adjustment, job evaluation and classification, premium pay, call-in pay, time study, cost-of-living increases, and any number of fringe benefits. This area is of crucial

---

[7] Several types of strikes are defined in *Appendix B.*

economic importance to both sides and the skill of negotiators is often evaluated on the basis of these quantifiable items. Obviously, too many considerations enter into wage and benefit determination to enumerate; financial position of the organization, general economic conditions, precedents, historic trends, and labor demand and supply are but a few.

Job rights are another key contract area. Unions attempt to provide security for their members by controlling transfer, promotion, demotion, termination, and layoff decisions. Seniority is usually the criteria unions seek to use for such decisions, but employers often feel strict seniority rules restrict their freedom to make decisions based on merit. Usually layoffs are made on the basis of seniority, while promotions are based on seniority and merit.

Grievance handling is the final important substantive area of contracts. Grievances can arise over any number of issues, such as disciplinary actions, promotions, pay, or work rules. The contract specifies a procedure used to resolve such grievances and thereby gives the aggrieved parties recourse. Typically, the grievance moves from the supervisor and shop steward or union committee person (where most are settled) to a shop committee consisting of members of labor and management, to an appeal committee consisting of higher-level officials of both sides, and finally perhaps to arbitration, where a third party decides the grievance. The filing of a grievance signifies that the aggrieved party feels the organization has not administered the contract faithfully, and the grievance procedure provides a means to decide how the contract should be interpreted.

Contract Administration. After a contract is ratified or accepted, both sides must conduct their affairs according to its provisions. However, no written contract can predict all of the problems that may be encountered as it is used. In order to administer the contract effectively, each side has certain responsibilities.

One such responsibility is communication and interpretation. The contract provisions must be communicated to all parties concerned and interpreted for them in everyday language to facilitate compliance. Next, consistency in interpretation and administration over time and across departments is vital to assure fairness. New interpretations should be publicized. Flexibility and adaptability are required—the contract must be somewhat pliable as it is applied. When novel situations arise for which there is no specific guideline, labor and management must cooperate to interpret the contract in a reasonable manner. Some-

times contracts contain reopening clauses which specify that during the term of the contract certain clauses may be renegotiated as situations warrant. Provisions and amendments are often necessary to allow the contract to realistically reflect the dynamic nature of the work setting.

Administration of a union contract is a difficult process for management and labor. Further, it is a day-to-day process, not a periodic one, as is contract negotiation. A spirit of cooperation is essential, but administration is certainly aided by negotiating a reasonable and thorough contract initially, and by making certain all parties, particularly union stewards and first-line supervisors, are very familiar with the contract.

The Impact of Labor Unions on Personnel Programs and Decisions: Some Examples. The union contract and the existence of the union itself influence the personnel function in many ways. They affect decisions personnel staffs and line managers are able to make, as well as basic personnel-program design and implementation. In regard to decision making, a union contract specifies precedent and standard procedure, and it is therefore difficult, for example, to overlook an infraction of a rule made by a long-standing employee with an excellent record or to administer a less-severe punishment to an employee who had an exceptionally valid reason for violating a contract provision. The personnel administrator's staff must advise managers to look at the rule, not the person. In practice, this is difficult and distasteful to some.

Union contracts typically rely heavily on seniority. Thus, the personnel administrator's staff must take seniority into account, often ignoring ability altogether, as it makes decisions. Accordingly, it may be impossible to give a promotion to a young, very able worker, or due to contract provisions regarding wage differentials, it may be impossible to give that same person a merit raise as a reward for performance. Such raises may only be possible with a certain seniority level. Finally, due to contract provisions, a supervisor may lose discretion in administering other bonuses, such as allowing someone to leave work early for a special occasion or as a reward. Hence, altruism must give way to due process or the rules and procedures specified in the contract.

Besides influencing various specific decisions made in regard to human resources, union contracts affect basic personnel programs. Seniority provisions influence performance-appraisal programs and bonus or motivation programs, such that the criteria for these programs become job tenure instead of merit. Selection procedures are also affected—for example, the contract may specify that vacancies be posted and filled from within whenever possible. Thus, selection procedures must be directed toward internal, rather than external, sources. Recruiting would also be affected, of course, as would human-resource plans and forecasts which attempt to predict future human-resource needs and their sources.

The union's existence and specific contract provisions do not necessarily make personnel programs less efficient or more difficult, but they must be taken into account as these programs are designed and implemented. In addition, since the various major personnel programs are so interdependent, a union's effect on one has an effect on others. Viable programs are possible if the union's impact is taken into account as the programs are designed and planned, not after implementation has begun, only to find a contractual provision that prohibits a specific practice.

Using the Union to Positive Advantage. The title of this exercise suggests that unions present constraints *and* opportunities for personnel administration. Such opportunities are often overlooked, especially if managers stereotype the union in a negative way. Opportunities are available in several areas. First, the union can share some of the record-keeping function of personnel, as it, too, keeps various records on its members which can serve as a check on company records. Second, the union's existence may help to bring some problems that otherwise would have been overlooked to the attention of proper officials. Real inequity between job types and their pay scales are an example. The union representative in the organization, the steward, can assist line managers by spotting problems. Third, the contract shifts some of the discipline burden to the union itself. Discipline takes considerable time and resources, as well as judgment, which can easily be attacked as capricious, subjective, or biased. With detailed grievance procedures and other rules, management can save the time and effort normally spent devising various disciplinary actions.

The union can also serve as an effectual communication link to employers, particularly through the steward, and the contract can facilitate the acceptance of certain management decisions that may be difficult for workers to understand and agree with. For example, the contract may specify holiday provisions or overtime rules—decisions management would otherwise have to justify to workers.

Although these advantages are possible, they are by no means assured or perhaps even typical. Many in personnel look upon unions as creating enormous problems, additional work, and expense. The degree to which a union presents constraints or opportunities to personnel depends on the individual situation and the posture of union-management relations in that situation. There are, however, potential advantages in almost every situation, and these benefits should be fully explored.

Summary. The *Introduction* was intended merely to introduce the topic of labor unions and their relation to personnel administration. As can be seen, the impacts are many and complex. Unions are now a fixed part of human-resource management. They remain viable in manufacturing, but are becoming increasingly large and powerful in the white-collar and professional jobs, both because the relative numbers of these jobs is increasing and because job holders have seen the effective results of collective action and power.

Organized labor in this country is still very much an emerging and changing movement, influenced heavily by general economic conditions, the political climate, public sentiment, and past precedent. Recent controversies, such as the right of public employees to strike, compulsory (forced) arbitration, and bargaining for such noneconomic issues as quality of working life, reflect these influences. The typical union member has also changed to reflect the demographic and value shifts in the country. Younger workers who are more mobile, more independent, better educated, and perhaps concerned with more than just economic gains, are now union members. Their job expectations are high and are channeled into areas typically not considered important in unions.

These trends may change, but the importance of organized labor and collective bargaining will no doubt remain and unions will continue to be a variable for personnel staffs to consider as they perform their duties. While some obvious impacts, both positive and negative, on personnel administration were discussed here, generalizations are tenuous in that their truth necessarily depends on each specific situation. However, a union's presence shifts some human-resource-program priorities, specifies the design and implementation procedures of others, amends others significantly, and necessitates and/or precludes others entirely. Personnel or human-resource decisions and programs are seldom effective if the presence of a labor union is not given its appropriate weight in personnel planning.

PROCEDURE

Overview. In this exercise, a set of review questions is given to assess your understanding of labor laws and terminology. Then, an example of the economic cost of a change in fringe benefits is presented. A questionnaire is designed to help you become familiar with actual labor-contract language and its possible effects on personnel programs. Next, several case studies of grievance situations are given. You are to analyze these cases and act as arbitrator. A simulated contract negotiation is also included in the exercise.

PART A

STEP 1: Review the *Introduction* and the *Appendixes* in this exercise and then answer the questions on Form 1. Discuss your answers in a small group and/or compare your answers with those your implementor reads.

TIME: About 35 minutes.

PART B

STEP 2: Read Form 2 carefully. Some background information and current contract provisions regarding benefits for an organization are given. Then, fill out Form 3 in order to compute the actual dollar costs of various changes in benefits written into a union contract. State any assumptions you made in computing the costs and decide whether or not it is feasible for the organization to proceed with a new project it has planned, based on its total anticipated labor costs.

TIME: About 40 minutes

STEP 3: Form 4 requires the use of a union contract. Obtain a current contract from a local or national union office, a union member you may know, the contract used where you work, a library, or use portions of one supplied by your implementor. Then, find the relevant articles in the contract which are noted on Form 4 and copy (or paraphase) these where indicated on the form. Familiarize yourself with the language used. Answer the questions posed after each contract article in order to become acquainted with the impact contract provisions might have on other personnel programs.

TIME: About 50 minutes.

PART C

STEP 4: Form 5 contains brief descriptions of four grievances. Read each one carefully and note that each grievance has gone to arbitration— that is, it could *not* be settled through the contract's normal grievance procedure. You are the arbitrator who must decide each case. Note the issue posed on the form. Decide whether the action taken by the organization was proper and justified. Decide whether or not you will allow the action to stand as is or will amend it in some way. Include your rationale in the space provided and state any assumptions about contract provisions or language you have made.

TIME: About 55 minutes.

PART D

STEP 5: Form 6 contains general instructions for participants in a simulated contract-renegotiation activity and Forms 7 and 8 contain background information pertinent to the activity. Form 9 contains a statement of current contract provisions for the newspaper around which the simulation is developed. Read these forms carefully.

TIME: About 35 minutes

STEP 6: Divide into groups of five or seven persons. Designate either two or three persons to be negotiators for the union and two or three to be negotiators for management. Remaining persons are observers/arbitrators. Once the roles have been assigned, management-negotiating-team members should read *only* Form 10, which contains a statement of their initial position and their roles. Union-negotiating-team members should read *only* Form 11, containing the same information for the union team. Observers should read Forms 10, 11, and 12. Negotiating-team members should be prepared to conduct a renegotiation of the union contract for the *Daily Post*. They should concentrate on the issues given to each on Forms 10 and 11 and use their role descriptions as a jumping off place for their behavior. Both sides, as well as the observer/arbitrator(s), should read Form 13, which contains some guidelines for negotiations, and should also be very familiar with the background data presented in earlier forms of Part D. The ultimate objective is to renegotiate the contract (see Step 7). Members of each team may want to meet to discuss their strategy and to formulate their initial proposal, which can be in writing.

TIME: About 25 to 75 minutes, depending on whether strategy meetings are held and their length.

STEP 7: The actual renegotiation should now begin, using the issues noted on Forms 10 and 11 as the primary agenda. Plan to negotiate for about one to two hours. The teams may want to break once or twice to confer or caucus amongst themselves as proposals are brought up and/or preliminary agreements are or are not made. Team members should attempt to bargain effectively in relation to the particular organization they represent (i.e., union or management) and to bargain in good faith (e.g., do not storm out of the room and refuse to bargain). Observers should note the answers to questions on Part I of Form 12 as they carefully observe the negotiation process. If the agreement is reached through bargaining, the observer should fill out Part III of Form 12 fully in the presence of negotiators.

The teams should then discuss the process and the fairness and appropriateness of their contract. The observer can provide feedback on their behavior during negotiations.

TIME: About one-and-one-half hours to two-and-one-half hours.

STEP 8: If the bargaining results in a deadlock over one or more issues, binding arbitration will be used to resolve the deadlock. The observer(s) then becomes the arbitrator and listens to both sides, weighs information and arguments, perhaps consulting other sources (see *For Further Reading*) for precedent and background information, and makes a final decision. The proposals of either side could be accepted, a compromise struck, or a new alternative developed and used. The arbitrator then fills out Part II of Form 12 and the discussion noted in the second paragraph of Step 7 above is conducted.

TIME: About 45 minutes (not including the discussion counted in the time estimate given in Step 7).

FOR FURTHER READING

Acuff, F. L., and M. Villere. "Games Negotiators Play." *Business Horizons* 19, no. 1 (February 1976): 70–76. (I)

Allen, D. A. "A Systems View of Labor Negotiations." *Personnel Journal* 50, no. 2 (1971): 103–114. (I)

Atwood, J. F. "Collective Bargaining's Challenge: Five Imperatives for Public Managers." *Public Personnel Management* 5 (January–February 1976): 24–32. (I)

Barbash, J. *American Unions: Structure, Government, and Politics.* New York: Random House, 1967. (I)

Beal, E. F., E. D. Wickersham, and P. Kienest. *The Practice of Collective Bargaining.* 3d ed. Homewood, Ill.: Irwin, 1973. (I)

Berquist, V. A. "Women's Participation in Labor Organizations." *Monthly Labor Review* 97, no. 10 (1974): 3–9. (I–R)

Black, J. M. *Positive Discipline.* New York: AMACOM, 1970. (I)

Blake, R. R., H. A. Shepard, and J. S. Mouton. *Managing Inter Group Conflict in Industry.* Houston: Gulf, 1964. (I)

Bloch, R. I. "Race Discrimination in Industry and the Grievance Process." *Labor Law Journal* 21 (1970): 627–644. (I)

Bowers, M. H. *Labor Relations in the Public Safety Services.* Chicago: International Personnel Management Assoc., 1974. (I)

Brown, M. A. Collective Bargaining on the Campus: Professors, Associations, and Unions. *Labor Law Journal* 21 (March 1970): 167–181. (II)

Bureau of National Affairs. *Grievance Guide.* 4th ed. Washington, D.C.: BNA, 1972. (I)

Chamberlain, N. W. *Collective Bargaining.* New York: McGraw-Hill, 1956. (I)

Davis, P. A. "Before the NLRB Election: What You Can and Can't Do." *Personnel* 44 (July–August 1967): 8–18. (I)

Derber, M., W. E. Chalmers, and R. Stagner. "The Labor Contract: Provisions and Practice." *Personnel* 54 (1958): 19–30. (I)

Dubin, R. "Power and Union-Management Relations." *Administrative Science Quarterly* 2 (1957): 60–81. (II)

Dubin, R. "Attachment to Work and Union Militancy." *Industrial Relations* 12 (1973): 57–64. (II–R)

Dunlop, J. T. *Industrial Relations Systems.* New York: Holt, 1958. (II)

Dunlop, J. T., and N. W. Chamberlain, eds. *Frontiers of Collective Bargaining.* New York: Harper, 1967. (II)

Ellis, D. S., L. Jacobs, and G. Mills. "A Union Authorization Election: The Key to Winning." *Personnel Journal* 51 (1972): 246–254. (I)

England, G. W., N. C. Agarwal, and R. E. Trerise. "Union Leaders and Managers: A Comparison of

Value Systems." *Industrial Relations* 10 (1971): 211–226. (II–R)

Fielly, A. C. *Interpersonal Conflict Resolution.* Glenview, Ill.: Scott Foresman, 1974. (I)

Frey, R. L., and J. S. Adams. "The Negotiator's Dilemma: Simultaneous In-Group and Out-Group Conflict." *Journal of Experimental Social Psychology* (1972): 331–346. (II–R)

Gilroy, T. P., and A. C. Russo. *Bargaining Unit Issues: Problems, Criteria, Tactics.* Chicago: International Personnel Management Assoc., 1975. (I)

Healy, J. J., ed. *Creative Collective Bargaining.* Englewood Cliffs, N.J.: Prentice-Hall, 1965. (I)

Heneman, H. G., and D. Yoder. *Labor Economics.* 2d ed. Cincinnati: South-Western, 1965. (I)

Herman, M. G., and N. Kogan. "Negotiation in Leader and Delegate Groups." *Journal of Conflict Resolution* 12 (1968): 332–344. (II–R)

"Public Sector Arbitration; Symposium." *Industrial Relations* 14 (October 1975): 302–326. (II)

Kennedy, R. F. *The Enemy Within.* New York: Harper, 1960. (I)

Kennedy, T. "Freedom to Strike Is in the Public Interest." *Harvard Business Review* 48, no. 4 (July–August 1970): 45–57. (I)

Klimoski, R. J., and R. A. Ash. "Accountability and Negotiator Behavior." *Organizational Behavior and Human Performance* 11 (1974): 409–425. (II–R)

McKelvey, J. T. "Sex and the Single Arbitrator." *Industrial and Labor Relations Review* 24 (1971): 335–353. (I)

Mills, C. W. *White Collar.* New York: Oxford, 1951. (I)

Mills, D. Q. "Wage Determination in Contract Construction." *Industrial Relations* 10 (1971): 72–85. (II–R)

Muench, G. A. "A Clinical Psychologist's Treatment of Labor-Management Conflicts." *Personnel Psychology* 13 (1960): 165–172. (I)

Myers, A. H., and D. P. Twomey. *Labor Law and Legislation.* 5th ed. Cincinnati: South-Western, 1975. (I)

Myers, M. S. *Managing with Unions.* Reading, Mass.: Addison-Wesley, 1976. (I)

Nash, A. N., and J. B. Miner, eds. *Personnel and Labor Relations. An Evolutionary Approach.* New York: Macmillan, 1973. (I)

National Industrial Conference Board. *White Collar Unionization.* New York: Conference Board, 1970. (I)

Paterson, L. T., and J. Liebert. *Management Strike Handbook.* Chicago: International Personnel Management Association, 1975. (I)

Pattefer, J. C. "Effective Grievance Arbitration." *California Management Review* 13, no. 2 (1970): 12–18. (I)

Robbins, S. R. *Managing Organizational Conflict.* Englewood Cliffs, N.J.: Prentice-Hall, 1975. (I)

Rubin, J. Z., and B. R. Brown. *The Social Psychology of Bargaining and Negotiation.* New York: Academic, 1975. (I)

Sayles, L. R., and G. Strauss. *The Local Union.* Rev. ed. New York: Harcourt Brace, 1967.

Selekman, B. M. *Labor Relations and Human Relations.* New York: McGraw-Hill, 1947. (I)

Sherman, V. C. "Unionism and the Nonunion Company." *Personnel Journal* 48 (1969): 413–422. (I)

Skibbins, G. J., and C. S. Weymur. "The 'Right to Work' Controversy." *Harvard Business Review* 44, no. 4 (July–August 1966): 6–19. (I)

Slichter, S. H. *Union Policies and Industrial Management.* Washington, D.C.: Brookings, 1941. (II)

Sloane, A. A., and F. Whitney. *Labor Relations.* 2d ed. Englewood Cliffs, N.J.: Prentice-Hall, 1972. (I)

Stagner, R., and H. Rosen. *Psychology of Union-Management Relations.* Belmont, Cal.: Wadsworth, 1965. (I)

Staudohar, P. D. "Results of Final-Offer Arbitration of Bargaining Disputes." *California Management Review* 18 (Fall 1975): 57–61. (I)

Thomas, K. "Conflict and Conflict Management." In M. D. Dunnette, ed., *Handbook of Industrial and Organizational Psychology.* Chicago: Rand McNally, 1976. (II)

Vidmar, N. "Effects of Representational Rules and Mediators on Negotiation Effectiveness." *Journal of Personality and Social Psychology* 17 (1971): 48–58. (II–R)

Vogel, A. "Your Clerical Workers Are Ripe for Unionism." *Harvard Business Review* 49, no. 2 (March–April 1971): 48–54. (I)

Walton, R. E., and R. B. McKersie. *A Behavioral Theory of Labor Negotiations.* New York: McGraw-Hill, 1965. (II)

Webb, S., and B. Webb. *Industrial Democracy.* London: Longmans, 1914. (I)

Weitzman, J. P. *The Scope of Bargaining in Public Employment.* New York: Praeger, 1975. (II)

Whyte, W. F. *Men at Work.* Homewood, Ill.: Dorsey, 1961. (I)

Wirtz, W. W. *Labor and the Public Interest.* New York: Harper, 1964. (I)

Wortman, M. S., and C. W. Randle. *Collective Bargaining: Principles and Practices.* 2d ed. Boston: Houghton Mifflin, 1966. (I)

APPENDIX A

Important Federal Labor Laws and Their Provisions (most terms used here are defined in Appendix B).

Title and Date	Major Provisions
A. Sherman "Anti-Trust" Act 1890	As applied to labor organizations through court interpretation, the act was used to show that certain union practices, such as the boycott, were illegal, as they restrained interstate trade.
B. Clayton Act 1914	Noted that the labor of humans was not a commodity or article of commerce. Therefore, unions were not illegal *per se*. No injunctions against unions could be made, unless necessary in order to prevent irreparable injury to property. The right to strike was also stated. Courts interpreted the law somewhat unfavorably as far as unions were concerned, limiting the use of boycotts and allowing unions to be sued even though they were not incorporated organizations.
C. Railway Labor Act 1926 (amended 1934, 1951)	Declared that employees have the right to bargain collectively through their own representatives. Yellow-dog contracts and closed shops were outlawed; union shops, check-off, elections of representatives were permitted. Extended to cover air carriers and subsidiary activities of railroads (e.g. deliveries, terminals).
D. Norris-LaGuardia Act 1932	Prohibits use of injunctions in labor disputes. (Injunctions, after the Clayton Act, had become very popular to prohibit picketing, etc.). Federal courts could still use injunctions if unlawful acts were threatened, occurred, or were likely and there was no adequate remedy for damages. Injunctions could not be used to restrain employees from refusing to work or from being members of unions. Parties seeking relief must have made reasonable efforts to settle disputes by negotiation.
E. National Industrial Recovery Act 1933	A foundation for the 1935 Wagner Act; states employees have the right to bargain collectively. Created National Labor Board as a temporary agency to deal with labor problems.
F. National Labor Relations Act (Wagner Act) 1935	Declared that public policy of United States was to encourage and facilitate collective bargaining. Employees had the right to join and form labor organizations and elect representatives. Prohibited "unfair labor practices" of employers, including the following: interfering in employees' rights noted above, dominating labor unions, discriminating against employees on the basis of union membership, refusing to bargain collectively, and discriminating against employees for filing charges under the Act. Created the National Labor Relations Board (NLRB) to administer the Act. The Board was to prevent unfair labor practices, certify unions as bargaining agents, and determine bargaining units.
G. Taft-Hartley Labor Management Relations Act 1947 (amended 1951)	Specified and changed Wagner Act Provisions and NLRB. NLRB increased to five members. Provisions for judicial review of Board decisions was made. Specified the following union unfair labor practices: restraining or coercing employees in exercise of their rights under the Act, causing or attempting to cause employer to discriminate against employee on basis of union membership, refusing to bargain in good faith, inducing or encouraging workers to stop working in order to force employer to bargain with a union when another union has been certified as bargaining agent, charging excessive or discriminatory fee for union membership, causing or attempting to cause an employer to pay for work not performed. Established the Federal Mediation and Conciliation Service (FMCS) as a separate agency to mediate disputes. Attempted to remove communists from positions of influence in unions; required financial statements of unions to be filed, including expense receipts and officers' salaries; forbade strikes against federal government.

APPENDIX A

Important Federal Labor Laws and Their Provisions (most terms used here are defined in Appendix B).

Title and Date	Major Provisions
H. Labor Management Reporting and Disclosure Act (Landrum-Griffin Act) 1959	Allowed states to act in situations where NLRB refused to act, in organizations NLRB did not cover, etc.; unions cannot coerce or boycott against a secondary employer; retailers of products of manufacturers with whom a union has a dispute cannot picket on this account; no group may be forced to agree not to handle products of a struck employer (hot-cargo agreements); closed shops were permitted in the construction industry.

Periodic public reports are demanded covering employers, unions, consultants, employees.

Title I, a "Bill of Rights" for union members, included provisions assuring members equal rights in nominating candidates, voting, and attending and participating in meetings. Procedures for dues, fees, and assessments are specified and disciplinary measures taken by unions against their members are limited by rules. Copies of the union agreement must be given to all members. Union elections are controlled in order to help assure democracy. Union internal affairs, such as financial affairs, use of trusteeships, and domination by racketeers, are controlled. |
| Other laws | Several other laws have direct or indirect impact on labor relations, but all were not specifically designed to apply to labor unions. They include the Davis-Bacon Act of 1931 (amended 1950), the Walsh-Healey Public Contracts Act of 1936, the Byrnes Anti-Strike-Breaking Act of 1938, the Hobbs Anti-Racketeering Act of 1946, the Lea Act of 1946, the Welfare and Pension Plans Disclosure Act of 1958 (amended 1962), Title VII of the Civil Rights Act of 1964 (amended 1972), The Fair Labor Standards Act of 1938 (amended 1955, 1961, 1963, 1966, 1967, 1969, 1972), the Service Contracts Act of 1965, and the Occupational Safety and Health Act of 1970. These laws, as well as others, affect labor practices and thus personnel policies. Several are explained in previous exercises [see also S. M. Myers, *Managing without Unions* (Reading, Mass.: Addison-Wesley, 1976), for a more detailed discussion]. |

APPENDIX B

A Glossary of Common Terms in the Areas of Labor Unions/Collective Bargaining

AFFILIATED UNIONS

Unions belonging to a larger, national organization, such as the AFL-CIO.

AFL-CIO

A large federation of several unions which was formed in 1955 from the Congress of Industrial Organizations (CIO) and the American Federation of Labor (AFL). The CIO was formed in 1938 to organize unskilled and semiskilled workers in mass-production industries and was the outgrowth of a minority faction of the AFL (founded in 1886). The AFL was primarily craft oriented.

AGENCY SHOP

All employees in the bargaining unit pay dues to the union, but do not have to join it.

APPEAL

The recourse available to a party when a decision is made against it; rules establish the appeal procedure for grievances, often resulting in arbitration.

ARBITRATOR

An impartial umpire both parties agree to use to resolve disputes by making an award or decision after weighing positions and facts; a judge.

AUTHORIZATION CARDS

Cards signed by workers and accepted by NLRB, indicating their intention to authorize the union to be their bargaining representative.

AUTOMATIC EXTENSION

A clause in a union contract which allows the contract to remain in effect after its expiration date as long as negotiations are in progress regarding its renewal.

AWARD

The decision rendered by an arbitrator; typically must be written.

BARGAINING AGENT

The union certified by the NCRB to represent a group of workers, jobs, etc. in negotiations with management.

BARGAINING UNIT

Those jobs, occupations, industries, locales, crafts, or organizations included in the representation of a union.

BILATERAL

Negotiated jointly with unions and management.

BUSINESS AGENT

The local union official in the business union who represents the members in matters of economic and political concern.

BUSINESS UNION

A union that emphasizes economic gains by collective action.

CERTIFICATION

State or federal labor relations boards' sanctioning, after a vote is taken according to various procedures, that a bargaining agent exists.

CHECK-OFF

Procedure whereby union dues are automatically deducted from workers' pay checks and forwarded to the union by the employer.

CLOSED SHOP

Only union members can be employed. The union agrees to supply workers.

CLOSED (ANTI-UNION) SHOP

An organization that refuses employment to union members; typically illegal.

COLLECTIVE BARGAINING

The process by which conditions of employment are determined by representatives of unions and management. The representatives are authorized to act as agents for the groups and the method of reaching agreement consists of each side offering proposals and counterproposals.

COMPANY UNIONS

A labor organization consisting of workers of only one company.

COMPULSORY ARBITRATION

Two parties are forced by law to submit their disagreements to an arbitrator who will decide them.

CONCILIATOR

A third party used to attempt to establish communications between union and management and help facilitate an agreement.

CONSENT ELECTION

An election to recognize a bargaining agent (union), held when the petition to hold a representation election is not contested; the election is held by secret ballot without a preelection hearing.

CONTRACT ADMINISTRATION

Interpreting and applying the terms of the union contract on a day-to-day basis; operating an organization under a union contract.

CRAFT UNION

A union consisting of members who all perform a single craft for their livelihood (e.g., typographers).

DECERTIFICATION

Not recognizing a union as a collective bargaining agent when it has been one.

DISCHARGE

Terminating an employees's association with an organization.

DUE PROCESS

The right given to someone to use the entire existing grievance procedure or other procedures established to resolve disputes before an action stands; typically used in reference to public-sector labor relations.

ECONOMIC STRIKE

Union members stop working in order to enforce their demands for higher wages or other benefits.

ESCALATOR CLAUSES

Contract articles that provide for automatic annual increases in a specified area if the index used to evaluate the area rises (e.g., escalator clauses for cost-of-living index changes are reflected in increased wages).

FEATHERBEDDING

Restriction of work output to maintain earnings and protect jobs.

GOOD FAITH

In bargaining, the tacit agreement that parties must communicate and negotiate, match proposal with counterproposals if they are not accepted, and agree to meet with the other party.

GRIEVANCE

A formal complaint filed by a worker against an organization due to any one of a number of actions it or a particular person has taken in regard to the worker.

GRIEVANCE PROCEDURE

The formal, agreed-on procedure for handling a grievance; usually consists of three or more sequential steps, beginning with a supervisor and a steward and perhaps ending in arbitration or mediation.

INDEPENDENT UNIONS

Unions without any larger affiliation, either by their own choosing or at the insistence of an affiliation.

INDUSTRIAL UNION

A union consisting of members with a variety of skills (as well as unskilled, semiskilled, and craft members) who are employed in a single industry (e.g., automobile industry).

INJUCTION

Legally precluding a union (or management) from certain acts or activities (e.g., picketing).

JUST CAUSE

The circumstances under which an organization's action (e.g., discharge) is considered permissible, according to the terms of an agreement and other considerations involving the particular situation.

KNIGHTS OF LABOR

An organization of craft, skilled, and semiskilled labor formed in Philadelphia in 1869. It had over 700,000 members by 1886, but declined very rapidly in power and size due to unsuccessful strikes and the diverse interests of its member unions.

LABOR CONTRACT

A written statement of provisions and terms of employment which represents the outcome of the collective-bargaining process.

LABOR MOVEMENT

The development and rise to power of labor unions which has accompanied the long-term process of industrialization or partial industrialization.

LOCKOUT

The shutting down of an organization by its management or their refusal to permit union members to work in order to force a union to cease certain tactics or to preclude the acceptance of certain demands made by a union.

MANAGEMENT RIGHTS

Those conditions management initially sets either unilaterally or bilaterally (i.e., with the union) as the status quo; these areas are precluded from negotiation and are reserved exclusively for management control.

MASS PICKETING

Large groups of people attempting to block the way of those wishing to enter a building; a protest tactic.

MASTER CONTRACT

A union agreement negotiated with several employers and an employer's association within an industry and/or area.

MEDIATOR

A third party who attempts to resolve conflict and impasse between union and management by actively suggesting compromises (overlaps with conciliation in practice).

NEGOTIATION

The process of making proposals and counterproposals, bargaining, and arriving at an eventual agreement, if possible.

NO-STRIKE CLAUSE

A union agreement clause forbidding work stoppage and lockouts for the duration of the contract.

OPEN SHOP

Organizations who refuse to recognize any union as a bargaining agent and insist on dealing with employees individually; typically illegal.

ORGANIZED LABOR

Labor unions and their members; formal groups of workers.

PICKETING

Placing persons with signs noting a strike is in progress at locations around an organization and at entrances; the picketers publicize the strike and hope to prevent workers (and others) from entering the building(s).

POLITICAL ACTION (UNION)

Union's degree of participation and initiative in the political process; includes support of candidates and issues with human resources and financial assistance, educational material, endorsements, etc.

POSTING

Notifying workers of new job openings, transfer and promotion opportunities, etc., by placing written notice in a conspicuous place (e.g., bulletin boards); place and duration of posting are typically fixed by contract provisions.

PREFERENTIAL SHOP

Organization in which management gives first chance or opportunity for employment to union members.

PRIMARY BOYCOTT

The refusal of a union to allow its members to purchase goods or services of an organization involved in a labor dispute.

PUBLIC SECTOR

Organizations belonging to federal, state, or municipal governments, agencies, administrative boards, etc., which are essentially "public" organizations and are nonprofit.

RANK AND FILE

Union membership.

REOPENING CLAUSE

An article in a union contract which permits one or more opportunities to renegotiate specified terms throughout the duration of the contract.

SECONDARY BOYCOTT

Unions' attempts to influence various third parties, such as suppliers, customers, and the public at large, to cease purchasing products or services from an organization involved in a labor dispute; generally illegal.

SENIORITY SYSTEM

The procedure for deciding preferences in the assignment of jobs, vacation selection, transfer, promotion, shifts, etc. based on job tenure; longer tenure indicates higher seniority.

SIT-DOWN STRIKE

Union members cease working but do not leave their work stations.

SLOW-DOWN STRIKE

Union members limit or restrict output while at work.

SWEETHEART CLAUSE

A general policy statement, typically included at the beginning of an agreement, that indicates the spirit with which each side enters into the contract; specific responsibilities are spelled out and each side may promise to cooperate.

SYMPATHETIC STRIKE

Union members stop working to support other union members on strike in the same or another organization.

VOLUNTARY CHECKOFF

Procedure whereby employer deducts union dues (and often other fees) from paychecks and forwards these amounts to the union, only if the worker gives his or her approval to do so.

UNFAIR LABOR PRACTICES

Practices relating to labor management relations, contract negotiation and administration, and the relationships management and unions each have with their employees and members, respectively, which are strictly prohibited by various labor laws.

UNILATERAL DECISION

Decided independently by either the union or by management.

UNION

A continuing, long-term formal association of workers formed to advance their interests.

UNION SECURITY

A union's degree of strength and/or susceptibility to undermining and weakening; provisions in a contract designed to help assure the continuation and power of a union; right of a union to speak for its members; the assurance the employer will recognize the union.

UNION SHOP

An organization in which all employees in the bargaining unit must become union members within a certain period of time after they are hired.

UNION STEWARD

The counterpart of an organization's supervisor or foreman; he or she works on the job with union members and represents them in disputes or grievances with the organization.

WILDCAT (OUTLAW) STRIKE

A cessation of work by union members undertaken without proper authorization from union officials; often occurs quickly, without warning.

WORK RULES

Those rules specifying the pace of work and the amount of human resources to be assigned to various tasks.

YELLOW-DOG CONTRACT

A contract workers sign as they begin employment, stating they will not join a union; typically illegal.

Name _____ Group Number _____

Date _____ Class Section _____ Hour _____ Score _____

PART A

Form 1 A Review of Your Understanding of Labor Laws and Terminology

As a review of labor laws and terminology, answer the questions below very briefly.

A. Labor Laws

1. List each of the laws discussed in *Appendix A* of the *Introduction* by its identifying letter and tell whether each was favorable, unfavorable, or neutral from the unions' point of view. Indicate very briefly why you answered as you did.

2. Regarding their application to labor unions, what were the differences between the Sherman and Clayton Acts?

3. List employer and union unfair labor practices.

4. What types of disclosures did unions and management have to make under the Landrum-Griffin Act? Why do you feel these disclosures and provisions had to be legislated?

B. Terminology

1. Distinguish between wildcat, sit-down, sympathetic, and slow-down strikes.

2. Distinguish between conciliation, mediation, arbitration, negotiation, and bargaining.

3. Distinguish between business, craft, industrial, company, affiliated, and unaffiliated unions.

4. Distinguish between the AFL-CIO and the Knights of Labor.

5. Distinguish between closed, open, union, agency, preferential, and closed (antiunion) shops.

6. What does the term "bargain in good faith" actually mean in practice?

7. Why do you suppose primary boycotts are typically legal and secondary boycotts are typically illegal?

PART B

**Form 2 Computation of Benefits Costs Due to Changes Anticipated in Union Contract:
The Built Fast to Last Corporation**

The Built Fast to Last Construction, Development, and Real Estate Corporation, a large company in the Northwest, employs several types of workers, including skilled and craft laborers, clerical workers, professionals (e.g., such as accountants and architects), salespersons, etc. It is deciding whether or not to purchase and develop an 850-acre plot of land in an ideal suburban location. Condominiums and some single-family detached houses are planned for the land.

Built Fast to Last must consider several factors as they make their decision. Among these are the current local supply and demand for housing, the location, interest rates on construction loans, zoning and sewer permits, future plans for building a shopping area, and attracting light industry to the area. One significant consideration, of course, is labor cost. Because so many different types of workers are required over the two-year period of development, wage, salary, and fringe-benefit costs are difficult to project. However, since the vast majority of the potential workers will be unionized, current union contracts, coupled with historical company accounting data, are quite helpful.

Of all the types of workers needed, Built Fast to Last is most concerned with plumbers and pipefitters. Very shortly after the project is scheduled to begin, the current labor contract with the plumbers expires. (The company is large enough to maintain its own permanent force of plumbers who work on whatever project is ongoing.) After the new contract is negotiated, Built Fast to Last will certainly have increased labor costs, for the plumbers have been publicizing their need for substantially improved benefits. They argue their real income has declined considerably due to inflation over the last three years, but perhaps more important, their demand for a significant pay increase three years ago was fulfilled at the expense, they feel, of fringe benefits. They make it very clear that they are going to "catch up" on benefits this time!

Built Fast to Last will operate on a small profit margin in the proposed project due to projected increases in materials and labor costs during the two years of the project. The plumber's new contract could add enough to the company's fixed labor costs to make the project only marginally profitable. Since no other major group of unionized workers required for the project will need to renegotiate their contract during the term of the project and since Built Fast to Last needs to use ninety of its plumbers for two years, any additional costs resulting from the new contract could be very large and could therefore affect the decision to proceed with the project. To make matters worse, these costs can only be estimated—the contract expires three months after the project is to begin and thus exact costs are unknown.

Built Fast to Last has reliable information concerning what the plumbers will ask for in the new contract in the way of wage and benefit increases. It also knows its current benefit cost per plumber, based on figures from a project just completed. The relevant figures for current benefit costs and anticipated changes being sought by the unions are given below. Built Fast to Last has decided that if the anticipated benefit costs for plumbers are estimated at lower than $2,200,000 for all of the plumbers over the two years of the project (one-and-three-fourths years after the new contract would take effect), it would go ahead with the project. If the figure is higher than $2,200,000, it must reconsider and perhaps attempt to look over its estimates of overtime, other salary costs, material costs, interest payments, etc., to be sure they are accurate before it makes a final decision.

Look over the figures and data below, compute the benefits costs for the plumbers asked for on Form 3, and tell whether the additional benefit costs are within the guidelines given above.

Current Benefits Costs for Plumbers Hired by Built Fast to Last*

Specific benefit	Dollar amount	Proposed contract change anticipated by Built Fast to Last (increases over present dollar amounts, in percent)
Employee Security and Health		
Life, health, and accident insurance	469.00	Increase an average of 5%
Workman's compensation	272.00	Increase an average of 4%
Sick leave	593.00	Increase an average of 8%
Pension plan	550.00	Increase an average of 3%
Social security	708.00	No effect
Unemployment insurance	32.00	Increase an average of 4%
Supplemental unemployment benefits	321.00	Increase an average of 4%
Severance pay	187.00	No effect

* These are average costs per worker per year. Built Fast to Last employs plumbers year-round. The costs are based on $18,750, the average yearly wage of the plumbers employed on a current project. The wage does not include overtime. The contract changes will go into effect three months after the two-year construction project will begin. The plumbers work seven-hour days, five days a week. Two week vacations are average, as are ten paid holidays.

Specific benefit	Dollar amount	Proposed contract change anticipated by Built Fast to Last (increases over present dollar amounts, in percent)
Time Not Worked		
Vacations	3474.00	Increase an average of 10%
Holidays	800.00	Increase an average of 10%
Personal excused absences	92.00	Increase an average of 10%
Grievances and negotiations	117.00	No effect
Reporting time	156.00	No effect
Employee Services		
Christmas bonuses	475.00	No effect
Social and recreational opportunities	45.00	No effect
Educational opportunities and subsidies	70.00	Increase an average of 11%
Total	*8361.00*	
Basic wage per hour	11.08	Increase 6% first year
		Increase 8% second year
Average overtime hours/worker/year (overtime rate = $1\frac{1}{2}$ regular rate)	72	No effect
TOTAL	_____	

Name _____   Group Number _____

Date _____   Class Section _____   Hour _____   Score _____

PART B

Form 3 Computation of Anticipated Change in Cost of Benefits for Built Fast to Last Plumbers*

Anticipated New Cost of Benefits and Wage Increase Per Plumber:

Employee Security and Health

    Life, health, and accident insurance   _____

    Workman's compensation   _____

    Sick leave   _____

    Pension plan   _____

    Social security   _____

    Unemployment compensation   _____

    Supplemental unemployment benefits   _____

    Severance pay   _____

Time Not Worked

    Vacations   _____

    Holidays   _____

    Personal excused absences   _____

    Grievance and negotiations   _____

    Reporting time   _____

Employee Services

    Christmas bonus   _____

    Social and recreational opportunities   _____

    Educational opportunities and subsidies   _____

TOTAL   _____

Total per plumber over two-year period of project   _____

Total for ninety plumbers over project period   _____

Should Built Fast to Last reconsider the project based on its anticipated benefit and wage cost? Why or why not?

---

* Not accounting for inflation

Name _____   Group Number _____

Date _____   Class Section _____   Hour _____   Score _____

PART B

Form 4 Contractual Language of Union Agreements and Its Impact on Other Personnel Programs

In order to familiarize yourself with the language of union contracts, secure one or more actual agreements from local unions. (These can be easily obtained by calling the union and explaining the reason for the request). Once a few contracts are obtained, or some sample contract language is given to you by your implementor, find the articles or specific paragraphs dealing with each of the issues listed below and copy or paraphrase the articles in the spaces provided. Then, answer each of the questions posed about each issue in order to consider how such issues would impact various management decisions.

Article 1:   Seniority

Copy or paraphrase contract articles/paragraphs here:

Questions:

1. What impact might the seniority article have on layoff and promotion decisions?

2. What impact might the seniority article have on job evaluation and classification?

3. What impact might the seniority article have on scheduling vacations?

4. What impact might the seniority article have on performance appraisal?

Article 2:   Layoff and Rehire

Copy or paraphrase contract article/paragraphs here:

Questions:

1. What impact might the layoff/rehire article have on selection programs?

2. What impact might the layoff/rehire article have on human-resources planning and forecasting?

Article 3:   Rates and Wages

Copy or paraphrase contract article/paragraphs here:

Questions:

1. What impact would the rates-and-wages article have on wage and salary administration?

2. What impact would the rates-and-wages article have on piece-rate and bonus-plan administration?

Article 4:   Hours of Work

Copy or paraphrase contract article/paragraphs here:

Questions:
1. What impact might the hours-of-work article have on wage and salary administration?

2. What impact might the hours-of-work article have on training programs?

Article 5:   Duration and Termination

Copy or paraphrase contract article/paragraphs here:

Questions:
1. What impact might the duration-and-termination article have on human-resource-planning programs?

2. What impact might the duration-and-termination article have on selection programs?

Name _____   Group Number _____

Date _____   Class Section _____   Hour _____   Score _____

PART C

Form 5 Grievance Issues and Analyses

Read each of the following sets of facts pertaining to a situation in which a grievance was filed. Then, read the issue of the grievance—it is stated as a question. Assume each grievance has progressed through the entire normal grievance procedure and, according to contract provisions, must be settled by an arbitrator. Assume the role of the arbitrator and write out your decision and a rationale for it. If you assume there are specific contractual agreements that would have a direct bearing on your decision, state these assumptions.

Grievance Situation 1:

Facts: A seven-day suspension was imposed on a grievant for failing to return to his assigned duties at the request of his supervisor. Due to various previous disputes, the grievant would not assume his regular duties until he was able to meet with the assistant plant manager. When called in for a meeting with his supervisor, the grievant allegedly made offensive remarks and was subsequently discharged. The discharge came one month after the suspension. The supervisor reported harassment and threats by the grievant. Insubordination justifies suspension according to the contract. The supervisor, during the month between the initiation of the suspension and the discharge, did not act on continued derogatory remarks, threats, and failure to assume assigned duties on the part of the grievant. These were ignored. The grievance was filed after the discharge. According to the contract, discharge is considered a last-resort action after "every reasonable effort is made" to restore proper attitudes.

Issue: Was there just cause for the suspension?

Was there just cause for the discharge?

Decision and Rationale:

Grievance Situation 2:

Facts: The grievant reported to work late after calling her supervisor at 10:15 A.M. and claiming she overslept. She was advised to wait until 1:00 P.M. to report to work (at a loss of one-half-day's pay), as she was reporting more than thirty minutes late. She questioned the rule and the supervisor explained it. When the grievant appeared at work at 11:00 A.M., the supervisor noted the grievant's unsteady manner, belligerence, and strong odor of alcohol. The grievant was then suspended and ultimately discharged. The grievant had been suspended in the past for intoxication and for possession of intoxicants. She had spurned all offers (by the supervisor and others) of assistance for this problem. The supervisor claimed the grievant was unable to properly perform her duties. Previous suspensions were severe enough in length of time and in number to warrant dismissal under the contract. The union claimed that the grievant, a fourteen-year employee, was unduly punished, based on the particular circumstances.

Issue: Was the grievant discharged for sufficient cause?

Decision and Rationale:

Grievance Situation 3:

Facts: While working at his desk, a general foreman observed the grievant operating a nearby transactor. (This machine is used to record workers' attendance. Each worker has a badge that is to be inserted into the transactor at the end of each day. The worker's number, as well as the time of insertion, is recorded electronically by the machine). He heard two distinct operations of the transactor. The grievant had his back to the foreman and thus the foreman did not actually see the grievant record two badges, although his motions and the machine's noises indicated he had. The computer printout subsequently obtained indicated that the grievant had rung out another worker's badge, as well as his own. This was concluded because two ring-outs were shown at exactly the same time and the foreman observed no one use the machine for several minutes before and after the grievant had. Ringing out two badges was prohibited by the contract and up to a one-month suspension was indicated as a punishment. The foreman prepared a written signed statement of his observations and conclusions, which he turned over to the grievant's immediate supervisor. The grievant was not questioned or notified by the foreman at the time of the alleged offense or at any time subsequent to it. The supervisor did not question the grievant or conduct an investigation, a procedure he is obligated to perform under the contract. The statement showed that the foreman suspended the grievant for one month and the supervisor initiated the punishment. It was put into effect immediately and when the grievant was notified, the grievance was filed. During the course of the normal grievance procedure initiated after the grievance was filed, two workers testified that they had been with the grievant at the time and that he had not committed the offense. However, on several other significant matters, when questioned alone, their testimony conflicted both with each other and with the grievant. The union argued that the suspension was not warranted, based on the fact that the foreman did not see the grievant commit the alleged offense. The foreman agreed, upon questioning, that alternative explanations for what he saw and heard the grievant do did exist and that the evidence was circumstantial.

Issue: Was the grievant suspended for just cause?

Decision and Rationale:

Grievance Situation 4:

Facts: The grievant contacted an acting supervisor (but not her own supervisor), advised the supervisor that she would be absent the following day, and requested emergency annual leave. The acting supervisor did not report the request to the grievant's immediate supervisor until the day the grievant returned to work. The grievant's immediate supervisor then denied the request and charged the grievant with being AWOL. The grievant's reason for the request was to move household goods. These had to be moved on the day specified due to the moving company's schedule. The grievant had a previous record of being AWOL two times. A letter of warning and a record of a counseling session were found in the grievant's personnel file. Emergency leave had not been granted in the past in the organization for moving household goods. Emergency leave, according to the contract, was to be determined by the immediate supervisor, and several guidelines for what constituted such leave were enumerated in the contract. The grievant was suspended for five days and the union argued both that the reason was legitimate and the penalty was too severe.

Issue: Was the grievant suspended for just cause?

Decision and Rationale:

PART D

Form 6 Labor Contract Renegotiation: A Skill-Building Session

General Instructions: This activity requires groups of from five to seven persons. A management and a union negotiating team of two or three persons each are formed, and one to three observers/arbitrators are also required. Roles for all participants follow this introduction. Choose one of the following five craft unions whose contract with the *Daily Post* will expire in one month: typographical, pressmen, stereotypes, photoengravers, mailers (see Forms 7 and 8). You will renegotiate this union's contract. Once you have chosen one of the five unions and have been given a role as either a member of the management or union negotiating team or an observer/arbitrator, read *only* your appropriate role information (and the role information for the other member(s) of your team). (Observers/arbitrators can read all role descriptions.) Also carefully read the background information about the *Daily Post* (Form 7), the current agreement information, the newspaper-craft-union facts, the guidelines for negotiators, and the bargaining strategy and roles for your side *only*. This information follows as Forms 7–13.

Once you have looked over the information, you are to prepare for a contract-renegotiation session. Formulate your strategy, your proposals, etc. Then, conduct the session for a period of one to two hours. Each side will use its strategy or position (Form 10 or 11) as a jumping-off point in this bargaining activity. The objective is to renegotiate with the *Daily Post* the contract of the craft union you chose above. You may meet and exchange initial proposals, dismiss to study them, and meet again to negotiate or conduct the entire renegotiation in one meeting. Assume that both sides are interested in the issues contained on the list of Current Agreement Provisions (Form 9) and that the union members will ratify the contract negotiated. The observer watches the negotiations carefully and fills out everything applicable on Form 12. Also see the *Procedure* to this exercise for instructions.

If, after a few hours, certain issues cannot be resolved, the observer(s) becomes an arbitrator (or arbitration panel). The arbitrator(s) listens to the arguments, views, and positions of each side; weighs all factors he, she, or they feel relevant, including how other issues were decided; and makes decisions that are binding—that is, each side must accept them. The arbitrator could adopt a win-lose strategy and accept the demands of either side on any issue in arbitration, or could compromise.

Members of both negotiating teams, as well as the observer/arbitrator or panel, may want to gather additional background data on union contracts in the newspaper industry or on the craft union they select. This information can be obtained by asking for a copy of the current contract from a local union, by visiting a newspaper and interviewing various industrial-relations staff members, by interviewing local union officials, and/or by looking up information about the newspaper industry's labor relations and the craft unions in the library. *For Further Reading* contains relevant general references. As much of contract administration relies on past precedent, having such precedents in mind, in addition to that data given in the exercise, would improve the effectiveness of the negotiating activity. Further, certain characteristics of your own local newspaper and craft unions and their contract negotiations can be obtained via the fact-finding methods noted above (e.g., a history of strikes, etc.) and can be incorporated into your negotiations to add realism. Remember to read all of the material carefully and to formulate your strategy and an initial position before negotiations begin.

PART D

Form 7 Background Information for the Daily Post

The *Daily Post* is a daily newspaper with a current circulation of 460,000. It is located in a large metropolitan area in the Great Plains region of the country. The *Post* is a morning paper and, except for a few weekly papers and suburban papers, it has no major competition at this time in the area. The *Post* is also one of twelve papers owned by a very large communications holding company. Like most newspapers in this country, it began many years ago as a family business. The paper was bought by the holding company about seven years ago.

The *Post* has a conservative editorial policy. Some have accused it of favoring big business; its editors, however, deny such charges. The paper has backed the incumbent governor of its state, a Republican, and has generally opposed Democratic political candidates. Syndicated columnists include very well-known "moderates" based in New York and Chicago. The paper has won a few Pulitzer prizes for reporting and its Sunday editions are considered excellent in the industry.

The *Post* has had a somewhat stormy relationship with its various craft unions over the years. The founders of the paper were very antiunion. Unions only made a significant incursion into the work force about fifteen or twenty years ago. Now, virtually all employees are unionized. However, the contract negotiations, particularly with the craft unions (e.g., pressmen, stereotypers), have been very bitter and several strikes have resulted. On a few occasions in the early 1960s, some violence accompanied these strikes—for example, presses were destroyed and several fights occurred. Since the holding company purchased the paper, the negotiations have been somewhat more peaceful, although the *Post* certainly still has a reputation for antiunionism, which it feels is undeserved. It locked out the pressmen three years ago for eleven weeks and threatened to replace its photoengravers with nonunionized persons a few years ago when they struck, but could not locate enough nonunion skilled labor to do so.

The management of the *Post* has gone on record as saying that while the unionized workers are competent and individually are good workers, the unions' leaders are threatening to ruin the country financially by demanding exorbitant wage increases, costly benefits, and inefficient work rules. A few of the descendents of the founding family, who still hold high positions in the paper, were recently forbidden by the paper's parent company from taking any direct part in contract negotiations due to their past behavior at the bargaining table. The unions were able to capitalize on such lack of control and emotional involvement in the past, according to the parent company.

Financially, the *Post* is only in fair shape. Inflation has hurt it in the past few years. In addition, high cost overruns on the estimates for its newly completed printing facilities and expanded office facilities forced it to add additional short- and long-term debts it had not anticipated. With high interest rates, these debt repayments are causing somewhat of a strain on cash flow. Advertising revenue is holding steady, but the large retail establishments and chains are putting more and more of their advertising in a few small suburban papers, most of which are printed once or twice weekly. As more and more people move to the suburbs, the *Post* fears this trend may grow.

The stock of the *Post*, the majority of which is held by its parent company, is doing reasonably well, considering the current volatile market. New presses and other equipment, a good year for the parent company, and some favorable publicity from excellent investigative reporting and an exposé of corrupt Democratic state political officials have all helped the stock price.

There is pressure on the *Post's* management from the parent company to go to a smaller, tabloid-size paper, to soften editorial rhetoric somewhat, to hire a few nationally known reporters, and generally to modernize the look and image of the paper. As yet, these changes have been resisted, but with circulation only holding steady for the past two years, no rise in advertising revenue, and the talk of another (evening) newspaper looking for a new location in the area, these changes may be pushed through by the parent company soon.

The management of the *Post* feels that the residents of the area are not ready for a "slick Eastern" paper. The current round of union negotiations may be crucial to the paper's financial stability and its management is already indicating that pay raises demanded by unions could ruin it. The financial statements, however, show that profit has held steady in the past three years and is the highest in the history of the paper, adjusting for inflation. In addition, dividends to shareholders are above the average declared for newspapers of the *Post's* size.

PART D

Form 8 Newspaper Craft Unions Supplemental Data

Table 1. Duration of Union Contracts (percentage comparisons)

Craft	Less than 1 year	1 year	18 mos.	2 years	30 mos.	3 years	More than 3 years
Typographical	0.0	10.8	2.2	42.0	8.0	35.7	1.3
Pressmen	0.3	9.2	2.6	35.8	4.2	37.6	10.3
Stereotypers	0.0	10.2	4.1	29.7	8.4	38.0	9.6
Photoengravers	0.0	7.2	0.4	34.5	9.8	40.9	7.2
Mailers	1.0	8.0	4.0	26.6	10.2	44.2	6.0

Table 2. Hours Constituting a Work Week (by number of contracts reviewed)

Craft	30	31	32	33	34	35	36	37	38	39	40	41
Typographical	0	0	5	4	6	70	41	250	18	2	22	0
Pressmen	3	0	4	5	6	73	31	216	14	1	31	2
Stereotypers	7	4	4	0	2	42	24	121	2	5	4	1
Photoengravers	0	0	0	0	0	27	12	47	0	0	0	0
Mailers	1	1	3	0	1	1	32	19	79	1	8	0

Table 3. Average Hourly Wage Scales since 1965 (in dollars per hour)

Craft	1965	1966	1967	1968	1969	1970	1971	1972	1973	1974	1975	1976	1977	1978
Typographical	3.73	3.83	3.99	4.16	4.20	4.69	4.99	5.37	5.62	5.84	6.01	6.22	6.43	6.61
Pressmen	3.79	3.90	4.03	4.20	4.45	4.70	5.05	5.37	5.68	5.87	6.13	6.31	6.42	6.69
Stereotypers	3.99	4.09	4.23	4.44	4.71	4.99	5.40	5.80	6.17	6.32	6.71	6.83	6.91	7.04
Photoengravers	4.31	4.39	4.57	4.75	5.04	5.32	5.65	6.13	6.37	6.41	6.62	6.84	6.97	7.21
Mailers	3.43	3.68	3.91	3.99	4.26	4.57	4.99	5.38	5.61	5.80	5.96	6.17	6.21	6.41

Table 4. Holiday Provisions Paid when not Worked—Holidays, Birthdays, Floating Days, etc. (percentage comparisons)

Craft	0 day	1 day	2 days	3 days	4 days	5 days	6 days	7 days	8 days	9 days	10 days	11 days	12 days
Typographical	2.3	0.7	0.0	0.0	0.5	1.6	29.2	42.1	15.0	4.2	4.0	0.4	0.0
Pressmen	6.7	0.8	0.0	0.0	0.0	1.5	24.3	41.0	16.7	4.4	4.0	0.0	0.6
Stereotypers	4.5	1.0	0.0	0.0	0.0	3.4	20.7	41.5	17.0	5.0	5.9	1.0	0
Photoengravers	8.8	0.8	1.0	1.0	0.0	5.0	16.7	44.3	14.7	6.3	1.4	0	0.0
Mailers	0.0	0.0	0.0	0.0	1.2	2.4	20.4	47.4	12.1	9.3	5.0	1.2	1.0

Table 5. Vacation Maximums (by number of contracts reviewed)

Crafts	Max. vacation less than 3 wks.	Max. vacation equals 3 wks.	Max. vacation equals 4 wks.	Max. vacation equals 6 wks.	Max. vacation greater than 6 wks.
Typographical	4	61	309	44	4
Pressmen	1	58	259	47	4
Stereotypers	0	19	160	26	2
Photoengravers	1	3	70	18	0
Mailers	0	17	105	15	1

Table 6. Analysis of Contracts' Provisions for Pension—Employer's Contribution (by number of contracts surveyed)

Crafts	No provision	3% of wage	4% of wage	5% of wage	$0.50/shift	$5.00/week
Typographical	50	42	21	3	74	11
Pressmen	32	18	24	7	83	21
Stereotypers	11	97	12	6	142	81
Photoengravers	21	37	27	8	110	42
Mailers	67	7	10	14	131	11

Table 7. Average Amount of Wage Scale Differential for Night vs. Day Shifts (in dollars per hour; craft averages)

Craft	
Typographical	0.183
Pressmen	0.192
Stereotypes	0.203
Photoengravers	0.179
Mailers	0.194

Table 8. Strike Activity (per 100 contracts)

Craft	
Typographical	1.22
Pressmen	1.53
Stereotypers	0.21
Photoengravers	3.92
Mailers	1.31

PART D

Form 9 Current Agreement Provisions and Other Relevant Facts for Contract Renegotiation

	Craft				
	Typographical	Pressmen	Stereotypers	Photoengravers	Mailers
Duration of present (expiring) contract	1 yr.	2 yrs.	2 yrs.	30 mos.	18 mos.
Hours constituting a workweek	36.5 hrs.	37 hrs.	37 hrs.	36 hrs.	38 hrs.
Average hourly wage scale	$6.42	$6.60	$7.01	$6.82	$6.19
Holiday provisions paid	6 days	8 days	9 days	7 days	6 days
Vacations maximum	4 wks.	4 wks.	3 wks.	4 wks.	3 wks.
Provision for pension	5% wage	none	3% wage	0.50/shift	$5.00/wk.
Average wage scale differential for night shift	$.162/hr.	$.190	$.167	$.166	$.183

Discharge Appeal Procedure (all crafts):

All discharge cases shall be disposed of under the following procedure: A discharged employee may first appeal his or her case to the manager of the office from which discharged. Both the foreman and the discharged employee shall appear at the manager meeting, and failure to do so shall constitute forfeiture of the case by the party failing to appear. If the appeal is sustained, the President of the Union at the direction of the Union's Executive Committee and the Publisher of the newspaper, or their authorized representatives, shall constitute an Appeal Board. This Board shall consider the case and make all reasonable efforts to decide it. In the event of failure to agree, a third member shall be added to the Appeal Board, and the decision arrived at by the three (3) person Board shall be final. The third member shall be a qualified person, who must be agreed upon by both union and management, and who is not affiliated in any way with either group or related groups. Fees charged by such a person will be shared equally by union and management. The time factor in cases before this Board shall be as follows: The manager meeting shall be held within five (5) days. The time for consideration by the two (2) person Board shall be within five (5) days, and the time allowed for the three (3) person Board decision shall be twenty (20) days. The time limits established in the foregoing may be extended by mutual agreement. It is the intent of both parties to this agreement that the entire procedure specified herein shall be consummated within thirty (30) days from the date of discharge. The Appeal Board, either two (2) or three (3) persons, may provide compensation to the discharged greivant for time lost. In no case shall reimbursement be in a sum greater than the working time actually lost, multiplied by straight-time rates.

Transfer Policy (all crafts):

All employees have the right to file for a transfer if a vacancy or new job occurs. All employees with satisfactory performance ratings, providing they have been on the job at least one year prior to the transfer request, may be considered for the transfer. The final decision tests with the immediate superiors of the two positions in question. All vacancies or new job openings are to be posted for at least five (5) working days on a centralized bulletin board. Only bids made during the time of posting shall be considered.

PART D

Form 10 Information for Management Negotiating Team

Initial Management Position*—to Be Read by Management Negotiating Team Only

The management of the *Post* has instructed the negotiators to remain firm on all issues, particularly those regarding the wage increase, the benefits demands, and the workweek. While it realizes it must give up some things and move off its first position, it has yet to draft a specific set of initial proposals, or answers to the union's initial position. The management of the *Post* is always geared up to give the unions a battle on "principle," but this time the paper's precarious financial position must be considered in planning a negotiation strategy.

Roles for Contract Renegotiation—to Be Read by Management Negotiating Team Only

Management Negotiator No. 1:   Robert Deals, personnel administrator, *Daily Post*

Robert Deals is a very well-respected and experienced personnel administrator who has been with the *Post* for fifteen years. He almost single-handedly managed the personnel changes required after the takeover of the *Post* by its current parent company, and was able to staff the *Post* with the parent company's management without disrupting operations or hurting feelings. He is tactful and very knowledgeable in the area of personnel. Despite its alleged antiunion stance, the *Post* has been a leader in affirmative-action programs and has never had an EEOC complaint filed against it, largely due to Deals' efforts. The union regards him as an honest, skillful, and tough negotiator; it respects him.

Management Negotiator No. 2:   Perry White, managing editor, *Daily Post*

Perry White is an "old-school" editor and a very close friend of one of the sons of the founder of the *Post*. He began his fifty-two-year career in journalism with the *Post* as an office boy. He is a firm believer in free enterprise and freedom of the press and a conservative Republican of considerable power in the state. He makes no attempt to hide his contempt for unions; according to him, they are restricting management's right to manage and leading us toward socialism. His knowledge of contract negotiations is very limited, but his knowledge of the newspaper business and what is best for the *Post* is extensive. He is not an extremely able negotiator, but is reserved and thoughtful. He never loses his temper and respects Robert Deals.

Management Negotiator No. 3:   Lois Lain (use only if there are three negotiators on each team)

Lois Lain is the assistant personnel administrator. She has been at this position for three years, but has been with the *Post* for ten years. Deals considers her his successor and an able one. She has had an enormous impact on the *Post*'s affirmative-action programs and has dealt with grievances and other union matters skillfully. Lain is a very popular speaker at women's groups in the state and has done much to enhance the image of the *Post*. She is working on a doctorate in industrial relations and is very interested in contract negotiations, although she has little experience in that area. The management of the paper considers her to be an extremely valuable employee for many reasons. However, Perry White and she have one large point of disagreement. Her husband is a newscaster and commentator for a local TV station and has in the past criticized the editorial stance the *Post* has taken on various political and community issues.

---

* Also see Form 13.

PART D

Form 11 Information for Union Negotiating Team

Initial Union Demands (all crafts) in order of Priority*—to Be Read by Union Negotiating Team Only

1. An across-the-board wage increase of 9.3 percent the first year of the contract, 8.2 percent the second year, and 7.6 percent the third year.
2. A three-year contract.
3. A change in the following benefits:
    a) Maximum vacation should be five weeks.
    b) Holidays paid should be ten.
    c) Pension contribution should be 5 percent of wage.
4. Workweek should be 36 hours.
5. Discharge cases should go directly to an arbitrator if they are appealed.
6. Transfers should be made completely according to seniority, providing the applicant meets the job specifications of the new job.
7. Job vacancies must be posted for ten working days and applications or bids for jobs must be accepted for an additional ten days.
8. Bids for transfer can also be accepted up to ten days after the posting period.

The local unions (of all five crafts) are prepared to bargain in good faith; however, realizing the reputation of the *Post*, they are determined to make up for what they consider to be less-than-adequate contract benefit provisions in the past.

Roles for Contract Renegotiation—to Be Read by Union Negotiating Team Only

Union Negotiator No. 1:   Samuel Stompers, president, local union (whichever craft union is chosen)

Samuel Stompers is forty years old and has been president of the local for one year. He is considered a reform and liberal president, having recently defeated the president of long-standing in a very rough election. The newer and younger workers identify with him. He is interested in economic gains, of course, but also talks a great deal about the "quality of work life." He is an able administrator and has won the respect of the national union leaders through his ability to run the local efficiently (and profitably) and by his knowledge and skill in negotiations and membership drives. He had been on the local negotiating team for three years prior to his election. Stompers is a very liberal Democrat and a local school-board member. He is quite ambitious and seriously considering running for city council; most agree he would win easily.

Union Negotiator No. 2:   Susan B. Abel, representative of national union (use whichever union is chosen)

Susan B. Abel is a very experienced union negotiator and high-level officer in the national union. She is typically sent to help in local negotiations with especially tough managements. Abel, an appointed union official, is a former administrator in the United States Department of Labor under two different Democratic administrations. She is a woman who literally grew up with unionism, as her father was for many years the national president of a very large union during the stormy period of the 1920s and 1930s. She feels that economic gains are vital in helping to reduce the differences between socioeconomic classes in the United States. Abel knows Stompers only by reputation. As this is one of the first local contracts in the national union to be renegotiated, she is hoping to set a precedent for sizable gains.

Union Negotiator No. 3:   Louis D. Lewis, executive vice president, local union (use only if there are three negotiators on each team)

Louis Lewis is a very experienced negotiator and has been in various union positions for several years. He has been employed at the *Daily Post* for over twenty years. In fact, many consider him to be the key worker at the *Post* responsible for the success of the union's early organizing efforts. Lewis, of course, has never been a favorite of the *Post*'s management, but no one doubts his skill at his job, his loyalty to the union, or his integrity. Several years ago, Lewis and one of the sons-in-law of the founder of the *Post* appeared on a local TV show and ended up losing their tempers, verbally attacking one another, and generally creating a scene on live local television which the station, the paper, and the union have yet to forget.

---

* Also see Form 13.

Name _____ Group Number _____

Date _____ Class Section _____ Hour _____ Score _____

PART D
Form 12 Worksheet for Observer(s)/Arbitrator(s)

Observer(s)/Arbitrator(s) Roles:

As observer and possibly arbitrator, you need to prepare carefully for the renegotiation by studying the facts of the case and all other material presented here. As observer, your objective will be to analyze and evaluate the renegotiation by answering the questions below in Part I. This information should then be fed back to the team members and discussed after the renegotiation is settled (see also the *Procedure*). If an arbitrator is needed due to the inability of the parties to reach agreement on one or more issues, you will hear and decide these issues alone, or as a member of a panel. Remember: you are an outside, "objective" third party. As an arbitrator, fill out Part II below. After the renegotiation is completed, write down the final new contract provisions and language, with the assistance of both teams, in Part III. Be sure all issues are settled before you fill out Part III.

PART I: Observation of Renegotiation

1. Summarize each side's initial position briefly.

2. Comment on the "reasonableness" of these initial positions. Were they simply set up as bargaining positions from which to move to compromises?

3. Comment on the cohesiveness and singularity of purpose within each team. Did intrateam conflicts deter efficient negotiation?

4. Did the negotiators work from a basis of logic, reason, and fact, or from emotion and ideology?

5. Were the teams flexible? Did they "move off their first position" in the spirit of good-faith bargaining?

6. Which team was the most skillful? Why?

7. Was there a "winner" in the renegotiation? If so, who was it and why?

PART II: Arbitration

1. State each issue that could not be settled in negotiation and each side's final position on the issue.

2. For each issue, indicate your decision as arbitrator and the rationale used for your decisions.

3. Why was binding arbitration necessary in this situation? What could or should each team have done to eliminate the need for binding arbitration?

PART III: Final Contract Provisions

Write each provision that will be in the new contract below.

PART D

Form 13 Some General Guidelines for Negotiators*

1. Carefully prepare for the negotiations. Study all relevant data and have it at your fingertips.
2. Formulate an initial position on each issue; develop a rationale and gather facts to support your positions.
3. Consider objectives of your organization, past practices, trends, etc. as you develop a strategy.
4. What management "rights" does management feel cannot be surrendered?
5. What principles and gains must be maintained according to the union?
6. What are the real desires of the employees?
7. Use clear and concise language.
8. Do not allow emotions and anger to interfere with your negotiating effectiveness.
9. Clear up any misunderstandings or conflicts within your negotiating team before the negotiations begin.
10. Prepare a three-way comparison: management proposal, union proposal, and present contract. Bargain weighing all three.
11. Present evidence for your positions clearly and have copies for all concerned. Evidence in writing is perhaps more persuasive than evidence given verbally.
12. Do not make demands that have no real advantage for your organization, as you may have to concede something valuable in order to get them.
13. Prioritize your demands. Decide what you will probably not give up, what you will give up if pressed, and what you will demand which you are actually using as a bargaining point or "stalking horse" for trading purposes.
14. Retain flexibility; be ready to change your course if it becomes necessary; try not to "burn bridges" behind you.
15. When agreement is reached on an item, make sure the exact language is developed and the item is initialed by the other team before you proceed.
16. Do not violate a confidence by using "off-the-record" conversations held away from the bargaining setting to undercut the position of another (opposing) negotiator.
17. Do not mislead the opposition by promising what you cannot or will not deliver, or by hinting you will reciprocate when you will not. Your credibility is important and cannot be destroyed.
18. Do not leave the bargaining table after an agreement is reached until you have gone over the entire agreement and reviewed its language, etc. It may be late and you may be tired, but a quick review just to make sure is wise.
19. Negotiating is an art and a science. Further, experience is valuable, as is knowledge of the opposing team members personalities, positions, and views, as well as relevant information about your own and the other organization. However, despite the importance of facts, objectives, precedents, financial reports, etc., much of what happens at the bargaining table gets down to personalities and interpersonal relations. Drama also plays a part—feigning anger, bluffing, putting on a show for the press or rank-and-file, and hedging are all used, sometimes very effectively. The important point to remember with regard to your behavior at the bargaining table is that the behavior should be instrumental to attaining the objectives you seek, as well as consonant with your own and the organization's personal philosophy, values, and position.
20. Negotiating does not necessarily involve "defeating" the other side. When negotiations are put in a win-lose context, neither side may be successful and the "winner" may gain a very hollow victory. The dictionary definition of negotiate is "confer with" or "parley," not "do battle with."

---

* Can apply to union and management negotiators.

Name _____ Group Number _____

Date _____ Class Section _____ Hour _____ Score _____

ASSESSMENT OF LEARNING IN PERSONNEL ADMINISTRATION
EXERCISE 19

1. Try to state the purpose of this exercise in one concise sentence.

2. Specifically what did you learn from this exercise (i.e., skills, abilities, and knowledge)?

3. How might your learning influence your role and your duties as a personnel administrator?

4. How might you evaluate the effectiveness or performance of a negotiator (for unions or management)?

5. Given the current economic conditions in this country and the political environment, what trends do you foresee regarding labor relations and unionism? Will unionism grow in the next decade? Why or why not? What types of employees and jobs are "ripe" for unionization? Why?

6. What positive effects would the existence of a union in an organization have on the operation of the personnel or human-resource-management functions of the organization?

7. Additional questions given by your implementor:

Index

Acme Precision Planter Co., 13, 14, 16
Adverse impact, 456–458, 473
Affirmative action, 459–461
  goals, timetables, quotas, 460–461
  illustrative court cases, 461
  plans, 501–510, 511
Age Discrimination in Employment Act, 453
Albemarle Paper Co. v. *Moody*, 79, 267, 451, 461
American Federation of Labor (AFL), 517
American Psychological Association (APA), 258, 261, 451, 452
Application blanks. *See* Biographical data
Assessment centers, 222–225
AT&Tn 451. *See also* Assessment centers
AT&T experiences, 223
  design of, 223–224
  management reports, 227, 238–240
  procedure in, 224–225
  simulation types, 224

Behavior modification
  cost/benefit analyses, 405–406
  definition of, 396
  implementation of, 397
  as a motivation strategy, 397
  and performance improvement, 395–398
  problems with, 398
  schedules of reinforcement, 396–397
  in training programs, 311
Behaviorally anchored rating scales (BARS), 103–152, 341

developmental procedure for, 106–107
and MBO, 156
retranslation in, 106–107, 111–112
uses of, 104
Benefits, 416, 535–537
  cafeteria style, 416
Biographical data, 177–206
  application blanks, 178–179
  categories of, 183–184
  hard vs. soft items, 178
  as a predictor of job success, 178
  uses of, 177
  verifiable items, 178
Bona fide occupational qualification (BFOQ), 453–454
Brito versus *Zia,* 461
Built Fast to Last Construction, Development, and Real Estate Corp., 535–537

Career development, 27
City of Eastern Shore, 419, 427, 431–436
Civil Rights Act of 1964, 9, 266, 451, 453*ff.*
Classification method, 417, 418
Clayton Act, 518, 526
Collective bargaining. *See* Unions
Congress of Industrial Organizations (CIO), 517
Criteria, 19, 258, 261, 295, 330, 459

Daily Post, 523, 545–547
Davis-Bacon Act, 418

Dictionary of Occupational Titles (DOT), 57
Disadvantaged workers, 325, 456-460
Discrimination. *See* Equal Employment
    Opportunity; Affirmative action
Douglas versus *Hampton*, 461

Edward Bedframe Co., 325
Equal Employment Opportunity (EEO),
    450-513
  and BFOQ, 453
  and enforcement agencies, 454-456
  and federal agencies, 454-456
  lawful and unlawful practices, 458-459
  legal and scientific terms, 466-470
  legislation and executive orders, 452-461
Equal Employment Opportunity (EEO) Act of
    1972, 453-454*ff.*
Equal Employment Opportunity Commission
    (EEOC), 262, 266, 267, 450-459
  Guidelines, 451-461
  work record of, 451
Equal Employment Opportunity Coordinating
    Council (EEOCC), 452
Equal Pay Act, 419, 453-455
Executive orders. *See* Equal Employment
    Opportunity
Experiential Learning, 5

Factor comparison method, 417
Fair Credit Reporting Act, 179
Fair Labor Standards Act, 419
Farmhelper Mfg. Corp., 423
Functional job language, 57

Grievances. *See* Unions
Griggs versus *Duke Power Co.*, 267-452

Happyday Corp., 32-33
Herzberg, F., 351, 370, 375
Human-resource development. *See* Training
    and development
Human-resource planning, 23, 24
  assessment of potential, 45, 47
  forecasts, 26-27, 41-43, 47, 49, 51
  sequential model of process, 26-27
  skill inventories, 36-37

In-basket test, 224, 226, 241-246
  and affirmative action, 453, 482-493

Interviewing, 10, 207-220, 224
  in assessment center, 224
  effectiveness of, 209-210
  interviewer accuracy, 210-211
  interviewer reliability, 210-211
  interviewer report form, 215-218
  model of, 211
  skills in, 209
  tapping social and motivational factors, 210
  validity problems, 208

Job analysis
  guidelines for conducting, 58-60
  methods of, 56-57
  position audit form, 69
  sample job dimensions, 89
  in training needs assessment, 287-288
Job behavior, 55, 105
Job descriptions, 56
  uses of, 57
Job Descriptive Index (JDI), 349, 353, 359,
    360-361
Job enrichment, 369-394
  applicability of, 370
  implementation of, 370-371
  job potential diagnosis and, 379-380
  vertical job loading, 370
Job evaluation, 415*ff.*
  methods of, 417-418
  and wage structure, 417
Job Instruction Training (JIT), 333
Job performance, 56, 105
Job relatedness, 461
Job satisfaction-dissatisfaction, 350-368
  causes of, 351
  consequences of, 351-352
  definitions, 350-351
  expectations and, 351
  remedies for, 352

Knights of Labor, 517

Labor legislation, 517-518, 526-527
Labor Management Reporting and Disclosure
    Act. *See* Landrum-Griffin Act
Labor relations. *See* Unions
Landrum-Griffin Act, 518-527
Leaderless group discussion (LGD), 224, 225,
    226-227, 247*ff.*
Learning. *See* Training and development

Leon and Sons Co., 409–410
Littleco, 462, 475–476

Management by Objectives (MBO), 153–174, 343
  and behaviorally anchored rating scales (BARS), 156
  history of, 154
  performance review session, 158–171
  problems with, 155
  steps in, 154–155
  varieties of, 154
Manpower Training and Development Act, (MTDA) of 1962, 9, 28
Myart v. *Motorola,* 261, 267

National Industrial Recovery Act, 526
National Labor Relations Act. *See* Wagner Act
National Labor Relations Board, 518
Norris-LaGuardia Act, 518, 526

Occupational Safety and Health Act (OSHA) of 1970, 9
Organization development (OD), 285
Organizational effectiveness, 2
Office of Federal Contract Compliance (OFCC), 208, 266

Palms Pacific Corp., Inc., 193–194, 212, 225
Pay. *See also* Wage and salary administration
  salary structure, 441
  satisfaction with, 416–417
Perfect Tool Corp., 462–463, 481, 494–495, 511
Performance appraisal, 38–39, 45, 77, 78–102
  dimensionalized scale, 92, 94–95
  forced distribution scale, 93
  format types, 79, 81–82
  giving feedback to ratees, 83
  global scale, 91
  and the law, 79
  objectives of, 78, 81–82
  problems in, 83
  raters in, 80
  ratees in, 80
  trait scale, 80, 90
Personnel administration
  definition, 1
  demands facing, 2
  model of, 3
  as opposed to personnel management, 1

Personnel administrator, 7
  background, training, and experience of, 10
  challenges for, 10
  influence of external environment on, 8–9
  job duties of, 8–21
  new roles for, 9
  traditional role of, 8
Point method, 418, 429
Position Analysis Questionnaire (PAQ), 57
Productivity, 349

Railway Labor Act, 518, 526
Ranking method, 418
Recruitment, 179–180
Reference checks, 179
Reinforcement. *See* Behavior modification
Reliability
  alternate forms, 262
  interviewer, 210–211, 262
    Kuder-Richardson formula, 321–322
    Spearman-Brown formula, 273
    test-retest, 262
Resumes, 177–178. *See also* Selection

Selection, 175*ff. See also* Biographical data; Interviewing; Work sampling; Simulation; Personnel testing
  model of, 176
Sherman Anti-Trust Act, 517, 526
Simulations. *See* Assessment centers
Skill building, 5, 285*ff.*
Skinner, B. F., 396
Statistics, 277–282. *See also* Reliability; Testing; Validity
Supercity, 477, 478

Taft-Hartley Act, 518
Testing, 257–284. *See also* Reliability; Validity
  accuracy, 264–266
  construction, 262–263
  cutting scores, 260
  and discrimination, 451
  perspectives on, 258
  practical usefulness of, 263–264
  standard error of the estimate (SEE), 264–265
  standard error of the mean (SEM), 269, 273, 277, 279
  statistical index of efficiency, 263
Title VII, 262, 451, 452*ff.*

Training and development, 285–348
  assessment of training needs, 287–289
  behavioral objectives, 310
  cost/benefit analysis of, 345
  feedback, 311. *See also* Behavior
    modification
  importance of, 309–310
  as learning, 310, 311–312
  methods of, 312
  model of, 332
  practice, 311
  program design, 312
  program evaluation, 329–348
  transfer of, 310, 311
  overseas selection, 288, 310

Uniform Selection Guidelines, 208, 262, 267,
    452
Union contract. *See* Unions
Unions, 515–558
  collective bargaining, 518–519
  central administration, 520
  contract negotiation, 519–520
  contract. *See* Labor agreement; Union
  development of, 517

glossary of terms, 528–532
grievances, 521, 543–544
impact on personnel administration, 521–522
labor agreement, 520–526, 539–541
using to positive advantage, 522
why workers join, 516–517

Validity, 3, 208, 258–262
  concurrent, 258–259
  coefficient, 263–265, 267, 279
  definition of, 258
  differential, 260
  and equal employment opportunity, 457–459
  logical models, 260–262
  models of, 259
  predictive, 258–259
  predictors, 258, 261

Wage and salary administration, 415*ff.*
  federal legislation and, 418–419
Wagner Act, 518, 526
Walsh-Healey Act, 418
Washington versus *Davis,* 267
Weighted application blank, 178
Work sampling, 221–222